ECONOMICS, INFORMATION SYSTEMS, AND ELECTRONIC COMMERCE: EMPIRICAL RESEARCH

ECONOMICS, INFORMATION SYSTEMS, AND ELECTRONIC COMMERCE: EMPIRICAL RESEARCH

ROBERT J. KAUFFMAN
PAUL P. TALLON
EDITORS

ADVANCES IN MANAGEMENT
INFORMATION SYSTEMS
VLADIMIR ZWASS SERIES EDITOR

M.E.Sharpe
Armonk, New York
London, England

Copyright © 2009 by M.E. Sharpe, Inc.

All rights reserved. No part of this book may be reproduced in any form without written permission from the publisher, M.E. Sharpe, Inc., 80 Business Park Drive, Armonk, NY 10504.

Library of Congress Cataloging-in-Publication Data

References to the AMIS papers should be as follows:

Sougstad, R., and Bardhan, I. R. Empirical analysis of information technology project investment portfolios. Robert J. Kauffman and Paul P. Tallon, eds., *Economics, Information Systems, and Electronic Commerce: Empirical Research. Advances in Management Information Systems,* Volume 13 (Armonk, NY: M.E. Sharpe, 2009), 89–112.

ISBN 978-0-7656-1532-9
ISSN 1554-6152

Printed in the United States of America

The paper in this publication meets the minimum requirements of American National Standards for Information Sciences Permanence of Paper for Printed Library Materials, ANSI Z 39.48-1984.

∞

IBT (c) 10 9 8 7 6 5 4 3 2 1

ADVANCES IN MANAGEMENT INFORMATION SYSTEMS

AMIS Vol. 1: Richard Y. Wang, Elizabeth M. Pierce, Stuart E. Madnick, and Craig W. Fisher
Information Quality
ISBN 978-0-7656-1133-8

AMIS Vol. 2: Sergio deCesare, Mark Lycett, and Robert D. Macredie
Development of Component-Based Information Systems
ISBN 978-0-7656-1248-9

AMIS Vol. 3: Jerry Fjermestad and Nicholas C. Romano, Jr.
Electronic Customer Relationship Management
ISBN 978-0-7656-1327-1

AMIS Vol. 4: Michael J. Shaw
E-Commerce and the Digital Economy
ISBN 978-0-7656-1150-5

AMIS Vol. 5: Ping Zhang and Dennis Galletta
Human-Computer Interaction and Management Information Systems: Foundations
ISBN 978-0-7656-1486-5

AMIS Vol. 6: Dennis Galletta and Ping Zhang
Human-Computer Interaction and Management Information Systems: Applications
ISBN 978-0-7656-1487-2

AMIS Vol. 7: Murugan Anandarajan, Thompson S.H. Teo, and Claire A. Simmers
The Internet and Workplace Transformation
ISBN 978-0-7656-1445-2

AMIS Vol. 8: Suzanne Rivard and Benoit Aubert
Information Technology Sourcing
ISBN 978-0-7656-1685-2

AMIS Vol. 9: Varun Grover and M. Lynne Markus
Business Process Transformation
ISBN 978-0-7656-1191-8

AMIS Vol. 10: Panos E. Kourouthanassis and George M. Giaglis
Pervasive Information Systems
ISBN 978-0-7656-1689-0

AMIS Vol. 11: Detmar W. Straub, Seymour Goodman, and Richard Baskerville
Information Security: Policy, Processes, and Practices
ISBN 978-0-7656-1718-7

AMIS Vol. 12: Irma Becerra-Fernandez and Dorothy Leidner
Knowledge Management: An Evolutionary View
ISBN 978-0-7656-1637-1

AMIS Vol. 13: Robert J. Kauffman and Paul P. Tallon
Economics, Information Systems, and Electronic Commerce Research: Empirical Research
ISBN 978-0-7656-1532-9

Forthcoming volumes of this series can be found on the series homepage.
www.mesharpe.com/amis.htm

Editor in Chief, Vladimir Zwass (zwass@fdu.edu)

Advances in Management Information Systems

Advisory Board

Eric K. Clemons
University of Pennsylvania

Thomas H. Davenport
Accenture Institute for Strategic Change
and
Babson College

Varun Grover
Clemson University

Robert J. Kauffman
Arizona State University

Jay F. Nunamaker, Jr.
University of Arizona

Andrew B. Whinston
University of Texas

CONTENTS

Series Editor's Introduction
 Vladimir Zwass — ix
Acknowledgments — xviii

1. Opportunities and Challenges for Information Systems Research:
 Beyond the Bounds of Statistical Inference—An Introduction
 Robert J. Kauffman and Paul P. Tallon — 3

**Part I. Strategies for Empirical Advances in Information Systems
and E-Commerce Research** — **29**

2. Research Strategies for E-Business: A Philosophy of Science View
 in the Age of the Internet
 Robert J. Kauffman and Charles A. Wood — 31

3. A Potential Outcomes Approach to Assess Causality in Information Systems Research
 Sunil Mithas, Daniel Almirall, and Mayuram S. Krishnan — 63

**Part II. Understanding the Dynamics and Outcomes Associated
with Information Technology Investments** — **87**

4. Empirical Analysis of Information Technology Project Investment Portfolios
 Ryan Sougstad and Indranil R. Bardhan — 89

5. Evaluating Information Technology Industry Performance:
 A Stochastic Production Frontier Approach
 Benjamin B.M. Shao and Winston T. Lin — 113

6. Using Accounting-Based Performance Measures to Assess the Business Value
 of Information Technologies and Systems
 Bruce Dehning, Vernon J. Richardson, Rodney E. Smith, and Robert W. Zmud — 135

Part III. New Approaches for Studying Mechanism Design in Online Auctions   **155**

  7. Modeling Dynamics in Online Auctions: A Modern Statistical Approach
      Galit Shmueli and Wolfgang Jank   157

  8. Empirical Design of Incentive Mechanisms in Group-Buying Auctions
      Her-Sen Doong, Robert J. Kauffman, Hsiangchu Lai, and Ya-Ting Zhuang   181

Part IV. New Empirical Approaches to the Analysis of Weblogs and Digital Community Forums   **227**

  9. Empirical Advances for the Study of Weblogs: Relevance and Testing of Random Effects Model
      Kai-Lung Hui, Yee-Lin Lai, and Shun-Jian Yee   229

 10. Choice-Based Sampling and Estimation of Choice Probabilities in Information Systems and E-Commerce Research
      Jungpil Hahn and Chen Zhang   249

Part V. Looking Forward: Challenges, Transformations, and Advances   **271**

 11. Debating the Nature of Empirical E-Commerce Research: Issues, Challenges, and Directions
      Vijay Gurbaxani, Henry C. Lucas, Jr., and Paul P. Tallon   273

Editors and Contributors   297
Series Editor   305
Index   307

SERIES EDITOR'S INTRODUCTION

Vladimir Zwass

This is the first of the *AMIS* volumes devoted to the economics research brought to bear on Information Systems (IS) and Electronic Commerce (EC) disciplines—and to the new economics research methods enabled by the developments in information technology (IT). You should find unsurprising that this is only the first volume: this is a very busy disciplinary intersection indeed. The methods and the thinking of economics permeate a large swath of the IS discipline. Reciprocally, the newly emerging research methods relying on the IT-enabled treatment of massive data aggregates feed economics research. As vital resources, information technology and digital goods and services increasingly define the landscape of production and consumption, and are thus a substrate of economic research. Economic analysis has a firm and broad grounding in the IS and EC disciplines, which are driven by technological innovation. When analyzed from the economic perspective, the understanding, and sometimes prediction, of IT- and EC-related developments in marketplaces and organizations offer an important dimension of managerial planning and control.

The editors of this *AMIS* volume—Robert J. Kauffman, a well-established thought leader in the field, and Paul P. Tallon, a rising one—are in an excellent position to present this well-selected set of research papers that demonstrate how the approaches of economic empirics can serve to generate new knowledge in our disciplines. It is particularly important to this research program that the editors offer strong methodological guidance in their own contributions here. This meets the essential objective of *AMIS,* as the serial is becoming a research codification of the IS discipline, is setting milestones, and is leading to ever new advances.

As mentioned, economics research in the Information Systems discipline, and in the more recent Electronic Commerce field, has a solid tradition. A notable synthesis of economic research in EC has been carried out by the co-editor of this volume, Robert Kauffman, and Eric Walden (2001). In the present brief tour d'horizon, I would like to identify several research streams prominent in the economic research on IS and EC. The streams overlap (at least *research* streams can), as well they should. In this concise narrative, encompassing both the deductive and inductive methodologies, I can mention only a few representative works. This survey of the general problematic should make the vibrancy of the overall research program abundantly clear. Here are these eleven themes as I see them.

IT-ENABLED AND IT-PRECIPITATED CHANGES IN THE COORDINATION OF ECONOMIC ACTIVITY

As the deployment of IT lowers the transaction costs of going to a market system, there is an economic opportunity for firms to externalize the appropriate functions and processes. The range of possible arrangements significantly widens the market-hierarchy spectrum of coordination possibilities. The phenomenon was analyzed by Malone, Yates, and Benjamin (1987) and has received much attention since. The countervailing economic force of lowered agency costs and the general tendency of firms to become larger, seeking economies of scale and scope, lowering some of the risks, and increasing their market power, is evident as well in the continuing mergers and acquisitions. However, outsourcing, some of it by offshoring to external suppliers, is an evident global phenomenon. Process specialists grow in such areas as IT services, logistics, and travel, among others. This move to the market is certainly evidenced in the lowered entry barriers for entrepreneurial activity in countries where entry-level capital is available and institutional barriers are low. However, in search of lower costs and the benefits of committed relationships, firms limit the breadth of their market activities by dealing with a limited number of suppliers over a long term. The "move to the middle," sometimes severely limiting the number of suppliers, which leads to mutual accommodation and investments in mutually beneficial innovation, has been analyzed as an attractive point in the spectrum (Clemons, Reddi, and Row, 1993). Under the prevailing conditions of incomplete contracting (stemming largely from the unknowns in future markets, including those for IT), the incentives for suppliers to invest in incontractibles, such as, for example, innovation that benefits the specific buyer, require close collaboration will well-selected and well-monitored suppliers (Bakos and Brynjolfsson, 1993). Internally, it has been found empirically that firms extensively using IT evolve a complementary set of organizational designs and practices (Hitt and Brynjolfsson, 1997).

New business models emerge and are tested by the marketplace, are often rejected and sometimes reemerge with new technologies and changed market configurations. The opportunity to introduce incentive-compatibility in organizational solutions offers new ways to substitute market solutions for the hierarchical ones in business governance (Ba, Stallaert, and Whinston, 2001a). Event studies are used to assess equity markets' reactions to strategic corporate moves in the IT domain; for example, it is one way to assess the effects of IT outsourcing (Oh, Gallivan, and Kim, 2006).

As new ITs that in certain cases lead to disruptive innovation emerge, questions of contingent development are asked anew. Many fundamental questions remain to be answered in a more fine-grained manner. What activities are best contracted, or acquired in spot markets? What are the long-term economic effects of outsourcing on the firm? Is the average firm size indeed decreasing? How can business models be evaluated a priori?

BUSINESS VALUE OF INFORMATION TECHNOLOGY AND INFORMATION SYSTEMS

The economic contribution of IT and of IS organized around IT has been studied intensely at various levels of analysis. Of greatest interest to researchers—and practitioners—has been the firm level of analysis, as this is where the decisions to invest in infrastructural technology are made. The contribution of IT to firm—or strategic business unit—productivity has been researched intensely, with the earliest empirics published over twenty years ago (Bender, 1986). The "productivity paradox," the coinage attached to Robert Solow's self-declared inability to find the effects of IT in productivity statistics, has been laid to rest. The work of Brynjolfsson and Hitt (1998) deserves much credit in the analysis. Solow himself, in the same unobvious venue where he made his original statement, wrote about "the rather sudden and unexpected acceleration of productivity in the U.S. in 1995, which was not shared by other industrial countries. Very likely some of it was the late-arriving benefits of information technology" (Solow, 2003, p. 51). As does any other capital input, IT renders benefits only when deployed well and appropriately to the organizational and marketplace contexts. As was the case with other transformational technologies, from the railroad to the telephone, their economic impacts are perceived after a multi-decade lag. An analytical review of the relationships between IT and organizational performance has been performed, among others, by Melville, Kraemer, and Gurbaxani (2004).

A large number of questions regarding the effective deployment of IT fall into the economic domain. Here are just a few instances. Depending on the nature of the markets served by firms, their effective strategies for investments in IT, technologies with sharply decreasing costs, should differ as well (Demirhan, Jacob, and Raghunathan, 2005–2006). Increasingly finer and more textured levels of analysis, such as process or team level, lead to actionable recommendations for managers. Process-level investigation is particularly important (Davamanirajan et al., 2006). Real options theory has been introduced into IS research on IT investments by Dos Santos (1991). It has been fruitfully adapted for use in project management (Fichman, Keil, and Tiwana, 2005) and its use in the practical managerial decision making has been advocated as a component of corporate risk management (Benaroch, Lichtenstein, and Robinson, 2006).

ECONOMICS OF ELECTRONIC AND MULTICHANNEL MARKETS

The advent of the Internet–Web compound has brought about vast opportunities for creating marketplaces of differing capabilities and features, whose comparative advantages are a subject of equally extensive investigation. A great variety of newly emerging intermediary roles, disintermediation in certain (more limited than originally thought) contexts, greatly lowered search costs over far larger and diverse search spaces, and the inherent trust deficit requiring economically efficient compensation are some of the major research subjects. Lowered menu costs in search markets give rise to various schemes of dynamic pricing. Auction marketplaces, featuring price discovery, which are particularly compatible with EC technologies of wide reach and controllable parameters, have proved too seductive and thus failed when a spot-market approach was unsuitable. Some of them, of course, have succeeded spectacularly: eBay has become, besides its primary functions, an excellent research lab (Ward and Clark, 2002). Multimodal all-in-one marketplaces, offering the possibility of negotiating, search buying, and auctioning, have emerged. Market microstructure alternatives need further close study (Anandalingam, Day, and Raghavan, 2005). Market design has fallen into the domain of economists in the case of various specialized online auction marketplaces.

Several general questions are open. Which markets are characterized by network externalities and what are their effects in those specific markets? What are the economic outcomes of large generalizable classes of bidding strategies, in the tradition of Vickrey (1961)? The maturation of the Web-based business-to-consumer (B2C) marketplaces appears to lead to lower prices and smaller price dispersion, as forecast in the early days of EC and not found empirically in those early days (Bock, Lee, and Li, 2007). The pricing strategies in some online markets have been found empirically to be distinct from those in the physical ones (Oh and Lucas, 2006). Novel pricing schemes can be introduced in the Internet–Web infrastructure environment; one of these is liquid pricing allowing for temporary bandwidth expansion at a price, which is analyzed in Bandyopadhyay and Cheng (2006).

Electronic commerce has brought the consumption side of economics within our disciplinary compass. The product variety available on the Web has been established as a significantly larger source of the gains in consumer surplus than the efficiency of the selling channel (Brynjolfsson, Hu, and Smith, 2003). Niche markets have become profitable, and the economics of the "long tail" are being investigated (Brynjolffson, Hu, and Smith, 2006). The economic effectiveness of investment in consumer switching costs on the Web has been studied (Xue, Ray, and Whinston, 2006). The economic aspects of services produced with IT and delivered electronically have been gaining attention lately.

ECONOMICS OF DIGITAL PRODUCTS

The subject of digital goods and services (or performances) is studied in conjunction with electronic markets, and as a topic in itself. A number of specific properties have long been identified and the effective tradability of these products in e-marketplaces where they are vulnerable to alienation and adulteration (or—depending on the point of view—enhancement) are studied (Shapiro and Varian, 1999). The variety of these products and their corresponding properties is large, ranging from massively multiplayer online role-playing games to software. The proper pricing of digital products, in view of the available options and often unforeseen consequences, is vital. As they are introduced to the market, digital goods can benefit from low fixed-fee penetration pricing, but usage-based pricing options may be beneficially combined with this as those markets mature (Sundararajan, 2004). Economically effective delivery options for digital products require identification and study; bundling and versioning are among the well-researched options. The bundling of digital products has been found advantageous under many circumstances (Bakos and Brynjolfsson, 1999). The vast opportunities for customization and personalization introduce further complexity as a race against profits may develop (Dewan, Jing, and Seidmann, 2000). Network externalities are present in the case of some products (although claimed excessively for others) and their impact has to be assessed, notably in the domains of interpersonal communication and social networking. Customer lock-in may result when learning or switching costs are high. Findings concerning the real values of the apparently low marginal prices of digital products are needed. The impacts of collective production by volunteers on the economics of digital products await further research findings. Thus, effective vendor postures in markets combining open-source and proprietary software are being determined (Sen, 2007).

VALUE OF KNOWLEDGE AND INFORMATION

The research stream aiming to determine the contingent value of information and knowledge as factors of production is distinct from that addressing productized digital goods and services. The findings of this research are related to the computation of the value of IS and IT in an organizational context, yet findings here are directed at the systems' outputs within a specific decision-making environment.

The distinction between information and knowledge is important (Foray, 2004; Machlup, 1983; Zwass, 2008). In an organizational context, information is an increment to knowledge, it is a flow, as it were, with its value in part relative to the recipients, and in part with such general attributes as timeliness or expressiveness. Knowledge is an organized body (stock) of facts, relationships, experience, and skills that produces a capacity for action. It is, in the aggregate, provisional, partly tacit, and in a sense collective (Zwass, 2008). Elements of knowledge may be congealed in patents and other intellectual property, and productized.

Optimal levels of investment in knowledge by a firm are studied (Ba, Stallaert, and Whinston, 2001b). The economics of multichannel delivery in expertise have been analyzed in the context of health care (Ozdemir, 2007). Organizational knowledge creation is vital to economies—and economically risky as well; an economic decision analysis of this creation is being investigated on the fundamental level of knowledge work, for example, by Chen and Edgington (2005). Reputation mechanisms are devised for e-commerce sites to lower the trust deficit by reducing information asymmetry between sellers and buyers (Dellarocas, 2005). Information about the sellers' reputations affects the value of companies such as eBay; incentive compatibility among the parties requires third-party providers of this information to step in (Clemons, 2007).

ECONOMICS OF RESILIENCE AND FLEXIBILITY

Globalized economies and global supply chains, relying on the Internet–Web infrastructure, bring major new benefits to business. They also bring new vulnerabilities and threats. Investment in counteracting these exposures is an economic decision for companies, many of which used to treat a simple-minded security as a cost center.

The broad outlines of this research stream include the economics of flexible supply-chain management, responsive to changing economic conditions as well as disruptions. Many research questions arise in security economics. What type of protection scheme is worth paying for? How should risk be apportioned among several possible means of its mitigation? Redundancy economics brings questions related to the costs of replication of facilities and the interconnections among them, as well as the costs of qualified human resources. Risk management, an established field of finance and economics, is now being targeted by the fields of IS and EC. The value of IS security to firms is being determined with event studies (Campbell et al., 2004). The comparative costs and benefits of proactive and reactive responses in IS intrusion prevention have been analytically assessed (Yue and Çakanyildirim, 2007).

ECONOMIC REGIMES OF INFORMATION TECHNOLOGY EVOLUTION

As IT has become a key capital item in world economies and in individual firms, broad issues of the assimilation and evolution of these technologies have been studied using both formal modeling and data-based empirics. Among the questions asked by researchers are the following: What are the economically effective regulatory regimes and player postures in the licensing of intellectual property involving IT? Who benefits by introducing IT standards and how do these actors benefit? What are the economics of the absorption of emerging technologies and what timing leads to the best financial outcomes? What are the economic outcomes and how are revenues distributed when computing is provided as a utility, and when software functions are delivered as a service?

Among the specific research issues are the comparative incentives to software vendors to invest in continuing software enhancement under a software-as-a-service regime versus a perpetual-use license (Choudhary, 2007). The existence of a large standardization gap in EC technologies has been established based on the economic network effects theory, and the means of ameliorating this situation have been proposed (Weitzel, Lamberti, and Beimborn, 2006). Incentive-compatible strategies for establishing standard consortia for EC that would lead to increased social welfare are being studied (Zhao, Xia, and Shaw, 2007).

MACROECONOMIC EFFECTS OF THE DIGITAL ECONOMY

The emergence of the Internet–Web compound as a source of multilayered technological as well as socioeconomic opportunities—and challenges—has led and continues to lead to profound changes in the way we work, live our private lives, govern our societies, and organize our supranational entities. Ever new innovation waves—m-commerce and ubiquitous computing, for instance, bring new waves of profound transformation. Economic analysis of e-government, regulation and fiscal policies, incipient and potential e-money, regional transformation, and global redistribution of labor markets are some of the areas that require continuing research attention.

In the United States, productivity growth from 1996 to 2006 was double that in the years 1973 to 1995 (2.7 percent growth in the output per worker-hour in the non-farm business sector versus 1.35 percent).

Between one-half and two-thirds of this productivity acceleration in the several years after 1995 has been ascribed to the deployment of IT, as both a product and a capital input of production (Slaughter, 2007). At the macroeconomic level, the contribution of telecommunications and EC has been shown to lead to a country's development (Dutta, 2001). Some of the less developed countries can in theory—and some have in practice—avail themselves of the "advantages of backwardness" articulated by Gershenkron (1962) and leapfrog the older and far more expensive technologies to move to IT-intensive economies. A resource-based view is used to analyze methods of effective diffusion of EC in developing economies (Shalhoub and Al Qasimi, 2006).

The above are the prominent established research directions. New research streams emerge as IT evolution takes us into new realms of possibility. Some important emerging research streams as well as some that will be required are addressed in the following three subsections.

THE ECONOMICS OF CO-PRODUCTION

The Internet–Web compound has vastly amplified the change in the relationship between producers and their customers, and in particular between producers and consumers. Consumers have become active participants in that relationship, and also as co-producers. Consumers own the means of production and many also possess the knowledge needed to contribute to the production of digital goods and electronically delivered services—the ever increasing component of total product assortment. The multiple aspects of the compound generate various opportunities that, when combined, can transform the competitive landscape (Zwass, 2003). Thus, the Web–Internet is also a medium of interaction among numerous consumers and producers, and the means of aggregation of their work. Many organizations take advantage of co-production processes in a great variety of forms. Indeed, open modes of production (such as open-source and free software) generate their own organizational forms, most prominently exemplified by the evolving Linux collective and the greater Linux ecosystem. The roles played by consumers on behalf of the traditional producers vary across a spectrum that ranges from product design and content creation to the forming of reputations and trust, and on to active experience-based promotion. Several of these roles have been explored by Benkler (2006), who sets out some of the parameters of the "economics of social production." By opening parts of their content for modification by consumers, for example, video-game firms are able to effectively outsource some of the game development to their customers—at low cost and binding the gamers more tightly to the games in the process (Arakji and Lang, 2007). Novel cultural valorization of active consumption has emerged.

The co-production trend generates a large number of research questions. How is value generated and distributed to maintain incentive compatibility? What is the long-term economically effective spectrum of co-production? What are the economics of disruptive innovation, predicated on a totally different cost structure, often free-riding on externalities left on the table by others? What are the mutual economic dependencies between "social production" and the predominant traditional production mode? Innovation rates, new institutional arrangements, the division (if not the redefinition) of consumer surplus are some of the issues requiring new findings.

THE ECONOMICS OF MUTUAL PENETRATION OF THE PHYSICAL AND VIRTUAL WORLDS

Related to the preceding theme is the needed investigation of the economic nature and effectiveness of business activity undertaken in virtual "worlds," such as Linden Lab's Second Life, and the symmetric phenomenon of objects valorized in the virtual world acquiring economic value in the physical world. Indeed, you can buy Linden's pixel-based properties on eBay for real dollars, and expand the branding for British Petroleum by setting up virtual gas stations in the Second World. Google Earth is moving toward enabling my avatar to have a conversation with yours in the already available three-dimensional digital world of our neighborhoods' replicas (McConnon, 2007). Although some of the economic characteristics of the goods and services traversing the virtual–physical boundary can be cast into traditional forms, interesting new regularities may be discovered as well. Virtual worlds will serve as the laboratories for studying the fluctuation of physical–virtual currency exchange rates, the appropriation of continually created value by producers versus consumers, and the economics of standardization enabling the "worlds" to interoperate.

ECONOMICS OF RAPID-RESPONSE ORGANIZATIONS

Relatively inexpensive and ubiquitous IT, progressively spreading IPv6 (Internet Protocol Version Six) with its vast number of addresses, and the proliferation of sensor technologies such as RFID (radio frequency identification device), will result in an avalanche of data, much of it coming from autonomously operating devices. Vast data generated as by-products of organizational processes call for absorption in real time to effectively respond to environmental requirements. Algorithmic methods of data absorption are being devised, as stream-processing database management systems (such as StreamBase) emerge, with rule-based in-memory processing. The organizations that are able to cope best by converting massive real-time data into strategic, tactical, and operational decisions, will enjoy competitive advantage. What are the institutional arrangements and economic consequences of coordination suited for rapid response? What are the economically justified transformations of business processes that take advantage of the data availability (or avalanche)? How do we keep our sights on the long-term objectives while responding in the short term?

This brief synthesis aims to show the richness and vibrancy of IS and EC research with the economic perspective rather than to offer an exhaustive categorization. Economics research is vital to our field, as it both opens and closes the loops in, what we hope, is an ascending spiral of organizational performance on various levels. It opens the loop by helping us assess the value of IT investments, and closes it by helping assess the economic outcomes. It does the same for the second-level loop, by helping our organizations learn from the IT investments made and the expanded organizational capabilities gained. Consequently, it is very important to the aims of *AMIS* and to the further development of these research streams that the editors of this volume provide assessment and guidance on research methodologies, exemplified by the chapters included here. The present volume is devoted, broadly speaking, to the results obtained with inductive methods. As the editors stress and the chapters illustrate, analysis of voluminous data leads to new scientific and managerial insights. The complementary next volume featuring the crossroads of IS, EC, and economics, will center on deductive work and will continue this ambitious project.

REFERENCES

Anandalingam, G.; Day, R.W.; and Raghavan, S. 2005. The landscape of electronic market design. *Management Science,* 51, 3 (March), 316–327.

Arakji, R.Y. and Lang, K.R. 2007. Digital consumer networks and producer-consumer collaboration: Innovation and product development in the video game industry. *Journal of Management Information Systems,* 24, 2 (Fall), 195–219.

Ba, S.; Stallaert, J.; and Whinston, A.B. 2001a. Introducing a third dimension in information systems—The case for incentive alignment. *Information Systems Research,* 12, 3 (September), 225–239.
———. 2001b. Optimal investment in knowledge within a firm using a market mechanism. *Management Science,* 47, 9 (September), 1203–1219.
Bakos, Y. and Brynjolfsson, E. 1993. Information technology, incentives, and the optimal number of suppliers. *Journal of Management Information Systems,* 10, 2 (Fall), 37–53.
Bakos, Y. and Brynjolfsson, E. 1999. Bundling information goods: Pricing, profits, and efficiency. *Management Science,* 45, 12 (December), 1613–1630.
Bandyopadhyay, S. and Cheng, H.K. 2006. Liquid pricing for digital infrastructure services, *International Journal of Electronic Commerce,* 10, 4 (Summer), 47–72.
Benaroch, M.; Lichtenstein, Y.; and Robinson, K. 2006. Real options in information technology risk management: An empirical validation of risk-option relationships. *MIS Quarterly,* 30, 4 (December), 827–864.
Bender, D.H. 1986. Financial impact of information processing. *Journal of Management Information Systems,* 3, 2 (Fall), 22–32.
Benkler, Y. 2006. *The Wealth of Networks: How Social Production Transforms Markets and Freedom.* New Haven: Yale University Press.
Bock, G.W.; Lee, S.-Y.T.; and Li, H.Y. 2007. Price comparison and price dispersion: Products and retailers at different Internet maturity stages. *International Journal of Electronic Commerce,* 11, 4 (Summer), 101–124.
Brynjolfsson, E. and Hitt, L.M. 1998. Beyond the productivity paradox. *Communications of the ACM,* 41, 8 (August), 49–62.
Brynjolfsson, E.; Hu, Y.; and Smith, M.D. 2003. Consumer surplus in the digital economy: Estimating the value of increased product variety at online bookstores. *Management Science,* 49, 11 (November), 1580–1596.
———. 2006. From niches to riches: Anatomy of the long tail. *MIT Sloan Management Review,* Summer, 67–71.
Campbell, K.; Gordon, L.A.; Loeb, M.P.; and Zhou, L. 2004. The economic cost of publicly announced security breaches: Empirical evidence from the stock market. *Journal of Computer Security,* 11, 3, 431–448.
Chen, A.N.K. and Edgington, T.M. 2005. Assessing value in organizational knowledge creation: Considerations for knowledge workers. *MIS Quarterly,* 29, 2 (June), 279–309.
Choudhary, V. 2007. Comparison of software quality under perpetual licensing and software as a service. *Journal of Management Information Systems,* 24, 2 (Fall), to appear.
Clemons, E.K. 2007. An empirical investigation of third-party seller rating systems in e-commerce: The case of buySAFE. *Journal of Management Information Systems,* 24, 2 (Fall), 43–71.
Clemons, E.K.; Reddi, S.P.; and Row, M.C. 1993. The impact of information technology on the organization of economic activity: The "move to the middle" hypothesis. *Journal of Management Information Systems,* 10, 2 (Fall), 9–35.
Davamanirajan, P.; Kauffman, R.J.; Kriebel, C.H.; and Mukhopadhyay, T. 2006. Systems design, process performance, and economic outcomes in international banking. *Journal of Management Information Systems,* 23, 2 (Fall), 65–90.
Dellarocas, C. 2005. Reputation mechanism design in online trading environments with pure moral hazard. *Information Systems Research,* 16, 2 (June), 209–230.
Demirhan, D.; Jacob, V.S.; and Raghunathan, S. 2005–6. Information technology investment under declining technology cost. *Journal of Management Information Systems,* 22, 3 (Winter), 321–350.
Dewan, R.; Jing, B.; and Seidmann, A. 2000. Adoption of Internet-based product customization and pricing strategies. *Journal of Management Information Systems,* 17, 2 (Fall), 9–28.
Dos Santos, B.L. 1991. Justifying investments in new information technologies. *Journal of Management Information Systems,* 7, 4 (Spring), 71–90.
Dutta, A. 2001. Telecommunications and economic activity: An analysis of Granger causality. *Journal of Management Information Systems,* 17, 4 (Spring), 71–95.
Fichman, R.G.; Keil, M.; and Tiwana, A. 2005. Beyond valuation: "Options thinking" in IT project management. *California Management Review,* 47, 2, 74–96.
Foray, D. 2004. *The Economics of Knowledge.* Cambridge, MA: MIT Press.
Gershenkron, A. 1962. *Economic Backwardness in Historical Perspective.* Cambridge, MA: Harvard University Press.

Hitt, L. and Brynjolfsson, E. 1997. Information technology and internal firm organization: An exploratory analysis. *Journal of Management Information Systems,* 14, 2 (Fall), 81–101.

Kauffman, R.J. and Walden, E.A. 2001. Economics and electronic commerce. *International Journal of Electronic Commerce,* 5, 5 (Summer), 5–116.

Machlup, F. 1983. Semantic quirks in studies of information. In F. Machlup and U. Mansfield, eds., *The Study of Information: Interdisciplinary Messages.* New York: Wiley, pp. 641–671.

Malone, T.W.; Yates, J.; and Benjamin, R.I. 1987. Electronic markets and electronic hierarchies. *Communications of the ACM,* 30, 6, 484–497.

McConnon, A. 2007. Just ahead: The Web as virtual world. *Business Week,* August 13, 62–63.

Melville, N.; Kraemer, K.; and Gurbaxani, V. 2004. Information technology and organizational performance: Integrative model of IT business value. *MIS Quarterly,* 28, 2 (June), 283–322.

Oh, W. and Lucas, H.C., Jr. 2006. Information technology and pricing decisions: Price adjustments in online computer markets. *MIS Quarterly,* 30, 3 (September), 755–775.

Oh, W.; Gallivan, M.J.; and Kim, J.W. 2006. The market's perception of the transactional risks of information technology outsourcing arrangements. *Journal of Management Information Systems* 22, 4 (Spring), 271–303.

Ozdemir, Z.D. 2007. Optimal multi-channel delivery of expertise: An economic analysis. *International Journal of Electronic Commerce,* 11, 3 (Spring), 89–105.

Sen, R. 2007. A strategic analysis of competition between open source and proprietary software. *Journal of Management Information Systems,* 24, 1 (Summer), 233–257.

Shalhoub, Z.K. and Al Qasimi, S. 2006. *The Diffusion of E-Commerce in Developing Economies.* Cheltenham, UK: Elgar.

Shapiro, C. and Varian, H.R. 1999. *Information Rules: A Strategic Guide to the Network Economy.* Boston: Harvard Business School Press.

Slaughter, M.J. 2007. Happy birthday ITA. *Wall Street Journal,* July 17, 22.

Solow, R.M. 2003. Mysteries of growth. *New York Review of Books,* July 3, 49–51.

Sundararajn, A. 2004. Nonlinear pricing of information goods. *Management Science,* 50, 12 (December), 1660–1673.

Vickrey, W. 1961. Counterspeculation, auctions, and competitive sealed tenders. *Journal of Finance,* 16, 1 (May), 8–37.

Ward, S.G. and Clark, J.M. 2002. Bidding behavior in on-line auctions: An examination of the eBay Pokemon market. *International Journal of Electronic Commerce,* 6, 4 (Summer), 139–155.

Weitzel, T.; Lamberti, H.-J.; and Beimborn, D. 2006. The standardization gap: An economic framework for network analysis. In M.J. Shaw, ed. *E-Commerce and Digital Economy, Advances in Management Information Systems,* Vol. 4. Armonk, NY: M.E. Sharpe, 54–73.

Xue, L.; Ray, G.; and Whinston, A.B. 2006. Strategic investment in switching cost: An integrated customer acquisition and retention perspective. *International Journal of Electronic Commerce,* 11, 1 (Fall), 7–35.

Yue, W.T. and Çakanyildirim, M. 2007. Intrusion prevention in information systems: Reactive and proactive responses. *Journal of Management Information Systems,* 24, 1 (Summer), 329–353.

Zhao, K.; Xia, M.; and Shaw, M.J. 2007. An integrated model of consortium-based e-business standardization: Collaborative development and adoption with network externalities. *Journal of Management Information Systems,* 23, 4 (Spring), 247–271.

Zwass, V. 2003. Electronic commerce and organizational innovation: Aspects and opportunities, *International Journal of Electronic Commerce,* 7, 3 (Spring), 7–37.

———. 2008. Series editor's introduction. In I. Becerra-Fernandez and D. Leidner, eds., *Knowledge Management: An Evolutionary Approach, Advances in Management Information Systems,* Vol. 12. Armonk, NY: M.E. Sharpe, vii–xi.

ACKNOWLEDGMENTS

We would like to thank the authors of the various chapters in this book for their innovative ideas in research, and their willingness to write and then write *again* under our guidance. The ideas that they have offered related to information systems, electronic commerce, and economics will provide a treasure trove for readers who are looking for the motivation to find new paths to research innovation and fresh thinking. Our role as editors of their work permitted us to participate in their discovery and creation of new knowledge. Very often, the process of figuring out what you are thinking in a new research effort is hastened and made clearer when a curious editor asks questions about "Why this?" and "What do you mean to argue here?" and "Have you thought of such and such?" In this enterprise, we never were short of questions (and suggestions) for the authors, and they were outstanding in their willingness to participate in the dialogues that led to the final products that you see here. Indeed, we have learned a great deal about a variety of new economics approaches to empirical research in information systems and electronic commerce through these rich and varied interactions.

We also thank Vladimir Zwass of Fairleigh Dickinson University, the series editor, and Harry Briggs, executive editor, M.E. Sharpe, Inc., for their guidance of our work on this project from conceptualization to completion. In addition, Rob Kauffman gratefully acknowledges the even earlier discussions with Vladimir Zwass, when the "AMIS Series" was still being thought through. We sincerely hope that the good vision that led to its initiation has come to fruition through the high-quality contributions to research that we have brought together in this new volume in the series.

Robert J. Kauffman
Arizona State University

Paul P. Tallon
Boston College

ECONOMICS, INFORMATION SYSTEMS, AND ELECTRONIC COMMERCE: EMPIRICAL RESEARCH

CHAPTER 1

OPPORTUNITIES AND CHALLENGES FOR INFORMATION SYSTEMS RESEARCH

Beyond the Bounds of Statistical Inference—An Introduction

ROBERT J. KAUFFMAN AND PAUL P. TALLON

PROLOGUE

Recent issues that have arisen in empirical research on information systems (IS) and e-commerce have created the necessity for researchers to reevaluate their knowledge of how they approach applicable theoretical knowledge, research design approaches, and statistical analysis and other evaluative methods. This volume presents new research that reflects recent advances in empirical analysis for the IS and e-commerce context. Based on our experience organizing and attending a variety of recent conferences—the INFORMS Conference on IS and Technology, the International Conference on Information Systems, the Hawaii International Conference on Systems Science, and the International Conference on Electronic Commerce—it has become increasingly clear to us that IS and e-commerce researchers are especially in need of guidance on how to extract knowledge from large and nontraditional data sets. The situation that we increasingly face in our research is akin to what has happened previously in molecular biology and bioinformatics, where the research questions that are being asked have begun to reflect a whole new paradigm of scientific inquiry in the presence of truly large-scale data.

For example, microbiologist Martin Vingron (2001, p. 389) has written in *Bioinformatics* magazine:

> Until a couple of years ago, a typical question from my colleagues on the biological workbench would be phrased something like: "I have this [genetic] sequence here and cannot find out anything about it. Can you help?" From today's standpoint two things are remarkable about this question. First, it deals with only *one* sequence. Today, the question might be: "I have got 2,500 sequences . . ." Secondly, even when using updated terms, the question is rarely asked. More typically, I now get asked questions like: "I have 17 hybridisations of such-and-such material versus an array of 10,000 genes. Can you help me interpret the data?"

Still others, such as Smyth (2000), have argued that it is necessary to bring data mining techniques to bear to help researchers and analysts make sense of the patterns which they are seeing in bioinformatics data and other massive data sets which require special techniques for analysis

(Abello, Pardalos and Resende, 2002; Kamath, 2001). Moreover, some useful meta-statistical observations have been offered about the inappropriate applications of statistics in some contexts and the need to make better decisions about which tools to use, as evidenced by the following statement:

> Instead of sorting out precisely what questions researchers need to ask, and then finding ways to answer those questions, many statisticians are guilty of pursuing mathematically tractable alternatives which are potentially misleading to the researcher. This is not merely an issue of using simplifying models because the full reality is too complex to cope with. .... It is a question of ambiguously or incorrectly stated research aims—of making "errors of the third kind" (giving the right answer to the wrong question). (Hand, 1994, p. 317)

Quite a bit of the research in IS up to now has been shaped by the exploration of relatively simple or straightforward research questions that have been studied in fairly accessible spaces for data collection with models of only limited complexity and statistical analyses that have been appropriate. For example, over the years one of our field's key theoretical perspectives has been the *technology acceptance model* (TAM) (Davis, 1989). Empirical research on TAM and its variants has been largely carried out through the validation of survey instruments that get at issues of perceived ease of use and usefulness of technologies that people can adopt. Researchers typically attempt to identify a set of key factors that reflect different aspects of the theory that they bring to a given setting to study technology adoption. The factors are built up to form a *structural equation model* whose links and connections can be evaluated as a means to develop an overall theoretical picture of how a given set of forces in a specific technology setting are interrelated and ultimately load on or create a unique *path of influences* on the desired outcomes—such as higher observed levels of adoption.

A similar story can be told for information technology (IT) value research, where the goal has mostly been to determine the extent to which investments in IT can be linked to the performance outcomes of a business process, a product or service, a strategic business unit or the firm (Melville, Kraemer, and Gurbaxani, 2004). Researchers who pursue this kind of research often use econometric methods, which can be tuned to reflect the *information structure* of a research setting (e.g., the representation of simultaneity and endogeneity, cross-equation error term correlations, limited dependent variables, etc.), and provide the best support for obtaining meaningful evidence of IT investment value. Although many readers of this literature may find that the methods used in this stream of research belong more in the domain of statistics and econometrics, the sizes of the data sets used remain small relative to the microbiology and genetics example cited above, and so the nature of the research questions found in the literature continue to be somewhat obvious and direct, and we daresay, uninspiring.

In parallel with Vingron's characterization of the new "massive" experimental methods in molecular biology and the emergence of bioinformatics as a separate discipline, we are also seeing a migration to much larger data sets in business disciplines. Ironically, as a research community, we have long struggled to make sense of data sets involving small sample sizes (Hoyle, 1999). An entire network of research methods has grown up around small sample sizes but with the advent of the Internet, the problems facing IS research involve not small sample sizes but *very large* sample sizes. When sample size is so large that the statistical power curve is flat or asymptotic, the dilemma facing researchers concerns not just the management of computer processing requirements but whether our traditional battery of statistical tests is meaningful (Kline, 2004). Wegman (2000) provides an even broader overview, in the presence of historically large data sets,[1] by characterizing the necessity for a move to new "computational statistics" from traditional mathematical statistics as a "completed theory." Wegman goes on to argue his belief that there are "computational and inferential implications" of different size data sets, and as we go from smaller to much, much larger data sets, it will be necessary to have different new tools to support "numerical tractability" in lieu of "mathematical tractability," and "statistical robustness" instead of "statistical optimality."[2] Elsewhere, in an analysis of data mining, Weiss and Indurkhya (1998, pp. 12–13) report:

> At the heart of statistics are models of data and methods of prediction that are supported by formal statistical theory. These enormous strengths may also be weaknesses. Classical statistical models, dominated by linear models, are now seen as models for modest, not big, data. Setting rigorous standards for modeling and statistical proof, statistical methods may have restricted the horizons of data mining to easily computable approaches. In a computer age, statistical models can be too efficient, often coming at the expense of too many simplifying assumptions.

Some brief examples should lock in these ideas with the reader. Fraud detection in online markets has become an increasing concern, and analysis for fraud detection requires working with huge data sets (Cahill, Lambert, Pinheiro and Sun, 2002; Clemons, 2007). Financial risk management is another case in point. Fifteen years ago, the lack of systems integration largely prohibited the acquisition of real-time data so that financial services firms would be able to economically and actively manage their intraday and overnight financial risks. They hoped to do so with respect to the key indicators in the financial environment (e.g., exchange rates and interest rates), financial instruments (loans, derivative securities), customers and counterparties, and business sectors and global regions. The rise of intrafirm networking and systems integration in the early to mid-1990s changed all of that, however, and made it economical to bring data together on a daily basis, permitting the transformation of business practices in the management of financial and operations risks (Han, Kauffman, and Nault, 2004). As a result, the demand for such data skyrocketed, in parallel with the use of increasingly sophisticated statistical methods for financial economic analysis of trends in the stock and derivatives and the current and energy markets.[3]

Although it still is nothing like the stock market or microbiology, which have focused global efforts and a well-established infrastructure for collecting and sharing data, empirical research in IS and electronic commerce today nevertheless is made much easier by the ready availability of data, due to new secondary data sets as well as new opportunities to collect primary data from the Internet. For those of us who graduated from IS doctoral programs in the late 1980s and 1990s (as did the editors of this research volume), our training on how to extract useful information from data in empirical research designs was largely founded on methods such as cross-sectional, time-series, and panel data analysis from econometrics for secondary data. We also became proficient and comfortable with analyzing data using factor analysis, structural equation modeling (LISREL, EQS, AMOS, PLS), analysis of variance and mean differences, and other approaches that are historically associated with organizational research and survey methods. Our methods choices were largely informed by statistics based on small-scale research with human subjects in a laboratory setting, surveys that never had much more than 500 or 600 respondents,[4] and firm and industry-level data sets that would go into the low four-figures (e.g., 1,200 or 2,500 observations) at the maximum.

Today, the business and technology landscape for our research is greatly changed. No longer are we short on data; instead, we are awash in it, to the point where we are forced to make appropriate choices about what is worthwhile to study and how best to study those things that we determine are important. In addition, we have access to all sorts of data that many of us never contemplated would be available when we wrote our dissertations and first journal articles. What is even more interesting is that we can access these new data in ways that we never thought possible—in our hands via PDAs (personal digital assistants) and cell phones, on our notebook PCs (personal computers) via wireless connections to the Internet, and on desktop computers with broadband connections to remarkable archival sources of data. Some of those sources are online auctions, online catalogs, Weblogs (blogs) and community forums, digital filings of corporate and industry data—even the electronic details of IT outsourcing contracts, corporate procurement purchases in business-to-business electronic markets, and lawsuits. It has become apparent, after all, that the world of the IS and e-commerce researcher is a bold, new research environment that has been reshaped by technological transformations, and for which the related "scientific stage" is now set to undergo its own significant revolution in methodology and research know-how.

In this context, it is natural to wonder what the next type of advance in empirical methodologies for research in this space will be. Our interest in this topic both guides our exploration and encourages us to be leaders in that revolution. As one might expect, the breadth of relevant ideas and methods goes far beyond the fields of IS and e-commerce mentioned so far. Included are marketing, operations, financial, accounting, and even strategy—all of which have been buffeted by the changes brought on by the emerging technologies of the Internet over the past decade. In addition, we have the opportunity to engender a new dialogue and participation from people in other fields including economics, statistics, biostatistics, medicine, regional science and geography, and computer science. To the extent that all these fields have some stake in creating and applying empirical advances for the study of new phenomena and new theories, many disciplines will contribute to one another's growth, development, and innovation.

In this introductory chapter of this research volume, we discuss a number of issues that arise in the consideration of empirical advances in IS and e-commerce, and that have broad influences from multiple disciplines, but specific tie-ins to economics and the methods that economists use to analyze data in empirical research. We first consider the general challenges that the new environments for data collection in e-commerce present to us. They include historically large data sets, p-values that imply the nearly complete fit of a data set to an empirical model, the meaning of the related inference tests, and what current statistical knowledge tells us about how to approach these kinds of problems in this research space.[5] We next argue on behalf of a new synthesis that blurs the demarcating lines between statistics, data mining, and computer science. The main idea that we present is one of "paradigm stretching": each of the three disciplines has its own procedures and norms for understanding what data have to say. Nobody that we know of (up until now) is adequately trained for research at the doctoral level in a way that creates unusual facility with a combination of these methods, and ends up with the capacity to flexibly select and apply the "right" data analysis methods from the appropriate discipline for a problem of a given description.[6] We outline our current thoughts on that, since they offer the mindset for research that will lead us to real discovery and innovation in our own IS and e-commerce research involving large data sets. We also consider the range of opportunities that a new synthesis of knowledge will open up for us and our research colleagues in the exploration of what the data have to say to us. Indeed, there is much untouched ground to be explored. Such exploration will: support our development of new knowledge with methods that are still largely unknown or underexploited; permit us to visualize, extract, and map new relationships and correspondences in our data; and support the creation of a "new frontier" style of analysis in our research that will mirror the innovations that we seek to achieve.

In the following sections of this introductory essay, we share our thoughts on each of these three aspects—challenges, synthesis, and opportunities—and then lay out the contents of this volume, and illustrate the various ways that the contributing authors' research reflects steps along the new paths that we have described. Putting this research volume together was an interesting challenge, since we knew from the start what we hoped to accomplish in terms of showcasing new ideas. We also had a sense of who we could invite to participate and share their research, based on our knowledge of the kind of work that they have been doing and the innovations and empirical advances that are implicit in their investigations. We leave it to readers to make their own judgments about the usefulness of the ideas that are offered, and to join in this dialogue of innovations and empirical advances in economics, IS, and e-commerce research.

CHALLENGES

In a recent research project with one of the coeditors' colleagues (Kauffman and Wood, 2007), we had an interesting experience exploring the relationships that were present in a very large data set. The application involved studying the price-leading and price-following behaviors of e-tailers of books and music CDs at leading firms such as Amazon.com, Barnes and Noble.com, and some less well-known sites. The data were collected in 2000, and consisted of 123,680 daily prices from 169 products and 53 unique Internet-based sellers—a historically large data set for the fields of IS and e-commerce at that time. We assembled the data on best-selling books and music CDs using a software tool developed for that specific purpose called the "Time-Series Agent Retriever" (or TSAR, for short). Our colleague, Chuck Wood (now of Notre Dame University), had great facility in software development and he created a number of inventive techniques and solutions to make it possible to repetitively "scrape" product and price data off of the e-tailers' Web sites, and dump it to a database. TSAR ran every night in the Carlson School of Management at the University of Minnesota for as long as was necessary to cull the necessary data.

The data for the study came from two sources: MySimon.com (www.mysimon.com) and DealPilot.com (now Dealtime, at www.dealtime.com). Although it sounds as if this would have taken quite a bit of time given the size of the data set, in fact the data were assembled over a relatively short period of time: from February 21, 2000, to March 29, 2000. From these data, we were able to extract 1,793 unique price changes, including 871 price increases and 922 price decreases. Later it would be necessary for us to remove all observations related to firms that displayed no more than 300 prices during that period of time, since our sense was that these Internet-based sellers would be less apt to be participating in and subject to the dynamics of price change competition in this segment of Internet sales. Also, we wondered whether the data that we captured would be sufficient to represent these firms' pricing behavior. This resulted in a data set of 1,674 price changes, which formed the basis for our modeling and analysis of interfirm price leadership and followership dynamics.

We used a *vector autoregression model* (VAR) in this research, a technique from macroeconomic econometrics pioneered by Sims (1980), an econometrician at Princeton University. The method supports the discovery of associational patterns over time, but does not impose any underlying theoretical relationships on the data before an analyst is able to specify an explanatory theory (Lutkepohl, 1990). A VAR model is a system of equations that includes lagged values of the dependent variable for each equation; these are included as the independent variables. In our case, each equation was intended to represent the predicted price of a given firm's product at a given point in time, conditional on the observation of prior prices.

Our use of this kind of model challenged the popular wisdom that existed in the IS field at the time we did the work. We did not wish to prespecify the theory and test it with our data. Instead, we wished to let the data speak for themselves. We did not use a panel data model, which in contrast, is useful for the analysis of cross-sectional data for which the observations are made across different points in time. Such models are often used to evaluate the effects of discrete changes of state, so we normally model the data as being period-specific, and we do not permit the values at a given time to carry across many time periods (Greene, 2000). VAR models are different though. They are time-series models and they usually involve two or more endogenous variables. Also with VAR models, it is not meaningful to think of the independent variables as explanatory variables. Instead, the typical approach is to use *variance decomposition* to decompose the error terms and then to study the extent to which large changes in the error terms—or "shocks"—tend to be associated with other factors in the environment around the time the shocks seem to occur.

We used VAR econometric methods to understand the extent to which we could consistently associate next-day price change reactions by an Internet bookseller or music CD seller to the price-change actions of its competitor the day before—or within a range of days following a vendor's initial price change. This is an interesting problem to evaluate in statistical terms. It was obvious as we did this research, for example, that price series for individual e-tailers across different products would be likely to be highly correlated over time—in other words, *autocorrelated,* a typical defect that makes it difficult to produce reliable parameter estimates in simple regression models. In fact, it is also likely that price changes will be fairly rare (and possibly Poisson-distributed, as we see with rare events and count data models) and that similar prices will tend to dominate.[7] The design of the econometric model and our sampling of the data set were specifically tuned to identify those periods when it was likely to see one event associated with the occurrence of another—something that Hui, Lai, and Yee (Chapter 9 in this volume) and Hahn and Zhang (Chapter 10 in this volume) have called *dyadic relationships* or *dyadic events.*

In our modeling analysis, we were able to determine that a number of booksellers were extreme price followers (with p-values → 0), while others exhibited no apparent reactions to their competitors' price changes (with p-values → 1), as illustrated in Table 1.1.

The results are interesting because they portray estimated R^2s for variance explained, F-statistics for model likelihood, and p-values for price reactions that tell a compelling story. In this case, we see evidence that something is tying the prices of first-movers in price changes to others who seem to make price changes within one day. In this sense, a high p-value is helpful in indicating that the connection is very strong—almost as though some kind of revenue yield management is occurring. We were not interested in the usual marginal effects, as is normally the case with regression models. Also, in the case of bookselling, based on the recent results of Bergen, Kauffman, and Lee (2005), there is no evidence that booksellers are reactive to small changes in demand and supply. Nevertheless, it is possible that there are other external events that provide an external means for coordination in the marketplace. One example is the movement of a book onto or off of the *New York Times* "best-seller list." Also, there may be enough price comparisons occurring among competitors, and a good number of them appear to be able to detect price changes and react to them swiftly. By the same token, for some other Internet booksellers who have p-values that are close to 1, it is also obvious that there is absolutely no leader and follower association.

In research that we have done on the use of "9"-ending prices and the quality image that Internet-based sellers wish to achieve (Bergen, Kauffman, and Lee, 2007), we have seen other examples where very large data sets produce a mix of highly significant and highly insignificant coefficients (see Table 1.2).

The "NineCents" and "NineDollars" models employ a set of regressors that describe stores and products over time, with the intention of predicting whether a given item's prices tend to end in 9¢ or $9. As the table shows, for this analysis we had 1,718,508 data points—data that were collected

Table 1.1

Sample: VAR for One-Day Reaction to Competitor Price Changes for Books

Bookseller	Adj-R^2 (%)	F-stat.	p-value	Bookseller	Adj. R^2 (%)	F-stat.	p-value
Amazon.com	11.9	8.51	0.000***	A1Books	0.0	0.12	0.999+
BN.com	25.4	19.46	0.000***	AllDirect	0.0	0.03	0.999+
Borders.com	8.0	5.18	0.000***	AlphaCraze	0.0	0.03	0.999+
Big Words	0.0	0.06	0.999+	Books Now	5.4	2.92	0.000***
BooksAMillion	0.0	0.13	0.999+	BookVariety	0.0	0.22	0.999+
Varsitybooks	2.1	1.64	0.020**	Harvard Book	21.8	10.07	0.000***
eCampus	0.0	0.80	0.767	Kingbooks	0.0	0.02	0.999+
Powell's	0.0	0.01	0.999+	Page One	3.6	2.14	0.000***
Efollet	0.0	0.03	0.999+	Rainy Day Books	21.0	9.03	0.000***
Buy.com	8.1	4.43	0.000***	Rutherford's	14.3	5.90	0.000***
10base.com	0.0	0.05	0.999+	Wordsworth	0.0	0.75	0.886
1bookstreet	6.6	3.70	0.000***				

Source: Adapted from Kauffman and Wood (2007), by authors' permission.
Note: ***$p < 0.001$; **$p < 0.01$; *$p < 0.05$; +$p > 0.999$.

Table 1.2

Sample: Seemingly Unrelated Probit Model Estimation for 9¢ and $9 Price Endings

	NineCents Model			NineDollars Model		
Variable	Coeff.	Std. err.	$p > |z|$	Coeff.	Std. err.	$p > |z|$
Store Rating	−0.1237***	0.1486	0.405	−0.0061***	0.0764	0.936
Relative Price	−1.0010***	0.3412	0.003	0.4783***	0.6188	0.440
Popularity	0.1491***	0.4756	0.002	−0.0010***	0.0288	0.972
Price Length	−0.2612***	0.1181	0.027	0.3932***	0.0670	0.000
Channel Used	0.5776***	0.3128	0.065	0.7410***	0.1628	0.000
Constant	0.1160***	0.5681	0.838	−2.7024***	0.6822	0.000

Source: Adapted from Kauffman and Wood (2007), by authors' permission.

Note: Model: Bivariate probit with maximum likelihood estimation. 1,718,508 data points. Wald test of $\rho = 0$: $\chi^2(1) = 3.1978$, $P[>\chi^2(1)] = 0.0737$. $-2LL = 4,101,583$. Standard errors assume clustering at the store level. Signif. levels: ***$p < 0.01$; **$p < 0.05$; *$p < 0.10$.

over about two years from March 2003 to April 2005. In contrast to our VAR model example where the expectation was for very high levels of significance for the variables, here in the context of a bivariate probit model for predicting price-endings, the "NineCents" model produces estimation outcomes (run separately) that are traditional in terms of the tightness of fit of the parameter estimates. In probit modeling, fit can be evaluated based on the likelihood that the dependent value equals 1, which would indicate the presence of either a 9¢ or $9 price-ending, captured by z-scores relative to a cumulative normal distribution. We see that the p-values associated with the z-scores for the different explanatory variables range between 0.002 to 0.003 on the low end indicating high significance, and 0.838 on the high end suggesting no association with other intermediate values. Based on our experience, such outcomes are common when we work with data sets of modest sizes, and so we conclude that there is nothing really out of the ordinary for the "NineCents" model.

The "NineDollars" model offers a somewhat different view of the data set relative to statistical significance though. Note that *Store Rating* and *Popularity* are highly insignificant at $p > |z| = 0.936$ and 0.972, respectively. Similarly, further note that two variables—*Price Length* and *Channel Used*—are highly significant, all with $p > |z| = 0.000$, which comes closer to the story that we told earlier about arbitrarily strong model fit. Even though these parameter estimates are not at the 0.000⁻ or 0.999⁺ levels, we still need to approach their interpretation with caution due to the size of the data set. With a large data set, the standard errors of the parameter estimates tend to become very small, which permits accurate estimation and high model fit.

These small examples point to the interesting differences in perspective that need to be operative for this kind of analysis. In some of the data sets that are described in the chapters in this book, it is almost certainly the case that the researchers obtained substantially *all* of the observable behavior that was available to be studied via the Internet under the research design conditions that are stated (e.g., Hahn and Zhang, Chapter 10 in this volume). This further challenges our standard practices about the usefulness of statistical inference tests and econometric analysis.

SYNTHESIS

With these observations in mind, our next steps involve contemplating some new ways of thinking about how to proceed with these kinds of analysis. In his book *Visualizing Data,* Cleveland distinguishes between two components for visualizing the structure of statistical data: graphing and fitting. He notes that:

> Graphs are needed, of course, because visualization implies a process in which information is encoded on visual displays. Fitting mathematical functions to data is needed too. Just graphing raw data, without fitting them and without graphing the fits and residuals, often leaves important aspects of data undiscovered. (Cleveland, 1993, preface)

In work that we have done with our coauthors (Kauffman and Lee, 2007), we have recognized not only the strengths that statistical analysis offers, but also its limitations in certain kinds of settings and with specific kinds of research questions. Lambert's (2000) exhortation to think about statistics as an information extraction process from noisy data is an important perspective, especially in contexts that are subject to substantial degrees of stochasticity (e.g., electronic auction bidding processes, airline revenue yield management-related prices based on changing demand, transaction making in market intermediation, and blog posting in dyadic response relationships), and is a good reminder about the "bigger picture":

> Simply stated, statistics is about extracting information from data that are noisy or uncertain. The unstated position is that all data are noisy. Twenty measurements from a small experiment are noisy, and zillions of transaction records in a data warehouse are noisy. The twenty observations are noisy because measurement errors are unavoidable. Transactions have noise because individuals generating them vary, and transactions for even one individual vary. In statistician's terms, transactions vary across individuals and vary within any one individual over time and space. If the data arise by sampling, so not all individuals are included, then errors and variability are introduced by the process that determines which individuals or population units are included in the sample. Additionally, the data many have errors or be incomplete (even in the U.S. Census). Statistics, then, is about overcoming the uncertainty, errors, and variability (noise) in the data to reveal the information hidden within (Lambert, 2000, pp. 217–218).

Statistics, however, is not the only mechanism that can effectively reveal underlying patterns in noisy data. Smyth (2001) has pointed out the opportunities associated with data mining at the intersection of statistics and computer science. The world of Internet auctions, computer networks, and electronic social networks (as we see with Facebook, MySpace, and LinkedIn, among others) are all settings in which there is great variability in the phenomena that we observe. Data mining and pattern recognition mechanisms will be especially appropriate (Smyth, 2000). With auctions, for example, in addition to understanding bidding dynamics with statistical concepts in mind, it may also be possible to develop representations of bidding behavior both within and across auctions that are quite a bit different—that demonstrate variability in the patterns of relationships among bidders and sellers within individual auctions, and for bidders across the auctions of multiple sellers over time. In lieu of the bid price paths that we see with studies of electronic auctions, there are other relationships that can be studied from a social networks perspective, and for relatedness of groups and subgroups.

We see this phenomenon in e-mail networks, too, such as what Adamic and Adar (2005) have studied for the e-mail communication social network of HP Labs relative to the structure of its organizational hierarchy (see Figure 1.1).

The figure shows that the pattern of e-mail communication tends to follow the general paths

Figure 1.1 **HP Labs E-mail Communication Patterns Map onto the Organizational Hierarchy**

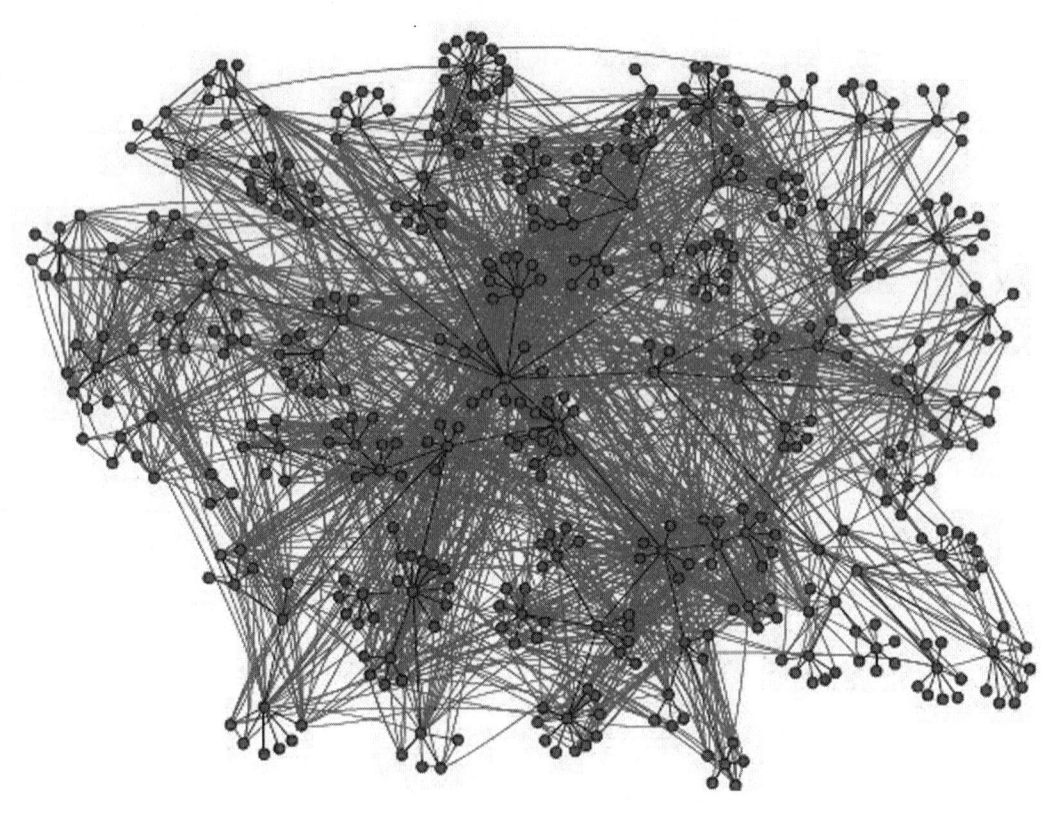

Source: Adamic and Adar (2005). Copyright © Elsevier 2005. Reprinted by permission.
Note: The light gray lines represent the e-mail communication between different people, represented by the black dots. The black lines represent connections in the organizational hierarchy.

that are established for the organizational hierarchy, relating one group of people to another group of people. Economic and strategy questions arise in such contexts, though the statistical analysis methods to answer them are not immediately obvious based on the traditional methods that most business school-trained IS, marketing, and supply-chain management faculty might think of.

Are the observed patterns of communication by e-mail value-maximizing for the organization? Do these patterns depict communication in an organization that has a healthy and effective information exchange environment for its employees? To what extent is there stochastic variation in the patterns of communication relative to on-hierarchy and off-hierarchy paths? How do the observed communication patterns adjust as different strategy requirements arise? How can they be predicted to adjust when senior management takes different actions? Although it would be hard to write down statistical models that would be of immediate use for estimation and assessment of these questions, we do envision that methods of pattern recognition from computer science will be extraordinarily useful—especially for the purposes of making comparisons between communications types and communication richness.

It may be possible to compare the communications patterns across similar business processes in different organizations, and to assess the strengths and weaknesses of their performance related

OPPORTUNITIES AND CHALLENGES FOR INFORMATION SYSTEMS RESEARCH 13

to it. In addition, it may be possible to compare business units within one organization as a means to gauge the efficacy of the units' business performance on some appropriately selected dimensions. Another possible assessment would be to evaluate for the purposes of prediction, as Lambert (2000) reminds us, the impacts on the organizational communication patterns of stochastic shocks that affect an organization.[8]

Another important point to make about this is that the kinds of data visualization and pattern recognition approaches that are possible involving a blend of statistics and computer science approaches are increasingly understood to be representative of a new toolkit of *hybrid methods*. Kauffman and Wang (2007) have recently written about the usefulness of such approaches in complex systems:

> A benefit of the use of data visualization approaches comes in the study of aspects of observed behavior in complex systems . . . that seem to defy human capacity to write down simple models and representations of likely outcomes in the presence of the dynamics of such systems. Studies of the movement of leading indicators in the macroeconomy are difficult to predict due to the underlying complexity and dynamics of the economic system. . . . Similar to this is the difficulty of predicting future prices of financial assets, given the inherent complexity of the processing of relevant information in the financial markets to yield specific asset price outcomes. In such settings, data visualization techniques offer researchers, investors and public policy-makers the equivalent of three-dimensional images that simplify the true-form n-dimensional images of the phenomena that we wish to understand. This can be said, for example, for the vast number of pharmacology studies that have been conducted to ascertain the effects of new pharmaceuticals on the human body, where the complexity of the underlying biochemical and biophysics processes can only be understood in greatly simplified form—as if the analysts were only studying several of many possible dimensions of a problem.

We can foresee many uses of such hybrid methods, and the rationale for the joint study of statistics, data mining, and pattern recognition methodologies from computer science. Continuing with the example involving e-mail communication, we present another graphical representation from Adamic, Buyukkokten, and Adar (2003) in Figure 1.2. The figure depicts the social network that occurs for one e-mail network user at one point in time, a person named Oliver, who has arrayed around him his most direct contacts via e-mail (e.g., Rika, Martina, Andres, Sergio, etc.). On the second ring of e-mail ID names, we see the contacts of Oliver's contacts, and so on out to the third ring and beyond.

The interesting and very general aspect of this representation of the e-mail network's social network is that it will have some persistence over time, with some stochastic changes. For example, some users will no longer communicate with other specific users. Friends of friends will become friends themselves, and other entirely new relationships will be established—and so on. The evolution of LinkedIn.com and similar professional networking sites reflects the ability of these new methods to study how communications vary according to the number of degrees of separation between individuals at different levels in a firm.

Although the representation in Figure 1.2 is for an e-mail network with no particular business aspects implied, it is possible to conceptualize many different settings in e-commerce in similar terms. For example, electronic procurement markets have buyers and suppliers, some of whom have close relationships that may strengthen or diminish in economic importance over time. One may also imagine edges on the social network graphs that are defined in economic terms by transac-

Figure 1.2 **A Single User's Perspective on the Club Nexis Network at Stanford, 2001**

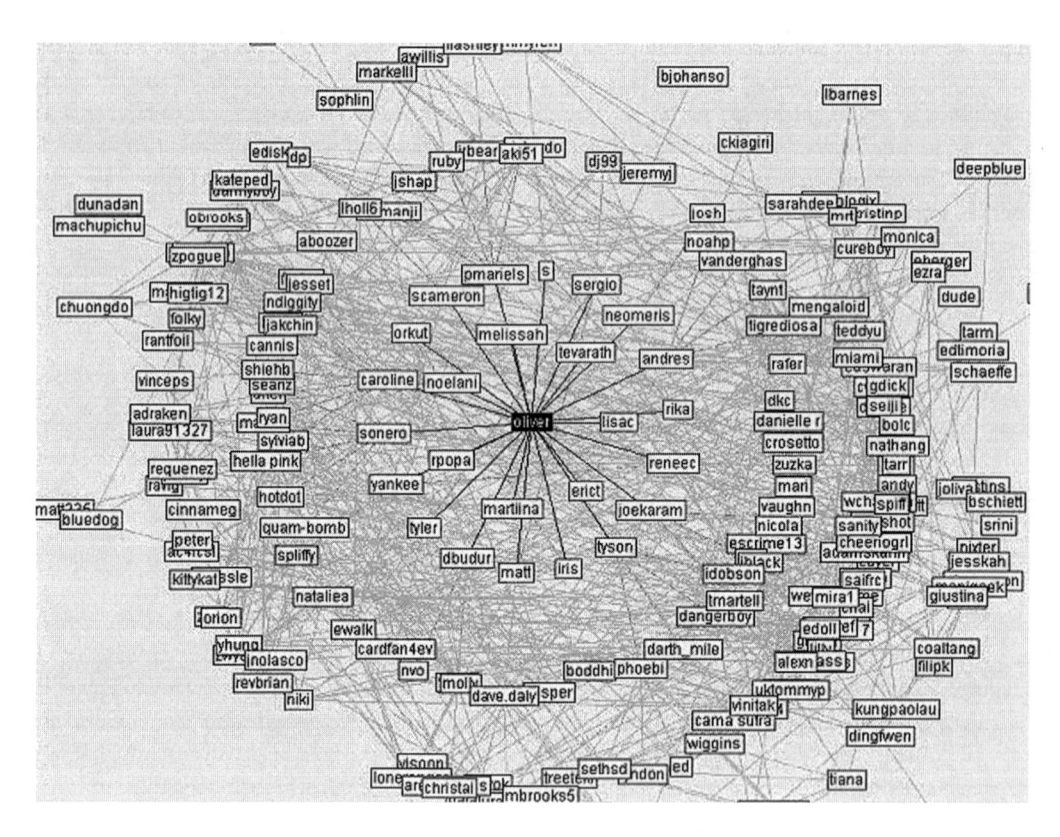

Source: Adamic et al. (2003). Reprinted by permission of the authors.

tion levels, dollar values of economic exchange, frequency of transactions, and so on. Similar to the simpler setting that we described, where users in an e-mail network continue, stop, or begin communicating, we also expect to see related dynamics at work in procurement networks. The difference though is that the participants and the e-market intermediary may have an interest in delving into the dynamics aspect of the underlying relationships, in order to find ways to support the relationships most effectively. The network of buyers and sellers that any individual buyer or supplier will see will be different—just as each user in an e-mail system will see a different group of users with whom they have contact easily reachable around them.

Understanding the underlying dynamics of these kinds of relationships puts a premium on the application of a blend of methods. Descriptive statistics will give us a toehold, and help us to answer simple factual questions regarding behavior in the network (e.g., participants, relational density, changes over time, etc.). Tools that permit the viewing of patterns in the data will be especially useful as a basis for thinking through what kinds of explanatory or predictive statistical models might be appropriate, but they are also subject to the creativity and insights of the analyst, as well as the analyst's ability to render them in a meaningful visual form (Tufte, 1990, 2001).

OPPORTUNITIES

A third area of opportunity comes with the recognition that statistical and econometric analysis in IS research should be able to be conducted with a number of alternative elucidating perspectives, as Churchman (1971) has argued from a philosophy of science perspective. It is appropriate to include the typical Leibnizian-deductive *theorize–hypothesize–test sequence,* as well as other more Lockean-inductive approaches that permit a Sherlock Holmes–like consideration of evidence in advance of choosing a theory, or testing data against a set of hypotheses (Mason and Mitroff, 1973). The former is most often referred to as *theory-testing research,* while the latter is called *theory-building research* (Kauffman and Wood, 2007). Churchman (1971) and Mason and Mitroff (1973) have also suggested other approaches that involve countertesting one theory against another in Kantian-inductive *theory verification,* and Hegelian-deductive *hybrid theory research* via the assessment of theories that provide different predictions in the same context. Nevertheless, very often, we find that IS researchers and IS journal article reviewers and associate editors are asking questions that seem mostly associated with the theorize–hypothesize–test sequence, with little regard for how their strategies might be adjusted to suit the circumstances of a given research inquiry. They are likely to ask, for example: What is the theory? Why are your hypotheses not tied to a specific theory? Is the theory true or false? Has the model been effectively specified to deliver answers about the efficacy of the theory in the particular context?

Although *structural equation modeling* is most often associated with theory testing, the use of *modification statistics,* such as the Wald and Lagrange multiplier tests, can point to the existence of paths whose removal from or insertion into a model would help to improve the overall fit of the model to the data. It has been argued that researchers who use such tests to improve their models are embarking on nothing more than a fishing expedition and yet within the Lockean-inductive approach, such moves are openly welcomed as a way to advance and build theory. In certain respects, we in the broader IS community are being held captive by a proclivity toward theory testing as the *only* way to conduct valid research with large pools of data. An interesting diversion from this line of reasoning has appeared in recent years with the introduction of TETRAD (www.phil.cmu.edu/projects/tetrad/). TETRAD uses path analysis techniques, in effect, to mine complex models from large pools of data. Often, multiple models can be produced. The challenge is then for the researcher to select and defend one of these models on the basis of theory and generalizability to a larger population. What may be remarkable about TETRAD is its potential use in conjunction with other structural modeling and even regression estimation techniques—the goal being to *trap* the most empirically and theoretically defensible model.

Historically large data sets open up the possibility of having enough degrees of freedom to partition a data set to use a portion of it to establish observed *empirical regularities* in advance of specifying the chosen theory and the hypotheses associated with it. This kind of approach has most often been observed with research in macroeconomic econometrics, especially among macroeconomic policy and rational expectations theory economists, who examine large data sets on a variety of economic indicators and do not wish to inappropriately rule out theoretical explanations prior to working with their data. This is especially true of their use of vector autoregression and Bayesian vector autoregression approaches, where the analyst specifically tries to hold off from developing a structural model or a causal model of the phenomenon of interest (Sims, 1980). Instead, the emphasis is on the residuals, and in particular, the decomposition of the variance of the residuals, so that it becomes possible to see what information they bear for the analysis. In addition, statisticians often use *data set partitioning* so that they can establish some knowledge of the analysis setting with one data set, then test an appropriate theoretical model with a second data set, and finally to validate it with additional so-called *out-of-sample data*.

In a recent study of human sleep data (exploring the effects of caffeine on sleep as well as how sleep apnea and other sleep disorders affect sleep patterns, Laxminarayan Alvarez, Ruiz, and Moonis (2006) employ a novel series of association data mining steps to uncover variables for use in later logistic regression modeling. Traditional regression analysis of large-scale data sets can reach a point where *every* variable that is included in the regression equation is significant. The point that this study makes is that a preliminary series of steps can be taken to uncover interesting patterns in the data—patterns that even if not theoretically derived can be used to identify variables for inclusion in follow-on regression analysis.

Recent research conducted by Jank, Shmueli, and their coauthors at the University of Maryland offers some path-finding new ideas on the relevance of next-generation methodologies in the pursuit of knowledge from large data sets (Hyde, Jank, and Shmueli, 2006; Jank and Shmueli, 2005, 2006). These authors have been exploring the usefulness of data visualization techniques for assessing the patterns and extracting new knowledge from large data sets in various e-commerce domains, especially online auction bidding behavior (Shmueli and Jank, 2005; Shmueli, Jank; Aris; Plaisant; and Shneiderman, 2006).

Researchers who study auctions know that there are a number of underlying determinants of how people bid, including: their level of personal utility for an item—essentially how badly they want to own it; the level of experience with auctions and dynamic pricing mechanisms that they bring to the setting; the point in time at which they are bidding prior to the close of an auction; the number of competitors that they believe are contesting their ability to purchase the item; the reservation price or maximum willingness-to-pay that they bring to the auction; and other psychological and interaction-related factors that add to the dynamics of the auction process. Figure 1.3 depicts bidding behavior that is observed in an eBay electronic auction. This figure is drawn from a joint faculty–MBA project conducted by Jank and Malu (2005) at the University of Maryland.

We can see from this innovative representation of the bidding behavior that the experienced sellers, represented by the larger squares, tend to make lower opening bids, as represented by the dark colors to the north and west in the figure. We also see that the most inexperienced bidders, represented by the smallest squares, tend to make higher opening bids, as represented by the lighter colors. Presented this way, information about the relationship between bidder experience and willingness-to-pay becomes rather apparent—even though it may be able to be generalized to other product settings. In this case, the auction item is a Bausch and Lomb microscope, which is likely to have different characteristics as a sale item on eBay than such things as consumer electronics, automobiles, collectible stamps, or Tiffany lamps. In the first two cases, it may be difficult to verify the quality of the items, but they are typically well known to potential buyers based on *Consumer Reports* information and hearsay about model quality. In the case of collectible stamps, it takes some expertise to know what is actually being offered and to know the market for collectible stamps to figure out what to bid. In the final case, Tiffany lamps, it may be hard to ascertain any particular value since most of the Tiffany items sold on eBay are known to be fakes.

Nevertheless, the sort of data visualization that is possible here seems to open up new directions for new thinking with respect to analytical style for understanding information that is embedded within data obtained in a given setting. Here we see the possibility of asking questions that are typically not contemplated in the context of statistical analysis. For example, what are the typical patterns of opening bids associated with different kinds of sale items on eBay and other electronic markets? Commodity products? Collectibles? Expensive vs. cheap items? New vs. used

OPPORTUNITIES AND CHALLENGES FOR INFORMATION SYSTEMS RESEARCH   17

Figure 1.3   **eBay Bidding in 2001 for a Bausch & Lomb Microscope**

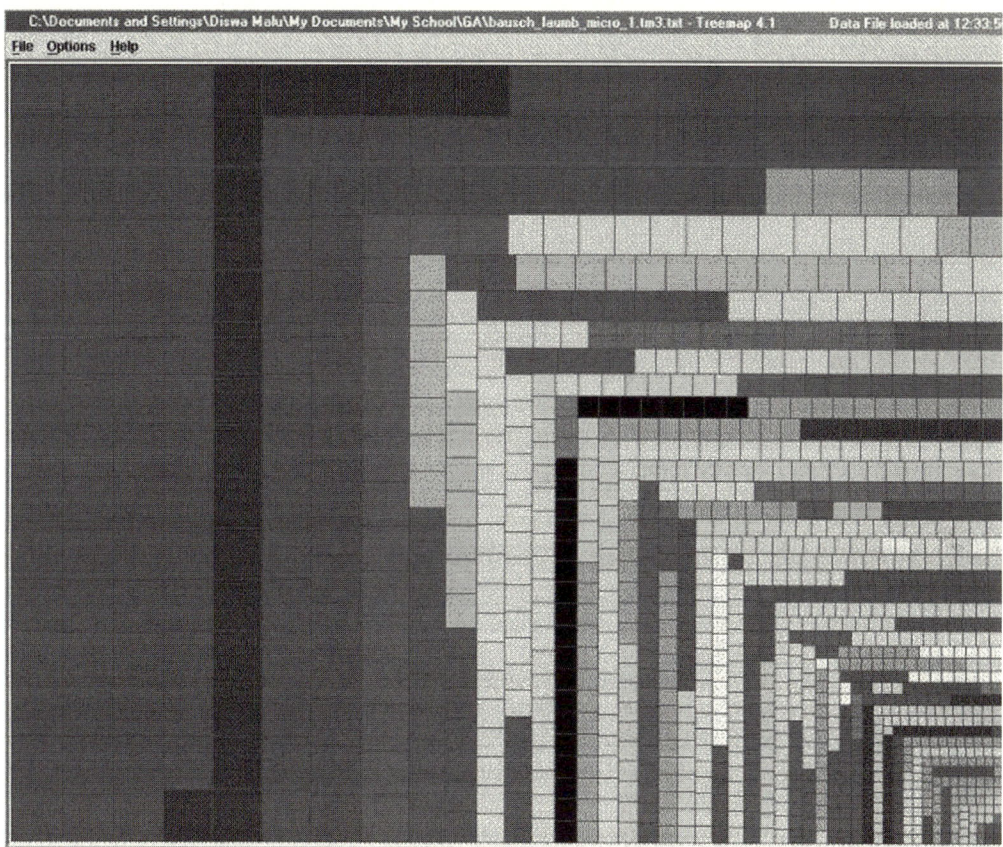

Source: www.devsmith.umd.edu/dit/infovis/analysis/treemap_ebay_analysis.htm. Reprinted by permission of the author.

Note: Seller experience is depicted by the size of the squares in the figure. Smaller squares represent sellers with less experience, and larger squares represent sellers with more experience. Experience declines from the northwest to the southeast in the figure. The different shades represent different levels of opening bids for the bidders. The authors, Jank and Malu (2005), conclude that "[m]ore experienced bidders (the largest squares) tend to start their bid process with low[er] bid[s] for this product." No conclusion is drawn that this is general behavior for experienced bidders. For additional information, see www.devsmith.umd.edu/dit/infovis/.

products? Branded vs. nonbranded products? Information goods vs. physical goods? And so on. Based on Jank and Malu's representation for opening bids, we can also imagine doing similar kinds of analysis for other aspects of online auctions. For example, what about bidding behavior at auction closing time? How can dyadic bidding interactions be captured and examined through this kind of data visualization lens?

More generally, what can we learn about time-wise changes in bidding behavior, and what happens in auctions of different mechanism designs, different durations, and different sale item contents? Figure 1.4 shows another eBay bidding example, from Jank and Shmueli (2005), this

Figure 1.4 **Bid Velocity and Bid Acceleration**

1.4a. Bid Velocity, 1st Differences

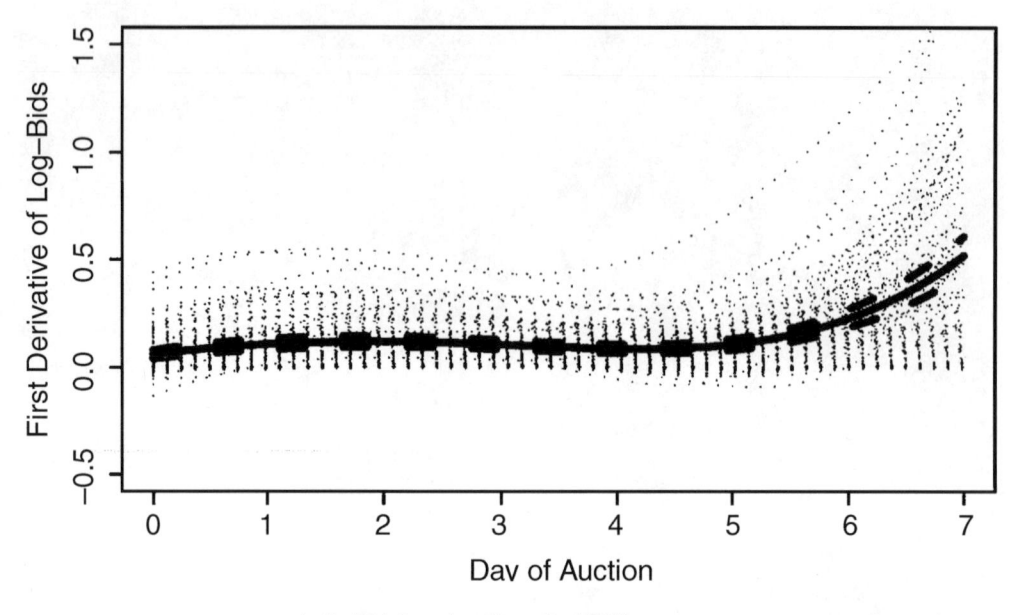

1.4b. Bid Acceleration, 2nd Differences

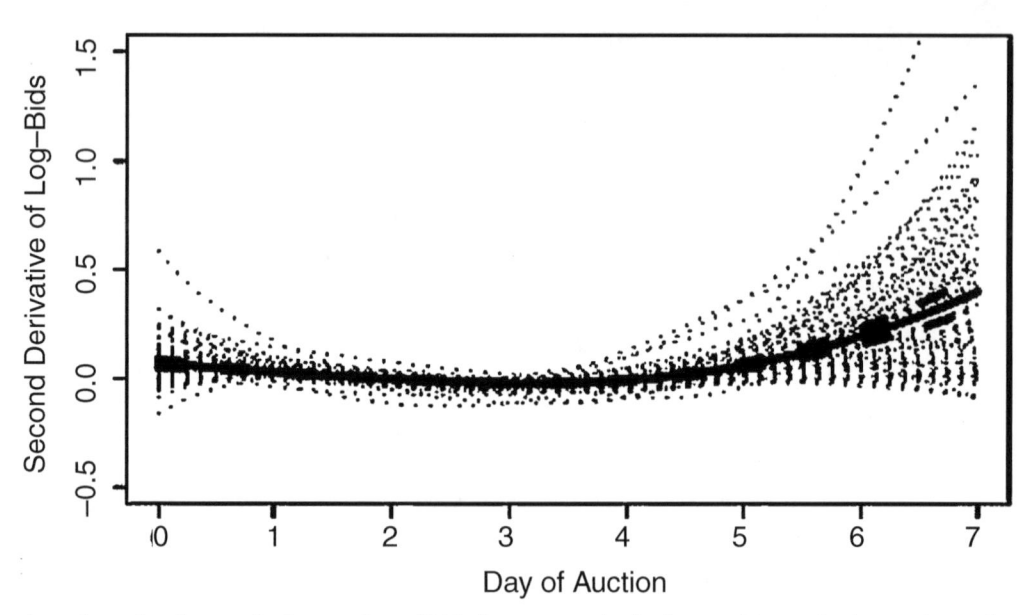

time about the changes in the number of bids from one point in time to the next in the auction—the *velocity,* and the change in the changes in the number of bids—the *acceleration.*

These measures are first derivatives and second derivatives on bid volume for a class of auctions run over seven days. Each line represents a unique auction. The measures help to surface information about the underlying bidding dynamics in an auction, and provide unusually informative visual cues about where most of the action is occurring. In Figure 1.4a, we can see that the greatest variation in bids over time appears to be occurring toward the end of the auction, when auction participants' attention needs to be most directed toward the bidding action. Note the dark trend line to capture the bid change performance across the auctions in the data set. Though the main weight of the observed change behavior appears to be occurring toward the end of the auction, examination of the behavior over time of the second derivative of the bid volume sheds light on another aspect of this data set.

Figure 1.4b shows that there is additional interesting activity occurring at the beginning of the auction also. We see an initially wide set of bid volume acceleration changes, trending both upward and downward, but this variability suggests a randomness in the behavior that appears to resolve itself in a fairly flat trend line after the first day. We are likely to be seeing evidence of unobserved heterogeneity in some explanatory variable that might help us to further understand why this kind of behavior is occurring.[9] After the bidding in this eBay auction gets going and before it comes to the closing, we see a zone of stable bid volumes, in which there is apparently less price discovery activity occurring. Building on our prior observations related to Jank and Malu's (2005) work, we might expect there to be some underlying explanations for the stability of bidding volumes during the second day up through the fifth day of the auction. For example, one explanation is that there just may not be much happening—a few bids may be received, but there is no additional volume to push away from the baseline volume. From this, one might conclude that there is a period of caution, with few bidders wanting to push prices higher, until such a time as they feel that they have to—in the sixth and seventh days—in order to be able to secure the item.

Of course, this kind of observed behavior for bid velocity and bid acceleration is likely to be specific to different e-auction sale item settings. Some auctions will be affected by the discovery of new information that may lead to much different bidding dynamics during the middle period after the opening and prior to the close. An example will illustrate this well. We are baseball fans, and when we wrote a prior draft of this chapter, the San Francisco Giants baseball player, Barry Bonds, hit a spectacular flurry of home runs in April 2007, bringing him closer to the 755 home-run record of Henry Aaron faster than most observers would have guessed. During this time, baseball memorabilia sale items that relate to the legendary home-run hitters of the sport are attracting greater interest by the day, leading up to when a new all-time record is established. It may not be surprising, as a result, to see price level and valuation changes, as well as auction bid volume adjustments occurring in the wake of the new information that comes to market.

Indeed, a vast amount of hidden information is waiting to be uncovered before we can be satisfied that we truly know how some of these e-commerce–related phenomena work. We have argued that there are great steps forward to be taken, driven by the new availability of data and by the even greater opportunities that await us to understand what these can tell us. The different approaches that we have discussed relate to how to work with theory in these data-rich contexts, how to apply post-traditional statistical methods and new data visualization techniques, and how to reinvigorate our thinking about what will be the most effective analytical style for achieving innovations in our research.

The birth of new methods and approaches to data analysis has an obvious bearing on our responsibility to train the next generation of research professors and doctoral students. More advanced training is necessary beyond the current battery of methods courses taken by the majority of students. We hope that the foregoing discussion and the chapters that form the core of this volume will provide a foundation for future coursework in advanced empirical methods.

AN OVERVIEW OF THE CHAPTERS IN THIS VOLUME

The chapters in this research volume examine some of the issues that we have discussed. They are organized into five separate sections, each of which develops a topic that relates to the overarching theme of empirical advances in economics, information systems, and electronic commerce research, and which contributes fresh perspectives on how to carry out innovative and managerially insightful work. The chapters offer innovative perspectives, fresh methods, and useful approaches that our discussion in the first four sections of this opening essay suggested as appropriate and necessary next steps. We now briefly introduce each of the remaining chapters of the book to orient the reader to their high-level contributions and their coverage of the issues that we have previously identified.

Part I. Strategies for Empirical Advances in Information Systems and E-Commerce Research

We begin with two chapters that explore new ways to think about doing research in e-commerce and information systems based on an evaluation of various philosophy of science approaches to inquiry, and emerging statistical thinking that aids in the development of stronger causal arguments about the relevant underlying effects.

Chapter 2: Research Strategies for E-Business: A Philosophy of Science View in the Age of the Internet—Robert J. Kauffman and Charles A. Wood

Kauffman and Wood provide a broad consideration of how the Internet has the potential to change current research practice in economics, information systems, and electronic commerce. The authors explore changes from the point of view of the philosophy of science in research, and show the different roles for induction, deduction, extension, and synthesis in the creation of theory in these areas. They also discuss the way that research practice is being transformed, based on the changing underlying costs of conducting research on the Internet—either by data collection with software agents, by electronic survey, or with experimental "e-testbeds" for research. The authors examine the empirical literature in e-commerce that applies a range of economic theories and econometric methods, and offer some impressions of how the new approaches are being put to good use.

Chapter 3: A Potential Outcomes Approach to Assess Causality in Information Systems Research—Sunil Mithas, Daniel Almirall, and Mayuram S. Krishnan

Mithas, Almirall, and Krishnan offer an interesting new perspective on a problem of long-standing research and managerial interest in the IS field: how to assert causality in empirical analysis involving real world data (e.g., IT investment valuation problems, systems deployment and impact analysis, and market events analysis and changing behaviors on the part of IT-adopting firms and consumers). The authors observe that the literature has had very few instances of empirical research designs that exploit near-experimental treatment conditions that give researchers significant control over their tests of theory through the manipulation of different elements of the environment. The authors' contribution to this research volume is to provide a survey of the background literature on the new methods and theories in statistics that help to get at causality without experimental controls in empirical research. They emphasize new concepts, including the idea of the *average causal effect,* and demonstrate a method that is not yet well known in IS and e-commerce research

OPPORTUNITIES AND CHALLENGES FOR INFORMATION SYSTEMS RESEARCH

circles, the *propensity score subclassification analysis* method. They illustrate how their proposed analysis approach works in the context of an empirical illustration related to causal effects in the deployment of e-customer relationship management systems.

Part II. Understanding the Dynamics and Outcomes Associated with Information Technology Investments

The issue of IT value has been one of enduring interest among senior management and IS researchers. This section of the book presents three chapters that offer new thinking about three different levels of analysis that are common in this area of research: the project, the firm, and the industry and country level. This section offers new ideas about the use of portfolio-based thinking for IT projects, revisits the application of accounting methods for identifying IT investment contributions to firm performance and value, and demonstrates a new aggregate level approach that employs stochastic production frontiers to compute the Malmquist total factor productivity index for the performance evaluation of IT industries.

Chapter 4: Empirical Analysis of Information Technology Project Investment Portfolios—Ryan Sougstad and Indranil R. Bardhan

Sougstad and Bardhan have recently been working to pioneer new techniques that combine portfolio analysis for the management of multiple IT project investments with real option analysis. The result is an interesting new methodology that creates an opportunity for managers to figure out how to time investments in specific technology projects while considering the complementarities and constraints that exist across portfolio projects. In this chapter, the authors focus on interrelated IT project portfolios and develop a new methodology that employs the log-transformed binomial option model. They illustrate their ideas using data from a health care management organization that is pursuing an e-commerce initiative. The kind of empirical analysis that the authors demonstrate is at the leading edge of new theory and methods for prospective evaluation of IT investments, and offers new ways for managers to think through the underlying conditions for the production of high business value for interrelated projects, especially those that create complex support infrastructure, interdependent software functionality, and nested real options for follow-on investments.

*Chapter 5: Evaluating Information Technology Industry Performance:
A Stochastic Production Frontier Approach—Benjamin B.M. Shao and Winston T. Lin*

The productivity and performance of IT industries relative to other traditional manufacturing and services industries is a topic of significant importance to business leaders, venture capitalists, investors, and government business policymakers. In this chapter, Shao and Lin contribute a new empirical approach for IT value that explores the use of the Malmquist total factor productivity index as a means to evaluate the extent to which IT industries in eight Organization of Economic Cooperation and Development nations outperform other indigenous industries. The authors explore the use of a stochastic production frontier model that is robust to random variation in the underlying conditions of the economy (e.g., consumer demand, economic growth, price changes, etc.) and the firm, as well as errors in the measurement of inputs and outputs. They also decompose the Malmquist index into two elements: a technological progress component and an industry efficiency component. This decomposition approach is useful because it permits the identification of efficiency levels for the production of IT capital goods in the countries under review, as well as a reading on some of the underlying reasons for why different levels are achieved.

Chapter 6: Using Accounting-Based Performance Measures to Assess the Business Value of Information Technologies and Systems—Bruce Dehning, Vernon J. Richardson, Rodney E. Smith, and Robert W. Zmud

Dehning, Richardson, Smith, and Zmud's contribution emphasizes that there are still new ideas to be explored and developed from the field of accounting that can guide senior management evaluation of IT investments. Their chapter argues that financial market measures of firm value, especially *return on equity* (ROE), should be examined in greater detail so as to find effective means to decompose ROE to show the role of IT in improving the performance of business processes. The authors propose *value chain analysis* and a *residual income model* to assess the impact of IT investments on business processes and the selection of appropriate accounting-based process measures. The residual income model is then used to link ROE directly to firm value. The framework is demonstrated using thirty-two high-tech manufacturing firms that adopted IT-based supply chain management systems. Their empirical contribution is to illustrate how ROE decomposition methodology can be used to find value from IT investments. In particular, this methodology integrates disparate parts of the business value framework into a comprehensive model for empirical analysis of the performance changes around the adoption of new IT investments.

Part III. New Approaches for Studying Mechanism Design in Online Auctions

Chapter 7: Modeling Dynamics in Online Auctions: A Modern Statistical Approach— Galit Shmueli and Wolfgang Jank

Shmueli and Jank are statisticians with a penchant for innovation in e-commerce research. In this chapter, they highlight how new statistical methods, especially functional data analysis, can offer some useful tools for creating deeper insights into the dynamic behavior of bidders in Internet auctions. Functional data analysis permits the analyst to estimate families of functions that can be used to describe different kinds of phenomena, as opposed to the estimation of individual coefficients for specific parameters. The authors illustrate their ideas with an application that encourages readers to try these new methods out for themselves. More generally, this kind of research has opened up a rich new dialogue involving statistics researchers and their colleagues in marketing, economics, IS, operations management, and computer science who are interested in the study of technology and e-commerce problems involving historically large data sets.

Chapter 8: Empirical Design of Incentive Mechanisms in Group-Buying Auctions— Her-Sen Doong, Robert J. Kauffman, Hsiangchu Lai, and Ya-Ting Zhuang

Doong, Kauffman, Lai, and Zhuang motivate and demonstrate the application of experimental research design methodologies in the development of new results on mechanism design and the use of participation incentives for group-buying auctions on the Internet. Although the authors apply their methods to a specific context, the broader context of mechanism design research offers many opportunities for the application of experimental methods. A key feature of this research is the stepwise methodology that is employed to sequentially understand the impacts of different participation incentives. The inclusion of bidder participation incentives in mechanism design is a general problem for which new managerial knowledge will be welcome. An interesting related aspect of the work on which the authors report is the contribution of a new experimental test bed on the Internet for the study of many different aspects of group-buying auctions.

Part IV. New Empirical Approaches to the Analysis of Weblogs and Digital Community Forums

As we were concluding the work on this research volume, there was much news in the background on the increasing importance of Weblogs, user-to-user Internet forums, and the freedom of information exchange made possible by the World Wide Web. This penultimate section explores some proposed empirical advances for the study of large data sets from Weblogs and community forums, and suggests the importance of two very useful methods from econometrics and statistics: random effects modeling and choice-based sampling with weighted exogenous sampling maximum likelihood estimation.

Chapter 9: Empirical Advances for the Study of Weblogs: Relevance and Testing of Random Effects Models—Kai-Lung Hui, Yee-Lin Lai, and Shun-Jian Yee

Hui, Lai, and Yee observe that much is already known about the motivation for participation in Weblogs that make it possible for people to share their political opinions as well as their innermost personal secrets. We know much less, however, about how people engage in the dyadic exchange of communications—from blogger to blog visitor and vice versa—and how this may lay the foundation for the creation of new knowledge for advertising and organizational communication. The authors propose and demonstrate the use of random effects econometric models as a means to answer research questions about the social and technological factors that underlie interpersonal information exchange with blogs. They argue that the heterogeneity of blog-based communications follows a statistical distribution, and that the use of a random effects model permits the assessment of a set of independent variables that vary across the data set but may be invariant for certain blogs in the data set. They do this by not trying to estimate parameters for the blog-level effects of certain independent variables, conserving degrees of freedom for estimation of the independent variables' effects across the entire sample.

Chapter 10: Choice-Based Sampling and Estimation of Choice Probabilities in Information Systems and E-Commerce Research—Jungpil Hahn and Chen Zhan

Zhang and Hahn continue the theme of this part of the book by proposing another empirical advance for the study of dyadic relationships in community forums and other analogous e-commerce settings (e.g., customer service via the Web, Internet-based advertising interactions, etc.). They focus on a new technique called *choice-based sampling,* which specifically treats dyads, or pairs of entities, especially when a rare event happens involving both of them. Examples of rare events involving dyads occur when a person makes the highest bid for a sale item in an online auction, or when a blog visitor replies to a blog posting by another visitor or the blog site host. Choice-based sampling involves the selection of observations according to observed values of the dependent variable; for example, an indicator for the highest bidder in an online auction, or someone who replies to a particular question in an operating system's technical support forum. To tease out the impacts of main effects variables in the applied settings that the authors are studying—in particular, open source software development forums on SourceForge.net—they show why it is statistically inappropriate to use standard maximum likelihood methods, and instead, they recommend the use of a weighted estimator that takes into account the fraction of the events that are sampled for which the dependent variable takes on a specific value. We expect the methods that are discussed in this chapter—similar to the new thinking of Kauffman and Wood, and Mithas, Almiral, and Krishnan that are showcased in Part I of this book—to have an important impact on the methods choices of IS researchers in the years ahead.

Part V. Looking Forward: Challenges, Transformations, and Advances

Chapter 11: Debating the Nature of Empirical E-Commerce Research: Issues, Challenges, and Directions—Vijay Gurbaxani, Henry C. Lucas, Jr., and Paul P. Tallon

No research volume that claims to offer insights on empirical advances in a research area is complete without some consideration and evaluation of whether the contributions of work are likely to be meaningful. In this chapter, Gurbaxani and Lucas were interviewed by Tallon, who crafted a set of questions that get at the heart of these issues. Are IS and e-commerce researchers studying the right problems? Are they doing the research in an appropriate manner? Are the results meaningful in the sense of our field's cumulative scientific tradition? Is the work of high managerial relevance? What about the theoretical ideas that have been created along the way? How does this help us to make an impact on MBA education? And to what extent can we expect to succeed as a discipline in the pursuit of this kind of knowledge? The good news is that the authors offer high-spirited dialogue, insightful commentary, and meaningful conclusions in lieu of "questions for future research." We are fortunate to have input from these academic leaders to wrap up this volume on such a thoughtful and practical note.

CONCLUSION

The chapters that comprise this research volume reflect the spirited dialogue that the editors encouraged, leading to high-quality contributions of new knowledge to empirical research on IS and e-commerce. We think this book will be a valuable contribution that provides useful reading materials for doctoral students in seminars in these areas, and informs active researchers who wish to expand their methodological repertoire and broaden their understanding of the range of theoretical perspectives that may be appropriate to driving their future research.

The difficulty in this kind of editorial enterprise always comes with when to bring the project to a close. We know quite a few others who are conducting pathfinding works in IS and e-commerce who also demonstrate empirical advances. As such, our choices of the authors and works that we have included can only be indicative of the true scope of innovation that is currently under way; it can never represent all of the ongoing developments. In spite of this, the samples that we have selected for development and presentation in this research volume should be useful in terms of the theoretical ideas they offer, the models they discuss, and the methods they showcase. They capture the spectrum of approaches in empirical research in the discipline, with multiple bases in survey research, experimental design, empirical analysis methods, case study approaches, and simulation of analytical models. Although we have tended to put greater emphases on research designs that involve large-scale data collection from the Internet, the reader should recognize that the richness of research in the areas that we have covered is largely driven by their diversity of scientific inquiry.

NOTES

1. The interested reader should see Wegman (1995) and Huber (1992, 1994) for additional information on the relative sizes of different kinds of data sets, and especially the sizes of the largest ones, as viewed in the 1990s. The data one can store on a piece of paper is about 10^2 bytes, with a hard disk having about 10^{10} (about 80 gigabytes) or 10^{11} bytes (400 gigabytes), to huge and massive storage solutions of between 10^{12} by 10^{15} bytes (terabytes and petabytes). The largest sizes occur in the context of government and very large corporate operations, and the physical sciences, including physics, meteorology, astronomy, and so on.

2. Stokes (2004) makes a related point about recent discussions of the move from traditional econometrics to *computational econometrics,* and the new role it will find as a research tool for building and testing theory in economic contexts where large amounts of data are available and the setting is characterized by complex relationships.

3. Intraday access to data has now reached the point where over two-thirds of all New York Stock Exchange trades are triggered by computer algorithms. So-called program-trades detect arbitrage opportunities between the current price of a security and the futures price of a portfolio containing this same security. As securities markets have become increasingly electronic, real-time data access and complex portfolio pricing models have emerged as a source of competitive advantage—and the firms with the faster capabilities will have an advantage.

4. Anecdotal evidence suggests that it is becoming increasingly difficult to collect survey data. Not only are survey respondents among groups such as the Fortune 500 surveyed too often, but firms seem increasingly unreceptive and even resistant to academic data collection efforts. This factor is particularly acute in research involving *matched surveys.*

5. Interesting supplemental reading to the chapters in this book is Galit Shmueli's (2006) blog, "BZST—Musings on Business and Statistics (Oops, Data Analysis)." She writes from the perspective of a statistician who is challenged to find meaning for statistical knowledge in her MBA teaching. Although there are humorous entries, most of them are *seriously* good, especially one entry on "*p*-values in LARGE data sets."

6. Although many doctoral programs, particularly in North America, employ a breadth requirement for students to take courses in disciplines outside their immediate area of study, the methods that will undoubtedly be important in the analysis of large data sets will almost certainly emerge from the intersection of disciplines. Analysis of customer relationship management data in a marketing context, for example, not only calls for a broad understanding of data mining techniques but also crosses into computer science and IS. Similarly, an understanding of real options and value-at-risk models in IS requires more than a rudimentary knowledge of financial portfolio analysis. The challenge of redesigning doctoral seminars to address the need for cross-disciplinary methods will not be trivial.

7. We actually showed that this was the case by finding only 1,793 price changes among 123,680 total daily price observations by firm by product and by day in our data set (Kauffman and Wood, 2007).

8. Imagine, for example, the changes in the patterns of communications (e-mail and otherwise) that have occurred in organizations that have been affected by some leading news events in 2007: inappropriate personnel actions for federal court justices by the leadership at the United States Department of Justice; the "troop surge" to boost military strength in Baghdad, Iraq and its impacts on communications in the Department of Defense; and the unfortunate killings at Virginia Tech, and the echoing shocks that have occurred across the safety and security departments and senior administrations of many American universities.

9. Anecdotal evidence from the stock market, and the daily start-up of trading in different equities, is subject to similar randomness in the bidding, and has been recognizing that trading will be more orderly in the presence of an appropriate start-up mechanism (e.g., the supply–demand call market mechanism that has been used by the New York Stock Exchange at the opening of the market every day).

REFERENCES

Abello, J.; Pardalos, P.M.; and Resende, M.G.C. 2002. *Handbook of Massive Data Sets.* Norwell, MA: Kluwer Academic.

Adamic, L., and Adar, E. 2005. How to search a social network. *Social Networks,* 27, 3, 187–203.

Adamic, L.A.; Buyukkokten, O.; and Adar, E. 2003. A social network caught in the Web. *First Monday,* 8, 6. Available at www.firstmonday.org/issues/issue8_6/adamic/index.html (accessed May 20, 2007).

Bergen, M.; Kauffman, R.J.; and Lee, D.W. 2005. Beyond the hype of frictionless markets: Evidence of heterogeneity in price rigidity on the Internet. *Journal of Management Information Systems,* 22, 2, 57–89.

———. 2007. Evaluating theories of image effects and rational inattention: An empirical study of price points in Internet-based selling. Paper presented at the Twentieth Anniversary Symposium on Competitive Strategy, Economics and Information Systems, at the Hawaii International Conference on Systems Science, Kona, HI, January 3.
Cahill, M.H.; Lambert, D.; Pinheiro, J.C.; and Sun, D.X. 2002. Detecting fraud in the real world. In J. Abello, P.M. Pardalos, and M.G.C. Resende, eds., *Handbook of Massive Data Sets,* Norwell, MA: Kluwer Academic, 911–929.
Churchman, C.W. 1971. *The Design of Inquiring Systems.* New York: Basic Books.
Clemons, E.K. 2007. An empirical investigation of third-party seller-rating systems in e-commerce: The case of buySAFE. *Journal of Management Information Systems,* 24, 2, 43–71.
Cleveland, W.S. 1993. *Visualizing Data.* Summit, NJ: Hobart Press.
Davis, F.D. 1989. Perceived usefulness, ease of use, and user acceptance of information technology. *MIS Quarterly,* 13, 3, 319–340.
Greene, W. 2000. *Econometric Analysis,* 4th ed. New York: Macmillan.
Han, K.; Kauffman, R.J.; and Nault, B.R. 2004. Information exploitation and interorganizational systems ownership. *Journal of Management Information Systems,* 21, 2, 109–135.
Hand, D.J. 1994. Deconstructing statistical questions. *Journal of the Royal Statistical Society Series A,* 157, 3, 317–356.
Hoyle, R.H. 1999. *Statistical Strategies for Small Sample Research.* Thousand Oaks, CA: Sage, 1999.
Huber, P.J. 1992. Issues in computational data analysis. In Y. Dodge and J. Whitaker, eds., *Computational Statistics: Proceedings of the Tenth Symposium on Computational Statistics,* 2. Heidelberg: Physica Verlag.
Huber, P.J. 1994. Huge data sets. In R. Dutter and W. Grossmann, eds., *Computational Statistics: Proceedings of the Twelfth Symposium on Computational Statistics.* Heidelberg: Physica Verlag.
Hyde, V.; Jank, W.; and Shmueli, G. 2006. Investigating concurrency in online auctions through visualization. *American Statistician,* 60, 3, 241–250.
Jank, W. and Malu, D. 2005. Information visualization. Web site-based presentation with slides, Smith School of Business, University of Maryland, College Park. Available at www.devsmith.umd.edu/dit/infovis/ (accessed May 20, 2007).
Jank, W. and Shmueli, G. 2005. Profiling price dynamics in online auctions using curve clustering. Working paper, Smith School of Business, University of Maryland, College Park.
———. 2006. Functional data analysis in electronic commerce research. *Statistical Science,* 21, 2, 155–166.
Kamath, S. 2001. On mining scientific data sets. In R. Grossman, C. Kamath, W. Kegelmeyer, V. Kumar, and R. Namburu, eds., chapter 3, *Data Mining for Scientific and Engineering Applications.* New York: Kluwer Academic, 1–22.
Kauffman, R.J. and Lee, D.W. 2007. Should we expect less price rigidity in Internet-based retailing? Working paper, Center for Advancing Business through Information Technology, W.P. Carey School of Business, Arizona State University, Tempe.
Kauffman, R.J. and Wang, B. 2007. Developing rich insights on public Internet firm entry and exit based on survival analysis and data visualization. Working paper, Center for Advancing Business through Information Technology, W.P. Carey School of Business, Arizona State University, Tempe.
Kauffman, R.J. and Wood, C.A. 2007. Price change timing in Internet-based selling. *Managerial and Decision Economics,* 28, 1–22.
Kline, R.B. 2004. *Beyond Significance Testing: Reforming Data Analysis Methods in Behavioral Research.* Washington, DC: American Psychological Association.
Lambert, D. 2000. What use is statistics for massive data? In J. E. Kolassa and D. Oakes, eds., *Crossing Boundaries: Statistical Essays in Honor of Jack Hall,* Lecture Notes Monograph Series, Volume 43, Institute for Mathematical Sciences, Beachwood, OH, 217–226.
Laxminarayan, P.; Alvarez, S.A.; Ruiz, C.; and Moonis, M. 2006. Mining statistically significant associations for exploratory analysis of human sleep data. *IEEE Transactions on Information Technology in Biomedicine,* 10, 3, 440–450.
Lutkepohl, H. 1990. Asymptotic distributions of impulse response functions and forecast error variance decompositions of vector autoregressive models. *Review of Economics and Statistics,* 72, 1, 116–125.
Mason, R. O. and Mitroff, I.I. 1973. A program for research on management information systems. *Management Science,* 19, 5, 475–487.

Melville, N.; Kraemer, K.L.; and Gurbaxani, V. 2004. Information technology and organizational performance: An integrative model of IT business value. *MIS Quarterly* 28, 2, 283–322.
Shmueli, G. 2006. *p*-values in LARGE data sets. Blog: BZST—Musings on Business and Statistics (Oops, Data Analysis), April 27. Available at bzst.blogspot.com/2006/04/p-values-in-large-datasets.html (accessed May 20, 2007).
Shmueli, G. and Jank, W. 2005. Visualizing online auctions. *Journal of Computational and Graphical Statistics,* 14, 2, 299–319.
Shmueli, G.; Jank, W.; Aris, A.; Plaisant, C.; and Shneiderman, B. 2006. Exploring auction databases through interactive visualization. *Decision Support Systems,* in press.
Sims, C. 1980. Macroeconomics and reality. *Econometrica,* 48, 1, 1–48.
Smyth, P. 2000. Data mining: Data analysis on a grand scale. *Statistical Methods in Medical Research,* 9, 309–327.
———. 2001. Data mining at the interface of computer science and statistics. In R. Grossman, C. Kamath, W. Kegelmeyer, V. Kumar and R. Namburu, eds., *Data Mining for Scientific and Engineering Applications,* chapter 3. New York: Kluwer Academic, 35–62.
Stokes, H.H. 2004. Econometric software as theoretical research tool. In C.G. Renfro, ed., *Computational Econometrics: Its Impact on the Development of Quantitative Economics.* Amsterdam: IOS Press, 183–188.
Tufte, E.R. 1990. *Envisioning Information.* Cheshire, CT: Graphics Press.
———. 2001. *The Visual Display of Quantitative Information,* 2d ed. Cheshire, CT: Graphics Press.
Vingron, M. 2001. Bioinformatics needs to adopt statistical thinking. Editorial, *Bioinformatics,* 17, 5, 389–390.
Wegman, E.J. 1995. Huge data sets and the frontiers of computational feasibility. *Journal of Computational and Graphical Statistics,* 4, 4, 281–295.
———. 2000. Visions: New techniques and technologies in statistics. *Computational Statistics,* 15, 133–144.
Weiss, S.M. and Indurkhya, N. 1998. *Predictive Data Mining: A Practical Guide.* San Francisco: Morgan Kaufmann.

PART I

STRATEGIES FOR EMPIRICAL ADVANCES IN INFORMATION SYSTEMS AND E-COMMERCE RESEARCH

CHAPTER 2

RESEARCH STRATEGIES FOR E-BUSINESS

A Philosophy of Science View in the Age of the Internet

ROBERT J. KAUFFMAN AND CHARLES A. WOOD

Abstract: *Just as the Internet has changed the way many businesses conduct business, it can also change the way that academic researchers design and execute research in e-business management. We present a series of revolutionary research strategies that employ six new data-collecting methodologies that can be used in conjunction with Internet technology. Data-collecting agents can gather very large amounts of data from the World Wide Web in a fraction of the time and the cost required to gather data using traditional research methodologies. Online experiments, online judgment tasks, and online surveys expand the reach of the researcher and reduce the cost when compared with traditional experiments, judgment tasks, and surveys. Because of the vast amount of data available online, research designs such as massive quasi-experiments can be conducted that allow the researcher to find subjects who meet some predetermined requirements without taking them out of their own environment, or some data that match a set of experimental or empirical test conditions. Finally, log files can be used to track a person's movements and actions through a Web site. We investigate these relatively new tools from a philosophy of science perspective. Using Runkel and McGrath's three-horned dilemma model for traditional research methodologies as a basis, we develop a framework that illustrates the strengths and weaknesses of these new tools relative to the research design flexibility that they permit. We find that they enable advances in empirical research that would be otherwise difficult to implement using traditional research methods.*

Keywords: *Data Collection, Electronic Commerce, Empirical Research, IT, Philosophy of Science, Research Methodologies, Online Surveys, Software Agents*

INTRODUCTION

The United States Census Bureau defines *e-business* as any process that a business organization conducts over an information technology (IT) or computer-mediated network, such as the Internet (Mesenbourg, 2004). This includes e-commerce transactions, reputation system postings, and other activities that businesses may conduct over the Web. There has been tremendous growth in e-business transactions over the past several years, despite the burst of the "dot-com bubble," and this growth trend is likely to continue. For example, comScore (www.comscore.com), an online business tracking company, reports that business-to-consumer (B2C) e-commerce spending increased 20.1 percent from US$67.2 billion in January–June 2005 to US$80 billion during the same period in 2006 (Lipsman, 2007). The U.S. total for 2006 is expected to be $170 billion, with about $102 billion of that coming in the non-travel category. Travel e-commerce will account for about 45 percent of the total, with $30.3 billion in January–June 2005 growing to $34.7 billion in January–June 2006, a 14.7 percent growth rate. Non-travel spending is growing faster at 24.6 percent. Online auctions are included in the B2C surge. For example, in 2005, eBay, the premier online auction retailer with a dominant market share of the online auction market share, reported record net revenues of US$4.55 billion, up 39.1 percent from 2004 (Securities Exchange Commission, 2006). Reports for business-to-business (B2B) e-commerce sales are even more impressive. The most recent actual statistics suggest that the U.S. economy's B2B e-commerce sales reached about $1.8 trillion in 2004, representing about 20 percent of the total of all B2B sales of $9.1 trillion (Lenard and Britton, 2006).

For researchers, the growth over the past ten years in e-business has produced a wealth of data that few might have imagined would become available to study online shopping. The research now includes books (Ghose and Sundararajan, 2006), pharmaceuticals (Stylianou, Kumar, and Robbins, 2005), digital music (Tang and Lu, 2001), and videos (Dellarocas, Awad, and Zhang, 2004), as well as other kinds of consumer behaviors related to brand preferences (Chu, Choi, and Song, 2005), price dispersion (Baye, Morgan, and Scholten, 2004; Baylis and Perloof, 2002), distribution channels (Tang and Xing, 2001), peer-to-peer (P2P) networks (Asvanund et al., 2004; Gopal, Bhatacharjee, and Sanders, 2006), cross-national differences (Mahmood, Bagchi, and Ford, 2004), digital music sampling (Tu and Lu, 2006), shopbot performance (Smith, 2002; Smith and Brynjolfsson, 2001), and consumer trust (Urban, Sultan, and Qualls, 2000). For example, most online auctions are public and viewable by researchers and the research has produced studies on bidding behaviors (Ariely and Simonson, 2003; Bapna et al., 2004; Shmueli and Jank, 2005; Shmueli et al., 2006), and fraud (Gregg and Scott, 2006). Today, online portals and Internet retailers, such as Yahoo (www.yahoo.com), Google (www.google.com), Amazon (www.amazon.com), and Barnes and Noble.com (www.bn.com), list all kinds of search information and prices online, allowing researchers to track price changes and competition (Ghose, Smith, and Telang, 2006; Walter et al., 2006), book sales and the influence of online reviews (Chevalier and Mayzlin, 2003), and evidence of portal use (Lee, Zufryden, and Drèze, 2003). The same is true in the digital music and digital entertainment arena, where the availability of harvestable data is also rapidly growing (Bockstedt, Kauffman, and Riggins, 2006). Meanwhile, the UseNet newsgroup lists have messages that number in the trillions. Moreover, online comments are available on everything from reactions to transactions with "bricks and mortar" business to reactions to online auction sales to growth projections from stock analysts. Finally, the growth in use of radio frequency identification (RFID) technologies will give rise to even more data, as data collection capabilities move in the mobile organizational systems and technology arena (Curtin, Kauffman, and Riggins, 2007).

While much has been written about the benefits that the Internet will have on the ease of commerce, very little has been written on the benefits that the Internet will have on research data collection and research design, and the academic facilitation of a more advanced managerial understanding of key e-business phenomena. Some notable exceptions are Kauffman, March, and Wood (2000), Wood and Ow (2005), and Allen, Burk, and Davis (2006). In many different disciplines, researchers have been faced with problems involving inadequate sample size, unrealistic representation of constructs, faulty time constraints, and unacceptable cost constraints. In this article, we discuss revolutionary strategies for research design and data collection for e-commerce and e-business-related research in a way that reflects a maturing awareness of the new capabilities of IT and the World Wide Web. We do this from a *philosophy of science* perspective, so that it is possible to see how current advances have the capacity to conceptually change the way we think about conducting research. We also consider some of the newer approaches to data collection and hypothesis testing where there are new opportunities and emerging techniques that make it possible to obtain more subjects in a population sample. This, in turn, will support more valid and statistically significant findings and new depths of managerial insight. Some of the new research tools that we will discuss also reflect somewhat different approaches, making substitution of new research designs possible. Data collection on the Internet has the potential to provide virtually equivalent data collection capabilities that can generate more subjects with lower costs, fewer strict assumptions, greater realism, and less contamination of research subjects' response capabilities.

We develop theory-based arguments and illustrations that are intended to answer the following research questions:

- How can data collection be enhanced through the use of Internet-based tools? What are its strengths and weaknesses?
- What research designs are facilitated when using the new tools that were previously infeasible with traditional research methodologies? Where will the new tools probably not have an impact?
- How can we understand the nature of the underlying changes in research from the multiple points of view that are present in the philosophy of science? What predictions will they enable us to make that affect use of the new tools?

We answer these questions by examining the use of new tools for data collection in the context of existing literature, and the research designs that are particularly applicable in the presence of the new data collection methodologies. We develop a framework that illustrates the strengths and weaknesses of these new tools from a philosophy of science perspective. The articles that we will examine employ these data collection techniques with respect to *theory generalization, theory building, theory verification,* and *hybrid theory construction* to address specific research design challenges in e-business research. Overall, our conclusions point to the revolutionary nature of the advances that are occurring in research design and data collection, and how to think about them to develop the most effective designs for research on a variety of e-business management problems.

LITERATURE

Before we discuss how the new Internet-based data collection techniques change our capabilities to develop effective research designs, we first consider the basis for this kind of inquiry in philosophy of science terms, and with respect to the current measurement models that are typically used in information systems (IS) and e-commerce-related research. Our assessment is based on existing literature and it points out a new way for researchers to think about how to answer key research questions that can improve the process of e-business management.

Inquiry Systems and Empirical Research

C. West Churchman (1971), the leading commentator on the practice and process of management science research in the past generation, defines *inquiry* as an activity that uses observational data to produce knowledge. The approach to developing new knowledge in the Singerian-Churchmanian view allows for the possibility of behavioral adjustments to be made by researchers when the circumstances of scientific inquiry necessitate change or evolve. This occurs, for example, when new technologies allow the investigation of emerging research questions and the undertaking of innovative research designs when these would be difficult or impossible without the new technology. Churchman describes five different *inquiring systems*—lenses or means for understanding what is true in different research inquiries—that can be used for research: the Leibnizian, Lockean, Kantian, Hegelian, and Singerian-Churmanian inquiring systems. The first four inquiring systems are named for different philosophers of science, each of whom viewed knowledge acquisition through a particular inquiring system lens. The fifth, Singer, was Churchman's doctoral adviser, and someone who had a great personal impact on Churchman's view of inquiring systems. See Table 2.1.

Mason and Mitroff (1973) have suggested that Churchman's models of inquiry are useful as a basis for creating evidence in the context of management IS research. We believe that this is also true for research designs and data collection involving, e-commerce, e-business management, and the Internet. In this section, we describe each of the *inquiring systems* in terms of their key characteristics and approaches in research, as a basis for understanding what opportunities Internet-based tools offer for research via the literature.

Theory Generalization Research

Leibnizian inquiry involves theorizing first through deduction and then collecting data to support an appropriate theory. This is done by forming hypotheses based upon widely accepted theories and models, or from theories and models that are used in similar situations. In this way, researchers are able to confirm existing theory and extend accepted theory into new areas. We will refer to research that examines data from the point of view of theory with a Leibnizian perspective as *theory generalization research,* since research articles of this type tend to generalize theory to show its applicability in other areas.

Theory Building Research

Lockean inquiry involves data collection or observation first, and then development of theories through induction that describe the observations. From a research perspective, Lockean analysis involves developing theories when there is a wide consensus about an unexplained relationship. It also involves testing the limits of existing theoretical models based upon observations, especially when these observations do not fit within an existing theoretical framework. The existing theoretical models, then, are adjusted to accommodate the new observations. When contrasted with Leibnizian inquiry, Lockean inquiry is used to understand a situation where there is no argument about the observations of the phenomenon, but little in the way of explanatory theory. Leibnizian inquiry, in contrast, is used when theory exists to explain this phenomenon or similar phenomena. If opposing theory already exists, then the Lockean approach cannot be used, which points out the need for more in-depth induction. We will refer to research that examines data using Lockean inquiry as *theory building research.*

Theory Verification and Falsification Research

Building on our prior comments, we next come to *Kantian inquiry.* This approach is used to delve more deeply into a research phenomenon of interest through *induction.* In contrast to Lockean inquiry—which is also inductive by nature—Kantian inquiry is not concerned with preserving exist-

Table 2.1

An Overview of Churchman's Five Inquiring Systems

Inquiring system	Approach	Main features
Leibnizian	Theory generalization	Information derived from axioms or models; formal, symbolic, mathematical representations; theorem and proof; best models developed; well-defined problems
Lockean	Theory building	Experimental; raw data, empirical approach used; inductive methods applied to well-defined problems
Kantian	Theory verification/ falsification	Multimodel, synthetic systems; interaction between theory and data; blend Leibnizian and Lockean inquiry; assume alternative theoretical explanations; applicable to moderately ill-structured problems
Hegelian	Hybrid theory construction	Antithetical representations of a problem, opposing theories; focus is on underlying theoretical assumptions; applicable to "wickedly" ill-structured problems
Singerian-Churchmanian	Meta-research	Flexible approach, emphasizing continual learning and adaptation through feedback; involves conversion of ill-structured problems into structured ones, and vice versa; other inquiring systems nested within it

Note: Adapted from Mason and Mitroff (1973, pp. 480–483).

ing theory. Instead, it seeks to rigorously test existing theory and either verify or falsify it. Then, if needed, the next step is to develop new theory to explain the new observations. Kantian analysis is mainly concerned with maintaining objectivity in the face of existing explanatory theory. It tends to be employed when researchers think an existing theory proves itself to be inadequate based on inconsistent research, or is fatally flawed in its explanatory power based upon new observations. We call this kind of inquiry *theory verification and falsification research.*

Hybrid Theory Construction Research

Hegelian inquiry involves conflicts and clashes between theoretical interpretations of similar phenomena in research. The Hegelian approach is to combine two or more conflicting theories to arrive at an explanatory combination of theories. This process encourages the researcher to assess conflicting theories through *deduction* to determine the range of their appropriateness. Thereafter, it is appropriate for the researcher to collect data to see whether it supports the new *hybrid theory*—or, as Poole and van de Ven (1989) have suggested, to identify the degree of the paradox in the explanations offered by alternative theories in the presence of the same data. Hegelian research, then, concentrates on bringing conflicting theories together as it examines limitations that exist for each theory, and when each might be appropriately used. We will refer to Hegelian inquiry as *hybrid theory construction.*

Meta-Research

Singerian-Churchmanian inquiry is a meta-research approach. It directs the researcher toward the selection of the proper inquiring system that will support advances in the acquisition of knowledge related to some problem or phenomenon of interest. Since Singerian-Churchmanian research does not analyze data, we will not concentrate on this mode of inquiry. However, the reader should recognize that this chapter might be considered as an instance of *Singerian-Churchmanian inquiry*, since it discusses how other inquiring systems can be flexibly implemented in e-business research, and what synthesis is possible to shed light on how e-business research insights are acquired with new data-collecting tools and research designs.

All these inquiring systems eventually involve some sort of data collection. But at their heart lay either the process of induction or process of deduction. *Induction* stresses the importance of data and observation. Data and observation enable the researcher to develop new theories. However, one concern with induction is that, when a small sample is used, its results cannot be generalized to an entire population. As a result, theories developed through induction are suspect for their lack of validity across other samples in the relevant population. *Deduction* conversely uses logic to arrive at a theory and then tests that theory using data and analysis. To support deductive efforts, data collection is also required. With the use of appropriate statistical analysis tools, the larger the data set, the less likely that the researcher will draw misleading conclusions from the analysis of the data (Beutler, 1996; Kendall and Flannery-Schroeder, 1998). In the past, Churchman (1971) has stressed that researchers should pursue ways to automate the collection of data, or some means to assist human researchers with data collection, so that they will be freed up to concentrate on research design and the interpretation of the research results.

The challenge with deduction is that the initial theory must be reasonably "fully formed," because otherwise empirical researchers will exclude essential aspects of the phenomenon under study (Mitroff and Mason, 1982). Induction answers this problem by allowing the examination of data to find patterns or relationships that may exist. Induction requires even more data than deduction though. When induction is used, researchers will often split their data sets into two or more portions. One portion of a data set is used to develop an initial reading on what relationships may exist. Then deduction is used to develop theories as to why these relationships exist. Thereafter, other portions of the data set can be used to statistically verify the new theoretical relationships that are asserted. As the reader might guess, each data set must be large enough so that the statistically significant relationships can be observed. In addition, the size of each data set is especially important when using modern statistical analysis techniques. The tension that exists, however, is that we have rarely—and usually only with some difficulty and cost—been able to develop data sets large enough to afford a researcher the necessary degrees of freedom to make this process of testing, deduction, and retesting easy to accomplish.

A Philosophy of Science Assessment of Alternative Research Methods

Data collection plays an intrinsic role in the execution of the inductive and deductive research methodologies in empirical research. It involves not only retrieving data but also interpreting and coding data. When introducing new ways to collect data, it is appropriate to review and assess existing research methodologies to see how they compare. McGrath (1982) helps us to put this comparison in a philosophy of science assessment perspective by discussing how alternative research methodologies may have recognizable strengths in one area but may be flawed in other areas. See Runkel and McGrath (1972) for a graphical representation of the *three-horned dilemma* of precision, generality, and realism. We show its main elements in Table 2.2, with a somewhat different interpretation.

The "three horns" of Runkel and McGrath's framework are *realism, generality,* and *precision*. Because of limitations of the traditional ways to collect data, no research methodology can be general, realistic, and precise all at the same time. Runkel and McGrath describe these research

Table 2.2

Three-Horned Dilemma for Research Methodologies of Runkel and McGrath (1972)

Methodology	Setting type	Emphasis	Precision	Behavior discovery
Field study	Natural setting	Realism	Low	Particular behavior system
Field experiment	Natural setting	Realism	Medium	Particular behavior system
Experimental simulation	Altered setting	Realism, some precision	Medium high	Tending to particular behavior system
Lab experiment	Altered setting	Precision	High	Tending to universal behavior system
Judgment task	Unaltered setting	Precision	Medium high	Universal behavior system
Sample survey	Unaltered setting	Generality	Medium	Universal behavior system
Formal theory	Free of setting	Generality	Medium	Tending to universal behavior system
Computer simulation	Free of setting	Generality, some realism	Medium low	Tending to particular behavior system

metrologies as *dilemmatic*, because of the choices that relate to the data collection performed in each research approach to establish truth and consistency with a proposed theory.

Consider the following research methodologies in terms of the manner in which they enable the researcher to collect data:

- *Formal theory, analytical modeling, and computer simulations.* These methods require no data collection. Instead, they generate their own data and results based on theories they assert, and, as a result, can be used to test ways of thinking about relationships between and among constructs.
- *Field studies.* These involve primary data collection and case studies, for which a researcher collects data from a research site or multiple sites.
- *Experiments* involve testing the effects of some stimulus against some control. Runkel and McGrath mention three types of experiments:
  - Laboratory experiments allow researchers to examine situations stripped of their complicating environmental context.
  - Field experiments are often undertaken in the context of workgroups, software development teams, or the firm. Therefore, they are more realistic, but they are also less precise than laboratory experiments, since the latter attempt to control every aspect of an environment to eliminate "noise" in the theorized relationships.
  - Experimental simulations try to mimic the content of the real world without actually placing the subject in the context of the real world, also to avoid complications in the research design (for example, reducing the requirements to control for certain environmental conditions).
- *Judgment tasks* are types of experiments that involve interviews and verbal protocols to be used when subjects possess data (such as mental processes, inside information on historical events, etc.) that are not readily available for retrieval by the researcher.
- *Sample surveys* are used to collect data about specific characteristics of a sample population to inductively test a theory.

Data-collecting agents on the Internet permit the pursuit of new types of field study research. They can change the dilemmatic nature of the applicable research methodologies, as we shall point out in the next section of this chapter. They also can affect the choices a researcher makes when choosing which among a set of alternative research methodologies will be most effective for the creation of new knowledge in a given research context.

DATA COLLECTION APPROACHES FOR E-BUSINESS RESEARCH

We have stressed how data collection is important to theoretical development, and how different traditional research methodologies used to collect data have strengths and weaknesses that can cause some research to be dilemmatic when investigating certain topics. Now we turn to a more in-depth discussion of new ways to collect data and the research design capabilities that are made possible through Internet technology. (See Appendix 2.1 for guidance on agent development.) We frame our discussion in terms of how these new methodologies can resolve some of the dilemmas of traditional research that Runkel and McGrath (1972) pointed out. However, these new research methodologies also have strengths and weaknesses. We conclude this section with an extension of Runkel and McGrath to address this issue.

New Approaches Made Possible by the Internet

We next consider five new approaches that are now possible because of the wide availability of Internet technology. They include two new data collection techniques—data-collecting agents and Web log files—and three new research approaches that extend existing methodologies—online experiments, online judgment tasks, and online surveys. Our overall argument is that the new capabilities offered by Internet technology require a shift in our thinking about what is possible in research design terms, as well as some reconsideration of how we approach making choices about the kinds of inquiring systems that empirical analysis involving the Internet can support for e-commerce and e-business management. We next discuss the five new approaches in greater detail, focusing on what they allow the researcher to do in e-business management research that is different from before. We begin by discussing the new ways to collect data.

Data-Collecting Agents

Data-collecting agents are software tools that are implemented when researchers want to collect data by examining Web pages that are available to the public on the Internet (Kauffman and Wood, 2007). Data-collecting agents are sometimes referred to as *shopbots,* or just *bots* for short, and *spiders* or *spyders*. They tend to be heavily automated, allowing direct downloading from the Web into a database, spreadsheet, or data file, based on the specifications that a researcher designs into the tool for collection of specific kinds of data (e.g., product prices and discounts, shipping costs, number of participants in an electronic auction, and so on). Also in this category, however, are the tools used by researchers who implement existing and publicly available software agents. These include the major search engines (e.g., Google, www.google.com), shopbots (e.g., MySimon, www.mysimon.com), and searches for products or comments within a single company.

The latter capability, available through several online retailers, such as Amazon (www.amazon.com) or eBay (www.ebay.com), utilizes Internet browsers such as Internet Explorer or Netscape to discover a smaller data set that can be manually entered into a database, spreadsheet, or data file to support a research investigation. It turns out that much information is available publicly and is readily accessed online (Wood and Ow, 2005). This includes auction transactions, and comments and evaluations about products, people, and companies. Also available are data related to prices charged by B2C vendors, and on the available bundles of information goods. Kauffman et al. (2000) point out how data-collecting agents can gather copious amounts of information for relatively little cost compared to traditional data collection methodologies. Such large data sets allow specialized data analysis techniques to be applied with real world data. The methods include large-scale time-series or panel data econometrics, structural equation modeling, paired-observations duration modeling, social network analysis, data mining and pattern recognition, and so on, that would be challenging to implement with traditional experiments due to sample size limitations.

Web Log Files

Companies use Web log files to track the navigational, transaction-making, and decision behavior of human users throughout their systems. These log files usually contain more information than would ever be made available publicly on the Web. For example, log file traces of user navigation on a Web site can include sites visited before and after reaching the company's site, movements (such as mouse movement and clicks or selections) while on the site, and indications of the patterns of use of the organizational hierarchy of information that is available on a Web site. In practice, such data may reach into the tens of thousands or even millions of records. Occasionally, vendors and firms make these log files available to researchers, giving them data analysis opportunities that heretofore have not been available. As with data-collecting agents, the acquisition of such large data sets allows analysis of realistic situations in e-commerce and e-business that would be difficult to implement with most of the traditional assisted data collection techniques, and would be infeasible for manual data collection. We now turn to a discussion of three other research approaches that have resulted from recent applications of Internet technology.

Online Experiments

Researchers also now have the capability to conduct online experiments over the Internet to set up different situations in which subjects can respond. Even though the researcher is bound to lose some control over the subjects that participate in these tests (e.g., eBay auction participants, customers of an electronic grocer's Web site, or users of an online search engine) when compared to traditional experiments, access to subjects is much greater, and data acquisition costs are considerably lower.

Online Judgment Tasks

Online judgment tasks can be used to examine motivations for actions on the part of human subjects. Often, judgment tasks are done within a context that most observers might interpret to be experimental research settings (e.g., involving decision making and discrimination, interpretation of the conditions that are present in some context, reactions to various stimuli, materials, or other contextual elements, etc.). By their nature, these judgment tasks often take on an experimental quality. We note that typical judgment tasks will often be presented with the realistic context stripped out of the data collection, so that the researcher can more clearly examine some relationship of interest. Thus, online judgment tasks are typically used inside hypothetical environments, hypothetical decision-making settings, or contrived situations where the researcher is looking for specific kinds of reactions and responses. In addition, these judgment tasks cannot be used to directly examine actions, but only to infer actions from examination of task results and the questioning of the participants in the study.

Figure 2.1 **Trade-Offs in E-Business Research Methodologies**

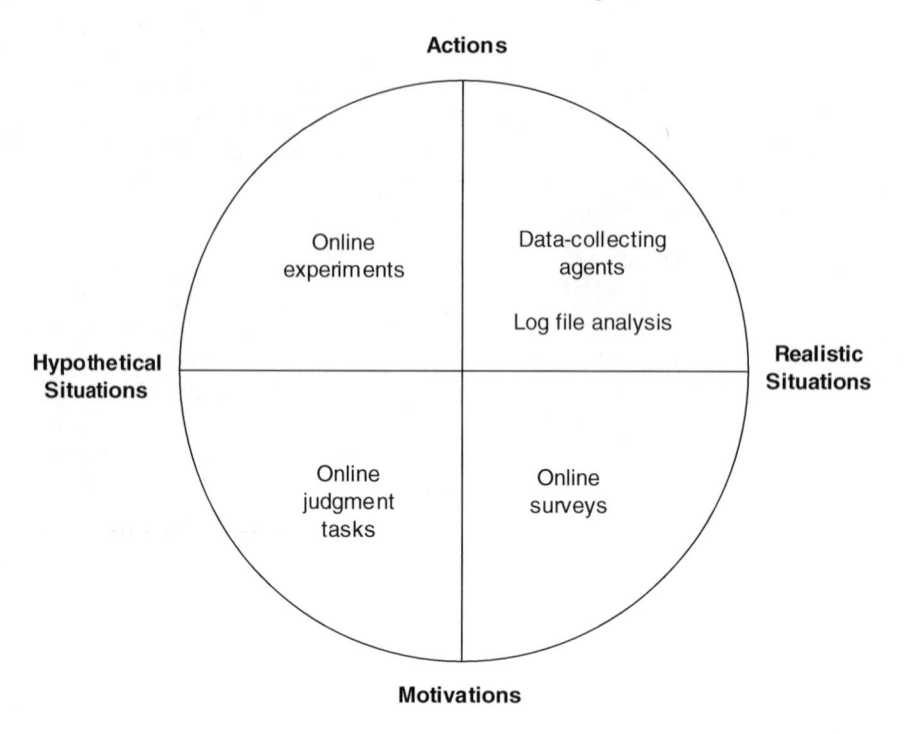

```
                        Actions
            Online              Data-collecting
         experiments               agents
                             Log file analysis
Hypothetical                                    Realistic
 Situations                                     Situations
            Online               Online
           judgment              surveys
             tasks
                       Motivations
```

Online Surveys

Online surveys, including surveys done by e-mail and surveys that are presented using data collection tools embedded in a Web site, can be used to question potential respondents about their actions and motivations. Online surveys can usually be done more quickly and cheaply than traditional surveys, and often with a broader reach for subjects and participants. However, like online judgment tasks, online surveys cannot be used to directly examine actions. One can only infer actions from survey responses, since the data collected are subjective rather than objective. There have been many studies that compare responses in online surveys or e-mail surveys to traditional surveys (e.g., Church, 2001; Mehta and Sivadas, 1995) or even between different online implementations of the same survey, such as with an embedded or attached survey (Dommeyer and Moriarty, 1999–2000). Most of these studies show little or no significant change in response, thus allowing researchers to pick a survey instrument on the basis of ease of implementation rather than on the basis of data quality.

Assessment of the Five New Approaches to Research in E-Business

In keeping with Runkel and McGrath's three-horned dilemma model, we contend that Internet technology has altered the process of data collection. For instance, the low cost to implement an Internet agent or a Web log allows observations that span across different companies (e.g., Brynjolfsson and Smith, 2000; Clay et al., 2002a, 2002b; Kauffman and Wood, 2007), making these field studies more generalizable. We concentrate on how the strengths and weaknesses of online data collection methodologies compare with each other and with traditional research methodologies. Figure 2.1 shows how these research methodologies compare with each other.

We note that:

- data-collecting agents and log files are best suited for e-business research in realistic situations where data are available;
- online experiments are useful for studying human actions inside hypothetical environments or when realistic data are unavailable; and
- online surveys and judgment task experiments support the examination of the motivations behind human actions in realistic situations, and the motivation for human actions inside hypothetical environments.

Table 2.3 shows the strengths and weaknesses of each research approach.

Just as in Runkel and McGrath's original framework, a researcher may use a research methodology that is not necessarily suggested by the above framework. For example, while a decision maker's or a consumer's motivations usually cannot be directly examined with data-collecting agents or log file analysis, they can be inferred in situations where surveys or judgment tasks are impractical or where the participant may wish to hide her actions or motivations, such as in the case of fraud or opportunism (e.g., Kauffman and Wood, 2005; Wood, Fan, and Tan, 2003).

Runkel and McGrath point out that it is important for the researcher to understand and acknowledge the research dilemma and its implications when justifying the approach that is to be employed. Weaknesses notwithstanding, the strengths of these relatively new techniques allow examination of research questions that were previously impossible or impractical to answer due to costs, contamination of subjects' responses, and so on.

Other Methods to Extend E-Business Management Research Capabilities

There are likely to be new ways to conduct research that will be very useful, given the nature of electronically available data. This section describes two other new approaches, in particular, that we believe are likely to have an especially salient impact on e-business research.

Massive Quasi-Experiments

Quasi-experiments in IS and e-commerce research aim to take advantage of naturally occurring conditions in the real world to capture data that enable a researcher to distinguish between outcomes associated with different levels of influence, access, or use of IT. In the case of the Internet, many natural settings permit quasi-experimental research designs to be developed for the study of human decision making, business processes, and organizational performance outcomes in the presence of technology. The sources of data for quasi-experimental research designs include log files or customized data from a data-collecting agent. They permit researchers to restrict the data they collect to support quasi-experimental research designs.

In our experience (e.g., Kauffman and Wood, 2005, 2007), when so many data become available, it is relatively easy to find individuals who meet multiple control and stimulus conditions. As a result, we think of quasi-experimental research designs in the context of very, very large data sets as *massive quasi-experimental designs*. It may be the case that it is necessary to sift through a very large data set (for example, a year's worth of daily prices on 1,000 products among 20 online booksellers, or two years' worth of eBay auction data for all of the bidders on auctions involving U.S. cent coins) to find just those observers that meet a set of predefined experimental conditions

Table 2.3

Strengths and Weaknesses of E-Business Research Approaches

Research approaches	Strengths	Weaknesses
New ways to collect data		
Data-collecting agents	• Inexpensive to get large transaction data sets • Realistic, actual transactions, observations	• Can be burdensome to host computer • Data must be present online; not all types of data are available • Can only infer motivations
Log file analyses	• Nonintrusive and easily repeatable • Multiple simultaneous data sources available • Does not require vendor cooperation • More data types (buyer identity, etc.) available • Extremely large data sets, nonintrusive process • Realistic, actual transactions/observations	• Usually single data source • Can only infer motivations • Requires cooperation from vendor
New extensions to existing research methodologies		
Online experiments	• Far-reaching experiments • Cheap compared to traditional experiments • Can test hypothetical environments • Can be used to examine motivations	• Technology may bias results • Controls may not be as strong • Responses are not made in context • Can be biasing, corrupting, unrealistic due to IT involved
Online judgment tasks	• Can be used with hypothetical environments • Inexpensive compared to the setup of traditional judgment tasks	• Actions only inferred from questions (self-reporting bias, memory bias) • Task training may be problematic
Online surveys	• Can be used to examine motivations • Less expensive than traditional surveys • Faster than traditional surveys	• Actions only inferred from responses • Realism of results can be questionable

RESEARCH STRATEGIES FOR E-BUSINESS   43

Table 2.4

Contents of a Representative Description Column for Dell Product Listing

Description
DELL WIN2K LATITUDE C600 750MHz 128MB TEST DO NOT BID
DELL Optiplex GX110/MT 933MHz TEST DO NOT BID
DELL WIN2K LATITUDE C600 750MHz 128MB TEST DO NOT BID
DELL Optiplex GX110/MT 933MHz TEST DO NOT BID
DELL WIN2K LATITUDE C600 750MHz 128MB TEST DO NOT BID
DELL Optiplex GX110/MT 933MHz TEST DO NOT BID
TEST ONLY DELL (NO O/S) Latitude C600 750MHz 256MB 20GB 24X 56K 10/100 NIC
TEST DO NOT BID DELL WIN2K LATITUDE C600 750MHz 128MB 20GB 24X 56K
TEST DO NOT BID DELL WIN2K Latitude C600 750MHz 128MB 20GB 24X 56K
TEST DO NOT BID DELL (NO O/S) Latitude C600 850MHz 512MB 20GB 24X 56K
TEST DO NOT BID DELL (NO O/S) Latitude CPXJ 750GT 750MHz 256MB 20GB 24X No Modem
TEST DO NOT BID DELL (NO O/S) Latitude C600 750MHz 320MB 20GB 24X 56K
TEST DO NOT BID DELL (NO O/S) Latitude C600 750MHz 256MB 20GB 24X 56K
DELL (No O/S) Dimension L1000 1000MHz 128MB 20GB 48X
DELL (No O/S) Optiplex GX110/L 866MHz 128MB 15GB DVD
DELL (No O/S) Optiplex GX110/MT 800MHz 128MB 20GB 48X
DELL (No O/S) Optiplex GX150/SDT 933MHz 256MB 10GB 24X
DELL (No O/S) Optiplex GX150/SMT 1000MHz 256MB 20GB ZIP DVD
DELL (No O/S) Dimension 4300 1500MHz 256MB 20GB 32X
DELL (No O/S) Optiplex GX110/L 866MHz 192MB 15GB DVD

Source: www.dell.com (accessed September 14, 2004).

(e.g., when price change reactions are apparent, or when there is some need to identify whether fraudulent bidding might be occurring).

Moreover, these individuals can remain in their own context and need not be taken to a laboratory setting for an experimental test. This is important given that other research process observers (e.g., Lave, 1988; Scribner, 1984) have pointed out that subjects do not behave as they normally would when taken out of their own context. However, such realism necessitates acceptance of somewhat less control over the subjects. A countervailing consideration is that the collection of extremely large data sets may permit the collection of data that represent substantially all of the behavior or firm actions that the researcher wishes to observe or track.

Use of Artificial Intelligence and Expert Systems Approaches

There has been much research on the use of artificial intelligence to solve business problems, especially when using Web-based data (e.g., Metaxiotis, Askounis, and Psarras, 2002; Srivastava and Cooley, 2003). The problem with Web data is that it is often in text form and there are thousands, hundreds of thousands, or millions of records. Using an expert system or computer-aided processing approach to deal with this text, with some type of pattern-matching algorithm, allows the researcher to identify items with less difficulty, lower cost, and a higher rate of precision, than by reading each item and determining item characteristics. For example, Table 2.4 contains 20 records of actual data retrieved from Dell Computer (www.dell.com) laptop auctions.

If the data set consisted of only 20 records, a researcher could easily identify each item being sold "by hand." However, if a software agent retrieves 10,000 records for such computers that are for sale *each day* for several months *from several different computer sites,* a researcher would be hard-pressed to identify or match similar items for sale without some sort of automated assistance. This problem, however, is readily solved by using simple pattern-matching algorithms. For example, the pattern recognition algorithm can be written in Visual Basic for Applications (VBA), which comes bundled with various Microsoft products, or using a stored procedure that most databases implement. To illustrate, consider the following VBA code that can be used to process SQL (structured query language) commands inside a Microsoft Access table called *Dell-Computer*. The code removes test records, and then finds the chip speed and stores it inside the *mhz* column in the database:

```
` Remove test data
DoCmd.RunSQL  "Delete   from   DellComputer   WHERE InStr(Description),'TEST')>0"

` Process MHz
For x = 700 to 2000
MySQL = "UPDATE DellComputer SET mhz = " & x & " WHERE mhz is null AND "
MySQL = MySQL + " InStr(Description, '" & x & "MHz')>0"
DoCmd.RunSQL MySQL
Next
```

Such processing can be somewhat complicated when the decisions about the data become more complex. This is likely to require an expert system that discriminates among the text-based data using rules and determines the order of execution of those rules. In addition, an artificial intelligence capability may be appropriate, so that the program is able to actually change its own decision processes without any human intervention, based upon new information it receives. When finding simple patterns in the data, the code required to identify items can be quite simple, as illustrated above. Automation often reduces the human error that can accompany many hours of scanning through data. Incorporation of such tools is part of the research design when implementing powerful data collection techniques.

UNDERSTANDING E-BUSINESS RESEARCH THROUGH THE INQUIRY SYSTEMS

The grid shown in Table 2.5 crosses the first four of Churchman's five types of inquiry systems in research with the five research approaches. This will give the reader examples of how a methodology was implemented in the context of various problem and topic areas in e-business research. As shown by the distribution of the literature that we have sorted according to the dimensions in Table 2.5, certain approaches appear to be predisposed to support research investigations within specific types of theory development. Based upon this literature review, it also appears, for example, that data-collecting agents seem to be the methodology most used for data collection in e-business research. This is understandable. Data-collecting agents are inexpensive to run and can gather large amounts of data. We will next survey the literature according to our framework's classification to discuss theory development and how researchers have designed research and used new data-collecting tools for empirical e-business management research.

A word is in order on the methodology that we used to select the papers and to place them in the framework. We identified candidate articles from the leading journals and conferences in the IS field, and then expanded our coverage to include the fields of economics and marketing. The articles included in this chapter are representative, and not truly exhaustive of *all* of the available research on e-commerce during the past ten years involving Internet-based data collection. To have pursued this latter task would have been a very great effort, indeed, and one that would not have served our ultimate purpose of illustrating the revolutionary new approaches and empirical advances that are seen in e-commerce research. Moreover, many of the articles that we identified, as it turned out, either did not collect data in the manner that we have described, or did not collect data at all. The most common instance for rejecting the inclusion of an article came when the authors used manual techniques (e.g., making queries on the Web via a search engine, manually clicking through Web pages, or obtaining secondary data in a traditional manner).

We also screened out papers that we believed did not have "significant" results in terms of contributions to new knowledge. Thereafter, the coauthors split the load of "bucketing" the various papers in the different boxes of the framework. We then discussed our separate assignments, especially checking for discrepancies. In some cases, it made sense to position a study in more than one box, because of the different research approaches that were demonstrated. When we disagreed on the assignment of a paper, we considered one another's arguments in favor of one bucketing or another, and eventually reached a consensus.

Theory Generalization Research

As is shown in Table 2.5, online experiments are not often used to generalize existing theory in different areas in the e-business research context. The nature of experiments is to apply a stimulus and a control to a subject, and the impersonal nature of e-business often makes such application difficult. However, other ways to collect data are more apt to facilitate theory generalization in e-business research.

Data-collecting agents can be used to examine existing theory in the context of the new e-business environment. Bajari and Hortacsu (2003a) examine how the typical empirical economic regularities from a sample match the observed patterns in data found in other samples of online auctions. The authors also examine the exact effects of the *winner's curse* (where the auction winner overpays) in online auctions (Bajari and Hortacsu, 2003b). Brinkmann and Seifert (2001), Dewan and Hsu (2001), and Livingston (2002) all find that trust increases the consumer's willingness-to-pay, as predicted by trust theory. Ba and Pavlou (2002) also find a trust effect. They conduct an online judgment task for students to complete, and follow it by analyzing data that have been collected online using a data-collecting agent. Hahn and Kauffman (2003) and Murphy, Hofacker, and Bennett (2001) apply different theories that explain the efficacy of Web design to develop hypotheses about Web site performance. In both cases, the authors show how the analysis of log files helps to shed light on optimal Web site design. More recently, Doong, Kauffman, Lai and Zhuang (Chapter 8 in this volume) explored the efficacy of different participation incentives for online group-buying auctions using on online experimental design approach with multiple treatments.

Online surveys can also be used for theory generalization. Chen and He (2003) develop a theory of online technology adoption with respect to a specific retailer. Then they validate this theory using online survey responses that are evaluated via structural equation modeling. Lederer et al. (2000) apply a similar technique and validate the *technology acceptance model* (TAM) for work-related tasks and Web applications. They also employ a survey with structural equation modeling to test TAM in this environment. Ferl and Millsap (1992) also conduct an online survey to show how technology acceptance is dependent upon ease of use, as predicted by the TAM model.

Table 2.5

Inquiring Systems, Data Collection Approaches, and E-Business Research

Research approach	Theory generalization	Theory building	Theory verification/ falsification	Hybrid theory construction
New ways to collect data				
Data-collecting agents	Ba and Pavlou (2002)	Ariely and Simonson (2003)	Bapna, Goes, and Gupta (2000)	Alpar, Poremski, and Pickerodt (2001)
	Bajari and Hortacsu (2003a, 2003b)	Asvanund et al. (2004)	Bergen, Kauffman, and Lee (2004)	Baye, Morgan, and Scholten (2004)
	Bergen, Kauffman, and Lee (2006a, 2006b)	Bapna, Goes, and Gupta (2001b, 2003)	Bergen et al. (2007)	Clemons, Hann, and Hitt (2002)
	Brinkmann and Seifert (2001)	Bergen, Kauffman, and Lee (2005)	Brynjolfsson and Smith (2000)	Dellarocas and Wood (2007)
	Dewan and Hsu (2001)	Brynjolfsson, Hu, and Smith (2003)	Chevalier and Mayzlin (2003)	Easley and Tenorio (2004)
	Granados, Gupta, and Kauffman (2005)	Dans (2002)	Clay et al. (2001, 2002a)	Kauffman and Lee (2004, 2006)
	Livingston (2002)	Dellarocas and Wood (2007)	Ghose, Smith, and Telang (2006)	Kauffman and Wood (2003, 2007)
		Eaton (2002)	Houser and Wooders (2000)	Levy et al. (2006)
		Ederington and Dewally (2003)	Hyde, Jank, and Shmueli (2006)	Resnick and Zeckhauser (2002)
		Gilkeson and Reynolds (2003)	Jank and Shmueli (2005, 2006)	Ward and Clark (2002)
		Gopal, Bhatacharjee, and Sanders (2006)	Jap (2003)	
		Kauffman and Wang (2001)	Kauffman and Lee (2004, 2006)	Yamagishi (2003)
		Kauffman and Wood (2005, 2006)	Levy et al. (2006)	
		Lucking-Reiley et al. (2000)	Lucas and Oh (2006)	
		Lynch and Ariely (2000)	Lucking-Reiley (1999)	
		Massad and Tucker (2000)	Melnik and Alm (2002)	
			Ow and Wood (2003)	

Research approach	Theory generalization	Theory building	Theory verification/ falsification	Hybrid theory construction
		Oh (2002)	Pan, Ratchford, and Shankar (2003)	
		Park and Kim (2003) Roth and Ockenfels (2002)	Smith (2002) Smith and Brynjolfsson (2001)	
		Segev, Beam, and Shanthikumar (2001) Standifird (2001) Wang, Jank, and Shmueli (2006) Wood, Fan, and Tan (2003)	Wilcox (2000)	
Log file analyses	Hahn and Kauffman (2003)	Catledge and Pitkow (1995)	Brynjolfsson and Smith (2000)	Clay, Krishnan, and Wolff (2001) Clay et al. (2002a, 2002b)
	Murphy, Hofacker, and Bennett (2001)	Hahn and Kauffman (2003)	Hahn and Kauffman (2003)	
		Lee, Zufryden, and Drèze (2003) Tillotson, Cherry, and Clinton (1995)	Lee (1998)	
New extensions to existing research methodologies				
Online experiments	None	Bapna, Goes, and Gupta (2001a) Jin and Kato (2002)	Doong (Chapter 8 in this volume) List and Lucking-Reiley (2000)	None
		Kamis (2006) List and Lucking-Reiley (2002) Rafaeli and Noy (2002)	Resnick et al. (2003)	
Online judgment tasks	Ba and Pavlou (2002) Chen and He (2003) Ferl and Millsap (1992)	Bapna (2003) Earp and Baumer (2003) Sheehan (2002)	None	None
Online surveys			Gardyn (2003) Gordon and Lima-Turner (1997)	None
	Lederer et al. (2000)	Yin (2002)		

Note: This table provides a more exhaustive list than the articles that are discussed in the body of the chapter.

Theory Building Research

Theory building is the area where most of the activity has concentrated in e-business research. This is understandable since e-business is a relatively new phenomenon, and it thus presents many challenges in our attempts to understand business relationships within e-business.

Data-collecting agents have been shown to be useful tools for building theory because of the large amounts of data that can be collected from a multitude of sources to test relationships that provide a basis for establishing new theory. Ariely and Simonson (2003) show that bidders undersearch, and, therefore, overpay in online auctions. They also suggest that high starting bids are likely to lead to higher prices only if competing items are not available. Bapna, Goes, and Gupta (2001b, 2003) examine bidder types and bidder behavior in online auctions, especially bidding behavior related to the prices paid and the timing of bidders' bids. Dans (2002) discusses new business models that are made possible by Internet technology.

In addition, Dellarocas and Wood (2007) evaluate factors that influence bidder participation levels in online auctions using an extensive data set collected on eBay's Web site. Wood, Fan, and Tan (2003) examine how sellers with higher reputations evaluate and react to positive buyer comments from transactions. Jin and Kato (2002), Eaton (2002), and Park and Kim (2003) analyze eBay data and show how additional information can reduce the information asymmetry inherent in e-business transactions, resulting in a buyer's willingness to pay more for an item and increasing a buyer's commitment to a seller.

In a similar vein, Kauffman and Wang (2001) analyzed the effects of buyer arrival rates and price plateaus in group-buying Web sites. Chevalier and Mayzlin (2003) evaluate the impact of word of mouth from online book reviews on book sales. Ederington and Dewally (2003), Lucking-Reiley et al. (2000), Gilkeson and Reynolds (2003), and Standifird (2001) use data collected with data-collecting agents to examine factors that affect the final price bid in online auctions. Kauffman and Wood (2005) examine the possibility of shilling through the examination of a massive data set that examines bidder behavior during concurrent auctions selling the same item. Massad and Tucker (2000) compare online auctions and traditional auctions, and find, surprisingly, that online auctions lead to higher dollar values in initial bid prices and in final bid prices, when compared with physical auctions. Segev, Beam, and Shanthikumar (2001) develop a new theoretical model for prediction of final auction price, and test this model using auction data collected with a data-collecting agent. Catledge and Pitkow (1995) and Tillotson, Cherry, and Clinton (1995) were among the first researchers to examine Internet browsing behavior through the use of log files.

Online experiments are also extensively used in e-business theory building, especially in hypothetical situations. In a laboratory experiment, List and Lucking-Reiley (2000) show how bundling items within auctions can result in large price premiums. Bapna, Goes, and Gupta (2001a) also use a laboratory experiment to analyze different price-setting processes in online auctions. Rafaeli and Noy (2002) developed experimental results to show that interpersonal additions to online auctions that mimic face-to-face contact increase transaction amounts.

Quasi-experiments can also be useful in finding relationships that are difficult to examine in traditional environments. Kauffman and Wood (2006) establish controls and stimuli for weekend and weekday buying, and buying with and without a picture of the trade item. They find that there is a *weekend effect*, and that pictures and reputation scores also affect the final price. Roth and Ockenfels (2002) examine *bid sniping*, or bidding at the last possible moment, with auctions on Amazon and eBay, and find that the fixed closing time on eBay motivates more sniping than the variable closing time on Amazon. By examining judgments in an online environment, Bapna (2003) is able to propose a new auction microstructure designed to eliminate sniping behavior.

Earp and Baumer (2003) and Sheehan (2002) use online surveys to test the privacy concerns of online shoppers. Both find some skepticism among users about providing personal information in online transactions, although Sheehan finds that education levels will mollify privacy concerns. Yin (2002) surveys and tests the effects of price dispersion with selling price. Geographical differences and the norms associated with the sharing of private information will also influence the efficacy of the approaches that we have discussed. For example, European Web site operators are precluded from sharing data with e-commerce researchers due to European Union data protection laws. In the United States, in contrast, by default consumers and users of various Web sites "opt in" for the use of their data, and need to express their desire to "opt out." In Europe, the opposite is true: the default is to "opt out," with the result that far less consumer and user data are available for study by a third party. Paul Tallon, a coeditor of this research volume, pointed out that such fundamentally different assumptions could pose a barrier to some forms of data collection—even though the relevant data will probably be there, somewhere in an inaccessible database.

Theory building is extremely data intensive, involving induction from observations, and then, to test the theories, empirical examination to determine whether the new theories are applicable to an environment. We show here how new data collection techniques, especially data-collecting agents, Weblog file analysis, and online surveys, are useful in collecting the data needed for the task of theory building.

Theory Verification Research

Often, theory verification results in the questioning of some theory's validity within the context of a given environment of research interest. Because of the easy access to data that the new data-collecting tools support, theory verification has become more attractive. For example, Bapna, Goes, and Gupta (2000) used data in online auctions to reject the often-used auction theory assumption that bidders are homogeneous. They then go on to illustrate different bidder types. Ow and Wood (2003) explore the effect that the winner's curse has in online auctions and find that buyer experience leads to an increase in willingness-to-pay in online auctions. This is the opposite of the findings that have been obtained in traditional markets. Houser and Wooders (2000) examine both online auctions and online reverse auctions, which involve contract bids where the lowest bid wins. They find that although a seller's reputation affects the final price in online auctions, a buyer's reputation does not affect price in reverse auctions. List and Lucking-Reiley (2000) examine several theoretical auction models advocated in economic theory, yet find no significant difference in revenue between these different types of auctions. Similarly, Lucking-Reiley (1999) finds that Dutch auctions generate approximately 30 percent higher revenues in e-mail and newsgroup auctions than in traditional first-price and second-price auctions, contrary to theoretical predictions. Melnik and Alm (2002) analyze eBay data to determine the effect a seller's reputation has on price, and find only a small effect, contrary to other theory on this topic. Wilcox (2000) examines the timing of bids, and finds that experienced bidders bid in a way that is more consistent with theory over time than inexperienced bidders.

Using log file analysis, Brynjolfsson and Smith (2000) find evidence of friction in e-commerce markets, which is also the opposite of what was expected as predicted by prior armchair theory builders. Also using log files, Lee (1998) examines Aucnet in Japan, a used automobile online auction, and finds that quality guarantees from a third-party auditor tend to increase willingness-to-pay in an e-market.

Resnick et al. (2003) examine what happens when they take a well-established eBay seller, and then set up a new eBay seller, and observe how they interact in terms of buyers' willingness-to-pay.

Their research design involves having each seller sell the exact same item. They found an 8.1 percent positive difference in willingness-to-pay for the reputable seller. In another quasi-experiment, Jap (2003) investigates how price competition mechanisms affect buyer–supplier relationships. He finds that reverse auctions can increase the supplier's belief that the buyer will act opportunistically. Gardyn (2003) conducts an online survey of 871 children, ages eight to fifteen. She finds, contrary to conventional wisdom, that older girls are more active computer users than their male counterparts. A survey by Gordon and Lima-Turner (1997) indicates that social contract theories may be somewhat limited in areas of e-business.

Verifying existing theory requires much evidence, especially if the verification process yields a result that is contrary to the prevailing conventional thought on a topic. As such, these new research technology-based techniques are ideal for reexamining conventional theory, especially as this theory applies to e-business phenomena. Here, we show how theory verification can be accomplished using new research methodologies.

Hybrid Theory Construction

Rather than attempting to verify or validate a theory, hybrid theory construction techniques allow the researcher to examine theories that are often diametrically opposed. This permits the determination of the circumstances in which one theory is suited to a situation and when another theory would be more appropriate. Often, hybrid theory construction requires larger sets of data, and so it is understandable that data-collecting agents and log files—the techniques that are best able to generate the largest data sets—are observed to be the most suitable for this type of inquiry. For example, when examining competition and tacit collusion, which are opposing actions in competitor interaction, Kauffman and Wood (2003) find that market leaders often dictate the dynamics of price competition for the rest of the industry, and that the same online companies react to competitors differently as members of different industries. Resnick and Zeckhauser (2002) examine reputation systems in online auctions and report that feedback was left despite incentives to free ride, that feedback is almost always positive, and that feedback does predict a seller's future performance in online auctions. Also, contrary to other literature, they find that higher reputation scores do not result in higher prices paid for an item. Easley and Tenorio (2004) find that experienced bidders tend to bid in higher increments, which they call *jump bidding,* and they theorize about the cost of repeat bidding compared against the cost of jump bidding. Clay et al. (2002b) describe that firm reactions to competitor price changes do occur, but not as often as one would expect. Yamagishi (2003) examines the effect of open versus closed auctions. Although the theory that he uses states that closed auctions will be less prone to opportunism and generate higher prices, Yamagishi still finds that a reputation system can make an open market outperform a closed auction.

Of all the theory development research we have discussed so far, hybrid theory construction can be the most data intensive. When there are conflicting theories, with each applying to different segments of a market or population (such as competition and collusion), data are required to examine the theories to gain an accurate picture of how they interact. The data can be used to evaluate the extent of the "paradox" that is created, in the words of Poole and van de Ven (1989). These authors have championed and applied this kind of thinking to build new management and organizational theories—something that the new approaches to research for e-commerce can support as well, only with as much data as are needed. Clearly, the new data collection techniques greatly simplify the task of data collection, and thus facilitate hybrid theory construction.

We now have illustrated how different types of theoretical development are accomplished with typically less time, less cost, and more ease than when doing traditional data collection. We have shown that these techniques are particularly well suited to e-business research by demonstrating how researchers have successfully implemented them to accomplish their research objectives.

CONCLUSION

This research delves into the newest frontier of research design approaches and data collection techniques for e-business management. We examine these new approaches from a philosophy of science perspective, and extend Runkel and McGrath's (1972) framework to illustrate different facets of these new techniques that extend beyond traditional research approaches. Leveraging Churchman's (1971) insights, we also illustrate how e-business researchers implement these approaches when developing theory that investigates important e-business problems. The result of this examination is that we call attention to several research directions that can facilitate empirical advances in e-business research.

Contributions

We investigated the strengths and weaknesses of these new approaches. We pointed out, echoing the long-standing insights of others who have written on research approaches from a philosophy of science perspective, how these tools can be used in theory building, theory generalization, theory verification, and theory combination. For this reason, we claim that it is critically important to appreciate how much impact they ought to have on the way in which researchers conceptualize and go about designing their research approaches for the exploration of current problems in e-business management. We found in our exploration that these new technology-based tools are able to resolve several issues associated with traditional data collection methodologies. This appears to be occurring because of researchers' new ability through Internet-based tools to inexpensively collect megabytes of data on individuals' actions. As a result, it is possible to use these approaches to mimic the data collection outcomes of traditional methods, without having to face up to their inherent limitations.

Research Directions

With these preliminary findings in mind, we think it is worthwhile to suggest some research directions involving the new data collection methodologies that may be appropriate for future research on the spectrum of e-business management topics.

Massive Quasi-Experiments

With so much data available, it is relatively easy to find individuals who meet multiple control and stimulus conditions, as we have seen in our prior discussion. These individuals remain in their own context and need not be taken to a laboratory setting for an experimental test. Lave (1988) and Scribner (1984) describe how subjects behave differently inside laboratories, even with tasks as simple as bowling or buying milk, and show how this lack of realism can give erroneous results. Traditionally, however, quasi-experiments are difficult to conduct due to the exorbitant costs involved in achieving a sample size of sufficient power, and are also difficult due to the possible contamination of subject behavior. Internet data, however, cannot be captured *without* the express knowledge of the participant, otherwise it will lead to significant ethical issues. This helps to resolve some of the unattractive features and difficulties of traditional quasi-experiments.

However, it also leaves some issues that will require additional study from university and research organization-based institutional review boards for research.

Fast, Cheap Surveys

Often, surveys can take months to implement. Pretesting and revising a survey instrument can be costly and laborious. With online surveys, the deployment is less expensive, the reach is greater, and the time required for the collection of responses is greatly compressed. Although we are not advocating a "quick and dirty" approach, we think it is important to point out that the fundamental cost-to-results quality relationship is undergoing significant and beneficial changes in favor of the researcher. The usual battery of nonresponse bias tests is still needed though, as are tests to assess the generalizability of the results to the population of interest.

Time-Series and Longitudinal Research Designs

Many of these new techniques, such as online surveys or data-collecting agents, can be easily reimplemented as time passes. Thus, researchers can more easily gather time-series data on individuals as well as panel data for a cross-section of individuals over time. Such data typically are not available when traditional data collection is done, other than in the most extraordinary circumstances. Indeed, longitudinal research designs place the greatest cost and feasibility pressures on traditional data collection techniques, so it is likely that opportunities for Internet-based longitudinal research designs will dramatically change the cost-to-research quality relationship.

Theory Building and Empirical Data Analysis

Many theories have not yet been tested extensively with realistic data. For example, Bapna, Goes, and Gupta (2000) investigate popular economic theories using online data, and find that many of them are not supported. In more recent research, Kauffman and Wood (2007) investigate the appropriateness of the Bertrand competition assumption in online markets, a long-standing truism in the IS literature, and find that Bertrand competition is not sufficient to explain competitive interaction.

"Hidden" Phenomena

One of the main concerns with traditional data collection is that some behavior (such as opportunism) is hardly ever exhibited when these techniques are used. This is because individuals can maintain control over the data that are presented to the researcher. Thus, a non-invasive data collection methodology is required to more closely examine the actions of individuals without having those individuals change their behavior because they know that they are being examined—the well-known *Hawthorne effect*. Data-collecting agents and log file analysis are natural tools for such investigation, coupled with new methods of data visualization (Shmueli and Jank, 2005; Shmueli et al., 2006). For example, Kauffman and Wood (2005) investigate online shilling by observing which bidders make bids on items that have characteristics different than the normal bid. Then these bidders are examined for shilling-like behavior. Such a technique would be extremely difficult or impossible to duplicate using traditional data collection. In addition, Jank and Shmueli (2005, 2006) and Shmueli, Russo, and Jank (2004) use curve clustering and functional data analysis to reveal a variety of online auction bidder behavior phenomena through innovative statistical analysis.

We have shown how cost effective and time-saving these new research approaches can be. A data-collecting agent can be developed by a single capable programmer in less than a month. If it is designed properly, it can collect literally hundreds of thousands of records in a single day. Surveys can be rapidly deployed with no mailing or materials costs, and with a twenty-four-hour response window. Also, it is often possible to retest results from analysis of agent data or online survey data repeatedly or to gather additional data or to gather data that were omitted early in a study. With other research approaches, such as traditional surveys, experiments, or field studies, collecting new data may be extremely problematic. Indeed, the new ways to collect data for e-business research are so effective that researchers can now spend the majority of their time thinking through the elements of the best research design, determining what data to collect, analyzing the available data, and figuring out how to best present the findings. As Churchman (1971) seems to have foreseen, this is all in sharp contrast to traditional data collection, for which the majority of the researcher's time must be spent on the data collection effort itself.

Transforming Our Thinking for Empirical Advances in E-Business Research

The technologies that have made e-business possible simultaneously have transformed many industries, but thus far academic researchers have shown little scientific awareness of the manner in which these technologies are also transforming the underlying processes of research design and data collection—at least not in philosophy of science terms or in a way that systematically lays out how we should proceed. Many companies, such as General Electric, Dell, Microsoft, and Cisco Systems, have recognized through their IT investments, how the efficiencies achieved through the Web can allow them to function with greater responsiveness and with far less expense, supporting higher levels of profitability than otherwise might be possible. At the same time, many consumers recognize how the Web allows them to more easily search for information and to shop electronically.

So too, we argue, will our thinking about research design and data collection in empirical research for e-business management have to be transformed. The new technologies will permit us to investigate emerging areas of e-business management for far lower cost and in far less time than we probably expected even five years ago. We predict that, in time, researchers will come to think of the World Wide Web as a data source and a research context where they can research their topics of interest with perspectives on research design and methodologies for data collection that are as new as the technologies of the Internet themselves. We recognize, of course, that some variables (especially intention-based and perceptual variables) will never be observable in the Web environment.

Limitations

Surely, however, the use of traditional approaches to research design and data collection will remain appropriate for many types of projects. It is unlikely, for example, that the use of Internet-based tools will be able to replace the depth of insight that can be obtained from interviewing real people (e.g., consumers, senior managers, Web-based systems designers, or e-commerce pricing strategists about their decision-making approaches) who have to deal with real-world risks and outcomes in their organizational and business environments. In addition, we recognize that no real-world quasi-experiment—undertaken on a limited basis or with a massive data collection approach—can approach the degree of control that a researcher can assert in a more controlled laboratory environment. Yet, even with powerful controls, it will be necessary to extrapolate the validity of the findings to the real world. Clearly, situations in which human motivation (i.e., on the part of an individual, a manager, or group of managers relative to a firm's strategy or performance) is the key variable are less apt to be effectively understood with Internet-based techniques for data collection.

In addition, it is appropriate to point out that some aspects of e-business management research will require joint Internet technology-based and traditional approaches to be effective in yielding meaningful managerial insights. For example, most investigations into the business value of Web-based technologies in e-business processes will continue to require data on investment levels, the timing of expenditures, and other behind-the-scenes data that capture the key drivers of organizational performance. No doubt, Internet-based data collection should be able to provide important information about the business processes themselves, how they have been configured, the output levels and performance dimensions associated with them, as well as the extent of the use of a given software application and the information associated with it (Straub, Limayem, and Karahanna-Evaristo, 1995). Constructing the "full picture" will remain costly and challenging nevertheless.

In conclusion, we also challenge researchers in e-business management to give more thought to whether they will be able to justify total reliance upon the new techniques. In the future, researchers will not only need to understand the best ways to design e-business research to build, test, and validate theory. They will also need to be aware of the best ways to construct and direct a data-collecting agent, how to incorporate data-collecting agents into research designs that also involve traditional data collection, and gauge the potential impact that data-collecting agents will have on what now becomes possible in e-business management research. In spite of the likely growing pains that we expect to experience as we gain confidence with these new empirical advances, we nevertheless see a bright and productive future for the application of new technologies in support of the creation of new e-business management knowledge.

APPENDIX 2.1. AGENT-BASED DATA COLLECTION

It is worthwhile to briefly consider some natural questions that will be asked relating to this research. They include: When a researcher is interested in developing software agents for Internet-based data collection, what are the key design issues? How do the design issues relate to the likely success a researcher will have with the use of the agent-based data collection methodology? What advice is available in the current research literature to guide this kind of work, and where might a novice begin? In this Appendix, we briefly answer these questions, and point the reader to the appropriate literature.

A good starting point for the interested reader is an article by Kauffman, March, and Wood (2000) on the design of *long-lived Internet agents.* The primary contrast with respect to data-collecting software agents lies in the length of time that they operate on behalf of the user. Consumers and buyers typically employ transaction agents to retrieve small amounts of data related to transaction events. Managers and researchers are more likely to use long-lived Internet agents, which provide the capability to retrieve, store, process, and analyze large amounts of data over a long period of time. When undertaking a project involving Internet-based agent-led data collection, it is important for the researcher to recognize the issues and difficulties that are associated with this approach. Kauffman, March, and Wood (2000) noted five issues that must be appreciated. First, there is still no single standard for the presentation of data on Web pages on the Internet. Second, HTML (hypertext markup language) has no standard elements related to the underlying data, and so it does not readily map to what is needed for effective data collection agent design.

XML (extensible markup language) is somewhat better in that data definitions can be discovered or created, however, in practice there has not been enough effort put toward the standardization of XML data in different business and e-commerce contexts. Third, conducting longitudinal data collection requires some tolerance to the typical faults that occur in the natural conduct of organizational and business processes involving computers, including Web site downtime, network and system crashes, data with errors, high usage loads, and so on—all of which result in faults, outages, and an impaired ability to conduct high quality automated data collection.

Fourth, part of the problem that the researcher will face involves identifying the Web pages from which to extract data. This consideration implies that appropriate software for the purpose of Internet-based data collection should also have the capacity to conduct *search* and *navigation*. Fifth, even though many, many Web servers are available on the Internet now—the places from which one could possibly collect data are thus endless—nevertheless, researchers must have some sensitivity to the propriety and impact of their automated search-and-extract activities on the Internet. Allen, Burk, and Davis (2006) point out that a code of conduct for data collection on the Web is yet to be established—what is admissible, what is not, and how to determine what available data and information should properly be treated as private property.

These issues are likely to affect the success that researchers will have in extracting the kind of research data that they wish to obtain from the Internet. Kauffman, March, and Wood (2000, p. 219) note that recovery from an abnormal terminal for a data collection agent on the Internet "typically requires context sensitivity and varies according to the history of work previously performed." So data collection agents need to demonstrate *persistence*, in that they are not only able to restart their processes of data collection, but also do so in a manner that restores the *state* of the software agent prior to the abend. Kauffman, March, and Wood (2000, p. 220) further point out that "Internet agents are *data-centric*" in that "[t]hey must acquire, interpret and transfer data, possibly modifying their behavior based on the data that they acquire."

These observations led the authors to argue that there are five dimensions of *agent sophistication* necessary (beyond the typical performance requirements for good computer programs) that Internet agents must demonstrate. They include intelligence, concurrency, validation, recovery, monitoring, and interactivity. *Intelligence* is the ability, similar to artificial intelligence, to use rules to mimic the responses of humans, and for the software agent to identify the conditions associated with its data extraction query, and adjust its data collection targets and behavior accordingly. *Concurrency* in a software agent is the capability to do several things at once, and is implemented through multithreaded processes that make it possible to take advantage of available CPU (central processing unit) time. *Validation* capability in an Internet agent is the means to ensure that the data are of the proper type and identity, and match the rules associated with their extraction. *Recovery* is the capacity of a software agent to recover from problems that cause data collection to fail. Klein and Dellarocas (1999) have pointed out that it is burdensome to program agents with exception handling code, and that it may help to rely on "generic" recovery routines that can be called upon as reusable external software objects. *Monitoring* is the capability of a software agent to periodically track events that give rise to new data on Web sites that are targeted for data collection. The capability is in contrast to the one-and-done approach; scheduled monitoring and continuous monitoring are both possible. Finally, *interactivity* is a software agent's ability to modify its data collection behavior based on the data it collects.

Kauffman, March, and Wood (2000) provide an interesting demonstration of a tool for Web-based data collection called, eDRILL, an *electronic data retrieval lexical agent*. Their demonstrational application is to eBay electronic auctions for collectible coins. The authors placed the agent sophistication constructs in the context of the Unified Modeling Language (UML), as a means to effectively express the key design concepts that go along with the dimensions of agent sophistication. Overall, however, these capabilities suggest that truly longitudinal data collection-based research designs on the Internet will be subject to multiple threats. They include missing data, incompletely collected data, data collected under inappropriately specified conditions, invalid data, and other problems that lie in the domains of the capabilities of the software agent and its interaction with a dynamic computing and networking environment. Other issues that may arise involve changes in Web site designs made by Internet-based sellers, requests to "cease and desist" from data collection at a particular site, difficulties in manipulating the very large gigabyte databases that are collected to extract the appropriate data (a special problem with log files), and so on.

We would like to recommend three additional resources that may be helpful for beginners in their use of this means of data collection. The most basic things to know about in this area are some software tools that will help to extract material from Web pages. An example is ListGrabber (www.egrabber.com), and other associated software, which permits a user to identify the kinds of data that are targeted for collection as lists. Although the software is sold with an emphasis on "grabbing" contact information, resumes, and response data from the Web, it can be adapted to pull list data and port it to Excel, so it can then be further "massaged" and cleaned to port to database software and to statistics packages. This tool works directly with HTML. A second example involves the extraction of data from XML pages on the Web. Microsoft Access 2002 and 2003 have had the capability to support importing XML. Microsoft states that "[w]ithout XML, this task might involve exporting the data [from a Web site] to a text-based file (assuming that the various data sources supported this), manipulating the data files by adding delimiters to separate the data into discrete parts, importing the data into SQL Server or Access, and then spending a considerable amount of time cleaning up the data. Using XML allows you to minimize this kind of time spent reformatting and cleaning up your data" (office.microsoft.com/en-us/access/HA010345601033.aspx?pid=CL100570041033).

Wood and Ow (2005) offer another useful source for beginners to gain specific insights into the technical side of the process of Web-based data collection based on an article published in the *Communications of the ACM*. They focus on extracting Web-based data using SQL extensions and a tool called WebView that supports open database connectivity (ODBC) for database programs such as Microsoft Access, Oracle, and SQL Server. Wood and Ow's innovation is to create the basis for dynamic "Web views" for Web page data in a relational database joined with dynamic organizational and user views of a corporate database. This innovation is founded on prior work by Lakshmanan, Sadri, and Subramanian (2001). These authors identified a means to achieve database interoperability through the creation of SchemaSQL. This is an extension of SQL that permits queries to database schemas and databases, the transformation of data in database structures that are different from the original database, the creation of database views that are dependent on input values related to the query, and additional facilitation of relational database interoperability and data/schema manipulation. Wood and Ow (2005, pp. 101–102) note five requirements for an effective WebView SQL extension: "(1) it must have expressive power that is independent of HTML, XML, or other Web-based markup languages; (2) it must allow the restructuring of Web data to conform to a database schema; (3) it must be shown to be sufficient to capture any Web data, including XML or HTML; (4) it must function like existing database constructs to allow transparency for the database developer; and (5) it must be efficiently implemented." The interested reader should see this article for additional details on an application of these ideas to data collection in eBay auctions.

ACKNOWLEDGMENTS

The authors thank Mark Bergen, Jungpil Hahn, Wolfgang Jank, Dongwon Lee, Sourav Ray, Galit Shmueli, Rahul Telang, and Bin Wang, who encouraged us to consider the range of applications of these ideas. We also appreciated the reactions to these ideas offered by doctoral students Pallab Sanyal, Ajay Kumar, and Ryan Sougstad—and especially Gordon Davis in the context of the IDSc 8511 Doctoral Seminar—at the University of Minnesota. Also, our doctoral students at Arizona State University—Yong-Jick Lee, Arti Mann, Greg Schymik, and Trent Spaulding—helped us to vet some of these ideas, through comments and in-class discussions. Finally, Chris Dellarocas, Roberto Evaristo, Mark Nissen, Terence Ow, Paul Tallon, Ron Weber, and Weidong Xia also offered helpful advice on earlier drafts.

REFERENCES

Allen, G.N.; Burk, D.L.; and Davis, G.B. 2006. Academic data collection in electronic environments: Defining acceptable use of Internet resources. *MIS Quarterly*, 30, 3, 599–610.

Alpar, P.; Poremski, M.; and Pickerodt, S. 2001. Measuring the efficiency of Web site traffic generation. *International Journal of Electronic Commerce*, 6, 1, 53–74.

Ariely, D. and Simonson, I. 2003. Buying, bidding, playing, or competing? Value assessment and decision dynamics in online auctions. *Journal of Consumer Psychology*, 13, 1–2, 113–123.

Asvanund, A.; Karen, C.; Krishnan, R.; and Smith, M.D. 2004. An empirical analysis of network externalities in peer-to-peer music sharing networks. *Information Systems Research*, 15, 2, 155–174.

Ba, S. and Pavlou, P.A. 2002. Evidence of the effect of trust building technology in electronic markets: Price premiums and buyer behavior. *MIS Quarterly*, 26, 3, 243–268.

Bajari, P. and Hortacsu, A. 2003a. Are structural estimates of auction models reasonable? Evidence from experimental data. Working paper, Department of Economics, Stanford University, Stanford, CA.

———. 2003b. The winner's curse, reserve prices and endogenous entry: Empirical insights from eBay auctions. *Rand Journal of Economics*, 34, 2, 329–355.

Bapna, R. 2003. When snipers become predators: Can mechanism design save online auctions? *Communications of the ACM*, 46, 12, 152–158.

Bapna, R.; Goes, P.; and Gupta, A. 2000. A theoretical and empirical investigation of multi-item on-line auctions. *Information Technology and Management*, 1, 1–2, 1–23.

———. 2001a. Comparative analysis of multi-item online auctions: Evidence from the laboratory. *Decision Support Systems*, 32, 2, 135–153.

———. 2001b. Insights and analysis of online auctions. *Communications of the ACM*, 44, 11, 42–50.

———. 2003. Replicating online Yankee auctions to analyze auctioneers' and bidders' strategies. *Information Systems Research*, 14, 3, 244–268.

Bapna, R.; Goes, P.; Gupta, A.; and Karuga, G. 2004. Predicting bidders' willingness-to-pay in online multi-unit ascending auctions: Analytical and empirical insights. Working paper, School of Business, University of Connecticut, Storrs.

Baye, M.R.; Morgan, J.; and Scholten, P. 2004. Temporal price dispersion: Evidence from an online consumer electronics market. *Journal of Interactive Marketing*, 18, 4, 101–115.

Baylis, K. and Perloff, J. 2002. Price dispersion on the Internet: Good firms and bad firms. *Review of Industrial Organization*, 21, 3, 305–324.

Bergen, M.; Kauffman, R.J.; Kim, H.K.; and Lee, D.W. 2007. Customer antagonism-driven price rigidity in Internet-based selling. Paper presented at the Twentieth Anniversary Research Symposium on Competitive Strategy, Economics and Information Systems, Fortieth Hawaii International Conference on Systems Science, Big Island, January.

Bergen, M.; Kauffman, R.J.; and Lee, D.W. 2004. Store quality image and the rational inattention hypothesis: An empirical study of the drivers and $9 and 9¢ endings. Paper presented at *INFORMS Conference on Information Systems and Technologies,* Denver, October.

———. 2005. Discovering price rigidity and price adjustment patterns on the Internet: Evidence from the e-bookselling industry. *Journal of Management Information Systems*, 22, 2, 57–90.

———. 2006a. From quality to competition: The role of economic factors to explain digital prices. Working paper, Carlson School of Management, University of Minnesota, Minneapolis, June.
———. 2006b. Price points and price rigidity on the Internet: A massive quasi-experimental data mining approach. Working paper, Carlson School of Management, University of Minnesota, Minneapolis, June.
Beutler, L.E. 1996. The view from the rear: An editorial. *Journal of Consulting and Clinical Psychology,* 64, 5, 845–847.
Bockstedt, J.; Kauffman, R.J.; and Riggins, F.J. 2006. The move to artist-led music distribution: Explaining market structure changes in the digital music market. *International Journal of Electronic Commerce,* 10, 3, 7–38.
Brinkmann, U. and Seifert, M. 2001. Face to interface: Zum problem der vertrauenskonstitution im Internet am beispiel von elektronischen auktionen (Face to interface: the establishment of trust in the Internet—the case of electronic auctions). *Zeitschrift für Soziologie,* 30, 1, 23–47.
Brynjolfsson, E.; Hu, J.; and Smith, M. 2003. Consumer surplus in the digital economy: Estimating the value of increased product variety. *Management Science,* 49, 11, 1580–1596.
Brynjolfsson, E. and Smith, M. 2000. Frictionless commerce? A comparison of Internet and conventional retailers. *Management Science,* 46, 4, 563–585.
Catledge, L.D. and Pitkow, J.E. 1995. Characterizing browsing strategies in the World-Wide Web. *Computer Networks and ISDN Systems,* 27, 6–14, 1065–1073.
Chen, R. and He, F. 2003. Examination of brand knowledge, perceived risk and consumers' intention to adopt an online retailer. *Total Quality Management and Business Excellence,* 14, 6, 677–694.
Chevalier, J.A. and Mayzlin, D. 2003. The effect of word of mouth on sales: Online book reviews. Working paper ES-28, School of Management, Yale University, New Haven.
Chu, W.; Choi, B.; and Song, M.R. 2005. The role of on-line retailer brand and infomediary reputation in increasing consumer purchase intention. *International Journal of Electronic Commerce,* 9, 3, 115–127.
Church, A.H. 2001. Is there a method to our madness? The impact of data collection methodology on organizational survey results. *Personnel Psychology,* 54, 4, 937–969.
Churchman, C.W. 1971. *The Design of Inquiring Systems.* New York: Basic Books.
Clay, K.; Krishnan, R.; and Wolff, E. 2001. Prices and price dispersion on the Web: Evidence from the online book industry. *Journal of Industrial Economics,* 49, 4, 521–539.
Clay, K.; Krishnan, R.; Wolff, E., and Fernandes, D. 2002a. Retailer strategies on the Web: Price and non-price competition in the online book industry. *Journal of Industrial Economics,* 50, 3, 351–367.
Clay, K.; Ouyang, S.; Smith, M.; and Wolff, E. 2002b. Leader follower behavior? Evidence from online book markets. Working paper, Heinz School of Public Policy and Management, Carnegie Mellon University, Pittsburgh.
Clemons, E.; Hann, I.; and Hitt, L. 2002. Price dispersion and differentiation in online travel: An empirical investigation. *Management Science,* 48, 4, 534–549.
Curtin, J.; Kauffman, R.J.; and Riggins, F.J. 2007. Making the "MOST" out of RFID technology: A research agenda for the study of the adoption, use and impacts of RFID. *Information Technology and Management,* 8, 2, 87–110.
Dans, E. 2002. Existing business models for auctions and their adaptation to electronic markets. *Journal of Electronic Commerce Research,* 3, 2, 23–31.
Dellarocas, C.N.; Awad, N.; and Zhang, X. 2004. Using online reviews as a proxy of word-of-mouth for motion picture revenue forecasting. Working paper, Sloan School of Management, MIT, Cambridge, MA.
Dellarocas, C. and Wood, C.A. 2007. The sound of silence in online feedback: Estimating trading risks in the presence of reporting bias. *Management Science,* in press.
Dewan, S. and Hsu, V. 2001. Trust in electronic markets: Price discovery in generalist versus specialty online auctions. Working paper, University of Washington Business School, University of Washington, Seattle.
Dommeyer, C.J. and Moriarty, E. 1999–2000. Comparing two forms of an e-mail survey: Embedded versus attached. *Journal of the Market Research Society,* 42, 1, 39–52.
Earp, J.B. and Baumer, D. 2003. Innovative Web use to learn about consumer behavior and online privacy. *Communications of the ACM,* 46, 4, 81–83.
Easley, R.F. and Tenorio, R. 2004. Jump-bidding strategies in Internet auctions. *Management Science,* 50, 10, 1407–1419.
Eaton, D.H. 2002. Valuing information: Evidence from guitar auctions on eBay. Working paper, Department of Economics and Finance, Murray State University, Murray, KY.

Ederington, L.H. and Dewally, M.A. 2003. Comparison of reputation, certification, warranties, and information disclosure as remedies for information asymmetries: Lessons from the online comic book market. Working paper, Price College of Business, University of Oklahoma, Norman.

Ferl, T.E. and Millsap, L. 1992. Remote use of the University of California MELVYL Library System: An online survey. *Information Technology and Libraries,* 11, 3, 285–303.

Gardyn, R. 2003. Born to be wired. *American Demographics,* 25, 3, 14–15.

Ghose, A.; Smith, M.D.; and Telang, R. 2006. Internet exchanges for used books: An empirical analysis of product cannibalization and welfare impact. *Information Systems Research,* 17, 1, 3–19.

Ghose, A. and Sundararajan, A. 2006. Evaluating pricing strategy using e-commerce data: Evidence and estimation challenges, *Statistical Science,* 21, 2, 131–142.

Gilkeson, J.H. and Reynolds, K. 2003. Determinants of Internet auction success and closing price: An exploratory study. *Psychology and Marketing,* 20, 6, 537–566.

Gopal, R.; Bhatacharjee, S.; and Sanders, L. 2006. Do artists benefit from online music sharing? *Journal of Business,* 79, 1503–1533.

Gordon, M.E. and Lima-Turner, K.D. 1997. Consumer attitudes toward Internet advertising: A social contract perspective. *International Marketing Review,* 14, 5, 362–375.

Granados, N.; Gupta, A.; and Kauffman, R.J. 2005. Market transparency in Internet-based selling: Modeling and empirical analysis. Paper presented at INFORMS Main Conference, San Francisco.

Gregg, D.G. and Scott, J.E. 2006. The role of reputation systems in reducing on-line auction fraud. *International Journal of Electronic Commerce,* 10, 3, 95–120.

Hahn, J. and Kauffman, R.J. 2003. Measuring and comparing the effectiveness of e-commerce Web site designs. Working paper, MIS Research Center, Carlson School of Management, University of Minnesota, Minneapolis.

Houser, D. and Wooders, J. 2000. Reputation in auctions: Theory and evidence from eBay. Working paper, Eller School of Business, University of Arizona, Tuscon.

Hyde, V.; Jank, W.; and Shmueli, G. 2006. Investigating concurrency in online auctions through visualization. *American Statistician,* 60, 3, 241–250.

Jank, W. and Shmueli, G. 2005. Profiling price dynamics in online auctions using curve clustering. Working paper, Smith School of Business, University of Maryland, College Park.

———. 2006. Functional data analysis in electronic commerce research. *Statistical Science,* 21, 2, 155–166.

Jap, S.D. 2003. An exploratory study of the introduction of online reverse auctions. *Journal of Marketing,* 67, 3, 96–107.

Jin, G. and Kato, A. 2002. Blind trust online: Experimental evidence from baseball cards. Working paper, Department of Economics, University of Maryland, College Park.

Kamis, A. 2006. Search strategies in shopping engines: An experimental investigation. *International Journal of Electronic Commerce,* 11, 1, 63–84.

Kauffman, R.J. and Lee, D. 2004. Price rigidity on the Internet: New evidence from the online bookselling industry. In R. Agarwal, L. Kirsch and J.I. DeGross, eds., *Proceedings of the 25th International Conference on Information Systems.* Washington, DC, December.

———. 2006. Should we expect less price rigidity in the digital economy? Working paper, University of Minnesota, Minneapolis, November.

Kauffman, R.J.; March, S.T.; and Wood, C.A. 2000. Design principles for long-lived Internet agents. *International Journal of Intelligent Systems in Accounting, Finance and Management,* 9, 4, 217–236.

Kauffman, R.J. and Wang, B. 2001. New buyers' arrival under dynamic pricing market microstructure: The case of group-buying discounts on the Internet. *Journal of Management Information Systems,* 18, 2, 157–188.

Kauffman, R.J. and Wood, C.A. 2003. Analyzing competitive and tacitly collusive strategies in electronic marketplaces. Working paper, MIS Research Center, Carlson School of Management, University of Minnesota, Minneapolis.

———. 2005. The effects of shilling on final bid prices in online auctions. *Electronic Commerce and Research Applications,* 4, 1, 21–34.

———. 2006. Doing their bidding: An empirical examination of factors that affect a buyer's utility in Internet auctions. *Information Technology and Management,* 7, 3, 171–190.

———. 2007. Follow the leader? Strategic pricing in e-commerce, *Managerial Decision and Economics,* in press.

Kendall, P.C. and Flannery-Schroeder, E.C. 1998. Methodological issues in treatment research for anxiety disorders in youth. *Journal of Abnormal Child Psychology,* 26, 1, 27–39.

Klein, M. and Dellarocas, C. 1999. Exception handling in agent systems. In *Proceedings of the Third International Conference on Autonomous Agents,* Seattle, WA. New York: ACM Press, 62–68.

Lakshmanan, L.V.S.; Sadri, F.; and Subramanian, S.N. 2001. SchemaSQL: An extension to SQL for multi-database interoperability. *ACM Transactions on Database Systems,* 26, 4, 476–519.

Lave, J. 1988. *Cognition in Practice: Mind, Mathematics and Culture.* Cambridge: Cambridge University Press, 1988.

Lederer, A.L.; Maupin, D.J.; Sena, M.P.; and Zhuang, Y. 2000. The technology acceptance model and the World Wide Web. *Decision Support Systems,* 29, 3, 269–282.

Lee, H.G. 1998. Do electronic marketplaces lower the price of goods? *Communications of the ACM,* 41, 1, 73–80.

Lee, S.; Zufryden, F.; and Drèze, X. 2003. A study of consumer switching behavior across Internet portal Web sites. *International Journal of Electronic Commerce,* 7, 3, 39–63.

Levy, D.; Lee, D.; Chen, A.; Kauffman, R. J.; and Bergen, M. 2006. Making sense of ignoring cents: Price points and price rigidity under rational inattention. Working paper, MIS Research Center, Carlson School of Management, University of Minnesota, Minneapolis, November.

Lenard, T.M. and Britton, D.B. 2006. *The Digital Economy Factbook,* 8th ed. Washington, DC: Progress and Freedom Foundation.

Lipsman, A. 2007. comScore forecasts total e-commerce spending by consumers will reach approximately $170 billion in 2006. comScore.com. Reston, VA. Available at www.comscore.com/press/ release.asp?press=959 (accessed May 20, 2007).

List, J.A. and Lucking-Reiley, D. 2000. Demand reduction in multi-unit auctions: Evidence from a sportscard field experiment. *American Economic Review,* 90, 4, 961–972.

———. 2002. Bidding behavior and decision costs in field experiments. *Economic Inquiry,* 40, 44, 611–619.

Livingston, J.A. 2002. How valuable is a good reputation? A sample selection model of Internet auctions. Working Paper, Department of Economics, University of Maryland, College Park.

Lucas, H.C., Jr. and Oh. W. 2006. Information technology and pricing decisions: Price adjustments in online computer markets. *MIS Quarterly,* 30, 3, 755–775.

Lucking-Reiley, D. 1999. Using field experiments to test equivalence between auction formats: Magic on the Internet. *American Economic Review,* 89, 5, 1063–1080.

Lucking-Reiley, D.; Bryan, D.; Prasad, N.; and Reeves, D. 2000. Pennies from eBay: The determinants of price in online auctions. Working paper, Department of Economics, University of Maryland, College Park.

Lynch, J.G. and Ariely, D. 2000. Wine online: Search costs affect competition on price, quality and distribution. *Marketing Science,* 19, 1, 83–103.

Mahmood, M.A.; Bagchi, K.; and Ford, T.C. 2004. On-line shopping behavior: Cross-country empirical research. *International Journal of Electronic Commerce,* 9, 1, 9–30.

Mason, R.O. and Mitroff, I.I. 1973. A program for research on management information systems. *Management Science,* 19, 5, 475–487.

Massad, V.J. and Tucker, J.M. 2000. Comparing bidding and pricing between in-person and online auctions. *Journal of Product and Brand Management,* 9, 5, 325–332.

McGrath, J.E. 1982. Dilemmatics: The study of research choices and dilemmas. In J.E. McGrath, J. Martin, and R. Kula, eds., *Judgment Calls in Research.* Beverly Hills, CA: Sage, 69–102.

Mehta, R. and Sivadas, E. 1995. Comparing response rates and response content in mail versus electronic mail surveys. *Journal of the Market Research Society,* 37, 4, 429–439.

Melnik, M.I. and Alm, J. 2002. Does a seller's e-commerce reputation matter? Evidence from eBay auctions. *Journal of Industrial Economics,* 50, 3, 337–349.

Mesenbourg, T.L. 2004. Measuring electronic business: Definitions, underlying concepts, and measurement plans. Research report, assistant director for Economic Programs, Bureau of the Census, United States Government, Washington, DC. Available at www.census.gov/epcd/www/ebusines.htm (accessed May 20, 2007).

Metaxiotis, K.S.; Askounis, D.; and Psarras, J. 2002. Expert systems in production planning and scheduling: A state-of-the-art survey. *Journal of Intelligent Manufacturing,* 13, 4, 253–260.

Mitroff, I.I. and Mason, R.O. 1982. Business policy and metaphysics: Some philosophical considerations. *Academy of Management Review,* 7, 3, 361–371.

Murphy, J.; Hofacker, C.F.; and Bennett, M. 2001. Website-generated market-research data: Tracing the tracks left behind by visitors. *Cornell Hotel and Restaurant Administration Quarterly,* 42, 1, 82–91.

Oh, W. 2002. C2C Versus B2B: A comparison of the winner's curse in two types of electronic auctions. *International Journal of Electronic Commerce,* 6, 4, 115–138.

Ow, T. and Wood, C.A. 2003. The conflicting effect of experience on buying and selling in online auctions: An empirical examination of the effect of trust in electronic markets. In A. Bharadwaj, S. Narasimhan, and R. Santhanam, eds., *Proceedings of the Fall 2003 Conference for Information Systems and Technology.* Atlanta, October.

Pan, X.; Ratchford, B.; and Shankar, V. 2002. Can price dispersion in online markets be explained by differences in e-tailer service quality? *Marketing Science,* 30, 4, 433–445.

Park, C. and Kim, Y. 2003. Identifying key factors affecting consumer purchase behavior in an online shopping context. *International Journal of Retail and Distribution Management,* 31, 1, 16–29.

Poole, M.S. and van de Ven, A.H. 1989. Using paradox to build management and organizational theories. *Academy of Management Review,* 14, 4, 562–578.

Rafaeli, S. and Noy, A. 2002. Online auctions, messaging, communication and social facilitation: A simulation and experimental evidence. *European Journal of Information Systems,* 11, 3, 196–207.

Resnick, P. and Zeckhauser, R. 2002. Trust among strangers in Internet transactions: Empirical analysis of eBay's reputation system. In M.R. Baye, ed., *Advances in Applied Microeconomics,* 11. Amsterdam: Elsevier Science, 127–158.

Resnick, P.; Zeckhauser, R.; Swanson, J.; and Lockwood, K. 2003. The value of reputation on eBay: A controlled experiment. Working paper, School of Information, University of Michigan, Ann Arbor.

Roth, A.E. and Ockenfels, A. 2002. Last-minute bidding and the rules for ending second-price auctions: Evidence from eBay and Amazon auctions on the Internet. *American Economic Review,* 92, 4, 1093–1103.

Runkel, P.J. and McGrath, J.E. 1972. *Research on Human Behavior: A Systematic Guide to Method.* New York: Holt, Rinehart and Winston.

Scribner, S. 1984. Studying working intelligence. In B. Rogoff and J. Lave, eds., *Everyday Cognition: Its Development in Social Context.* Cambridge: Harvard University Press.

Securities Exchange Commission. 2006. eBay 2005 annual report, U.S. Government, Washington, DC. Available at www.sec.gov/Archives/edgar/data/1065088/000095013406003678/ f17187e10vk.htm (accessed May 20, 2007).

Segev, A.; Beam, C.; and Shanthikumar, J.G. 2001. Optimal design of Internet-based auctions. *Information Technology and Management,* 2, 2, 121–163.

Sheehan, K.B. 2002. Toward a typology of Internet users and online privacy concerns. *Information Society,* 18, 1, 21–31.

Shmueli, G. and Jank, W. 2005. Visualizing online auctions. *Journal of Computational and Graphical Statistics,* 14, 2, 299–319.

Shmueli, G.; Jank, W.; Aris, A,; Plaisant, C.; and Shneiderman, B. 2006. Exploring auction databases through interactive visualization. *Decision Support Systems,* 42, 3, 1521–1536.

Shmueli, G.; Russo, R.P.; and Jank, W. 2004. Modeling bid arrivals in online auctions. Working paper, Smith School of Business, University of Maryland, College Park.

Smith, M.D. 2002. The impact of shopbots on electronic markets. *Marketing Science,* 30, 4, 442–450.

Smith, M.D. and Brynjolfsson, E. 2001. Customer decision making at an Internet shopbot: Brand still matters. *Journal of Industrial Economics,* 49, 4, 541–558.

Srivastava, J. and Cooley, R. 2003. Web business intelligence: Mining the Web for actionable knowledge. *INFORMS Journal on Computing,* 15, 2, 191–198.

Standifird, S.S. 2001. Reputation and e-commerce: eBay auctions and the asymmetrical impact of positive and negative ratings. *Journal of Management,* 27, 3, 279–296.

Straub, D.; Limayem, M.; and Karahanna-Evaristo, E. 1995. Measuring system usage: Implications for IS theory testing. *Management Science,* 41, 8, 1328–1344.

Stylianou, A.C.; Kumar, R.L.; and Robbins, S.S. 2005. Pricing on the Internet and in conventional retail channels: A study of over-the-counter pharmaceutical products. *International Journal of Electronic Commerce,* 10, 1, 135–152.

Tang, F. and Lu, D. 2001. Pricing patterns in the online CD market: An empirical study. *Electronic Markets,* 11, 3, 171–185.

Tang, F. and Xing, X. 2001. Will the growth of multi-channel retailing diminish the pricing efficiency of the Web? *Journal of Retailing,* 77, 3, 319–333.

Tillotson, J.; Cherry, J.; and Clinton, M. 1995. Internet use through the University of Toronto Library: Demographics, destinations, and users' reactions. *Information Technology and Libraries,* 14, 3, 190–198.

Tu, Y. and Lu, M. 2006. An experimental and analytical study of on-line digital music sampling strategies. *International Journal of Electronic Commerce,* 10, 3, 39–70.

Urban, G.L.; Sultan, F.; and Qualls, W. 2000. Placing trust at the center of your Internet strategy. *Sloan Management Review,* 24, 1, 39–48.

Walter, Z.; Gupta, A.; and Su. B. 2006. The sources of online dispersion across product types: An integrative view of on-line search costs and price premiums. *International Journal of Electronic Commerce,* 11, 1, 37–62.

Wang, S.; Jank, W.; and Shmueli, G. 2006. Explaining and forecasting online auction prices and their dynamics using functional data analysis. *Journal of Business and Economic Statistics,* in press.

Ward, S.G.; and Clark, J.M. 2002. Bidding behavior in on-line auctions: An examination of the eBay Pokemon card market. *International Journal of Electronic Commerce,* 6, 4, 139–155.

Wilcox, R.T. 2000. Experts and amateurs: The role of experience in Internet auctions. *Marketing Letters,* 11, 363–374.

Wood, C.A.; Fan, M.; and Tan, Y. 2003. An examination of the reputation systems for online auctions. Working paper, Mendoza College of Business, University of Notre Dame, Notre Dame, IN.

Wood, C.A. and Ow, T. 2005. WebView: A SQL extension for joining corporate data to data derived from the Web. *Communications of the ACM,* 48, 9, 99–104.

Yamagishi, T. 2003. The role of reputation in open and closed societies: An experimental study of Internet auctioning. Working paper, Department of Behavioral Science, Graduate School of Letters, Hokkaido University, Sapporo, Japan.

Yin, P. 2002. Information dispersion and auction prices. Working paper, Harvard Business School, Harvard University, Boston, MA.

CHAPTER 3

A POTENTIAL OUTCOMES APPROACH TO ASSESS CAUSALITY IN INFORMATION SYSTEMS RESEARCH

SUNIL MITHAS, DANIEL ALMIRALL, AND MAYURAM S. KRISHNAN

Abstract: Difficulties in conducting experiments in commercial settings make it necessary to use observational data to study the effect of technological interventions. Since assignment to treatment group cannot be assumed to be random in observational data, the challenge lies in assessing when one can infer causality in such quasi-experimental studies. This chapter reviews recent theoretical and methodological advances in econometrics and statistics to suggest applicability of a potential outcomes approach to assess the causal effect of a particular treatment on outcomes of interest in the information systems literature.

Keywords: *Analytical Methods, Causality, Empirical Research, IS Research, Potential Outcomes Approach, Propensity Scores, Quasi-Experiments, Statistical Methods, Technology Interventions, Theory Testing*

INTRODUCTION

The ultimate purpose of scientific inquiry is to uncover causal relationships among variables of interest. However, discussions of causality often turn philosophical, offering little guidance for applied researchers. The traditional solutions to deal with causality either make strong and unverifiable assumptions, as in the instrumental variable (IV) approach (Angrist, Imbens, and Rubin, 1996) or may require the collection of longitudinal data that may not be feasible. The problem of causality is particularly severe in applied fields such as information systems (IS) and electronic commerce because of the difficulty or the infeasibility of carrying out experiments using randomization, or of collecting longitudinal data on most phenomena of interest. The question then arises: Can researchers infer causality if they use cross-sectional data sets in an observational study? More specifically, we may ask: What are the explicit assumptions researchers must make in order to assess causality using observational cross-sectional data sets, and what tools are available to authenticate such assumptions?

IS researchers have grappled with the problem of inferring causality and have debated this issue for many years. While many researchers agree that randomized experiments are important for establishing cause-and-effect relationships, conducting experiments with real firms is quite difficult in most cases in the IS domain (Lucas, 1975, 1980). For example, Banker, Kauffman, and Morey (1990) observe "it will continue to be a challenge to collect large and rich samples of data, and to identify instances where a simulated IT value experiment can be carried out with a control group and a test group" (p. 50).

The following extract from a panel discussion among senior scholars at the 1991 International Conference on Information Systems (ICIS) meeting suggests dissatisfaction with the narrow repertoire of techniques being used for data analysis in the IS domain. This exchange also recognizes the difficulty of conducting randomized field trials involving actual firms to study business value of IT (Banker, Kauffman, and Mahmood, 1993, pp. 582–583):

> Benn Konsynski: I challenge each one of you to make sure that you have exercised the full spectrum of analytics. You might consider trying out laboratory research. . . .
> Rajiv Banker: . . . can you explain how one can use lab experiments to study business value?
> Benn Konsynski: With that exception in mind, I find it very difficult (except for microcosmic impacts assessments) to find out how I can leverage lab experiments to look at the business value. . . .

Given the difficulty of conducting randomized field trials in IS research, one option is that researchers analyze and make causal inferences from data that have been generated in a way that *approximates* a randomized experiment; see Rosenbaum (1999) for a description of how to achieve randomization through careful control of research design. As an example of such a field design in IS research, Banker, Kauffman, and Morey (1990) study the effect of deployment of a new cash-register point-of-sale and order-coordination technology called "Positran" on material cost savings at Hardee's. Their study uses data on eighty-nine randomly selected restaurants, of which forty-eight had deployed Positran for more than a quarter. They note: "The design of the study is of special interest, because it approximates a controlled experiment" (p. 30). However, many observational studies do not have data that approximate an experimental design and yet researchers are interested in estimating causal effects.

The goal of this chapter is to review theoretical and methodological advances in econometrics and statistics to point to a framework for investigating causal relationships for such situations (Heckman, 2005; Rubin, 1974, 1977; Rubin and Waterman, 2006). This framework uses the language of *potential outcomes* to define the causal parameters of interest. This is accomplished, in large part, by focusing on a simple causal effect—the most common, in fact—known as the *average causal effect* (ACE). (Appendix 3.1 describes some other causal effects that may be of interest to IS researchers.) We also describe the steps to carrying out a *propensity score subclassification analysis* in the context of a substantive research problem in the IS domain: the effect of *customer relationship management* (CRM) systems on customer satisfaction (Fornell et al., 2006; Mithas, Krishnan, and Fornell, 2005). This is one of many methods available to the IS researcher for estimating the ACE. In addition, we point to an approach for judging the robustness of an analysis to unobserved/unknown confounder bias that will appeal to IS researchers interested in causal analysis (Rosenbaum and Rubin, 1983a, 1983b).

Although several excellent reviews of the causality literature are available (Angrist, Imbens, and Rubin, 1996; Angrist and Krueger, 1999; Dehejia and Wahba, 2002; Heckman, 2005; Imbens, 2004; Little and Rubin, 2000; Rosenbaum, 2002; Rubin, 2005; Winship and Morgan, 1999), this chapter's contribution lies in discussing the statistical and econometric issues from an IS perspective and describing a practical approach for applying these ideas within empirical IS research. We expect that after reading this chapter, IS researchers will have an intuitive understanding of the potential outcomes framework for causality, and understand the role of confounding bias and why this is the primary obstacle in estimating causal effects. We hope that this chapter encourages IS researchers to couch their causal questions in terms of potential outcomes that put questions of causality on a firm footing.

This chapter provides a relevant set of definitions and a conceptual framework; describes the application of the causal approach using propensity scores and sensitivity analysis; compares the potential outcome-based causal approach with ordinary least squares approach commonly used by IS researchers; discusses the role of theory in causal analysis; and ends with concluding remarks.

DEFINING A CAUSAL QUESTION AND TERMINOLOGY

The approach underlying the causal reasoning and methods adopted in this chapter is based on the *potential outcomes framework for causation,* sometimes known as the *counterfactual framework for causal inference.* In this section, we (1) conceptualize the basic building blocks for causation under the potential outcomes framework, (2) define *individual* and *average* causal effects using potential outcomes, (3) discuss the *fundamental problem of causal inference,* (4) relate potential outcomes to observed data, (5) define the *standard estimator,* (6) discuss the role of randomization in causal inference, and (7) define and discuss *confounding bias,* the main obstacle to obtaining estimates for causal effects in observational studies.

Historical Perspective and the Building Blocks of the Potential Outcomes Approach

The origin of the *counterfactual view* of causality can be traced back to the insightful critique of Hume (1740) in the eighteenth century and subsequent work by Lewis (1973). Independently, Neyman, Dabrowska, and Speed (1990) introduced *potential outcomes* to analyze the causal effect of different crop varieties on crop yield using experimental data. Rubin (1974, 1978) extended Neyman's work to deal with the analysis of causal effects in observational studies. Since then, the approach has received considerable attention from statistical (Holland, 1986), epidemiological (Little and Rubin, 2000), and econometric (Heckman, Ichimura, and Todd, 1997) researchers seeking a formal language for the study of causation using both experimental and observational data. In parallel, the philosophy community also provided analyses of counterfactual reasoning for causation (Glymour, 1986). Holland (1986) provides an excellent introduction of the potential outcomes model for causality, which he calls *Rubin's model,* and compares it with causal thinking in philosophy, statistics, medicine, economics, and social science.

Notation

Under the potential outcomes framework, defining a causal question involves essentially two things: (1) an entity with two or more levels of a hypothesized or putative cause, and (2) a notion for the response or effect at every possible level of the putative cause.

We define a population Q that has its individuals or units denoted by i. We denote the treatment (i.e., the putative cause) by lowercase z, where z can take at least two distinct values or levels. Typically, $z = 0$ represents the standard, baseline, low, or no treatment. For every unit i under study and corresponding to each fixed value of treatment z, we conceptualize a potential response (or outcome), $Y_i(z)$, a random variable that may be either continuous or discrete. Refer to Appendix 3.2 for a list of key terms and notation used in this chapter.

For example, consider studying the causal effect of investing in CRM systems within the past year on customer satisfaction among the population of Fortune 500 firms. In this case, z is dichotomous depending on whether a firm has implemented CRM ($z = 1$, the treatment) or not ($z = 0$, the control) within the past year. Suppose further that customer satisfaction is measured on a

Table 3.1

Hypothetical Data for Ten Fortune 500 Companies Used to Describe Concept of a Potential Outcome

Company	Potential customer satisfaction $Y(z)$ $z = 1$ (CRM)	$z = 0$ (No CRM)	Individual Causal Effect (ICE)
A	72	56	16
B	70	65	5
C	44	49	−5
D	81	43	38
E	65	70	−5
F	70	80	−10
G	80	75	5
H	75	80	−5
I	75	70	5
J	75	70	5
Population averages	$E[Y(1)] = 70.7$	$E[(0)] = 65.8$	ACE = 4.9

continuous scale. For each of the Fortune 500 firms under study, we conceptualize two potential responses for the *customer satisfaction index:* $Y_i(0)$ and $Y_i(1)$. For a particular firm, say Firm A, $Y_A(1)$ refers to the customer satisfaction score if A had invested in CRM ($z = 1$), whereas $Y_A(0)$ refers to the customer satisfaction score if A had not invested in CRM ($z = 0$). The set $[Y_A(0), Y_A(1)]$ is known as the *set of potential outcomes* for A. Using the *potential outcomes framework,* every company in our population Q—for example, every Fortune 500 company—is said to have a set of potential outcomes.

Notice that lowercase z does not have a unit-specific index i; it does not represent a random variable. It merely describes the possible treatment values. Also, there is no requirement that treatment (the hypothesized cause z) be binary. If z were a trichotomous variable (e.g., high [$z = 2$], medium [$z = 1$], low [$z = 0$] IT investment), then each firm would have three potential outcomes, one under each level of the treatment. Likewise, if z were continuous (e.g., amount of investment in IT as a percentage of revenue) then each firm would have a separate trajectory of response values along the interval of possible values for z.

DEFINING CAUSAL EFFECTS

Under the above conception, contrasts between potential outcomes for the same unit represent *individual causal effects* (ICE). The causal effect of a treatment z on the outcome $Y_i(z)$ for unit i is defined as the difference between the two potential outcomes at different levels of z. In our hypothetical example, in which z is dichotomous, the difference in customer satisfaction, $Y_A(1) − Y_A(0)$, represents the Firm A-specific causal effect of implementing CRM versus not implementing CRM on customer satisfaction. We call this the *individual causal effect* for Firm A and denote it by ICE_A.

To fix these ideas, we ask that the reader consider Table 3.1, a hypothetical data set of ten Fortune 500 firms, in which we pretend to know the potential outcomes describing customer satisfaction (a continuous measure between 0 and 100) had the companies implemented CRM ($z = 1$) or not ($z = 0$). The final column describes the individual causal effect for each company, which is simply the difference in the level of customer satisfaction among the two treatment settings. Table 3.1

reveals that Firm A will not benefit from implementing CRM as much as Firm D will ($ICE_A = 16$ versus $ICE_D = 38$). We also see that for Firm C, implementing CRM actually hurts the company in terms of customer satisfaction ($ICE_C = -5$).

More generally, for any type of treatment z—whether binary, discrete, or continuous—*individual causal effects* are defined as contrasts between potential outcomes at two fixed values of the treatment. Thus, $ICE_i = Y_i(z_1) - Y_i(z_2)$ represents the individual causal effect of z_1 relative to z_2, where z_1 and z_2 are fixed values in the domain of z.

Fundamental Problem of Causal Inference

Note that *ICE* is a firm-specific quantity. This firm-specific quantity can never be observed because, in actuality (i.e., for real observed data), each firm undergoes only one of the possible treatment values. In other words, we cannot calculate *ICE* and this problem has been termed as the fundamental problem of causal inference (Holland, 1986). In our hypothetical example, each firm will experience either CRM implementation or not, but not both. Thus, only one of the potential outcomes is observed for any given firm under study. Textbox 3.1 provides a discussion of how physical sciences avoid this fundamental problem of causal inference by making *homogeneity* and *temporal invariance* assumptions (Holland, 1986). Unfortunately, these assumptions are untenable in the context of social sciences.

Rubin's insight was to recognize and reformulate the *fundamental problem of causal inference* as a problem of missing data (Holland, 1986). For simplicity of notation, we omit the subscript i from further discussions, and assume that treatment z is binary and the response is continuous. Thus, from this point onwards, $Y(z)$ refers to a continuous unit-specific potential outcome that takes only two values: $Y(0)$ and $Y(1)$. Although we cannot estimate *ICE* for each firm, we can estimate the *average causal effect* (ACE) in the population Q, defined as $ACE = E[Y(1) - Y(0)]$, where the expectation operates on the potential outcomes over all units (recall, subscript i has been omitted) in the population of interest Q (e.g., all Fortune 500 firms). Under our hypothetical scenario presented in Table 3.1, for example, the average causal effect of implementing CRM on customer satisfaction is 4.9.

The *fundamental problem of causal inference* applies in this setting as well (naturally, if we cannot observe each *ICE*, then we cannot observe the *ACE*), but it has a statistical solution based on assumptions relating potential outcomes to actual observed (i.e., measured) data.

The *ACE* is an example of a causal *estimand*, defined in terms of the potential outcomes; it is the thing we wish to estimate (Rubin, 2005). Many estimators for the causal estimand *ACE* can be used (some of these are discussed below; they include the standard difference in observed means, regression, propensity score estimators, etc.). Estimators produce estimates of the *ACE* based on observed data. One important goal, for example, is to find an estimator that is unbiased for the *ACE* and to understand the conditions under which the unbiasedness can be achieved. We describe next the relationship between potential outcomes (which are used to define causal estimands) and observed data, followed by a presentation of the main assumption needed to identify causal parameters such as *ACE*.

Potential Outcomes and Observed Data

The key innovation in the definitions of causal effects described above is the notion of multiple values of the response (i.e., the potential outcomes) for each unit, under different levels of the treatment (Rubin, 2005). In fact, the nonstandard notation presented above embodies this fact.

Box 3.1

Getting Around the Fundamental Problem of Causal Inference? The Role of Homogeneity and Temporal Invariance Assumptions

In the physical sciences, the solution to the fundamental problem of causal inference is found by invoking various homogeneity or invariance assumptions about the units under study (Holland, 1986). For example, suppose we are interested in understanding how a hydrogen atom responds to the presence ($z = 1$) or absence ($z = 0$) of a certain condition (e.g., temperature, pressure, presence of some other chemical element, etc.). Suppose further that the physicist has two hydrogen atoms available to her in the laboratory. The physicist can safely assume that Hydrogen Atom 1 and Hydrogen Atom 2 will respond to the presence or absence of the condition in exactly the same way; this is known as the homogeneity assumption. In symbols, the assumption says that $Y1(0) = Y2(0)$ and $Y1(1) = Y2(1)$, which implies that the individual causal effect will be the same for both atoms; that is, $CE = Y1(1) - Y1(0) = Y2(1) - Y2(0)$. Further, this implies that $Y1(1) - Y2(0) = Y2(1) - Y1(0)$, which gives us a way to "estimate" the individual causal effect. All that the physicist needs to do is to expose Atom 1 to the condition to observe $Y1(1)$, and withhold the condition from Atom 2 in order to observe $Y2(0)$. Then, by the homogeneity assumption, the difference between the two observed responses gives a causally valid estimate of the individual causal effect: $Y1(1) - Y2(0)$, which is equal to CE. An implicit assumption here is that all other variables different from the "condition" (i.e., the treatment or exposure of interest) are kept fixed (the same) for both atoms. For example, if treatment refers to the presence or absence of oxygen, then Atom 1 and Atom 2 only differ in their exposure to oxygen—the two atoms do not differ in their exposure to temperature, pressure, the presence of other chemicals, and so on.

Another assumption often employed in the physical sciences has to do with temporal invariance. Consider studying how length of flight time is affected by wing size (small $z = 0$ versus large $z = 1$) in a robotic unmanned helicopter. The idea is to use the same unit (just one helicopter) to observe both potential outcomes: the helicopter's flight time with the small wings $Y(0)$, and flight time with the large wings $Y(1)$. Since the helicopter is exposed to each condition sequentially, then in reality what we observe are the potential outcomes indexed by both wing size and time Y(wing size, time). If the helicopter is exposed to large wing size first (time = 1) and small wing size second ($t = 2$), then the actual observed potential outcomes are $Y(1,1)$ and $Y(0,2)$, respectively. The temporal invariance assumption says that there can be no effect of time ($Y(z,1) = Y(z,2)$), so that the difference between the two observed responses is a valid estimate of the causal effect of the individual causal effect of small versus large wing size on flight—that is, $Y(1,1) - Y(0,2) = Y(1) - Y(2)$. Another way to state the assumption is that there are no carry-over effects, or that the response at time 2 is in no way affected by the exposure at time 1.

The homogeneity assumption is usually untenable in the context of units (such as firms or individuals) that are of interest to IS and e-commerce researchers. Any two Fortune 500 companies, for instance, are likely to respond differently to CRM implementation. The effect of CRM on customer satisfaction can depend, perhaps, on a firm's business sector, its location within the continental United States, or type of ecommerce (e.g., B2B or B2C). This fact has nothing to do with confounding, which can be seen as alternate explanations of observed effects. Even in an ideal setting, in which the presence or absence of CRM is randomly assigned to all Fortune 500 companies so that confounding is eliminated or reduced substantially, heterogeneous causal effects are still likely to exist.

Like the homogeneity assumption, the temporal invariance assumption also can be indefensible in IS and e-commerce research. A company's exposure to CRM at the present time may have prolonged or delayed effects on customer satisfaction (or other outcomes of interest) at later points in time, whether or not the company continues to implement CRM. As a result, it is not clear whether taking the difference in responses at two points in time (one exposed and the other not exposed) represents the true effect of CRM, a temporal effect, or some combination of the two.

Lowercase z is not a random variable. It is conceived as an *index of the response Y(z)*, which is assumed to exist for each unit under every possible value of z. Neither z nor Y(z) represents observed data.

The observed data analogs of z and Y(z) are represented by the random variables uppercase Z and Y, respectively. Z and Y are the actual observed (measured and collected) data. The relationship between [z, Y(z)] and (Z, Y) is best seen through an example. Consider Table 3.2, an augmentation of Table 3.1 that includes uppercase Z and Y, the observed values of treatment and the response, respectively. Uppercase Z is a binary random variable that denotes whether a company actually has implemented CRM within the past year (Z = 1) or not (Z = 0). Uppercase Y refers to the actual observed value of the response; it corresponds to the potential outcomes that are "said to exist" according to the observed value of Z.

Under this very simple hypothetical scenario, in which the treatment is binary, the mapping

$$Y = Z \cdot Y(1) + (Z - 1) \cdot Y(0) \tag{3.1}$$

is what relates the potential outcomes, under which causal effects are defined, to the observed data. The distinction between the *two potential values of the response variable Y(1) or Y(0)* and the *observed response variable Y* is very important in this causal framework and is rarely made in associational studies involving observed data in which causality is inferred. In fact, all statistical methods (observed data contrasts, regression methods, random effects models, fixed effects models, selection models, etc.) are *studies of association*—not causality—among observed random variables. The power of the distinction made above (or the notion of potential outcomes, more generally) is that it allows us to disentangle causal quantities that we wish to understand from statistical methods that we know how to carry out. We have defined the ACE, a data-independent causal parameter that we wish to understand. The question then becomes: How do we utilize the associational observed data methods that we know so well to estimate these structural causal quantities or, equivalently: What are the explicit assumptions that we need to make in order to infer causality from statistical methods that utilize observed data? Before we shed light on the answer to these questions, we review an assumption that has been implicit in our discussion of potential outcomes thus far.

Stable-Unit Treatment-Value Assumption

Equation 3.1 makes an implicit assumption regarding the existence of the set of potential outcomes [Y(0), Y(1)], the treatments received by others in the population Q, and the mechanism by which units in Q might receive their treatment. The assumption is known formally as the *stable-unit treatment-value assumption* (SUTVA) (Rubin, 1986). The first part of SUTVA is commonly known in the social sciences as the *no interference assumption*, which goes as far back as Neyman's work in the 1920s (discussed in Neyman, Dabrowksa, and Speed, 1990) and with a subsequent articulation by Cox (1958). It says that one unit's treatment assignment does not interfere with another unit's potential outcome. It is easy to see how this assumption may be violated in settings in which treatments are administered to groups of firms in a particular industry or time frame, such as mandated use of electronic data interchange (EDI) systems or Y2K systems. Economists refer to such effects as *social interaction* or *general equilibrium effects* (Heckman, 2005). Equation 3.1 and the first part of SUTVA assume that such effects do not exist.

The second part of SUTVA is more subtle; it concerns itself with variations in treatment. More specifically, it concerns itself with variations in treatment that are unrepresented—that is, versions

Table 3.2

Augmented Hypothetical Data Set That Includes the Observed Treatment Z for Ten Fortune 500 Companies

Company	Potential customer satisfaction Y(z) z = 1 (CRM)	Potential customer satisfaction Y(z) z = 0 (No CRM)	Observed treatment Z	Observed response Y	Individual causal effect (ICE)
A	(72)	56	0	56	16
B	70	(65)	1	70	5
C	44	(49)	1	44	−5
D	81	(43)	1	81	38
E	(65)	70	0	70	−5
F	(70)	80	0	80	−10
G	80	(75)	1	80	5
H	(75)	80	0	80	−5
I	75	(70)	1	75	5
J	75	(70)	1	75	5
Averages	Shaded[a] corresponds to observed Z = 1 $E[Y(1) \mid Z=1]$ = 70.8	Shaded[a] corresponds to observed Z = 0 $E[Y(0) \mid Z=0]$ = 71.5	π = proportion (Z = 1) = 0.6	T = the standard estimator = $E[Y(1) \mid Z=1]$ − $E[Y(0) \mid Z=0]$ = 70.8 − 71.5 = −0.7	ACE = average causal effect = $E(Y=1) - E(Y=0)$ = 4.9
	$E[Y(1) \mid Z=0]$ = 70.5	$E[Y(0) \mid Z=1]$ = 62			

Notes: Adapted from Little and Rubin (2000).
[a]Only bold values are observed and values in parentheses are not observed for a given firm.

$E[Y(1) \mid Z = 1] = (70 + 44 + 81 + 80 + 75 + 75)/6 = 70.8$
$E[Y(1) \mid Z = 0] = (72 + 65 + 70 + 75)/4 = 70.5$
$E[Y(1)] = 70.7$ (see Table 3.1)
$E[Y(0)] = 65.8$ (see Table 3.1)
$E[Y(0) \mid Z = 1] = (65 + 49 + 43 + 75 + 70 + 70)/6 = 62$
$E[Y(0) \mid Z = 0] = (56 + 70 + 80 + 80)/4 = 71.5$

APPROACH TO ASSESS CAUSALITY IN INFORMATION SYSTEMS RESEARCH   71

of the treatment that were not considered part of the causal model, or definition of treatment.

The Standard Estimator

The simplest estimate of *ACE* is the observed average difference in the response between the two observed treatment groups: $T = E(Y|Z=1) - E(Y|Z=0)$. This is the observed treatment effect estimate comparing the observed average level of customer satisfaction between companies that implemented CRM versus companies that did not. Unlike *ACE*, *T* can be estimated using the observed data. For example, we can calculate *T* using the hypothetical data presented in Table 3.2; here, $T = -0.7$. As we can see, however, *T* does not accurately reflect the true *ACE* in our made-up example. In fact, it is quite far off.

To see why *ACE* and *T* are not necessarily equivalent, first note that $E[Y(1)]$ and $E(Y|Z=1)$ are not the same thing. Whereas $E[Y(1)]$ is the expected value of $Y(1)$ over *all units* in *Q*, $E(Y|Z=1)$ refers to the expected value of $Y(1)$ for *units that are exposed to treatment;* that is, $E(Y|Z=1) = E(Y(1)|Z=1)$. We can see this relation using Equation 3.1, since $E(Y|Z=1) = E[Z \cdot Y(1) + (Z-1) \cdot Y(0) | Z=1] = E[1 \cdot Y(1) + (1-1) \cdot Y(0) | Z=1] = E(Y(1) | Z=1]$.

Likewise, $E[Y(0)]$ and $E(Y|Z=0)$ differ in that the former is an average of $Y(0)$ over *all units* in *Q*, whereas the latter is an average of the potential outcomes conditional on *units exposed to no treatment:* $E(Y|Z=0) = E(Y(0) | Z=0)$. For instance, in the hypothetical scenario of Table 3.2, the quantities of interest are: $E[Y(1)] = 70.7$; $E(Y(1) | Z=1] = 70.8$; $E[Y(0)] = 65.8$ and $E(Y|Z=0) = 71.5$. Based on these quantities, $ACE = E[Y(1)] - E[Y(0)] = 70.7 - 65.8 = 4.9$.

Second, consider the following decomposition of *ACE* (Winship and Morgan, 1999) based on the *proportion of the population assigned to the treatment group* $\pi = P(Z=1)$.

$$ACE = \pi \cdot E[Y(1) - Y(0) | Z=1] + (1-\pi) \cdot E[Y(1) - Y(0) | Z=0]$$
$$= \pi \cdot E[Y(1) | Z=1] + (1-\pi) \cdot E[Y(1) | Z=0] - (\pi \cdot E(Y(0) | Z=1]$$
$$+ (1-\pi) \cdot E[Y(0) | Z=0)]. \qquad (3.2)$$

Equation 3.2 shows that the true average causal effect *ACE* is a weighted average of the average causal effect for companies implementing CRM and the average causal effect for companies not implementing CRM. From Table 3.2, for instance, we can see that $ACE = (0.6 \cdot 70.8) + (0.4 \cdot 70.5) - (0.6 \cdot 62) + (0.4 \cdot 71.5) = 4.9$.

The Role of Randomization

Observe that if we assume

$$E[Y(1) | Z=1] = E[Y(1) | Z=0], \text{ and}$$
$$E[Y(0) | Z=1] = E[Y(0) | Z=0],$$

then the standard estimator *T* consistently estimates the true average causal effect *ACE*. However, the standard estimator *T* does not always estimate the true causal effect as defined using potential outcomes. Equivalently, the coefficient of *Z* in a regression of *Y* on *Z* does not always estimate the true causal effect.

The above fact and the relationships described in Equation 3.2 begin to underscore the importance of understanding the association of treatment exposure *Z* to the unobserved potential outcomes *Y*(0) and *Y*(1); which, as we shall see later, corresponds to understanding the *process* by which units in Q are assigned to Z. In fact, a sufficient condition for the equality conditions (i) and (ii) to hold is that the potential outcomes (Y(0), Y(1)) and Z are independent of each other. Formally, randomization ensures that, on average,

$$Y(1), Y(0) \perp Z, \qquad (3.3)$$

where the symbol $\perp$ denotes independence.

If Z and the potential outcomes Y(0) and Y(1) were independent of each other—for instance, if the Fortune 500 companies under study were randomized to implement (or not implement) CRM—then $ACE = E[Y(1) - Y(0) \mid Z = 1] = E[Y(1) - Y(0) \mid Z = 0]$, so that $T = ACE$. Thus, under randomization (and given a sufficiently large sample size), we would have a situation in which the standard observed treatment effect estimate T is equal to the average causal effect ACE. Note that this result would hold even if randomization to implement or not implement CRM was not balanced—that is, the result would hold even if π was not equal to 0.50.

The developments described above are encouraging to the extent that our new language for causal effects is consistent with common knowledge that randomizing the treatment Z allows for valid estimation of causal effects using T. We have not yet addressed, however, estimating causal effects in the observational setting in which Z is not randomized—the primary focus of this chapter. Fortunately, the potential outcomes framework will also assist us in the task of making explicit the assumptions necessary in order to identify causal effects in observational studies. Once these assumptions are made explicit, statistical methods that capitalize on these alternative assumptions can be developed in order to estimate causal parameters such as ACE in observational studies.

Confounding Bias in Observational Studies

The reason randomization works, as we have seen above, is because it ensures that both the treatment group ($Z = 1$) and the control group ($Z = 0$) are balanced across all measured and unmeasured (e.g., unknown) pretreatment covariates. This means that there can be no over- (or under-) representation of any other variable, measured or unmeasured, in the composition of the treatment or control groups. Randomization would ensure, for example, that companies randomized to implement CRM do not underrepresent the manufacturing sector. As a result of this balance, there can be no alternate explanations of the apparent (estimated) average treatment effect of Z on the response. In other words, T, by itself, captures the full effect of Z on Y.

In observational studies, on the other hand, T may reflect a combination of the true average causal effect ACE plus another quantity that reflects a noncausal association between Z and the potential outcomes Y(0) and Y(1). This quantity is known as the *confounding bias B:*

$$T = ACE + B \qquad (3.4)$$

The bias B is due to confounders of the causal effect of treatment on the response. Confounders are measured and unmeasured pretreatment variables C that are related to both treatment and the response. In the absence of randomization, confounders are likely to exist. Consider again the study of the causal effect of CRM on customer satisfaction. Manufacturing companies, for instance, which typically have higher levels of customer satisfaction (Fornell et al., 1996) may have less probability of investing in CRM systems. Without the benefits of randomizing CRM, then, the association between participating in the manufacturing sector and implementing CRM cannot be broken. As a result, the observed average treatment effect T will reflect the noncausal association between Z and the response as a result of participating (or not) in the manufacturing sector, in addition to the true causal effect of CRM on customer satisfaction. In this case, a firm's industry sector confounds (that is, confuses or distorts) the observed effect of CRM on customer satisfaction. Confounding bias B is one of the primary obstacles to obtaining valid causal effect estimates using observational data (Rubin, 2005).

All is not lost to bias B, however, in an observational studies context. One solution to help reduce or eliminate the confounding bias problem is to utilize measured pretreatment covariates to adjust for B. In particular, the pretreatment covariates that will be useful are those that are confounders of the causal effect of CRM on customer satisfaction. Confounders are those variables that both influence the assignment to treatment (e.g., CRM adoption) and are related directly to the outcome (e.g., customer satisfaction). Whether adjusting for measured pretreatment covariates thought to be confounders of the causal effect of z on $Y(z)$ is sufficient to eliminate confounding bias relies on an assumption, called *strong ignorability,* which implies that assignment to a treatment group is independent of potential outcomes conditional on observed pretreatment covariates (more details on this are provided in the next section) (Rosenbaum and Rubin, 1983b). This assumption can be seen as an alternative to the act of randomization that is characteristic of experimental studies. The assumption is also the basis for the propensity score methods we present in the next section for estimating causal effects using observational data (Rosenbaum and Rubin, 1983b).

A PROPENSITY SCORE-BASED APPROACH FOR ESTIMATING CAUSAL EFFECT

The propensity score-based matching estimator relies on the assumption of *strong ignorability.* Essentially, this assumption says that selection (and thus, confounding bias) takes place only on the observables X; that is, given information on X alone, we can obtain causal effect estimates as we would in a randomized experiment (Dehejia and Wahba, 1999; Rosenbaum and Rubin, 1983b).

Treatment Selection on Observables: The Strong Ignorability Assumption

Let X denote all measured pretreatment covariates, and let U denote the complement of X—all other unmeasured pretreatment covariates. U may include pretreatment factors that are unknown, not available to the researcher, or too expensive to measure. Thus (X, U) makes up the entire universe of pretreatment (pre-Z) covariates; note that the set of *confounders* C is a subset of (X, U).

The assumption that ensures adjusting for X is sufficient to control for confounding bias says that given X (i.e., within levels of X), the set of unmeasured confounders U is independent of the "assigned" (observed) treatment Z. In other words, this means that adjusting for X is sufficient to account for confounding bias—and thereby sufficient to estimate ACE—if the set of measured covariates X includes all confounders of the effect of z on $Y(z)$. Another way to say this is that once X is taken into account, U and Z are not correlated.

In symbols, the assumption of strong ignorability says that

$$U \perp Z \text{ given } X, \tag{3.5}$$

where the symbol $\perp$ denotes independence. Equation 3.5 is known as the assumption of *strong ignorability* (Rosenbaum and Rubin, 1983b, 1984; Rubin, 1978) and it is more often presented in its more technical form using potential outcomes

$$Y(0), Y(1) \perp Z \text{ given } X, \tag{3.6}$$

which says that "the potential outcomes $Y(0)$ and $Y(1)$ are independent of the treatment assignment Z given X." Equations 3.5 and 3.6 are equivalent.

When strong ignorability holds, it is possible to obtain a valid (i.e., unbiased) estimate of ACE by computing T within levels of X and then averaging over these strata—perhaps in a weighted fashion, depending on the contribution of each strata to the overall causal effect. The methods presented below for assessing causal effects in observational studies utilize measured pretreatment covariates to adjust for confounding in this way. The innovation in the methods presented below, however, is in the way the strata are defined.

Overcoming Confounding Bias with Propensity Scores

Under the assumption of strong ignorability, matching on observed measured confounders X can be used to overcome the confounding bias problem. However, the problem with matching is that sample sizes are often not big enough to achieve matching on all observed covariates. As a result, researchers are often constrained to match on a relatively small set of variables (Bharadwaj, 2000; Mukhopadhyay and Kekre, 2002). This problem of matching applies if one has several discrete covariates but becomes particularly severe if the covariates are of a continuous nature and is known as the curse of dimensionality. Rosenbaum and Rubin (1983b) propose an ingenious solution to this problem. The idea is based on a *propensity score,* which is the probability of being treated given X—that is, the probability that a firm has implemented CRM given the covariates X. We denote the propensity score by $e(x) = P(Z = 1 \mid X = x)$. Rosenbaum and Rubin (1983b) show that if it suffices to control for a vector of covariates X, then it suffices to control for the estimated propensity scores based on observed Xs (Joffe and Rosenbaum, 1999).

The propensity score approach offers certain advantages compared with conventional regression analysis in terms of reduced dimensionality of the problem of matching on multiple covariates, better visibility of the extent to which treatment and control groups are similar, and avoidance of reliance on strong functional form assumptions (linear effect of covariates) that are implicit in regression analysis (Dehejia and Wahba, 1999; Rubin, 1997). This approach is nonparametric in that it does not require a model for the mean of the potential outcomes $Y(z)$ given X.

Traditional matching methods based on propensity scores pair each treatment subject with a single control subject, where pairs are chosen based on similarity in the estimated probabilities of selection into the treatment. An alternative approach relies on forming subclasses $S(x)$ based on propensity scores (Rosenbaum and Rubin, 1984). Cochran (1968) has shown that five strata or subclasses are usually enough to remove more than 90 percent of the bias due to subclassifying on covariates. Recent work in econometrics has extended traditional pair-wise matching methods to accommodate use of multiple control subjects[1] to compute the missing potential outcomes leading to a reduction in variance of the matching estimator (Heckman et al., 1998; Heckman, Ichimura, and Todd, 1997).

Unfortunately, strong ignorability is an untestable assumption because we do not observe the unmeasured covariates U. This has two main implications for the planning and analysis of observational studies. The first is a proactive one: researchers should brainstorm and anticipate all possible confounders of the treatment effect of z on $Y(z)$ and then collect data on all such confounders. However, it may often be quite expensive or infeasible to collect data on all the potential confounders. Hence, the second implication is that researchers should test the sensitivity of their results subject to violations of the strong ignorability assumption (Rosenbaum, 1999). The need for such a sensitivity analysis is quite critical in applied fields such as IS and e-commerce, where an outcome such as customer satisfaction may be influenced by a multitude of factors other than information systems (such as market orientation, reputation, firm size, strategy, previous firm performance, etc.) and it may not be practical to collect data on all these relevant variables.

Steps to Achieving Estimation Robustness When the Ignorability Assumption Is Violated

Fortunately, methods exist that allow researchers to assess the robustness of their results to violations of the strong ignorability assumption and to evaluate the uncertainty of the estimated treatment effect due to selection on *unobservables*. For a lucid description of one way to conduct such a sensitivity analysis, refer to Rosenbaum and Rubin (1983a). In order to conduct the sensitivity analysis, we now assume that treatment assignment is not strongly ignorable when given Xs but it is strongly ignorable when given both s (subclass) and u. One can then calculate the sensitivity of estimates of the average treatment effect to several sets of assumptions about α (the increase in the log odds of treatment associated with $u = 1$ rather than $u = 0$), δz (the increase in the log odds of improvement under treatment z associated with $u = 1$ rather than $u = 0$) and π (probability of $u = 0$). Such an analysis will help quantify the extent to which a hypothetical unobserved covariate u would have to significantly increase the odds of treatment and the odds of improvement before altering the conclusion about the estimated causal effect of the treatment on the outcome of interest.

We have just seen how to obtain average treatment effect estimates from observational data using matching techniques. Subject to a particular assumption about the selection process—namely, strong ignorability—the treatment effect estimates we obtain are said to be *causally valid*. The strong ignorability assumption says, essentially, that we have "controlled" for or "adjusted" for all the possible confounders of the effect of treatment on response. As we have seen in the previous section, "adjustment" came in the form of matching so that pairs of treatment and control firms used in the contrasts that make up the causal estimator are said to be "very close" in their pretreatment (confounding) characteristics.

Figure 3.1 shows the steps involved in causal analysis and Table 3.3 provides a more detailed description of these steps.

We next discuss how the potential outcomes approach presented in the preceding section compares with the traditional regression-based approach.

CLASSICAL REGRESSION USING THE LANGUAGE OF POTENTIAL OUTCOMES

The most common form of adjustment in most scientific disciplines using observational data, however, utilizes the method of *regression*. Under this formulation, researchers posit models for the observed response Y given observed treatment Z *and* observed pretreatment covariates X. Let us suppose that the response Y is continuous, Z is binary, and X may be a vector of discrete or continuous covariates. Regression models typically take the form

$$E(Y \mid Z = z, X = x) = \beta_0 + z\beta + x\gamma, \tag{3.7}$$

although more complicated forms for the systematic component are often posited (e.g., treatment-covariates interaction terms, a cubic or quadratic term in X, etc.). An ordinary least squares (OLS) estimate of β is typically said to describe an estimate of the treatment effect of Z on Y.

Figure 3.1 **Six-Step Procedure for a Causal Analysis**

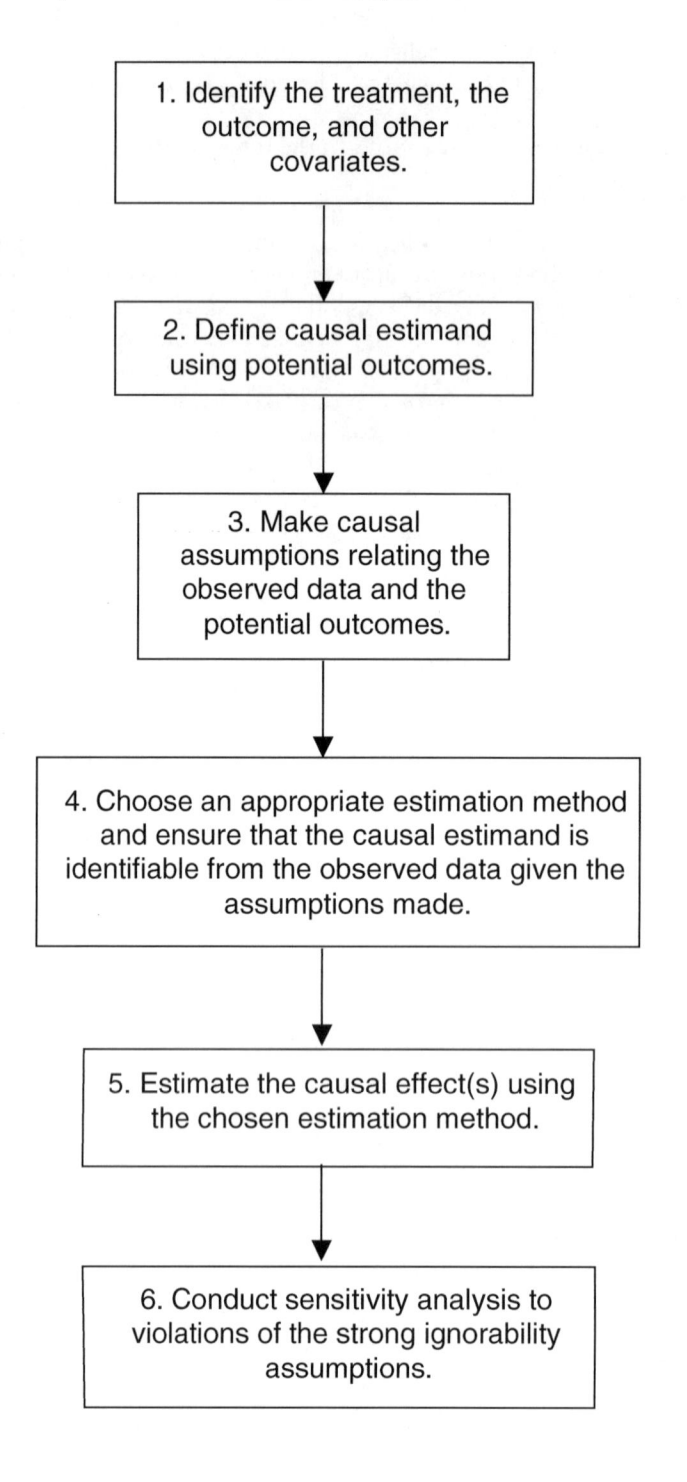

1. Identify the treatment, the outcome, and other covariates.

2. Define causal estimand using potential outcomes.

3. Make causal assumptions relating the observed data and the potential outcomes.

4. Choose an appropriate estimation method and ensure that the causal estimand is identifiable from the observed data given the assumptions made.

5. Estimate the causal effect(s) using the chosen estimation method.

6. Conduct sensitivity analysis to violations of the strong ignorability assumptions.

Table 3.3

Detailed Steps for Carrying Out a Propensity Score Subclassification Analysis to Estimate ACE Using Observational Data

Steps	Description	Hypothetical example
1. Identify the treatment, the outcome, and other covariates	Identify the observed data: Z (the treatment), Y (the response), X (pre-Z covariates); Ensure appropriate temporal ordering: X must occur before Z and Z must occur before Y (see Mithas, Almirall, and Krishnan, 2006; Mithas and Krishnan, 2004b; Rubin and Waterman, 2006)	Z is a binary variable indicating whether a firm adopts CRM systems in 1999; Y is a continuous measure of customer satisfaction in 2000; X is a vector of 5 covariates measured prior to Z.[a]
2. Define causal estimand using potential outcomes	The potential outcomes are $Y(1)$ and $Y(0)$; the parameter of interest is the average causal effect, $ACE = E[Y(1) - Y(0)]$ (see Rubin and Waterman, 2006)	The ACE is the average causal effect of implementing versus not implementing CRM systems in 1999 on customer satisfaction levels in 2000.
3. Make causal assumptions relating the observed data and the potential outcomes	Assume strong ignorability, that is, $[Y(1), Y(0)]$ are independent of Z given X (see Rosenbaum and Rubin, 1983b)	Strong ignorability assumes that we have at our disposal, as part of the vector X, all the possible pre-CRM covariates that are directly related to both CRM adoption (Z) and customer satisfaction levels (Y).
4. Choose an appropriate estimation method and ensure that the causal estimand is identifiable from the observed data given the assumptions made	Choose propensity score subclassification (see Mithas, Almirall, and Krishnan, 2006; Rosenbaum and Rubin, 1983b)	Instead of trying to adjust for the vector of 5 covariates in a regression model of Y on Z and X, for instance, we employ propensity score subclassification.
5. Estimate the causal effect(s) using the chosen estimation method	(a) Model propensity score $e(x) = Pr(Z = 1 \mid X = x)$ (see Mithas, Almirall, and Krishnan, 2006; Mithas and Krishnan, 2004b)	Run a logistic regression or probit regression model (or any other prediction method for binary outcomes) to get the propensity to adopt CRM systems given X.
	(b) Create propensity score strata to ensure balance for each covariate in each strata. Revisit the propensity score model in step (a) and iterate until a balance is achieved (see Mithas, Almirall, and Krishnan, 2006; Rubin, 2001)	Use charts or diagnostics to assess covariate balance for all Xs in each strata formed on the basis of propensity score.
	(c) Estimate causal effect (see Rubin, 2001)	One can estimate overall causal effect or strata-wise causal effects to assess treatment effect heterogeneity.
6. Conduct sensitivity analysis to violations of the strong ignorability assumptions	Calculate the sensitivity of estimates of the average treatment effect to several sets of assumptions about α (the increase in the log odds of treatment associated with $u = 1$ rather than $u = 0$), δz (the increase in the log odds of improvement under treatment t associated with $u = 1$ rather than $u = 0$) and π (probability of $u = 0$) (see Rosenbaum, 1999; Rosenbaum and Rubin, 1983a)	Report results of sensitivity analyses.

[a] One of the advantages of the propensity score approach is that it is highly scalable and one can use this approach even if one has hundreds of pretreatment covariates.

But when does β have a valid interpretation as the causal effect of treatment on the response? That is, when does conditioning (i.e., "adjusting") on observed confounders X as in Equation 3.7 allow valid causal inference according to β?

The language of potential outcomes can help us answer this question (Sobel, 1995). To understand how, let us first consider the conditional expectation that β represents according to Equation 3.7. The model in Equation 3.7 *implies* that β is the difference in conditional expectations of the response given X for Z = 1 versus Z = 0:

$$\beta = E(Y \mid Z = 1, X = x) - E(Y \mid Z = 0, X = x). \tag{3.8}$$

As stated, Equation 3.8 does not represent a contrast in Y(0) and Y(1). Thus, within the potential outcomes framework, Equation 3.8 does not represent a causal effect. In fact, it appears to be quite different from the causal effect β is typically said to describe—the average causal effect of the binary treatment z on Y(z): $ACE = E[Y(1) - Y(0)]$.

Interpreting β causally requires making additional assumptions about the relationship between the observed data X, Z, Y, and the potential outcomes Y(0) and Y(1). It can be shown that if we assume strong ignorability, as we did using the matching estimators in the preceding section, then β from the regression model in Equation 3.7 is equivalent to ACE.

So how does the regression formulation differ from the matching estimators in the preceding section? The key difference is that with regression we make the additional modeling assumption that we know the true model for the mean of Y conditional on the past (e.g., Equation 3.7). The obvious problem with this approach is that we may misspecify the model for the mean of Y given the past, thereby producing biased estimates for the causal effect. This problem would persist even if the strong ignorability assumption were satisfied. Therefore, not only is the choice of covariates crucial (in order to satisfy the strong ignorability assumption), but also the choice or correctness of the presumed model for the conditional mean of Y given Z and X. The matching and stratification-based estimators of the previous section did not require models for the conditional mean of Y.

The results presented above also provide some insight into the meaning and purpose of "adjustment" in regression models. For the purposes of causal inference, it is not necessary to include in X in Equation 3.7 model all possible covariates that are thought to generate Y in order to arrive at a valid causal effect. The researcher will be content to include in X only those covariates that are said to be related to both Z and the response Y—that is, confounders of the effect of z on Y(z)—so as to satisfy the strong ignorability assumption. It is erroneous to assume that X must contain all other predictors of Y in order to make causal inference according to β.

In this sense, the use of regression for causal inference as we have conceived of it thus far differs from the structural approach of causal modeling in which an attempt is made to model the full structure of the system that generates the response Y. We are not interested in adjusting for X because we are interested in how it affects Y; instead, we are interested in adjusting for X because it may be an alternate explanation of the apparent (observed, unadjusted) effect of Z on Y. As we have described in the section above defining a casual question, in order for X to be an alternate explanation (confounder) of the apparent effect of Z on Y, X must be related to both Z and Y.

THE ROLE OF THEORY IN CAUSAL ANALYSIS

The role of theory is as important for the potential outcomes framework for causal inference as it is in other modes of scientific inquiry (Gregor, 2006). Here we give at least three ways in which theory provides useful guidance for causal analysis and also how the potential outcomes framework clarifies the theoretical reasoning. For concreteness, let us consider again the hypothetical example concerning the average causal effect (ACE) of implementing CRM systems on levels of customer satisfaction. First, theory is indispensable because it provides the reasoning for "why" CRM systems will have an effect on customer satisfaction (Mithas, Krishnan, and Fornell, 2005). For example, Mithas, Krishnan, and Fornell (2005) argue that CRM systems affect customer satisfaction because of the impact of CRM systems on customer knowledge. Although such theoretical reasoning is not directly incorporated into the analysis in terms of estimation of structural parameters that one typically encounters in mediation[2] or other types of structural models (Freedman, 1997), it is nevertheless useful for identifying other contexts for testing this theoretical reasoning for further validation and testing as Rosenbaum (1999) suggests. In other words, the absence of structural parameters in the potential outcomes framework does not relieve a researcher from the responsibility of articulating the pathways for causal effects so that these are testable and falsifiable (Popper, 1959). In some cases, the language of potential outcomes may even make null results compelling to the extent that a theory might predict otherwise (Fornell et al., 2006; Rosenbaum, 1999).

Second, theory plays an important role when estimating the ACE and considering what variables are potential confounders of the effect of implementing CRM systems on levels of customer satisfaction. For example, if theory (based on prior knowledge or empirical work) suggests that the industry sector of a firm and the extent of supply chain integration of a firm are likely to influence both CRM adoption and customer satisfaction, then one should control for these variables in the propensity score models for CRM (Mithas, Krishnan, and Fornell, 2005). Inclusion of all the variables suggested by theory in the propensity score model will likely satisfy the *strong ignorability* assumption discussed earlier.

Finally, a third reason for the use of theory lies in the identification of variables that one may have missed in the propensity score model. As noted earlier, in a comprehensive causal analysis (that includes a sensitivity analysis), theory can help in the identification of missing variables that affect both the treatment assignment and outcome variable. In particular, if the use of sensitivity analysis in a study of the effect of CRM systems on customer satisfaction reveals that the estimated causal effect is not sensitive to assumptions about the presence or absence of market orientation among CRM firms versus non-CRM firms, then one will have greater confidence in the estimated effect (Mithas and Krishnan, 2004a).

CONCLUSION

Our goal in this chapter was to provide an overview of some of the recent advances in statistics and econometrics that can help researchers to assess causal effects of a certain treatment from observational data. While traditional regression-based methods are extremely useful for analyzing cross-sectional data, we believe that many researchers will find the potential outcomes approach attractive to answer well-posed causal questions. The most attractive feature of the methods used in this chapter is that a researcher can assess the sensitivity of his or her causal estimates to unobserved selection biases (Boulding et al., 2005). We also described the use of propensity score-based matching and sensitivity analysis. We hope that IS researchers will try some of the methods enumerated in this chapter to answer interesting research questions and make their studies more compelling, by taking steps to move from associational inference to causal inference and to quantify the degree of uncertainty involved through sensitivity analysis.

APPENDIX 3.1. THE AVERAGE TREATMENT EFFECT AMONG THE TREATED PLUS ANOTHER WAY TO LOOK AT CONFOUNDING BIAS

This chapter has devoted a great deal of effort to explicating and acquainting the reader with the potential outcomes framework in the context of the average causal effect (ACE). The decision to focus heavily on the ACE has been largely pedagogic and it is a good place to start because (1) the issues of confounding bias (the main obstacle in estimating causal effects using observational data) are easy to describe and are given meaning quite readily; (2) many IS researchers will be interested in estimating the ACE in their own work; (3) various propensity score estimation methods have been developed to estimate the ACE (among them: propensity score matching, propensity score subclassification, and propensity score weighting); and (d) because the ACE is intuitive and easy to understand—in fact, it is the effect that the majority of randomized clinical trials are designed to estimate.

It is important to understand, however, that this is just the tip of the iceberg. Many more causal effects can and have been defined using the language of potential outcomes. For substantive reasons and from a policy perspective, the average treatment effect ACE is not always of theoretical interest. Heckman (1997) and Heckman, Smith, and Clements (1997) have argued that in many situations, it is the average treatment effect *among the treated* that is of substantive interest. An intuitive way to understand their key argument is that we are less interested in knowing whether an intervention was beneficial for all individuals on average but more interested in knowing whether intervention was beneficial for those who were assigned to the treatment. For instance, we are more interested in knowing if the firms implementing CRM systems benefited from such systems after subtracting the costs of implementing CRM, instead of posing a hypothetical question about the effect of a CRM system on a firm picked at random from a population. The same reasoning applies to answering managerial concerns about usefulness of other IT systems such as ERP (enterprise resource planning) systems or RFID (radio frequency identification device) implementation.

In symbols using potential outcomes, *the average treatment effect among the treated*, which we denote by *ATT* is given by:

$$ATT = E[Y(1) - Y(0) \mid Z = 1],$$

where the symbol "|" means "given."

We have already seen *ATT* in the discussion above when the *ACE* was decomposed in Equation 3.2. Here, we offer a more detailed analysis of the ways *ACE*, *ATT*, and *T* relate in order to further understand the bias *B* that may result from using the standard estimator (Winship and Morgan, 1999). Consider the following relation (see below for a proof):

$$T = ACE + E[Y(0) \mid Z = 1] - E[Y(0) \mid Z = 0)] + (1 - \pi) \cdot (ATT - ATC) \quad (A3.1\text{-}1)$$
$$T = ACE + B1 + B2$$

where, as above, $\pi = P(Z = 1)$; and where *ATC* denotes the *average treatment effect for those assigned to control*: $ATC = E[Y(1) - Y(0) \mid Z = 0]$. Using Equation A3.1–1, we can see that *B* from Equation 3.4 has been decomposed into two parts, *B1* and *B2*. *B1* is referred to as *baseline difference* (sometimes called *heterogeneity bias*), or the differences in potential outcomes in the treated and control groups in the absence of treatment. It can be seen as the *heterogeneity bias due to differences in baseline potential outcomes*. *B2* is known as the *endogeneity bias*, which is proportional to the difference between the *average treatment effect for those assigned to treatment* (*ATT*) and the *average treatment effect for those assigned to control* (*ATC*) [Winship and Sobel 2004, Xie and Wu 2005].[3]

From Equation A3.1-1 we can see that the bias in estimating *ACE* using the standard estimator *T* is zero if the following two conditions hold:

a. If the subjects in the treatment group had not been treated, they would have had the same mean outcome as the subjects in the control group; and
b. If the subjects in the control group had instead been treated, their average treatment effect would have been the same as the average treatment effect of those who were in fact in the treatment group.

In other words, the conditions say that (1) both treatment and control groups have the *same mean on potential outcomes in the absence* of any treatment, and (2) subjects in both the treatment and control groups stand to *gain equally* from exposure to treatment.

To further clarify *B2* in Equation A3.1-1, assume that those who implemented CRM ($Z = 1$) and those who did not implement CRM ($Z = 0$) had the same mean initial customer satisfaction. Assume further that only those firms that implemented CRM would have seen an increase in their customer satisfaction. If treated and control groups are of equal size, then the standard estimator *T* would overestimate the true causal effect by a factor of two (Winship and Morgan, 1999). Note carefully, however, that in this example, the standard estimator *T* will yield a consistent estimate of the average treatment effect for the treated (i.e., *ATT*), not the average treatment effect for the entire population (i.e., *ACE*).

Proof of Equation A3.1-1

Notation

Using the notation developed in the section above defining a casual question, we again define

π = $P(Z = 1)$, the proportion of treated units in the population *Q*,
ACE = $E[Y(1) - Y(0)]$, the true *average causal effect* of the binary treatment *z* on the continuous response *Y*,
T = $E[Y(1) | Z = 1] - E[Y(0) | Z = 0]$, the *standard treatment effect* estimate,
ATT = $E[Y(1) - Y(0) | Z = 1]$, the treatment effect among the treated, and
ATC = $E[Y(1) - Y(0) | Z = 0]$, the treatment effect among those in the control group.

Proposition

We wish to prove that $T = ACE + B1 + B2$, where

$B1 = E[Y(0) | Z = 1] - E[Y(0) | Z = 0]$, the *heterogeneity bias* term, and
$B2 = (1 - \pi) \cdot (ATT - ATC)$, the *endogeneity bias* term

Proof

First, observe that using this notation, Equation 3.2 decomposes the true average causal effect according to *Z* and weighted by the proportion of treated units π.

$$ACE = \pi \cdot ATT + (1 - \pi) \cdot ATC, \qquad (A3.1\text{--}2)$$

Second, adding and subtracting $E[Y(0) | Z = 1]$ to T, we have that the standard estimator equals the *ATT* estimand plus *B1*:

$$T = E[Y(1) | Z = 1] - E[Y(0) | Z = 0]$$
$$T = E[Y(1) | Z = 1] - E[Y(0) | Z = 0] + E[Y(0) | Z = 1] - E[Y(0) | Z = 1]$$
$$T = E[Y(1) | Z = 1] - E[Y(0) | Z = 1] + E[Y(0) | Z = 1] - E[Y(0) | Z = 0]$$
$$T = ATT + B1. \qquad (A3.1\text{--}3)$$

Now, add and subtract the true causal effect *ACE* to Equation A3.1–3 to get

$$T = ACE + B1 + ATT - ACE. \qquad (A3.1\text{--}4)$$

Replacing the second *ACE* in Equation A3.1–4 with Equation A3.1–2 we arrive at

$$T = ACE + B1 + ATT - \pi \cdot ATT - (1 - \pi) \cdot ATC,$$
$$T = ACE + B1 + (1 - \pi) \cdot ATT - (1 - \pi) \cdot ATC,$$
$$T = ACE + B1 + (1 - \pi) \cdot (ATT - ATC),$$
$$T = ACE + B1 + B2,$$

as desired.

APPENDIX 3.2. NOTATION AND DEFINITIONS IN POTENTIAL OUTCOMES FRAMEWORK

Symbol	Full form	Definition
Q	Population of firm under study	Q refers to the population of interest, or the population of firms for which causal inferences are made. In this chapter, the population of interest and the sample are equivalent.
i	Unit index for firms in Q	
z	Treatment index	Lowercase z symbolizes the levels of the putative treatment variable, "independent" variable, or cause. Lowercase z must have at least two levels. It may be discrete or continuous, and depends on the causal question being answered. Lowercase z is not a random variable; thus, it is not indexed by i. If z were binary, then it may could the values 0 and 1, for instance.
$Y_i(z)$	[or $Y(z)$] potential outcome (response) indexed by z	The set of potential outcomes for one firm i in the population Q. For each unit i in the population Q, there are as many potential outcomes as there are levels of lowercase z. They are indexed by z. If z were binary, then the potential outcomes are $Y(0)$ and $Y(1)$.
ICE_i	(or *ICE*) individual (unit-specific) causal effect	This is the firm-i-specific causal effect. This is an unobservable quantity. For binary z, then $ICE_i = Y_i(1) - Y_i(0)$.
ACE	Average (over Q) causal effect	This is the population average causal effect. This is an unobservable quantity. For binary z, then $ACE = E[Y_i(1) - Y_i(0)]$ where the expectation acts over the firms i in the population Q.

Symbol	Full form	Definition
Z_i	(or Z; uppercase) observed treatment	Uppercase Z is the observed treatment (or putative cause) for firm i in the population Q. Z takes on as many levels as the index lowercase z. Z is a random variable.
Y_i	(or Y) observed outcome (response)	Y is the observed (realized) response or outcome. It is only one of at least two potential outcomes.
T	Standard estimator	$E(Y \mid Z=1) - E(Y \mid Z=0)$
π	Marginal proportion assigned to treatment group	$P(Z=1)$
C	Set of confounders	A confounder is a pretreatment variable that is directly associated with both observed Z and the outcome Y.
B	Confounding bias	The bias that results from the presence of confounding variables. This is sometimes referred to as selection bias.
ATT	Average treatment effect among treated firms	
ATC	Average treatment effect among control firms	
B1	Endogeneity bias	Treatment effects are different across treatment and control units.
B2	Heterogeneity bias	Treatment and control units differ systematically due to predetermined unobservables.
X	Measured pretreatment (pre-Z) covariates	
U	Unmeasured pretreatment (pre-Z) covariates	
$\perp$	Independence	
$e_i = e(x_i)$ [or $e = e(x)$]	propensity score given X at x	
$s_i = s(x_i)$ [or $s = s(x)$]	Subclass $(1, 2, \ldots, J)$ unit i belongs to; subclass is defined according to the propensity score	

ACKNOWLEDGMENTS

We thank Robert Kauffman and Paul Tallon for their guidance and detailed comments, which improved this chapter. The chapter complements and draws on some of our related work cited herein. We thank the anonymous reviewers of these chapters and participants in conferences where we have presented our related work. They helped to clarify our thinking on many of the concepts that we point to in this chapter and how they are relevant to IS researchers. We also thank the faculty of and participants in the winter 2004 "causality seminar" at the University of Michigan for stimulating discussions on some of the themes covered in this chapter. In particular, we acknowledge Yu Xie, Ben Hansen, and Steve Raudenbush for sharing their insights on the use of the potential outcomes approach during seminar discussions.

NOTES

1. For example, a kernel matching estimator uses all controls on support to compute the missing outcome variable by weighting these controls in proportion to the closeness of observables of these controls with respect to a treated unit.

2. These mediation theory arguments do not actually play themselves out in the *analysis* or *estimation* of the *ACE* of CRM on customer satisfaction—they are simply not necessary for *estimating* the total causal effect of CRM on customer satisfaction. As we have described in previous sections, other things are practically

more important when assessing this effect, such as eliminating the bias due to confounders. These arguments do, however, play a more direct role in the analysis if, instead of the *ACE,* the researcher is interested in substantiating the intervening variable theory (by this we mean estimating direct and indirect effects) using observational data. At this time, this is a very active, complex and controversial area of methodological research.

3. The term "endogeneity bias" was suggested by Yu Xie.

REFERENCES

Angrist, J.D.; Imbens, G.W.; and Rubin, D.B. 1996. Identification of causal effects using instrumental variables. *Journal of American Statistical Association,* 91, 434, 444–455.

Angrist, J.D. and Krueger, A.B. 1999. Empirical strategies in labor economics. In O. Ashenfelter and D. Card, eds., *Handbook of Labor Economics.* Vol. 3a. Amsterdam: Elsevier, 1277–1366.

Banker, R.D.; Kauffman, R.J.; and Mahmood, M.A. 1993. Measuring the business value of IT: A future oriented perspective. In R. D. Banker, R. J. Kauffman, and M. A. Mahmood, eds., *Strategic Information Technology Management: Perspectives on Organizational Growth and Competitive Advantage.* Harrisburg, PA: Idea Group, 595–605.

Banker, R.; Kauffman, R.; and Morey, R. 1990. Measuring gains in operational efficiency from information technology: A case study of the Positran deployment at Hardee's Inc. *Journal of Management Information Systems,* 7, 2, 29–54.

Bharadwaj, A. 2000. A resource-based perspective on information technology capability and firm performance: An empirical investigation. *MIS Quarterly,* 24, 1, 169–196.

Boulding, W.; Staelin, R.; Ehret, M.; and Johnston, W.J. 2005. A customer relationship management roadmap: What is known, potential pitfalls, and where to go. *Journal of Marketing,* 69, 4, 155–166.

Cochran, W.G. 1968. The effectiveness of adjustment by subclassification in removing bias in observational studies. *Biometrics,* 24, 205–213.

Cox, D.R. 1958. *The Design and Planning of Experiments.* London: Chapman and Hall.

Dehejia, R.H. and Wahba, S. 1999. Causal effects in nonexperimental studies: Reevaluating the evaluation of training programs. *Journal of American Statistical Association,* 94, 448, 1053–1062.

———. 2002. Propensity score-matching methods for nonexperimental causal studies. *Review of Economics and Statistics,* 84, 1, 151–161.

Fornell, C.; Johnson, M.D.; Anderson, E.W.; Cha, J.; and Bryant, B.E. 1996. The American customer satisfaction index: Nature, purpose, and findings. *Journal of Marketing,* 60, 4, 7–18.

Fornell, C.; Mithas, S.; Morgeson, F.; and Krishnan, M.S. 2006. Customer satisfaction and stock prices: High returns, low risk. *Journal of Marketing,* 70, 1, 3–14.

Freedman, D. 1997. From association to causation via regression. *Advances in Applied Mathematics,* 18, 59–110.

Glymour, C. 1986. Comment: Statistics and metaphysics. *Journal of the American Statistical Association,* 81, 396, 964–966.

Gregor, S. 2006. The nature of theory in information systems. *MIS Quarterly,* 30, 3, 611–642.

Heckman, J.J. 1997. Instrumental variables: A study of implicit behavioral assumptions used in making program evaluations. *Journal of Human Resources,* 32, 3, 441–462.

———. 2005. The scientific model of causality (with discussion). *Sociological Methodology,* 35, 1, 1–150.

Heckman, J.J.; Ichimura, H.; Smith, J.; and Todd, P. 1998. Characterizing selection bias using experimental data. *Econometrica,* 66, 5, 1017–1098.

Heckman, J.J.; Ichimura, H.; and Todd, P. 1997. Matching as an econometric evaluation estimator. *Review of Economic Studies,* 65, 2, 261–294.

Heckman, J.J.; Smith, J.A.; and Clements, N. 1997. Making the most out of programme evaluations and social experiments: Accounting for heterogeneity in programme impacts. *Review of Economic Studies,* 64, 4, 487–535.

Holland, P. 1986. Statistics and causal inference (with discussion). *Journal of the American Statistical Association,* 81, 396, 945–970.

Hume, D. 1740. *A Treatise of Human Nature.* London: J.M Dent & Sons (republished 1977).

Imbens, G.W. 2004. Nonparametric estimation of average treatment effects under exogeneity: A review. *Review of Economics and Statistics,* 86, 1, 4–29.

Joffe, M.M. and Rosenbaum, P.R. 1999. Invited commentary: Propensity scores. *American Journal of Epidemiology,* 150, 4, 327–333.

Lewis, D. 1973. *Counterfactuals.* Oxford: Blackwell.

Little, R.J. and Rubin, D. 2000. Causal effects in clinical and epidemiological studies via potential outcomes: Concepts and analytical approaches. *Annual Review of Public Health,* 21, 121–145.

Lucas, H.C. 1975. Performance and the use of an information system. *Management Science,* 21, 8, 908–919.

———. 1980. The impact of the mode of information presentation on learning and performance. *Management Science,* 26, 10, 982–993.

Mithas, S.; Almirall, D.; and Krishnan, M.S. 2006. Do CRM systems cause one-to-one marketing effectiveness? *Statistical Science,* 21, 2, 223–233.

Mithas, S. and Krishnan, M.S. 2004a. "Causal effect of CRM systems on cross selling effectiveness and sales-force productivity by bounding a matching estimator." Presented at the Ninth INFORMS Conference on Information Systems and Technology, Denver, CO, October 23–24.

———. 2004b. "Returns to managerial and technical competencies of IT professionals: An empirical analysis." Working paper, University of Michigan, Ann Arbor.

Mithas, S.; Krishnan, M.S.; and Fornell, C. 2005. Why do customer relationship management applications affect customer satisfaction? *Journal of Marketing,* 69, 4, 201–209.

Mukhopadhyay, T. and Kekre, S. 2002. Strategic and operational benefits of electronic integration in B2B procurement process. *Management Science,* 48, 10, 1301–1313.

Neyman, J.S.; Dabrowska, D.M.; and Speed, T.P. 1990. On the application of probability theory to agricultural experiments. Essay on principles. Section 9. *Statistical Science,* 5, 4, 465–472.

Popper, K.R. 1959. *The Logic of Scientific Discovery.* London: Hutchinson of London.

Rosenbaum, P. 1999. Choice as an alternative to control in observational studies. *Statistical Science,* 14, 3, 259–304.

———. 2002. *Observational Studies.* New York: Springer.

Rosenbaum, P.R. and Rubin, D.B. 1983a. Assessing sensitivity to an unobserved binary covariate in an observational study with binary outcome. *Journal of Royal Statistical Society Series B,* 45, 2, 212–218.

———. 1983b. The central role of the propensity score in observational studies for causal effects. *Biometrika,* 70, 1, 41–55.

———. 1984. Reducing bias in observational studies using subclassification on the propensity score. *Journal of the American Statistical Association,* 79, 387, 516–524.

Rubin, D.B. 1974. Estimating causal effects of treatments in randomized and nonrandomized studies. *Journal of Educational Psychology,* 66, 5, 688–701.

———. 1977. Assignment to treatment group on the basis of a covariate. *Journal of Educational Statistics,* 2, 1, 1–26.

———. 1978. Bayesian inference for causal effects: The role of randomization. *Annals of Statistics,* 6, 1, 34–58.

———. 1986. Which ifs have causal answers? *Journal of the American Statistical Association,* 81, 961–962.

———. 1997. Estimating causal effects from large data sets using propensity scores. *Annals of Internal Medicine,* 127, 8, Pt. 2, 757–763.

———. 2001. Using propensity scores to help design observational studies: Application to the tobacco litigation. *Health Services & Outcomes Research Methodology,* 2, 3–4, 169–188.

———. 2005. Causal inference using potential outcomes: Design, modeling, decisions. *Journal of the American Statistical Association,* 100, 469, 322–331.

Rubin, D.B. and Waterman, R.P. 2006. Estimating the causal effects of marketing interventions using propensity score methodology. *Statistical Science,* 21, 2, 206–232.

Sobel, M.E. 1995. Causal inference in the social and behavioral sciences. In G.A. Arminger, C.C. Clogg, and M.E. Sobel, eds., *Handbook of Statistical Modeling for the Social and Behavioral Sciences.* New York: Plenum Press, 1–35.

Winship, C. and Morgan, S.L. 1999. The estimation of causal effects from observational data. *Annual Review of Sociology,* 25, 659–706.

Winship, C. and Sobel, M. 2004. Causal inference in sociological studies. In Melissa Hardy and Alan Bryman, eds., *Handbook of Data Analysis.* London, UK: Sage, 481–503.

Xie, Y., and Wu, X. Market premium, social process, and statisticism. *American Sociological Review,* 70, October (2005), 865–870.

PART II

UNDERSTANDING THE DYNAMICS AND OUTCOMES ASSOCIATED WITH INFORMATION TECHNOLOGY INVESTMENTS

CHAPTER 4

EMPIRICAL ANALYSIS OF INFORMATION TECHNOLOGY PROJECT INVESTMENT PORTFOLIOS

RYAN SOUGSTAD AND INDRANIL R. BARDHAN

Abstract: We analyze a class of information technology (IT) investment decisions, interdependent projects in a portfolio, which can be informed by the application of real option analysis from financial economics. We specifically identify the attributes unique to IT investments, both within and across projects. We examine previous literature in real option analysis of IT investments and extend the methodology with a log-transformed binomial model to a portfolio of interdependent IT projects. Using data from a representative portfolio of a large health care company's Internet initiatives, we model complex interdependencies between the e-health projects in our portfolio as a series of nested options. We frame our analysis in light of current research and address ongoing issues on managerial tractability of real options analysis in IT investments.

Keywords: Empirical Model, E-Health, Investment Evaluation, IT Value, Log-Transformed Binary Model, Option-Adjusted Value, Project Portfolios, Real Options

INTRODUCTION

The rate of growth of spending on information technology (IT) has been steadily increasing in every part of the world during the past decade. The rate of increase has ranged from an average of 1.5 percent in Asia to an average of 7 percent in America and Canada (Gartner Group, 2004). In the United States alone, IT spending accounted for a full third of total corporate spending in 1998, comprising 7 percent of the gross national product (Lentz and Henderson, 1998). Yet for the magnitude of this investment, the analysis of the IT investment remains a daunting challenge. The direct benefits and costs are difficult to quantify. IT investments often encompass a myriad of interdependent risk factors, both endogenous and exogenous to the firm. These risk factors include financial risk, project risk, and political risk, as well as competitive risks and environmental uncertainties (Benaroch, 2002). Although IT investment evaluation remains complex, managers nonetheless must make investment decisions with real dollars subject to real budget constraints. This chapter addresses the problem with a real option method for evaluating a portfolio of interdependent IT initiatives that incorporate managerial flexibility (Luehrman, 1998).

Managers are often left with few alternatives to analyze their IT investment decisions in light of uncertainty (Amram and Kulatilaka, 1999; Dutta, 2004). Companies often employ traditional methods to evaluate the financial impact of IT investments, such as net present value (NPV), internal rate of return, and payback period (Ballantine and Stray, 1998). However, as various researchers, such as Clemons (1991) and Kauffman and Kriebel (1988), have noted, these traditional capital budgeting techniques often fail to accurately capture the benefits and risks associated with IT investments.

The problem is compounded when multiple IT projects are considered. Managers must allocate funds to competing projects. Often these projects encompass shared technologies and risk factors. One project may provide leverage for another. To evaluate each project independently on an NPV basis will not capture the total value of the projects in aggregate. For example, a database upgrade may enhance or enable an enterprise resource planning (ERP) system, which may enable a high value interorganizational supply chain module. However, the NPV of the database project may be unfavorable—and thus overlooked—if it is a favorable investment when viewed in the context of the aggregate supply chain solution. Likewise the database project may enhance the capability of the same firm's high-value customer interface system, and should be valued accordingly.

A key component to the IT investment is flexibility. IT investments can be strategically staged to offer management the option to delay, cancel, or undertake subsequent decisions (Benaroch, 2002). Returning to the example of the ERP investment, the initial ERP modules could be implemented first. The firm then can wait to see whether the market conditions for the interorganizational system materialize. Thus, the firm benefits from the new information it receives, mitigating the market risk by delaying the commitment to the interorganizational information system (IS) investment. However, managerial flexibility is ignored in traditional methods of financial evaluation.

In today's environment the issue of uncertain and interdependent IT investment projects is not going away. New service-delivered IT solutions add to the complexity faced by managers. Service-oriented architectures (SOAs) enable firms to develop Web services that offer specialized capabilities at a low development cost. These services are often on the edge of the enterprise (Hagel, 2002), thus enabling greater collaboration between firms. SOAs increase the number of investment considerations for firms while also allowing firms to decouple IT solutions based on business processes. As the number of investment decisions grows, a portfolio view is necessary to manage the menagerie of IT projects under consideration.

Portfolio management techniques in IT have traditionally focused on qualitative strategic factors. Weill and Broadbent (1998) developed a framework that consists of informational, strategic, transactional, and infrastructure variables. Verhoef (2002) developed a quantitative model of analysis for a portfolio of software development projects. He uses function points as a software output variable for valuation analysis and incorporates these variables in an advanced portfolio analysis with elements of sophisticated financial theory. Dickinson, Thornton, and Graves (2001) incorporated portfolio analysis techniques into Boeing's existing portfolio management tools to optimize the company's investment strategy in enabling technologies.

Unfortunately, these approaches have not fully recognized the nuances of strategic flexibility and the interdependent risk factors inherent in many IT investments. A stream of research in the application of real options analysis to IT has emerged that enables managers to identify and quantify the strategic risk factors among IT investments. We draw upon previous research in real options analysis to present a methodology: the log-transform binomial analysis of nested IT investments in a portfolio. This methodology addresses the key issues of interdependency, managerial flexibility in IT investments, and the prioritization of project portfolios under budget considerations.

Real Options in IS Research

An option gives the bearer the right, but not the obligation, to purchase (call) or sell (put) an asset at a predetermined price at a future date. Black and Scholes (1973) developed a model to price op-

Table 4.1

Primary Parameters and Notation in Real Option Pricing Models

Parameter	Description
V	Asset value
I	Strike price or cost of underlying asset
r_f	Risk-free rate of return
σ	Standard deviation of project returns
T	Exercise date
X	Log of asset value, V

tions. The core components of the option pricing model are variance of returns, time to expiration, exercise price, and underlying asset value. Margrabe (1978) extended this work by introducing a European option pricing model. Cox, Ross, and Rubinstein (1979) extended the field of options pricing with the binomial options model, which accommodates estimations of complex risk. All of these models derive the price of the option from five basic parameters; see Table 4.1, which also includes modeling notation.

Dixit and Pindyck (1994) identify three characteristics that investments share. (1) The investment is partially or completely *irreversible*. (2) There is *uncertainty* over the future rewards from the investment. (3) There is some leeway to *timing* of the investment. These factors complement the use of options analysis to real investments. Real options have been used in several industries for investment valuation, including mining, pharmaceuticals, financial services, manufacturing, and oil and gas exploration (Dixit and Pindyck, 1995). Kogut and Kulatilaka (1994) applied real options analysis to value flexibility in manufacturing. Trigeorgis (1993) modeled interacting options, and found that options to defer, abandon, and contract can exist within a project, but the value of such options in aggregate is not a strictly additive function.

Real options analysis represents a relatively mature application of financial economics concepts in IS research. Several different types of options can be considered in the IT investment scenario such as the option to defer, stage, explore, alter scale, abandon, outsource, and lease (Benaroch, 2002). Clemons and Weber (1990) were among the first to identify the components of the IT investment decision that laid the ground for the current IS research stream. They cited the major characteristics that are unique to IT investment decisions—first and foremost, the inability of traditional discounted cash flow (DCF) modes to capture the complexity and the ambiguity of IT investments. They also identified the value of timing and sequential nature of IT investments and identified the fit with option theory. Their work suggested the need for managerial considerations of these elements when making the IT investment decision.

Dos Santos (1991) presented a model to justify investments in integrated services digital network (ISDN) technologies using real options. He used the Margrabe (1978) model of asset-to-asset exchange to value the second-stage projects that were enabled by a first-stage investment in ISDN capabilities. The ISDN investment provided management with the option, but not the obligation, to pursue follow-on projects. Management had the flexibility to wait on market conditions before allocating capital to the second-stage investment. Likewise, Kambil, Henderson, and Mohsenzadeh (1993) utilized the Cox-Rubenstein binomial model to analyze a hospital's investment in IT infrastructure.

These early models led to more sophisticated work in terms of rigor and relevance. Taudes (1998) examined the role of software growth options inherent in an IS investment platform. He used a geometric Brownian motion to model the stochastic nature of the underlying asset value, and explored variations on the options modeled. They are the traditional, European exchange and pseudo-American exchange models. Benaroch and Kauffman (1999) offered a comparative analysis between the Black-Scholes and binomial models of option valuation. They also presented a case study of point-of-sale debit card systems in the banking industry and developed a rigorous sensitivity analysis-based first derivative analysis ("the Greeks"), as well as a comparison of the American call-option-enabled decision and the actual decision undertaken by management. They later expanded the analysis to include comparisons between American and European deferral options in the same case (Benaroch and Kauffman, 2000). In addition, they demonstrated the viability of real option analysis for options that were not explicitly purchased or traded.

Taudes, Feurstein, and Mild (2000) presented a real option analysis model that evaluated the investment decision of an SAP R2 to R3 upgrade. In this analysis, a negative NPV ERP investment was shown to have a positive NPV due to the options for follow-on projects (including electronic data interchange, workflow, e-commerce), which would be enabled by the ERP platform investment. Schwartz and Zozaya-Gorostiza (2003), extending Benaroch and Kauffman's research, developed a model incorporating a stochastic cost function for technical and input cost uncertainties in software project development. Kumar (2002) introduced active risk hedging in IT investments by using real options analysis. Fichman, Keil, and Tiwana (2005) presented a real option model for evaluating IT platform adoption.

Researchers have developed models based on real options thinking with new theoretical considerations from decision sciences, economics, and finance. Kauffman (in Tallon et al., 2002) has referred to this as the "third image" of real options research in IS. Examples of such work are the game-theoretic approaches identified by Dai (2004) and Zhu (1999) in their respective doctoral dissertations. Lin and Whinston (2003) introduced contract and pricing theory to real options analysis research. Au and Kauffman (2003) have proposed a number of related theories, including theories of optimal technology adoption timing as an extension to the option-type analysis. Kauffman and Li (2005) examined the role of competition investment timing. Additional work has been done to apply real options theory to create an optimal IT investment portfolio and to assess the business value associated with breaking budget constraints when new technology investment opportunities are identified in such managerial contexts (Bardhan, Kauffman, and Narapanawe, 2006; Bardhan, Sougstad, and Bagchi, 2004) More recent research on the business value of flexibility (Lee and Xia, 2002) and the latent effects of IT investments (Goh and Kauffman, 2005) may also be reconsidered with options-type analysis in mind. The fusion of theoretical insights, unique to the economics of IS, holds promise to both inform managerial thinking and improve the tractability of real option applications to IT (Sambamurthy, Bharadwaj, and Grover, 2003).

A Real Options Approach to IT Portfolio Prioritization

We extend current methodology to develop a *nested log-transformed binomial model of IT portfolio prioritization* using a case study of a health care company, hereafter referred to as HealthCo, to protect its identity and its projects. (For an overview of the impact areas for IT investments in health care, see Table 4.2. For additional background on HealthCo, and the hard and soft benefits of IT investments in health care settings, see Figure 4.1.) The data presented in this chapter have been disguised by using a constant to scale the data. We use the HealthCo data purely as an illustrative example to demonstrate the validity of our proposed real options model. In this approach we address the need for managers to assess and quantify the interdependence between projects and prioritize these valuations under a budget constraint. The methods that we describe provide

Table 4.2

Components of the E-Health Domain Affected by IT Investments

Content	Connectivity	Community	Commerce	Care
• Information presentation	• Public health management information systems	• P2P networks	• e-Commerce	• Self-help reference information
• Information query	• Health services		• Billing and payment systems	• Information portability/HIPAA
• Health data	• Systems integration			• Shared clinical decision making
• Distance learning	• Research			• Disease management
• Decision-making guidelines	• Administrative services			
	• Telemedicine			

Source: Adapted from Eng (2001).

managerial insights related to the impact of uncertainty and interdependency on project valuation and prioritization along with the flexibility of deferring investments, or making follow-on investments to existing problems.

As health care companies increasingly use the Internet to conduct critical business process transactions and disseminate information to their key stakeholders, it is becoming more important for them to plan, structure, and prioritize their technology investments in a successful manner (Levit and Cowan, 2000). U.S. health care companies are facing mounting pressure from other insurers as well as from commercial banks and agents. To counter the resulting decline in profitability, many health care companies are looking to IT as a way to boost operational efficiency and effectiveness and reduce costs (Oakes, 2004). In addition health care companies utilize technology to reengineer business processes and improve quality (Devaraj and Kohli, 2000).

A real option-based methodology is especially relevant to Healthco's current situation. Many projects, such as the Cross Data Center Access Initiative, incorporate a significant amount of technology implementation risk; see Table 4.3 for a description of HealthCo's projects.

HealthCo can choose to abandon the project in case of failure or excessive cost overruns. Perhaps more relevant is the ability to evaluate market conditions at the end of each project before proceeding to a later stage investment. If the expected functional capabilities—such as the ability to integrate data across multiple data centers—do not materialize, decay in the value of follow-on projects may result. For example, competitors may poach customers or projected costs may escalate and outweigh expected benefits. Hence, flexibility in structuring such investments includes an option to delay under negative conditions, and a growth option if conditions improve over time.

In addition, the portfolio of projects under consideration contains numerous interdependencies. Based on a thorough understanding of HealthCo's proposed projects that we developed during the course of a field study, we identified several interdependencies between the projects; see Figure 4.2.

Hard dependencies between two projects exist when a capability developed for one project is

Figure 4.1 **Background on HealthCo**

In the late 1990s, HealthCo was facing several challenges to its core health care insurance business from several fronts. Competition from Internet health care startups, which were able to provide more cost-effective alternatives for health insurance, were identified as a major threat to HealthCo's business. The passage of the Health Insurance Portability Act (HIPAA), in the late 1990s, was a key environmental factor that required HealthCo to address major deficiencies in the way it processed and disseminated health care data of its members and providers.

    The company embarked on a major initiative to fundamentally improve its business operations by leveraging the Internet to reduce the cost of doing business by reducing overall administrative and transaction costs, improving the delivery of health information to its stakeholders (employers, members, and medical providers), and improving its brand image. Senior IT and business executives, working jointly, proposed a portfolio of projects to improve the e-business capabilities of the firm and enable it to compete more effectively in the e-health arena. The figure below provides a high-level summary of HealthCo's objectives in the context of its decision to invest several millions of dollars into the proposed e-health projects.

Hard and Soft Benefits from E-Health Projects at HealthCo

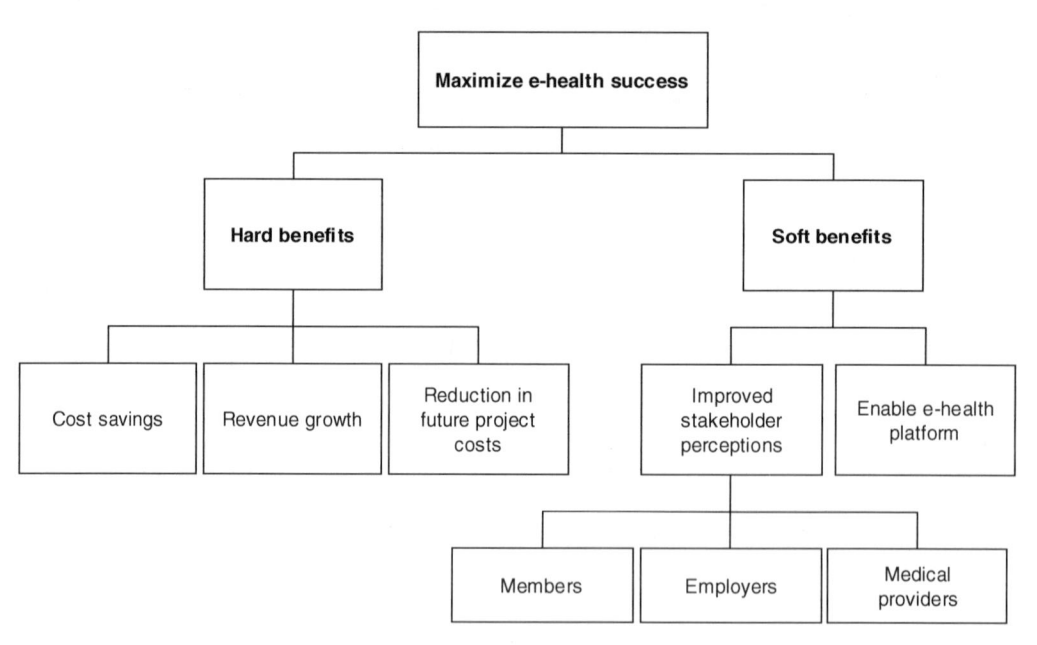

```
                    Maximize e-health success
                    /                        \
            Hard benefits                 Soft benefits
           /     |        \                /           \
    Cost    Revenue   Reduction in    Improved      Enable e-health
   savings   growth   future project  stakeholder      platform
                          costs       perceptions
                                      /     |      \
                                 Members Employers  Medical
                                                   providers
```

also required by one or more of the other project(s). *Soft dependencies* exist when a capability from one project supports or enhances capabilities required by other projects. For example, the infrastructure initiatives of Cross Data Center Access build the network foundations for future value-added initiatives, such as development of a Common Payment Engine, Enhanced Provider Database, and Centralized Authorization Database. In addition, the latter two projects further enable the high-return on investment Auto Adjudication projects. The framework allows for studying the impact of managerial flexibility in implementing HealthCo's IT initiatives.

    Most managers realize that IT projects provide leverage to launch future value-added services and take them into consideration when evaluating technology decisions (Fichman, 2004; Fichman, Keil, and Tiwana, 2005). This works well when there are few options to consider. However, when dozens of projects with complex interdependencies are considered, this decision is not as clear and the risks of making suboptimal decisions are high. Hence, identification of the interdependencies

Table 4.3

Project IDs, Names, and Descriptions

ID	Project name	Description
1	Auto Adjudication I	Modify claim systems to incorporate claims processing business rule.
2	Auto Adjudication II	Modify claim systems to incorporate business rules for adjudication of more complicated claims, and so on.
3	Cross Data Center Access	Build infrastructure/connectivity that enables data sharing across two separate data centers. Applications to get to one common view, move data from one location to another.
4	Centralized Authorization Database (CAD)	Consolidate patient authorizations from multiple databases into a single database. Joint work with the business units to address workflow redesign, development and redefinition of policies, and rule simplification to increase auto-adjudication.
5	Product Database and Services	Develop centralized data stores with a flexible product structure that enables a high degree of customization.
6	Strategic Claims Receipt	Do the work involved in developing a single, strategic claim receipt and router system. The strategic receipt/router would handle simple eligibility edits and route claims to the appropriate claim engine, with support for batch and real-time adjudication.
7	Automated Provider Pricing	Align provider contracts with automated pricing rules.
8	Enhanced Provider Database (EPD)	Make changes required to incorporate new types of provider relationships, provider profile changes, connectivity methods, and so on, to serve as the strategic solution for provider information.
9	Web-Enabled Plan Setup	Provide Web-enabled small group plan selection through a set of external services, and automation of the plan setup process through its entire work flow. Provide an Internet-accessible point of entry for all new business and renewal quotation activities.
10	Common Payment Engine (CPE)	Enable payments to pay providers electronically via electronic fund transfers (EFTs). This engine would handle payments for claims and capitation across multiple product lines.
11	Plan Sponsor Services	Do the work involved in rethinking how to support plan sponsors who operate in an e-health environment, and retool and prepare support staff, along with the Web-enabled tools for supporting plan sponsors.
12	Web Access to Disease Management	Web-enabled disease management program to improve the quality of care and quality of life for members, avoid the development of complications through intensive member education, and fostering physician compliance with accepted guidelines for treatment of these diseases.
13	Provider Web Pilot	Develop value-added features for the provider Web site, lab test ordering/results, and member alerts.
14	Provider Web Site	Develop the provider Web site to record provider-specific information and an appropriate partner solution for transaction processing.
15	Content Management	Define process/organization to maintain content on firm's Web site.
16	E-Integration with Providers	Business process infrastructure to establish full electronic integration of transactional data with providers, including claims submissions, inquiries, and so on.

(continued)

Table 4.3 *(continued)*

ID	Project name	Description
17	e-Commerce Infrastructure Support	Suite of e-health infrastructure tools to support the development of member, provider, and plan sponsor Web sites and electronic integration.
18	Architecture Database	Hardware and software components to support development of strategic databases.
19	Application Infrastructure	Suite of applications to support development of enhanced functionality for member, provider, and employer services, including claims, payments, information dissemination, and sales and marketing.
20	Information Security Layer	Building the Web servers, public key infrastructure, firewall servers, and so on, required in Web environment. Includes building and implementing the application and database servers, along with infrastructure (hardware, software, network connectivity).

between projects must be undertaken in a consistent and repeatable manner that scales well with the number of projects (Jeffery and Leliveld, 2004).

METHODOLOGY

We now describe our proposed option model to account for the series of nested options between predecessor and successor projects, and the impact of hard and soft dependencies on project value. We first describe the parameters of the basic model before moving on to an illustrative example.

The Log-Transformed Binomial Model

The log-transformed binomial model allows mangers to incorporate interproject embedded options (Benaroch, 2002). For example, consider an IT investment embedding an option to defer. Holding the option is similar to holding an investment opportunity, and exercising the option is akin to converting the opportunity into an operational investment.

We utilize this approach to model *interproject embedded options*. Managers can consider strategic embedded options, such as the option to delay, abandon, or reinvest, along with subsequent projects enabled by the initial investment. The distinction between inter- and intraproject options is important because the underlying risk of the options across projects will be different than the risk when considering *intraproject embedded options*. Cross-project nested options must be analyzed under separate diffusion processes (Benaroch, Shah, and Jeffery, 2006).

A financial call option on an underlying asset with value, V, gives its holder the right to buy the asset for an agreed-upon exercise price, I, at a fixed expiration date, T. Hence, the payoff function modeling the terminal value of a call option is equal to $\max(0, V_T - I)$ (Benaroch, 2002). The present value of a call option, C, is determined primarily by the variance of the underlying asset's value, σ^2, and its time to maturity, T, in the presence of the time value of money. The higher the value of σ^2, or the longer the time to expiration T, the higher the value of the call option C. See Table 4.1 again for modeling notation.

We note that two broad categories of models have been developed for valuing financial options: the binomial model and the Black-Scholes model. They can be readily adapted to the context of valuing IT projects using real options (Benaroch, 2002). Benaroch and Kauffman (1999) offer a comparative analysis of these models, showing that they make the same key assumptions. The

Figure 4.2 **Portfolio of E-Health Initiatives with Interdependencies**

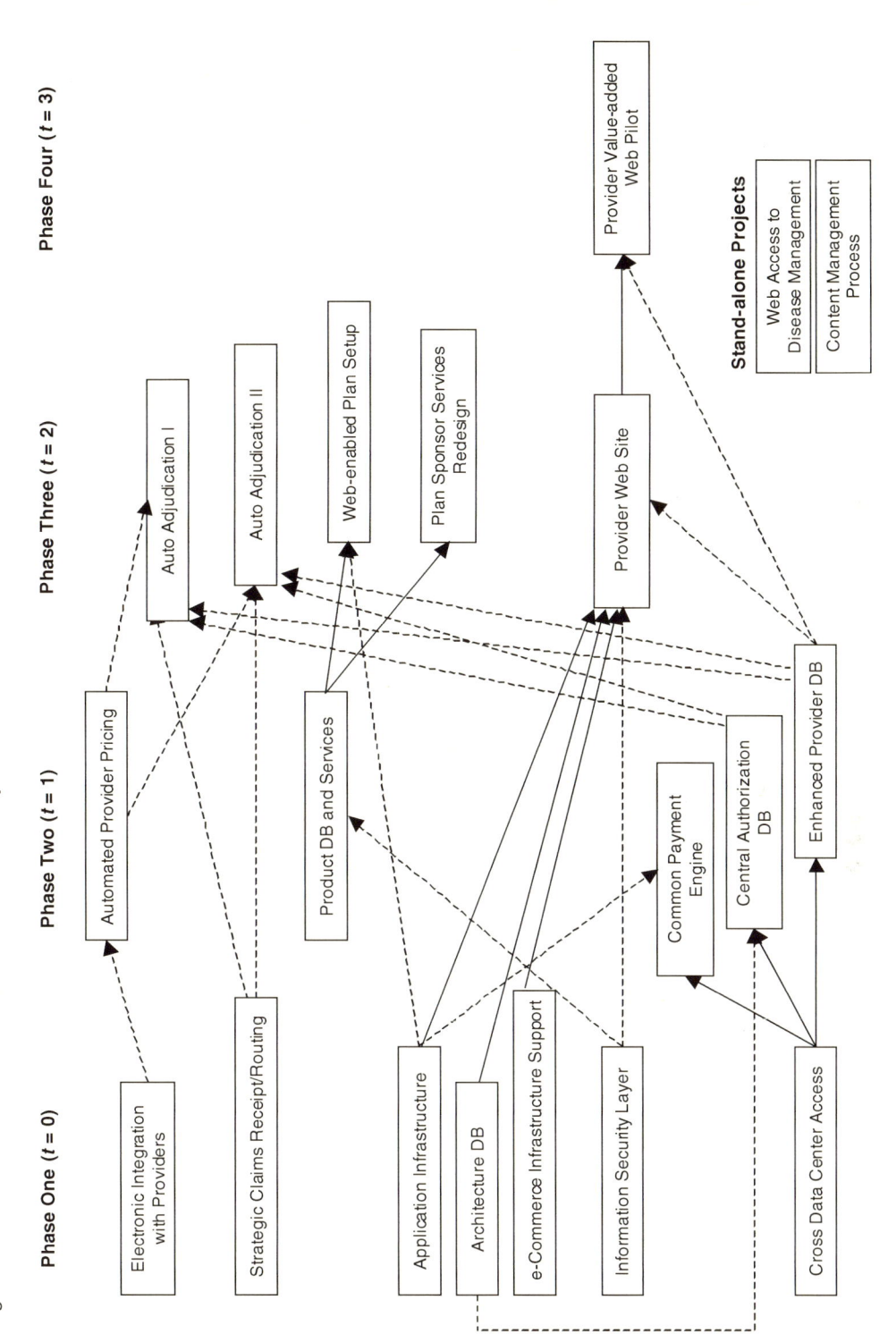

Figure 4.3 The Basic Binomial Model Representation of Asset Value Movement over Time

Underlying Asset Value, V, over Time

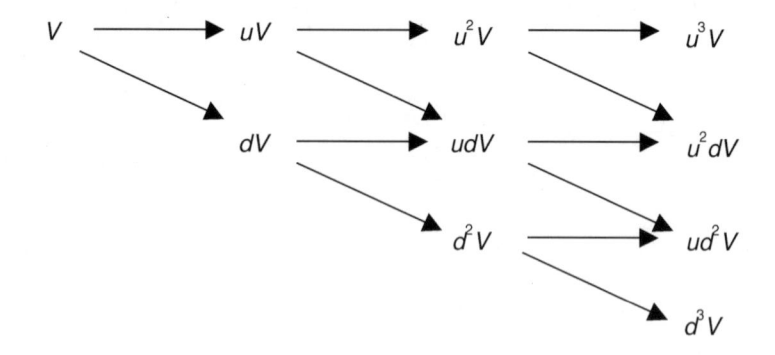

$$V \to uV \to u^2V \to u^3V$$
$$\to dV \to udV \to u^2dV$$
$$\to d^2V \to ud^2V$$
$$\to d^3V$$

Call Option Value C of Asset V

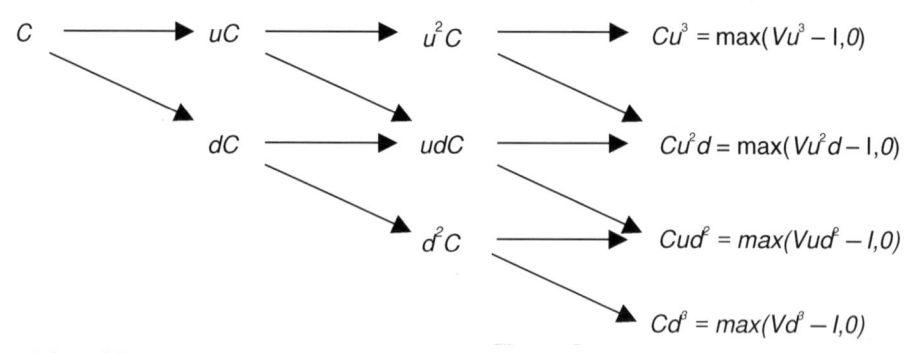

$$C \to uC \to u^2C \to Cu^3 = \max(Vu^3 - I, 0)$$
$$\to dC \to udC \to Cu^2d = \max(Vu^2d - I, 0)$$
$$\to d^2C \to Cud^2 = \max(Vud^2 - I, 0)$$
$$\to Cd^3 = \max(Vd^3 - I, 0)$$

Source: Adapted from Benaroch (2002).

binomial model assumes that V, the value of the option's underlying risky asset (or present value of expected investment payoffs), is governed by a binomially distributed multiplicative diffusion process (Cox, Ross, and Rubinstein, 1979; Hull, 1993). Starting at time zero, in one time period t, V may rise to uV with probability p, or fall to dV with probability $1 - p$, where $d < 1$, $u > 1$ and $d < r < u$, with r equal to $1 + r_f$ and r_f is the risk-free interest rate. The variables u and d represent the respective magnitudes of the rise and fall in asset value. For the multiperiod case, V can be modeled in this fashion using a binomial tree. See Figure 4.3.

The value of the call option, C, is shown on the lower tree in Figure 4.3. If I is the exercise price, the terminal value of a call option on V is calculated as $C_u = \max[0, uV - I]$, or $C_d = \max[0, dV - I]$ with probabilities p and $1 - p$, respectively.

In the context of our research, several nested dependencies exist among a project and its set of follow-on projects, wherein the follow-on projects leverage the functional capabilities provided by their predecessors. Bardhan, Sougstad, and Bagchi (2004) proposed a nested options model, using the Black-Scholes model formulation, to value and prioritize a portfolio of e-business projects in the energy industry. Benaroch, Shah, and Jeffery (2006) developed a model to evaluate multi-

Figure 4.4 Asset Value Movement with the Log-Transformed Binomial Model Technique

Value of Project R with Option Value C

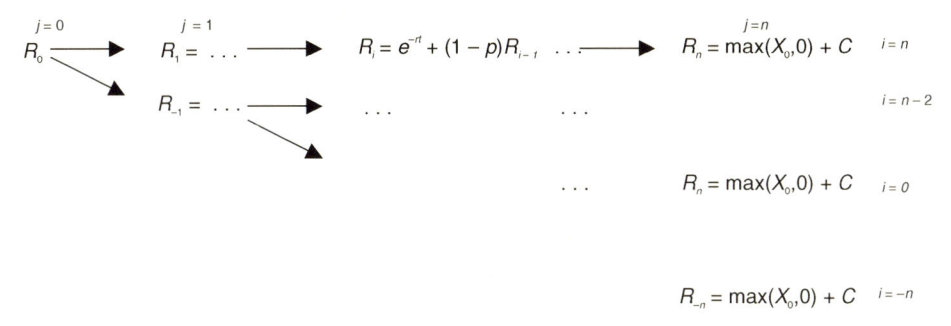

$$j=0 \quad\quad j=1 \quad\quad\quad\quad\quad\quad\quad\quad\quad\quad\quad j=n$$

$R_0 \longrightarrow R_1 = \ldots \longrightarrow R_i = e^{-rt} + (1-p)R_{i-1} \ldots \longrightarrow R_n = \max(X_0, 0) + C \quad i = n$

$\quad\quad\quad R_{-1} = \ldots \longrightarrow \quad\quad\quad\quad\quad\quad\quad\quad\quad\quad\quad\quad\quad\quad\quad\quad i = n-2$

$$\quad\quad\quad\quad\quad\quad\quad\quad\quad\quad\quad\quad\quad\quad\quad\quad\quad\quad\quad R_n = \max(X_0, 0) + C \quad i = 0$$

$$\quad\quad\quad\quad\quad\quad\quad\quad\quad\quad\quad\quad\quad\quad\quad\quad\quad\quad\quad R_{-n} = \max(X_0, 0) + C \quad i = -n$$

Value of Asset State Variable

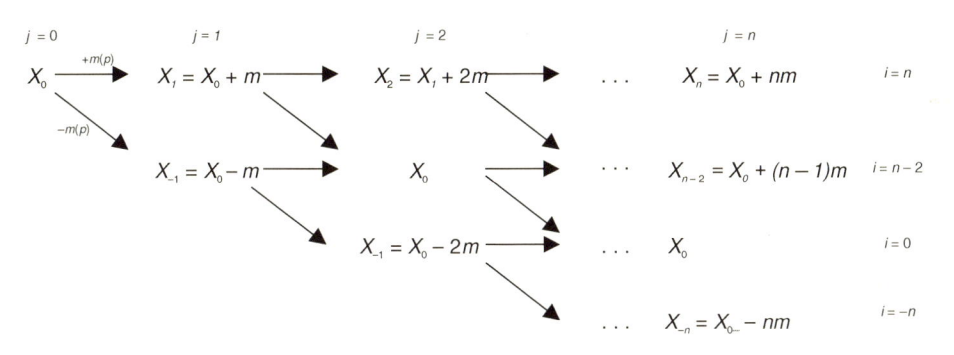

$$j = 0 \quad\quad j = 1 \quad\quad\quad j = 2 \quad\quad\quad\quad\quad\quad j = n$$

$X_0 \xrightarrow{+m(p)} X_1 = X_0 + m \longrightarrow X_2 = X_1 + 2m \longrightarrow \ldots \quad X_n = X_0 + nm \quad i = n$

$\quad\xrightarrow{-m(p)} X_{-1} = X_0 - m \longrightarrow \quad X_0 \quad\quad\quad\quad\quad \ldots \quad X_{n-2} = X_0 + (n-1)m \quad i = n-2$

$\quad\quad\quad\quad\quad\quad\quad\quad\quad\quad X_{-1} = X_0 - 2m \longrightarrow \ldots \quad X_0 \quad\quad\quad\quad\quad\quad\quad i = 0$

$$\quad\quad\quad\quad\quad\quad\quad\quad\quad\quad\quad\quad\quad\quad\quad\quad\quad\quad \ldots \quad X_{-n} = X_0 - nm \quad i = -n$$

Note: R_i represents the total investment value, including embedded options, at state i. $X = \log V$ is governed by the additive diffusion process as shown above. Adapted from Benaroch (2002).

stage embedded real options. In the present context, we extend the work of Benaroch (2002) and Benaroch, Shah, and Jeffery (2006) with the development of a log-transformed binomial model incorporating a portfolio of multistage nested real options.

The log-binomial model can be represented by a decision tree. Figure 4.4 provides an illustrative example of an asset transformed in the log state variable X ($= \log V$), which also enables a further option (C) on a separate asset; see Figure 4.4.

A project reaps payoffs in the upstate for its performance with a known probability, p, and the downstate payoffs for lesser performance occur with a probability of $1 - p$. We adapt the log-transformed binomial model of Trigeorgis (1991, 1996) to evaluate such a portfolio of nested options in the e-health sector (Eng, 2001). In our context, since we have a relatively short exercise time for these options (varying between one and three years), the log-transformed binomial approach is appropriate (Benaroch, 2002; Trigeorgis, 1991). In addition, the log-transformed binomial model allows for intraproject real options to be considered. Appendix 4.1 contains a more detailed overview of the log-transformed binomial model. Readers should refer to Trigeorgis (1991) for a complete proof of the model.

The change in asset value is measured in an increment of magnitude m with a probability p.

Given two serially dependent call options, C_1 and C_2, each will have its own underlying asset price and exercise price (V_1, I_1) and (V_2, I_2). *The option value for the second asset is attributed to the terminal nodes of the asset value option, V_1. Since C_2 changes the size of the underlying asset of C_1, then C_2 should be incorporated into the binomial tree for C_1.*[1] Hence, the call option value of the terminal node is calculated as $\max(u^2 V_1 + C_2 - I_1, 0)$ [10].

Illustrative Example

For illustration purposes, consider the cluster of projects enabled by Cross Data Center Access (CDCA). This project provides critical infrastructure and connectivity capabilities that enable data sharing across two separate data centers. Its purpose is to provide a common view of the data to allow decision makers greater transparency of data across different lines of business. It provides infrastructure capabilities for three follow-on projects in Phase I, namely, Common Payment Engine (CPE), Centralized Authorization Database (CAD), and Enhanced Provider Database (EPD). The CPE enables HealthCo to pay providers electronically via electronic funds transfers (EFTs) and handles electronic payments for claims and capitation products. Hence, CPE depends on the functional "data transparency" capabilities provided by CDCA in order to enable EFT payments across multiple product lines.

In a similar manner, CDCA provides data management capabilities that can be leveraged by other follow-on projects, including CAD and EPD. For instance, the purpose of the CAD is to enable the consolidation of patient authorizations from multiple databases into a single one. By building the connectivity capabilities required for sharing data, CDCA provides the basic foundation capabilities required for the consolidation of patient authorization data (referrals, precertifications, notifications) from multiple databases. In the same vein, CDCA provides the data management capabilities required to support the changes needed to incorporate new types of provider relationships and provider profile changes that are part of the EPD strategic initiative.

Hence, the portfolio of project investment decisions that comprise CDCA can be represented as a *nested options model* (Luehrman, 1998; Panayi and Trigeorgis, 1998) that consists of a series of cascading options that yield an NPV for the project:

$$\text{NPV(CDCA)} = \text{PV(CDCA)} + \textit{Option Value of } \text{CPE} + \textit{Option Value of } \text{EPD} \\ + \textit{Option Value of } \text{CAD} \qquad (4.1)$$

Since both CAD and EPDB provide data management capabilities that support future follow-on projects, their net present values should include the option values associated with these follow-on projects. These are shown as soft dependencies. Hence, we have:

$$\text{NPV(CAD)} = \text{PV(CAD)} + \textit{Option Value of Auto Adjudication I} \\ + \textit{Option Value of Auto Adjudication II} \qquad (4.2)$$

$$\text{NPV } \textit{of } \text{EPD} = \text{PV(EPDB)} + \textit{Option Value of Auto Adjudication I} \\ + \textit{Option Value of Auto Adjudication II} \\ + \textit{Option Value of Provider Web Site} \\ + \textit{Option Value of (Provider value-added Web Pilot)} \qquad (4.3)$$

Hence, the NPV of CDCA can be expressed as a series of cascading options, and calculated using the log-transformed binomial model, which was transformed into an additive model, as described earlier.

Since the CPE project does not enable other follow-on initiatives, its option value can be computed by using a simple log-normal binomial analysis. We calculate the option value of CPE attributable to CDCA to be equal to $8.364 million.

As we observed earlier, the option values of the Auto Adjudication projects (AA I and AA II must be incorporated in calculating the overall NPV of their relevant enabling project. For example, the EPD project has a projected NPV of $3.982 million, but when considering the option value that EPD provides to CDCA, the benefits enabled by its follow-on projects (AA I, AA II, Provider Web Site, and Provider Web Pilot) must be factored into the terminal node of the EPD binomial tree. The option to exercise these follow-on projects in future years changes the underlying asset value of EPD.

Hence, the steps to calculate the value for HealthCo's IT initiatives are given below.

- *Step 1.* Transform the underlying asset value into a state variable.
- *Step 2.* Calculate the probabilities of an upstate or downstate shift in asset values and the magnitude of the upstate shift.
- *Step 3.* Calculate the value of the state variable at time *t*.
- *Step 4.* Transform the state variable to the logarithmic form. Any follow-on option values determined by this method are added to the state variable. The state variable values are weighted by probabilities and summed to give an expected value at time zero.
- *Step 5.* Subtract the initial investment *I* from the expected value at time zero to provide the value of the real option.

The option values associated with the other projects that leverage the capabilities provided by CDCA, namely, EPD and CPE, are calculated in a similar manner. The overall value of Cross Data Center Access is given by:

$$[PV(CDCA) + \textit{Option Value } CAD + \textit{Option Value } EPD + \textit{Option Value } CPE] =$$
$$-\$7.556 \textit{ million} + \$51.465 \textit{ million} = \$59.020 \textit{ million} \qquad (4.4)$$

We observe that the nested options approach allows managers to consider the options enabled by future follow-on projects leveraged by a necessary infrastructure investment, which, on the surface, appears to have little direct benefit.

EMPIRICAL RESULTS

We calculated the option-adjusted NPVs for the entire portfolio of twenty e-health projects. Of these twenty projects, two were stand-alone projects. Six others did not have an option value associated with them since they did not provide a foundation to leverage follow-on projects (at the present time). In other words, the value of each of these eight projects is the same as their NPV as calculated using discounted cash flow analysis. We calculate the option values associated with the remaining twelve projects using the nested options methodology described in the previous section. The option NPVs of these projects are shown in Table 4.4, in descending order of NPV, along with the NPVs of projects that do not have an option value; see Table 4.4.

We note that several e-health projects exhibit low NPVs but high option-adjusted NPVs. For instance, the CDCA project is a classic example in that it exhibits an NPV of –$7.556 million when calculated using traditional DCF, but when the option values associated with its follow-on projects are taken into consideration, it exhibits a large NPV of $59.020 million. The large swing

Table 4.4

Option-Adjusted Net Present Values (NPVs) for the Projects

Project name	NPV	Option NPV
Auto Adjudication I	$111,988,079	$111,988,079
Cross Data Center Access	($7,555,915)	$59,020,275
Auto Adjudication II	$49,968,748	$49,968,748
Centralized Authorization Database	$21,945,150	$39,862,342
Product Database and Services	$13,239,383	$27,663,227
Enhanced Provider Database	$3,982,823	$24,127,671
Architecture Database	($277,923)	$20,489,450
Strategic Claims Receipt	$993,288	$17,391,882
Automated Provider Pricing	($2,257,164)	$16,330,882
Web-Enabled Plan Setup	$11,506,789	$11,506,789
Application Infrastructure	($4,250,504)	$9,247,250
Common Payment Engine	$6,962,403	$6,962,403
Electronic Integration with Providers	($2,866,172)	$5,374,779
Plan Sponsor Services	$5,302,484	$5,302,484
Web Access to Disease Management	$4,927,601	$4,927,601
Provider Web Site	$218,941	$2,769,812
Provider Web Pilot	$2,336,389	$2,336,389
e-Commerce Infrastructure Support	($256,190)	$2,152,242
Content Management	$293,555	$293,555
Information Security Layer	($17,103,935)	($3,498,956)

Note: All portfolio option values were calculated using a project variance value of $\sigma^2 = 0.2$.

in its NPV can be attributed to the core capabilities that CDCA provides in terms of data management and connectivity across multiple data centers that can be leveraged by its dependent projects, namely, EPD, CPE, and CAD. In a similar vein, we note that other projects that change from a negative NPV to positive status include the Architecture Database, Automated Provider Pricing, Application Infrastructure, and Electronic Integration with Providers.

Upon closer examination, we note that each of these projects provides important functional capabilities that can be leveraged by their dependent projects. For example, the Architecture Database provides the hardware and software components to support the development of strategic provider and member databases, which is required for successful rollout of the Provider Web Site project. The Automated Provider Pricing project enables alignment of provider contracts with automated pricing rules. This is a critical requirement for successful implementation of Auto Adjudication projects (I and II). These allow large volumes of claims to be processed without human intervention, based on preestablished business rules. Similarly, Electronic Integration lays the necessary connectivity and business process infrastructure to establish full electronic integration of transactional data with providers, and thereby supports implementation of follow-on projects such as Automated Provider Pricing.

Based on the results of our real options analyses, we eliminate projects that have a negative NPV. In this context, we observe that the Information Security Layer project has an NPV of –$3.499 million, which, although smaller than its NPV computed through DCF, is still negative and does not merit investment at the present time. Hence, we drop the Information Security Layer project from consideration. The remaining projects form the *feasible consideration set* of projects for funding during the budgeting cycle. Next, we identify any hard and soft dependencies between the project that was eliminated and those that remain in the consideration set. Eliminating the Information Security Layer project has a direct material impact on two projects: Product DB and

Table 4.5

Portfolio after Removal of Negative Net Present Value (NPV) Projects ($)

Project name	Option NPV
Auto Adjudication I	111,988,079
Cross Data Center Access	58,057,312
Auto Adjudication II	49,968,748
Centralized Authorization Database	39,491,048
Product Database and Services	24,533,088
Enhanced Provider Database	23,517,088
Architecture Database	20,414,766
Strategic Claims Receipt	17,703,667
Automated Provider Pricing	16,330,934
Web-Enabled Plan Setup	11,506,789
Application Infrastructure	9,180,373
Common Payment Engine	6,962,403
Electronic Integration with Providers	5,374,779
Plan Sponsor Services	5,302,484
Web Access to Disease Management	4,927,601
Provider Web Site	2,570,511
Provider Web Pilot	2,336,389
e-Commerce Infrastructure Support	2,069,073
Content Management	293,555

Note: All portfolio option values were calculated using a project variance value of $\sigma^2 = 0.2$.

Services, and Provider Web Site; see Table 4.5. Their project benefits are reduced by 25 percent, and their revised option NPVs are calculated to be $24.533 million and $2.570 million.

Although the Information Security Layer project is not funded at the present time due to its negative NPV, one must recognize that future conditions could have a significant impact on its NPV. For instance, the loss of private member health care data to hackers (due to IT security breaches) or the passage of government-imposed regulations may increase the expected benefits of building a dedicated information security layer. The negative NPV on this project may be explained by the fact that since the project data were set in the late 1990s, IT security was not of as much concern as it is today. Hence, this project should be carefully monitored to ensure that its projected benefits and costs are aligned with HealthCo's strategic objectives and that any changes in these estimates are accurately represented in our model.

We also note that adjustments in the option values of the Product DB and Services and Provider Web Site projects create a ripple effect on other feasible projects that support some or all capabilities provided by these projects. For instance, since a portion of the NPV of the Application Infrastructure, Architecture DB, e-Commerce Infrastructure Support, and Enhanced Provider Database projects can be attributed to their call option on the Provider Web Site project, a reduction in the NPV of Provider Web Site entails a corresponding reduction in its call option value attributed to its parent projects. Hence, it results in a decrease in the option values attributed to these Phase I and II projects; see the entries in Table 4.5.

Sensitivity Analysis

To verify the sensitivity of the real option model to our project-specific volatility estimates, we conducted a sensitivity analysis using a range of values for σ^2 from 0.10 to 0.50, with increments of 0.1. This method is similar to other approaches that utilize ranges of σ^2 to assess the impact of the volatility of returns on project values. For example, see Benaroch and Kauffman (2000) and Taudes, Feurstein, and Mild (2000). At very low volatilities, Electronic Integration with Providers (EIP) has a slightly lower value than Plan Sponsor Services (PSS), whereas EIP has a higher value than PSS at higher volatilities; see Table 4.6.

If management were forced to choose between the two projects, this analysis would signal the managers to carefully examine the risk factors surrounding both products. However, as the results show, the rankings do not change for the remaining nineteen projects across different volatility scenarios. These results provide a measure of consistency to our overall project rankings. We note that the variance in project returns may be more significant in other settings related to HealthCo's services and the environmental factors in its industry, which we do not explore here.

Project Prioritization

Our real options model captures portfolio effects where project values are related to other projects, and cancellations or delays have a ripple effect on other projects. Table 4.7 provides an initial prioritization of the feasible projects, after incorporating the effect of real options associated with projects that they leverage. For each phase, we have prioritized the projects, based on their overall option NPV value, along with a representation of their one-time investment and the ongoing cost of operations.

We note that we can incorporate additional considerations imposed by budget constraints on our prioritization framework in a manner similar to the approach described in Bardhan, Sougstad, and Bagchi (2004). For example, if HealthCo has a budget constraint of $15 million in the first year, then some of the Phase I projects will be delayed to future years. This delay, in turn, may create additional delays on follow-on projects, which will result in a change in the option values of these dependent projects. In Bardhan, Sougstad, and Bagchi (2006), we propose an integer programming model to incorporate time-wise project interdependencies in developing an optimal prioritization model using real options valuation.

APPLICATION AND MANAGERIAL IMPLICATIONS

Managerial ease of use remains a challenge to researchers who apply real options methodologies. Thus far there has not been widespread use of these methods by practitioners, outside of specialty consulting firms and business analytics services providers. However, the concepts have been gaining wider consideration. Real option analysis has been a subject in the popular press (Mayer, 2002) and has been cited by management consultants. Matheis and Dickson (2005) cite a case of managers utilizing real options analysis in an RFID context, and cite the benefits of a portfolio approach to real options analysis in IT investments.

Application

One of the major obstacles is the estimation of volatility of returns to IT investments. Modern financial theory depends upon frictionless, arbitrage-free markets where assets are traded with liquidity. No such market exists for IT assets. Gustafson and Luft (2002) found that managers have limited ability to estimate volatility of IT investments. Thus, the estimation of risks and

Table 4.6

Sensitivity Analysis ($)

Project name	$\sigma^2 = 0.1$	$\sigma^2 = 0.2$	$\Sigma^2 = 0.3$	$\sigma^2 = 0.4$	$\sigma^2 = 0.5$
Auto Adjudication I	111,988,079	111,988,079	111,988,079	111,988,079	111,988,079
Cross Data Center Access	58,068,061	59,020,275	60,651,986	63,009,441	66,160,361
Auto Adjudication II	49,968,748	49,968,748	49,968,748	49,968,748	49,968,748
Centralized Authorization Database	39,596,358	39,862,342	40,318,129	40,976,636	41,968,748
Product Database and Services	27,414,364	27,663,227	28,089,675	28,705,794	29,529,281
Enhanced Provider Database	23,823,859	24,127,671	24,648,279	25,400,436	26,405,749
Architecture Database	20,173,576	20,489,450	21,030,733	21,812,766	22,858,016
Strategic Claims Receipt	17,151,212	17,391,882	17,804,291	18,400,126	19,196,503
Automated Provider Pricing	16,064,953	16,330,934	16,786,716	17,445,215	18,325,346
Web-Enabled Plan Setup	11,506,789	11,506,789	11,506,789	11,506,789	11,506,789
Application Infrastructure	9,090,243	9,247,250	9,516,473	6,962,403	10,426,038
Common Payment Engine	6,962,403	6,962,403	6,962,403	6,962,403	6,962,403
Electronic Integration with Providers	5,241,789	5,374,779	5,602,670	5,931,919	5,302,484
Plan Sponsor Services	5,302,484	5,302,484	5,302,484	5,302,484	5,302,484
Web Access to Disease Management	4,927,601	4,927,601	4,927,601	4,927,601	4,927,601
Provider Web Site	2,728,192	2,769,812	2,841,130	2,944,170	3,081,889
Provider Web Pilot	2,336,389	2,336,389	2,336,389	2,336,389	2,336,389
e-Commerce Infrastructure Support	2,111,997	2,152,242	2,221,207	2,320,846	2,454,020
Content Management	293,555	293,555	293,555	293,555	293,555
Information Security Layer	(3,629,754)	(3,498,956)	(3,274,822)	(2,951,000)	(2,518,189)

Table 4.7

Prioritization of Feasible Portfolio of E-Health Projects ($)

	Option value	Costs						
		t = 0	t = 1	t = 2	t = 3	t = 4	t = 5	t = 6
Phase I projects								
Cross Data Center Access	59,020,275	(7,593,463)	(789,847)	0	0	0	0	0
Architecture Database	20,498,450	(277,923)	0	0	0	0	0	0
Strategic Claim Receipt	17,391,882	(2,547,209)	0	(255,600)	0	0	0	0
Web Access to Disease Mgmt	4,927,601	(378,480)	0	0	0	0	0	0
Application Infrastructure	9,247,250	(4,250,504)	0	0	0	0	0	0
Electronic Integration	5,374,779	(1,125,000)	0	(1,125,000)	(1,080,000)	0	0	0
e-Commerce Infrastructure Support	2,152,242	(256,190)	0	0	0	0	0	0
Total costs		**(16,428,769)**	**(789,847)**	**(1,350,600)**	**(1,080,000)**	**0**	**0**	**0**
Phase II projects								
Centralized Authorization DB	39,862,342		(1,088,556)	(18,900)	(18,900)			
Product Database and Services	27,663,227		(3,499,960)	(371,460)	(221,460)	0	0	0
Enhanced Provider Database	20,679,831		(899,448)	0	0	0	0	0
Automated Provider Pricing	16,330,934		(2,768,567)	0	(600,480)	(57,600)	(57,600)	(57,600)
Common Payment Engine	6,962,403		(634,066)	0	(10,740)	(10,740)	0	0
Total costs			**(8,890,598)**	**(390,360)**	**(851,580)**	**(68,340)**	**(57,600)**	**(57,600)**
Phase III projects								
Auto Adjudication I	111,988,079			(1,720,141)	0	(1,599,000)	0	0
Auto Adjudication II	49,968,748			(1,916,576)	(1,918,733)	(299,159)	(299,159)	(299,159)
Web-Enabled Plan Setup	11,506,789			(2,180,118)	0	0	0	0
Plan Sponsor Services	5,302,484			(150,000)	0	0	0	0
Provider Web Site	2,769,812			(940,851)	0	(18,000)	(18,000)	0
Total costs				**(6,907,686)**	**(1,918,733)**	**(1,916,159)**	**(317,159)**	**(299,159)**
Phase IV projects								
Provider Web Pilot	2,336,389				(376,601)	0	(190,472)	(190,472)
Content Management	293,555				(833,440)	0	(360,000)	(360,000)
Total costs				**(6,907,686)**	**(3,128,774)**	**(1,916,159)**	**(867,631)**	**(849,631)**
Total portfolio costs		**(16,428,769)**	**(9,680,444)**	**(8,678,646)**	**(5,060,354)**	**(1,984,499)**	**(925,231)**	**(907,231)**

volatilities associated with the techniques of risk management are subject to scrutiny. However, several techniques have been outlined to address this obstacle. Proxies for IT assets can be modeled from proxy market data or other sources of liquidity. As service-driven technology solutions emerge, market prices may provide proxies for volatility. Simulation techniques can be utilized to model IT risks. Robust methods of sensitivity analysis have also been proposed by Benaroch and Kauffman (1999). Manaster and Koehler (1982) developed a method for calculating implied variance, the instantaneous variance for a stock's return, which could help overcome the lack of a liquid market for certain assets.

The true impact from the real options IS research may come from the strategic managerial insight offered by such analysis (Tallon et al., 2002). The methods proposed in this chapter—as well as the works cited—provide opportunities for new managerial insight into strategic investment decision making for IT. Managers can strategically embed options in their projects in a future-oriented way (Benaroch, 2002). Such an approach has the capability to help managers more effectively direct strategic decisions, such as investments in a service-oriented architecture, to enable option-like IT capabilities. In an environment where adaptability and flexibility are paramount to a firm's success, real options analysis can help firms reach a higher level of agility. In addition, managers can utilize real options analysis to inform themselves about the appropriateness and optimal timing of technology adoption decisions (Kauffman and Li, 2005).

Further, options thinking can help managers overcome project biases and strategically abandon failing initiatives before the damage becomes significant. To sum up, the IT investment decision comprises many contingencies, and not all of them are financial. Therefore, managers must always weigh other quantitative factors when making a decision. Techniques such as the balanced scorecard of Kaplan and Norton (1992) can be utilized, along with real option analysis, for this purpose. Managers can incorporate real options analysis in the context of economic value added (Mayer, 2002), rather than straight NPV project evaluation.

Managerial Implications

We propose the following takeaways for senior managers in their use of real options analysis of IT investments, relative to the analysis approach we have presented in this chapter:

Recommendation 1: Build Strategic Embedded Options into Large IT Investments

Managers should deliberately consider embedded options, such as the option to abandon, expand, and defer, when they are analyzing an IT investment. IT investments can be partitioned by management into specific stages. Not only does such an approach yield quantitative insights via option analysis, but such thinking also forces managers to pay close attention to a project's implementation.

Recommendation 2: Utilize Risk-Based Partitioning of Investments
to Limit Unnecessary and Risky IT Exposures

Managers should identify major risk factors in an IT investment and create options around those risks. In addition, risk factors that spawn multiple IT investments can be partitioned and considered as separate option-enabling investments. For example, a CRM initiative in health care may depend on the same market risks that might also affect a payment processing system. Managers can build options to delay around the resolution of such risk factors.

Recommendation 3: Consider the Timing Decision of Investments and Upgrades

Often IT project timing is a function of a firm's budget or operating cycle. Managers should consider all relevant risk factors and look toward optimal timing for project initiation. In addition, firms should work with vendors in planning upgrades around strategic option-enabled decision making, rather than external factors such as vendor development time.

Recommendation 4: Leverage Interdependencies among IT Project Investments

As illustrated in the examples of nested options regarding the HealthCo databases, managers should scrutinize current and existing IT investments to identify interdependencies between projects. Infrastructure may be the source of "low-hanging fruit" in this area. A common integration backbone, for example, such as an enterprise service platform, can be leveraged by many follow-on projects. Infrastructure should be viewed at a portfolio, rather than at a project level of analysis.

Recommendation 5: Do Not Be Afraid to Execute the Option to Abandon

Unfortunately, IT investments, like other business decisions, are not always governed by rational managerial actions. IT investments often become "pet" projects of individuals or coalitions within a firm. This is partly due to the fact that IT benefits are often hard to quantify and may affect different constituencies within a firm. In addition, cost overruns and project shortcomings are often not realized until after the fact. Real options analysis brings attention to specific stages or "go/no-go" points within the IT investment decision.

Recommendation 6: Use Sensitivity Analysis to Test the Results of Options Analysis

As we mentioned previously, options theory relies on the assumption of a traded, liquid market for the asset in question (Benaroch and Kauffman, 1999, 2000). IT investments do not have such a market, so any proxy for volatility of IT asset returns is suspect. Therefore, managers must consider a range of alternatives for each identified risk factor. Any decision or project sequence that changes significantly in the sensitivity analysis should serve as a signal for greater managerial scrutiny of the decision.

Recommendation 7: Real Options Analysis Is Just One More Tool; Consider Strategic and Other Quantitative Factors in the Decision

Many variables in an IT investment simply cannot be quantified. For example, firm culture can be a major factor in the success of an IT initiative. Hidden costs may emerge as firms face resistance to adoption of a technology. Long-term firm strategy should also be considered when considering between alternatives. As mentioned in the previous recommendation, many of the numbers used are estimates, so managers must feel comfortable with outcomes across a broad range of scenarios. Angelou and Economides (2005) have proposed a hybrid model where the nested options model is combined with an analytic hierarchy process method to evaluate the impact of qualitative factors on project valuation decisions.

CONCLUSION

We presented an overview of the issues involving IT portfolio investment decisions and examined how research in IS real option analysis addresses the difficulties facing decision makers. Then, using a real-world case study of a health care company, we showed that projects that provide e-health capabilities to build the platform for future success have higher option values that are not evident if projects are evaluated using DCF analysis. We further observed that several IT infrastructure projects, which have negative NPV values, also have significant positive NPVs since they provide the foundation to conduct more effective business transactions with HealthCo's key stakeholders. Indeed, many of these projects have high soft benefits since they provide stakeholders with greater ownership of the business processes, thereby improving their perception of HealthCo.

We extended prior research by providing a new method for making IT valuation and investment decisions for project portfolio management. Although prior studies have used real options to value a single project and ignored the effect of project interdependencies, our model accounts for the complexities involved in valuing a portfolio of projects while considering the impact of interdependencies and sequencing constraints. A key contribution involves the development of a nested real options model, within which we use a log-transformed binomial model to calculate the nested option values. Our research extends prior work described in Bardhan, Sougstad, and Bagchi (2004), whose article used a simpler Margrabe options model, and our choice of the log-transformed binomial model corrects for possible overvaluations of project option values, as discussed in Benaroch, Shah, and Jeffery (2006). In addition, the use of the log-transformed binomial option in the technology portfolio view offers the possibility for managers to consider both within- and across-project real options.

IT portfolio investment decisions will continue to constitute complex and uncertain decisions. With service-delivered offerings and architectures, the problem space is only expanding and becoming more complex. However, by analyzing project risk factors and interdependencies, managers can make better-formed decisions in light of the bustling and chaotic environments in which they must manage. The methods described in this chapter provide a powerful tool to address the challenges of IT investment in an uncertain world.

APPENDIX 4.1. OVERVIEW OF THE LOG-TRANSFORMED BINOMIAL OPTION PRICING MODEL

The approach derived by Trigeorgis (1993) relies on the common assumption in derivative pricing that the asset value, V, follows a Wiener diffusion process:

$$dV/V = \alpha dt + \sigma\, dz \qquad (A4.1-1)$$

Mathworld.com defines a *Weiner process* as a continuous-time stochastic process $W(t)$ for $t \geq 0$ with $W(0) = 0$, such that the increment $W(t) - W(s)$ is Gaussian with mean 0 and variance $t - s$ for any $0 \leq s < t$, and increments for non-overlapping time intervals are independent. The first term on the right-hand side refers to drift of the asset returns. The second represents the diffusion where dz follows the Wiener process. For a small interval $K \equiv \Delta t$, $X \equiv \ln V$ follows an arithmetic Brownian motion. With the assumption of risk neutrality, it follows that $\alpha = r$.

Hence, the dynamics of X can be expressed as:

$$\Delta X = \ln(V_{t+\Delta t})/V_t = (r - \tfrac{1}{2}\sigma^2)\Delta t + \sigma dz \qquad (A4.1-2)$$

Now we have the increments ΔX, which are normally distributed with a mean of $(r - \frac{1}{2}\sigma^2)\Delta t$, and a variance of $\sigma^2 \Delta t$. We then introduce the length of each time step, $k = \sigma^2 \Delta t$ and $\mu = r / \sigma^2 - \frac{1}{2}$, and we can represent $E(\Delta X) = uk$ and $Var(\Delta X) = k$. We let m represent the magnitude of the state step, which is given by

$$\sqrt{k + (uk)^2}$$

The probability of an upward movement, p, is $0.5(1 + uk / m)$.

If m represents the magnitude of upward or downward movement in asset value, and p represents the probability of an upward movement, we can represent the discrete time Markov process (Benaroch, 2002) of this asset as:

$$E(\Delta X) = p(+m) + (1 - p)(-m) = 2pm - m, \qquad (A4.1-3)$$

and

$$VAR(X) = E(X^2) - [E(\Delta X)]^2 = [p(+m)^2 + (1-p)(-m)^2] - [2pm - m]^2 = m^2 - [E(\Delta X)]^2 \qquad (A4.1-4)$$

Since the discrete time process must be consistent with the continuous time Weiner process, we conclude that $2pm - m = uk$. Therefore, $p = \frac{1}{2}(1 + uk / m)$ and $m^2 - (uk)^2 = k$, so we know that $m = \sqrt{[k + (uk)^2]} \geq uk$.

NOTE

1. It would be incorrect to use $C_1 = BS(V_1 + C_2, I_1)$, where BS is the Black-Scholes call option value. By assuming that the underlying asset of C_1 is $V_1 + C_2$, the terminal nodes in the binomial tree of C_2 would be represented inaccurately as max $[u^3(V_1 + C_2) - I_1, 0]$. We thank Michel Benaroch for making this suggestion.

REFERENCES

Amram, M. and Kulatilaka, N. 1999. *Real Options: Managing Strategic Investment in an Uncertain World.* Cambridge, MA: Harvard Business School Press.

Angelou, G.N. and Economides, A.A. 2005. A decision analysis framework for prioritizing a portfolio of ICT infrastructure projects. Working paper, University of Macedonia, Thessaloniki, Greece.

Au, Y.A. and Kauffman, R.J. 2003. What do you know? Rational expectations in information technology adoption and investment. *Journal of Management Information Systems,* 20, 2, 49–76.

Ballantine, J. and Stray, S. 1998. Financial appraisal and the IS/IT investment decision making process. *Journal of Information Technology,* 13, 1, 3–14.

Bardhan, I.R.; Kauffman, R.J.; and Narapanawe, S. 2006. Optimizing an IT project portfolio with time-wise interdependencies. In R. Sprague, ed., *Proceedings of the 39th Hawaii International Conference on Systems Science,* Kauai. Los Alamitos, CA: IEEE Computing Society Press.

Bardhan, I.R.; Sougstad, R.; and Bagchi, S. 2004. Prioritization of a portfolio of information technology projects. *Journal of Management Information Systems,* 21, 2, 33–60.

Benaroch, M. 2002. Managing information technology investment risk: A real options perspective. *Journal of Management Information Systems,* 19, 2, 43–84.

Benaroch, M. and Kauffman, R.J. 1999. A case for using real options pricing analysis to evaluate information technology project investments. *Information Systems Research,* 10, 1, 70–86.

———. 2000. Justifying electronic network expansion using real option analysis. *MIS Quarterly,* 24, 2, 197–225.

Benaroch, M.; Shah, S.; and Jeffery, M. 2006. On the valuation of multi-stage IT investments: Embedding nested real options. *Journal of Management Information Systems*, 23, 1, 239–261.

Black, F. and Scholes, M. 1973. The pricing of options and corporate liabilities. *Journal of Political Economy*, 81, 3, 637–659.

Clemons, E.K. 1991. Evaluating strategic investments in information systems. *Communications of the ACM*, 34, 1, 22–36.

Clemons, E.K. and Weber, B. 1990. Strategic information technology investments: Guidelines for decision making. *Journal of Management Information Systems*, 7, 2, 9–28.

Cox, J.C.; Ross, S.A.; and Rubinstein, M. 1979. Option pricing: A simplified approach. *Journal of Financial Economics*, 7, 3, 229–263.

Dai, Q. 2004. Understanding the performance of B2B e-markets. Ph.D. dissertation, Carlson School of Management, University of Minnesota, Minneapolis.

Devaraj, S. and Kohli, R. 2000. Information technology payoff in the healthcare industry: A longitudinal study. *Journal of Management Information Systems*, 16, 4, 41–67.

Dickinson, M.; Thornton, A.; and Graves, S. 2001. Technology portfolio management: Optimizing interdependent projects over multiple time periods. *IEEE Transactions on Engineering Management*, 48, 4, 518–527.

Dixit, A.K. and Pindyck, R.S. 1994. *Investment under Uncertainty*. Princeton, NJ: Princeton University Press.

———. 1995. The options approach to capital investment. *Harvard Business Review*, 73, 3, 105–115.

Dos Santos, B. 1991. Justifying investment in new information technologies. *Journal of Management Information Systems*, 7, 4, 71–89.

Dutta, A. 2004. Putting numbers on intangible benefits. In V. Sambamurthy, R. Watson, and J. DeGross, eds., *Proceedings of the Twenty-Fifth International Conference on Information Systems*. Washington, DC, 387–398.

Eng, T.R. 2001. *The E-Health Landscape: A Terrain Map of Emerging Information and Communication Technologies in Health and Health Care*. Princeton, NJ: Robert Wood Johnson Foundation.

Fichman, R.G. 2004. Real options and IT platform adoption: Implications for theory and practice. *Information Systems Research*, 15, 2, 132–154.

Fichman, R.G.; Keil, M.; and Tiwana, A. 2005. Beyond valuation: Options thinking in IT project management. *California Management Review*, 47, 2, 74–96.

Gartner Group. 2004. IT investment trends. White paper, Stamford, CT.

Goh, K. and Kauffman, R.J. 2005. Towards a theory of value latency for IT investments. In R. Sprague (Ed.), *Proceedings of the 38th Annual Hawaii International Conference on Systems Science*, Kailua-Kona, January 2005. Los Alamitos, CA: IEEE Computing Society Press.

Gustafson, N. and Luft, J. 2002. Valuing strategic flexibility in information technology investments: When do subjective valuation and real options analysis differ? Working paper, Eli Broad School of Business, Michigan State University, East Lansing.

Hagel, J., III. 2002. *Out of the Box: Strategies for Achieving Profits Today and Growth Tomorrow through Web Services*. Boston: Harvard Business School Press.

Hull, J.C. 1993. *Options, Futures, and Other Derivative Securities*. 2d ed. Englewood Cliffs, NJ: Prentice Hall.

Jeffery, M., and Leliveld, I. 2004. Best practices in IT portfolio management. *MIT Sloan Management Review*, 45, 3, 41–49.

Kambil, A.; Henderson, C.J.; and Mohsenzadeh, H. 1993. Strategic management of information technology investments. In R. Banker, R.J. Kauffman, and M.A. Mahmood, eds., *Strategic Information Technology Management: Perspectives on Organizational Growth and Competitive Advantage*. Harrisburg, PA: Idea Group, 161–178.

Kaplan, R.S. and Norton, D.P. 1992. The balanced scorecard: Measures that drive performance. *Harvard Business Review*, 70, 1, 71–79.

Kauffman, R.J. and Kriebel, C.H. 1988. Modeling and measuring the business value of information technologies. In P. Strassmann, P. Berger, B. Swanson, C. Kriebel, and R. Kauffman, eds., *Measuring the Business Value of IT*. Washington, DC: ICIT Press.

Kauffman, R.J. and Li, X. 2005. Technology competition and optimal investment timing: A real options perspective. *IEEE Transactions on Engineering Management*, 52, 1, 15–30.

Kogut, B. and Kulatilaka, N. 1994. Options thinking and platform investments: Investing in opportunity. *California Management Review*, 36, 4, 52–71.

Kumar, R. 2002. Managing risks in IT projects: An options perspective. *Information and Management,* 40, 1, 63–74.
Lee, G. and Xia, W. 2002. Development of a measure to assess the complexity of information systems. In L. Applegate, R. Galliers, and J. DeGross, eds., *Proceedings of the 23rd International Conference on Information Systems,* Barcelona, 79–88.
Lentz, C.M. and Henderson, J.C. 1998. Aligning IT investment and business strategy: A value management capability. Working paper, School of Management, Boston University.
Levit, K. and Cowan, C. 2000. Health spending in 1998: Signals of change. *Health Affairs,* 19, 1, 124–132.
Lin, L. and Whinston, A.B. 2003. Contracts for information technology: Uncertainty, timing and asymmetric information. In *Proceedings of the Eighth INFORMS Conference on Information Systems and Technology,* Atlanta, GA, October 18–19.
Luehrman, T.A. 1998. Strategy as a portfolio of real options. *Harvard Business Review,* 76, 5, 89–99.
Manaster, S. and Koehler, G. 1982. The calculation of implied variances from the Black and Scholes model: A note. *Journal of Finance,* 37, 1, 227–230.
Margrabe, W. 1978. The value of an option to exchange one asset for another. *Journal of Finance,* 33, 1, 177–186.
Matheis, M. and Dickson, D. 2005. Real options = real value. White paper, AT Kearney, Chicago. Available at www.atkearney.com (accessed May 21, 2007).
Mayer, T. 2002. A buyers' guide to IT valuation methodologies. *CIO Magazine,* July 15. Available at www.cio.com (accessed May 21, 2007).
Oakes, P.R. 2004. Life insurers look to IT. *McKinsey Quarterly,* November. Available at www.mckinsey.com (accessed May 21, 2007).
Panayi, S. and Trigeorgis, L. 1998. Multi-stage real options: The case of information technology infrastructure and international bank expansion. *Quarterly Review of Economics and Finance,* 38, Special Issue, 675–692.
Sambamurthy, V.; Bharadwaj, A.; and Grover, V. 2003. Shaping agility through digital options: Reconceptualizing the role of information technology in contemporary firms. *MIS Quarterly,* 27, 2, 237–263.
Schwartz, E. and Zozaya-Gorostiza, C. 2003. Investment under uncertainty in information technology: Acquisition and development projects. *Management Science,* 49, 1, 57–70.
Tallon, P.P.; Kauffman, R.J.; Lucas, H.C., Jr.; Whinston, A.B.; and Zhu, K. 2002. Using real option analysis for evaluating uncertain investments in information technology: Insights from the ICIS 2001 debate. *Communications of the Association of Information Systems,* 9, 136–167.
Taudes, A. 1998. Software growth options. *Journal of Management Information Systems,* 15, 1, 165–185.
Taudes, A.; Feurstein, M.; and Mild, A. 2000. Options analysis of software platform decisions: A case study. *MIS Quarterly,* 24, 2, 227–243.
Trigeorgis, L. 1991. A log-transformed binomial numerical analysis method for valuing complex multi-option investments. *Journal of Financial and Quantitative Analysis,* 26, 3, 309–326.
———. 1993. The nature of options interactions and the valuation of investments with multiple real options. *Journal of Financial and Quantitative Analysis,* 28, 1, 1–20.
———. 1996. *Real Options.* Cambridge, MA: MIT Press.
Verhoef, C. 2002. Quantitative IT portfolio management. *Science of Computer Programming,* 45, 4, 1–96.
Weill, P. and Broadbent, M. 1998. *Leveraging the New Infrastructure: How Market Leaders Capitalize on Information Technology.* Cambridge, MA: Harvard Business School Press, 1998.
Zhu, K. 1999. Strategic investment in information technologies: A real-options and game-theoretic approach. Ph.D. dissertation, School of Industrial Engineering, Stanford University, Stanford, CA.

CHAPTER 5

EVALUATING INFORMATION TECHNOLOGY INDUSTRY PERFORMANCE

A Stochastic Production Frontier Approach

BENJAMIN B.M. SHAO AND WINSTON T. LIN

Abstract: We apply a stochastic production frontier approach to evaluate the productivity of information technology (IT) industries for eight Organization for Economic Cooperation and Development countries. We employ a translog production function to examine the performance patterns of these IT industries along three dimensions—productivity, technological change, and efficiency change. The analysis approach that we use is based on the Malmquist total factor productivity (TFP) index. Our empirical results indicate that the IT industries of the different countries in our sample demonstrate distinctive patterns in the three performance metrics. Overall, we find that the IT industries tend to be more productive than other industries when compared with previous research findings. Further analyses that we conducted reveal that technological progress is the main driver of productivity growth for the IT industries, and efficiency change actually has a negative impact (yet on a smaller scale) on productivity growth. We conclude with a discussion of policy implications from our results and identify related issues for future research. The empirical advance made by this chapter to the field of information systems is the application of stochastic production frontiers to the computation of the Malmquist TFP index for the performance evaluation of IT industries in a cross-country context.

Keywords: Economic Analysis, Empirical Methods, Information and Communications Technology, Malmquist Productivity Index, Stochastic Production Frontier, Technical Efficiency, Technological Progress, Translog Production Function

INTRODUCTION

Over the past two decades, researchers in the field of information systems (IS) have become more and more interested in the impacts of information technology (IT) on performance. The metrics of performance used to assess the contributions of IT include *productivity* (Brynjolfsson and Hitt, 1996; Dewan and Kraemer, 2000), *efficiency* (Lin and Shao, 2000; Shao and Lin, 2002), *profitability* (Hitt and Brynjolfsson, 1996; Tam, 1998), *quality* (Davamanirajan et al., 2006; Mukhopadhyay, Rajiv, and Srinivasan, 1997), *cost* (Mitra and Chaya, 1996), and *variety* (Thatcher and Oliver, 2001), among others. There have been few studies so far, however, that have looked at the production of IT capital goods—on the foundation of which subsequent IT contributions are based. In this chapter, we showcase some new and innovative ways to study IT business value from a different angle. Rather than measuring the returns from IT adoption and IT usage, we focus instead on evaluating the production processes of IT-producing industries in a cross-country context. This shift in research focus is not trivial, as IT production has grown into a $500 billion worldwide industry (Dedrick and Kraemer, 1998) and IT investment in the United States is now equal to the amount of expenditure on offices, warehouses, and factories combined (McAfee, 2006). Even with the recent cutbacks in investments that have been reported in the press, IT still accounts for the lion's share of current capital investment by businesses.

The specific research question that we address is: How can we empirically ascertain whether IT industries, as defined by the Organization for Economic Cooperation and Development (OECD), are productive, efficient, and technologically progressive in their production processes? The OECD (2002) actually refers to these industries as *information and computer technology industries*. However, we prefer to use *IT industries* in lieu of *information and computer technology industries* because of the confusion the latter creates with the widely used term for ICT—*information and communication technologies*—which includes telecommunications technologies. Several factors make the proposed research question a topic of importance for both a country's economy and the global economy. First, IT industries provide various IT products for other industries in an economy, so their performance in this regard is likely to affect the adoption rate of these IT products by IT-using industries. This IT adoption rate will then impact the consequent productivity gains enabled by IT. Second, the share of IT industries in many country's economies continues to rise; the increases constitute a key factor for determining their aggregate output productivity. Finally, because IT has become a much stronger segment in international trade, its significance extends beyond country boundaries in the form of job transfers, value added, and trade imbalances, according to Kraemer and Dedrick (1998). Indeed, as noted by Tallon and Kraemer (2000) in the case of Ireland's Celtic Tiger economy, IT production can be an important source of employment for an emerging economy.

In this chapter, we apply the *parametric stochastic production frontier method* to construct *Malmquist total factor productivity* (TFP) *indices* for eight OECD countries' IT industries. We prefer to use a translog production function over the Cobb-Douglas function to relax the inherent assumptions of fixed returns to scale and unitary elasticity of substitution (Shao and Lin, 2001); see Appendix 5.1 for definitions and explanations of the terms and concepts that we use. We then decompose the Malmquist TFP index into two components—*technological change* and *efficiency change*. Technically, the former represents the shift in the production frontier over time, and the latter refers to the adjustment in the relative distance of the actual output to the ideal output specified by the production frontier. Economically, technological progress reflects the degree of innovative potential, and efficiency change reveals the capacity of a production unit to catch up with its leading peers (Arcelus and Arozena, 1999). This study aims to find out whether IT capital goods are created in an effective manner by these OECD countries and, if so, to specify what sources can best explain their productivity growth over a specified period.

Our intention is to identify the productivity patterns of these countries and then break down the Malmquist productivity index into its two components, one as technical change and the other as efficiency change. A decomposition of the Malmquist TFP index is informative, as it assists us in both evaluating the performance of these IT countries and identifying sources of productivity (or causes of underperformance). Our empirical results have considerable implications for formulating an IT industry policy at the government level. The analysis can help a country to better understand its competitiveness in the global IT market and, accordingly, develop and implement more sustainable strategies to advance its IT industry.

Table 5.1

Comparisons of Stochastic Production Frontiers and Data Envelopment Analysis (DEA)

Stochastic production frontiers	Data envelopment analysis (DEA)
Characteristics	
• Parametric	• Nonparametric
	• Based on management science and operations research
• Based on production theory in microeconomics	
• Utilizes the technique of statistical estimation	• Utilizes the technique of linear programming
Strengths	
• Accounts for measurement error and random noise	• No need to assume a distributional form for the inefficiency term
	• No need to specify a functional form for the production function
• Can be used to conduct hypothesis testing	
• No need to assume constant or variable returns to scale	• Can accommodate multiple outputs
Weaknesses	
• Need to specify a distributional form for the inefficiency term (e.g., half-normal, truncated normal, etc.)	• Does not account for measurement error and random noise
• Need to specify a functional form for the production function (e.g., Cobb-Douglas, translog, etc.)	• Cannot be used to conduct hypothesis testing directly
	• Need to assume constant or variable returns to scale
• More difficult to accommodate multiple outputs	
Applicable contexts	
• Measurement error and random noise are present	• Multiple-output production
• Single-output production	• Nonprofit service sector
• Hypothesis testing regarding inefficiency and/or production structure	• Behavioral assumptions are difficult to justify

In terms of empirical advances for IS research, this chapter notably applies the technique of stochastic production frontiers, instead of the more conventional data envelopment analysis (DEA) (Banker, Charnes, and Cooper, 1984; Charnes, Cooper, and Rhodes, 1978), to compute the Malmquist TFP index in the context of evaluating IT industry performance across countries. Although the use of stochastic production frontiers for measuring *technical efficiency* in place of DEA is well documented in the literature, its application to the Malmquist TFP index is a recent novel proposition (Fuentes, Grifell-Tatje, and Perelman, 2001; Orea, 2002). Thus it is also our intention to introduce this analytical technique to empirical IS researchers. To highlight the methodological contribution of the chapter, Table 5.1 compares the stochastic production frontiers approach with DEA based on their characteristics, strengths, weaknesses, and applicable contexts (Coelli et al., 2005). Given the research problem addressed by this study, it is evidently more appropriate to employ the stochastic production frontiers over DEA for our empirical analysis.

The next section of the chapter reviews the literature on the productivity impacts of IT and explains the link between this study and prior research. The third section presents the stochastic production frontier model for computing the Malmquist TFP index and its two deciding components. The country-level data used in our analysis are described and the empirical results are presented next. The fifth section discusses our results and evaluates issues addressed by our methodology. The conclusion presents some comments about the overall contribution of the research. We also discuss policy implications, limitations, and topics for future research.

LITERATURE REVIEW

IT is a major enabler of economic change, since it can essentially reshape the way a business operates and competes. Specifically, IT can help reduce both production costs and transaction costs for a firm. The traditional view of IT economic value is to treat IT as a substitute for common factors of production in the production process. In particular, advances in IT-based computing power have helped to reduce the need for expensive labor and cut back on employee headcount (Gordon, 2000). On the other hand, IT also plays a dual role when it can be used as a facilitator of coordination. Interconnected computer networks shrink the time it takes to gather, analyze, store, and disseminate information. The abilities of IT to support information exchange across functional, geographical, and temporal barriers facilitate firm-specific management approaches that are difficult to imitate. In this respect, IT is a powerful tool for decreasing the transaction costs of coordinating economic activities, both within and across organizations (Gurbaxani and Whang, 1991; Malone, Yates, and Benjamin, 1987). Taking both views into account, we can see that IT represents a unique opportunity to both enhance output productivity and enable fundamental change in the production process. Using the resource-based view of firms, Melville, Kraemer, and Gurbaxani (2004) argue that IT has potential value, but the extent and dimensions of its realized value rely on several internal and external factors, including complementary organizational resources of the firm, its trading partners and the competitive environment.

Studies of IT impacts on productivity can be categorized into three main clusters. The first cluster examines IT productivity gains using the production function framework. Most of the studies that fall into this category employ traditional factors of production such as capital and labor and include IT capital as a separate factor of production. They assume certain production functional forms (either parametric or nonparametric) to measure the marginal product, output elasticity, and output/input ratio for IT (e.g., Dewan and Min, 1997; Hitt and Brynjolfsson, 1996). Typically, this group of studies attempts to ascertain whether the investments in IT lead to a favorable outcome of total output. A well-known debate in this area during the 1990s and early 2000s is the *productivity paradox*. Based on a now-famous observation made by economist Robert Solow (1987) in the late 1980s, doubts were cast on the productivity returns expected from IT, which seemed absent from data on economic growth and performance around that time. The paradox was later resolved in the minds of many observers by Brynjolfsson and Hitt (1996), as well as by convincing evidence of a significant IT-led productivity revival experienced by many countries in the late 1990s (Gordon, 2000). Willcocks and Lester (1999) provide a review of the origin, evolution, and assessment of this subject for the interested reader.

The second approach to examining IT productivity effects centers on the connection between IT capital accumulation and economic growth. Neoclassical growth theory posits that the rate of change in capital accumulation, called *capital deepening*, is a critical factor in determining an economy's growth. Jorgenson and Stiroh (1999) applied neoclassical growth models and found evidence that IT capital deepening has been instrumental in spurring economic growth over the past forty years. By the same token, Oliner and Sichel (2002) found that the increasing use of IT capital after 1995 contributed to the recent acceleration of U.S. labor productivity but non-IT capital per worker did not increase. Triplett and Bosworth (2004) also reported that increasing IT capital per worker contributed about 0.8 percent to growth in labor productivity after 1995 and

0.5 percent to its acceleration. The implication here is that although IT may account for a small portion of capital, its contribution to an economy's output productivity can still be significant as long as the economy experiences sustained increases in IT capital accumulation. However, Dewan and Kraemer (1998, 2000) note that that such increases in IT capital accumulate on an established base of education and non-IT infrastructure. Without that core base of investment, it would be difficult to reap and sustain the potential productivity benefits from IT capital.

The third and relatively newer viewpoint is to look at the role of IT capital production in the productivity revival: the production of IT capital goods. Researchers who have been working with this perspective ask the following question: Do IT industries contribute to economic growth? Both Oliner and Sichel (2000) and Gordon (2000) found that two-thirds of the total factor productivity acceleration in the United States after 1995 is accounted for by the acceleration in the industries that produce IT investment goods. They concluded that the acceleration in technological progress of IT industries and the increased expenditures in purchasing their products were the main drivers of the recent growth in U.S. productivity. Stiroh (2002) also reported that a significant part of recent U.S. productivity growth was due to IT industries, as well as to those industries that utilize IT intensively and creatively. We further note that while IT use and IT production are linked, they are also different. They are linked since IT industries supply IT capital goods used by other industries in an economy. In other words, IT usage happens after IT production and this link between the two phenomena is well reflected in the concept of "production close to use" for IT products (Dedrick and Kraemer, 1998). On the other hand, industries that supply IT are expected to display their own performance in terms of productivity, efficiency, and technical progress that affect the overall productivity of an economy through IT capital accumulation.

We seek to study the value of IT from the second and third points of view by measuring the productivity of IT industries in producing IT capital goods. For most sectors in an economy, IT has a *substitution effect,* barring some extrinsic factors like unions (Melville, Kraemer, and Gurbaxani, 2004). With the persistent price decline of IT products (especially in comparison to labor), it is sensible for firms to take advantage of any cost advantages associated with IT (Mukhopadhyay, Lerch, and Mangal, 1997), which in turn leads to higher demand for IT capital products. If, as claimed by prior research (Gordon, 2000; Oliner and Sichel, 2000), IT capital accumulation actually helps enhance the aggregate productivity of an economy's output, then to meet the higher demand created by IT capital deepening, IT industries should exhibit better performance than most other industries in terms of productivity, efficiency, and technological progress. In other words, IT industries should possess unique performance characteristics in their own production processes that influence an economy's aggregate productivity growth. Our objective is to answer this question based on empirical advances that yield interesting and novel insights. The empirical advances are made possible by the new methodologies of stochastic production frontiers, recently proposed in the field of production economics (Fuentes, Grifell-Tatje, and Perelman, 2001; Orea, 2002). To our knowledge, this research is the first time that these methodologies have been applied in an IS domain, and particularly within the economics of IS in order to study the productivity performance of IT industries.

SPECIFICATION OF THE MODEL

We use the *Malmquist total factor productivity index* (MPI) (Caves, Christensen, and Diewert, 1982) to measure the productivity of IT industries for a set of eight OECD countries for which data are available. Several reasons prompted us to choose the MPI over other productivity indices such as Törnqvist and Fisher. First, the MPI does not require data on prices of inputs. Second, the MPI can combine multiple inputs and outputs without having to specify how to aggregate them. Third, the MPI does not make any behavioral assumptions (e.g., cost minimization or profit maximization) for the economic units under consideration. Finally, the MPI can be decomposed into two factors—technical change and efficiency change—that represent specific sources of productivity growth (Färe et al., 1994). While the computations of the Törnqvist and Fisher indices do not involve distance functions and are less demanding, the MPI index is more informative because of its ability to separate and identify sources for explaining productivity growth. In addition, the decomposition capability of the MPI index represents an innovative empirical advance, in terms of analysis and modeling, and it separates our study from earlier research based on the Törnqvist index (e.g., Oliner and Sichel, 2000; Triplett and Bosworth, 2004).

The MPI was initially proposed by Malmquist (1953) to define a distance function on a consumption space. The distance function is similar to the Shepard input function of producers and is used to develop a quantity index (Färe, Grosskopf, and Russell, 1998). This distance function was then extended to production theory where it was tasked with a different economic undertaking of productivity measurement. Notably, the distance function on which the MPI is based results in a value that happens to be the technical efficiency defined by Farrell (1957). As a result, we can apply the related methodologies for measuring technical efficiency, including stochastic production frontiers and DEA, to the computation of the MPI.

Distance Functions and the Malmquist Productivity Index

A production unit at time t employs input vector X^t to produce output vector Y^t. In production theory, this production process is defined using an output set:

$$P^t(X^t) = \{Y^t : X^t \text{ can produce } Y^t\}. \quad (5.1)$$

The output set $P^t(X^t)$ is assumed to be closed, bounded, and convex. It also satisfies the axiom of *strong disposability of inputs and outputs* (Coelli et al., 2005). The output distance function is defined on the output set as:

$$D^t(X^t, Y^t) = min\{\theta : (Y^t/\theta) \in P^t(X^t)\} \quad (5.2\text{--}1)$$

$$= [max\{\rho : (\rho Y^t) \in P^t(X^t)\}]^{-1}. \quad (5.2\text{--}2)$$

The maximum of the output distance function $D^t(X^t, Y^t)$ is 1, meaning the production unit is operating on the production frontier and hence is perfectly efficient. When it is less than 1, the production unit is producing somewhere below the production frontier and is technically inefficient (Goh and Kauffman, 2007). Based on the output distance function $D^t(X^t, Y^t)$, the Malmquist productivity index is defined as (Färe et al., 1994):

$$M^t(\mathbf{X}^t, \mathbf{Y}^t, \mathbf{X}^{t+1}, \mathbf{Y}^{t+1}) = \sqrt{\frac{D^t(\mathbf{X}^{t+1}, \mathbf{Y}^{t+1})}{D^t(\mathbf{X}^t, \mathbf{Y}^t)} \times \frac{D^{t+1}(\mathbf{X}^{t+1}, \mathbf{Y}^{t+1})}{D^{t+1}(\mathbf{X}^t, \mathbf{Y}^t)}} \quad (5.3\text{--}1)$$

$$= \frac{D^{t+1}(\mathbf{X}^{t+1}, \mathbf{Y}^{t+1})}{D^t(\mathbf{X}^t, \mathbf{Y}^t)} \sqrt{\frac{D^t(\mathbf{X}^{t+1}, \mathbf{Y}^{t+1})}{D^{t+1}(\mathbf{X}^{t+1}, \mathbf{Y}^{t+1})} \times \frac{D^t(\mathbf{X}^t, \mathbf{Y}^t)}{D^{t+1}(\mathbf{X}^t, \mathbf{Y}^t)}} \quad (5.3\text{--}2)$$

In Equation 5.3–2, the leading ratio of D^{t+1} to D^t outside the square root is equivalent to the change in technical efficiency between periods t and $t + 1$. This ratio represents the change in the relative distances from the observed output to the potential maximum output at time t and $t + 1$. On the other hand, the parts associated with the square root of Equation 5.3–2 represent the geometric mean of two productivity indices and correspond to technical change (or the shift in the production frontiers from time t to $t + 1$). To summarize:

$$\text{Technical efficiency change (TEC)} = \frac{D^{t+1}(X^{t+1}, Y^{t+1})}{D^t(X^t, Y^t)} \tag{5.4}$$

$$\text{Technical change (TCH)} = \sqrt{\frac{D^t(X^{t+1}, Y^{t+1})}{D^{t+1}(X^{t+1}, Y^{t+1})} \times \frac{D^t(X^t, Y^t)}{D^{t+1}(X^t, Y^t)}} \tag{5.5}$$

$$\text{Malmquist productivity index (MPI)} = \text{TEC} \times \text{TCH} \tag{5.6}$$

We further note that the MPI as well as its two components, TEC and TCH, are each calculated as an index and have a threshold value of 1. In other words, if a certain index value is equal to 1, then it indicates that the performance of a country's IT industry remains unchanged with regard to that measure from one period to the next. On the other hand, an index value greater than 1 represents an improvement, and a value less than 1 indicates a decline.

Stochastic Production Frontiers

Equation 5.2–2 suggests that the output distance function $D^t(X^t, Y^t)$ corresponds to Farrell's output-oriented technical efficiency. This linkage enables the computation of an output distance function $D^t(X^t, Y^t)$ through the methods of efficiency measurement like parametric stochastic production frontiers or nonparametric DEA (Goh and Kauffman, 2007). In this study, we use the stochastic production frontier approach with a translog functional form to measure the technical efficiency of each country's IT industry (i.e., the output distance function $D^t(X^t, Y^t)$), TEC, TCH, and finally the MPI. According to Table 5.1, there are a number of reasons for us to choose stochastic production frontiers over DEA for the computation of the Malmquist TFP index. First, given the *aggregate* nature of the data set used for our empirical analysis, we expect the data set to have measurement errors and random noise, as is the case with most empirical studies. Second, the data set we use has one output variable. Third, the translog production function does not impose assumptions of fixed returns to scale and unitary elasticity of substitution. A translog stochastic production frontier is defined as follows (Fuentes, Grifell-Tatje, and Perelman, 2001; Orea, 2002):

$$\ln Y_{it} = \beta_0 + \beta_K \ln K_{it} + \beta_L \ln L_{it} + \beta_{KK} \ln K_{it} \ln K_{it} + \beta_{LL} \ln L_{it} \ln L_{it} \\ + \beta_{KL} \ln K_{it} \ln L_{it} + \beta_T T + \beta_{TT} T^2 + \beta_{TK} T \ln K_{it} + \beta_{TL} T \ln L_{it} + v_{it} - u_{it} \tag{5.7}$$

where Y_{it} is the output of the ith country's IT industry in the tth year;
K_{it} denotes the capital of the ith country's IT industry in the tth year;
L_{it} denotes the labor of the ith country's IT industry in the tth year;
T is a time variable (1 for year 1, 2 for year 2, etc.);
β are unknown parameters to be estimated;
v_{it} are random errors, assumed to be i.i.d. with $N(0, \sigma_v^2)$ distribution; and
u_{it} are technical inefficiencies, assumed to be $|N(\mu_{it}, \sigma_u^2)|$.

The truncated normal distribution $|N(\mu_i, \sigma_u^2)|$ indicates that technical inefficiency u_{it} is nonnegative and depends on some country-specific characteristics (Shao and Lin, 2001). In addition, the stochastic frontier model in Equation 5.7 has the time variable T, which interacts with the input variables K_{it} and L_{it}, which allows for nonneutral technical change (Coelli et al., 2005).

The technical efficiency score, TE, for each country i in each year t can be derived as:

$$TE_{it} = E[exp(-u_{it}) \mid e_{it} = v_{it} - u_{it}] \tag{5.8}$$

Because u_{it} is a nonnegative random variable, the technical efficiency score TE_{it} falls between 0 and 1, with a higher value indicating a higher technical efficiency. After we obtain TE_{it} (and hence the output distance function D^t), the *technical efficiency change, TEC*, in Equation 5.4 can be obtained as:

$$TEC = TE_{i(t+1)} / TE_{it} \tag{5.9}$$

However, this approach for TE_{it} does not help with the calculation of $D^t(X^{t+1}, Y^{t+1})$ and $D^{t+1}(X^t, Y^t)$ in Equation 5.5 for *technical change, TCH*. Instead, TCH between the year t and $t+1$ for the ith country needs to be calculated directly from the estimated parameters β (Coelli et al., 2005). We first evaluate the partial derivatives of the production function with respect to time using the data for the ith country in year t and $t+1$. Then we calculate the technical change, TCH, as the geometric mean of these two partial derivatives. For our translog functional specification, this is equivalent to the exponential of the arithmetic mean of the log derivatives, computed as follows:

$$\text{Technical change (TCH)} = \exp\left\{\frac{1}{2}\left[\frac{\partial h\, Y_{i(t+1)}}{\partial(t+1)} + \frac{\partial h\, Y_t}{\partial t}\right]\right\} \tag{5.10}$$

Finally, as specified by Equation 5.6, the Malmquist TFP index (*MPI*) can be derived by multiplying TEC of Equation 5.9 and TCH of Equation 5.10.

DATA AND RESULTS

The country-level data set was collected from two sources—the *OECD STAN Database for Industrial Analysis* (OECD, 1998) and the OECD *International Sectoral Database* (OECD, 1999). The data were obtained under the category "Office and Computing Machinery" with an International SIC code of 3825. There are two inputs, Capital and Labor. *Capital (K)* is defined as the "Gross Fixed Capital Formation—Current Price" deflated using the "Producer Price Index—Commodities." *Labor (L)* is defined as the "Labor Compensation—Current Price" deflated using the "Labor Price—1982 Price." *Output (Y)* is defined as the "Office and Computing Machinery Production—Current Price" deflated using the "Computer and Peripheral Price—1992 = 100" (a price index of National Income and Product Accounts from BEA). Thus, output Y is the real gross output of an IT industry. Since our focus of analysis is the IT industry, it only includes the computer hardware and peripheral equipment and does not cover the output of software and telecommunications sectors.[1]

All of the variables were retrieved directly from the OECD publications. The unit of measurement for K, L, and Y is expressed in 1992 U.S. dollars. Data availability allowed us to include eight countries in the data set. They are Finland, Germany, Japan, Korea, the Netherlands, Norway, the United Kingdom, and the United States. The time period covered is from 1978 to 1993, inclusive. Table 5.2 summarizes the descriptive statistics for the variables.

Table 5.2

Averages of Key Variables, 1978–1993 (data in millions of 1992 US$)

Country	Output Y	Capital K	Labor L
Finland	395.2	87.8	12.6
Germany	12,489.4	3,549.2	971.3
Japan	48,006.8	6,964.0	3,908.2
Korea	825.3	95.9	67.6
Netherlands	738.8	148.5	43.8
Norway	243.5	63.0	16.3
United Kingdom	7,922.6	1,390.9	261.1
United States	48,217.6	12,817.6	2,548.3
All countries	14,854.9	3,139.6	978.6

Technical Efficiency

Because the MPI and its two components are based on the computations of output distance functions that are equal to Farrell's output-oriented technical efficiency, we first present technical efficiency TE_{it} in Equation 5.8 for every country across the various years in Table 5.3. A higher score in Table 5.3 indicates a higher technical efficiency for that country in a given year. To be consistent with the way the MPI is defined, country averages across years are calculated as geometric means. However, yearly averages across countries are still computed as arithmetic means.

As can be seen from Table 5.3, Japan and the UK are the two countries with the highest averages for technical efficiency across the period, indicating that both countries are the "best practices" countries in producing their outputs using a fixed set of inputs with a given production technology. Thus, Japan and the UK seem to have the most technically efficient IT industries according to our analysis. Figure 5.1 plots technical efficiencies over the period for the eight countries.

The Malmquist Productivity Index and Its Components

After obtaining technical efficiency TE_{it} (and hence the output distance function D^t) for each country i in year t, we then proceed to compute the corresponding technical efficiency change (TEC), technical change (TCH), and the Malmquist index (MPI) according to Equations 5.6, 5.9, and 5.10. Table 5.4 presents the geometric means of the MPI, as well as its components of TEC and TCH over the years for each country. The decimal figures may be interpreted as the corresponding percentages. Thus, 1.161 should be interpreted as 16.1 percent growth, while 0.975 should be interpreted as a decline of 2.5 percent.

The results shown in Table 5.4 summarize the MPIs across years for each of the eight countries. The average MPI provides a snapshot of the overall changes from 1978 to 1993. Thus it would be interesting to observe the fluctuation patterns of these MPI values over time. Table 5.5 (see p. 125) presents the MPIs over the entire period from 1979 through 1993 for each country.

For the TFP growth, all eight countries experienced an increase in their MPIs, with Finland exhibiting the highest average TFP growth rate of 21.9 percent. Only three countries did not register a TFP growth greater than 10 percent: the Netherlands with 9.3 percent, Japan with 2.2 percent, and Korea with 1.6 percent. Overall, the Malmquist TFP indices for the eight countries

Table 5.3

Technical Efficiency

Country	1978	1979	1980	1981	1982	1983	1984	1985	1986	1987	1988	1989	1990	1991	1992	1993	Avg.
Finland	0.799	0.916	0.876	0.575	0.633	0.464	0.430	0.419	0.758	0.769	0.641	0.593	0.709	0.761	0.954	0.964	0.710
Germany	0.459	0.415	0.423	0.458	0.460	0.483	0.543	0.596	0.559	0.509	0.501	0.461	0.386	0.466	0.604	0.587	0.478
Japan	0.925	0.893	0.839	0.868	0.841	0.877	0.871	0.813	0.869	0.863	0.858	0.823	0.705	0.753	0.687	0.639	0.822
Korea	0.986	0.910	0.889	0.576	0.803	0.807	0.584	0.477	0.617	0.968	0.911	0.891	0.928	0.625	0.637	0.678	0.771
Netherlands	0.663	0.618	0.533	0.486	0.473	0.527	0.806	0.642	0.673	0.800	0.907	0.723	0.548	0.595	0.642	0.367	0.602
Norway	0.315	0.372	0.619	0.571	0.678	0.695	0.493	0.483	0.453	0.584	0.413	0.627	0.558	0.462	0.667	0.495	0.518
United Kingdom	0.823	0.848	0.776	0.626	0.764	0.734	0.895	0.782	0.855	0.957	0.947	0.962	0.981	0.797	0.883	0.736	0.824
United States	0.629	0.677	0.657	0.644	0.669	0.694	0.693	0.660	0.692	0.747	0.743	0.717	0.687	0.619	0.613	0.614	0.669
All countries	0.699	0.706	0.701	0.600	0.665	0.660	0.664	0.609	0.684	0.774	0.740	0.724	0.687	0.634	0.710	0.635	0.674

Note: Country averages across years are geometric means; yearly averages across countries are arithmetic means.

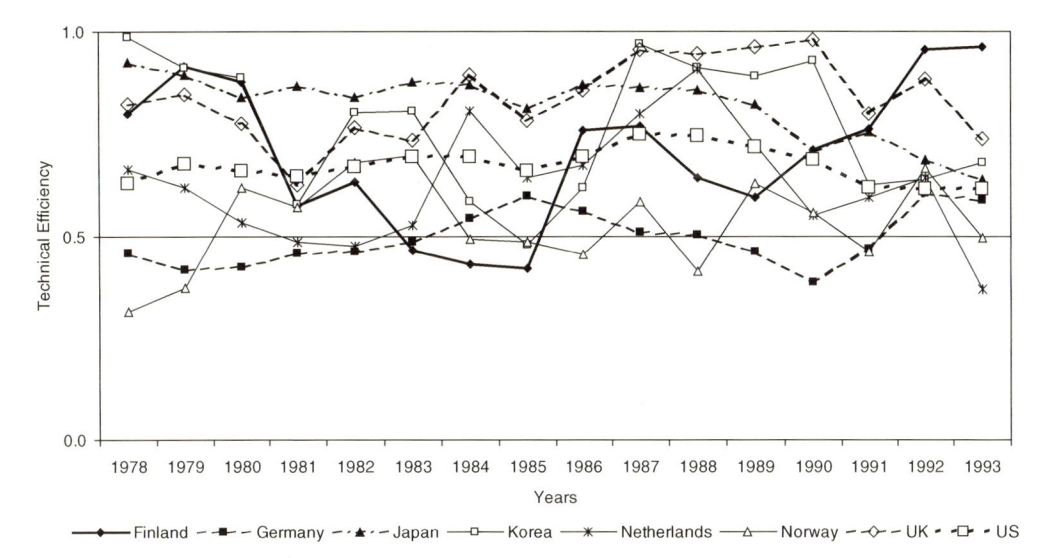

Figure 5.1 Technical Efficiency for Eight OECD Countries During 1978–1993

[Line chart showing Technical Efficiency (0.0 to 1.0) on the y-axis versus Years (1978–1993) on the x-axis for Finland, Germany, Japan, Korea, Netherlands, Norway, UK, and US.]

we examined grew at an impressive annual rate of 12.5 percent from 1978 to 1993. This figure is quite significant, considering that Arcelus and Arozena (1999) found the overall manufacturing sector of fourteen similar OECD countries enjoyed only a TFP growth of 0.6 percent from 1970 to 1990, and Färe et al. (1994) reported output productivity growth of just 0.7 percent for a larger set of seventeen OECD countries from 1979 through 1988.

Table 5.4 also shows the two components of the MPI that can help identify the sources of the growth of TFP. First, technological change TCH refers to the extent to which the MPI growth is due to the shifts in the production frontiers over time. Thus, TCH implies the innovation capability of an IT industry for a country. Second, technical efficiency change TEC represents the ability of an IT industry to catch up with other more efficient IT industries defined by the translog production frontier over time. Although technical efficiency change TEC in Table 5.4 is derived from technical efficiency TE_{it} in Table 5.3, these are two different performance measures, each with a different economic meaning. Technical efficiency in Table 5.3 is measured as the *relative proximity of an IT industry's actual output to its ideal output,* and its value has an upper bound of 1. On the other hand, technical efficiency change TEC in Table 5.3 measures the *change in technical efficiency over time* and can have an index value greater than, equal to, or less than 1, indicating improvement, stagnation, or deterioration in technical efficiency, respectively.

As can be seen in Table 5.4, overall across countries, technological change TCH (1.130) contributes 13.0 percent to the increase of the MPI, while technical efficiency change TEC (0.995) actually hurts MPI by 0.5 percent. The overall average productivity growth MPI (1.125) is equal to the product of these two components. Consequently, the TFP growth measured for these IT industries is mainly driven by the innovation of their production technologies (i.e., advancement of their production processes), and the effect of technical efficiency change on the MPI is negative (albeit on a relatively small scale). This finding is consistent with Romer's (1990) argument that technological progress is the *key* force driving the growth of an industry or economy.

Table 5.4

Malmquist Productivity Index Geometric Means and Its Components, 1978–1993

Country	MPI	TCH	TEC
Finland	1.219	1.203	1.013
Germany	1.146	1.127	1.016
Japan	1.022	1.047	0.976
Korea	1.016	1.042	0.975
Netherlands	1.093	1.137	0.961
Norway	1.204	1.169	1.030
United Kingdom	1.156	1.164	0.993
United States	1.161	1.163	0.998
All countries	1.125	1.130	0.995

Notes: MPI = Malmquist productivity index; TCH = technical change; TEC = technical efficiency change.

Some interesting observations can be seen across countries in Table 5.4. First, consistent with the aggregate finding, technical change TCH also plays a critical role in enhancing the TFP growth for each of the countries. This finding suggests that IT industries are capable innovators at improving their production technologies, and that technological innovation is the main source of their productivity. It is known that IT industries provide IT products that are typically used to advance the production processes for other industries. So it is not surprising to see that IT industries themselves are quite innovative at improving their own production processes, by incorporating the IT capital goods they themselves produce.

As for the average technical efficiency change TEC, three countries—Finland, Germany, and Norway—demonstrated an improvement in their technical efficiency change, which in turn also helped their MPIs. A review of Tables 5.3 and 5.4 shows that Finland was more efficient than Germany and Norway, but Germany had a much smoother pattern of efficiency change over the years. On the other hand, the remaining five countries—Japan, Korea, the Netherlands, the UK, and the United States—all displayed deterioration in their efficiency over time. This deterioration, in effect, affected their respective TFP growth in an adverse way.

Finally, a decomposition of the MPIs reveals that each country's IT industry has its particular aspects to work on for performance improvement. Japan and Korea had the lowest productivity growth among the countries studied (MPI = 1.022 and 1.016, respectively). Table 5.4 shows that these two countries have registered the second and third lowest technical efficiency change (TEC = 0.976 and 0.975, respectively) and also their technological change levels (TCH = 1.047 and 1.042) were not as significant as those of the other countries. Therefore, their MPIs turn out to be the lowest among all the countries. Finland and Norway had the highest productivity growth (MPI = 1.219 and 1.204, respectively) but Norway actually benefited more from technical efficiency change TEC (1.030) than did Finland (1.013). Regardless of the difference in TEC, both countries exhibited the highest technological progress (TEC = 1.203 and 1.169 for Finland and Norway), which put the two countries on top for their productivity growth. The Netherlands had good technical progress (TCH = 1.137) but its technical efficiency change TEC was the lowest (0.961). As a result, its MPI (1.093) did not fare well.

To summarize our findings, Table 5.6 presents the rankings of the countries by their MPIs and

Table 5.5

Malmquist TFP Index

Country	1979	1980	1981	1982	1983	1984	1985	1986	1987	1988	1989	1990	1991	1992	1993	Avg.
Finland	1.194	1.027	0.715	1.220	0.827	1.031	1.086	2.102	1.208	0.999	1.150	1.649	1.581	1.819	1.418	1.219
Germany	0.910	1.038	1.109	1.047	1.119	1.223	1.217	1.066	1.049	1.147	1.086	1.016	1.496	1.568	1.280	1.146
Japan	0.976	0.957	1.058	0.998	1.076	1.025	0.960	1.112	1.053	1.060	1.024	0.905	1.127	0.980	1.040	1.022
Korea	0.925	0.986	0.650	1.418	1.050	0.742	0.799	1.211	1.513	0.987	1.067	1.179	0.779	1.184	1.157	1.016
Netherlands	0.940	0.879	0.941	1.013	1.167	1.620	0.848	1.154	1.389	1.394	1.003	0.947	1.363	1.439	0.727	1.093
Norway	1.183	1.710	0.972	1.268	1.132	0.773	1.025	0.987	1.459	0.843	1.907	1.202	1.099	2.063	1.159	1.204
United Kingdom	1.051	0.949	0.851	1.312	1.043	1.338	0.966	1.225	1.291	1.174	1.226	1.262	1.062	1.569	1.218	1.156
United States	1.095	1.004	1.029	1.108	1.129	1.104	1.068	1.216	1.292	1.213	1.198	1.209	1.170	1.311	1.337	1.161
All countries	1.034	1.069	0.916	1.173	1.068	1.107	0.996	1.259	1.282	1.102	1.208	1.171	1.210	1.492	1.167	1.125

Note: Country averages across years are geometric means; yearly averages across countries are arithmetic means.

Table 5.6

Country Rankings of MPI and Its Components

MPI	Country	TCH	Country	TEC	Country
1.219	Finland	1.203	Finland	1.030	Norway
1.204	Norway	1.169	Norway	1.016	Germany
1.161	United States	1.164	United Kingdom	1.013	Finland
1.156	United Kingdom	1.163	United States	0.998	United States
1.146	Germany	1.137	Netherlands	0.993	United Kingdom
1.093	Netherlands	1.127	Germany	0.976	Japan
1.022	Japan	1.047	Japan	0.975	Korea
1.016	Korea	1.042	Korea	0.961	Netherlands

Notes: MPI = Malmquist productivity index; TCH = technical change; TEC = technical efficiency change.

the two components. Overall, our empirical results support the findings of other researchers. Jorgenson and Stiroh (1999), Oliner and Sichel (2000, 2002), Gordon (2000), and Jorgenson (2001) all contend that accelerating technological progress in IT industries is the driving force for overall productivity growth. Our study finds that IT industries show significant technological progress and such technical advance is the main driver behind their impressive productivity growth. As a consequence, these earlier research conclusions are fully supported by, and consistent with, the empirical results of this study.

INTERPRETATION AND EVALUATION

The results presented in the previous section can be interpreted from several angles and have the potential for economic and governmental policy considerations. In addition, our results embody the empirical advance made possible by the use of the Malmquist TFP index and the translog stochastic production frontier. We discuss both points in the following subsections.

Country-Level Interpretation and Policy Considerations

From our empirical results, practical implications can be drawn to assist governmental agencies in formulating effective policies for their IT industries. Clearly, a government ought to be aware of its competitive position in the global IT market, understand the strengths and weaknesses of its IT industry compared with other countries, and make continued efforts to enhance its productivity. Even if a country lacks an indigenous IT industry, Tallon and Kraemer (2000) show the value of using incentives to pursue a policy of *industrialization by invitation,* as occurred with Ireland's pursuit of firms such as IBM, Dell, and Intel. To extract useful implications from this study that might apply to countries trying to establish or improve their industrial IT base, several insights can be obtained from the countries examined in the study.

First, Japan and the UK are two countries with the highest average technical efficiency TE_{it} defined by the translog stochastic production frontier. Both countries have technical efficiency scores greater than 0.80 and experience relatively small technical efficiency change TEC. This suggests that, in comparison with other countries in the sample, Japan and the UK are very good at what they do. This better performance of both countries in efficiency may be attributed to effective governmental policies for their IT industries. Consistently they are able to utilize a given set of input resources to produce the greatest amount of outputs with a given production technology. As a result, for *best practice frontier countries* like Japan and the UK to improve their IT industry productivity levels, the logical approach for them is to emphasize other drivers of technical change and encourage continuous innovations that will help to advance their production technologies.

Next, for some other countries like Germany, the Netherlands, and Norway, Table 5.3 shows that they were not as efficient as the frontier countries. This implies that to become more productive, they should first attempt to be more efficient in their production processes (i.e., to produce more outputs using the same amount of inputs or to produce the same amount of outputs using less inputs with a given production technology). This action of efficiency improvement amounts to catching up with frontier countries like Japan and the UK. Usually making efficiency improvements is less costly for them to implement than any other approach that would achieve a similar impact. After gaining higher efficiency, they can proceed to revamp their production processes to enhance their MPIs. Alternatively, they can try to make efforts to improve their efficiency levels and their production technologies simultaneously, but we note that this combined undertaking is typically costly and that countries' respective progress will be difficult to evaluate and isolate in terms of the specifics of the drivers of improvements.

Finally, we found that the United States had a technical efficiency change (TEC = 0.998) that *barely* made a difference in its productivity growth. In other words, the IT industry of the United States seems to have depended solely on technological progress to boost its productivity, as evidenced by the fact that the United States has a high technical change (TCH = 1.163). This further suggests that the United States has more resources that allow its IT industry to advance its production technology—perhaps sometimes before the industry even becomes efficiently skilled with a given production technology. This conjecture is further supported by the lackluster average of 0.672 for technical efficiency in the United States; see Table 5.3.

Researchers have been engaged in a debate regarding the success of *market-driven strategies vs. plan-directed strategies* for the development of a country's IT industry (Dedrick and Kraemer, 1998; Tam, 1998). Among the countries that we have studied in our analysis, Japan and Korea are considered plan-directed (Kraemer and Dedrick, 1998). The argument for a government to institute a national IT policy and to take the lead in building a viable IT industry is that the government will make better resource allocations and develop an IT industry that fits well with its national characteristics. For that reason, it is particularly important for these plan-directed countries to carefully assess their own performance in technological progress, efficiency change, and productivity before drawing up their IT policies. However, for market-driven countries, our analysis should also offer useful insights into the competitive advantages of different parts of the world when their IT firms, in the hope of remaining competitive on a global stage, contemplate investing in, or outsourcing their operations to, these foreign countries (Tallon and Kraemer, 2000).

Process Evaluation: MPI and Translog Production Function Analysis as an Empirical Advance

The results of this study are obtained using the Malmquist TFP index as the measurement unit and the translog stochastic production frontier as the estimation technique. In comparison with their conventional counterparts, both approaches that we adopted in the study *together* represent an empirical advance in the performance evaluation of a production process. They also suggest some promising directions for future empirical IS research.

First, the choice of the Malmquist TFP index over other common TFP indices (e.g., Törnqvist and Fisher) is justified because it can be decomposed into two components of technical change and efficiency change. This helps us to identify the source of productivity growth or pinpoint the cause of underperformance. As a consequence, our results based on the Malmquist TFP index are more insightful than they would be if based on the Törnqvist and Fisher indices. Second, the use of a translog production function also assists us in overcoming the inherent constraints of unitary elasticity of substitution and fixed returns to scale associated with the popular Cobb-Douglas production function. Finally, stochastic production frontiers are parametric and can account for measurement errors and random noise frequently encountered in empirical studies. On the other hand, DEA is nonparametric and typically does not consider measurement errors and random noise, which eventually are absorbed into technical efficiency measures, thus biasing the true efficiency score (although there is also a stochastic form of DEA).

Dedrick and Kraemer (1998) profiled the historic development of the global computer industry with a focus on the Asia-Pacific region. They criticized the two economic models commonly used to describe the growth and evolution of industries. One relates to the roles of national industrial policy and market forces. The other compares competition among countries with competition within industries. They argued that neither model fully explains the global IT industry's structure, and proposed a third force called the *global IT production network*. Although we do not directly address the gap identified by these authors, our study incorporates both economic models (i.e., plan vs. market and country vs. industry) and, in a cross-country context, can be extended to examine the third force—the global IT production network—that they suggested. In other words, at the macro and industry level of analysis used in this study, we are looking for ways to generate empirical results that have meaningful implications for both national industry policy considerations and company competitive strategy interpretations.

Looking to the future, we believe there are many interesting things on the horizon that will reshape the process evaluation of IT productivity impacts for empirical IS research. Several innovative forces have already been at work in the IT domain. Globalization (Kraemer and Dedrick, 1998), offshore outsourcing (Shao and David, 2007), contract manufacturing (Kraiselburd, Narayanan, and Raman, 2004), deregulation (Roach, 1998), and business process outsourcing (Willcocks et al., 2004) are just some examples. To explain these new innovations and assess their impacts on IT productivity, conventional theories and methods are likely to be insufficient because the environment for IT production and IT use would be dramatically changed by these new phenomena. We need theories and methods that are either emerging or well-established but that may be unfamiliar to IS researchers. Possible theory sources include supply chain management, competitive strategy, and organization behavior. Methodology-wise, we should utilize new advances that are likely to be made in the fields of production economics and operations research, especially when the new methodologies of performance evaluation are proved to be effective. Doing so will help strengthen the depth of the IS research perspective for this kind of analysis. Fortunately, many IS researchers have been aware of this requirement and are making necessary adjustments. For example, IS researchers have increasingly recognized the limitations of the Cobb-Douglas production function due to its underlying constraints and lack of flexibility (Han, Kauffman, and Nault, 2007). Another case can be found in the study of Banker et al. (2006) on modern manufacturing plants involving IT. They emphasized the importance of manufacturing and organizational capabilities in studying the impact of IT and found evidence that manufacturing capabilities mediate the impact of information systems on plant performance. The performance of producing intermediate outputs turns out to be as important as the production of final outputs.

Some remarks on data collection for conducting empirical research are also called for in this context. Empirical researchers have encountered a persistent problem in collecting accurate data and identifying reliable data sources for the production and consumption of goods. This data problem becomes even more severe for IS research, because IT goods—as they are generally defined—include not only tangible computer and communication equipment but also intangible software services, whether bought in packaged form from a software vendor or written for internal use. The intangible side of IT services has been underestimated, and hence the output measures derived for them tend to underreport true economic activities or miscalculate the input level required to carry out these activities. Although the use of an improved methodology (e.g., the stochastic production frontiers employed in the study) can account for such measurement errors and alleviate this problem to some degree, the real solution lies in the collection of accurate data from reliable sources. Recently the U.S. government has made noticeable progress in its statistical system to expand the range of surveys of services-producing industries for measuring both the output of services and the contribution of new IT products (Triplett and Bosworth, 2004). The availability of such new government data offers ample opportunities for empirical IS researchers to measure IT productivity impacts at the level of individual industries.

CONCLUSION AND LIMITATIONS

We have applied the stochastic production frontier method to a comparative study of IT industries for eight OECD countries. We used the Malmquist TFP index to measure their productivity performance. All eight countries displayed impressive productivity growth for their IT industries. In addition, we found these IT industries to be more productive than other industries when compared with the findings of previous studies. We also decomposed the MPI into two components: technical efficiency change and technological change. Our empirical results suggest that the IT industries possess unique patterns with regard to the performance measures of productivity, efficiency change, and technical change. We also learned that technological progress in the production process is the major driver of productivity growth for these IT industries. Further, we observed that technical efficiency change seems to have only a small effect on the countries' productivity growth. Finally, based on our findings, we presented practical implications for formulating IT policies. In conclusion, we now discuss some limitations of our approach and identify several topics for future research.

Most of the existing studies using the Malmquist TFP index for productivity evaluation rely on the more conventional DEA to calculate the underlying distance functions. An alternative to DEA for measuring efficiency is stochastic production frontiers, but the latter has not been applied to the Malmquist TFP index until recently (Fuentes, Grifell-Tatje, and Perelman, 2001; Orea, 2002). However, there are situations where stochastic production frontiers are more appropriate than DEA for this task. This study demonstrates such use of stochastic production frontiers in a cross-country context to evaluate IT industry performance. Thus, the empirical advance of this chapter for IS research is the introduction of this novel analytical tool for IS researchers who are interested in the impacts of IT on organizational performance as measured by productivity, efficiency, and technical progress, but who have concerns about measurement errors and random noise in the data collection procedure and do not know how to account for them.

Although this study represents one of the first attempts to analyze productivity, technical change, and efficiency change of IT industries across countries, several limitations should be pointed out to help the reader to interpret the results properly. The limitations are mainly associated with the lack of available data and could be addressed in future research. First, in this study we focused our attention on the traditional factors of production—capital and labor—to evaluate the outputs of IT industries. There are some characteristics associated with IT industries that we have not considered. For instance, we have not incorporated any meaningful treatment of *complementarities* or *substitution effects between countries,* as suggested by Kim, Chang, and Shocker (2000). In addition, significant differences also exist in labor costs and the quality of inputs between countries, and they can further complicate these effects. Among the countries that we considered in our analysis, Japan and Korea are both major suppliers and competitors in the DRAM sector. The United States also competes with Japan on the design and development of several cutting-edge IT components, but at the same time it cooperates with other East Asian countries for production. Such complementarities and substitution effects for IT production can provide further insights into the relative strengths and weaknesses of a country's IT industry in terms of productivity, technical advances, and efficiency. We can also incorporate these effects in the stochastic production frontier model in our study using the approach suggested by Battese and Coelli (1995). As a result, with the availability of additional data on these characteristics, future research can investigate these effects and determine whether similar results can be obtained.

Second, subject to the limitations on available data, we are restricted to *just* these eight OECD countries. We were not able to find and include in our analysis data on other *newly industrialized economies* (NIEs) such as Singapore, Taiwan, and Hong Kong. These NIEs have been key suppliers for a number of essential IT products since the early 1990s. For example, Singapore has been a principal provider of hard drives and sound cards. Taiwan assumes a similar role for notebook computers and motherboards. Most of these NIEs are plan-directed countries and have devised specific national policies that their economic leadership has deemed critical in developing their successful IT industries (Wong, 1998). It would be insightful and important for future research to examine these NIE countries and assess how they perform along these three dimensions. Furthermore, Kraemer and Dedrick (1998) claim that since the 1990s, the United States has retained only the activities with increasing returns to scale but outsourced most of the activities with decreasing returns to scale to these East Asian NIEs, China, India, and parts of Europe. This division of labor results mostly in a mutually beneficial situation for the countries involved. A cross-country study that includes NIEs should be able to generate empirical results to substantiate such claims.

In keeping with the theme of this research volume on empirical advances in IS research, our study looks at the accumulation of IT capital goods with a new methodological perspective and by considering only *essential* IT hardware products. The IT industry as defined by the OECD does not cover telecommunications, as described earlier, and this is an important sector of IT hardware equipment. Although the OECD (1999) does have another International SIC 3832 for "Radio, TV and Communication Equipment," telecommunication products make up only part of this category because typically radio and TV are not categorized as part of the IT domain. In addition, the OECD does not report data on software. Software, however, has grown to be a very critical sector that warrants our attention and analysis (Slaughter, Harter, and Krishnan, 1998). Kemerer (1998), for instance, argues that software costs have persistently risen but we have little understanding about how to control costs of software development. Hence, another direction for future research is to examine the software sector among the IT industries across country boundaries (e.g., India and the United States), to measure and compare their productivity patterns, and to identify the reasons for their successes or failures.

APPENDIX 5.1. KEY TERMS, CONCEPTS, AND THEIR DEFINITIONS

Terms and concepts	Definitions and comments
Production process	The process used by a producer to transform factors of production (or inputs) into outputs for the provision of goods and services
Production function	A functional specification that describes the relationship between inputs and outputs in the production process, also called "production frontier"
Factors of production (or inputs)	Resources consumed to produce outputs; typically include capital, labor, material, and so on
Outputs	Goods and services produced by the production process
Stochastic production frontier	A parametric estimation technique based on production functions with a stochastic term specified for technical inefficiency
Data envelopment analysis	A nonparametric technique based on linear programming to establish a piece-wise linear convex production frontier
Productivity	The ratio of outputs produced to the inputs consumed
Productivity growth	The change in productivity between two time periods
Total factor productivity	A productivity index that incorporates all factors of production
Labor productivity	A productivity index that considers only the input of labor
Technical efficiency	The ratio of the actual output produced to the maximum possible output specified by the production frontier
Efficiency change	The change in technical efficiency between two time periods
Technical change	The shift in the production frontier between two time periods, also called "technological progress"
Malmquist productivity index	A compound measure of productivity change that can be attributable to efficiency change and technical change
Returns to scale	The degree to which output is increased by a proportional change in all inputs. Suppose $\alpha > 1$, for a production function f using two inputs K and L, it is: • Constant returns to scale, if $f(\alpha K, \alpha L) = \alpha f(K, L)$ • Increasing returns to scale, if $f(\alpha K, \alpha L) > \alpha f(K, L)$ • Decreasing returns to scale, if $f(\alpha K, \alpha L) < \alpha f(K, L)$
Elasticity of substitution (σ)	A measure of the substitution behavior between the inputs: • $\sigma = 0$ occurs when the inputs must be used in fixed proportions • $\sigma = \infty$ occurs when the inputs are perfect substitutes
Cobb-Douglas functional form	A conventional production functional form. For a production process that employs two inputs K and L, the Cobb-Douglas functional form is specified as $f(K, L) = AK^b L^c$ • Its returns to scale (b + c) are fixed irrespective of input amounts used • Its elasticity of substitution $\sigma = 1$
Translog functional form	A generalized flexible production functional form that relaxes the inherent assumptions of the Cobb-Douglas functional form and includes it as a special case
Truncated normal distribution	A generalization of the half normal distribution; obtained by the truncation at zero of the normal distribution with mean μ

ACKNOWLEDGMENTS

This research is supported by the Dean's Award for Excellence Summer Program funded by the Dean's Council of 100, the Economic Club of Phoenix, and the Alumni of the W.P. Carey School of Business at Arizona State University. The authors would like to thank the volume editors, Rob Kauffman and Paul Tallon, and an anonymous reviewer for their valuable comments and insightful suggestions, which have greatly improved the quality and presentation of this chapter. Any errors that remain are the sole responsibility of the authors.

NOTE

1. See www.oecdwash.org/PUBS/ELECTRONIC/epsti.htm#stan for more details on the data set.

REFERENCES

Arcelus, F.J. and Arozena, P. 1999. Measuring sectoral productivity across time and across countries. *European Journal of Operational Research*, 119, 2, 254–266.

Banker, R.D.; Bardhan, I.R.; Chang, H.; and Lin, S. 2006. Plant information systems, manufacturing capabilities, and plant performance. *MIS Quarterly*, 30, 2, 315–337.

Banker, R.D.; Charnes, A.; and Cooper, W.W. 1984. Some models for estimating technical and scale inefficiencies in data envelopment analysis. *Management Science*, 30, 9, 1078–1092.

Battese, G.E. and Coelli, T.J. 1995. A model for technical inefficiency effects in a stochastic frontier production function for panel data. *Empirical Economics*, 20, 2, 325–332.

Brynjolfsson, E. and Hitt, L.M. 1996. Paradox lost? Firm-level evidence on the returns to information systems spending. *Management Science*, 42, 4, 541–558.

Caves, D.W.; Christensen, L.R.; and Diewert, W.E. 1982. The economic theory of index numbers and the measurement of input, output, and productivity. *Econometrica*, 50, 6, 1393–1414.

Charnes, A.; Cooper, W.W.; and Rhodes, E. 1978. Measuring the efficiency of decision-making units. *European Journal of Operational Research*, 2, 6, 429–444.

Coelli, T.; Rao, D.S.P.; O'Donnell, C.J.; and Battese, G.E. 2005. *An Introduction to Efficiency and Productivity Analysis*. 2d ed. Norwell, MA: Kluwer Academic.

Davamanirajan, P.; Kauffman, R.J.; Kriebel, C.H.; and Mukhopadhyay, T. 2006. Systems design, process performance, and economic outcomes in international banking. *Journal of Management Information Systems*, 23, 2, 65–90.

Dedrick, J. and Kraemer, K.L. 1998. *Asia's Computer Challenge: Threat or Opportunity for the United States and the World?* New York: Oxford University Press.

Dewan, S. and Kraemer, K.L. 1998. International dimensions of the productivity paradox. *Communications of the ACM*, 41, 8, 56–62.

———. 2000. Information technology and productivity: Evidence from country-level data. *Management Science*, 46, 4, 548–562.

Dewan, S. and Min, C. 1997. The substitution of information technology for other factors of production: A firm-level analysis. *Management Science*, 43, 12, 1660–1675.

Färe, R.; Grossskopf, S.; Norris, M.; and Zhang, Z. 1994. Productivity growth, technical progress, and efficiency change in industrialized countries. *American Economic Review*, 84, 1, 66–83.

Färe, R.; Grossskopf, S.; and Russell, R.R. 1998. *Index Numbers: Essays in Honor of Sten Malmquist*. Norwell, MA: Kluwer Academic.

Farrell, M.J. 1957. The measurement of technical efficiency. *Journal of the Royal Statistical Society Series A*, 120, 3, 252–267.

Fuentes, H.J.; Grifell-Tatje, E.; and Perelman, S. 2001. A parametric distance function approach for Malmquist productivity index estimation. *Journal of Productivity Analysis*, 15, 2, 79–94.

Goh, K.G. and Kauffman, R.J. 2007. An industry-level analysis of the potential and realized value of IT. Working paper, Carlson School of Management, University of Minnesota.

Gordon, R.J. 2000. Does the "New Economy" measure up to the great inventions of the past? *Journal of Economic Perspectives*, 14, 4, 49–74.

Gurbaxani V. and Whang S.J. 1991. The impact of information systems on organizations and markets. *Communications of the ACM,* 34, 1, 59–73.
Han, K.; Kauffman, R.J.; and Nault, B. 2007. Returns to IT outsourcing. Working paper, Carlson School of Management, University of Minnesota, Minneapolis.
Hitt, L.M. and Brynjolfsson, E. 1996. Productivity, business profitability, and consumer surplus: Three different measures of information technology value. *MIS Quarterly,* 20, 2, 121–142.
Jorgenson, D.W. 2001. Information technology and the U.S. economy. *American Economic Review,* 91, 1, 1–32.
Jorgenson, D.W. and Stiroh, K.J. 1999. Information technology and growth. *American Economic Review,* 89, 2, 109–115.
Kemerer, C.F. 1998. Progress, obstacles, and opportunities in software engineering economics. *Communications of the ACM,* 41, 8, 63–66.
Kim, N.; Chang, D.R.; and Shocker, A.D. 2000. Modeling intercategory and generational dynamics for a growing information technology industry. *Management Science,* 46, 4, 496–512.
Kraemer, K.L. and J. Dedrick. 1998. Globalization and increasing returns: Implications for the U.S. computer industry. *Information Systems Research,* 9, 4, 303–322.
Kraiselburd, S.; Narayanan, V.G.; and Raman, A. 2004. Contracting in a supply chain with stochastic demand and substitute products. *Production and Operations Management,* 13, 1, 46–62.
Lin, W.T. and Shao, B.B.M. 2000. Relative sizes of information technology investments and productive efficiency: Their linkage and empirical evidence. *Journal of the Association for Information Systems,* 1, 7, 1–35.
Malmquist, S. 1953. Index numbers and indifference surfaces. *Trabajos de Estatistica,* 4, 4, 209–242. Reprinted in *Journal of Productivity Analysis,* 4, 3, 251–260.
Malone, T.; Yates, J.; and Benjamin, R.I. 1987. Electronic Markets and Electronic Hierarchies. *Communications of the ACM,* 30, 6, 484–497.
McAfee, A. 2006. Mastering the three worlds of information technology. *Harvard Business Review,* 84, 11 (November), 141–149.
Melville, N.; Kraemer, K.L.; and Gurbaxani, V. 2004. Information technology and organizational performance: An integrative model of IT business value. *MIS Quarterly,* 28, 2, 283–322.
Mitra, S. and Chaya, A.K. 1996. Analyzing cost-effectiveness of organizations: The impact of information technology spending. *Journal of Management Information Systems,* 13, 2, 29–57.
Mukhopadhyay, T.; Lerch, F.J.; and Mangal, V. 1997. Assessing the impact of information technology on labor productivity: A field study. *Decision Support Systems,* 19, 2, 109–122.
Mukhopadhyay, T.; Rajiv, S.; and Srinivasan, K. 1997. Information technology impact on process output and quality. *Management Science,* 43, 12, 1645–1659.
Oliner, S.D. and Sichel, D.E. 2000. The resurgence of growth in the late 1990s: Is information technology the story? *Journal of Economic Perspectives,* 14, 4, 3–22.
———. 2002. Informational technology and productivity: Where are we now and where are we going? *Economic Review,* 87, 3, 15–44.
Orea, L. 2002. Parametric decomposition of a generalized Malmquist productivity index. *Journal of Productivity Analysis,* 18, 3, 5–22.
Organization for Economic Cooperation and Development (OECD). 1998. *The OECD STAN Database for Industrial Analysis 1978–1997.* Paris.
———. 1999. *International Sectoral Database.* Paris.
———. 2002. *The OECD Information Technology Outlook 2002.* Paris.
Roach, S.S. 1998. In search of productivity. *Harvard Business Review,* 76, 5, 153–158.
Romer, P.M. 1990. Endogenous technological change. *Journal of Political Economics,* 98, 5 (Part 2), 71–102.
Shao, B.B.M. and David, J.S. 2007. The impact of offshore outsourcing on IT workers in developed countries. *Communications of the ACM,* 50, 2, forthcoming.
Shao, B.B.M. and Lin, W.T. 2001. Measuring the value of information technology in technical efficiency with stochastic production frontiers. *Information and Software Technology,* 43, 7, 447–456.
———. 2002. Technical efficiency analysis of information technology investments: A two-stage empirical investigation. *Information & Management,* 39, 5, 391–401.
Slaughter, S.A.; Harter, D.E.; and Krishnan, M.S. 1998. Evaluating the cost of software quality. *Communications of the ACM,* 41, 8, 67–73.
Solow, R.M. 1987. We'd better watch out. *New York Times Book Review,* July 12, 36.

Stiroh, K.J. 2002. Information technology and U.S. productivity revival: What do the industry data say? *American Economic Review,* 92, 5, 1559–1576.

Tallon, P. and Kraemer, K.L. 2000. Information technology and economic development: Ireland's coming of age with lessons for developing countries. *Journal of Global IT Management,* 3, 2, 85–98.

Tam, K.Y. 1998. The impact of information technology investments on firm performance and evaluation: Evidence from newly industrialized economies. *Information Systems Research,* 9, 1, 85–98.

Thatcher, M.E. and Oliver, J.R. 2001. The impact of technology investments on a firm's production efficiency, product quality, and productivity. *Journal of Management Information Systems,* 18, 2, 17–45.

Triplett, J.E. and Bosworth, B.P. 2004. *Productivity in the U.S. Services Sector.* Washington, DC: Brookings Institution Press.

Willcocks, L.P.; Hindle, J.; Feeny, D.; and Lacity, M. 2004. IT and business process outsourcing: The knowledge potential. *Information Systems Management,* 21, 3, 7–15.

Willcocks, L.P. and Lester, S. 1999. *Beyond the IT Productivity Paradox.* Chichester, UK: Wiley.

Wong, P.K. 1998. Leveraging the global information revolution for economic development: Singapore's evolving information industry strategy. *Information Systems Research,* 9, 4, 323–341.

CHAPTER 6

USING ACCOUNTING-BASED PERFORMANCE MEASURES TO ASSESS THE BUSINESS VALUE OF INFORMATION TECHNOLOGIES AND SYSTEMS

BRUCE DEHNING, VERNON J. RICHARDSON,
RODNEY E. SMITH, AND ROBERT W. ZMUD

Abstract: In this chapter, we apply contemporary financial analysis methods to the measurement of information technology (IT) business value. IT contributes to business value by changing and enhancing business processes. Embedding IT in business processes or more effective uses of IT should show up in improved accounting measures of performance, which subsequently affect financial market measures of firm value. Thus, an assessment of IT's impact on firm performance must consider IT's effect on specific business processes and how those processes affect overall firm performance. First, we propose value chain analysis to assess the impact of IT investments on business processes and the selection of appropriate accounting-based process measures. Then, we describe the link between process performance measures and overall firm performance measures such as return on equity (ROE). ROE decomposition provides further insight into the contribution of IT to business value. The residual income model is then used to link ROE directly to firm value. The framework is demonstrated using thirty-two high-tech manufacturing firms that adopted IT-based supply chain management systems. Our empirical contribution is to illustrate how ROE decomposition methodology can be used to find value from IT investments. In particular, this methodology integrates disparate parts of the business value framework into a comprehensive model for empirical analysis of the performance changes around the adoption of new IT investments.

Keywords: Firm Performance, Firm Value, High-Tech Companies, Information Technology, Manufacturing, ROE Decomposition, Residual Income Model, Value Chain

INTRODUCTION

According to the U.S. Bureau of Economic Analysis 2006 estimates, annual information technology (IT) spending in the United States approaches $1 trillion (www.bea.gov), and for many firms, investments in information technology (IT) represent their single largest capital expenditure. Accordingly, managers naturally seek to understand how IT contributes to business value[1] and how to measure that contribution. In this chapter, we provide an illustration of how contemporary financial analysis methods may be used to highlight and measure the business value of information technologies and systems. In particular, we focus on measuring the impact of IT on the firm using accounting-based performance measures and data available from public sources such as annual financial statements and SEC 10K filings.

IT contributes to business value by changing business processes and practices within firms and across industries (e.g., Kaplan and Norton, 1996, 2000; Melville, Kraemer, and Gurbaxani, 2004; Smith and Fingar, 2003). Although well-targeted IT investments can positively affect accounting measures of firm performance and subsequently affect financial market measures of firm performance, the genesis of these effects invariably lies in the realization of greater efficiency, productivity, and/or effectiveness in a firm's business processes (operational, managerial, and/or entrepreneurial). Thus, realistic appraisals of the impact of specific IT investments on firm performance should first consider IT's effect on targeted business processes (Ray, Barney, and Muhanna, 2004) and then lay out how improvements in those processes affect firm performance metrics. The schematic shown in Figure 6.1 describes the relationship between IT investment, business processes, firm performance, and firm value, and will serve as a framework for our discussion of the measurement of IT's impact on business value.

As described in Figure 6.1, we begin with a value chain analysis of the impact of IT investments on associated business processes and the selection of appropriate accounting-based process measures. Then, we describe the link between specific process performance measures and overall firm performance measures, such as *return on assets* (ROA) and *return on equity* (ROE). We propose that ROE is the best measure of overall performance, because of the direct link between ROE and market measures of firm value. We also describe how the decomposition of firm ROE measures provides further insight into the contribution of IT to business value. Additionally, we discuss how IT investments affect risk and how risk links to overall firm value. Finally, we provide an example that assesses the impact of supply chain management (SCM) systems initiatives to illustrate the concepts.

Before we proceed, however, it is important to note that accounting-based performance measures often do not capture the direct effects of IT investment. For example, a new quality control system should result in improved quality, but quality measures are generally not reported in published financial statements. There are several variables reported on most companies' annual financial statements and Securities and Exchange Commission (SEC) 10K filings, however, that can serve as proxies for quality improvements, such as changes in estimated warranty expense and related warranty liabilities. The selection of appropriate proxy measures requires careful consideration of the link between the affected process(es) and the information contained in the accounting statements. Furthermore, IT investments do not affect selected accounting measures in a 1 : 1 manner; instead, these relations tend to be both N : 1 (i.e., multiple and distinct IT investments occurring within a window of time will directly and/or indirectly affect the selected accounting measure) and 1 : N (i.e., a specific IT investment will directly or indirectly affect multiple accounting measures). Accounting for such equifinality in the relationship between IT investment and accounting measures of firm performance can be very messy and invariably introduces considerable noise in statistical analyses.

In the next section, we apply value chain analysis to generic business processes and identify corresponding accounting-based performance measures. We then describe how process performance measures contribute to overall firm performance measures. In the third section, we link accounting-based firm performance measures to firm value. We describe firm value as the net present value of future residual income. In the fourth section, we present a specific example that applies the approach outlined in sections two and three. In the fifth section, we conclude by describing examples of the use of these techniques in the academic literature. We also highlight the limitations of these techniques.

Figure 6.1 **Framework for Measuring the Business Value of Information Technologies and Systems**

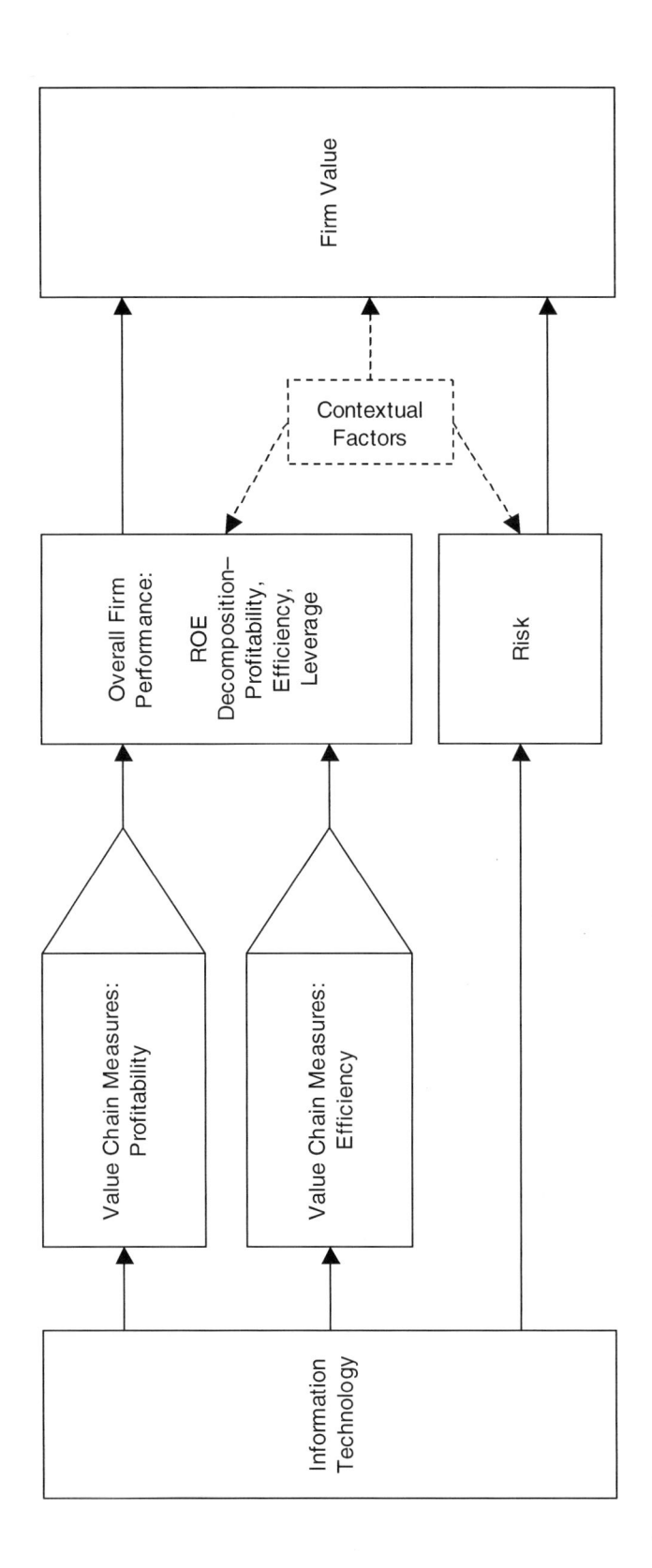

Figure 6.2 **The Value Chain Model**

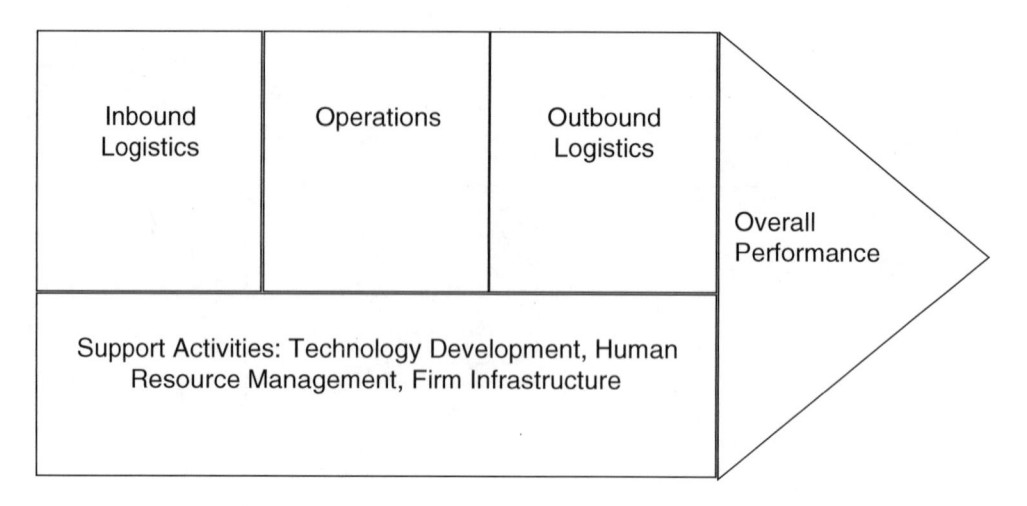

Inbound Logistics	Operations	Outbound Logistics

Overall Performance

Support Activities: Technology Development, Human Resource Management, Firm Infrastructure

Source: Adapted from Porter (1985).

VALUE CHAIN ANALYSIS AND PROCESS PERFORMANCE MEASURES

In this section, we use the generic value chain (Porter, 1985) to examine how IT investments contribute to business processes and how to measure those contributions. We then outline how individual process performance measures affect overall firm performance measures. We describe ROE decomposition techniques that provide further insight into process efficiency and effectiveness.

Value Chain Analysis

Value chain analysis helps in choosing the appropriate financial performance measures for a particular type of IT investment. As described by Porter (1985), a firm's value chain consists of a set of activities through which the firm creates and delivers its products or services. Value chain analysis provides a systematic approach to identifying sources of firm value in a competitive environment. For this chapter, we employ the *simplified value chain* shown in Figure 6.2, which depicts the operational processes associated with inbound logistics, operations, outbound logistics, and support activities. *Inbound logistics* include activities related to the acquisition and receipt of raw materials. *Operations processes* include the conversion activities by which the firm converts raw materials into finished goods. *Outbound logistics* include the marketing, sale, and delivery of the firm's products and services to its customers. *Support processes* include all other necessary activities, such as accounting, technology management, and research and development. The purpose of value chain analysis is to focus attention on appropriate performance measures for each value chain activity. This improves the likelihood of detecting and explaining changes in performance, while also reducing the chance of attributing spurious changes in performance to the IT investment under consideration.

As indicated in Figure 6.1, IT investments can affect both process profitability and efficiency. An IT investment can directly increase overall profitability by reducing process costs (e.g., auto-

Figure 6.3 **Value Chain Profitability Ratios**

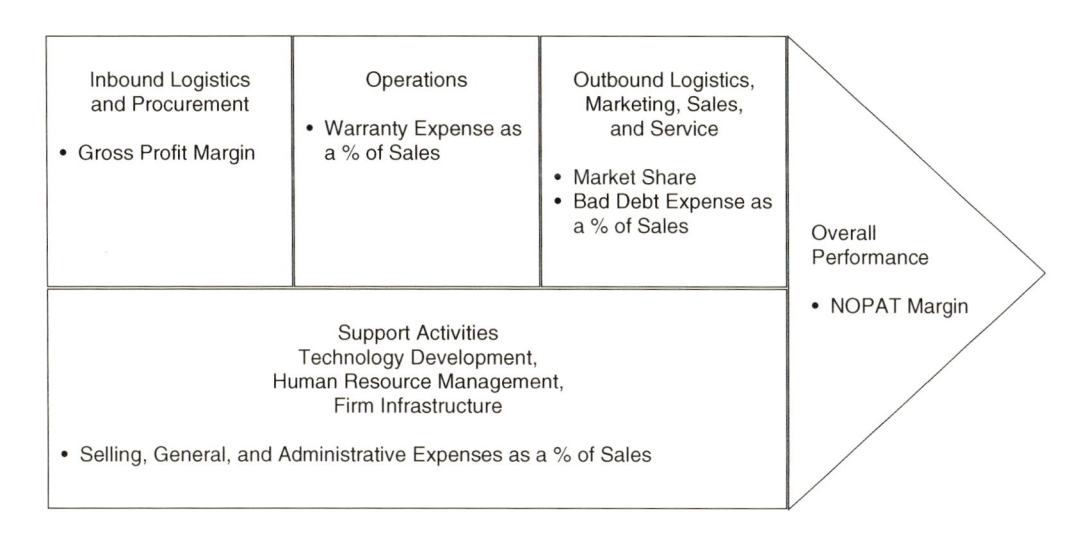

Inbound Logistics and Procurement • Gross Profit Margin	Operations • Warranty Expense as a % of Sales	Outbound Logistics, Marketing, Sales, and Service • Market Share • Bad Debt Expense as a % of Sales	Overall Performance • NOPAT Margin
Support Activities Technology Development, Human Resource Management, Firm Infrastructure • Selling, General, and Administrative Expenses as a % of Sales			

mation that eliminates labor costs) or improving processes so as to increase revenues (e.g., a Web site that broadens the reach of marketing programs, thus increasing the customer base). An IT investment can indirectly affect overall profitability by increasing efficiency, for example, a supply chain management system that improves raw material inventory turnover and reduces per-item product cost through the elimination of waste and inventory obsolescence.

Figure 6.3 presents an example of process profitability measures. For manufacturing companies, inbound logistics costs eventually appear in the financial statements as cost of goods sold. Thus, reductions in inbound logistics costs increase the firm's gross profit margin ([sales less cost of goods sold] divided by sales). For the Operations activities, an IT investment that improves manufacturing quality should mean fewer post-sale product failures and lower warranty expense. For Outbound Logistics, Marketing, Sales, and Service, IT investments that improve sales should correspondingly increase market share, and IT investments that allow better credit checks or induce a greater proportion of cash sales should lower bad debt expense (measured as a percentage of sales). For Support activities, IT investments that reduce administrative overhead should reduce the ratio of selling, general, and administrative expenses to sales. Collectively, one or more improvements in specific activity measures, holding other factors constant, should also result in improved overall profitability, measured as the ratio of net operating profit after tax (*NOPAT*) to sales (*NOPAT Margin*).

Figure 6.4 presents an example of process efficiency measures. Improved process efficiency allows the firm to produce the same level of output (e.g., sales) with fewer inputs (e.g., inventory, labor). Thus, efficiency measures relate resources to output, for example, inventory turnover, sales per employee, orders per purchase agent, or sales per square foot. Obviously, increased efficiency can also improve profitability, since the firm requires less investment in resources. Thus, the distinction between profitability and efficiency effects is often imprecise.

As we mentioned earlier, accounting-based process measures often apply to more than one value chain activity. We present a more complete list of generic process performance measures with definitions for calculations in Table 6.1. The selection of appropriate measures of IT impact depends on a robust appreciation of the direct effects of the focal IT investment on firm processes.

Figure 6.4 **Value Chain Efficiency Ratios**

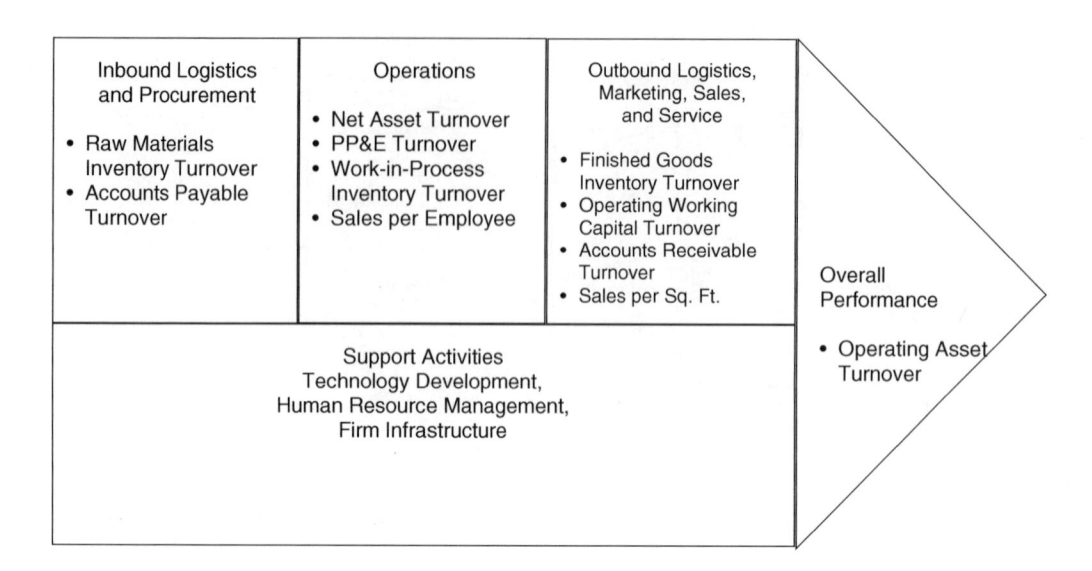

Inbound Logistics and Procurement	Operations	Outbound Logistics, Marketing, Sales, and Service
• Raw Materials Inventory Turnover • Accounts Payable Turnover	• Net Asset Turnover • PP&E Turnover • Work-in-Process Inventory Turnover • Sales per Employee	• Finished Goods Inventory Turnover • Operating Working Capital Turnover • Accounts Receivable Turnover • Sales per Sq. Ft.

Support Activities
Technology Development,
Human Resource Management,
Firm Infrastructure

Overall Performance
• Operating Asset Turnover

As an illustration of value chain analysis of IT impacts, we highlight a recent paper by Matolcsy, Booth, and Wieder (2005). Their study examines the economic benefits of enterprise resource planning (ERP) systems implemented by Australian firms from 1993 to 1999. They use the value chain approach to identify ratios for each area of the firm to reflect improvements due to new ERP systems. Financial performance measures for a group of companies that adopted ERP systems are compared with a group of companies that did not adopt ERP systems. They find that adopting ERP systems leads to increased efficiency and liquidity as measured by the *current ratio,* the ratio of current assets to current liabilities, and *inventory turnover,* the ratio of annual sales to inventory. They also find some support for improved accounts receivable management and increased profitability two years after the adoption of ERP systems.

Performance Analysis

Value chain analysis traces the impacts of a focal IT investment to specific business processes. The next step is to examine the cumulative impact on overall firm performance. One prominent measure of overall firm performance is *ROA,* defined as net income divided by total assets. However, there are three problems with using *ROA* as the single overall measure of firm performance. First, *ROA* is not directly related to firm value. Increases in *ROA* may or may not increase firm value if there are also changes in financial leverage. Second, *ROA* contains nonoperating items such as interest income and interest expense in the numerator and financial assets such as cash and short-term investments in the denominator. Thus, the firm's capital structure (debt vs. equity) affects *ROA,* making it difficult to isolate the impact of the IT investment. Third, *ROA* does not distinguish profitability effects from efficiency effects. In summary, the use of *ROA* as an overall firm performance measure obscures the logic behind an IT investment's direct impact on firm value.

ROE, defined as net income divided by total shareholders' equity, represents a much better measure of overall firm performance. First, *ROE* decomposition isolates financing and investing effects from operating effects and distinguishes between profitability and efficiency as follows (see Appendix 6.1 for derivation):

Table 6.1

Performance Measures and Formulas

$$ROE = \left(\frac{NOPAT}{Sales} \times \frac{Sales}{Net\ Assets}\right) + \left(\frac{NOPAT}{Net\ Assets} - \frac{Net\ Interest}{Net\ Debt}\right) \times \frac{Net\ Debt}{Equity}$$

Overall Performance

ROE	NI / SE (Net Income divided by Total Stockholder's Equity)
Operating ROA	NOPAT/Net Assets (Net Operating Profit After Taxes divided by Net Assets, where NOPAT = Net Income + Net Interest; Net Interest = (Interest Expense – Interest Income) × (1 – Tax Rate); and Net Assets = Total Noncurrent Assets minus Non-Interest-Bearing Noncurrent Liabilities

ROE Decomposition

NOPAT Margin	NOPAT / Sales (Net Operating Profit After Taxes divided by Sales)
Operating Asset Turnover	Sales / Net Assets (Sales divided by Net Assets)
Spread	NOPAT / Net Assets – Net Interest/Net Debt (NOPAT divided by Net Assets minus Net Interest divided by Net Debt, where Net Debt = Total Interest-Bearing Liabilities – Cash and Marketable Securities
Leverage	Net Debt / Equity (Net Debt divided by Total Stockholder's Equity

Components of the Value Chain

Inbound Logistics

Gross Profit Margin	(Sales – Cost of Goods Sold) / Sales (Sales minus Cost of Goods Sold divided by Sales)
Raw Materials Inventory Turnover	Cost of Goods Sold/Raw Materials Inventory (Cost of Goods Sold divided by Raw Materials Inventory)
Accts Payable Turnover	Purchases / AP (Purchases divided by Accounts Payable)

Operations

Warranty Expense as a % of Sales	Warranty Exp/Sales (Warranty Expense divided by Sales)
Net Asset Turnover	Sales / Net Long-Term Assets (Sales divided by Net Assets, where Total Noncurrent Assets minus Non-Interest-Bearing Noncurrent Liabilities)
PP&E Turnover	Sales / Net PP&E (Sales divided by Net Property, Plant, and Equipment, where Net Property, Plant, and Equipment = Total Property, Plant, and Equipment net of Accumulated Depreciation)
Work-in-Process Inventory Turnover	Cost of Goods Sold / Work-in-Process Inventory (Cost of Goods Sold divided by Work-in-Process Inventory)

Outbound Logistics

(continued)

Table 6.1 (continued)

Market Share	Sales / Total Industry Sales (Sales divided by Total Industry Sales)
Finished Goods Inventory Turnover	Cost of Goods Sold / Finished Goods Inventory Turnover (Cost of Goods Sold divided by Finished Goods Inventory)
Operating Working Capital Turnover	Sales / Operating Working Capital (Sales divided by Operating Working Capital where Operating Working Capital = Current Assets minus Cash and Marketable Securities minus Current Liabilities except Short Term Debt and the Current Portion of Long Term Debt)
Accounts Receivable Turnover	Sales / Accounts Receivable
Bad Debt Expense as a % of Sales	Bad Debt Expense / Sales (Bad Debt Expense divided by Sales)
Support Activities	
Selling, General, and Administrative Expenses as a % of Sales	Selling, General, and Administrative Expenses / Sales (Selling, General, and Administrative Expenses divided by Sales)
Other Ratios	
EBITDA	NI + Int + Taxes + Depr + Amort (Net Income plus Interest plus Taxes plus Depreciation plus Amortization)
EBITDA Margin	EBITDA/Sales (Net Income plus Interest plus Taxes plus Depreciation plus Amortization divided by Sales)
Quality of Income	CFO/NI (Cash Flow from Operations divided by Net Income)
Inventory Turnover	CoGS/Inventory (Cost of Goods Sold divided by Total Inventory)

$$ROE = \left(\frac{NOPAT}{Sales} \times \frac{Sales}{Net\ Assets}\right) + \left(\frac{NOPAT}{Net\ Assets} - \frac{Net\ Interest}{Net\ Debt}\right) \times \frac{Net\ Debt}{Equity} \qquad (6.1)$$

or equivalently:

$$ROE = NOPAT\ Margin \times Operating\ Asset\ Turnover = (Spread \times Leverage) \qquad (6.2)$$

or also:

$$ROE = Operating\ ROA = (Spread \times Leverage) \qquad (6.3)$$

where: *ROE* = Net Income / Stockholder's Equity
NOPAT = Net Operating Profit After Taxes = Net Income + Net Interest
Sales = Total Net Sales
Net Assets = Total Noncurrent Assets minus Non-Interest Bearing Noncurrent Liabilities
Net Interest = (Interest Expense-Interest Income) × (1 − Tax Rate)
Net Debt = Total Interest Bearing Liabilities minus Cash and Marketable Securities
Equity = Total Stockholder's Equity
NOPAT Margin = NOPAT / Sales
Operating Asset Turnover = Sales / Net Assets
Spread = Operating ROA (NOPAT / Net Assets) minus Cost of Borrowing (Net Interest / Net Debt)
Leverage = Net Debt / Equity
Operating ROA = NOPAT Margin × Operating Asset Turnover.

Equations 6.1 and 6.2 state *ROE* in terms of profitability (*NOPAT*), efficiency (*Operating Asset Turnover*), cost of debt capital (*Spread* considers the cost of borrowing), and financial leverage (*Leverage*). Equation 6.3 separates operating performance from the effects of financing. Using *ROE* decomposition separates out the impact of IT on operating profitability and efficiency and ties directly to the value chain analysis discussed earlier.

Additionally, *ROE* decomposition accounts for the effect of *Spread* and *Leverage* on *ROE*. If a company has no borrowing at all (is financed entirely with equity), then *ROE* equals *Operating ROA*. Increasing leverage, by borrowing or repurchasing equity, increases *ROE* if the firm's *Spread* is positive and decreases *ROE* if the *Spread* is negative. Thus, *Spread* indicates the firm's ability to earn a return on operating assets that is higher than the cost of borrowing. If *Spread* is positive, then firms can increase ROE by additional borrowing, and if *Spread* is negative, then firms will decrease ROE through additional borrowing. Thus, changes in financing can mask the impact of IT investments on ROE unless the assessment accounts for the separate effects of *Spread* and *Leverage*.

EMPIRICAL ADVANCES: LINKING PERFORMANCE ANALYSIS TO FIRM VALUE

In this section, we present the theoretical relationship between return on equity (*ROE*) and firm value through the residual income model. This model describes firm value as the net present value of future residual income, and future residual income can be stated in terms of future *ROE*.

Return on Equity and the Role of the Residual Income Model

ROE measures the return on the historical cost of contributed capital, but it does not directly measure firm value or the change in firm value. *ROE* links to market measures of firm value through the *Residual Income Model (RIM)* (Edwards and Bell, 1961; Feltham and Ohlson, 1995; Ohlson, 1995; Peasnell, 1982). The *RIM* denotes firm value as a firm's current book value of equity plus the discounted sum (via the cost of capital) of all future abnormal earnings, or residual income as follows:[2]

$$V_0 = BV_0 + \frac{I_1 - (r_e \times BV_0)}{1 + r_e} + \frac{I_2 - (r_e \times BV_1)}{(1 + r_e)^2} + \frac{I_3 - (r_e \times BV_2)}{(1 + r_e)^3} + \ldots \quad (6.4)$$

where: V_0 = Current Firm Value
BV_t = Book Value of the Firm at time t (total stockholder's equity at time t)
r_e = Cost of Equity Capital
I_t = Net Income at time t
$I_t - (r_e \times BV_{t-1})$ = Residual Income

To depict firm value in terms of accounting numbers, Equation 6.4 can be rewritten in terms of *ROE*, since:

$$\text{Residual Income} = I_t - (r_e \times BV_{t-1}) = (ROE_t - r_e) BV_{t-1}. \quad (6.5)$$

Substituting residual income written in terms of *ROE* into Equation 6.4 results in

$$V_0 = BV_0 + \sum_{t=1}^{\infty} (1 + r_e)^{-t} [(ROE_t - r_e) \times BV_{t-1}], \quad (6.6)$$

or equivalently:

$$V_0 = BV_0 + \frac{(ROE_1 - r_e) BV_0}{(1 + r_e)} + \frac{(ROE_2 - r_e) BV_1}{(1 + r_e)^2} + \frac{(ROE_3 - r_e) BV_2}{(1 + r_e)^3} + \ldots \quad (6.7)$$

Thus, a change in accounting performance due to investments in IT can be linked directly to firm value (V_0), because Equations 6.6 and 6.7 express firm value entirely in terms of accounting numbers.

Furthermore, variation in *ROE* links to variation in market value. IT investments can affect firm risk by increasing or decreasing variation in performance (Tanriverdi and Ruefli, 2004). For example, firms that replace labor costs with technology change their operating leverage, and a larger proportion of operating costs are fixed rather than variable. Higher operating leverage increases performance variation, since a greater percentage of costs remains fixed, and can result in higher market risk. A complete discussion of market risk measures is, however, beyond the scope of this article.

Relative Performance Comparison over Time

Industry or economy-wide factors can also affect firm performance and mask the impact of IT investments. Thus, we recommend measuring firm performance relative to performance for the *average* firm in the focal firm's industry, or the change in performance of a direct competitor. The former approach is preferable since finding a direct competitor with the appropriate characteristics is often difficult (Barber and Lyon, 1996).[3]

To measure the impact of IT on the firm, we compare firm performance after implementing IT to performance before implementing IT, and then subtract the change in average industry performance over the same time period, leaving the portion of firm performance attributable to the IT investment. For example, we calculate the change in *Operating ROA* (OROA) as follows:

$$(OROA_{FIRM.POST} - OROA_{FIRM.PRE}) - (OROA_{INDUSTRY.POST} - OROA_{INDUSTRY.PRE}) \quad (6.8)$$

where: $OROA_{FIRM.POST}$ = Operating ROA of the IT Investing Firm after Implementing New IT
$OROA_{FIRM.PRE}$ = Operating ROA of the IT Investing Firm before Implementing New IT
$OROA_{INDUSTRY.POST}$ = Industry Average Operating ROA after the IT Investing Firm Implements New IT
$OROA_{INDUSTRY.PRE}$ = Industry Average Operating ROA before the IT Investing Firm Implements New IT

If the average industry-adjusted change in performance for IT implementing firms is significantly different from zero, then the change in performance is probably due to the IT investment. It is possible, however, that the change in firm performance is simply due to reversion to the mean and not to the IT investment. Thus it may be advisable to test the performance of the IT implementing firms relative to the industry average prior to the implementation of IT as follows.

$$OROA_{FIRM.PRE} - OROA_{INDUSTRY.PRE} \quad (6.9)$$

If the industry-adjusted performance prior to implementing IT is significantly different from zero, then we cannot rule out reversion to the mean as the reason for the change. In that case, we prefer using a direct competitor with the appropriate characteristics (Barber and Lyon, 1996).

Additionally, firms may not immediately realize the full benefits of an IT investment. The nature of the IT investment, therefore, dictates the selection of the performance measurement period. Most IT investments require at least one to two years before the full benefits of the investment are realized (Brynjolfsson, 1993; Jasperson, Carter, and Zmud, 2005; Kohli and Devaraj, 2003; Peffers and Dos Santos, 1996). However, comprehensive IT investments such as ERP often require longer implementation periods and greater breadth and depth of business process changes before tangible benefits become apparent (Ranganathan and Brown, 2006). Therefore, it is important to understand the timing of the IT investment, the installation period, the adoption time frame, the implementation time, and the benefit realization period.

APPLICATION: A PERFORMANCE ANALYSIS EXAMPLE

To illustrate these concepts, we assembled a sample of high-tech firms that announced major supply chain management (SCM) system initiatives during the period 1995 to 2000. To identify major SCM system initiatives, we searched for announcements on the Lexis/Nexis and Factiva newswire services using the search terms "implement" or "choose" or "select" or "purchase" or "install" or "chosen" within twenty-five words of the words "supply chain" for all available years. We then examined each announcement or press release to verify that the announcement actually pertained to SCM systems implementations and to determine the implementation schedule, scope, and nature of the SCM software project. For the purpose of this example we limited this selection to high-tech firms[4] because we expected such firms to exhibit similar supply chain structures. In most cases, firms issued these announcements when they signed a contract with external SCM software vendors such as i2 or Manugistics and planned to begin implementation immediately.

After the Lexis/Nexis and Factiva searches, we eliminated firms that did not have complete financial data for six years surrounding the SCM announcement (three years before and three after). This produced a final sample of 32 firms and 192 annual financial observations around the announcements. The relatively small size of this sample obviously limits our ability to find significant changes in firm performance that are attributable to IT, but it provides an effective illustration of the concepts in a real world systems context.

For each announcement, we computed the change in firm performance over the period from one year before to either one or two years after the announcement using t-tests.[5] We adjusted each performance measure by subtracting the corresponding industry median value as described in Equations 6.8 and 6.9. Formulas for the performance measures are defined in Table 6.1.

Table 6.2 presents the value chain analysis as shown in Figures 6.3 and 6.4. The value chain analysis allows an evaluation of the contribution of the IT investment to firm performance at the process level. For these firms, the objective for their SCM systems was primarily to improve the management of their upstream supply chain (i.e., the interaction with their suppliers), and we note positive improvements in the Inbound Logistics process. Sample firms enjoyed significantly positive industry-adjusted changes in gross profit margins and raw material inventory turnover, prime indicators of a more efficient supply chain. As shown in Table 6.3, sample firms also enjoyed a corresponding improvement in overall inventory turnover.

The results for the Operations and Outbound Logistics process in this sample are mixed. The sample firms did not significantly improve either their work in process or finished goods inventory turnovers. They did, however, significantly increase their property, plant, and equipment (PP&E) turnover as well as their accounts receivable turnover, both of which are attributable to supply chain efficiency. Additionally, our sample firms made notable improvements in the ratio of selling, general, and administrative (SG&A) expense to sales, indicating improved efficiency relative to firms in their industries.

These process improvements contributed to improvements in overall performance. These firms significantly increased net operating profit after tax margin (*NOPAT Margin*) and *Operating ROA*. Thus, relative to other firms in their industries, these firms earned more on each dollar of sales and more on employed assets after the IT investment. From the value chain analysis, we see that it is likely that these overall improvements came primarily as a result of their improved inbound logistics process and improved overall efficiency of their support activities.

Table 6.3 presents additional performance calculations, including the *ROE* decomposition described at the top of Table 6.1, as well as other ratios for which data were available for this sample. As noted earlier, changes in *ROE* directly relate to changes in overall firm value; see Equation 6.5. For this example, there was a significant change in *ROE* over the period from one year before the implementation to two years after the implementation.

To see what contributed to this change, we can decompose *ROE* into pieces representing profitability, turnover, spread, and leverage, as shown in Equation 6.6. Table 6.3 shows that the primary drivers of the *ROE* improvement are (1) improved net operating profit after tax to sales ratio (*NOPAT Margin*), and (2) improved spread (*Operating ROA* minus the net interest rate on debt). There was little change in the overall operating asset turnover (sales divided by net assets), although the value chain analysis in Table 6.2 shows an improvement in raw material inventory

Table 6.2

Value Chain Profitability and Efficiency Measures Example Using Thirty-two High-Tech Firms That Announced Supply Chain Management System Initiatives

Changes in Industry-Median-Adjusted Measures Around Supply Chain Management System Initiative

Components of the value chain/measures	[–1 / +1][a]	[–1 / +2][b]
Profitability measures		
Inbound Logistics		
Gross Profit Margin	0.031**	0.044**
Outbound Logistics		
Market Share	0.004	–0.009
Bad Debt Expense (as a % of Sales)	–0.001*	–0.001
Support Activities		
SG&A as % of Sales	–0.032**	–0.047***
Overall Performance		
NOPAT Margin	0.026**	0.117**
Operating ROA	0.050***	0.083***
Efficiency Measures		
Inbound Logistics		
Raw Material Inventory Turnover [c]	9.401*	10.091**
Accounts Payable Turnover	0.007	0.464
Operations		
PPE Turnover [b]	0.532**	0.461*
Work-in-Process Inventory Turnover	–1.722	–3.745
Outbound Logistics		
Finished Goods Inventory Turnover	–3.089	–5.269
Accounts Receivable Turnover	0.525*	0.885***
Overall Performance		
Operating Asset Turnover	–0.061	0.021

Note: Measures defined in Table 6.1.
[a][–1 / +1] = change from one year before announcement to one year after.
[b][–1/+2] = change from one year before announcement to two years after.
[c]Influential outliers trimmed by winsorizing at 2 percent level.
Significance: * = $p < 0.01$, ** = $p < 0.05$, *** = $p < 0.10$.

turnover and Table 6.3 also shows an improvement in overall inventory turnover. This indicates that in general firms made little change to other operating assets (other than raw material inventories) as a result of their SCM systems initiatives. There was also little change in overall leverage (ratio of net debt to net equity), as would be expected, since such systems initiatives seldom affect overall debt levels. Thus, the *ROE* decomposition analysis enables us to eliminate alternative explanations (i.e., overall operating assets and leverage) and link the observed ROE improvement primarily to improved margins and thereby improved overall profitability relative to their direct competitors. The value chain analysis described above indicates that decreases in support costs

Table 6.3

Return on Equity (ROE) Decomposition and Other Measures Example Using Thirty-two High-Tech Firms That Announced Supply Chain Management System Initiatives

Changes in Industry-Median-Adjusted Measures Around Supply Chain Management System Initiative

Measures	[−1 / +1][a]	[−1 / +2][b]
***ROE* Decomposition [*ROE = NOPAT Margin × Operating Asset Turnover + Spread × Leverage*]**		
ROE	0.026	0.059*
Operating ROA [NOPAT Margin × Operating Asset Turnover]	0.050***	0.083***
NOPAT Margin	0.026**	0.117**
Operating Asset Turnover	−0.061	0.021
Spread[c]	0.157**	0.135**
Leverage	−0.018	−0.004
Other Ratios		
EBITDA Margin	0.038***	0.105***
Quality of Income	−0.915	0.156
Inventory Turnover	1.214***	1.300**

Note: Measures defined in Table 6.1.
[a][−1 / +1] = change from one year before announcement to one year after.
[b][−1 / +2] = change from one year before announcement to two years after.
[c]Influential outliers trimmed by winsorizing at 2 percent level.
Significance: * = $p < 0.01$, ** = $p < 0.05$, *** = $p < 0.10$.

(*SG&A as percent of sales*) and higher gross profit margins (*Gross Profit Margin*) drove the overall improvements in *NOPAT Margin*.

CONCLUSION

In this chapter, we applied contemporary financial analysis methods to the measurement of the business value of IT. The framework developed brings together previously disparate and often underutilized empirical tools into a method for appropriately determining the impact of IT on business processes and firm performance. Unlike most previous research approaches examining the IT-firm performance relationship, this framework does not suffer from problems of competing alternative explanations (such as industry or economy-wide effects or non–IT-related changes in asset levels or financial leverage), allows for specific targeting of performance measures, allows for an analysis of both efficiency and profitability effects, and demonstrates a direct link between performance and firm value.

Contributions

We focused on measuring the impact of IT on the firm using accounting-based performance measures and data available from public sources, such as annual financial statements and SEC 10K filings. Specifically, we outlined six steps for performing tests of the impact on firm performance of investments in IT. These six steps are summarized in Table 6.4.

Table 6.4

Six Steps in Performing the Analysis of the Performance Benefits from IT Investments

1. Understand the IT investment.
   a. Strategic reason for implementing the IT.
   b. Uses of the IT.
   c. Expected direct and indirect benefits.
   d. Where the expected benefits will appear.
   e. When the expected benefits should appear.

2. Choose performance measures.
   a. Overall performance measures Return on Equity (*ROE*) and Operating Return on Assets (*OROA*).
   b. Return on Equity (*ROE*) decomposition.
   c. Profitability versus efficiency.
   d. Value chain model.
   e. Leverage and risk measures.

3. Choose control group.
   a. Industry median.
   b. Matched sample.

4. Choose time period.
5. Perform empirical tests.
6. Conduct additional empirical analysis.

Using similar approaches, academic research by Mukhopadhyay, Kekre, and Kalathur (1995), for example, offers a rare glimpse at the specific changes in detailed financial performance measures by considering the effects of electronic data interchange on total inventory, obsolete inventory, and premium freight charges. Similarly, research by Barua, Kriebel, and Mukhopadhyay (1995) identifies relationships between various IT and non-IT inputs and business processes, and relations between these business processes and overall firm performance finding (a) a positive impact of IT on business processes, and (b) that certain business processes relate positively to overall firm performance.

Limitations

Of course, any methodology is subject to limitations, and the methodology presented in this chapter is no different. Recently, Davamanirajan et al. (2006) have shown that IT will not simply affect an isolated portion of the firm's value chain, but rather there will be many interrelated effects. Improvements in one process are likely to spill over into other processes. It is also possible that improvements in one process will come at a cost to another process. Thus, a clear trail linking IT investments to overall firm performance improvements through specific business process impacts might be identified through the value chain analysis presented here, but there are secondary impacts that could show up in other processes. It is important for researchers to consider these secondary impacts and not ignore these spillover effects.

Bardhan, Bagchi, and Sougstad (2004) examine another limitation of using accounting performance measures in the evaluation of IT investments. Because accounting performance measures do not consider the option value of IT investments, firm value is likely to increase in the short term, although the performance impacts of exercising future options will not be realized until the long term. Thus, *ROE* measured in the first few years after investing in new IT might not reflect the total increase in firm value from the IT project. This is particularly true when there are interdependencies among a portfolio of IT projects. Such value could be captured using market value measures such as stock returns or Tobin's q.

In summary, the nature of an IT investment and the business processes affected by that investment begin a logical chain of reasoning that traces through to the investment's impact on the firm's financial performance. Value chain analysis serves to guide this assessment process. *ROE* decomposition and relative performance analysis further isolate the effects of the investment from competing financing and macroeconomic effects. As illustrated in this chapter and throughout this book, it is through creative data capture strategies, thoughtful selection of appropriate performance metrics, and careful application of analysis techniques that account for alternative explanations of observed relationships that more useful insights into the relationship between IT investment and firm performance will emerge.

APPENDIX 6.1. OVERALL PERFORMANCE MEASURES VERSUS DIRECT MEASURES OF BUSINESS PROCESSES

It cannot be stated that IT might affect business processes and *not* overall firm performance. It can only be stated that IT might be observable in business processes and be unobservable in overall firm performance (Davamanirajan et al., 2006). The problem with using overall firm performance measures is not that IT will not have an effect on overall firm performance, but that due to noise in the measures the impact might be unobservable. This is an *errors-in-variables* problem, as the additional noise in overall performance measures biases coefficients toward zero. In the past, researchers have used overall firm performance measures to measure the benefits from investments in IT out of convenience or data availability, not because they saw these as the best measures for detecting the impact of IT on firm performance.

A simple illustration using the decathlon as an example might clarify the error in the belief that IT might improve business processes but not overall firm performance. The decathlon is made up of ten events, each with an individual score, which added together determine the winner. Suppose that a new type of pole is developed for the pole vault, and a researcher is interested in determining whether athletes using the new pole have improved performance.

A simple way to determine the impact of the new poles would be to examine the increase in the total score for athletes using the new poles, or the total score of athletes using the new poles compared with those using the old poles. The problem with this measure is that overall score is a very noisy measure. An increase in only one event out of the ten total will be observable only if there is a large enough sample size, and even then the true increase in performance will probably be underestimated. The best way to measure the impact of the new poles would be to directly measure the scores from only the pole vault event. The impact of the new poles can be measured by examining the increase in the pole vault score for athletes using the new poles, or the pole vault score of athletes using the new poles compared with those using the old poles. However, if this measure is unobservable then using the total score is acceptable, because the total score is a function of the underlying events. This is very important, because the overall firm performance measures that researchers use to gauge the impact of IT on firm performance are also a function of the underlying business processes. Ceteris paribus, it is not possible to improve a business process without also improving overall firm performance.

A linear relationship between two variables can be measured with a correlation coefficient (or the equivalent in regression analysis). If random error is added to one of the variables, then the coefficient is biased toward zero. This makes it difficult to find the relationship between two variables where one does exist, due to one or both variables being measured with error.

Analogously, the problem with accounting measures is that they contain both nonrandom error (bias) and random error (noise). First, accounting numbers are determined with the use of many estimates (depreciation, bad debts, etc.), and many accounting rules do not measure the true underlying economic reality (fair value, inventory, etc.). Second, accounting numbers are subject to manipulation, primarily through the use of accruals, but also due to fraud or other intentional misstatements. Third, accounting numbers are susceptible to random error due to incorrectly recorded transactions, unrecorded transactions, and human error.

So just using accounting numbers decreases the power of the tests, but it is exacerbated when overall business performance is used as a surrogate for business processes. Consider that overall firm performance is a function of the underlying business processes. When new IT is used to improve some of those processes, overall business performance by definition must improve as well. So why does it not show up in the statistical analysis? It is because IT does not improve underlying business processes. Therefore, what you have is some improved processes added together with several other processes. Any correlation between IT use and overall firm performance will be biased toward zero because changes in business processes not affected by IT add error in the measurement of firm performance.

We ran a simulation using 50 firms with 10 business processes per firm, equally weighted in determining firm performance. The simulation measures the correlation between performance and IT, with IT affecting 10 percent of business processes (1 out of the 10). IT improved the performance of the business process between 2 percent and 100 percent per firm (51 percent average improved performance). Running the simulation 100 times, the average correlation between IT and business process performance was 0.30, but between IT and overall firm performance 0.14. Out of 100 correlations, 97 were positive for the relationship between IT and business processes, and 87 were positive between IT and overall firm performance.

The simulation demonstrates the decline in power from using overall performance measures versus direct measures of business processes (from 0.30 to 0.14). Unfortunately, in many cases researchers do not have data for the underlying business processes and overall performance measures must be used. In these cases it is important to increase power through large sample size and using measures with the fewest confounding effects (*Operating ROA* instead of overall *ROA*, for example).

APPENDIX 6.2. ROE DECOMPOSITION

$$ROE = \frac{Net\ Income}{Equity} \tag{A6.2-1}$$

$$ROE = \frac{NOPAT - Net\ Interest}{Equity} \tag{A6.2-2}$$

$$ROE = \frac{NOPAT}{Equity} - \frac{Net\ Interest}{Equity} \tag{A6.2-3}$$

$$ROE = \left(\frac{Operating\ Assets}{Equity} \times OROA\right) - \left(\frac{Net\ Debt}{Equity} \times \frac{Net\ Interest}{Net\ Debt}\right) \qquad (A6.2\text{–}4)$$

$$ROE = \left(\frac{Equity + Net\ Debt}{Equity} \times OROA\right) - \left(\frac{Net\ Debt}{Equity} \times \frac{Net\ Interest}{Net\ Debt}\right) \qquad (A6.2\text{–}5)$$

$$ROE = OROA \times \left(1 + \frac{Net\ Debt}{Equity}\right) - \left(\frac{Net\ Debt}{Equity} \times \frac{Net\ Interest}{Net\ Debt}\right) \qquad (A6.2\text{–}6)$$

$$ROE = OROA + \left(\frac{Net\ Debt}{Equity} \times OROA\right) - \left(\frac{Net\ Debt}{Equity} \times \frac{Net\ Interest}{Net\ Debt}\right) \qquad (A6.2\text{–}7)$$

$$ROE = OROA + \frac{Net\ Debt}{Equity} \times \left(OROA - \frac{Net\ Interest}{Net\ Debt}\right) \qquad (A6.2\text{–}8)$$

$$ROE = OROA + Leverage \times Spread \qquad (A6.2\text{–}9)$$

$$ROE = OROA + Spread \times Leverage \qquad (A6.2\text{–}10)$$

$$ROE = \left(\frac{NOPAT}{Sales} \times \frac{Sales}{Net\ Assets}\right) + \left(\frac{NOPAT}{Net\ Assets} - \frac{Net\ Interest}{Net\ Debt}\right) \times \frac{Net\ Debt}{Equity} \qquad (A6.2\text{–}11)$$

where: *ROE* = Net Income / Stockholder's Equity
NOPAT = Net Operating Profit After Taxes = Net Income + Net Interest
Sales = Total Net Sales
Net Assets = Total Noncurrent Assets minus Non-Interest Bearing Noncurrent Liabilities
Net Interest = (Interest Expense minus Interest Income) × (1 – Tax Rate)
Net Debt = Total Interest Bearing Liabilities minus Cash and Marketable Securities
Equity = Total Stockholder's Equity
NOPAT Margin = NOPAT / Sales
Operating Asset Turnover = Sales / Net Assets
Spread = Operating ROA (*NOPAT / Net Assets*) minus Cost of Borrowing (*Net Interest / Net Debt*)
Leverage = Net Debt / Equity
OROA = Operating ROA = NOPAT Margin × Operating Asset Turnover

Source for Appendix 6.2: Adapted from Halsey (2001), pp. 261–262.

NOTES

1. *Business value* is a general term used to describe things (activities, assets, processes) that contribute to the value of a company. Firm value is the market value of a company, defined as the current market price per share times the number of shares outstanding.
2. The RIM assumes a clean surplus relationship. This requires that, except for transactions with owners, changes in book value (*BV*) are due to net income (*I*) and dividends (*D*): $BV1 = BV0 = I1 - D1$. This is the concept behind comprehensive income in the U.S. Generally Accepted Accounting Principles.
3. We use *average* to refer to both mean and median. We recommend industry median instead of industry mean in empirical tests because it is less subject to wide fluctuation due to small firms and outliers.
4. We defined high-tech firms using a list of three-digit SIC codes from Francis and Schipper (1999). Other alternatives for determining industry include the North American Industry Classification System codes, as well as industry classification systems used by Standard and Poor's.
5. We winsorized the data at the 2 percent cutoff level to reduce the effect of influential outliers in the analysis.

REFERENCES

Barber, B.M. and Lyon, J.D. 1996. Detecting abnormal operating performance: The empirical power and specification of test statistics. *Journal of Financial Economics,* 41, 3, 359–399.

Bardhan, I.; Bagchi, S.; and Sougstad, R. 2004. Prioritizing a portfolio of information technology investment projects. *Journal of Management Information Systems,* 21, 2, 33–60.

Barua, A.; Kriebel, C.H.; and Mukhopadhyay, T. 1995. Information technologies and business value: An analytic and empirical investigation. *Information Systems Research,* 6, 1, 3–23.

Brynjolfsson, E. 1993. The productivity paradox of information technology: Review and assessment. *Communications of the ACM,* 36, 12, 67–77.

Davamanirajan, P.; Kauffman, R.J.; Kriebel, C.H.; and Mukhopadhyay, T. 2006. Systems design, process performance and economic outcomes in international banking. *Journal of Management Information Systems,* 23, 2, 67–92.

Edwards, E.O. and Bell, P.W. 1961. *The Theory and Measurement of Business Income.* Berkeley: University of California Press.

Feltham, G. and Ohlson, J. 1995. Valuation and clean surplus accounting for operating and financial activities. *Contemporary Accounting Research,* 11, 2, 689–731.

Francis, J. and Schipper, K. 1999. Have financial statements lost their relevance? *Journal of Accounting Research,* 37, 2, 319–352.

Halsey, R. 2001. Using the residual-income stock price valuation model to teach and learn ratio analysis. *Issues in Accounting Education,* 16, 2, 257–272.

Jasperson, J.; Carter, P.E.; and Zmud, R.W. 2005. A comprehensive conceptualization of post-adoptive behaviors associated with information technology enabled work systems. *MIS Quarterly,* 29, 3, 525–557.

Kaplan, R.S. and Norton, D.P. 1996. *Balanced Scorecard.* Boston: Harvard Business School Press.

———. 2000. *The Strategy-Focused Organization.* Boston: Harvard Business School Press.

Kohli, R. and Devaraj, S. 2003. Measuring information technology payoff: A meta-analysis of structural variables in firm level research. *Information Systems Research,* 14, 2, 127–145.

Matolcsy, Z.; Booth, P.; and Wieder, B. 2005. The economic benefits of enterprise resource planning systems: Some empirical evidence. *Accounting and Finance,* 45, 3, 439–456.

Melville, N.; Kraemer, K.; and Gurbaxani, V. 2004. Review: Information technology and organizational performance: An integrative model of IT business value. *MIS Quarterly,* 28, 2, 283–322.

Mukhopadhyay, T.; Kekre, S.; and Kalathur, S. 1995. Business value of information technology: A study of electronic data interchange. *MIS Quarterly,* 19, 2, 137–156.

Ohlson, J. 1995. Earnings, book values and dividends in equity valuation. *Contemporary Accounting Research,* 11, 2, 661–687.

Peasnell, K.V. 1982. Some formal connections between economic values and yields and accounting numbers. *Journal of Business Finance & Accounting,* 9, 3, 361–381.

Peffers, K. and Dos Santos, B.L. 1996. Performance effects of innovative IT applications over time. *IEEE Transactions on Engineering Management,* 43, 4, 381–392.

Porter, M.E. 1985. *Competitive Advantage.* New York: Free Press.
Ranganathan, C. and Brown, C.V. 2006. ERP investments and the market value of firms: Toward an understanding of influential ERP project variables. *Information Systems Research,* 17, 2, 145–161.
Ray, G.; Barney, J.B.; and Muhanna, W.A. 2004. Capabilities, business processes, and competitive advantage: Choosing the dependent variable in empirical tests of the resource-based view. *Strategic Management Journal,* 25, 1, 23–38.
Smith, H. and Fingar, P. 2003. *Business Process Management: The Third Wave.* Tampa, FL: Meghan-Kiffer Press.
Tanriverdi, H. and Ruefli, T.W. 2004. The role of information technology in risk/return relations of firms. *Journal of the Association of Information Systems,* 5, 11–12, 421–447.

PART III

NEW APPROACHES FOR STUDYING MECHANISM DESIGN IN ONLINE AUCTIONS

CHAPTER 7

MODELING DYNAMICS IN ONLINE AUCTIONS

A Modern Statistical Approach

GALIT SHMUELI AND WOLFGANG JANK

Abstract: *In this work we propose a modern statistical approach to the analysis and modeling of dynamics in online auctions. Online auction data usually arrive in the form of a set of bids recorded over the duration of an auction. We propose the use of a modern statistical approach called functional data analysis that preserves the entire temporal dimension in place of currently used methods that aggregate over time, thereby losing important information. This enables us to investigate not only the price evolution that takes place during an auction but also the dynamics of the price evolution. We show how functional data analysis can be combined with cluster analysis and regression-type models for data exploration and summarization, and for testing hypotheses about relationships between price formation and other relevant factors.*

Keywords: *Functional Data Analysis, Price Evolution, eBay, Smoothing, Clustering, Regression*

INTRODUCTION

A growing body of empirical research in the fields of economics and information systems is concerned with the study of online auctions. A variety of questions are investigated, among them: What factors affect the final price of an auction? Why does last-minute bidding occur and why do people bid early in the auction? Is the phenomenon of Winner's Curse present in online auctions? Studies that employ statistical tools for answering such questions typically use a single measure, such as the final price, or total number of bids as the dependent variable of interest. These variables are static in the sense that they only give a snapshot taken at one particular time point, usually at the end of the auction.

However, they ignore the entire duration of the auction, and in particular the *dynamics* of the price formation or bidding process as it evolves throughout the auction. In this chapter, our aim is to study the entire price formation process and its dynamics in online auctions. By *price dynamics* we mean the progress of the price throughout the auction, its speed, changes in speed, and so on. An analogy is cars in a car race. Instead of focusing exclusively on the winner's score (or the winning price in an auction) as the dependent variable, we look at the route, speed, acceleration, and other dynamic characteristics specific to the choices the driver made. Clearly, there is a relationship between these dynamics and the winner's score. However, the race dynamics are interesting in themselves and can be useful for understanding other important phenomena. For instance, better acceleration performance of our driver can be an indication of a superior car. Thus, the dependent variable from our viewpoint is not a static point variable, but rather the price curve throughout the auction. We investigate how price increases throughout an auction: How fast does it increase at different stages of the auction? How fast does it move toward the final price? Which dynamics are common and which are different across various auctions? We also study factors that influence the price formation, in particular the minimum price, which is analogous to a reserve price in auction theory (Bajari and Hortacsu, 2004). Finally, we investigate relationships between the auction dynamics and other variables of interest such as final price.

From a data structure point of view, static variables call for aggregated data whereas dynamic data use the entire unaggregated sequence of bids. For this reason, previous studies tended to aggregate available information over the auction duration, over auctions, or over both. In the first case, an entire auction is reduced to a single time point, usually the end. Examples are modeling the closing price (a single point for each auction) as a function of various factors such as the number of bids, the auction duration, and the seller rating (Lucking-Reiley, 2000). Aggregation over auctions is the case where the data from a set of auctions are treated as one set of data points. For example, Roth and Ockenfels (2000) look at the empirical cumulative distribution function of bid times that are taken from multiple auctions but they combine them into a single sample. Finally, aggregation over time *and* auctions occurs when the object of interest is, for example, the final price, and all final prices are aggregated, so that they are represented by their mean.

This type of double-aggregation is widespread, and typically appears as a table of means. Although aggregation is convenient for summarizing data, it carries the risk of losing important information to the degree of arriving at wrong conclusions (this is also known as "Simpson's paradox"). Once data are aggregated, the information loss is usually unrecoverable. Clearly, it would be ideal to explore and model the information contained in the entire duration of each auction, and to aggregate as late as possible in the modeling process, and only when deemed necessary. One of the main reasons that such analyses are absent from the online auction literature is most likely the inadequacy of popular methods such as regression models and time-series analysis for fitting such data. Online auction data have a special form that is not traditional in the statistics literature. On the one hand, the bidding sequence in a single auction forms a time series with special features (such as unequally spaced observations over a finite interval). On the other hand, we have not a single series but multiple time series, which are not "aligned" or of the same length. Such a data structure is not common and thus commands special statistical methods.

It appears that there is a gap between online auction researchers, who are typically from the fields of economics and information systems, and researchers in the area of statistics. In part this is due to the new data collection mechanisms that have not swept the statistics academic community: In order to obtain online auction data (and other e-commerce-type data) software agents are commonly used. The software agents, also known as *spiders,* are typically written by the research team and the code is specific for the application at hand. Kauffman and Wood (Chapter 2, this volume) discuss the implications of these modern data collection mechanisms and how their availability enables empirical research that has not been possible earlier.[1] Statisticians usually do not have the knowledge or expertise to write such agents, and are therefore left outside of this rich world of data and the research opportunities that they create. This gap between disciplines certainly calls for collaboration between data collection gurus and data analysis masters!

Our main goal is to show how statistical thinking and modern statistical methodology can be useful for exploring, gaining insight into, and testing hypotheses with such data, in the sense of capturing processes and their dynamics. In the second section, we describe the special features and structure of online auction data, which make traditional statistical analysis methods such as regression and time-series models less adequate for exploring their dynamics. We also discuss

Table 7.1

Comparison of the Traditional Static Dependent Variable and Dynamic Variable

Issues	Static (point) response	Dynamic curve response
Examples	Final price, number of bids, number of bidders, average bidder rating	Sequence of bids over time, cumulative number of bids, number of distinct bidders over time, bidder rating over time
Data structure	Single measurement per auction	Time series for each auction
Research question format: How factors relate to ...	Increase/decrease in response	Shape, speed, acceleration of response curve
Typical summary statistics	Averages, percentiles, counts	Average and percentile curves
Typical plots	Histograms, scatterplots, bar charts	Profile plots, phase-plane plots
Statistical models	Regression-type models; cluster analysis	Functional regression models, functional cluster analysis

the data structure from a statistical perspective and define the sample-population relationship of interest. We then introduce the method of *functional data analysis* (FDA): we explain how FDA differs from classical statistical methods, and why we think it is suitable for exploring and analyzing online auction data. Table 7.1 summarizes the main differences between a "static" approach and our "dynamic" approach in terms of data structure, research questions, and statistical models.

In the third section, we illustrate how the method works using real data from eBay.com. We perform exploratory analysis and confirmatory analysis of the price formation process and tie our results with auction theory and the current literature on online auctions. We describe the different steps involved in FDA, and show what type of information and knowledge are gained at each step. Thus, our goal is to integrate our research question, statistical methodology, and data within this expository work. In the final section, we discuss additional aspects of auction dynamics and suggest future directions for applying modern statistical methods to auction data and more generally to e-commerce data.

DATA STRUCTURE AND STATISTICAL SETTING

We next discuss the features of bid histories and our statistical framework for this research.

Features of Bid Histories

Bid data from online auctions are very different from data used in traditional statistical analyses in several respects. In the following, we use the term *bid history* to denote the sequence of bids and time stamps for a single auction. In that sense, a bid history is a time series. In closed-end auctions such as eBay, the auction length is predetermined by the seller, and thus the time series takes place over a preset, finite interval. In open-ended auctions the duration could be, at least in theory, infinite. We focus here on closed-end auctions only.

Unlike traditional time-series analysis, where the problem at hand is to fit a model or forecast a single time series, the goal in analyzing auction data is to gain a better understanding of other (current or future) auctions that are not part of the data set. In contrast to traditional time-series analysis, which is concerned with a single time series at a time, we have multiple (typically several hundred) such series. Furthermore, in a single time-series analysis the unobserved population of interest is usually the future (i.e., times $t + 1, t + 2, \ldots$), whereas in the auction setting it is the unobserved population of all similar auctions that are not in the data set (and not the "future" since the auction is closed!). Thus the goals, the data structure, and the statistical setting are different from ordinary time-series analysis.

The three features that set bid histories apart from traditional time series are the unequally spaced observations within each auction, the different number, and the different time stamps across different auctions. Even if we "standardize" all the auctions to start at time 0 and end at time T, we have multiple time series with varying numbers of observations, which are unequally spaced and differ across auctions. This means that even from a data entry point of view we cannot store the data easily in a traditional matrix form.

Statistical Framework

In light of the objectives of our study, we define what we mean by a sample, by a population, and the relationship between the two. Treating each bid history as a time series, we view our sample of auctions as a sample from the entire population of all relevant auctions. Thus, our observation of interest is not a scalar but an entire function. We then use the sample information to investigate the dynamics of the entire population, in the sense of the price evolution throughout the auction, its speed, and more. In addition to exploring patterns of price dynamics, we also examine heterogeneity across auctions and aim to find factors that drive such heterogeneity. In particular, we strive to compare the price dynamics in auctions either for the same item, or even across auctions for different types of items (electronics, collectibles, etc.). On the one hand, it is possible that there are different patterns of price dynamics even among auctions for the same item. On the other hand, although prices are expected to be different across different items (for example, between a DVD and a collectible coin), the dynamics of the price formation can be similar. Thus, the population of all auctions need not necessarily be partitioned into subpopulations according to the item sold.

We approach the data analysis task from a statistical angle: we start by simple exploration before moving to more formal confirmatory analysis. The goal of the exploratory phase is simply to display the data for the purpose of familiarization with its structure, features, and complexity—a very important step that is often overlooked. At this point, we do not yet test hypotheses. We use graphical displays, summarization, and data reduction techniques. Since the data have special features, ordinary displays such as histograms, scatter plots, and bar charts lead to a loss of the temporal information. We thus strive to limit the loss of information as much as possible.

In many papers that analyze online auction data, aggregation of bids across time appears to be a commonplace practice (e.g., Bajari and Hortacsu, 2003). This means that instead of viewing an auction over its entire duration, it is reduced to merely a single time point. The dynamics of the auction, as it turns out though, are important for capturing, understanding, and evaluating phenomena that are found in the aggregated data. One example is the phenomenon of *last minute bidding*, which has been examined through looking at the number of bids during the last minute or so of the auction and comparing it with the overall number of bids in the auction (Bajari and Hortacsu, 2003; Wilcox, 2000). An alternative, which preserves the temporal information, is to look at auctions as time series. Shmueli, Russo, and Jank (2004) developed a three-stage model that describes the bid arrival process in closed-end auctions such as eBay. They treat the incoming bids as points in a continuous process, thereby maintaining the temporal information. Applying the model to real data, they show that the last minute bidding actually occurs over the last couple of minutes, and that the bid arrivals are actually more moderate than expected in light of the rapidly increasing bid arrivals until the last two minutes of the auction.

A Suitable Statistical Method: Functional Data Analysis

Since our object of interest is the sequence of bids (representing the price curve) throughout the entire auction, we choose to use the method of functional data analysis for exploring and analyzing online auction data.[2] FDA is a cutting-edge statistical method that was made popular by the monograph of Ramsay and Silverman (1997) and earlier work by the two authors and others. FDA has gained momentum in various fields of application such as the agricultural sciences (Ogden et al., 2002), the behavioral sciences (Rossi, Wang, and Ramsay, 2002), and medical research (Pfeiffer et al., 2002). The method has been used to analyze the dynamics of seasonally varying production indices (Ramsay and Ramsey, 2002) as well as to predict El Niño (Besse, Cardot, and Stephenson, 2000). An excellent collection of case studies involving functional data analysis can be found in Ramsay and Silverman (2002).

Unlike longitudinal methods that are suitable when the number of observations per unit is small, thereby requiring parametric assumptions, FDA is a flexible nonparametric method that can handle cases in which many observations per unit are recorded. The only requirement in FDA is a sufficiently large amount of data so that the curve can be adequately approximated (Faraway, 1997).

In the next section we show why FDA is suitable for handling online auction data, and how it is advantageous over static statistical methods.

FUNCTIONAL DATA ANALYSIS IMPLEMENTATION

The process of modeling data using functional data analysis is described in Table 7.2.

The process begins by representing each bid sequence by a curve. The assumption is that there is an underlying price curve that manifests itself as points over time. After the underlying curve is estimated, or "recovered," we follow the traditional statistical process of analysis: We start by plotting the raw data (which are the "curves"), then we compute summaries and characterize the overall features of the dependent variable. We continue the exploration using methods such as cluster analysis for learning about natural grouping of auctions. Finally, we perform more formal parametric or nonparametric modeling, thereby integrating factors of interest and examining their effect on the response. These steps and their functional implementation are described next. In order to illustrate each method and what is gained by it, we use a collection of data on 353 closed auctions that took place on eBay.com during November–December 2003. The auctioned items include a variety of popular items from several categories: children's items (e.g., books and posters), tickets for college football, collectible items (e.g., Morgan Silver Dollars), fashion items (e.g., Gucci bags), and electronics (e.g., computers and computer accessories).

Recovering the Functional Object and Data Smoothing

The first step in every functional data analysis consists of recovering, from the observed data, the underlying functional object. This functional object can be a continuous curve, a shape, an image, or an even more complicated phenomenon such as the movement of an object through space and time. Consider Figure 7.1, which displays bid histories for four selected auctions on exclusive

Table 7.2

Steps in Functional Data Analysis

Step	FDA implementation
1. Preprocess	Estimate/recover underlying curve from time series
2. Explore curves	Plot and summarize curves, cluster curves
3. Explore curve dynamics	Plot and summarize derivatives and the relations between derivatives
4. Model curves/derivatives	Regress curves/derivatives on factors of interest, or other statistical methods (e.g., principal components analysis, discriminant analysis, principal differential analysis)
5. Predict and interpret	Relate curve dynamics to domain theory; Real-time forecasting of curve continuation

women's fashion accessories. We can see that the price, as reflected by the bid histories in each of these four auctions, follows an underlying trend that can be described by a continuous curve.

In the top left panel of Figure 7.1, for instance, the bid amount quickly increases at the beginning of the auction, then slows down over the next several days, and finally increases rapidly at the end of the auction. Interestingly, the underlying trend is not identical for the four auctions. In the bottom right panel, for instance, the bid amount only increases gradually at the beginning, then picks up speed at the end of Day 5, only to slow down again near the end of the auction. Clearly, a very flexible class of models is required to accommodate these very different functional trends under one umbrella.[3]

There exist a variety of methods for recovering an underlying functional object from a set of data. The collection of all these methods is often referred to as *data smoothing*. For an introduction into smoothing methods see, for example, Simonoff (1996). Here, we focus on one particularly popular method that provides a lot of modeling flexibility, the *polynomial smoothing spline*. The polynomial smoothing spline applies the local smoothing effect of polynomials to a larger interval without the need to use high polynomial orders. Simply speaking, a *spline* is a piecewise polynomial function. The interval of interest is broken down into subintervals and within each subinterval a polynomial is fitted. This is done in such a way that the polynomial pieces blend smoothly, so that the resulting composite function has several continuous derivatives. The edges of the subintervals are called *knots*. More formally, a polynomial spline of degree p can be written in the form:

$$f(t) = \beta_0 + \beta_1 t + \beta_2 t^2 + \ldots + \beta_p t^p + \Sigma_{i=1\ldots L} \beta_{pi} [(t-\tau_i)_+]^p \quad (7.1)$$

where the constants $\tau_1, \ldots, \tau_L$ are a set of L knots and $u_+ = u I_{\{u \geq 0\}}$ denotes the positive part of the function u. The choices of L and p strongly influence the local variability of the function f, such that larger values of L and p result in a rougher (or more "wiggly") f, exhibiting a larger deviation from a straight line. While this may result in a very good data fit, a very wiggly function f may not recover or identify the underlying process very well.

One can measure the degree of departure from a straight line by defining a roughness penalty such as

$$PEN_m = \geq \{D^m f(t)\}^2 dt, \quad (7.2)$$

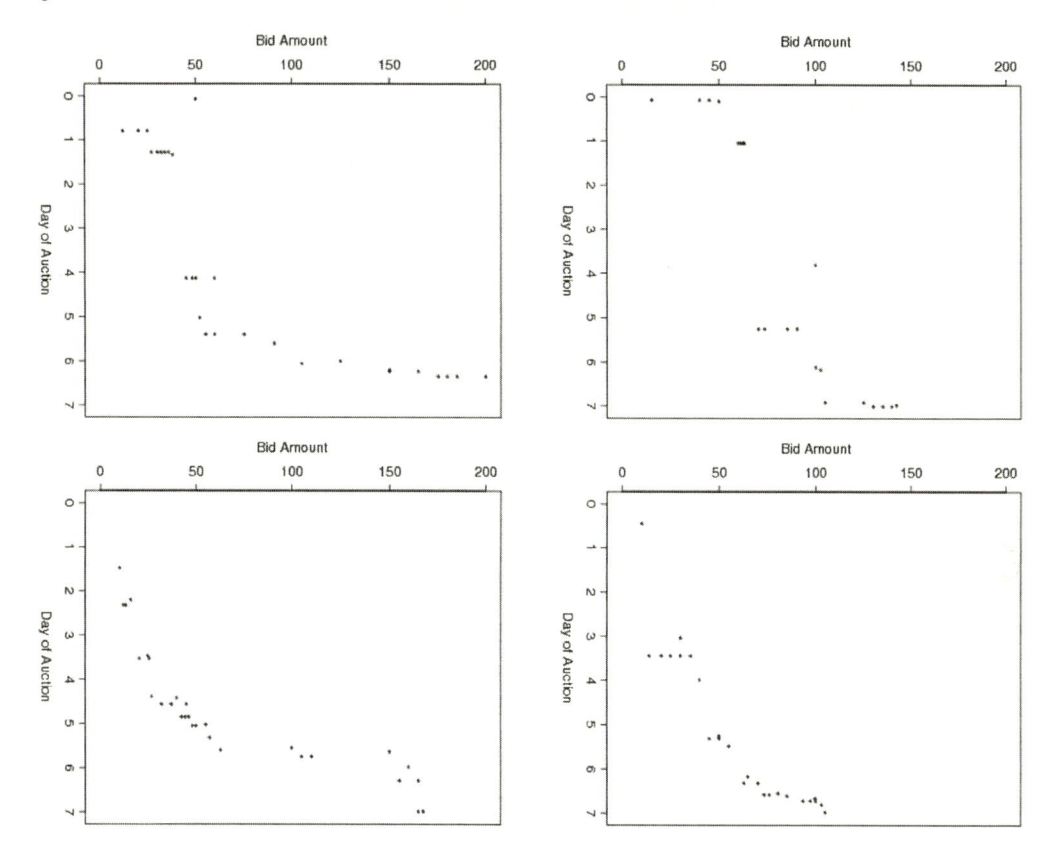

Figure 7.1 Bid Histories for Four Auctions on Women's Fashion Articles

where $D^m f$, $m = \{1,2,3, \ldots\}$ denotes the mth derivative of the function f. For $m = 2$, for instance, PEN_2 yields the integrated squared second derivative of f that is sensitive to the curvature of the function f. One reason for the popularity of polynomial smoothing splines is the compromise that they achieve between data fit and variance reduction. Another reason is the immediate availability of the curves' derivative functions.

Fitting a polynomial smoothing spline to the observed data $y_1, \ldots, y_n$ involves finding the coefficients $\beta_0, \beta_1, \ldots, \beta_p, \beta_{p1}, \ldots, \beta_{pL}$ of (1) that minimize the penalized residual sum of squares

$$Q_{\lambda,m} = \lambda P_m + \Sigma_{I = 1 \ldots n} \{y_i - f(t_i)\}^2, \qquad (7.3)$$

where the smoothing parameter $\lambda \geq 0$ controls the trade-off between the data fit, as measured by the summation on the right-hand side of equation 7.3, and the local variability of the function f, measured by the roughness penalty PEN_m in equation 7.2. Using $m = 2$ in equation 7.3, for instance, leads to the commonly encountered cubic smoothing spline, a polynomial of degree three. More generally, a smoothing spline of order m is a polynomial of degree $p = 2m - 1$. Figure 7.2 illustrates the effect of different values of m and λ on the smoothing function f.

Minimization of the penalized residual sum of squares is done in a way very similar to the minimization of the least squares operator in standard regression analysis; see Appendix 7.1.

Figure 7.2 **Different Smoothing of the Same Data**

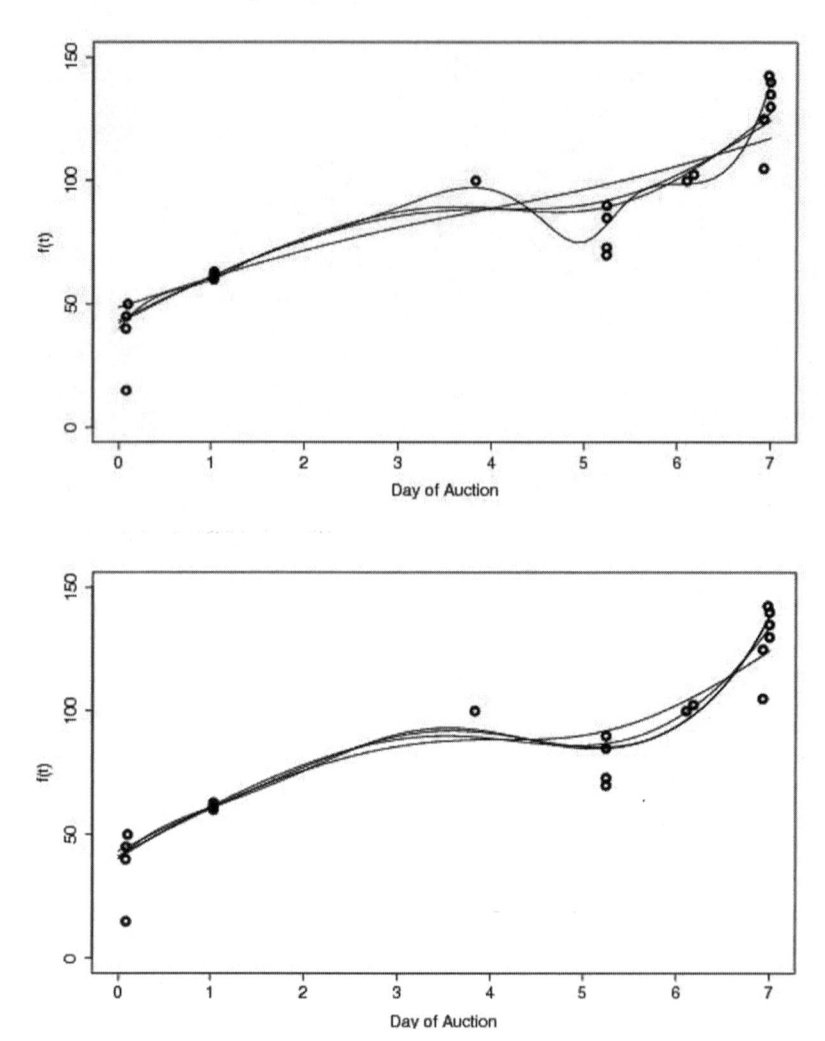

Note: The top panel compares smoothing splines of order $m = 2$ with values of $\lambda = 0, 0.5, 1, 10$. The spline becomes smoother as λ increases. The bottom panel compares smoothing splines of order $m = 2, 3, 4, 5$ using $\lambda = 1$. Higher-order splines produce smoother curves.

Many software packages exist to fit polynomial smoothing splines. In this work we use the *pspline* module. This and many more FDA functions are freely available online for R (2007), SPlus, and Matlab software (ego.psych.mcgill.ca/misc/fda/software.html).

Summarizing and Visualizing Functional Data

As in any classic statistical analysis, the first step in FDA consists of summarizing and visualizing the data (see Shmueli and Jank [2005] for online auction visualizations). Figure 7.3 shows the smoothing splines for the 353 completed eBay auctions described above. We fit the splines

Figure 7.3 **Summarizing Functional Data**

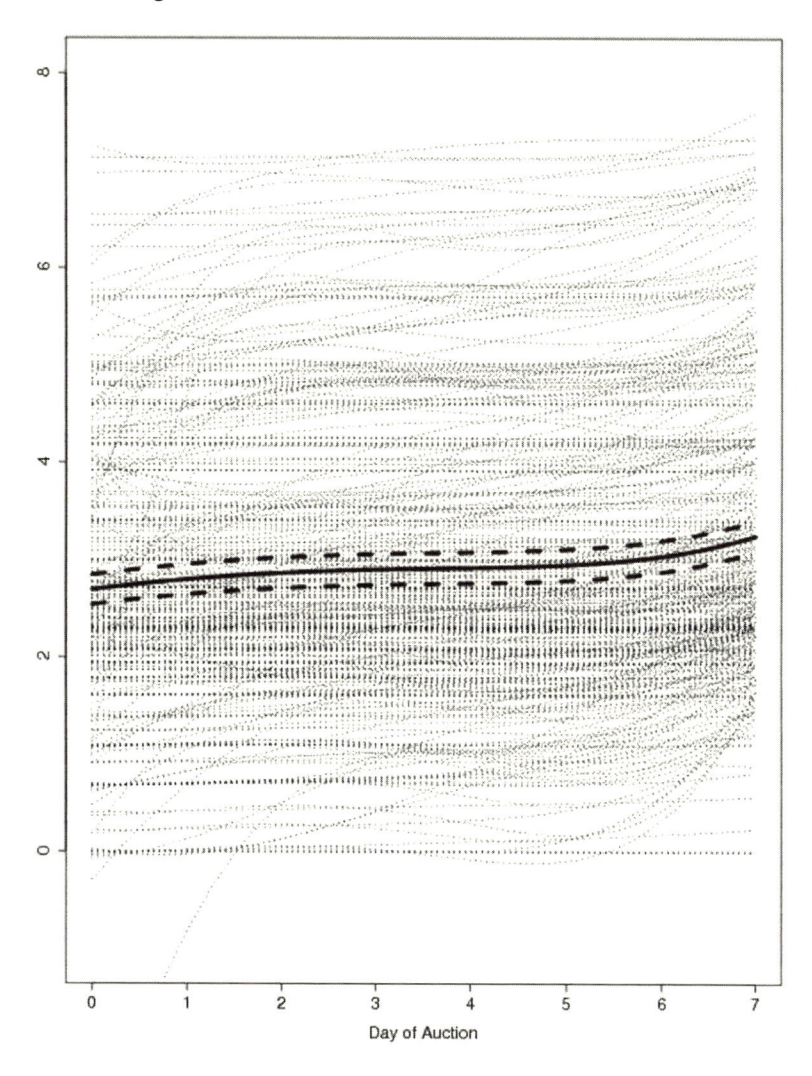

Note: The 353 smoothed price curves with their point-wise average (thick solid line) and 95 percent confidence bounds (thick dashed lines).

to logs of the bid amounts in order to capture periods of very quick increases in price, similar to growth curve models in economics or biology. We can see that there is a large amount of variability between the curves and that an overall pattern is hard to identify.

One way to summarize the information contained in functional data is in a point-wise manner. That is, let $f_i(t)$ denote the smoothing spline pertaining to auction i. Using an evenly spaced grid of points $t_1, t_2, \ldots, t_G$, we can sample the spline at each grid point, leading to a set of function values $f_i(t_1), f_i(t_2), \ldots, f_i(t_G)$ for each individual auction. Standard summary measures can now be applied to this grid directly. For instance, in order to determine the average trend in the functional data, the sample mean can be computed at each grid point.

$$\bar{x}(t_g) = \frac{1}{353}\sum_{i=1}^{353} f_i(t_g), \quad g = \{1, \ldots, G\} g = \{1, \ldots, G\}. \tag{7.4}$$

In a similar fashion, we can compute the sample standard deviation for each grid point, leading to a set of values, say, $s(t_G)$. Using standard statistical reasoning, we can now derive point-wise confidence bounds

$$\bar{x}(t_g) \pm z_{\alpha/2} \cdot s(t_g)/\sqrt{353} \tag{7.5}$$

where z_α denotes the α percentile of the standard normal distribution. After interpolation, these confidence bounds can be plotted and used as a visual summary of the functional data. Figure 7.3, for instance, shows the point-wise mean (thick solid line) and point-wise 95 percent confidence bounds (thick dashed lines) for the 353 auctions. We can see that, on average, the bid amount increases gradually over the duration of the auction. Toward the end of the auction, however, the rate of increase changes.

The information in the functional data can also be summarized in other ways. Using the median instead of the mean (together with confidence bands based on, say, the fifth and ninety-fifth percentiles), for instance, is a useful alternative that is robust to outliers. A completely different approach is to visualize the *dynamics* in the observed data. This is especially useful in the auction context, because we can think of the current highest (or second highest) bid as a moving object that travels at a certain pace throughout the auction. Attributes that are typically associated with a moving object are its *velocity* (or its *speed*) and its *acceleration*. Given an object with a certain mass, velocity is proportional to the object's *momentum*, while acceleration is proportional to its *force*. Velocity and acceleration can be computed for each auction via the first and second derivatives of $f_i(t)$, respectively.

Figure 7.4 shows the velocity and acceleration for the 353 auctions. First, notice the significantly smaller amount of variability compared with Figure 7.3.

The values of the products that are auctioned in these 353 auctions are highly variable and range from only a few dollars (e.g., a children's poster of the movie *The Lord of the Rings*) to several thousand dollars (e.g., a Dell Inspiron computer). So it is not surprising to see high variability in bid values/positions in Figure 7.3. On the other hand, the rate at which the current bid changes from one value to the next is often much less variable. This can be observed in Figure 7.4, which describes the velocity and acceleration of the price in these auctions.

Thus, summarizing the dynamics can be a very useful tool to learn about similarities and differences between auctions at different levels of their dynamics. It is also useful for comparing a variety of possibly very diverse auction categories, as will be seen next.

Functional Cluster Analysis

Exploratory statistics is typically concerned with detecting patterns within a large set of possibly high-dimensional data. In functional data analysis, since each data point consists of a continuous curve, the data are infinite-dimensional! This poses new challenges for the generalization of traditional exploratory tools like cluster analysis.

One way to handle the high dimensionality of functional data is to use a low-dimensional representation of the infinite-dimensional curve. Let $\hat{\beta}_i$ be the vector of estimated spline coefficients for the ith smoothing spline. Notice that $\hat{\beta}_i$ is of finite (and typically relatively low) dimension. Within

Figure 7.4 **Dynamics of Price**

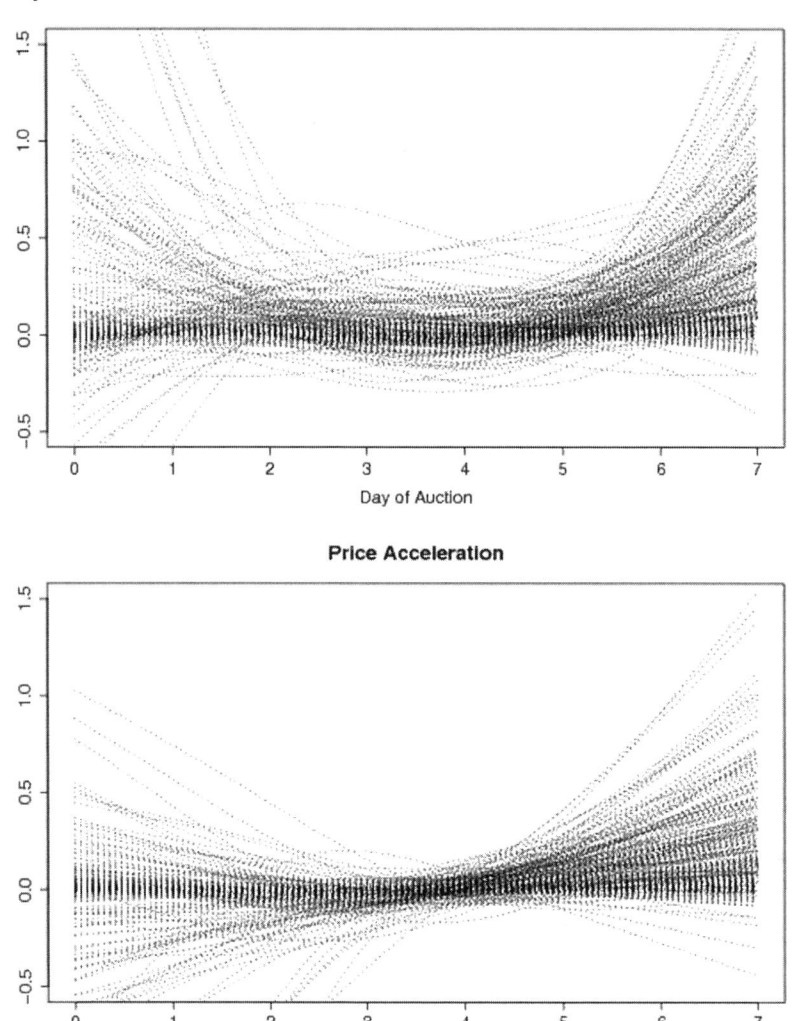

Price Acceleration

Note: There are 353 price velocity (first derivative) and price acceleration (second derivative) curves depicted.

the set of all splines of order m, $\hat{\beta}_i$ determines the shape of $f_i(t)$. Therefore, each spline (describing an auction) is exactly determined by its spline coefficients $\hat{\beta}_i$, and we use the set of coefficients as the low-dimensional representation of the infinite-dimensional spline.

Cluster analysis is a useful tool for exploring the natural grouping of observations in a data set. The *functional version of cluster analysis* searches for natural groupings of splines by using their coefficients. In particular, we use a variant of the well-known k-means algorithm called the *k-medoids algorithm,* which has the advantage of robustness to outliers; for details on the functional K-medoid clustering algorithm, see Appendix 7.2. Figure 7.5 shows the results of clustering the spline coefficients of the 353 auctions.

Figure 7.5 **Cluster-Specific Price Curves**

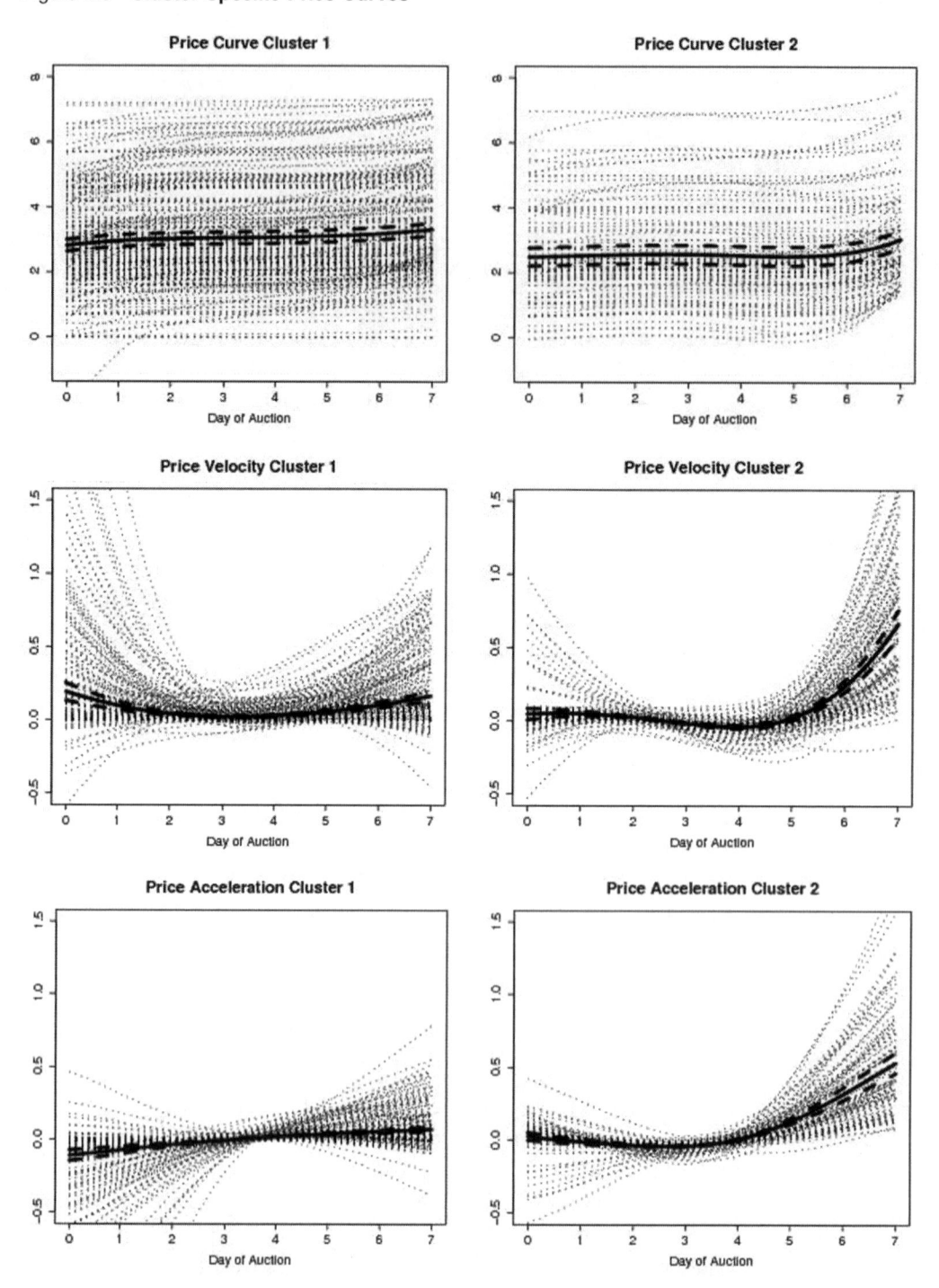

Note: Point-wise averages are shown with thick solid lines, and the 95 percent confidence bound is shown with thick dashed lines. Cluster 1 exhibits early dynamics, while Cluster 2 exhibits late dynamics.

Figure 7.6 **Cluster-Specific Distribution of Item Categories**

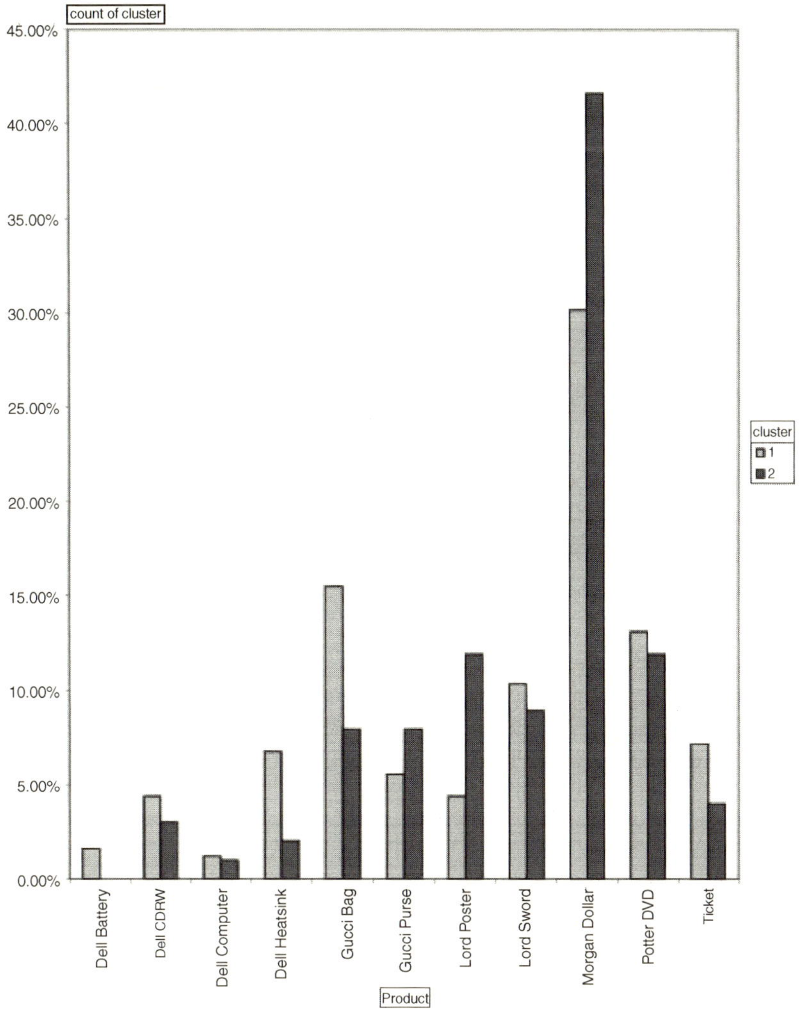

Note: The data set includes auctions on items of a variety of categories and a range of prices. The two clusters are similar with respect to category distribution.

Two very diverse auction clusters are recognizable: One exhibits early dynamics (left) and the other late dynamics (right). In the *early activity cluster*, price velocity is high at the beginning of the auction. However, its acceleration is negative during that time and hence the velocity drops to almost zero toward the middle of the auction. Toward the end of the auction velocity picks up again, although this increase is rather slow. The *late activity cluster* exhibits different dynamics: In this cluster, price velocity and acceleration are near zero at the beginning of the auction. Velocity remains low until about Day 5. From there on it increases sharply toward the end of the auction. The strong surge in price dynamics is even more visible in the price acceleration where the slope continues to increase until the very end.

Table 7.3

Mean and Standard Error (s / √n) for Five Auction Variables, by Cluster

Cluster	1n (OpeningBid)	1n (FinalAuctionPrice)	1n (SellerFeedback)	1n (WinnerFeedback)	1n (NumberofBids)
Early Activity	2.32 (0.113)	3.34 (0.10)	5.46 (0.12)	4.52 (0.10)	1.35 (0.07)
Late Activity	1.76 (0.123)	3.32 (0.11)	5.56 (0.15)	4.84 (0.13)	2.20 (0.05)

Note: Variables are logarithmically transformed, for example, ln(OpeningBid) and ln(FinalAuctionPrice).

The next step is to find what other features distinguish the clusters. Figure 7.6 compares the item categories between the two clusters. It can be seen that the two clusters are similar, indicating that similarities and differences in auction dynamics are global rather than category-specific.

Table 7.3 gives the mean and standard error of different numerical variables that are recorded in the bid histories, for each of the clusters.

From the five variables, two seem to differ significantly from one cluster to the other: the late activity cluster has a lower average opening bid and a higher average number of bids. This is in line with evidence and theory about lower opening prices attracting more bids (Bajari and Hortacsu, 2002; Lucking-Reiley, 2000; Roth and Ockenfels, 2000). We further examine the three-way relationship between opening bid, number of bids, and closing prices and compare the two clusters. Figure 7.7 shows a scatterplot of price vs. the opening bid by cluster, with circle size proportional to the number of bids.

We make the following observations:

1. Most of the auctions starting at $0.99–$1 are in the early dynamics cluster (cluster 1). Thus, although the late dynamic cluster has a lower average opening bid, the majority of "standard" $1 opening bid auctions fall in the early dynamic cluster. So a standard $1 opening bid is associated with early price dynamics.
2. The early activity cluster appears to have many auctions with low-price–low-opening-bid pairs (falling on a straight line), which attracted only 1–2 bids (small circles). None of the variables in our data set shed light on the reason for these "undesirable" items.
3. Auctions with many bids tend to have high closing prices in both clusters, as expected by the above three-way relationship. However, in the early dynamics cluster (cluster 1) the opening bid does not appear to play a role.

These are a few illustrations of the types of questions and insights that can be derived by exploring the relationship between auction design, auction dynamics, and auction results. Functional cluster analysis is especially suitable for exploring dynamic hypotheses where the price dynamics are described as a flowing process that is influenced by and/or has influence over traditional variables, such as the number of bids, the seller's rating, and the closing price.

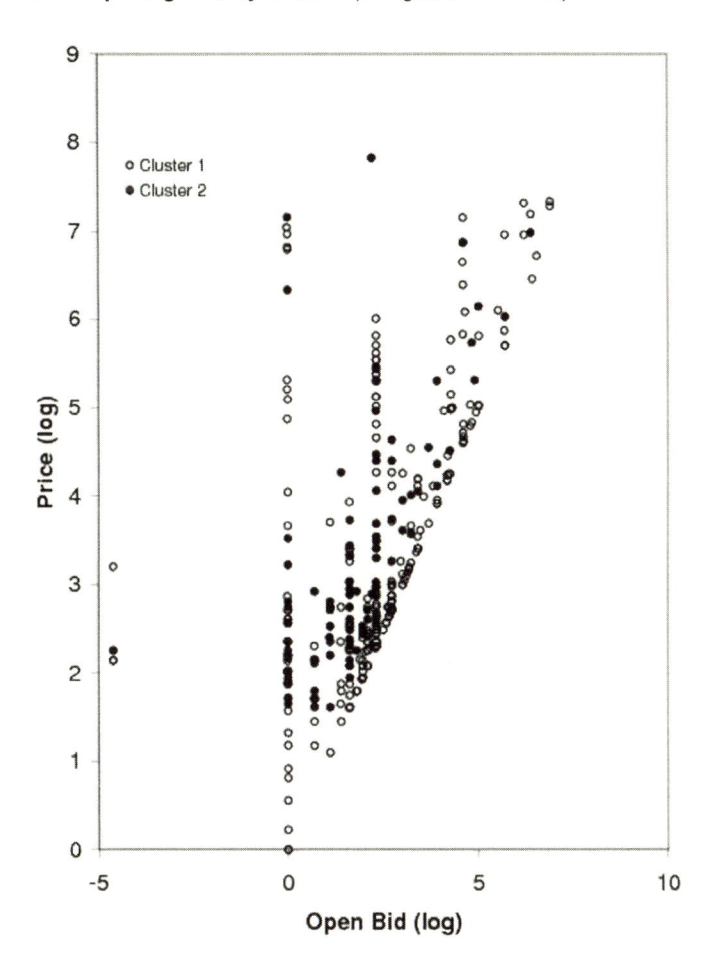

Figure 7.7 **Price vs. Opening Bid, by Cluster** (in logarithmic values)

Functional Regression Analysis

Much of the empirical work on online auctions uses regression-type models in order to find and explain the effect of different factors on a dependent variable. In the functional context we can use regression-type models to explain and predict the shape of a curve, or its dynamics, based on a set of input variables. This means that our dependent variable can either be the splines representing the price curves, or even their derivatives, that is, the price velocity, price acceleration, and so on.

A straightforward functional implementation of regression-type models is to fit point-wise models over a grid.[4] For instance, we can take snapshots of the splines and predictors at hourly intervals and fit a model to each snapshot. The sequence of regression coefficients is then combined by interpolation; for a more formal model, see Appendix 7.3.

To illustrate how functional regression can be used to investigate research questions of interest and its advantage over a static regression model, we examine the effect of the opening bid or minimum price that is set by the seller (equivalent to the *reserve price* in auction theory: Bajari and Hortacsu, 2004) on the price formation. According to auction theory, a revenue-maximizing seller should always set a reserve price that exceeds his or her value (Krishna, 2002). This is true as long as bidders' values are statistically independent. However, the theoretical derivations that lead to this strategy are based on a *fixed number of bidders N,* and it has been shown that the optimal minimum bid can be very different when bidders must incur a cost to acquire information on the auctioned item (Bajari and Hortacsu, 2002). This information is acquired by the bidders throughout the auction, and therefore we would learn much from examining the effect of the minimum price as information unveils to the bidders, or in other words, on the price dynamics.

The functional cluster analysis from the previous section has already highlighted the possible role of the opening bid in distinguishing between "early" and "late" activity auctions. We now continue to a more formal exploration of this relationship and its implications.

Before we fit a functional regression model, we start by fitting the standard static regression model where ln(*FinalAuctionPrice*) is regressed on ln(*OpeningBid*). The estimated coefficient for ln(*OpeningBid*) is 0.5118 (statistically significant, $p < 0.000$). This implies that a 1 percent increase in the opening bid is associated with an average increase of 0.5 percent in the final auction price. Let us compare this result and its usefulness with what the functional regression offers. Figure 7.8 illustrates the basic idea of functional modeling.

The three panels show the influence of the ln(*OpeningBid*) on the ln(*FinalAuctionPrice*) as well as on its velocity and acceleration. Specifically, using the smoothing spline as the response variable and the opening bid as the predictor variable, we fitted a simple linear regression model on an equally spaced grid $0 \leq t_j \leq 7$. For each of these grid points, we obtained an estimate for the coefficient of the ln(*OpeningBid*), $\hat{\beta}_j$, together with an estimate of its standard error. The solid line in the top panel shows the interpolation of these parameter estimates while the dotted lines correspond to the resulting 95 percent upper and lower confidence bounds. The rightmost regression (at time $t_j = 7$) is, in fact, almost equivalent to the static regression model of ln(*FinalAuctionPrice*) on ln(*OpeningBid*), except that the static model uses the actual final prices whereas the functional regression uses the smoothed values. We repeated this procedure twice, using the price velocity and the price acceleration as the response variable. The results are shown in the middle and bottom panels of Figure 7.8.

The positive coefficient in the model for *FinalAuctionPrice* indicates that the price at any point in the auction is positively associated with the value of *OpeningBid,* but its decreasing shape indicates the reduction in informativeness of the opening bid as the auction progresses. For price velocity the coefficient is negative and most pronounced at the start and end of the auction, indicating that during these times high opening bids are associated with reduced speed of price increase.

The top graph in Figure 7.8 shows that the *OpeningBid* coefficient estimate remains positive throughout the entire duration of the auction, implying a positive relationship between the opening bid and bid position. In other words, the higher the opening bid, the higher the value of the price at any time of the auction (as indicated by the static regression of *FinalAuctionPrice* on *OpeningBid*). Although positive, this estimate actually declines through the auction, especially after the start and even more so toward the end of the auction. This means that the impact of the size of the opening bid on the current bid drops after the first day of the auction by approximately 7.5 percent, then plateaus, and finally takes a steeper drop (~15 percent) as the auction approaches its end. The steep decline in the coefficient after Day 5 implies that *toward the end of the auction the information contained in the opening price loses its usefulness for explaining the current price.* This is expected by auction theory due to the information acquisition cost argument. The auction start does not contain much information on the value of the auctioned item and therefore the opening bid is more crucial to bidders early in the auction, whereas once bids are placed more information is revealed on the item's valuation and the opening bid becomes less central.

Figure 7.8 **Estimated Coefficients for ln(*OpeningBid*) in the Functional Regression Models**

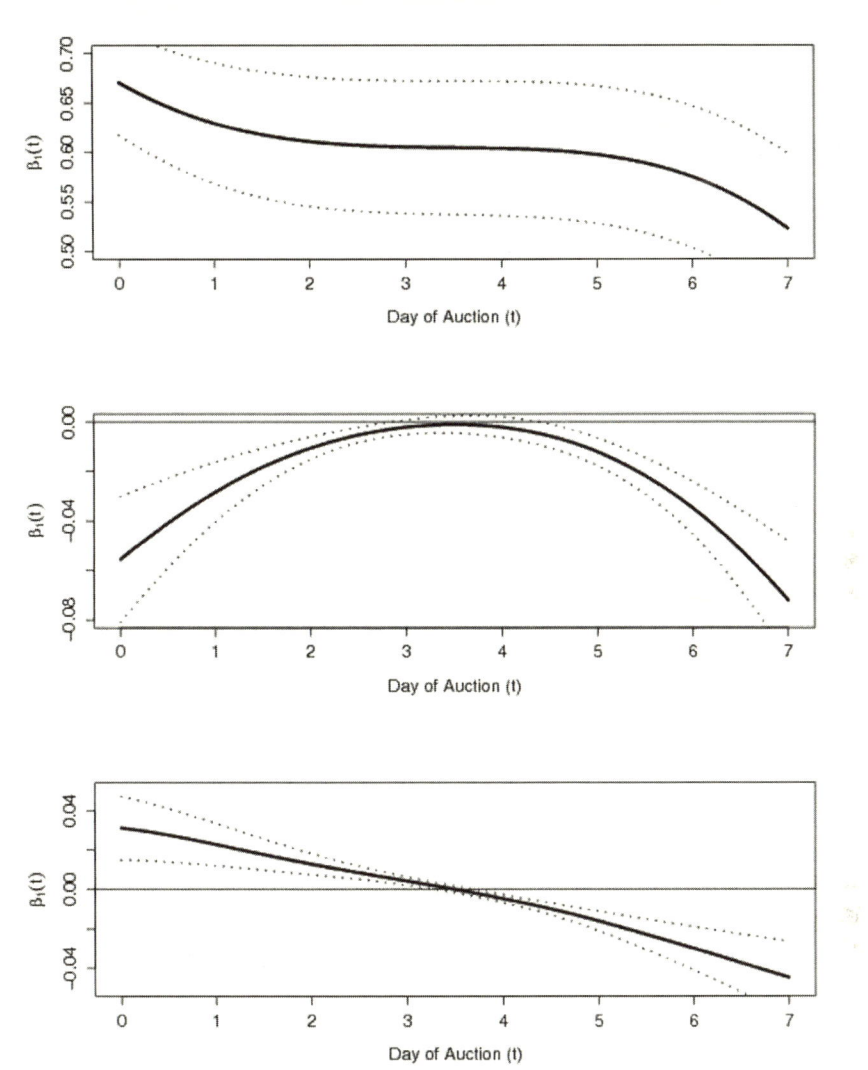

Note: The general model is of the form $y(t) = \beta_0(t) + \beta_1(t)$ for these figures. In the top panel, $y(t) = f(t)$ (*Price*), the middle panel uses $y(t) = f'(t)$ (the first derivative, *velocity*), and the bottom panel uses $y(t) = f''(t)$ (the second derivative, *acceleration*).

To learn about the effect of opening bid on the *dynamics* of the auction we regress the derivatives of the splines on *OpeningBid*. The middle graph in Figure 7.8 describes the influence of *OpeningBid* on the price velocity. Throughout the auction *OpeningBid* is (on average) negatively associated with the price velocity, and this relationship is statistically significant everywhere, except for a short period in the middle of the auction (between Days 3 and 4, the 95 percent confidence bounds for the parameter estimate include zero, indicating that the negative association is statistically insignificant). The negative relationship means that higher opening bids are associated with slower price increases. In addition to the sign, we see that the coefficient increases during the first third of the auction, then plateaus for a day or more, and finally decreases steeply toward the end of the auction, ending with the lowest value at the end of the auction. *This implies that during the last days of the auction higher opening bids are strongly associated with slowdown in the speed of price increase, whereas lower opening bids are associated with a speeding up of the price increase.* We also learn that the closing price has the strongest relationship with the opening bid among all bids in the auction. This explains why almost every study that looked at the impact of the opening bid on the final price, using a static regression model, found a statistically significant effect.

Finally, the bottom panel in Figure 7.8 describes yet another dimension of the price dynamics: the price acceleration. Here we see that the coefficient for the opening bid changes sign during the auction! The relationship between the opening price and price acceleration starts out positive and slowly decreases until it completely changes sign at the middle of the auction. It then continues to decrease, indicating an increasingly stronger negative relationship between the opening bid and the price acceleration. As in the velocity case, the strongest relationship with the opening bid is at the end of the auction. The interpretation of a positive relationship is that high opening prices are associated with price acceleration, whereas lower bids are associated with deceleration. During the start of the auction, it appears that higher opening prices drive the price up by accelerating the price increase. This changes during the second half of the auction, where the negative relationship indicates that high opening bids are associated with price deceleration, and low opening prices are associated with price acceleration. In other words, the *rate of change* in current price is most sensitive to the opening price during the start and end of the auction, but in opposite ways. This could also be attributed to the two clusters in the data, and therefore a regression that includes a dummy variable separating the two clusters would give a clearer picture.

To summarize the information from the three graphs, we can say that, in general, higher opening bids are associated with higher prices at any point during the auction, but this relationship weakens as the auction progresses. The dynamics of the relationship are such that high opening bids are associated with a slower increase in price compared with low opening bids, especially early in the auction and even more so toward the end of the auction. High and low opening bids also differ in the rates of change in price speed: The price increase process in auctions with high opening bids accelerates faster than in auctions with low opening bids during the first half of the auction, but slower during the second half.

If we think of this as a car race where each car (representing an auction) has a different head start (representing the opening bid), then cars with a large head start are generally ahead of cars with little head start at any point in the race, but they go slower. The head start cars accelerate faster during the first half of the race, but then accelerate slower during the second half.

This conveys a much richer picture of the forces and dynamics that are associated with the opening bid, compared with the ordinary static regression model. Some of the dynamics were captured by the cluster analysis, which pointed out the "early" and "late" activity clusters of auctions and their relationship to the opening bid. The regression helps to quantify these phenomena and can be used to test particular hypotheses of interest.

Further Functional Methods

Other popular functional methods that extend static analyses to functional data have been developed. One method that would be useful in the context of the price curve is functional principal components analysis (Ramsay and Silverman, 1997). The idea is to condense the time dimension across price curves in order to find times during the auction that explain most of the variability across auctions. Preliminary results suggest, as expected, that the first and last day in seven-day auctions contain most of the variation across price curves. Another method that can be useful for analyzing data from experiments on online auctions (e.g., Bapna, Goes, and Gupta, 2001; List and Lucking-Reiley, 2002; Rafaeli and Noy, 2002) is functional analysis of variance (ANOVA).

There are a variety of extensions to the analysis of functional data. Yu and Lambert (2000), for instance, develop a method to fit multivariate regression trees to functional data. In their approach, they consider a low-dimensional representation of the high-dimensional functional curves, either via the spline coefficients or the first several principal components of the smoothing spline. The authors then fit a standard multivariate regression tree to the low-dimensional data representation.

Approaches for nonnormal data have also been extended to the functional context. Ratcliffe, Heller, and Leader (2002) consider a model for binary responses that allows for the inclusion of functional covariates. Their approach is again based on a low dimension representation of the functional data that allows for an application of standard maximum likelihood methodology. A further interesting extension of FDA has been done by Ramsay and Ramsey (2002), using differential equations. The authors use functional data methodology to investigate the dynamics of the nondurable goods index. Most notably, they achieve this goal by developing and fitting differential equation models to a functional representation of the monthly production index for nondurable goods. Applying this methodology in the context of the price formation process in online auctions, we found that some types of auctions are indeed well captured by a second-order homogenous differential equation, while others do not; see Jank and Shmueli (2005) for details.

DISCUSSION

We have shown how functional data analysis is a useful statistical approach for modeling and analyzing online auction data. It meets the criteria of being able to address research questions of interest while maintaining most of the information contained in the raw data. Furthermore, it enables us to address questions about the dynamic aspect of the process and uncover such structures. In a sense, it generalizes analyses that are based on a snapshot of the data at a single time point. By treating an entire curve, such as the price over the entire auction, as the dependent variable, we can investigate not only the static closing prices but also their dynamics. We can also explore the curve separately in order to characterize it, and we can explore the effect of different factors on the curve.

As we pointed out above, a promising facet of functional data analysis is its relationship to differential equation models. In traditional auction theory many results are derived using differential equations. Our next step is to try to connect the two threads to see what relates or differentiates offline from online auction mechanisms using this approach. In this context we would like to be able to examine auctions in the broader context of the entire auction market. One step in this direction is to borrow the concept of "energy" from physics and to talk about "auction energy" and even "market energy." In common value auctions we can treat the common valuation of the item as the amount of potential energy that the auction has. This is a finite amount and at the start of the action is equally distributed over the auction duration. Within the market of auctions for such items, items that are of interest to buyers will "attract energy" from the market having a larger amount of initial energy. When an auction takes place, each placed bid "consumes energy" in proportion to its value or impact (higher bids consume more auction energy). Once a bid is placed, the remaining energy is "rebalanced" or reallocated so that it is again equally distributed across the remaining duration of the auction. Using the "energy" concept we can explain the results that we found regarding the relationship between the price formation and the opening bid. The opening bid, like any other bid, consumes auction energy. Therefore, a low opening bid consumes only a little of the auction energy, leaving more potential energy untouched compared with a high opening bid. Graphing the smoothed price curve over time (e.g., Figure 7.3) describes the "energy consumption meter" from the auction start to its end. The price velocity (e.g., Figure 7.4, top) describes the level of energy consumption at each point in the auction. This is where we would expect to see bouts of consumption when a high bid is placed. The price acceleration (e.g., Figure 7.4, bottom) reflects the changes in energy consumption throughout the auction. Further study of the concept of "auction energy" is needed in order to gain insights into the forces that drive the price evolution and other related processes.

The dynamic results are useful for various managerial applications. Currently eBay allows the seller in an auction to specify a *buy-it-now value*. This value is set before the auction start and does not change. Using the dynamic model for price dynamics throughout the auction, one could design a *dynamic buy-it-now* feature. The dynamic value would change to reflect the change in interest and willingness-to-pay as expressed by the price curve (Bapna et al., 2004).

Although our application is focused on online auction data, functional data analysis can be a valuable tool for modeling other Internet and e-commerce data. The online environment in many cases involves an ongoing process (such as user interaction or market change) that can be captured by a curve. In such cases the dynamics are central to design and decision making. One example of ongoing user interactions is online product ratings. Chevalier and Mayzlin (2003), who look at online book reviews, and Dellarocas, Awad, and Zhang (2004), who look at online movie ratings, both use ratings data to investigate word-of-mouth effects and their impact on sales. In particular, Chevalier and Mayzlin (2003) compare the number of book ratings, review lengths, and rating distributions of several books on Amazon vs. BN.com. Here the ratings are treated as static, in the sense that the rating evolution is not considered. Dellarocas, Awad, and Zhang (2004) compare ratings on the opening weekend of the movie to the second week and to later ratings and find interesting differences. However, their actual analyses are based on static versions of the ratings. In both applications it seems beneficial to capture the entire rating evolution. An FDA approach would treat the rating evolution or the cumulative number of ratings for a single event as a curve. Curves can then be compared and their dynamics explored and modeled.

Other examples where the online process evolution can contain insightful information and where the data are readily available are assessing Web site usability by *inspecting user browsing patterns* (e.g., the number of Web pages or clicks that a user goes through in order to complete an online transaction.) Another example is the *dynamics in newsgroups*, where we can track the number of new postings over the lifetime of a thread. A third type of process where dynamics are crucial to performance and design is *sales of time-sensitive goods*.[5] In the airline and hotel industries, for example, the prices of tickets or hotel rooms change over time as a function of demand and the deadline after which the goods are no longer valuable (e.g., when the flight leaves or the hotel fills up). In such cases, information about the dynamics can be integrated directly into the pricing to reflect the dynamic demand over time.

Finally, with the latest advances in software agent collection methods that will supply longitudinal or repeated auction data (Kauffman, March, and Wood, 2000), functional analysis will be especially useful because the collected data will be functional by nature. For example, the auction closing price for a certain item over time is no longer a single number, and can be described by a curve. We anticipate that FDA will play a major role in longitudinal analyses that will follow from such data.

APPENDIX 7.1 ESTIMATION OF THE SMOOTHING SPLINE

To describe the minimization of the penalized residual sum of squares in Equation 7.3, we define the $(L + p + 1)$ vector of spline basis functions

$$x(t) = (1, t, t^2, \ldots, t^p, [(t - \tau_1)_+]^p, \ldots, [(t - \tau_1)_+]^p) \qquad (A7.1-1)$$

and notice that we may write the spline in Equation A7.1–1 as $f(t) = x(t)\beta$, where $\beta = (\beta_0, \beta_1, \ldots \beta_p, \beta_{p1}, \ldots, \beta_{pL})'$ is the $(L + p + 1)$ parameter vector. The roughness penalty in Equation 7.2 can now be written as

$$PEN_m = \beta'D\beta, \qquad (A7.1-2)$$

where the symmetric positive semi-definite penalty matrix D is defined as

$$D = \int \{D^m x(t)\}' \{D^m x(t)\}\, dt. \qquad (A7.1-3)$$

We can now rewrite the penalized residual sum of squares in Equation 7.3 as

$$Q\beta_{,m} = \lambda\beta'D\beta + \Sigma_{i=1 \ldots n}\{y_i - x(t_i)\beta\}^2. \qquad (A7.1-4)$$

Let $y = (y_1, \ldots, y_n)'$ denote the vector of the prices and define the matrix of spline basis functions

$$X = \begin{pmatrix} x(t_1) \\ x(t_2) \\ \vdots \\ x(t_n) \end{pmatrix}. \qquad (A7.1-5)$$

Equation A7.1–4 can now be rewritten as

$$Q_{\lambda,m} = \lambda\beta'D\beta + (y - X\beta)'(y - X\beta). \qquad (A7.1-6)$$

Setting the gradient of the right-hand side of Equation A7.1–6 equal to zero and rearranging terms yields the estimating equations

$$(X'X + \lambda D)\beta = X'y. \qquad (A7.1-7)$$

Solving for β in Equation A7.1–7 gives the penalized spline estimator

$$\hat{\beta}_{ps} = (X'X + \lambda D)^{-1} X'y. \qquad (A7.1-8)$$

We note that the Hessian matrix of Equation A7.1–6 is

$$2(X'X + \lambda D). \qquad (A7.1-9)$$

Since the matrix $X'X$ is positive definite and λD is positive semi-definite, the Hessian matrix is positive definite and, hence, $\hat{\beta}_{ps}$ in Equation A7.1–8 indeed minimizes the penalized residual sum of squares in Equation 7.3.

APPENDIX 7.2. FUNCTIONAL K-MEDOIDS CLUSTERING ALGORITHM

For two vectors of coefficients $\hat{\beta}_i$ and $\hat{\beta}_{i'}$, let $d_{i,i'} = D(\hat{\beta}_i, \hat{\beta}_{i'})$ denote a measure of dissimilarity between them. A variety of dissimilarity measures exist. By far the most common measure is the Euclidian distance, $D(\hat{\beta}_i, \hat{\beta}_{i'}) = \| \hat{\beta}_i - \hat{\beta}_{i'} \|$. The K-medoids algorithm (e.g., Hastie, Tibshirani, and Friedman, 2001; Kaufman and Rousseeuw, 1987) is an iterative procedure whose goal is to find a partition of the set of all spline coefficients that minimizes the within-cluster dissimilarity

$$W_K = \sum_{k=1}^{K} \sum_{i \in I_k} d_{i,i'} \qquad (A7.2\text{–}1)$$

where I_k denotes the set of indices pertaining to the elements of the kth cluster, $k = \{1, \ldots, K\}$.

The K-medoids algorithm achieves this goal in iterative fashion, by alternating between two steps. In the first step, cluster centers are determined. That is, given a current data partition, one finds the observation in the kth cluster that minimizes the total distance to the other points in that cluster:

$$i_k^* = \arg \min_{i \in I_k} \sum_{i' \in I_k} d_{i,i'}. \qquad (A7.2\text{–}2)$$

Then, $c_k = \hat{\beta}_{i_k^*}$, $k = \{1, \ldots, K\}$, is the current estimate of the center of cluster k. The second step reassigns observations to their nearest cluster. That is, given a current set of cluster centers $\{c_1, \ldots, c_K\}$, one finds a new partition by assigning $\hat{\beta}_i$ to the cluster k for which

$$k = \arg \min_{1 \leq k \leq K} D(\hat{\beta}_i, c_k). \qquad (A7.2\text{–}3)$$

These two steps are repeated until the assignments do not change any further.

APPENDIX 7.3 FUNCTIONAL REGRESSION FORMULATION

We next let the following

$$Y(t) = \begin{pmatrix} y_1(t) \\ y_2(t) \\ \vdots \\ y_n(t) \end{pmatrix} \qquad (A7.3\text{–}1)$$

be a $n \times 1$ vector of curves that we wish to model. If we wish to model the position of the price, for instance, then these curves could be given by the smoothing splines themselves, $y_i(t) = f_i(t)$. On the other hand, if the goal is to find a suitable model for the velocity, then we can put $y_i(t) = f_i'(t)$. We define a q vector of parameter curves $\beta(t)$ as

$$\beta(t) = \begin{pmatrix} \beta_1(t) \\ \beta_2(t) \\ \vdots \\ \beta_n(t) \end{pmatrix} \quad (A7.3\text{--}2)$$

If Z denotes a suitable (and known) $n \times q$ design matrix, then the functional linear model attempts to find $\beta(t)$ such that the expected value of $Y(t)$ is $Z\beta(t)$ for each value of t.

The above problem can be written in a way very similar to the least squares minimization objective of ordinary regression. Let

$$ISSE(\beta) = \int \|Y(t) - Z\beta(t)\|^2 \, dt \quad (A7.3\text{--}3)$$

denote the integrated residual sum of squares, where $\|.\|$ denotes the Euclidian norm. The goal is to find $\beta(t)$ that minimizes *ISSE*. Since there is no particular restriction on the way in which $\beta(t)$ varies as a function of t, one can minimize *ISSE* by minimizing

$$\|Y(t) - Z\beta(t)\| \quad (A7.3\text{--}4)$$

individually for each t (Ramsay and Ramsey, 1997). In particular, the most straightforward method of finding an estimate $\hat{\beta}(t)$ is to find $\hat{\beta}(t_j)$ that minimizes Equation A7.3–4 for a suitable grid of values $t_1, t_2, \ldots$, and then to interpolate these values.

ACKNOWLEDGMENT

This research was partially funded by NSF Grant DMI-0205489.

NOTES

1. For recent advances and challenges in software agents development, see Kauffman, March, and Wood (2000).
2. For specialized visualizations for online auction data, see Shmueli and Jank (2005).
3. A slight enhancement is to transform the proxy bids, which can be nonmonotone, to the "current price" values that form a monotonically increasing step function. See Jank and Shmueli (2005) for further details.
4. In many cases we approximate the curves with a linear combination of *B*-splines. This permits us to apply linear operators (e.g., computing the mean, or fitting a linear regression model) directly to the *B*-spline coefficients, rather than to a grid of points. This is more computationally efficient.
5. Based on private communication with Dr. Michael Ball, University of Maryland.

REFERENCES

Bajari, P. and Hortacsu, A. 2002. Cyberspace auctions and pricing issues: A review of empirical findings. Working paper no. 02–005 (2002). Economics Department, Stanford University, Stanford, CA.
———. 2003. Winner's curse, reserve prices and endogenous entry: Empirical insights from eBay. *RAND Journal of Economics,* 34 , 2, 329–355.
———. 2004. Economic insights from Internet auctions. *Journal of Economic Literature,* 42, 2, 457–486.
Bapna, R.; Goes, P.; and Gupta, A. 2001. Comparative analysis of multi-item auctions: Evidence from the laboratory. *Decision Support Systems,* 32, 135–153.

Bapna, R.; Goes, P.; Gupta, A.; and Karuga, G. 2004. Predicting bidders' willingness-to-pay in online multi-unit ascending auctions: Analytical and empirical insights. Working paper. School of Business, University of Connecticut, Storrs.

Besse, P.C.; Cardot, H.; and Stephenson, D.B. 2000. Autoregressive forecasting of some functional climatic variations. *Scandinavian Journal of Statistics,* 27, 4, 673–687.

Chevalier, J.A. and Mayzlin, D. 2003. The effect of word of mouth on sales: Online book reviews. Working papers nos. ES-28 and MK-15. . School of Management, Yale University, New Haven, CT.

Dellarocas, C.N.; Awad, N.; and Zhang, X. 2004. Using online reviews as a proxy of word-of-mouth for motion picture revenue forecasting. Working paper. Sloan School of Management, MIT, Cambridge, MA.

Faraway, J.J. 1997. Regression analysis for a functional response. *Technometrics,* 39, 254–261.

Hastie, T.; Tibshirani, R.; and Friedman, J. 2001. *The Elements of Statistical Learning.* New York: Springer-Verlag.

Jank, W. and Shmueli, G. 2005. Profiling price dynamics in online auctions using curve clustering. Working paper. Smith School of Business, University of Maryland, College Park.

Kaufman, L. and Rousseeuw, P.J. 1987. Clustering by means of medoids. In Y. Dodge, ed., *Statistical Data Analysis Based on the L1-norm and Related Methods.* New York: Birkhauser, 405–416.

Kauffman, R.J.; March, S.T.; and Wood, C.A. 2000. Design principles for long-lived Internet agents. *International Journal of Intelligent Systems in Accounting, Finance, and Management,* 9, 4, 217–236.

Krishna, V. 2002. *Auction Theory.* San Diego, CA: Academic Press.

List, J.A. and Lucking-Reiley, D. 2002. Bidding behavior and decision costs in field experiments. *Economic Inquiry,* 40, 44, 611–619.

Lucking-Reiley, D. 2000. Auctions on the Internet: What's being auctioned and how? *Journal of Industrial Economics,* 48, 3, 227–252.

Ogden, R.T.; Miller, C.E.; Takezawa, K.; and Ninomiya, S. 2002. Functional regression in crop lodging assessment with digital images. *Journal of Agricultural, Biological, and Environmental Statistics,* 7, 3, 389–402.

Pfeiffer, R.M.; Bura, E.; Smith, A.; and Rutter, J.L. 2002. Two approaches to mutation detection based on functional data. *Statistics in Medicine,* 21, 22, 3447–3464.

R—The R Project for Statistical Computing. 2007. Department of Statistics and Mathematics, WU Wein, Vienna. Available at www.r-project.org/index.html (accessed October 29, 2006).

Rafaeli, S. and Noy, A. 2002. Online auctions, messaging, communications and social facilitation: A simulation and experimental evidence. *Journal of Information Systems,* 11, 3, 196–207.

Ramsay, J.O. and Ramsey, J.B. 2002. Functional data analysis of the dynamics of the monthly index of nondurable goods production, *Journal of Econometrics,* 107, 1–2, 327–344.

Ramsay, J.O. and Silverman, B.W. 1997. *Functional Data Analysis.* New York: Springer-Verlag.

———. 2002. *Applied Functional Data Analysis: Methods and Case Studies.* New York: Springer-Verlag, 2002.

Ratcliffe, S.J.; Heller, G.Z.; and Leader, L.R. 2002. Functional data analysis with application to periodically stimulated foetal heart rate data. II: Functional logistic regression. *Statistics in Medicine,* 21, 8, 1115–1127.

Rossi, N.; Wang, X.; and Ramsay, J.O. 2002. Nonparametric item response function estimates with the EM algorithm, *Journal of Educational and Behavioral Statistics,* 27, 3, 291–317.

Roth, A.E. and Ockenfels, A. 2000. Last-minute bidding and the rules for ending second-price auctions: Theory and evidence from a natural experiment on the Internet. Working paper no. 7729, National Bureau of Economic Research, Cambridge, MA.

Shmueli, G. and Jank, W. 2005. Visualizing online auctions. *Journal of Computational and Graphical Statistics,* 14, 2, 299–319.

Shmueli, G.; Russo, R.P.; and Jank, W. 2004. Modeling bid arrivals in online auctions. Working paper, Smith School of Business, University of Maryland, College Park.

Simonoff, J.S. 1996. *Smoothing Methods in Statistics.* New York: Springer-Verlag.

Wilcox, R.T. 2000. Experts and amateurs: The role of experience in Internet auctions. *Marketing Letters,* 11, 4, 363–374.

Yu, Y. and Lambert, D. 2000. Fitting trees to functional data, with an application to time of day patterns. *Journal of Computational and Graphical Statistics,* 8, 4, 749–762.

CHAPTER 8

EMPIRICAL DESIGN OF INCENTIVE MECHANISMS IN GROUP-BUYING AUCTIONS

HER-SEN DOONG, ROBERT J. KAUFFMAN,
HSIANGCHU LAI, AND YA-TING ZHUANG

Abstract: Experimental methodologies offer a unique lens through which to examine the dynamics of bidding behavior and consumer perceptions of the efficacy of mechanism design in group-buying auctions. Group-buying auctions permit participating consumers to leverage their numbers to achieve discounted prices for purchase. We examine three incentive mechanisms for group-buying with the goal of understanding which provide the greatest perceived value for participants, especially how the incentive mechanisms impact the participants' planned behavior and perceived value. They include time-based incentives, quantity-based incentives, and sequence-based incentives. We also examine the role of planned order sizes versus final order sizes across the models. To obtain our results, we developed an experimental test bed that permits group-buying supply procurement buyers to participate in specially developed auctions that implement the different incentive mechanisms. The empirical methods that we demonstrate suggest the efficacy of incremental refinements in the experimental design as a means for developing deeper insights into group-buying incentive mechanism design. We conclude with a discussion of the experimental methods as a means for studying a variety of mechanism design issues in the context of a larger family of group-buying mechanisms.

Keywords: Advanced Empirical Methods, Auction Markets, Consumer Participation, Experimental Methods, Group-Buying Auctions, Incentive Mechanisms, Price Curve Effects, Procurement

INTRODUCTION

Since the late 1990s, group-buying auctions have been the subject of experimentation and real-world application as one of the innovative business models associated with business-to-consumer (B2C) electronic commerce (Kauffman and Walden, 2001). These are among a number of new electronic intermediaries that have been predicted by savvy observers of the business landscape (O'Hara, 1997; Shapiro and Varian, 1999; Spulber, 1996, 1999), as well as technologists who have seen new ways to leverage technology in emerging marketplaces (Bakos and Kemerer, 1992; Smith, Bailey, and Brynjolfsson, 1999; Weber, 1998). A number of firms, including the "darlings" of group-buying auctions during the dot-com years, Mobshop.com and Mercata.com, and others have employed a variety of group-buying business models, and have explored the benefits that consumers are likely to obtain from participating in discount shopping clubs (e.g., Clark, 2001; Cook, 2001; and many others).[1] A *group-buying auction* involves a dynamic pricing mechanism that encourages shoppers to aggregate the power of their purchase activities (Andrews, 1999, 2000). This permits them to obtain lower prices than they would be able to obtain on their own. The rationale behind such quantity discount models is based on the economic advantage for the seller gained from customers who order larger quantities of products, resulting in greater profits with lower prices (Kotler, 1988; Sadrian and Yoon, 1994).

Unfortunately, however, companies with group-buying business models were not so successful in achieving effective or sustainable business models, as Kauffman and Wang (2002) explain in their comprehensive assessment of group-buying auction performance.

A Definition of an Internet-Based Group-Buying Auction

Group-buying is referred to as group-shopping, power-shopping, customer–seller coalitions, and co-buying, depending on where you read. Group-buying on the Internet enables consumers to obtain lower prices, as more people indicate a willingness to buy from the Internet-based seller (Lai, Doong, and Yang, 2006). There are two key aspects of group-buying auctions: they have a *fixed time period to completion* of a given auction, and there is a *set of prices* that are achieved only when enough consumers participate. We define *group-buying on the Internet* as a computer-based mercantile exchange mechanism that allows consumers to take advantage of volume discounts by shopping together, possibly coordinated by technological capabilities that support many new approaches to price curve specification and participation coalition formation (Kauffman and Wang, 2001). Group-buying auctions do not offer quantity discounts for individual customers' orders, but on the total of all customer orders (Anand and Aron, 2003). They contrast with a *Dutch auction* or *descending price auction,* which involves a mechanism in which the price begins high, and then falls until an auction participant indicates a willingness to accept the price. Another contrasting variant of this kind of auction that should not be confused with a group-buying auction is called a *multiunit English ascending auction,* which involves the sale of identical auction items to individual high price bidders.[2]

Lai (2002) proposed a number of generic group-buying models based on five different key dimensions: the initiator, the extent of product variety, the number of sellers, the size of the collective buying-power base, and the conditionality of the sales offers. Her classification suggests that there are different ways to interpret the meaning of the word "group" in this context. For instance, a *group* can be the total number of similar products that are being sold (e.g., they could all be Honda Accord EX cars, or different models such as the EX and LX), or it can be the number of similar or different products from the same seller (e.g., based on the monetary value rather than the number of products). A group can also be based on the bundles of different sets of products (e.g., bundled in such a way that individual consumers combine forces to pay for portions of the bundle that suit their interests), and so on.

In addition, group-buying can be initiated by either the consumer or the seller. So it is possible that there will be consumers who have similar intentions to buy a specific product, and need a means to do that. Another possibility is that one consumer wishes to bargain with the seller first, and then recruit other consumers to participate in group purchase. Still another possibility—and one that is much more likely to occur in reality—is that a specific buyer may act in the role of a group-buying intermediary, where the intention is to buy in quantity with the idea of reselling to others, using the same kind of group-buying approach that we have described. Another variant occurs when an intermediary represents the interests of buyers to create buying power and achieve the kinds of group discounts that are associated with shopping clubs. This role can be taken on by a *demand aggregation agent,* who never seeks to acquire or resell products.

According to Tsvetovat et al. (2000), most group-bargaining coalition protocols can be divided into two classes, *pre-negotiation* and *post-negotiation*, based on the order in which negotiation and coalition formation happen. This applies directly to the formation of group-buying auction coalitions. When coalitions are pre-negotiated, the leader will negotiate a deal with one or more suppliers using an estimated coalition size or order volume, and then advertise the creation of the coalition and wait for other members to join. It is also possible to create the group first, based on some admission criteria. Then, a designated group leader will negotiate with suppliers, and offer the resulting deal to the group. This leads us to a discussion of demand aggregation.

A Sampler of Demand Aggregation and Group-Buying Approaches on the Internet

Some of the well-known names of firms in this sector on the Internet at one time included Mercata.com, Mobshop.com, Etrana.com, CoShopper.com, C-Tribe.com, DemandLine.com, LetsBuyIt.com, OnlineChoice.com, PointSpeed.com, SHOP2gether, VolumeBuy.com, and Zwirl.com. Kauffman and Wang (2002) pointed out a number of problems with the business models underlying many of these Web sites, including the inability of consumers to engage in impulse shopping, the lack of guarantees to the consumer that the group-buying auction had previously acquired the auctioned goods, inconsistencies with delivery and fulfillment, and alternative channel "everyday low prices" for similar goods. A final issue, which we appreciate better from our current research and other related work, is the extent to which group-buying auctions provide basic communication between buyers and sellers around price and demand. They also have the capacity to more effectively support interbidder communication and coordination. For example, in Taiwan a popular means of recruiting group-buying participants by sellers and for consumers to communicate among themselves is through bulletin board systems, especially the popular "Ptt BBS" (批踢踢 in Chinese, www.ptt.cc/index.html), where over 300 posts per day pertain to group-buying.[3]

Since the fall of the group-buying dot-com firms, the focus has largely shifted to demand aggregation in the business-to-business (B2B) context. *Demand aggregation* is most often used to indicate the use of online collaboration approaches for the purposes of pooled buying across multiple companies with similar procurement needs. An example is the WorldWide Retail Exchange (WWRE) (www.worldwideretailexchange.org), which offers services that permit live negotiations in support of demand aggregation for corporate supply procurement; see Figure 8.1. Another similar business model is at work with PetroSilicon.com (www.petrosilicon.com), which now supports online demand aggregation for various crude oil and petroleum products.

In spite of the concerns that have been expressed about the efficacy of B2C group-buying auction business models, there nevertheless persists significant interest among entrepreneurs in many countries around the world, including China, India, the Netherlands, Taiwan, the United Kingdom, the United States, and elsewhere. Netherlands-based 52MarketPlace.com (www.52Marketplace.com) created the Open Source Auction Network (OSAN) in mid-2005, with the intent of bringing together more auction-based suppliers with larger groups of consumers. In 2005, the company's Web site commented: ". . . customers may post free reverse auctions by completing a short online form that is submitted to the OSAN database. The system then scours [the OSAN database] looking for buyers who want the same products. As matches are found, the system forms buyer groups, enabling sellers to submit their best price quote based on the total number of consumers. The results: Discounts for buyers and more sales for sellers a happy ending for both sides."

Another example in the United States is a well-known name in group-buying and consumer demand aggregation, OnlineChoice (www.onlinechoice.com), which provides a platform for

Figure 8.1 **Demand Aggregation at the WorldWide Retail Exchange** (WWRE)

WWRE Demand Aggregation LIVE!

Demand Aggregation Overview

Demand Aggregation is an online collaborative tool that allows multiple buyers to aggregate their sourcing needs. This collaboration can help buyers to standardize their items and terms, rationalize their supplier base, and lower their costs per item through increased volume leverage. These aggregated demand pools can be used as the input to future sourcing activities whether conducting an auction, issuing an RFI, RFQ, or RFP, or even the occasional spot buy. Demand Aggregation can also be leveraged to collect non-sourcing data from different divisions, distribution centers or stores. See below for examples.

Demand Aggregation can be used internally within a member company as well as externally between member companies.

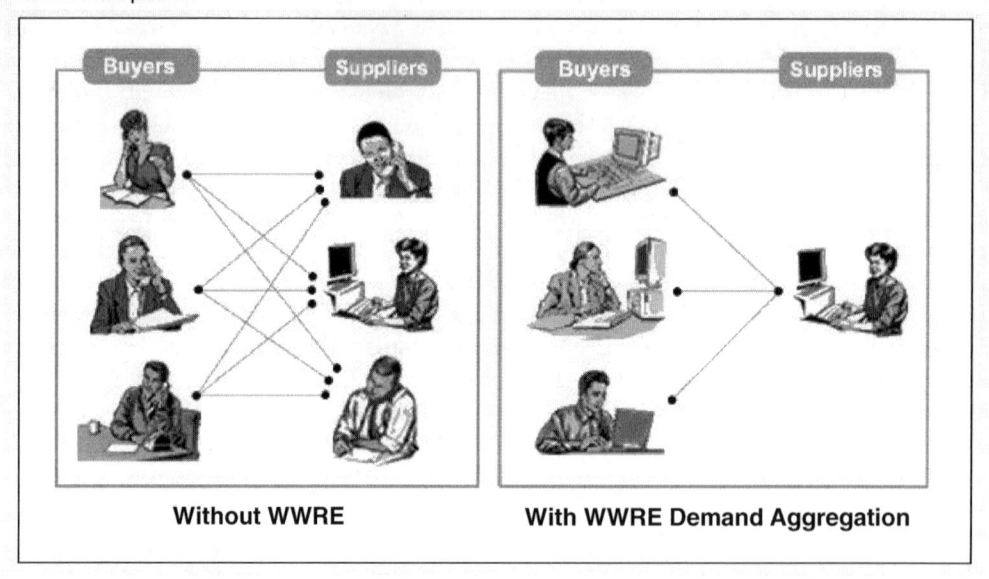

Without WWRE   **With WWRE Demand Aggregation**

Source: www.worldwideretailexchange.org/cs/en_US/exchange/wr3500_info_da.html (accessed March 8, 2006).

group-buying for telephone long distance services, home heating services, prescriptions for pharmaceuticals, various kinds of personal insurance, and other services; see Figure 8.2.

This Web site is not a group-buying auction site, but rather a pooled-buying subscription service, in which individuals can register to participate in "buying pools" for various kinds of goods and services. OnlineChoice then presents information about the extent of participation in various buying pools to encourage suppliers to offer discount prices. The business model works as a coordination mechanism that provides occasional broadcasts about buying-pool member opportunities to buy when new suppliers' offers become available.

Another well-known name in group-buying is LetsBuyIt.com, which was founded in 1999 in Sweden (www.letsbuyit.com). The company had business model and financial difficulties in the first half of the 2000s, but has since come back to the market with greater breadth and flexibility in its approach to Internet-based selling, though it is still in search of an effective business model. LetsBuyIt.com's current business model includes a "shopping centre" for everyday low prices, and

Figure 8.2 **Group-Buying via "Buying Pools" at OnlineChoice**

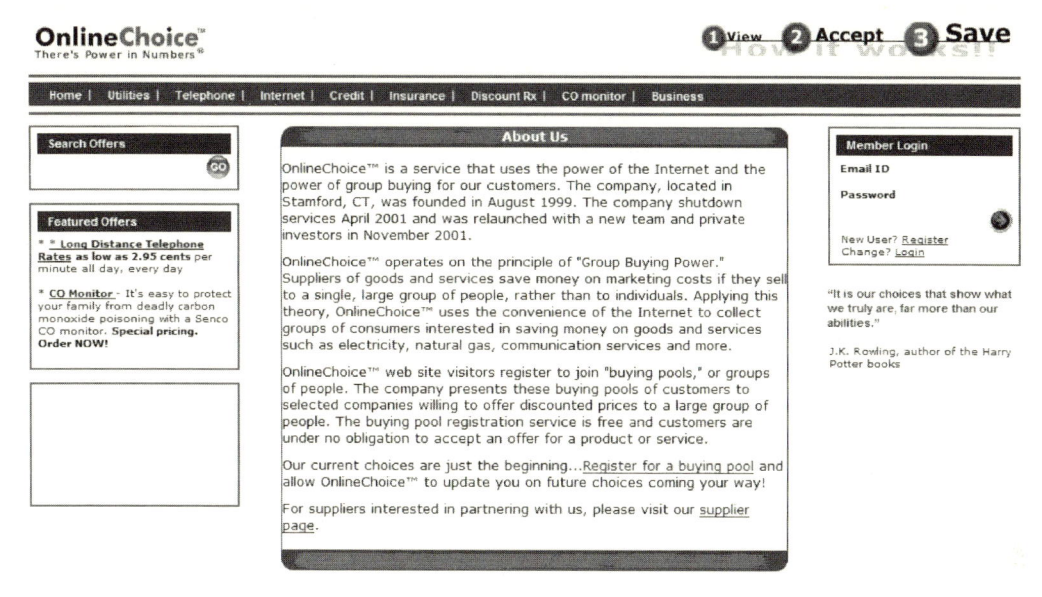

Source: www.onlinechoice.com/Home/Body/AboutUS.asp (accessed May 21, 2007).

an "outlet shop" that is outsourced to another Swedish provider, Priskrig, which offers competitive prices. Still another option for consumers is to participate in "co-buying," LetsBuyIt.com's term for group-buying. Consumers have an opportunity to select from among three different group-buying purchase price choices: the *current price* (a buy-it-now option), the *closing price* (when the co-buying auction closes), and the *best price* (which is the lowest stated price in the co-buying auction); see Figure 8.3.

Interestingly, the current approach that the firm appears to be taking is to offer a relatively limited number of co-buying opportunities. (For example, there were three different products on the day that we investigated the Web site.) However, the selected products appear to be ones that are likely to be highly popular, and thus will draw many interested bidders—in other words, probably the products that LetsBuyIt.com is selling. These seem to be products with homogeneous attributes that act like commodities and have the greatest liquidity. Another indication of this is that the price curves that the company has set for price improvement by bidding volume are relatively flat after the first price drop. For example, an Apple 60GB Photo iPod is posted with a £300.00 list price on LetsBuyIt.com's co-buying Web site.

The price curve for group-buying (with roughly a one-week duration to auction close) is £229.99 for 1 to 50 consumers, £223.99 for 51 to 150 consumers, £223.00 for 151–300 consumers, and finally £222.00 for 301–500 consumers. Such a flat price curve suggests that the site is going to attract people who will check to see if it is in their interest to make a bid, rather than to encourage others to attract friends and relatives to participate in co-buying. The flatness of the price curve offers is the seller's choice—in this case LetsBuyIt.com—and provides little in the way of price-drop incentive. The relatively flat curve may suggest the popularity of the sale item that is being offered, or it may reflect the fact that the seller is experimenting to determine price elasticity of demand with its potential consumers. We have also observed similar multitiered price curves in group-buying auction designs among American group-buying auction market providers.[4]

Figure 8.3 **The Co-Buying Market Mechanism at LetsBuyIt.com in 2006**

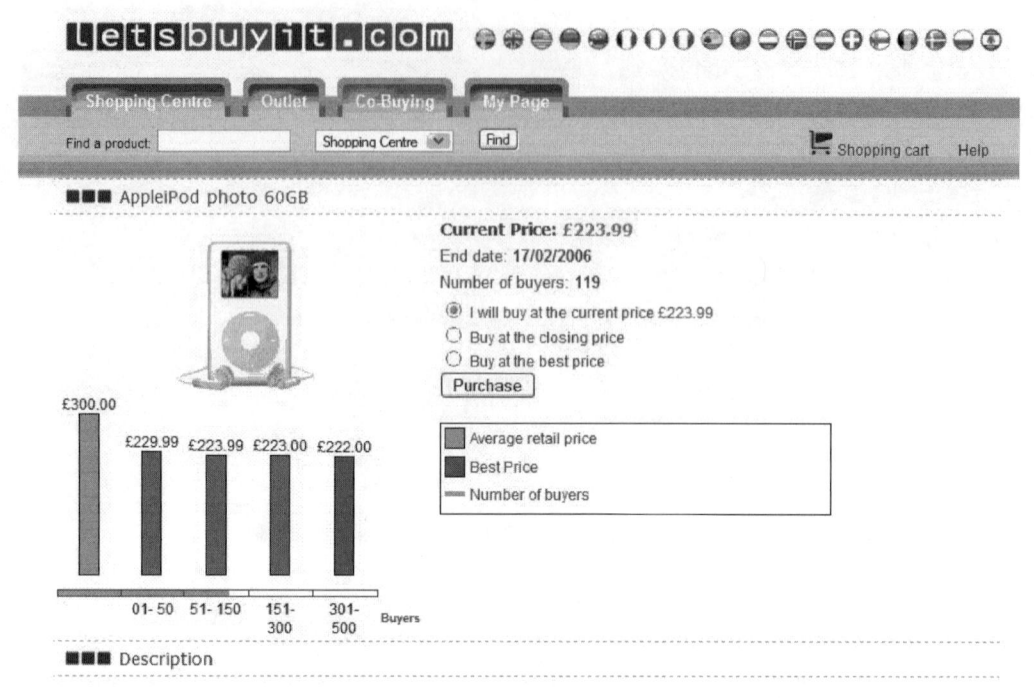

Source: www.letsbuyit.com/outlet_product~cobuyproduct_200-category_9.html (accessed February 13, 2006).

We believe that there is an opportunity to create novel methodological interest with new research approaches that can deepen our understanding of the group-buying auction mechanism. To our knowledge, few prior studies in the literature have attempted to experiment with group-buying auctions. Instead, most of the work is analytical modeling-based or uses secondary data obtained from group-buying Web sites. We also have not seen research in this area of study that involves the use of multiple comparative experimental treatments—our chosen approach in this research—that probe the inner workings of group-buying auction participation incentives.

The research approach that we will demonstrate shows that our approach—which emphasizes the modification of incentives in a test-and-retest manner—has the capacity to provide relatively fine-grained insights about the efficacy of the different kinds of incentives in group-buying auctions.[5] In addition, because our experiments can be carried out in a simulated, but relatively realistic Web setting with people who have some knowledge of the underlying purchase decisions (i.e., laser printer purchases in corporate procurement), there is a greater likelihood that we will be able to capture fairly realistic buyer purchase decision-making behavior. As this chapter progresses, we will further develop the argument that this is especially applicable to the study of a variety of mechanism design issues. They go beyond group-buying and include: various kinds of combinatorial and auction participation incentive mechanisms; pricing experiments with live customers in different market segments, to understand price elasticity and consumer sensitivity to price changes; and other kinds of procurement experiments with different information-sharing treatments in supply chain management. We also demonstrate the use of a range of *post hoc* mean difference tests, to provide comparative information on the results. This permits us to be clearer with respect to the appropriate degree of inference that can be drawn about the main results that we obtained.

In the next section, we will provide additional background on group-buying auction market mechanisms. In the third section, we explore how three different incentive mechanisms for group-buying auctions affect the participants' behavior. In the fourth section, we translate the theoretical findings from the prior literature into testable hypotheses concerning the performance of the different incentive mechanisms relative to a simpler base case. The fifth section discusses the details of our experimental design. The sixth section presents the results of our experimental analysis. We finish by tying the findings together to provide senior managers of group-buying auctions with actionable recommendations for improving their mechanism designs. The chapter concludes with a final section that provides an evaluative discussion of the power of experimental methods in the group-buying auction design context, as well as some of its limitations.

WHAT WE KNOW ABOUT HOW GROUP-BUYING WORKS

Academic research and entrepreneurial efforts with respect to group-buying have begun to turn to the issue of technological support for information sharing, group formation, bidding coordination, and other approaches that address some of the incomplete aspects of the group-buying auction mechanism. They emphasize the consideration of different mechanism design elements. Of critical interest is the development of appropriate incentive mechanisms to ensure that consumers are encouraged to demonstrate the appropriate kinds of participation and rational bidding behavior so that group-buying will work well.

Background

Normally, the value of a product depends on the subjective judgment of each consumer, and the consumer's inclination to purchase is influenced by the price level for the item. Bitran and Mondschein (1997) point out that although higher prices result in fewer consumer purchases (due to demand curve considerations), lowering the price may not increase the total profit to the seller even though there will be more consumers purchasing. As a result, designing an appropriate pricing scheme is critical to maximizing profits from the seller's perspective.

Kauffman and Wang (2002) found evidence for positive *participation externality effects* and an *expected price-drop effect* in group-buying on the Internet.[6] The positive participation externality effect indicates that the number of existing orders has a significant and positive effect on the number of new orders placed thereafter. The expected price-drop effect comes into play when the total amount of existing orders is approaching the quantity level that will invoke the next lowest price tier; the number of new orders will increase more quickly in this period. On the other hand, if the price is not expected to fall soon, fewer new orders will be placed.

As a result, determining how to encourage more orders, leading to an increase in the number of total orders, is an important tactical consideration for both sellers and group-buying auction intermediaries. Tsvetovat et al. (2000) believe that reducing purchase price and increasing utility are key incentives for customers to organize themselves to form group-buying coalitions. As a result, we believe that better performance will be obtained by using group-buying models with appropriate incentive mechanisms that encourage consumers to join and take advantage of the positive participation externality effect.

Recent research by Chen et al. (2006) proposed technology-based coordination of bidding ring formation, so that potential group-buying auction consumers are able to leverage their will to cooperate to achieve better outcomes than ones that are not coordinated. The authors show that group-buying auction mechanisms with support for cooperative bidding have the potential to dominate both group-buying without coordination and the more standard fixed-price purchase mechanisms that most physical stores and Internet-based sellers use.

Methods for Studying Group-Buying Mechanism Design

To date, a number of methods have been used to study group-buying auctions. They include case study methods, empirical analysis of group-buying auction data, analytical models, and experimental research approaches. Each of these methods offers different strengths for analysis.

The benefit of *case study* approaches in this context is to identify the effects of group-buying mechanism design decisions in the context of real-world applications, where senior managers are able to take stock of the strategy choices they make in pursuit of business profits. *Empirical analysis* offers somewhat different advantages. Chief among them is that they offer a means to discover regularities and patterns associated with consumer behavior in the presence of different design choices for group-buying auctions. It also permits the testing of hypotheses that represent theoretical assertions of how group-buying ought to work, and whether they square with observations that are made in the real world. In addition, analytical models offer other advantages. The primary advantage is the analyst's ability to focus on specific aspects of the group-buying auction process, by constructing models that focus on one aspect or another (e.g., the design of the price curve, or the means for coordinating bids among consumers).

Experimentation is the primary method used to examine a specific phenomenon or a certain cause-and-effect relationship more precisely (Carnevale and De Dreu, 2005; McGraw, 1993; Wilkenfeld, 2004). This is also the focus of our current efforts with group-buying auction research. *Controlled experiments,* involving the *random assignment of experimental subjects* to different *treatment groups* and *control groups,* allow researchers to isolate the effects of a crucial independent variable by controlling other extraneous factors, and then looking at the effects of key variables (Campbell and Stanley, 1963). We believe that experimental methods are especially useful for the purpose of studying issues involving group-buying auction mechanism design.

Based on the three criteria proposed by Runkel and McGrath (1972)—realism, generality, and precision—we can achieve higher precision with the observation of universal behavior. However, this is likely to come at the cost of realism. This is because the degree of precision in research design and experimental controls that we can implement for the study of specific aspects of the group-buying auction process will enable us to evaluate the efficacy of the current state of knowledge in this area. Some may view experimental designs for group-buying and the technical test beds that implement them to be contrived and not as realistic as real-world, for-profit group-buying auction Web sites. Nevertheless, experimental approaches to auction and lottery design permit the researcher to work toward understanding issues that arise with this electronic auction business model in a much more precise manner (Shavit, Sonsino, and Benzion, 2001). Experimental methods further provide the researcher with the capability to focus on just one element in group-buying auction design (e.g., price curve design or bidding ring formation), while holding the others fixed. This permits the researcher to focus on the variables or design elements of interest, for example, how well a given kind of price curve performs, or how consumers seem to respond to different dimensions of possible purchase incentives that a group-buying auction operator is able to offer.

Another concern is the possibility of biased adoption and use by customers who act as subjects in nonexperimental group-buying auction settings. Experimental methods permit some randomization of auction participants and the experimental conditions that they face, thus creating the basis for rich comparative analysis of their behavior as group-buying auction participants. Another possible weakness involves the possibility of inappropriate learning on the part of experimental subjects when an experiment is repeated. When an experiment is repeated, past participants may come to the experimental group-buying auction with a certain amount of knowledge about the process and expectations about the final price, so it is important to ensure that problems of this nature do not negatively impact the experimental results. (This has no real bearing on our research, since the experiments were the first of a kind.)

In spite of the limitations, we see a number of unique advantages associated with the application of experimental methods in the group-buying auction context. First, the questions that we have related to group-buying auction mechanisms are primarily driven by theory. Experimental methods will thus enable us to articulate some more definitive knowledge about how to make group-buying auctions work that is based on theory. Second, today there is not widespread venture capital interest in the marketplace to try out a range of group-buying auction mechanism design ideas that appear to have some theoretical merit. Experimental research designs will yield useful information without the corresponding high costs of trying out possibly unworkable market mechanisms. Third, we can build from simplicity of design toward greater complexity, by selectively introducing different group-buying auction design features. The utility of the experimental method in this context is to provide a means to test for improvements in the mechanism. Finally, we can use this approach to test variations of the same idea—in our case, the role of incentive mechanisms for group-buying.

Following the boom of e-commerce, many researchers conducted experimental research via the Internet (e.g., Anderhub, Müller, and Schmidt, 2001; Birnbaum, 2004; Shavit, Sonsino, and Benzion, 2001). We can obtain additional power by reflecting real-world aspects of group-buying auctions in our experimental approach. Group-buying auctions naturally occur in the online environments of the Internet. We can match this aspect exactly, by building an experimental test bed that also is implemented on the Internet and that is accessed by typical Internet users.

Compared with traditional laboratory experiments that provide significant capabilities for precision testing auction-related phenomena (e.g., Ferejohn, Forsythe, and Noll, 1979; Friedman and Sunder, 1994; Grether, Isaac, and Plott, 1981; Keppel, 1991), there are other advantages that make implementing experiments on the Internet attractive. They include larger, more heterogeneous subject pools with non–college-age participants, standardized procedures and experimental efficiency, experimenter and subject cross-anonymity, and easier replication (Anderhub, Müller, and Schmidt, 2001; Birnbaum, 2004). Furthermore, data can be collected from questionnaires as well as from the detailed online click-stream behavior of the experimental subjects. However, there are also some limitations, such as higher subject dropout rates, different dropout rates across groups, sampling and response bias, and experimenter bias (Anderhub, Müller, and Schmidt, 2001; Birnbaum, 2004).

Based on the three criteria proposed by Runkel and McGrath (1972)—realism, generality, and precision—conducting experiments over the Internet on group-buying issues seems to be an appropriate choice. Group-buying experiments on the Internet come close to reality because the group-buying business model was designed as an online business model. However, in group-buying, the participants will not buy until an item's price falls below their expected price (or reservation price). Off the Internet, it typically is not possible to have a laboratory experiment that goes for several days, but it is not a problem to do this on the Internet. Second, we can also use an experimental scenario involving business purchases, which makes the setting come even closer to the real world, further improving the realism and generality. In addition, because we wish to focus on how incentive mechanisms affect the group-buying behavior, we can design an Internet experiment to control for other differences so that the incentive mechanism is the only difference among the different group-buying models that are tested. Finally, we can effectively provide instructions to the experimental subjects on a Web page, so the precision of the experiment will not be adversely impacted.

INCENTIVE MECHANISM DESIGN FOR GROUP-BUYING AUCTIONS

The purpose of this study is to explore whether group-buying auction incentive mechanisms can effectively encourage participants to order earlier or order more, leading to *positive participation network externalities* that ultimately increase sales for the seller or auctioneer and lower price for the consumer. The consumers' perceptions of network externalities typically come from their access to information on existing orders, so they are able to gauge market interest in participating in the group-buying auction. Without access to information on existing orders, it would not be possible for consumers to have a sense of what level the final price will reach. From the above discussion, the reader should see that a group-buying auction's performance ultimately is a concern for the seller or group-buying auction intermediary, as well as for the consumer, since the primary outcome is the product price that must be paid.

We next summarize the features of group-buying auctions, and then provide some theoretical background for the related incentive mechanisms.

Features of Group-Buying Auctions

A number of key features are observed in group-buying auction designs. They typically involve a *bargaining power base* of participants that create the basis for volume-based discounting. Group-buying Web sites vary in their construction of buying groups from simple *consumer bid arrival mechanisms,* to more complex differential price level bid-as-you-arrive mechanisms, to more sophisticated technology-assisted bidding ring construction approaches. The seller also typically offers a *total quantity of sale items* or items that add up to some total value. There may be a *variety of products,* from a single product to any combination of unspecified products, to a bundle of specified products. The *initiator* of a group-buying auction can be a seller (the standard form), a consumer (indicating a *reverse group-buying auction*), or a third party (indicating a digitally intermediated group-buying auction). Also required is an *initiation procedure* that permits a price curve to be set and consumers to be recruited. A *price curve* defines the relationship between the price level and bargaining power base of consumers who bid, and is usually preset by the seller or the intermediary so that consumers know how the auction will work, and applies throughout the entire auction. Group-buying auctions sometimes include a communication mechanism for consumers to share information, giving them additional means to effectively coordinate their bids. Another feature of interest is the capability to identify *conditional consumer participation.* The variants of this span consumer participation without conditions on the final price, conditional participation when the *final price* is lower than the consumer's *reservation price,* as well as the capability to opt out, as with the popular buy-it-now option on eBay and Yahoo (Yoo, Ho, and Tam, 2006). Finally, some group-buying auctions provide further incentives beyond the regular volume discounts, such as additional discounts for early participation.

With these various features among the design choices, we can see that there are many different possible configurations of the group-buying auction mechanism. In this research, we also will explore how four different incentive mechanisms for group-buying auctions affect the participants' behavior. A *traditional mechanism* for group-buying uses the usual design features for group-buying on the Internet, including a descending series of price and volume buckets that define the price curve. In contrast, a *time-based mechanism* rewards the consumer with an additional discount beyond the group-buying discount the earlier she joins the auction. A *sequenced-based mechanism* gives the consumer an additional variable discount depending on her sequence of arrival (e.g., she is among the first ten participants, or she is among the second group of twenty participants, etc.). Finally, a *quantity-based mechanism* encourages the consumer to purchase more sale items to achieve a greater discount beyond the group-buying auction discount. In addition to these incentive mechanisms, we will apply the following mechanism design elements. First, price is based on the quantity of total orders for a single product. Second, the group-buying auction is initiated by the seller (or a third party on behalf of the seller). Third, consumers are recruited after the price curve has been set up by the seller (or the third party). Fourth, consumers join the group-buying auction without any conditions. And last, there is no communication permitted among consumers.

General Theoretical Background on Incentive Mechanisms in Group-Buying Auctions

In this research, we used two approaches to increase the volume of orders as early as possible in the auction cycle. One is to entice participants to join the auction as early as possible. The other way is to encourage participants to join and indicate their willingness to purchase more items. The problem, then, becomes how to induce the participants to exhibit this behavior. We think that several incentive mechanisms can be configured. One is based on the time that an arriving bidder joins the group-buying auction. The other is based on the size of the order that the arriving bidder is willing to place (i.e., assuming that it is possible for the person to buy more than one sale item). Group-buying Web sites often provide volume discounts, and some are designed to attract consumers who are willing to wait for the price to fall (Gottlieb, 2000).

Thaler (1985) developed the concept of *transaction utility* in relation to prospect theory and applied it to marketing and consumer behavior. He argued that the perceived gains and losses with respect to a transaction can be calculated on the basis of *reference points*. In other words, transaction utility will depend on the price that the individual pays compared to certain reference prices. These may be external reference prices or internal reference prices. In both cases a negative relationship obtains: the more the consumer pays, the less the transaction utility will be. In the process model of reference price effects proposed by Urbany, Bearden, and Weilbaker (1988), an increase in the perceived transaction utility will increase the likelihood of a purchase. Biswas and Blair (1991) considered that a higher perceived saving resulting from the comparison between the offered price and price beliefs will increase the shopping probability.

Anand and Aron (2003) have pointed out that the seller can stimulate and increase revenues by manipulation of the discount because prices fall with the number of bids, so customers who bid early will induce other consumers to bid. They argued that the creation of appropriate bidding incentives should benefit both the consumers and the sellers through Pareto-improving welfare gains.

Senior managers and researchers have indicated that price discounting is a very popular sales promotion tool (Bitran and Mondschein, 1997; Bonini and Rumiati, 1996; Feng and Gallego, 1995; Garretson and Burton, 2003). In B2B activities involving demand aggregation and procurement, how to make appropriate discount pricing decisions is of key concern. Buzzell, Quelch, and Salmon (1999) pointed out that when there are unanticipated excess inventories, suppliers often resort to the practice of offering a temporary discount in price to increase retailers' order quantities. Sadrian and Yoon (1994) developed a procurement decision support system to identify how to manipulate prices so as to improve purchases. Monahan (1984) further analyzed how a supplier can structure the terms of an optimal quantity discount schedule. In addition, Bitran and Mondschein (1997) demonstrated the effectiveness of volume discount as a coordination mechanism. They found that its effectiveness is higher with higher price sensitivity of demand on the part of consumers, while the effectiveness of a quantity discount is higher with lower price sensitivity of demand. In addition, Han, Gupta, and Lehmann (2001) and Kauffman and Wang (2001) have noted the sensitivity of consumers to price thresholds.

Based on the above observations, we conclude that a price discount can serve as a meaningful incentive to encourage consumer participation in group-buying auctions. In addition to the sequence and quantity-based incentive mechanisms, it is also possible to encourage consumers to join based on their time of arrival in general (in addition to just the earliest arrivals). A time-based incentive mechanism can be used to give a participant the incentive to join the group-buying auction in the early days of the auction, by offering an extra participation discount, in addition to the regular volume discount based on the price curve. For example, if the final price for a sale item based on the price curve is $100, a time-based incentive mechanism can be included that provides an extra 5 percent discount for anyone who joins the group-buying auction in the first three days. So, any participant who joins in the first three days will only have to pay $95.

A sequence-based incentive mechanism also is related to a consumer's time of joining the group-buying auction. However, the time the consumer joined can be compared to that of others, depending on the sequence of arrival of each participant. For example, with a sequence-based incentive mechanism, the first five participants might receive an additional 10 percent discount. Thus, if the final price (i.e., lowest price curve bucket) of the group-buying auction is $100, then the first five participants would only have to pay $90. Finally, for the quantity-based incentive mechanism, any extra discount that is offered will be based on the size of a single order. So if there is a quantity-based incentive mechanism that provides a 5 percent extra discount for any participants ordering more than ten sale items and the final price of the group-buying auction is $100, then a participant who orders twelve items will only have to pay $90 per unit for each of them.

THEORY ON INCENTIVE MECHANISMS FOR GROUP-BUYING AUCTIONS

We next present a series of hypotheses related to the four different group-buying models: traditional approach without incentive, and with a time-based incentive, a sequence-based incentive, and a quantity-based incentive. *Consumers* in our experimental procurement context are actually intended to be purchasing specialists, whom we refer to hereafter as *buyers.* We also think of them as *auction bidders,* even though their only action is to decide when to place an order. We discuss the role of planned versus final order sizes, and how participants perceive the value of the different incentive mechanisms and design choices.

Discovering how the various incentive mechanisms for group-buying auction support ought to work should be based on the application of existing theory or the development of new theory. For this research, we will draw upon a number of different theoretical perspectives that have helped us to establish a set of hypotheses about how we think incentive-enhanced group-buying auction mechanism designs will work. We expect that time-, sequence-, and quantity-related group-buying incentives should work differently based on the predictions of related theory.

Decision Time

A distinguishing characteristic of group-buying auctions is that the price falls as the number of buyers or participants increases. Since both the time-based and the sequence-based incentives encourage participants to join the group-buying auction as early as possible, the decision time for the participant to enter the auction should be short. Otherwise, others will be able to receive an extra discount. For the quantity-based incentive, in contrast, the extra discount is based on the size of the order rather than on the time that the participant joins. Cunningham (1967) and Cox (1967) claimed that there are two relevant components of cognitive risk, and we believe that both are likely to apply here: *uncertainty* and *consequence*. Related to the consequence of the person's time to decide to enter the auction, the extra discount will not change as long as the participant's order quantity fulfills the condition that is required for the person to receive an extra discount. However, the final price of the group-buying auction will be unknown until the end of the auction, which results in final price uncertainty for the procurement buyer. Moreover, the larger the number of sale items for which the buyer places orders, the more risky it will be due to the associated larger payment. As time goes on, however, the buyer's uncertainty will decrease, similar to the expiration of a financial option, where the owner is uncertain as to whether the option will be "in-the-money" or "out-of-the-money." Participants whose incentives are based on quantity will not join until they are satisfied by the price; this is a means they can use to control the risk that they will bear. Both the expected price-drop effect and the auction-ending effect demonstrate the nature of the participants' risk attitude. As a result, we believe that a quantity-based incentive mechanism may result in the longest average decision time for participants to enter a group-buying auction in terms of an absolute measure of time, which is counted from the day of first login to the experimental system to the day when the participant places an order. This leads us to assert our first hypothesis on group-buying mechanism design:

H1 (The Average Decision Time Hypothesis):
>Bidders in a group-buying auction involving the quantity-based incentive mechanism will have the longest average decision time in terms of an absolute measure of time.

Planned Order and Final Order Size Mean Differences

The quantity-based incentive is based on the ordered quantity while both the time-based and sequence-based incentives are based on the moment of joining the group-buying auctions. The rationale behind quantity discount models is derived from the economic advantage gained from customers ordering larger quantities of products. Sadrian and Yoon (1994) have shown that buyers who have quantity-based incentives are likely to buy more sale items than they originally planned. However, the overall economic advantage they obtain will depend on the trade-offs involving the quantity discount pricing schedule, the order processing cost, the inventory holding cost, and other relevant factors (Monahan, 1984; Sadrian and Yoon, 1994). As a result, how to determine the economic order quantities has been the focus of significant managerial interest on the buyers' side, with a quantity discount schedule set out by the supplier (Lee and Rosenblatt, 1986). Viswanathan and Wang (2003) demonstrated that the effectiveness of a quantity discount is higher with lower price sensitivity of demand.

Based on the above discussion, we cannot conclude immediately that a quantity-based incentive will induce buyers to order much more than the other incentive mechanisms, but we nevertheless believe that there may be some contrasts among the four models. This suggests a second hypothesis based on the mean difference of order sizes across different incentive structures.

H2 (The Planned Order and Final Order Size Mean Difference Hypothesis):
> The mean difference between the planned order size and the final order size for auction participants will differ across the incentive mechanisms of the different group-buying models.

Perceived Value by the Auction Participants

A consumer or buyer will perceive that there is an opportunity to save money when there is a price discount in the presence of a reference price. Grewal et al. (1998) suggested that a consumer's perception of value will be enhanced if the price paid is less than the buyer's reference price. Furthermore, Grewal, Monroe, and Krishnan (1998) measured the perceived value by asking buyers the following questions: Is the deal a bargain? Is the deal good? Will the deal save a lot of money? Based on the reference price process model proposed by Urbany, Bearden, and Weilbaker (1988), the perceived value will be the difference between the expected price and the price paid by the consumer. Hence, perceived value is similar to the concept of transaction utility. Both will be important reference value on which consumers can base their purchase decisions.

Because the final price at the close of a group-buying auction will not be known until the end of the auction, the buyer's perceived value at the moment of making the decision to join a group-buying auction may not be the difference between some reference prices and final group-buying price at the close of the auction. According to Lowengart (2002), the relevant reference prices, for example, might be the average market price, the list price, the lowest price, the expected price, the reservation price, or the aspiration price. The forecasted final price at the close of the group-buying auction should be consistent with the number of sale items that can transact at that price, consistent with the group-buying price curve. However, if there is an extra discount available to buyers due to an incentive mechanism that is used, then the final price—inclusive of the discount—may be less than the price associated with the quantity that is stated in the group-buying price curve. In other words, buyers who participate in a group-buying auction involving some incentive mechanism should perceive higher value than the buyers who make bids and transact under a group-buying model without an incentive mechanism. This leads to our final hypothesis on the difference in the perceived value between the group-buying with and without incentive mechanisms:

H3 (The Group-Buying Auction Participants' Perceived Value Hypothesis):
> Compared with group-buying models that offer no incentives, group-buying models with incentive mechanisms give higher perceived value to buyers.

We next discuss the details of the experimental design that we use to test the hypotheses.

THE EXPERIMENTAL APPROACH

Our experimental approach involves a number of considerations. They include the basic experimental design, the formulation of the group-buying auction price curve, and the nature of the incentive mechanisms that we apply. We will discuss our experimental subjects and materials, including the Web-based descriptions of the experimental group-buying scenario, and the questionnaires that we used. Finally, we also discuss the experimental procedures. The experiments that we describe were carried out during the period from April 13 to 17, 2004.

Figure 8.4 **Experimental Group-Buying Auction Web Site**

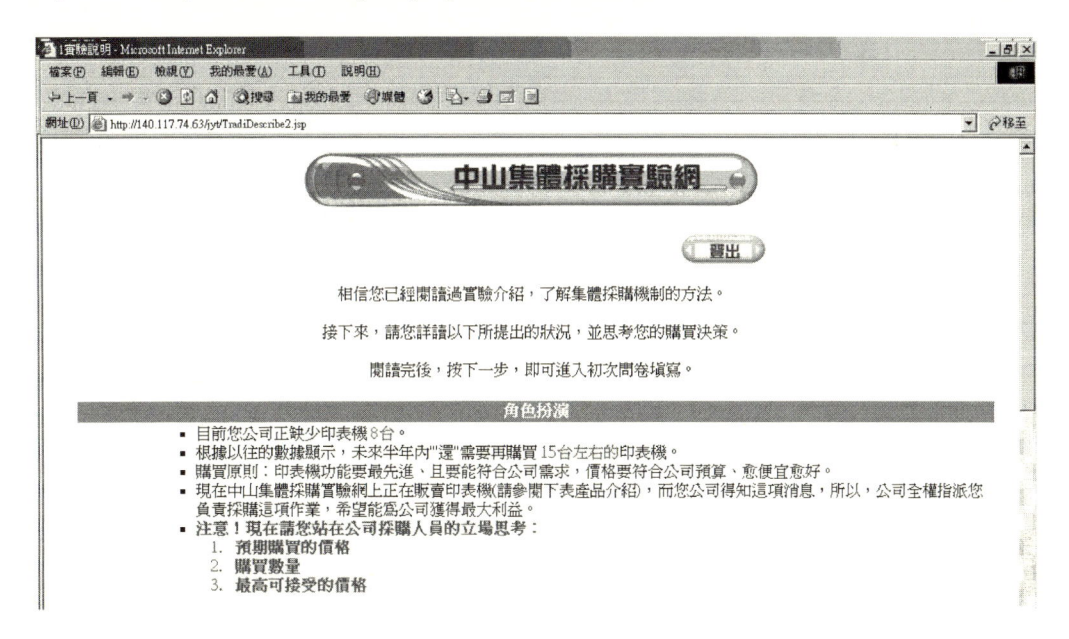

[Screenshot of web browser showing 中山集體採購實驗網 with Chinese role-playing scenario text listing:
- 目前您公司正缺少印表機 8 台。
- 根據以往的數據顯示，未來半年內"還"需要再購買 15 台左右的印表機。
- 購買原則：印表機功能要最先進、且要能符合公司需求，價格要符合公司預算、愈便宜愈好。
- 現在中山集體採購實驗網上正在販賣印表機(請參閱下表產品介紹)，而您公司得知這項消息，所以，公司全權指派您負責採購這項作業，希望能為公司獲得最大利益。
- 注意！現在請您站在公司採購人員的立場思考：
  1. 預期購買的價格
  2. 購買數量
  3. 最高可接受的價格]

Experimental Design

The Group-Buying Auction Experimental Scenario

The experimental design consists of a group-buying scenario, a price curve specification, and four incentive mechanisms, as discussed previously. This nonrepeating experiment attempts to simulate the practices of a normal business as closely as possible. The scenario we employ is a case of B2B procurement. Each subject plays the role of a procurement buyer who is in charge of printer purchasing in a company, and is provided with a scenario for a company's computer purchasing requirements. Printers are operating resources rather than input materials for the company's products. The scenario presented to the subject is shown in Figure 8.4 in Chinese, translated as:

> Currently, your company needs eight printers. Based on previous data, another fifteen printers will be needed in the coming half year. The basic principles of the company are to keep costs within budget, while acquiring advanced printers of good quality and price. Based on an advertisement, there is a group-buying auction going on in the marketplace. You are assigned to be in charge of purchasing printers. Please go to the group-buying auction marketplace and make your purchasing decision based on the company's policies.

We chose printers as the sales items to avoid the problem of insufficient product knowledge among subjects. Most people know about laser printers because they are commodity-like articles in daily use. In addition, printer procurement occurs in just about every company, so our experimental setting is a common real-world activity. Because all of the targeted experiment subjects work in companies, this kind of scenario should be very familiar. However, we set up our experiment so that participants could play the auction game over several days. The subjects usually logged into the system several times, expecting to see lower prices as time went by. However, we did not see

Table 8.1

The Experimental Group-Buying Auction Price Curve

Number of total orders	Unit prices for laser printers (NT$)
1–50	6,000
51–100	5,800
101–200	5,400
201–400	5,200
> 400	5,000

Table 8.2

Extra Discounts Provided by Different Group-Buying Incentive Mechanisms

Model	Extra discounts (beyond volume discount)
Traditional	No extra incentives.
Time	If a buyer joins the auction during its first three days (April 13 to 15), a 10 percent extra discount is applied to the final auction price.
	If a buyer joins the auction on the fourth or fifth day (April 16 to 17), a 5 percent extra discount is applied to the final auction price.
Sequence	The first five buyers will receive a 10 percent extra discount.
	The sixth through the fifteenth buyers will receive a 5 percent extra discount.
Quantity	Buyers purchasing more than twenty printers will receive a 10 percent extra discount.
	Buyers purchasing more than twelve printers will receive a 5 percent extra discount.

behavior that suggested learning was a problem in the experimental environment, which might otherwise make comparisons across individuals and treatment groups problematic.

Experimental Price Curve Specification

The regular price schedule is the same for every printer model that is offered, but different extra discounts are provided for different models; see Tables 8.1 and 8.2.

If there are 50 or fewer total orders, then the group-buying unit price will be NT$6,000. As the number of total orders increases, consumer anticipation of a price drop will grow, but the price will only drop once a *price bucket threshold* has been reached. Thus, the quantity thresholds for this price curve are 51, 101, 201, and 401 laser printer units. If the number of total orders is larger than 400, the unit price will drop to NT$5,000, the lowest auction price.

Incentive Mechanisms

Building on our earlier description and the purpose of this research, we constructed the following additional details for the group-buying models with different extra discounts based on the different incentive mechanisms that are applied; see Table 8.2 again.

We operationally define the *time-based mechanism* that operates in addition to regular volume discounts based on buyer arrival dates. This enabled a buyer who joined the auction between April 13 and 15, 2004 to earn an additional 10 percent discount. A second incentive was offered to buyers arriving between April 16 and 17, 2004, so they could earn an extra 5 percent discount. Our operational definition of the *sequence-based mechanism* called for the first five buyers to receive an extra 10 percent discount, while the next ten buyers only received an extra 5 percent discount. The remaining arriving buyers receiving discounts based on the traditional mechanism's price curve discounts. The *quantity-based mechanism,* operationally defined, benefited buyers who purchased in quantity. Those who purchased twenty or more printers received an extra 10 percent discount. A second quantity-based incentive is for the purchase of twelve or more printers, for which the buyer obtains another 5 percent discount. Beyond the traditional motivation for buying based on group discounts associated with the *traditional mechanism,* the time-based and sequence-based incentive mechanisms are designed to encourage buyers to join the group-buying auction as early as possible. The quantity-based mechanism is intended to encourage the buyers to buy more. All else being equal, we expect that all three mechanisms will help to increase the number of total orders by creating *positive participation externality effects.*

Data Collection, Subjects, and Implementation

Data Collection

In addition to collecting the information about the subjects' backgrounds prior to the experiment, we also used two other means to collect data: questionnaires and click-stream data on the buyers' online behavior. Once the subject had read the role script that they would play, then they were invited to participate in the group-buying auction, fill out the questionnaires, and make decisions that involve using an online group-buying auction test bed.

From the questionnaires, we were able to obtain each subject's planned order quantity. Beliefs about the forecasted final price were collected once the subject learned about her assigned purchasing task and the context of the group-buying auction. We also recorded each subject's online behavior by recording her actual purchasing decisions. We were further able to obtain information on whether the subject joined the group-buying auction, the printer order quantity, and the time that a purchase decision was made. Another key piece of data is the final price.

Subjects

In view of the procurement-related content of the experimental tasks, for this study we attempted to obtain subjects with business experience and knowledge of procurement of office supplies. We recruited our subjects via the Internet. An advantage with this approach is that we could send e-mail to former part-time students through an e-learning system that retained information about the enrollment of students in previous courses. We also sought participants who expressed an interest in this experiment and invited them to register as well. After examining the list of all of the people who registered for the group-buying experiment, we assigned them randomly to the four incentive-based group-buying models. The number of valid participant clickstream and questionnaire samples is 173, distributed as indicated in Table 8.3 among the four different incentive groups.

Implementation

We assigned every subject randomly to one of the four incentive-based group-buying models. In the experiment, each subject was asked to complete three questionnaires: the first one was ad-

Table 8.3

Valid Samples in the Group-Buying Experiment

Incentive Groups	Buyer action		Total
	No. buyers joining	No. buyers not joining	Invited buyers
Traditional	40	5	45
Time	39	5	44
Sequence	37	1	38
Quantity	43	3	46
Total	159	14	173

Note: When an experimental subject *joins* the group-buying experiment, the person places an order for a laser printer. When an experimental subject *does not join,* the group-buying auction does not receive the person's order. A key element of this experimental design is its capability to not only observe decision-making behavior by experimental subjects to join and not join the auction, but also to capture relevant information that may explain the rationale for the decisions based on the mechanism design.

ministered before the experiment started, the second just after making a decision about whether to join the group-buying auction, and the last after the entire experiment was finished (when the final results in terms of total number of orders and final price became available). To encourage the subjects to participate until the experiment ended, we gave them coupons after they completed the last questionnaire, which allowed them to participate in a lottery. Figure 8.5 describes the experimental procedure. Subjects received an explanation of the group-buying auction setup for the experiment, with a brief explanation, as shown in Figure 8.6. Figure 8.7 provides a description of the product that is used in the experimental design. (For additional information on the details of the experimental incentives presented on the experimental Web site, see materials in Appendix 8.1. For a translation of the questionnaire given to experimental subjects, see Appendix 8.2.)

The experiment lasted for ten days, during which time the system kept all subjects continuously informed about the progress of the group-buying auction. The rules of group-buying typically forbid a consumer to remove bids or to make a bid that is less valuable for the seller or the intermediary. We implemented a similar approach in this experience, by not permitting experimental subjects to take back their bids as time passed. The system also reminded them that they did not have to make a decision to buy unless they found an attractive price. The purpose of these reminders was so that the subjects did not make an immediate purchase decision at their first login and then never return. In practice, we know that most consumers usually do not make a decision when they first visit a real world group-buying auction.

RESULTS AND DISCUSSION

The experiments described above permitted us to collect interesting data for a large number of subjects who participated in group-buying auctions for the procurement of laser printers. In this section of the chapter, we will discuss the main findings of our experiments, with an emphasis on what we learned about the various theory-based hypotheses that we laid out. Our primary argument in the use of this methodological approach is that it permits a deliberate and stepwise analysis of different aspects of group-buying auction incentive mechanisms that help us to learn about their efficacy from the auction participants' standpoint.

Figure 8.5 **The Experimental Procedure**

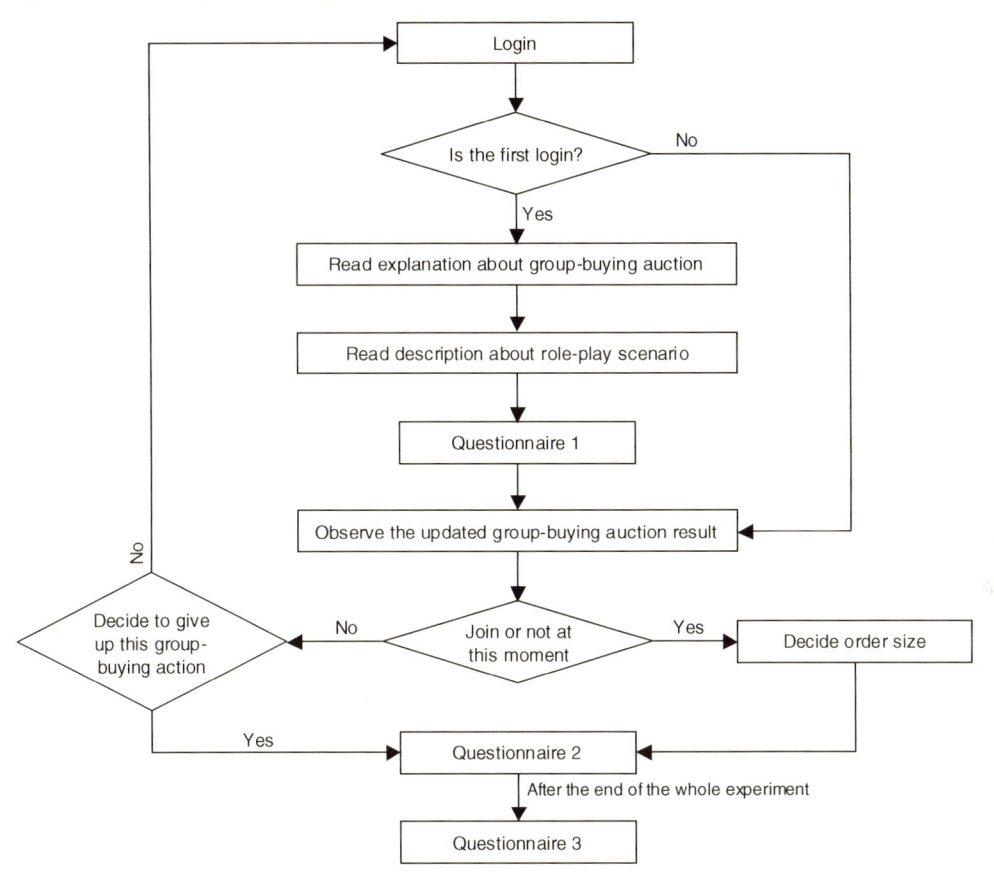

Main Findings: Summary of Results

Based on descriptive statistics of the data and additional analysis presented below, we discuss our main findings.

We obtained valid samples from 114 males and 59 females. Table 8.4 (see p. 202) lists the basic transactional results of the experiment. All of our experimental treatments reached the lowest price of the regular price schedule, NT$5,000, except the time-based treatment. The quantity-based model has the largest total number of orders at 593.

Table 8.5 (see p. 202) reveals that more buyers placed larger orders in the quantity-based model than in the other models. There were twenty-four orders for the purchase of more than eleven printers. Fourteen of these orders were for the purchase of more than nineteen printers in the quantity-based model. These preliminary data imply that the quantity-based model reached its goal of encouraging buyers to purchase more in order to get the extra discounts.

Another result we obtained involves the timing of when experimental subjects joined the group-buying auction. Table 8.6 (see p. 203) indicates that more buyers joined during the first four days with the time-based incentive model, while more buyers joining the group-buying auction in the first day in the sequence-based incentive model.

These results generally are as we expected. Although the sequence-based model had the largest number of buyers who joined the group-buying auction on the first day, only a few new buyers

Figure 8.6 Experimental Materials: Introduction of Group-Buying Auctions to Subjects

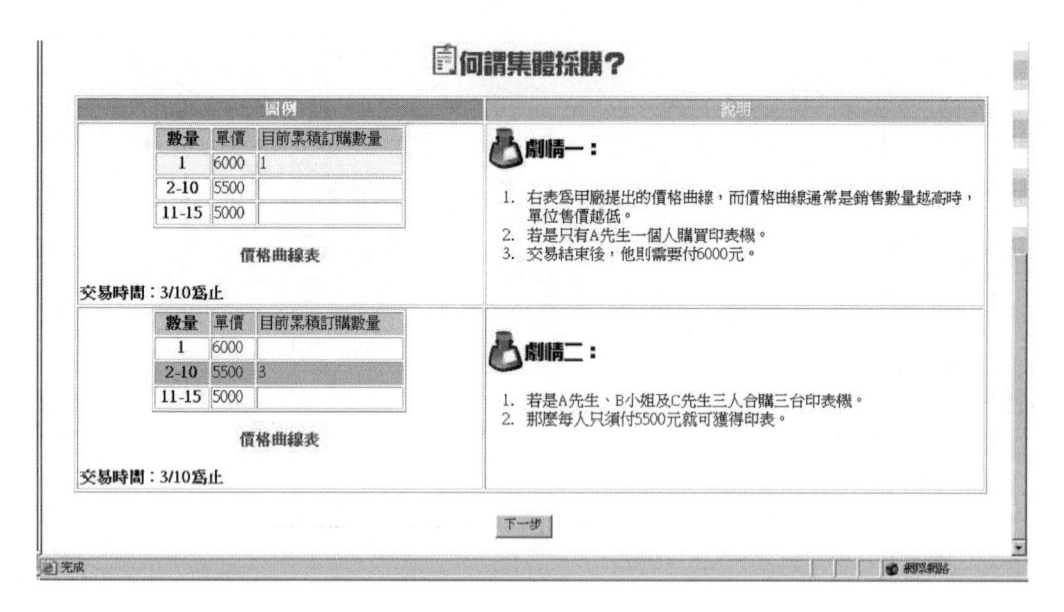

Note: The figure shows sample price curves and the quantity of orders at each price level, and provides related explanations for the experimental subject.

joined it thereafter. This is because only the first fifteen buyers can get extra discounts, and this number was reached during the first day. Similarly, for the time-based incentive model, most buyers joined the group-buying auction in the first four days, which corresponds to the period during which they could receive extra discounts. From these results, we can see that it is obvious that the experimental subjects are aware of and are responding to the opportunities for extra discounts that the different incentive mechanisms offer.

Testing the Hypotheses

Decision Time

Recall that the Average Decision Time Hypothesis (H1) argues that buyers who experience a quantity-based incentive mechanism will exhibit the longest average decision time. We operationalized *decision time* as the period from the buyer's login to the day she decides to join the group-buying auction. The analysis of variance (ANOVA) results in Table 8.7 (see p. 204) ($F = 2.827$; $p < 0.042$) suggest that decision time varies across the models.

Though the *F*-statistic tells us that the number of days subjects take to join the group-buying auction is not the same for the different incentives that we apply in the experiments, it does not pinpoint which group means are different from any other. A typical test is to run as many pairwise *t*-tests on the means as needed to cover all of the treatment groups. With this approach we run a risk of finding accidental significance, since there are six pairs of means altogether. The more pairs of means we test, the greater the likelihood that spurious significance will arise. They include: no

DESIGN OF INCENTIVE MECHANISMS IN GROUP-BUYING AUCTIONS   201

Figure 8.7   **Experimental Materials: Group-Buying Product Description**

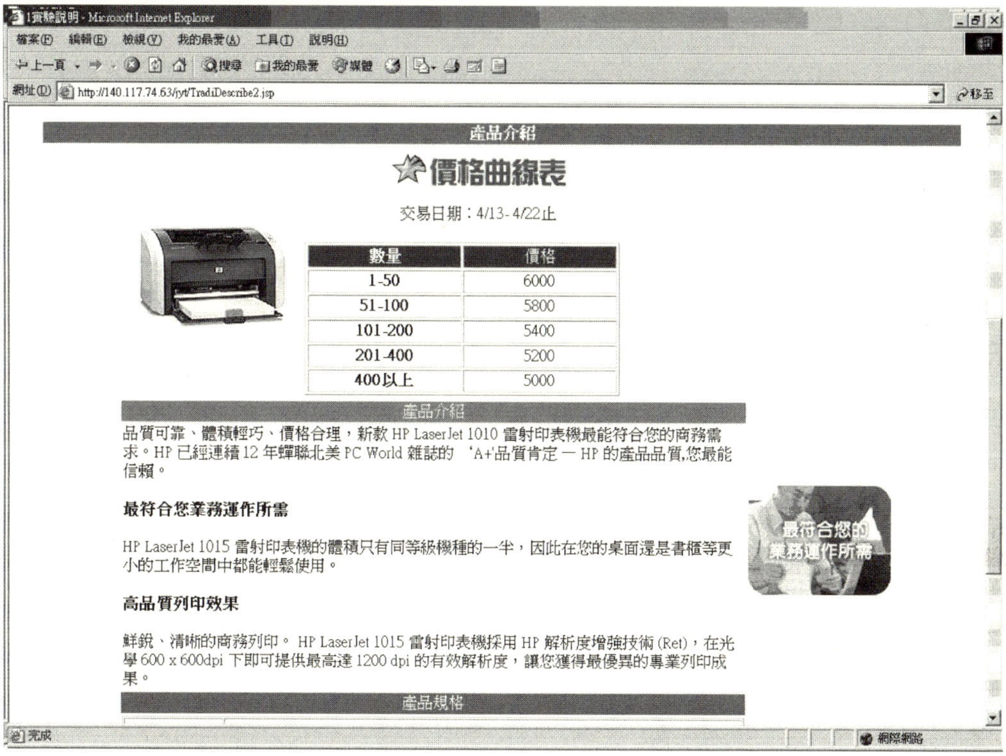

Note: The figure provides details on the price curve for the HP LaserJet 1015, and its capabilities.

treatment vs. time-based; no treatment vs. quantity-based; no treatment vs. sequence-based; time-based vs. sequence-based; time-based vs. quantity-based; and sequence-based vs. quantity-based. For this purpose, we need to use a specialized family of statistical tests that are called *treatment group post hoc mean difference tests* (Lomax, 2001; Wilcox, 1995).[7]

Determining whether it is appropriate to report statistical results on the basis of decision time treatment group means that have equal or unequal variances is a matter of judgment. For this purpose, we used Levene's (1960) test; see Table 8.8 (see p. 204).

Its null hypothesis is that the variances of all the treatment group means k are equal ($\sigma_1 = \sigma_2 = \ldots = \sigma_k$). Its alternative hypothesis is that there is one pair, i and j, which are not equal ($\sigma_i \neq \sigma_j$ for some $[i, j]$). We obtained mixed results. In two cases, we were unable to obtain evidence for group treatment means with unequal variances (for the Discrepancy between Planned and Final Order Sizes, and for the Perceived Value Difference between Group-Buying Incentives). However, in the third case (first and fourth entries in the table), we had consistent significant results (albeit at the 1 percent and 5 percent significance levels) to suggest that unequal variances across means are present (for the Number of Days Subjects Take to Join the Group-Buying Auction). With these mixed results, we decided to adopt a conservative approach, by reporting our main findings based on tests that assume the treatment group mean differences have unequal variances. The tests subsume the case of equal variances.[8]

Table 8.4

Basic Results of the Group-Buying Auction Experiments

Model	No. buyers joining	No. buyers not joining	No. total orders	Final price (NT$)
Traditional	40	5	462	5,000
Time	39	5	399	5,200
Sequence	37	1	422	5,000
Quantity	43	3	593	5,000

Note: N = 713. The experimental task was for business procurement of laser printers. Number of buyers joining identifies the number of people who made an order. Number of buyers not joining means that potential participants signed up by the experimenters never made an order and did not really participate.

Table 8.5

Summary of Individual Order Sizes

Model	< 12 orders	12–19 orders	≥ 19 orders	Total buyers	Average order size
Traditional	30	3	7	40	11.55
Time	31	3	5	39	10.23
Sequence	25	5	7	37	11.41
Quantity	19	10	14	43	13.79

Note: N = 173. Average order size applies to the number of laser printers that a group-buying participant ordered in the experiment.

Group Mean Test Results Under the Assumption of Unequal Variances[9]

The test results that we will describe involve the assumption of unequal variances for the means of the different treatment groups. These tests give us the opportunity to check for consistency in two ways. One is to see whether the group treatment means are different across the different tests that assume unequal variances of the means. A second is to compare the results from the unequal variances tests with other tests that assume equal variances of the treatment group means. This helps the researcher to establish confidence in the robustness of the statistical test results and the related experimental findings. *Post hoc group mean difference tests* that assume unequal variances of the group treatment means include *Dunnett's studentized maximum modulus distribution-based T3 test* and *Dunnett's studentized range distribution-based pairwise mean comparison C test* (SPSS Inc., 2003). They also include Tamhane's *T2 test* (Tamhane, 1979), which is based on pairwise mean difference *t*-tests, and another related pairwise mean comparison test by Games-Howell (SPSS Inc., 2003).

We previously noted in Table 8.6 that the average decision times for consumers to join the group-buying auction for traditional, time-, sequence-, and quantity-based incentive treatments was 2.96, 1.59, 2.13, and 3.35 days, respectively. According to the results in Table 8.9 (see p. 205), a

Table 8.6

Number of Days When Buyers Joined for Traditional and Incentive-Based Mechanisms

Day no.	No treatment — Buyers joining this day	No treatment — Cumulative number of buyers	Time — Buyers joining this day	Time — Cumulative number of buyers	Sequence — Buyers joining this day	Sequence — Cumulative number of buyers	Quantity — Buyers joining this day	Quantity — Cumulative number of buyers
1	13	13	10	10	15	15	5	5
2	3	16	8	18	2	17	4	9
3	5	21	7	25	3	20	7	16
4	1	22	3	28	0	20	1	17
5	0	22	0	28	0	20	7	24
6–10	18	40	11	39	17	37	19	43
Average time to join	2.96 days		1.59 days		2.13 days		3.35 days	

Note: N = 173. Three treatment groups and base case for experiment. The operational definition of *joining* the group-buying auction is the occurrence of a participant's order on the sale items offered.

Table 8.7

ANOVA Results: Number of Days Subjects Take to Join Group-Buying Auction

Treatments	Mean	Standard deviation	F-statistic
Traditional	2.956	3.618	
	(0.399)	(0.426)	
Time	1.591	2.499	2.854**
	(0.257)	(0.348)	(2.827**)
Sequence	2.132	2.924	
	(0.308)	(0.401)	
Quantity	3.348	3.308	
	(0.482)	(0.397)	

Note: Significance: ** = $p < 0.05$. Numbers outside parentheses in Mean and Standard deviation columns are raw values used for Levene's test. The numbers in parentheses are log-transformed values [with $\log(x + 1)$] to which Levene's test was also applied. See Table 8.8 for more details.

Table 8.8

Test of Homogeneity of Variances for the Group Treatment Mean Differences

Variables	Levene's statistic
Levene's Test Applied with Raw Data	
• Number of Days Subjects Take to Join Group-Buying Auction	4.820***
• Discrepancy between Planned and Final Order Sizes	1.291
• Perceived Value Differences between Group-Buying Incentives	2.141*
Levene's Test Reapplied to Transformed Data [$\log(x + 1)$]	
• Number of Days Subjects Take to Join Group-Buying Auction	2.645**

Note: d.f. = (3, 169) in all instances. The reasons for transforming the data for the "number of days" mean homogeneity of variance test are: (1) prior research (Hong, Thong, and Tam, 2004–2005) suggests that logarithmic and reciprocal transformation of the data may be helpful in obtaining meaningful test results in the presence of outliers, and (2) some subjects joined the group-buying auction immediately, so that the number of days to join was 0. We used a logarithmic transformation, and added 1 to the raw data, that is, $\log(x + 1)$. The similarity in results for the raw and transformed data permits us to use the raw data in reporting our results hereafter. Significance: * = $p < 0.10$, ** = $p < 0.05$, *** = $p < 0.01$.

quantity-based incentive results in a longer time for laser printer buyers to join the group-buying auction, in comparison with the time-based incentive, but shows no difference in comparison to sequence-based incentives or traditional group-buying without any participation incentives. To establish these results, in Table 8.9 we report the results of the treatment group mean difference tests for one test that assumes equal variances of the means (i.e., Fisher's least significant difference test), and several similar tests that assume unequal variances of the means (i.e., Tamhane's T2, Dunnett's T3, Games-Howell, and Dunnett's C tests). The time-based incentive seems to encourage consumers to decide to join the group-buying auction in a significantly shorter time. The quantity-based

Table 8.9

Post Hoc Test Results Comparison: Days before Deciding to Join Group-Buying Auction

Significance according to several *post hoc* mean difference tests

Incentive (*i*)	Incentive (*j*)	Mean Difference (*i-j*)	Fisher (LSD)	Tamhane (T2)	Dunnett (T3)	James-Howell	Dunnett (C) 95% Confidence Interval
Traditional	Time	1.365	0.041**	0.224	0.220	0.171	−0.393 3.122
	Sequence	0.824	0.233	0.829	0.822	0.662	−1.100 2.748
	Quantity	−0.392	0.551	0.995	0.995	0.949	−2.333 1.548
Time	Traditional	−1.365	0.041**	0.224	0.220	0.171	−3.122 0.393
	Sequence	−0.541	0.436	0.940	0.937	0.809	−2.166 1.085
	Quantity	−1.757	0.008***	0.033**	0.032**	0.028**	−3.402** −0.112**
Sequence	Traditional	−0.824	0.233	0.829	0.822	0.662	−2.748 1.100
	Time	0.541	0.436	0.940	0.937	0.809	−1.085 2.166
	Quantity	−1.216	0.078*	0.384	0.378	0.287	−3.039 0.606
Quantity	Traditional	0.392	0.551	0.995	0.995	0.949	−1.548 2.333
	Time	1.757	0.008**	0.033**	0.032**	0.028**	0.112** 3.402**
	Sequence	1.216	0.078*	0.384	0.378	0.287	−0.606 3.039

Note: Post hoc group treatment mean difference tests: Fisher's least significant difference (LSD) test assumes equal variances of the group treatment means; Tamhane's T2, Dunnett's T4, Games-Howell, and Dunnett's C all assume unequal variances of the group treatment means. Assuming unequal variances makes it more challenging to obtain significance, and thus leads to more conservative hypothesis tests. Significance: * = $p < 0.10$, ** = $p < 0.05$, *** = $p < 0.01$.

Table 8.10

ANOVA Results for Mean Differences between Planned and Final Order Size

Treatments	Mean	Standard deviation	F-statistic
Traditional	−2.267	8.603	
Time	−3.023	6.389	3.650**
Sequence	−1.395	7.012	
Quantity	1.978	8.694	

Note: Data: raw data used. Significance: ** = $p < 0.05$.

incentive does not relate to any specific time period. So consumers who decide to participate in our group-buying auction under this treatment tend to take a longer time to make a decision. This has a beneficial aspect: it reduces their financial risk. Interestingly, for traditional group-buying without incentives, the amount of time in terms of the number of days for a consumer to join is not significantly longer than for the other incentives, except when the incentive is time-based.

Order Size

We previously specified the Planned Order and Final Order Size Mean Difference Hypothesis (H2), which states that the mean difference between the planned order size and the final order size differs across the group-buying models. We operationally defined the *planned order size* to be the original number of laser printers that an experimental subject, acting as a buyer for a company, planned to buy. Our experiment was designed to permit us to determine whether the use of a group-buying auction model changes this. Table 8.10 indicates that the mean difference between the planned order size and the final order size differs significantly across the different incentive-based group-buying auction models. The ANOVA results for the mean differences between planned and final order sizes suggest that the quantity-based incentive tends to encourage a higher quantity than the planned purchase quantity, while the sequence-based, traditional, and timed-base mechanisms encourage lower and lower quantities, in that order. Again, the ANOVA-produced *F*-statistic does not specify which of the pairs of means are significantly different, just that there are significant differences in general. So we also present detailed analysis of paired comparisons in Table 8.11, based on *post hoc* group treatment mean difference tests.

We see that the discrepancy between the planned and final order sizes is significantly larger in the quantity-based incentive treatment than in either the traditional or the time-based incentive treatments. These results demonstrate that quantity-based incentives can encourage consumers to not only buy more, but also affect the consumer's original purchasing plans.

Perceived Value of Extra Discounts

The Group-Buying Auction Participants' Perceived Value Hypothesis (H3) argues that if there is an extra discount due to an incentive mechanism, the forecasted final price achieved by a consumer should be less. As a result, a consumer who receives an extra discount incentive should perceive higher value than a consumer in traditional group-buying without an incentive mechanism. We define a *consumer's perceived value* as the discrepancy between the reference price and forecasted final

Table 8.11

Post Hoc Test Results Comparison: Discrepancy between Planned and Final Order Size

Significance according to several *post hoc* mean difference tests

Incentive (I)	Incentive (J)	Mean difference (i − j)	Fisher (LSD)	Tamhane (T2)	Dunnett (T3)	Games-Howell	Dunnett (C) 95% confidence interval
Traditional	Time	0.756	0.647	0.998	0.998	0.965	−3.528 — 5.040
	Sequence	−0.872	0.612	0.997	0.996	0.957	−5.464 — 3.720
	Quantity	−4.245	0.010***	0.122	0.121	0.097	−9.084 — 0.594
Time	Traditional	−0.756	0.647	0.998	0.998	0.965	−5.040 — 3.528
	Sequence	−1.628	0.346	0.859	0.852	0.695	−5.626 — 2.370
	Quantity	−5.001	0.003***	0.015**	0.015**	0.013**	−9.281** — −0.721**
Sequence	Traditional	0.872	0.612	0.997	0.996	0.957	−3.720 — 5.464
	Time	1.628	0.346	0.859	0.852	0.695	−2.370 — 5.626
	Quantity	−3.373	0.050**	0.276	0.272	0.208	−7.961 — 1.215
Quantity	Traditional	4.245	0.010***	0.122	0.121	0.097	−0.594 — 9.084
	Time	5.001	0.003***	0.015**	0.015**	0.013**	0.721** — 9.281**
	Sequence	3.373	0.050**	0.276	0.272	0.208	−1.215 — 7.961

Note: Post hoc group treatment mean difference tests: Fisher's least significant difference (LSD) test assumes equal variances of the group treatment means; Tamhane's T2, Dunnett's T4, Games-Howell, and Dunnett's C all assume unequal variances of the group treatment means. Assuming unequal variances makes it more challenging to obtain significance, and thus leads to more conservative hypothesis tests. Significance: ** = $p < 0.05$, *** = $p < 0.01$.

Table 8.12

ANOVA Test Results: Mean Perceived Value Differences between Group-Buying Incentives

Treatments	Mean	Standard deviation	F-statistic
Traditional	−22.22	358.589	
Time	274.55	464.715	5.798***
Sequence	151.32	366.570	
Quantity	318.48	486.561	

Note: Data: raw values. Significance: *** = $p < 0.01$.

payment by the consumer. We also can operationally define the *consumer's reference price* as her *willingness-to-pay*. Thus, for a consumer who joins the experimental group-buying auction and obtains an extra discount, her *forecasted final payment* will be the net value that is obtained by deducting the extra discount from the forecasted final price resulting from the regular volume discount at the end of the group-buying auction. However, for the other consumers, their forecasted final payments will be determined by the forecasted final prices resulting from the regular volume discount. Table 8.12 shows the results of a third ANOVA test for the group treatment means. The results indicate that group-buying auction participants who have the various incentive mechanisms available perceive higher value than if they did not have them available. The *post hoc* treatment group mean difference test results provide additional finer-grained information about this general result, as shown in Table 8.13. Although we note some mixed significance levels across the tests that assume equal and unequal variances of the group treatment means, basing our statement of the results on the results of the unequal variance tests paints a consistent picture. First, time-based incentives appear to be more beneficial in terms of buyers' perceived value for the mechanism in comparison with traditional group-buying with no incentives beyond the standard discount price curve. Second, quantity-based incentives in group-buying also appear to win out over traditional group-buying without incentives in terms of consumers' perceived value. We now turn to a broader discussion of our results.

Interpretation and Managerial Implications

Overall, our results generally confirm the three hypotheses. First, quantity-based incentives in group-buying seem to result in the longest average decision time for buyers to place an order. Second, quantity-based incentives result in the largest discrepancy between the planned order size and the actual order size compared with all sequence-based incentives and no incentives in the traditional group-buying mechanism. Finally, additional incentive mechanisms seem to be attractive to buyers, because they appear to accord them higher perceived value. What are the interpretations and implications for group-buying auction mechanism designers and managers?

The first hypothesis, the Average Decision Time Hypothesis (H1), indicates that the quantity-based incentive treatment leads group-buying bidders to take the longest time to decide to join the group-buying auction. The original purpose of the incentive mechanism was to make the number of arriving orders as large in number as possible early in the auction cycle to try to create the basis for the positive participation externality effect. Our findings suggest that both the time-based and the sequence-based group-buying auction models encourage buyers to join the group-buying auc-

Table 8.13

***Post Hoc* Test Results Comparison: Perceived Value Difference between Group-Buying Incentives**

			Significance according to several *post hoc* mean difference tests				Dunnett (C) 95% confidence interval	
Incentive (*I*)	Incentive (*J*)	Mean difference (*i* − *j*)	Fisher (LSD)	Tamhane (T2)	Dunnett (T3)	Games-Howell		
Traditional	Time	−296.768	0.001***	0.007***	0.007***	0.006***	−532.191***	−61.344***
	Sequence	−173.538	0.066*	0.182	0.180	0.141	−387.905	40.829
	Quantity	−340.700	0.000***	0.002***	0.002***	0.002***	−579.441***	−101.960***
Time	Traditional	296.768	0.001***	0.007***	0.007***	0.006***	61.344***	532.191***
	Sequence	123.230	0.193	0.704	0.696	0.540	−123.015	369.474
	Quantity	−43.933	0.625	0.999	0.998	0.972	−311.663	223.798
Sequence	Traditional	173.538	0.066*	0.182	0.180	0.141	−40.829	387.905
	Time	−123.230	0.193	0.704	0.696	0.540	−369.474	123.015
	Quantity	−167.162	0.075*	0.380	0.374	0.284	−416.579	82.254
Quantity	Traditional	340.701	0.000***	0.002***	0.002***	0.002***	101.960***	579.441***
	Time	43.933	0.625	0.999	0.998	0.972	−223.798	311.663
	Sequence	167.163	0.075*	0.380	0.374	0.284	−82.254	416.579

Note: Post hoc group treatment mean difference tests: Fisher's least significant difference (LSD) test assumes equal variances of the group treatment means; Tamhane's T2, Dunnett's T4, Games-Howell, and Dunnett's C tests all assume unequal variances of the group treatment means. Assuming unequal variances makes it more challenging to obtain significance, and thus leads to more conservative hypothesis tests. Significance: * = $p < 0.10$, *** = $p < 0.01$.

tion early, but quantity-based incentives do not have the same effect. Our interpretation is that it is largely due to a consumer's perception of two different elements of cognitive risk: uncertainty and consequence (Cox, 1967; Cunningham, 1967). Uncertainty occurs in group-buying up to the time that the final price is known. The consequence of the final purchase price that obtains in a group-buying auction is based on transactional utility and monetary value.

In group-buying auctions, the earlier that a supplies procurement buyer makes a decision to join, the higher the risk will be. It is more difficult to predict the final price in the early stage of the auction and the forecasted final price will be an important factor to calculate the expected transaction utility or expected value. Based on our findings, it seems that an appropriate incentive mechanism should be time-related if the purpose is to encourage the largest number of orders as early as possible.

In addition, if a procurement buyer wants to purchase more sale items to qualify for an extra discount, the person will face a higher level of risk if she decides to participate early. There are two reasons for this. First, it is more difficult to forecast final price early in a group-buying auction, and second, the participants will face a loss of transactional utility if the order size is larger.

For the second hypothesis, the Planned Order and Final Order Size Mean Difference Hypothesis (H2), we learned that the quantity-based incentive mechanism influenced consumers to buy more laser printers than the order size they originally planned. However, this mechanism did not lead to more buyer participation early in a group-buying auction. We actually expected this result. The mean order size under a quantity-based incentive was larger than for the other two incentive mechanisms. Some additional comments on Hypotheses 1 and 2 are in order. Based on the Average Decision Time Hypothesis (H1), time-related incentives should encourage more participation and orders early in an auction. However, based on the result of our test of the Planned Order and Final Order Size Mean Difference Hypothesis (H2), individual order sizes will be larger and placed later in time in the auction if the incentive mechanism is based on quantity rather than the time the order is placed. This leads us to conclude that only the time-based and the sequence-based incentives are likely to have positive participation externality effects. Under quantity-based incentives, larger individual order sizes result from supplies procurement buyers who place orders involving more than their original planned order quantities so they can obtain the applicable extra discounts. The effectiveness of quantity discounts—even in group-buying auctions—is consistent with a lower price elasticity of demand (Viswanathan and Wang, 2003). From this, we conclude that it may be better for managers to apply quantity-based incentives in group-buying auctions that involve products with a lower price elasticity of demand.

Finally, for the Group-Buying Auction Participants' Perceived Value Hypothesis (H3), we obtained the result that our theory predicts: procurement buyers in group-buying treatment groups with incentive mechanisms perceive higher value than those who are assigned to participate in traditional group-buying without incentives. Interestingly, however, the results that we have presented do not indicate that group-buying auctions without incentives lead to the smallest number of orders. Instead, the order sizes that are observed depend on many factors, including the level of demand in the market, the procurement buyer's attitude toward risk and judgment about future markets (e.g., different demand levels in the future, temporal drift in prices, and so on), in addition to the perceived value of the sale item. Another reason that perceived value under a quantity-based incentive may be higher than under sequence-based incentives is that consumers are better able to correctly forecast final price because their decision time for participation is closer to the end of the auction.

The purpose of this research was to see the extent to which different incentive mechanism designs in group-buying auctions encourage earlier orders, resulting in an increase in the positive participation externality effect. However, we found that only time-related incentives can reduce the decision time resulting in earlier buyer participation. In other words, a quantity-based incentive was unable to influence a consumer's time to join the group-buying auction and submit an order. Somewhat contrary to what we expected to see, a quantity-based incentive seems to permit procurement buyers to delay their orders to reduce the risk they face. This is because order size, not time, is central to perceived utility. However, based on the Planned Order and Final Order Size Mean Difference Hypothesis (H2), we found that quantity-based incentives lead consumers to buy more than originally planned. From the results of the Average Decision Time Hypothesis (H1) and the Planned Order and Final Order Size Mean Difference Hypothesis (H2), we conclude that time-based and sequence-based incentives may influence order timing while quantity-based incentives may increase individual order sizes.

A final point pertains to whether the tested incentive mechanisms achieved the original intended purpose: to create the basis for positive participation externalities. Surprisingly, none of the group-buying auctions incentive treatments seemed to have the desired effects, based on the findings we presented in Tables 8.6 and 8.7. There may be several reasons for this. First, it may be due to the small number of experimental subjects in each treatment group (see Table 8.1 for details on the number of valid data points by treatment group). Second, we designed the experiment in a B2B procurement setting. It is possible that this context is less appropriate for testing our hypotheses than if we had conducted the research in a B2C consumer group-buying setting. Third, a possible confounding effect is our choice of a specific group-buying price curve, which is an important issue based on the findings of other group-buying research (e.g., Chen et al., 2006).

CONCLUSION

We conclude this chapter with a summary of its main findings and contributions. We will also discuss some key limitations and caveats related to this research. Finally, we will remind the reader about the aspects of this work that reflect empirical advances for information systems and e-commerce research in particular.

Main Findings and Contributions

In this chapter, we first provided a definition for group-buying on the Internet, and then discussed a number of different group-buying Web sites, emphasizing the main elements that are characteristic of this form of electronic market mechanism. We then discussed the nature of current methods that are used for studying group-buying mechanism design. We reviewed the different strengths and weaknesses for studying this context, including case studies, empirical analysis, analytical models, and experimentation. We focused on the dimensions of realism, generality, and precision. We argued in favor of using Internet-based experimental designs, rather than less realistic laboratory experiments.

To evaluate the performance of group-buying auctions, we designed three incentive mechanisms for group-buying auctions to evaluate the extent to which early participation externality effects develop. The three incentive mechanisms are time-based, sequence-based, and quantity-based group-buying auction participation incentives. We offered propositions related to the potential effects of each of the incentive mechanisms that we examined through our online experiments. The overall results generally confirm the three propositions that we offered. First, procurement buyers that were assigned to the quantity-based incentive mechanism treatment group took the longest average amount of time to join the group-buying auction. Second, the buyers in the quantity-based incentive model had the largest discrepancy between their planned order sizes and their actual orders compared with all of the other incentive mechanism models. Finally, buyers under all three incentive mechanism treatments in online group-buying perceived higher value compared with those in the traditional model without incentives.

Our original purpose in this research, in addition to showcasing the kinds of empirical advances that are possible with online experiments on the Internet, was to try to observe the extent to which different incentive mechanisms are successful in encouraging earlier orders from group-buying auction participants. Our development of the different treatments in this research was intended to tease out the related positive participation externality effects. However, even though we found that some time-related incentives may encourage group-buying auction participants to place orders in the early stages of a group-buying auction, we did *not* obtain evidence that was sufficient to permit us to claim that the participation externality effect was operative.

Limitations and Caveats

A number of limitations and caveats apply to this kind of research. Compared with lab experiments, online experiments are problematic in terms of precision, even if they provide more realism and general applicability. Although we tried to construct an experimental design that was as appropriate as possible, there were still some problems. Our experimental scenario is related to B2B e-commerce, so our experimental design has limitations insofar as its main thrust is on business buyer behavior. In addition, even though we chose a product for purchase (laser printers) that is well known to most people who use computers and the Internet, we still are not able to assert that this was a perfect experimental design choice. We recruited subjects who we believed had business purchasing responsibilities, but we still cannot be 100 percent certain that every subject knew about printers and the general customs associated with business purchasing.

Another concern that might be expressed about this research is that it has limitations with respect to group-buying settings where small variations in quality or product descriptions of the sale item are possible. Imagine, for example, that an artist would like to sell a series of engraved prints that are thematically similar, but have small variations. It is possible that the artist would like to sell these in lots that might not sell as a group to an individual, but instead to several different people who are interested in acquiring them, with the idea that this approach might bring higher aggregate revenue. The market mechanism that we have described may not be perfect for this scenario, as some buyers might be willing to pay more for certain individually distinguishable sale items in the group-buying lot. In this case, it may be appropriate to give auction participants the opportunity to "break the lot" by using some means of communication with the auctioneer to indicate some willingness-to-pay level for an individual item. This points out that the necessity for carefully defining the rules for a group-buying auction in advance. In the experimental context that we have evaluated in this chapter, we *only* consider indistinguishable commodity sale items. This limits the generalizability of our results.

Furthermore, we recognize the trade-offs that were present in our choices of incentive mechanisms in the experimental treatments and the overall setup. Our research design required the subjects to acquire laser printers through the group-buying channel, which is realistic in terms of real-world procurement. Another issue that deserves some comments is our price curve design. In our experiment, every group reached the lowest price bucket, except the one that received the time-based incentive treatment. This may not always occur in real-world group-buying auction settings, however. Clearly, there are other possible combinations of settings (e.g., multiple mechanisms with different likelihoods of the group reaching the lower price buckets, different products with different dollar values, pure B2C vs. B2B e-commerce group-buying, and so on). As a result, we admit that there are complexities and difficulties associated with ascertaining the behavioral differences across the different incentive models. For these reasons, it may be appropriate to incorporate additional simulation-based testing to provide evidence on the critical features of the group-buying auction experimental setups, and then use those findings for subsequent experimental design refinements. We further recognize that simulation combined with online experimentation will provide a limited means to determine group-buying auction participants' true intentions and cognitive processes (Kwasnica et al., 2005).

A final question that some may want to ask about this research is: To what extent is there anything uniquely "Chinese" about this research, the experimental design context, the bidding behavior of the buyers, or the results that we obtained? Of course, we cannot draw any true empirical conclusions on this question, because we lack cross-cultural empirical results as evidence. This does not prevent us from reflecting on what we have done in this research though, and how it may influence the experimental results. First, the choice of experimental subjects may be a limitation to the generality of the findings. Even if we cannot pinpoint the difference between Chinese and American experimental subjects in our research, for example, a reasonable assumption might be that cultural differences may matter in bidding behavior. If so, what might the differences be? Second, another possible consideration may arise with the perceived trust that an experimental subject might place in a university-run versus a business-run experimental study. Based on our observation of Chinese consumers in other Internet-based selling contexts, Chinese experimental subjects may be relatively more trusting of a university-run study than their American counterparts, since universities and their faculty are held in high esteem by most people in Taiwan, and Internet-based sellers are generally not viewed as trustworthy. In contrast, Americans may be less patient with university-run studies, since they are routinely bombarded with telephone advertising, Internet spam, and other trust-damaging actions by parties with whom they do not already have a trusted relationship. Americans may be less willing to participate in relative terms, and require even greater incentives to join. Clearly, such speculation is open to debate, although comparative research might provide additional useful evidence to support further understanding.

Empirical Advances: Last Words

It is always a challenge to argue on behalf of methodological advances that are not tried out in multiple contexts. In this chapter, we have sought to illustrate how it is possible to use an online experimental design approach to incrementally test and understand different phenomena associated with group-buying mechanism design in the presence of participation incentives. By focusing on just one aspect of this setting—the extent to which there are positive participation externalities—we are able to illustrate the application of experimental methods in a unique way.

Our use of experimental methods in the group-buying auction setting has been especially fruitful in the exploratory analysis of incentive mechanism design. In addition to providing evidence about how the different mechanisms create incentives for the participation of B2B procurement buyers, the results generally are suggestive of the important potential role for this methodology in the study of many other market mechanism design problems. Also, for business models such as group-buying where the participants need to keep track of updated information about accumulated orders before they decide to bid, the auctions usually take several days to carry out and bidders also may need to be able to lodge several bids to reflect their true valuation for the sales item. Without adopting the Internet for our experiment, it would be difficult to achieve an appropriate level of realism and generality. Our key insight from this work is the applicability of the iterative design approach to evaluating different incentive mechanisms. We believe that this approach has great generality and that it is possible to apply it in many other kinds of settings where mechanism design issues need to be informed with empirical testing.

A second key aspect of our work that is at the heart of the suggested empirical advances we are promoting lies in the specific use of contrasting mechanisms, and observing the extent to which they are able to outperform one another experimentally, while the costs of commitment to any one mechanism on the part of a firm need not be expended. This kind of stepwise approach to the refinement of group-buying auction market mechanism design revealed different issues and managerial questions that are key to determining the most effective design choices. Overall, this outcome is in line with what we have claimed at the outset that our experiment would be able to deliver: meaningful managerial guidance in decision-making related to market mechanisms. We hope that the reader will be motivated do similar kinds of research in other areas where managerial design choice for auction market mechanism design and participation incentives are important.

APPENDIX 8.1. GROUP-BUYING AUCTION EXPERIMENT ILLUSTRATIONS

The four screenshots below provide additional details on the manner in which the incentive-based group-buying auction models are presented to the experimental subjects.

Figure A8.1–1 **Experimental Materials: Traditional Group-Buying Price Curve**

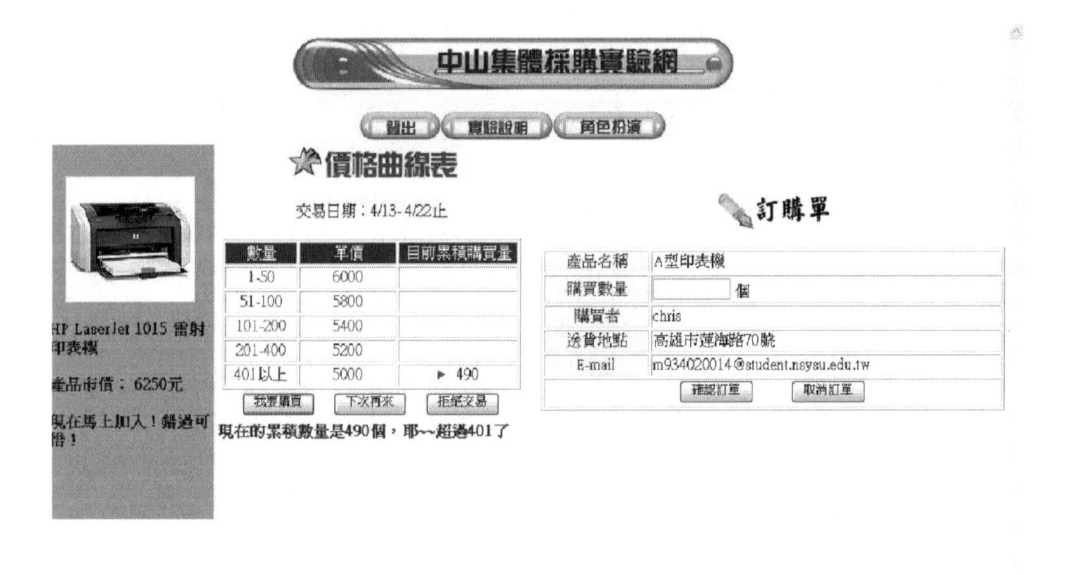

Note: In this illustration, a group-buying participant can purchase a laser printer for different prices, depending on the total number of laser printers that are sold in the group-buying auction. For example, for 1 to 50 printers, the price will be NT$6,000; for 51 to 100 it will be NT$5,800, and so on.

Figure A8.1–2 **Experimental Materials: Time-Based Incentive Model Illustration**

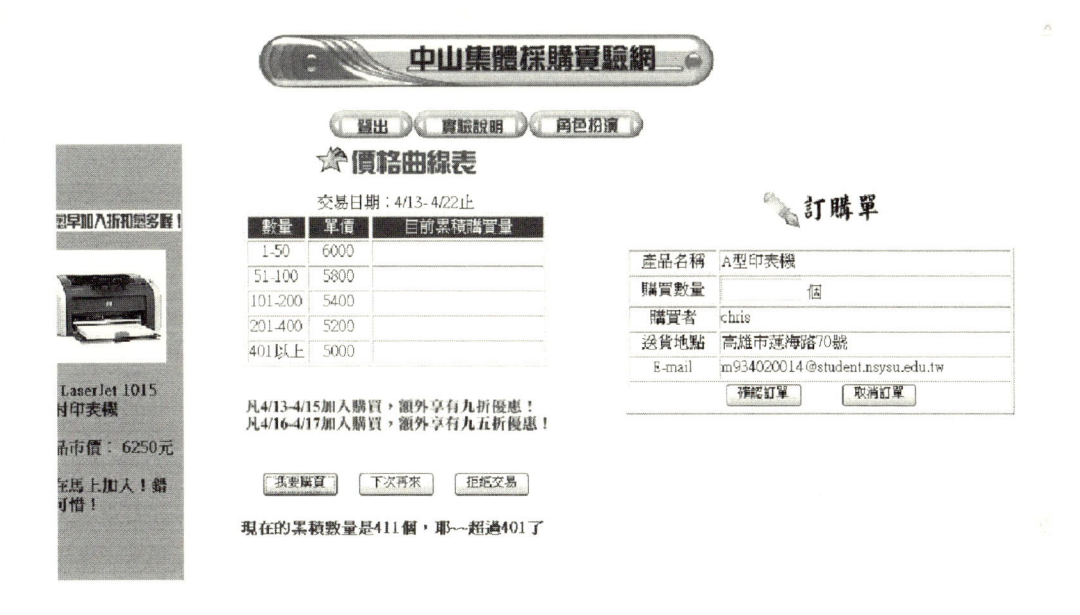

Note: The time-based incentive provides an extra 10 percent reduction to the final price if the buyer begins to participate in the group-buying auction on April 13 to 15, and a somewhat smaller 5 percent reduction in the final price if the buyer begins to participate on April 16 or 17. Other successful group buyers will receive the stipulated discount price—the final price—of the group-buying auction.

Figure A8.1–3 **Experimental Materials: Sequence-Based Incentive Model Illustration**

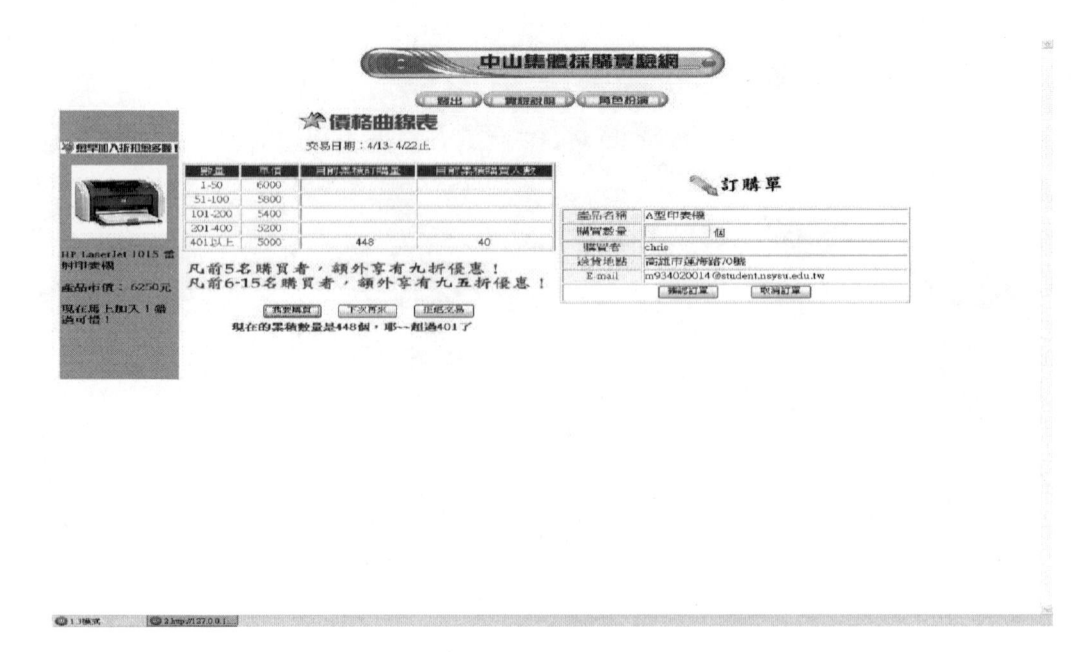

Note: The sequence-based incentive gives the first through fifth entering participants an extra 10 percent discount on the final price, and the sixth through fifteenth participants a somewhat smaller 5 percent discount on the final price. All other successful group-buying participants will receive the final price, which still reflects a discount from the list price for the items that are sold.

Figure A8.1–4   **Experimental Materials: Quantity-Based Incentive Model Illustration**

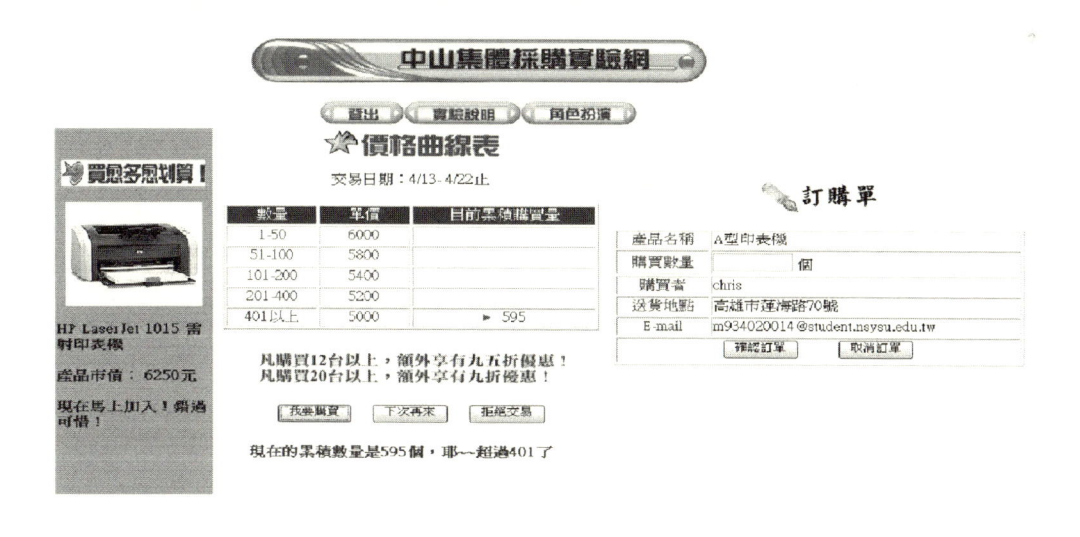

Note: In the quantity-based incentive scenario, there are additional discounts on the final price that are applied group-buying participants who purchase either more than 12 or more than 20 laser printers. Those who buy more than 12 and up to 20 laser printers will receive an extra 5 percent discount below the final group-buying auction price. Those who buy more than 20 laser printers will benefit even more with a price per printer that is an extra discount of 10 percent less than the final group-buying auction price.

APPENDIX 8.2. QUESTIONNAIRE FOR EXPERIMENTAL SUBJECTS

1. Company name: _____

2. Job title: _____

3. Gender: Male   Female

4. Educational level: Postgraduate   Undergraduate

5. In what way does your company mainly procure its supplies?
    By paper, telephone, or fax machine
    By e-mail or electronic document
    By e-procurement platform using the Internet, or an intranet or extranet

6. The capital base of your company in NT$ is:
    < 1 million
    1–5 million
    5–10 million
    10–50 million
    50–100 million
    100 million–1 billion
    > 1 billion

7. The total number of your company's employees is:
    < 100
    100–250
    250–500
    500–1,000
    1,000–2,000
    > 2,000

8. In the context of the company procurement,

    - At what price do you expect to get a printer? _____
    - To meet your company's demand, how many printers do you plan to buy? _____
    - What is the final group-buying auction price you expect for each printer? _____

9. At the end of the experiment, how many printers did you finally decide to buy? _____

Note: The median capital base of the experimental participants' companies was in the $NT50–100 million range. The median total number of employees in the subjects' companies was in the 250–500 people range. The exchange rate for New Taiwan Dollars (NT$) to U.S. dollars varied within the range of NT$32.970 per US$1 (April 1, 2004) to NT$33.444 (May 1, 2004). The source for this exchange rate data is the Economic Research Department, Federal Reserve Bank of St. Louis, for the data set EXTAUS, the Taiwan / U.S. Foreign Exchange Rate data series, available at research.stlouisfed.org/fred2/series/EXTAUS/downloaddata?&cid=15. For additional information, see the table below.

Responses to Questionnaire for Experimental Subjects

Variable		Frequency	Percentage
Gender	Male	114	65.90
	Female	59	34.10
Educational level	Postgraduate	44	25.43
	Undergraduate	129	74.57
Procurement methods	By paper, telephone, or fax machine	136	78.61
	By e-mail or electronic document	22	12.72
	By e-procurement platform on the Internet, or by intranet or extranet	15	8.67
Firm capital (NT$)	< 1 million	10	5.78
	1–5 million	19	10.98
	5–10 million	21	12.14
	10–50 million	17	9.83
	50–100 million	11	6.36
	100 million–1 billion	44	25.43
	> 1 billion	51	29.48
Number of employees	< 100	63	36.42
	100–250	23	13.29
	250–500	27	15.61
	500–1,000	16	9.25
	1,000–2,000	11	6.36
	> 2,000	33	19.08

ACKNOWLEDGMENTS

Rob Kauffman wishes to thank the MIS Research Center of the University of Minnesota and T.P. Liang and the E-Commerce Research Center of National Sun Yat-sen University for partial support. Hsiangchu Lai thanks the Taiwan Ministry of Education Program for Promoting Academic Excellence of Universities under Grant no. 91-H-FA08–1–4 and the Taiwan National Science Council under Grant no. NSC91–2416-H-110–018.

NOTES

1. There are a number of useful sources for the reader to establish an understanding of the group-buying auction marketplace in historical perspective, in addition to the references that we offer in the main text of this chapter. They cover general trends in the development of group-buying online, news about specific firms that is interesting for what it says about the efficacy of alternative mechanisms, new business models, adoption- and diffusion-related facts, and background on strategy changes and strategic alliances. The interested reader should see: *Apparel Industry Magazine* (2000); Belsie (2000); Browder (1999); *Business Wire* (1999, 2000a, 2000b, 2000c, 2000d); DeBono (2000); Dodge (2000); Eldridge (2000); Gambale (2000a, 2000b, 2000c); Gomez Advisors (2000, 2001); Guzzo (2000); Jidoun (2000); Juergens (2000); Kafka et al. (2000); Kane (1999); King (2000); LetsBuyIt.com (2000a, 2000b, 2001); Mara (2000); Olsen (2000a, 2000b); Patsuris (2000); *PR Newswire* (2000a, 2000b, 2000c); Regan (2001); Rugullies (2000); Sandoval and Kawamoto (2001); Scheraga (2001); Stelin (2000); Sullivan (2001); Tanaka (1999); United States Department of Energy

(1999); Van Horn (2000); Webby Awards.com (2000); and Wimpsett (2000). Also see Kauffman and Wang (2002), who survey other more recent developments for group-buying auctions.

2. For additional background on auction market mechanism design, see McAfee and McMillan (1987).

3. In the present research, we do not consider the possibility of communication among buyers and sellers, an obvious limitation of our research design.

4. The most popular approach to price curve design in Taiwan, based on our observation, involves a list price and one alternative discounted group-buying price. The logic of this is that if the number of orders exceeds a given quantity, then the price will be $NT\$_{DISCOUNT} \ll NT\$_{LIST}$. This approach maintains simplicity over all else, which makes sense in terms of making the mechanism effective from the viewpoint of inexperienced consumers.

5. For an assessment of cognitive efforts and incentives for strategy with assistance from a decision support system, the interested reader should see Todd and Benbasat (1999).

6. For additional background on the network externalities theory literature, which we do not have space to develop here, the interested reader should start with the article by Economides (1996) and the book by Shapiro and Varian (1999), and then consider more specific aspects. A relevant example is Dybvig and Spatt (1983), who show why adoption externalities act as public goods for others to benefit from, as we see with group-buying. Other more general examples treat technological compatibility (Katz and Shapiro, 1985), technology adoption with network externalities (Katz and Shapiro, 1986), intersystem and network competition (Katz and Shapiro, 1994), and shared network adoption benefits (Kauffman, McAndrews, and Wang, 2000).

7. Few papers in the information systems (IS) literature, including the journals *MIS Quarterly, Information Systems Research,* and *Journal of Management Information Systems,* have reported on the homogeneity of variances in group treatment mean differences before using ANOVA. We found only one article by Hong, Thong, and Tam (2004–2005) that used ANOVA *and* also checked the homogeneity of variances with Levene's test. Others by Lee and Kim (1999) and Fiedler and Grover (1996) also tested for the homogeneity of group treatment mean variances, but did not employ ANOVA. Application of group treatment mean different tests under the assumption of equal variances of the means is more common in the IS literature. Among these: Abdul-Gader and Kozar (1995) and Todd and Benbasat (1999) applied Sheffé's test; Kasper and Morris (1998) and Leithheiser and March (1996) applied the Bonferroni test; Mejias and Shepherd (1997) applied Tukey's test for an unbalanced sample; and Szajna and Scamell (1993), Sia, Tan, and Wei (2002), and Zhang et al. (2006) used Fisher's LSD test.

8. The authors thank Paul Tallon for specific guidance related to the handling of the treatment group mean differences tests, and contributing to our effort to demonstrate our methodological approach in the most general way so that it will be useful for other researchers. Hypothesis testing for treatment group mean differences in auction settings such as we have described should be prudently based on the assumption of unequal treatment group means.

9. A natural starting point for the group treatment mean difference tests is the assumption of *equal variances. Fisher's least significant difference* (LSD) *test* is one such approach that enables an analyst to identify the *smallest difference between the group means* that is statistically significant across two different treatments (Szajna and Scamell, 1993). Differences that are larger than the criterion differences at different significance levels will be more significant. Though Fisher's LSD test is a natural test to apply, it fails to incorporate information about the number of pairwise comparisons that are being made, so it is subject to spurious significance in the presence of a sufficient number of pairwise comparisons. To address this particular concern, we conducted a number of other *post hoc* statistical tests, including the Bonferroni test and the Sheffé test. These gave similar results to Fisher's LSD test, based on the assumption of equal variances of the group treatment means. For additional commentary on these tests, including computational issues, statistical power, equal and unequal error variances, sample size effects, and other issues, the reader should refer to Klockars, Hancock, and McAweeney (1995), Kromrey and LaRocca (1995), Lomax (2001), Olejnik, Supattathum, and Huberty (1997), Seaman, Levin, and Serlin (1991), Sheshkin (1997), and Wilcox (1995).

REFERENCES

Abdul-Gader, A.H. and Kozar, K.A. 1995. The impact of computer alienation on information technology investment decisions: An exploratory cross-national analysis. *MIS Quarterly,* 19, 4, 535–559.

Anand, K.S. and Aron, R. 2003. Group-buying on the Web: A comparison of price-discovery mechanisms. *Management Science,* 49, 11, 1546–1562.

Anderhub, V.; Müller, R.; and Schmidt, C. 2001. Design and evaluation of an economic experiment via the Internet. *Journal of Economic Behavior and Organization,* 46, 2, 227–247.

Andrews, W. 1999. The new laws of dynamic pricing. *Internet World,* 5, 35 (December 15), 27–34. Available at technews.acm.org/articles/1999–1/1215w.html#item13 (accessed May 21, 2007).

———. 2000. Dynamic pricing 101. *Internet World,* 6, 10 (May 15), 42. Available at www.iw.com/magazine.php?inc=051500/5.15ebusiness2.html (accessed May 21, 2007).

Apparel Industry Magazine. 2000. Web to help, not hurt traditional sales, 61, 1 (January), 14.

Bakos, J.Y. and Kemerer, C.F. 1992. Recent applications of economic theory in information technology research. *Decision Support Systems,* 8, 365–386.

Belsie, A. 2000. A power shift on energy prices. *Christian Science Monitor Electronic Edition,* September 25. Available at www.onlinechoice.com/us/home/body/about_us/ (accessed May 21, 2007).

Birnbaum, M.H. 2004. Human research and data collection via the Internet. *Annual Review of Psychology,* 55, 803–832.

Biswas, A. and Blair, E.A. 1991. Contextual effects of reference price in retail advertisements. *Journal of Marketing,* 55, 3, 1–12.

Bitran, G.R. and Mondschein, S.V. 1997. Periodic pricing of seasonal products in retailing. *Management Science,* 43, 1, 64–79.

Bonini, N. and Rumiati, R. 1996. Mental accounting and acceptance of a price discount. *Acta Psychologica,* 93, 149–160.

Browder, S. 1999. Paul Allen's e-commerce play: Bring the buying club to the net. *BusinessWeek,* May 13. Available at www.businessweek.com/bwdaily/dnflash/may1999/ nf90513c.htm (accessed May 21, 2007).

Business Wire. 1999. DealTime.com expands with new shopping categories and buying groups. October 14. Available at www.findarticles.com/cf_0/m0EIN/1999_Oct_14/ 56283870/ p1/article.jhtml (accessed May 21, 2007).

———. 2000a. MIT Sloan School of Management announces finalists for the 2nd Annual MIT Sloan eBusiness Awards; Monster.com, Ebay, iCanBuy, Freeserve and Red Hat among finalists. March 9. Available at www.findarticles.com/cf_0/m0EIN/ 2000_March_9/ 60017608/ p1/article.jhtml (accessed May 21, 2007).

———. 2000b. Mercara's television commercials honored in 21st Annual Telly Awards; Group-buying e-commerce company takes home silver and bronze awards for outstanding creative achievements. April 11. Available at www.findarticles.com/m0EIN/ 2000_April_11/61423048/p1/article.jhtml (accessed May 21, 2007).

———. 2000c. PointSpeed launches online purchasing centers for small business; Announces key partnerships with Concentric Network, Bizography.com. May 23. Available at www.findarticles.com/cf_0/m0EIN/2000_May_23/62257715/p1/article.jhtml (accessed May 21, 2007).

———. 2000d. C-Tribe, Inc. unveils the next generation of its web venture, C-Tribe.com, offering the complete clicks and mortar solution. June 1. Available at www.findarticles.com/cf_0/m0EIN/2000_June_1/62414978/p1/article.jhtml (accessed May 21, 2007).

Buzzell, R.D.; Quelch, J.A.; and Salmon, W.J. 1990. The costly bargain of trade promotion. *Harvard Business Review,* 68, 2, 141–149.

Campbell, D.T., and Stanley, J.C. 1963. *Experimental and Quasi-Experimental Designs for Research.* Boston: Houghton Mifflin.

Carnevale, P.J. and de Dreu, C.K.W. 2005. Laboratory experiments on negotiation and social conflict. *International Negotiation,* 10, 1, 51–65.

Chen, J.; Chen, X.; Kauffman, R.J.; and Song, X. 2006. Cooperation in group-buying auctions. In R. Sprague, ed., *Proceedings of the 39th Hawaii International Conference on System Sciences,* Kauai, January. Los Alamitos, CA: IEEE Computing Society Press.

Clark, D. 2001. Mobshop, a pioneer in group-buying on the Web, discontinues consumer service. *Wall Street Journal Online Edition,* January 15.

Cook, J. 2001. Venture capital: Where Mercata led, consumers were unwilling to follow. *Seattle Post–Intelligencer,* January 12. Available at seattlep-i.nwsource.com/business/vc122.shtml (accessed May 21, 2007).

Cox, D.F. 1967. Risk handling in consumer behavior: An intensive study of two cases. In D.F. Cox, ed., *Risk Taking and Information Handling in Consumer Behavior.* Boston: Harvard University Press.

Cunningham, S.M. 1967. The major dimensions of perceived risk. In D.F. Cox, ed., *Risk Taking and Information Handling in Consumer Behavior.* Boston: Harvard University, pp. 82–108.

DeBono, M. 2000. Playing the price is right: the Internet edition. *Gomez Wire, Shopping Tips*, January 17.
DeCeglie, P. 2000. It's negotiable: How to negotiate discounts on products and services. *Business Startups Magazine*, July. Available at www.entrepreneur.com/magazine/businesstartupsmagazine/2000/july/29186.html (accessed May 21, 2007).
Dodge, J. 2000. Strength in numbers? A look at what group-buying sites have to offer consumers in search of computer gear. *Inc. Magazine*, 3 (September 15), 135–136.
Dybvig, P.H. and Spatt, C. 1983. Adoption externalities as public goods. *Journal of Public Economics*, 20, 2, 231–247.
Economides, N. 1996. The economics of networks. *International Journal of Industrial Organization*, 14, 2, 673–699.
Eldridge, E. 2000. Web sites offer group car buying: Plans to use old-economy way of lowering prices. *USA Today, Auto Track*, June 22.
Feng, Y. and Gallego, G. 1995. Optimal starting times for end-of-season sales and optimal stopping times for promotional fares. *Management Science*, 41, 8, 1371–1391.
Ferejohn, J.A.; Forsythe, R.; and Noll, R.G. 1979. An experimental analysis of decision making procedures for discrete public goods: A case study of a problem in institutional design. Working paper, Division of the Humanities and Social Sciences, California Institute of Technology, Los Angeles.
Fiedler, K.D. and Grover, V. 1996. An empirically derived taxonomy of information technology structure and its relationship to organizational structure. *Journal of Management Information Systems*, 13, 1, 9–34.
Friedman, D. and Sunder, S. 1994. *Experimental Methods: A Primer for Economists*. London: Cambridge University Press.
Gambale, M. 2000a. Dynamic pricing: A beast in prince's clothes. *News Analysis, Gomez Wire*, February 24.
———. 2000b. Tips for getting the most from Internet buying services. *Auction Tips, Gomez Wire*, March 3.
———. 2000c. Group-buying space needs more than name changes to demonstrate consumer value. *News Analysis, Gomez Wire*, April 7.
Garretson, J.A. and Burton, S. 2003. Highly coupon and sale prone consumers: Benefits beyond price savings. *Journal of Advertising Research*, 43, 2, 162–192.
Gomez Advisors. 2000. Buying services: Group buyer. December 6.
———. 2001. Reviews of Mobshop, Inc. March 18.
Gottlieb, B. 2000. Does group-shopping work? The economics of Mercata and Mobshop. *MSN.com*, July 25.
Grether, D.; Isaac, M.; and Plott, C. 1981. The allocation of landing rights by unanimity among competitors. *American Economic Review*, 71, 2, 166–171.
Grewal, D.; Krishnan, K.; Baker, J.; and Borin, N. 1998. The effect of store name, brand name and price discount on consumers' evaluations and purchase intentions. *Journal of Retailing*, 74, 3, 331–352.
Grewal, D.; Monroe, K.B.; and Krishnan, R. 1998. The effects of price-comparison advertising on buyers' perception of acquisition value: Transaction value and behavioral intentions. *Journal of Marketing*, 62, 2, 46–59.
Guzzo, M. 2000. OnlineChoice.com, Mercata creates buying pool. *Pittsburgh Business Times*, September 6. Aavailable at pittsburgh.bcentral.com/pittsburgh/stories/2000/09/04/ daily11.html (accessed May 21, 2007).
Han, S.; Gupta, S.; and Lehmann, D.R. 2001. Consumer price sensitivity and price thresholds. *Journal of Retailing*, 77, 4, 435–456.
Hong, W.; Thong, J.Y.L.; and Tam, K.Y. 2004–2005. The effects of information format and shopping task on consumers' online shopping behavior: A cognitive fit perspective. *Journal of Management Information Systems*, 21, 3, 149–184.
Jidoun, G. 2000. Online shopping: When teaming up to buy pays off. *Money*, 29, 6 (June), 180.
Juergens, M. 2000. Making sense of buying services. *Gomez Wire, Shopping Tips*, August 16.
Kafka, S.J.; Temkin, B.D.; Sanders, M.R.; Sharrard, J.; and Brown, T.O. 2000. eMarketplaces boost B2B trade. *Forrester Research*. February. Excerpt available at www.forrester.com/ER/Research/Report/Excerpt/0,1338,8919,00.html (accessed May 21, 2007).
Kane, M. 1999. Web startup pushes volume shopping. *ZDNews*, March 3. Available at www.zdnet.com/zdnn/stories/news/0,4586,2219279,00.html (accessed May 21, 2007).
Kasper, G.M. and Morris, A.H. 1998. The effect of presentation media on recipient performance in text-based information systems. *Journal of Management Information Systems*, 4, 4, 25–43.
Katz, M.L. and Shapiro, C. 1985. Network externalities, competition, and compatibility. *American Economic Review*, 75, 3, 422–440.

———. 1986. Technology adoption in the presence of network externalities. *Journal of Political Economy,* 94, 4, 822–841.
———. 1994. Systems competition and network effects. *Journal of Economic Perspectives,* 8, 2, 93–115.
Kauffman, R.J. and Walden, E. 2001. Economics and electronic commerce: Survey and directions for research. *International Journal of Electronic Commerce,* 5, 4, 5–116.
Kauffman, R.J. and Wang, B. 2001. New buyers' arrival under dynamic pricing market microstructure: The case of group-buying discounts on the Internet. *Journal of Management Information Systems,* 18, 2, 157–188.
———. 2002. Bid together, buy together: On the efficacy of group-buying business models in Internet-based selling. In P.B. Lowry, J.O. Cherrington, and R.R. Watson, eds., *Handbook of Electronic Commerce in Business and Society.* Boca Raton, FL: CRC Press.
Kauffman, R.J.; McAndrews, J.; and Wang, Y.M. 2000. Opening the "black box" of network externalities in network adoption. *Information Systems Research,* 11, 1, 61–82.
Keppel, G. 1991. *Design and Analysis: A Researcher's Handbook.* 3d ed. Englewood Cliffs, NJ: Prentice Hall.
King, C. 2000. Small businesses get online help. *InternetNews.com.* August 11. Available at www.internet-news.com/ec-news/article/0,,4_436061,00.html (accessed May 21, 2007).
Klockars, A.J.; Hancock, G.R.; and McAweeney, M.J. 1995. Power of unweighted and weighted versions of simultaneous and sequential multiple-comparison procedures. *Psychological Bulletin,* 118, 300–307.
Kotler, P. 1988. *Marketing Management: Analysis, Planning, Implementation and Control.* 6th ed. New York: Prentice Hall.
Kromrey, J.D. and La Rocca, M.A. 1995. Power and Type I error rates of new pair-wise multiple comparison procedures under heterogeneous variances. *Journal of Experimental Education,* 63, 343–362.
Kwasnica, A.; Ledyard, J.; Porter, D.; and DeMartini, C. 2005. A new and improved design for multiobject iterative auctions. *Management Science,* 51, 3, 419–434.
Lai, H. 2002. Collective bargaining models on the Internet. Paper presented at the International Conference on Advances in Infrastructure for e-Business, e-Education, e-Science, e-Medicine on the Internet, L'Aquila, Italy, July 29–August 4.
Lai, H.; Doong, H.S.; and Yang, C.Y. 2006. The effect of price dispersion in e-markets on consumers' intentions to join group-buying. In R. Sprague, ed., *Proceedings of the 39th Hawaii International Conference on System Sciences,* Kauai, January. Los Alamitos, CA: IEEE Computing Society Press.
Lee, H.L. and Rosenblatt, M.J. 1986. A generalized quantity discount pricing model to increase supplier's profits. *Management Science,* 32, 9, 1177–1185.
Lee, J.N., and Kim, Y.G. 1999. Effect of partnership quality on IS outsourcing success: conceptual framework and empirical validation. *Journal of Management Information Systems,* 15, 4, 29–61.
Leitheiser, R.L. and March, S.T. 1996. The influence of database structure representation on database system learning and use. *Journal of Management Information Systems,* 12, 4, 187–213.
LetsBuyIt.com. 2000a. Offer price set at EUR 3.50. Corporate press release, Stockholm, June 2.
———. 2000b. LetsBuyIt.com applies for moratorium. Corporate press release, London, December 28.
———. 2001. LetsBuyIt.com back in control. Corporate press release, London, February 21.
Levene, H. 1960. Robust test for equality of variance. In I. Olkin, ed., *Contributions to Probability and Statistics.* Palo Alto, CA: Stanford University Press, pp. 278–292.
Lomax, R.G. 2001. *Statistical Concepts: A Second Course for Education and the Behavioral Sciences.* 2d ed. Rahway, NJ: Erlbaum.
Lowengart, O. 2002. Reference price conceptualizations: An integrative framework of analysis. *Journal of Marketing Management,* 18, 1–2, 145–171.
Mara, J. 2000. Good buys. *Adweek,* 41, 10 (March 6), 58–64.
McAfee, R.P. and McMillan, J. 1987. Auctions and bidding. *Journal of Economic Literature,* 25, 2, 699–738.
McGraw, K. 1993. Political methodology: research design and experimental methods. In R.E. Goodin and H.D. Klingemann, eds., *A New Handbook of Political Science.* New York: Oxford University Press, pp. 769–786.
Mejias, R.J. and Shepherd, M.M. 1997. Consensus and perceived satisfaction levels: A cross-cultural comparison of GSS and non-GSS. *Journal of Management Information Systems,* 13, 3, 137–161.

Monahan, J.P. 1984. A quantity discount pricing model to increase vendor profits. *Management Science*, 30, 6, 720–726.

Mullaney, T. 1999. Online shopping: Bargaining power. *BusinessWeek Online*, December 13. Available at www.businessweek.com/1999/99_50/b3659033.htm (accessed May 21, 2007).

Needle, D. 2001. Group-buying forges ahead despite Mercata shut down. *Internetnews.com*, January 4. Available at siliconvalley.internet.com/news/article.php/551521 (accessed May 21, 2007).

O'Brien, J. 2000. Cooperative commerce: Group-buying engines promise consumers strength in numbers. *Computer Shopper*, 78 (May).

O'Hara, M. 1997. *Market Microstructure Theory*. Malden, MA: Blackwell.

Olejnik, S.; Li, J.; Supattathum, S.; and Huberty, C.J. 1997. Multiple testing and statistical power with modified Bonferroni procedures. *Journal of Educational and Behavioral Statistics*, 22, 389–406.

Olsen, S. 2000a. Mercata's planned IPO highlight group-buying trend. *CNET News.com*, March 14. Available at news.com.com/Mercatas+planned+IPO+highlights+group+buying+trend/2100–1017_3–237972.html (accessed May 21, 2007).

———. 2000b. Accompany changes its name. *CNET News.com*, March 27. Available at news.cnet.com/news/0–1007–200–1591013.html (accessed May 21, 2007).

Patsuris, P. 2000. Group-buying boom. *Forbes.com*, March 3. Available at www.forbes.com/ 2000/03/29/mu1.html (accessed May 21, 2007).

PR Newswire. 2000a. Prandium announces alliance with C-Tribe.com; Koo Koo Roo and El Torito gift certificates to be marketed in cyberspace. January 11. Available at www.highbeam.com/doc.aspx?DOCID=1G1:58520838&ctrlInfo=Round20%3AMode20c%3ADocFree%3AResult&ao= (accessed May 21, 2007).

———. 2000b. SHOP2gether.com kicks off nationwide program to pool local vendors to serve education market. April 18. Available at www.findarticles.com/cf_0/m4PRN/ 2000_April_18/61721849/p1/article.jhtml (accessed May 21, 2007).

———. 2000c. Mobshop named fourth among top 50 private e-commerce companies. July 7. Available at www.highbeam.com/doc.aspx?DOCID=1G1:63190578&tab=lib (accessed May 21, 2007).

Regan, K. 2001. Allen-backed Mercata bows out. *E-Commerce Times*, January 5. Available at www.ecommercetimes.com/story/6492.html (accessed May 21, 2007).

Rugullies, E. 2000. Power to the buyer with group-buying sites. *e-Business Advisor*, 10 (February), 10–13. Available at www.highbeam.com/doc/1G1:59515109/Power+to+the+Buyer +With+Group+Buying+-Sites~R~(Industry+Trend+or+Event).html (accessed May 21, 2007).

Runkel, P.J. and McGrath, J.E. 1972. *Research on Human Behavior: A Systematic Guide to Method*. New York: Holt, Rinehart and Winston, 1972.

Sadrian, A.A. and Yoon, Y.S. 1994. A procurement decision support system in business volume discount environments. *Operations Research*, 42, 1, 14–22.

Sandoval, G. and Kawamoto, D. 2001. Group-buying site Mercata to shut its doors. *CNet News.com*, January 4. Available at news.cnet.com/news/0–1007–200–4372403.html (accessed May 21, 2007).

Scheraga, D. 2001. 2001: A sales odyssey. *Chain Store Age*, 77, 1, 96–106. Available at www.findarticles.com/p/articles/mi_g01459/is_200201/ai_n6744246 (accessed May 21, 2007).

Seaman, M.A.; Levin, J.R.; and Serlin, R.C. 1991. New developments in pairwise multiple comparisons: some powerful and practicable procedures. *Psychological Bulletin*, 110, 3, 577–586.

Shapiro, C. and Varian, H.R. 1999. *Information rules: A Strategic Guide to the Network Economy*. Boston, MA: Harvard Business School Press, 1999.

Shavit, T.; Sonsino, D.; and Benzion, U. 2001. A comparative study of lotteries: Evaluation in class and on the Web. *Journal of Economic Psychology*, 22, 4, 483–491.

Sheskin, D.J. 1997. *Handbook of Parametric and Nonparametric Statistical Procedures*. New York: CRC Press.

Sia, C.L.; Tan, B.C.Y.; and Wei, K.K. 2002. Group polarization and computer-mediated communication: Effects of communication cues, social presence, and anonymity. *Information Systems Research*, 13, 1, 70–90.

Smith, M.D.; Bailey, J.; and Brynjolfsson, E. 1999. Understanding digital markets. In E. Brynjolfsson and B. Kahin, eds., *Understanding the Digital Economy*. Cambridge, MA: MIT Press.

SPSS Inc. 2003. SPSS Advanced Models 12.0. Chicago, IL. This is a user manual that is widely available on the Internet.

Spulber, D.F. 1996. Market microstructure and intermediation. *Journal of Economic Perspectives*, 10, 3, 135–152.

———. 1999. *Market Microstructure: Intermediaries and the Theory of the Firm.* Cambridge: Cambridge University Press, 1999.

Stelin, S. 2000. Going abroad. *ZDNet InteractiveWeek,* November 27.

Sullivan, B. 2001. Paul Allen's Mercata.com to close. *MSNBC,* January 4. Available at news.zdnet.com/2100-9595_22-526836.html (accessed May 21, 2007).

Szajna, B. and Scamell, R. 1993. The effects of information system user expectations on their performance and perceptions. *MIS Quarterly,* 17, 4, 493–516.

Tamhane, A.C. 1979. A comparison of procedures for multiple comparisons of means with unequal variances. *Journal of the American Statistical Association,* 74, 471–480.

Tanaka, J. 1999. The never-ending search for the lowest price. *Newsweek,* 133 (June 7), 86.

Thaler, R.H. 1985. Mental accounting and consumer choice. *Marketing Science,* 4, 3, 199–214.

Todd, P. and Benbasat, I. 1999. Evaluating the impact of DSS, cognitive effort, and incentives on strategy selection. *Information Systems Research,* 10, 4, 356–374.

Tsvetovat, M.; Sycara, K.; Chen, Y.; and Ying, J. 2000. Customer coalitions in the electronic marketplace. In *Proceedings of the Third Workshop on Agent-Mediated Electronic Commerce,* Barcelona, 263–264.

United States Department of Energy. 1999. In Pennsylvania, ElectricityChoice.com becomes first in the nation to form Internet buying pools for electricity. *Weekly Update,* December 3.

Urbany, J.E.; Bearden, W.O.; and Weilbaker, D.C. 1988. The effects of reference pricing on consumer perceptions and price search. *Journal of Consumer Research,* 15, 1, 95–110.

Van Horn, T. 2000. Mercata files for $100 million IPO. *CNet News.com,* March 9. Available at news.com.com/2100-1017-237820.html (accessed May 21, 2006).

Viswanathan, S. and Wang, Q. 2003. Discount pricing decisions in distribution channels with price-sensitive demand. *European Journal of Operational Research,* 149, 571–587.

WebbyAwards.com. 2000. 2000 nominees and winners. The Webby Awards, May 11. New York. Available at www.webbyawards.com (accessed May 21, 2007).

Weber, B. 1998. Elements of market structure for online commerce. In C.F. Kemerer, ed., *Information Technology and Industrial Competitiveness: How IT Shapes Competition.* New York: Kluwer Academic, pp. 15–32.

Wilcox, R.R. 1995. *Statistics for the Social Sciences.* St. Paul, MN: Assessment Systems.

Wilkenfeld, J. 2004. Reflections on simulation and experimentation in the study of negotiation. *International Negotiation,* 9, 3, 429–439.

Wimpsett, K. 2000. CNet's ultimate guide to group shopping. *CNET Internet,* July 20. Available at www.cnet.com/4520-6022_1-105245-1.html (accessed May 21, 2007).

Yoo, B.; Ho, K.W.; and Tam, K.Y. 2006. The impact of information in electronic auctions: An analysis of buy-it-now auctions. In R. Sprague, ed., *39th Hawaii International Conference on Systems Science,* Kauai, January. Los Alamitos, CA: IEEE Computer Society Press, 2006.

Zhang, D.S.; Lowry, P.B.; Fu, X.L.; Zhou, L.; and Adipat, B. 2006. Culture and media effects on group decision making under majority influence. In R. Sprague, ed., *Proceedings of the 39th Hawaii International Conference on System Sciences,* Kauai, January. Los Alamitos, CA: IEEE Computing Society Press.

PART IV

NEW EMPIRICAL APPROACHES TO THE ANALYSIS OF WEBLOGS AND DIGITAL COMMUNITY FORUMS

CHAPTER 9

EMPIRICAL ADVANCES FOR THE STUDY OF WEBLOGS

Relevance and Testing of Random Effects Models

KAI-LUNG HUI, YEE-LIN LAI, AND SHUN-JIAN YEE

Abstract: The global blogging phenomenon has caught researchers by surprise. While past research has focused on the motivations behind blogging, since the number of Weblogs is growing at such an unprecedented rate, the roles played by their visitors should not be overlooked. This chapter presents an empirical analysis of Weblogs from a methodological perspective that demonstrates empirical advances in this research area. Owing to the large number of Weblogs in our sample and the persistent use of certain technological features in some of these Weblogs, accounting for individual blog-specific effects through traditional dummy-variable regression is infeasible. We introduce the use of random effects in empirical Weblog research. A random effects model allows researchers to encapsulate blog-specific effects in a regression without significant degree of freedom losses, as in typical dummy variable regressions. The modeling approach also allows the analyst to confront issues and problems with data singularity, which happens because of the linear dependency between blog-specific dummy variables and the persistent use of technological features. By developing and testing a random effects model that accounts for mutual influences between blog visits and comments, we show that blogger–visitor interactions play an important role in affecting blog popularity. Further, the use of technological features may not always raise the number of blog visits, and hence may not add value to bloggers in terms of increasing their blogs' popularity. We discuss some implications of these findings for research and practice.

Keywords: Blogs, Blog Entries, Comments, Dyadic Relationships, Economic Analysis, Empirical Analysis, Generalized Two-Stage Least Squares, Instrumental Variables, Random Effects Model

INTRODUCTION

The development of Web technology has been booming in recent years. For individuals, there is now a wide spectrum of tools and utilities that they can conveniently use to share their personal thoughts and opinions, and to engage in discussion and collaboration (McAfee, 2006). Among these new tools and utilities, *Weblogs*—often simply called *blogs*—are among the most popular, arousing the interest of people with different backgrounds and demographics. By late 2006, Technorati.com (www.technorati.com), an online blog portal and search engine, was tracking more than 63.2 million blogs, and its statistics indicate that bloggers (people who "blog") post more than 1.6 million messages per day, or an average of 18 updates per second (Technorati, 2006). Clearly, blogging has spawned an unprecedented amount of online traffic and communication exchange.

The majority of blog research to date has focused almost exclusively on the motivations of bloggers, specifically, why would people want to share with others intimate details of their daily lives, personal thoughts, views, and opinions (e.g., Herring et al., 2005; Nardi et al., 2004; Nardi, Schiano, and Gumbrecht, 2004; Trammell and Keshelashvili, 2005). There is very little research, however, on the traffic generated by blogs, and more important, the extent of communication exchanges between bloggers and visitors, and factors that stimulate such communication exchanges. It is important to undertake this research for the following reasons. First, it helps us to understand the nature of communication between mostly unrelated individuals in an online environment. In particular, recent research has found that the mere existence of an audience reading blog entries could be a sufficient motivation for people to maintain a blog (Menchen, 2005; Nardi et al., 2004). In a blog context, such reading is mostly reflected in a blog's visit statistics and the number of comments that it receives from visitors. Hence, blog visits and comments appear to play an instrumental role in sustaining the ever-expanding *blogosphere*. A better understanding of how this has come about may provide useful and practical insights toward analyzing similar online communities.

Second, the growing popularity of blogs implies that substantial consumer attention is being devoted to them, suggesting that blogs could become an important avenue for advertising. Prior studies have found that the sales of some products spiked after they were mentioned in popular blogs (Gruhl et al., 2005). Sony, as a result, once paid up to $25,000 per month to sponsor a new blog that focused on electronic gadgets (Advertising Age, 2005).[1] With the increasing popularity of online advertising and the emergence of new concepts such as sponsored links and cost-per-click or cost-per-impression pricing models, even casual bloggers can now earn advertising revenues simply by maintaining a blog. A prerequisite for this, however, is to build a substantial, recurring readership and contributor base.[2] How to achieve this recurring stream of readers and contributors has been a recurring research question.

Third, the study of some blog features, such as the categorization of entries, the use of tag boxes, and the posting of a personal profile, allows us to assess the relevance of some possible motivations for people to visit and read blogs (e.g., information seeking, community exchanges, etc.). These assessments could help individuals and enterprise decision makers determine whether a blog could be the right tool for them in facilitating structured information dissemination, the collection of feedback, or collaborative exchanges—or simply, in organizing social functions and activities.

Finally, since the majority of blogs are maintained as venues for expressing personal opinions, visitors will be interacting directly with the bloggers, as opposed to the case of business- and firm-centric e-commerce Web sites wherein they interact with a "system," and hence the interaction is less personal. It is interesting to determine whether the use of the technological features of blogs plays a significant role in affecting visits and communications in the more personal blog context. Further, because of the direct interaction with other people and the public nature of blogs, it is possible for people to give more attention to a popular blog because of its wide readership. In other words, there may be different social network effects in blogs of different popularity, and this will be reflected by the blogs' visit statistics and especially the number of comments that they are able to gather. Hence, it is important to study the relationship between blog visits and comments.

Given the above motivations and our observation that some popular blogs are getting thousands of visits per day, while many others suffer from poor hits and readership, we pose our research questions as follows:

- Are visits to individual blogs influenced by social and technological factors associated with the blogs, such as the number of comments made by visitors, the recency of blog updates, or the provision of content management and navigation tools?
- Do people make more comments, and hence, engage in more communication exchanges, in blogs that are more widely visited or that post more entries? Does the number of comments vary with blog entry characteristics?

We conducted an empirical study to address these research questions, and in the process, demonstrated the kinds of empirical advances that can be made in the presence of such Weblog data. Specifically, we randomly sampled 100 blogs and recorded their key features, visit rates, and the extent of communication exchanges exhibited in them (in terms of the number of entries made by bloggers and comments made by visitors) over a period of seven days in early 2006. Then, with this set of panel data, we constructed an econometric model to study the dynamics of blog visits and communication exchanges. Our model comprises two endogenous variables, one pertaining to *visit rate*,[3] and the other to the *number of new comments* written by visitors. The latter reflects the extent of communication exchanges exhibited in the blogs under consideration. We will formalize the definitions of both later in this chapter.

In specifying our econometric model, it is important to take account of time-invariant, blog-specific heterogeneity. Such heterogeneity could arise because of the quality of writing, being listed on different search engines or portals, consistent choices of topics by bloggers, and so on. A simple and often-employed way to capture such heterogeneity in traditional panel data analysis is to incorporate, in our context, blog-specific dummy variables (often called *fixed effects* to reflect their fixed, time-invariant nature). These dummy variables would extract the variations in the dependent variables due to unobservable blog characteristics, and by including them, the effects of other independent variables (often the ones that are of key research interest), can be estimated with better accuracy and precision.

However, the dummy variable approach is costly in terms of degrees of freedom, especially when the number of blogs is large relative to the number of time periods. This is likely to be the case in large-scale empirical blog research. In our case, the sample comprised 100 blogs but only seven time periods. Further, because a subset of the studied blogs may persistently use some technological attributes, there may be linear dependencies in the blog-specific dummy variables and the technological attributes, which prevent estimation of separate effects for the latter.

Hence, instead of using blog-specific dummy variables, we introduce the use of *random effects* in our empirical analysis. The random effects specification assumes that blog-specific heterogeneity follows a statistical distribution, which is reasonable given that the set of blogs that we studied were drawn from a population with a much larger size.[4] Because this approach does not parameterize individual blog effects, it conserves degrees of freedom and, at the same time, allows for estimating the effects of the full set of independent variables, even when the values of a subset of these variables did not vary within some of the sampled blogs during the studied time window.

There was one final estimation challenge that we needed to tackle. Although more comments on blog entries may enrich a discussion and hence lead more people to visit a blog, the number of new comments was correlated with number of visits, as it was likely that more visitors would have written more comments in a blog too. In other words, there was an endogeneity problem in our setting. It is well known that with endogeneity, ordinary least squares (OLS) or generalized least squares (GLS) estimations would produce biased parameter estimates (Greene, 2003).

Given that we simultaneously collected visit and new comment data on the blogs that we studied, and the fact that we were not able to manipulate the number of new comments written in these blogs, the most appropriate solution to this endogeneity problem was to conduct an *instrumental variable regression* (Angrist and Krueger, 2001). We compiled a set of instrumental variables for the *Number of New Comments* variable, and used them in a *generalized two-stage least squares* (G2SLS) procedure to estimate our model and identify its parameters (see Baltagi, 2001). This gave us information on the effects of the blogs and their technological attributes on visit rates and the number of new comments. We used the two-stage least squares procedure to address the endogeneity issue, while the estimation was "generalized" to incorporate the random effects.

Our results show that blog visit rates and the number of new comments are complementary. There were more comments in blogs that were more widely visited, and these new comments induced more people to visit the blogs. This may have occurred because the comments enriched the overall content contained in the blogs, or because people were interested in following interactive and recurrent blog discussions. These results suggest that blogs could form a new type of online community that features a closely knit one-to-many dyadic relationship. Further, we found that blogs that employed content management and navigation tools had higher visit rates. This is consistent with the view that some people visit blogs to seek targeted information.

The remainder of this chapter is organized as follows. The second section presents a brief history of Weblogs and a summary of prior research. The third section describes our research model. The fourth section reviews variable definitions and data collection procedures, leading up to the fifth section, which presents our main results. The sixth section discusses the implications of our research findings and, finally, the seventh section concludes the chapter with the contributions and limitations of this research.

BACKGROUND

A *blog* consists of multiple entries that are typically organized in reverse chronological order (Blood, 2002). Blogs differ from general Internet Web sites: they are frequently updated and interactive. Visitors or readers of blogs are allowed to leave comments on any particular entries, and bloggers often respond in turn to these comments. Blogs also differ from online communities such as discussion forums in that their exposition and content are primarily governed by the people who contribute content to them—the bloggers. Unlike online communities that empower all of their participants and visitors with almost equal ability to contribute to a community's contents or choices of specific topics, a blog's content is generally constructed by the blogger herself. Hence, the relationship between bloggers and visitors is highly asymmetrical. Bloggers determine the topics that they want to write on, and it is then up to visitors to determine whether to respond to an entry. Blog entries are often interconnected to each other. Also, bloggers tend to exhibit intimate self-expressions repeatedly over time (Herring et al., 2005; Trammell and Keshelashvili, 2005) including penning chronicles of their private lives and exhibiting personal self-portraits, which is not common in online discussion forums.

Figures 9.1 and 9.2 show some examples of blog entries. Some of these blog entries were merely exhibits of the bloggers' thoughts, or pictures of their own or their pets (as in Figure 9.1), whereas others were more informative and contained knowledge on a special topic (as in Figure 9.2).

Most blogs provide a few common tools or possess some common features, including the following:

- *Comment tools* allow visitors to respond to a blog entry. This facilitates interaction between bloggers and visitors.
- *Trackback capabilities* inform bloggers about who has referred to their original entries.
- *Archives* allow visitors to conveniently browse old entries.
- *Personal profiles* let visitors view personal data (e.g., age and gender) provided by bloggers.

EMPIRICAL ADVANCES FOR THE STUDY OF WEBLOGS   233

Figure 9.1   **Every Dog Has Its Day**

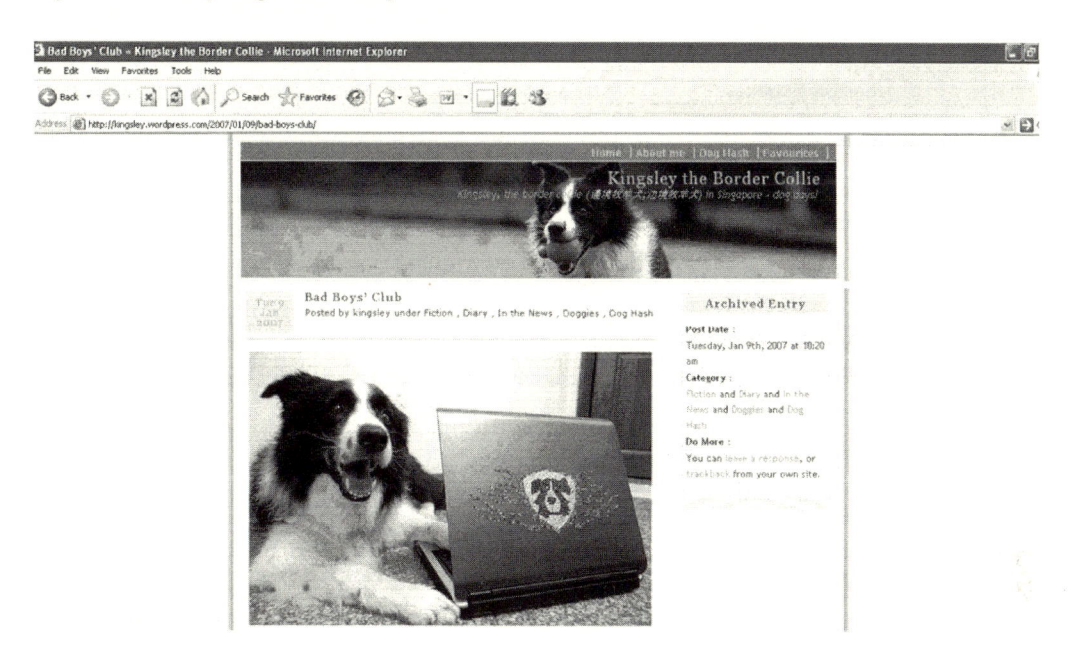

Note: Even canines are keeping up with technology, utilizing blogs as a tool to document their daily adventures and training routines.

Figure 9.3 shows a blog that contains various links to some of these features. Most of these features are directly accessible from the home page of the blog with just one mouse click.

Prior research has suggested that the number of unique inbound links from other Web sites is a good predictor of blog traffic (Hindman, Tsioutsiouliklis, and Johnson, 2004; Simmons, 2005). Other than inbound links, however, little research has focused on whether blog features affect popularity in terms of *actual visits*. Based on Technorati.com's ranking, Du and Wagner (2006) consider how blogging technologies are used. They considered blogging technologies ranging from basic content editing and linking tools to enhanced integrated applications for social interactions, such as workflow or project management tools. They specifically evaluated how the use of these capabilities affected the popularity of top "A-list" blogs. Technorati.com's ranking, however, was based on the number of inbound links from other *Web sites* rather than the actual number of visits by *people,* which is a more direct measure of popularity. Also, they only studied the use of blogging technologies and tools but did not consider how the dynamics of blogger–visitor communication exchanges might affect blog popularity.

The prior literature on system and Web site quality has focused on usability and design metrics (Bucy and Lang, 1999; Delone and McLean, 1992; McKinney, Yoon, and Zahedi, 2002; Palmer, 2002). The suggestions that emerge from these studies, however, pertain more to contexts in which end users or visitors to a Web site have a specific goal in mind. This is often not the case for a user's visit to a blog. Studies on human behavior and technology acceptance have advocated behavioral controls, and ease of use and usefulness of technologies (Ajzen and Fishbein, 1980; Davis, 1989). By contrast, marketing research on "flow" and online user experience is useful, since both are inevitably important in affecting a person's intent to read a blog. The prior research in this area has emphasized factors such as users' skills, motivations, and arousals when browsing a Web site to a

234 HUI, LAI, AND YEE

Figure 9.2 **No Secrets on the Web?**

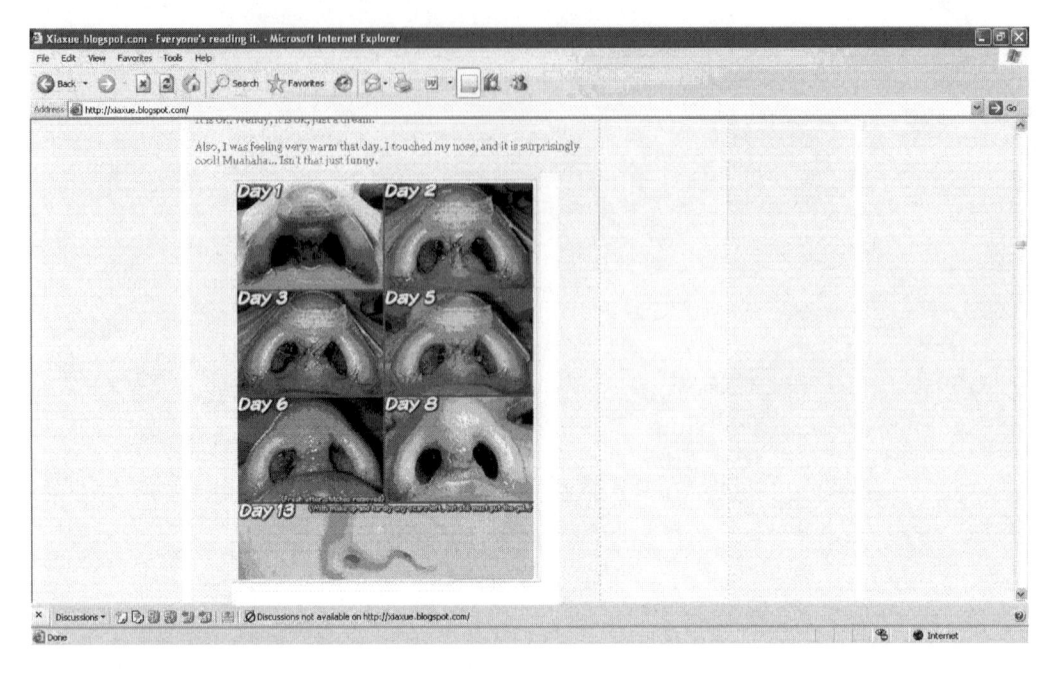

Note: Plastic surgery, which is conventionally kept secret, is openly disclosed and detailed by this blogger who underwent a rhinoplasty or "nose job" operation.

greater degree than other issues (Hoffman and Novak, 1996; Novak, Hoffman, and Yung, 2000). Clearly, in a blogging context—namely, a highly personal, selective, and casual environment that enables peer-to-peer communication exchanges—it is useful to consider whether design features, including those listed above and other less common ones, affect actual visits.

More important, previous blog research has mostly ignored the social communications and exchanges exhibited in blogs. As suggested in prior research, one possible motivation for blogging is to seek others' feedback or opinion (Menchen, 2005; Nardi et al., 2004), which may lead to future blogger–visitor communications. It is important to study how visitors respond to blog entries, and if their responses and interactions thereafter could trigger more follow-on blog visits.

THE MODEL

The characteristics of blogs, such as their use of content management and navigation tools, may increase the usability of blogs and hence reduce visitors' efforts in navigating and reading their entries (Du and Wagner, 2006; McKinney, Yoon, and Zahedi, 2002; Palmer, 2002). Further, the nature of blog entries, such as their length, their use of multimedia, or their hyperlinks to other Web sites, may affect the content quality of the blogs and lead to different visit rates over time (Lim and Benbasat, 2000). Hence, we posit that the visit rate of a blog may depend on two groups of factors—*persistent blog characteristics* (e.g., use of tag boxes or navigation bars) and *dynamic blog entry characteristics* (e.g., number of words or images included in new entries). This leads us to propose a model for the empirical research that we are conducting on blogs (see Figure 9.4, and in particular the arrows leading to *Visit Rate*).

Figure 9.3 **Components of a Typical Blog**

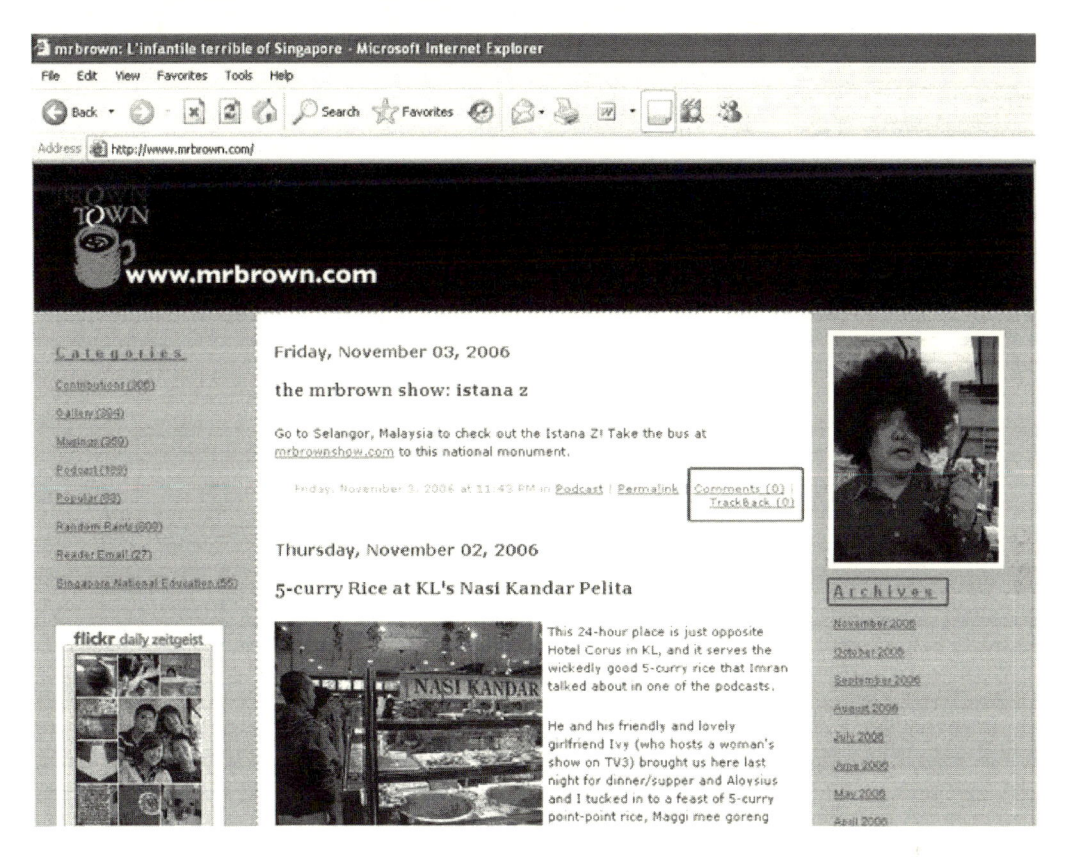

Note: Rectangles added by the authors for emphasis.

On the other hand, once a visitor has read the blog entries, she may decide to follow up a topic by posting her comments. In general, we expect a visitor's tendency to post comments to be correlated with blog entry characteristics (e.g., a longer entry or one that contains more images may provide more bases for blogger–visitor exchanges and discussions). These comments, in turn, are likely to expand the richness of the blog, thus increasing the likelihood that others will visit the blog also. This relationship is also depicted in Figure 9.4 (see the arrows related to the *Number of New Comments* variable).

Equations 9.1 and 9.2 below present the relationships depicted in Figure 9.4 in empirical form:

$$v_{it} = \alpha_i + x'_{it}\beta_v + z'_i\gamma + \rho c_{it} + d'_t\tau_v + \varepsilon_{it} \tag{9.1}$$

$$c_{it} = \lambda_i + x'_{it}\beta_c + \mu v_{it} + d'_t\tau_c + \varsigma_{it} \tag{9.2}$$

where v_{it} denotes the *Visit Rate* to blog i in day t, c_{it} denotes the *Number of New Comments*, x'_i is a vector of *temporal new blog entry characteristics,* and z'_i is a vector of *persistent blog characteristics* (including technological attributes, such as inclusion of search engines and tag boxes,

Figure 9.4 **Research Model**

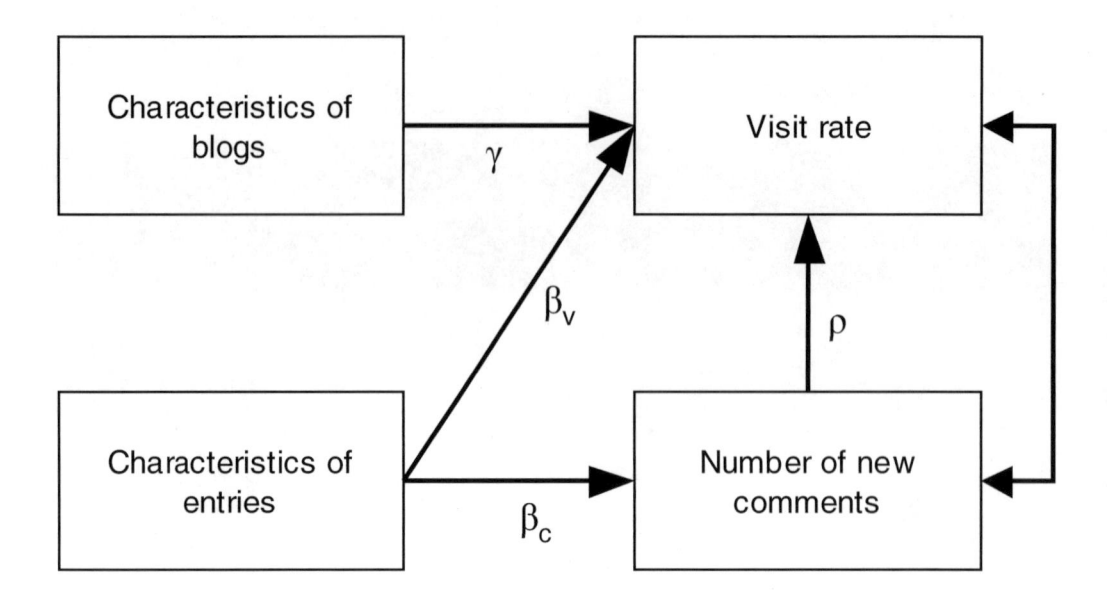

```
┌─────────────────┐                              ┌─────────────────┐
│ Characteristics │ ─────────── γ ──────────────▶│   Visit rate    │◀──┐
│    of blogs     │                              │                 │   │
└─────────────────┘       ╲                      └─────────────────┘   │
                           ╲ β_v                          ▲            │
                            ╲                             │ ρ          │
                             ╲                            │            │
┌─────────────────┐           ╲                  ┌─────────────────┐   │
│ Characteristics │ ───── β_c ──────────────────▶│  Number of new  │◀──┘
│   of entries    │                              │    comments     │
└─────────────────┘                              └─────────────────┘
```

and other features, such as inclusion of advertisements, recency of update, etc.). As we discussed in the previous section, the *Number of New Comments* and *Visit Rate* are inherently correlated (as more visitors will generate more comments), and hence we added an extra parameter μ in Equation 9.2 to extract such a priori correlations. Overall, β_v, γ, ρ, β_c, and μ are vectors of parameters, and τ_v and τ_c are vectors of period-specific fixed effects that will be estimated from the data; α_i and λ_i are blog-specific effects, d'_t is a vector of period-specific dummy variables, and ε_{it} and ζ_{it} are random error terms.

Realistically, the number of visits to a blog may be serially correlated. A blog may slowly build up its visitor base over time, and hence the number of visits today may be a function of the number of visits in the past. Our use of *Visit Rate*—defined as the number of new visits to a blog divided by its average number of daily visits—as the dependent variable effectively addresses such serial correlations. This step standardizes the *Visit Rate* variable. It essentially captures the percentage rather than the nominal growth in visits, and should be free from serial correlation since there is no a priori reason to expect the percentage change in visits to be correlated over time.

As also mentioned in the previous section, there could be unobserved time-invariant heterogeneity in blogs. Some bloggers may write better than others, some may get more comments because of their choice of topics or stories, or their general style of writing, and so on. It is important to control for such time-invariant heterogeneity in our estimation. To do that, we incorporated a blog-specific random effect in each of the two empirical model equations. Random effects could effectively capture the blog-specific heterogeneity without incurring heavy losses in degrees of freedom. Further, it is common for blogs to use some technological attributes continuously over time. It is infeasible to estimate blog-specific dummy variables and the effects due to these technological attributes separately. The use of random effects avoids this identification problem. Specifically, assuming random blog-specific effects, α_i and λ_i can be decomposed as:

$$\alpha_i = \alpha = u_i, \tag{9.3}$$

$$\lambda = \lambda + v_i, \tag{9.4}$$

In Equations 9.3 and 9.4, α and λ are then the overall constants from Equations 9.1 and 9.2, and u_i and v_i capture random heterogeneity specific to blog i. By applying standard regression assumptions on u_i and v_i (zero mean, constant variance, etc.), the parameters in Equations 9.1 and 9.2 can be efficiently estimated by *feasible generalized least squares* (FGLS) (Greene, 2003).[5]

There is one final caveat though. We have posited that the *Number of New Comments* may have increased the observed *Visit Rate*. These two variables may also correlate simply because a larger number of visitors will likely have posted more comments; in other words, there is a natural and positive association between these two variables. From our data it was impossible to distinguish which additional visitor had written a new comment, and which visits were attracted by the new comments. Therefore, the *Number of New Comments* was endogenous in Equation 9.1, and so it is important to account for such endogeneity in our estimation.

The standard solution to the endogeneity problem is to perform an instrumental variable regression (Angrist and Krueger, 2001). In our case, for Equation 9.1, what we need for this are variables that were highly correlated with the *Number of New Comments* (especially on its effect of attracting new visitors), and that have little or no correlation with the parts of *Visit Rate* that were not supposed to be influenced by the *Number of New Comments* (including the inherent positive association between *Visit Rate* and the *Number of New Comments*) (Greene, 2003).

We compiled a set of data on the *Average Time Spent per Visit* and the *Total Pages Viewed* by *all* visitors during the *new* visits, and used them as instrumental variables for c_{it}. These two variables were likely to be correlated with the *Number of New Comments*, since all three of these variables were related to the visitors' blog reading or browsing experience. *Time Spent per Visit* and *Total Pages Viewed* should not be related to *Visit Rate*, however, because they captured the depth rather than breadth of blog visits. Hence, they satisfy the conditions for suitable instruments.[6]

DATA

We randomly sampled 100 blogs from blo.gs and tracked their visit and comment statistics for seven days in February 2006.[7] The visit statistics were compiled from Site Meter (www.sitemeter.com), which provides the free Site Meter counter to track the visit statistics of a Web page. This tool has been recommended and used in a number of previous blog studies (e.g., Adamic and Glance, 2005; Gelder, Beijer, and Berger, 2002; Hindman et al., 2004). It provides a simple and standardized way to measure blog visits.

Specifically, the 100 blogs that we sampled fulfilled the following two criteria:

- They had publicly accessible visit statistics from Site Meter.
- They were not spam blogs that contain no meaningful content but rather an unusually large number of links for the purpose of distorting search engine results;

To focus the analysis on reasonably active blogs, we further restricted our sample to blogs that had at least two entries, and that were updated at least once in February 2006, prior to the data collection. These restrictions eliminated neophyte bloggers or dead blogs that could be expected to get few visits and hence were not of much interest to us. We also removed audio blogs because the nature of interaction in these blogs could be quite different from text blogs, which are the dominant type of blogs on the Internet.

Table 9.1

Definitions of Variables

Dependent variables

Visit Rate[+]	Total number of new visits to the blog (i.e., visits recorded since the previous day) divided by its average number of daily visits. As defined by sitemeter.com, a "visit" is a series of page views by a person with no more than thirty minutes in between the page views. If a visitor clicks on a link to another site but goes back to the blog within thirty minutes, then she would be considered as remaining in the same visit.
Number of New Comments[+]	Total number of new comments written based on all (old + new) entries since the previous day.

Independent variables

Cumulative Number of Entries[+]	Total number of entries in the blog in the previous day.
Number of New Entries[+]	The number of new entries added since the previous day.
Number of New Images[+]	Total number of images contained in the new entries.
Number of New Links[+]	Total number of links contained in the new entries.
Number of Words[+]	Total number of words in the new entries.
Number of New Visits[+]	The number of visits recorded since the previous day.
Blog Age	The age of the blog measured in months.
Recency of Update	Number of days before the first day of data collection when the blog was updated.
Group blog	Binary variable for blog maintained by a group or individual (1 = Group; 0 = Individual).
Top Navigation Bar	Binary variable for whether top navigation bar was used in the blog (1 = Y; 0 = N).
Bottom Navigation Bar	Binary variable for whether bottom navigation bar was used in the blog (1 = Y; 0 = N).
Sidebar	Binary variable for whether a sidebar was used in the blog (1 = Y; 0 = N).
Profile	Binary variable for whether a profile of the blogger was posted (1 = Y; 0 = N).
Photo	Binary variable for whether a photo of the blogger was posted (1 = Y; 0 = N).
E-mail	Binary variable for whether an e-mail address of the blogger was posted (1 = Y; 0 = N).
Archive	Binary variable for whether the blogger allowed visitors to view archives of entries (1 = Y; 0 = N).
Categorized Entries	Binary variable for whether blog entries were categorized by topic (1 = Y; 0 = N).
Tag Box	Binary variable for whether a tag box was used (1 = Y; 0 = N). Tag box is an interactive dialog box that allows bloggers and visitors to engage in message exchanges similar to those in online discussion forums.
Trackback	Binary variable indicating whether the Trackback feature was enabled (1 = Y; 0 = N). Trackback allows a person to keep track of who has referred to an entry.

Table 9.1 *(continued)*

Independent variables	
External Links	Binary variable for whether external links were placed on the blog site, but not within blog entries (e.g., on the top or bottom navigation bars) (1 = Y; 0 = N).
Link to Personal Photo Gallery	Binary variable for whether a link to the blogger's personal photo gallery was provided (1 = Y; 0 = N).
Number of Ads	Number of advertisements placed on the blog site, but not within the blog entries (e.g., on the top or bottom navigation bars).
Search Engine	Binary variable for whether a search engine was used in the blog (1 = Y; 0 = N).
Instrumental variables	
Average Visit Length[+]	Average time (in seconds) visitors spent reading the blog. Site Meter was able to track visit length only when visitors viewed at least two pages in the blog. It is difficult to capture time spent on a Web site if a person only views a page and then leaves.
Total Page View[+]	Number of pages viewed by all visitors during the new visits. The count was increased by one every time a visitor followed a link on the page.

[+]Variables that were measured daily for seven days during the data collection period.

Table 9.2

Blog Demographics

Demographic variable	Frequency[+]	Percentage
Gender (1 = Female; 0 = Male)	55 (*n* = 93)	59.14
Located in the United States	63 (*n* = 96)	65.63
Blogger age	Average = 29.64	Max. = 47
	Std. dev. = 7.85	Min. = 18

[+]Some blogs do not publish these data, and hence the total number, *n*, varies.

We collected the data for this research in early February 2006. For each blog, we recorded the following dynamic data on a daily basis for seven consecutive days: cumulative number of entries up to the previous day, number of new entries and comments, visit rate, and total number of images, links, and words in the new entries. We also collected some blog characteristics: demographics, inclusion of blogging tools and technologies (e.g., tag boxes and search engines) in the blog sites, inclusion of advertisements, and so on. These characteristics were persistent and did not vary over the period in which the data were collected. All blog and entry characteristics were recorded by directly traversing the blog sites. Table 9.1 presents definitions of all variables that are included in this study.

Generally, the demographics of the blogs that we sampled resemble those studied in previous research (e.g., Herring et al., 2005; Viegas, 2005). Table 9.2 presents demographic statistics of the blogs used for this study. There were more female bloggers in our sample than male, and the bloggers were primarily adults, with a minimum age of eighteen. The majority of the blogs were located in the United States.

Table 9.3

Descriptive Statistics of the Daily Measures

Variable	Mean	Std. dev.	Max.	Min.
Visit Rate	2.69	3.05	24.42	0.09
Number of New Comments	7.27	11.68	97	0
Cumulative Number of Entries	3.67	3.60	29	1
Number of New Entries	0.89	1.19	8	0
Number of New Images	0.63	1.63	14	0
Number of New Links	1.78	4.37	37	0
Number of Words	223.24	383.75	4,458	0
Number of New Visits	704.79	2,615.74	34,475	2
Average Visit Length (seconds)	99.76	65.11	356	2
Total Page Views	1,170.18	4,315.96	47,979	2

Table 9.4

Descriptive Statistics of Persistent Blog Characteristics

Variable	Mean	Std. dev.	Max.	Min.
Blog Age	21.50	16.31	86	1
Recency of Update	1.89	1.98	10	0
Number of Ads	0.92	1.30	5	0

	Frequency ($n = 100$)
Group Blog	7
Top Navigation Bar	15
Bottom Navigation Bar	33
Sidebar	98
Profile	85
Photo	58
E-mail	81
Archive	98
Categorized Entries	45
Tag Box	9
Trackback	32
External Links	96
Link to Personal Photo Gallery	37
Search Engine	40

Table 9.3 presents descriptive statistics of the variables that were recorded daily during the period of study. The statistics in Table 9.3 indicate that the blogs that we studied were active. On average, the bloggers posted close to one entry per day, and the entries were reasonably long (with more than 200 words on average). The entries also stimulated quite a lot of comments, and

Table 9.5

Estimation Results

Variable	Visit Rate[+]		Number of New Comments
	GLS	G2SLS	GLS
Constant	2.7824	1.8939	3.4090***
Cumulative Number of Entries	0.0181***	0.0132	0.0450
Number of New Entries	−0.0061	−0.1137	1.2445***
Number of New Images	0.0511	0.0836*	−0.1060
Number of New Links	−0.0340	−0.0503*	0.2521**
Number of Words	0.0004	−0.0000	0.0052***
Blog Age	0.0747***	0.0821***	
Recency of Update	−0.1133	−0.0490	
Number of Ads	−0.1411	−0.1654	
Group Blog	1.3845	1.1172	
Top Navigation Bar	0.6102	0.2860	
Bottom Navigation Bar	0.9643	0.8324**	
Sidebar	−1.3237	−1.7817*	
Profile	−0.8168*	−0.8505**	
Photo	0.4497	0.1294	
E-mail	0.1317	−0.1434	
Archive	1.2084	2.0434**	
Categorized Entries	0.4570*	0.8330***	
Tag Box	−0.7600**	−0.3685	
Trackback	0.1623	−0.1102	
External Links	−2.0768*	−1.6813*	
Link to Personal Photo Gallery	−0.5854	−0.7571**	
Search Engine	0.0058	0.0431	
Number of New Visits	—	—	0.0018***
Number of New Comments	0.0622***	0.1388***	
Adjusted R^2	0.4661	0.4093	0.3336

Notes: We do not report the period fixed effects and random blog-specific effects for brevity. The sample size of the data set was 700 (100 blogs × 7 days).
[+]We used Average Visit Length and Total Page Views as instruments for the Number of New Comments in the G2SLS estimation. Significance: *** $p < 0.01$, ** $p < 0.05$, * $p < 0.10$.

the high value of *Visit Rate* suggests that the blogs were becoming popular over time. Table 9.4 presents descriptive statistics of the persistent blog characteristics.

From Table 9.4, it is clear that several features were quite commonly used in blogs, such as a *Sidebar,* posting of personal *Profiles* and *E-mail* addresses, *Archives* of entries, and *External Links.* By contrast, the use of a *Top Navigation Bar* and *Tag Boxes* was not popular. The blogs that we sampled were reasonably mature, with an average age of close to two years, and most had only one identifiable author.

DATA ANALYSIS

We performed *generalized two-stage least squares* (G2SLS) to estimate Equations 9.1 and 9.2 (Baltagi, 2001). In general, the idea is to perform two sets of OLS regressions, one on the pooled data with an overall constant, and the other on mean-adjusted data, and then use the residuals from these regressions to compute estimates for the error variances (i.e., the variances of ε_{it}, ζ_{it}, u_i, and v_i). These error variance estimates can then be used to transform the variables in a standard weighted least squares fashion (Greene, 2003). The transformed variables would account for the error components in the random effects models. They can then be used directly in a *two-stage least squares* (2SLS) procedure to obtain consistent parameter estimates.[8]

Table 9.5 presents the G2SLS estimation results of Equation 9.1, and the GLS estimation results of Equation 9.2. For comparison, we also report the GLS estimates of the simple random effects model for Equation 9.1 (i.e., without instrumenting for the number of new comments).

We first conducted a Lagrange multiplier test to see if the random effects specification fits the data that we collected. According to (Greene, 2003), the test statistic is computed as:

$$LM = \frac{nT}{2(T-1)} \left[\frac{\sum_{i=1}^{n} (T\bar{e}_i)^2}{\sum_{i=1}^{n}\sum_{t=1}^{T} e_{it}^2} - 1 \right]^2$$

where e_{it} are the residuals obtained from an OLS regression with only one overall constant, and $\bar{e}_i$ are the means of the OLS residuals that can be computed from e_{it}. In our case, LM equals 12.27 for the *Visit Rate* Equation 9.1. This exceeds the 99 percent critical value of a χ^2 distribution with one degree of freedom, 6.63. Hence, we conclude that the random effects specification is appropriate for the *Visit Rate* equation.[9]

On the other hand, LM equals 0.57 for the *Number of New Comments* Equation 9.2, which is not statistically significant ($p = 0.45$). Apparently, allowing for random effects did not significantly improve the fit of the *Number of New Comments* equation. However, given the large number of blogs in this study, it is reasonable to free up the constant of the equation. Thus, we will continue to focus on the results with random effects for the *Number of New Comments*.[10]

Comparing the GLS and G2SLS estimation results for the *Visit Rate* equation, it is clear that after instrumenting for the *Number of New Comments*, all of the coefficients changed considerably, and the coefficient for the *Number of New Comments* almost doubled in G2SLS. This suggests that failing to account for endogeneity could lead to misleading inferences on the effect of comments on blog visits. In the remaining discussion we will focus on the G2SLS results.

The G2SLS results show that the *Number of New Images, Blog Age*, use of *Bottom Navigation Bars*, provision of *Archives* and *Categorized Entries*, and the *Number of New Comments* had a positive impact on *Visit Rate*. On the other hand, the *Number of Links in New Entries*, use of *Sidebars*, publishing of personal *Profiles* and *External Links*, and *Links to Personal Photo Galleries*, all had a negative impact on *Visit Rate*. The adjusted R^2 was 40.93 percent, which suggests that our model was able to explain a reasonable amount of the variance in *Visit Rate*.

For the *Number of New Comments* equation, in general, the characteristics of blog entries affected the extent to which visitors submitted comments. The *Number of New Entries* and the *Number of Links* and *Number of Words* in the new entries had a positive effect on the *Number of New Comments* written by visitors. Also, *Visit Rate* was positively correlated with the *Number of New Comments*. The adjusted R^2 was 32.24 percent.

DISCUSSION AND IMPLICATIONS

There are several interesting results in Table 9.5. First, the visit rate of blogs increased with the number of new comments posted by visitors. This implies that new visitors are interested in the comments written by other people, and blogs may possibly help to facilitate social communications, which may be an important motivation behind the blogging phenomenon as previously noted by Nardi, Schiano, and Gumbrecht (2004) and Nardi et al. (2004). On the other hand, the increased visits were also coupled with more new comments. We found a systematic complementarity between blog visits and comments, which implies that although blogging is primarily meant for asymmetric sharing of personal stories or opinions, it could also form a new type of online community in which discussion and interaction is anchored on blogger-driven topics.[11] Many blog hosts now allow bloggers to create "friends lists." These "friends" often do not know each other before joining the blogs, but they interact frequently by making comments and responses, which over time may attract other people to visit their blogs and expand their social network.

Clearly, the presence of an audience and feedback could be a key to success of Internet Web sites, including those that aim to share information. Our findings also imply that, similar to personal blogs, it is possible for new knowledge or enterprise systems to enjoy greater success or more widespread adoption if users are encouraged to provide feedback or responses. Feedback or responses may make a new system more interesting and "lively," which may increase people's interest in "taking a look" at the system and possibly posting an opinion.

Second, the results in Table 9.5 show that older blogs tended to have a higher visit rate too. This implies that older blogs receive more visits, which could have been due to improved search engine indexing over time, the loyalty of visitors, or diffusion through word of mouth since older blogs have a larger base of visitors. In any case, older or more well-established blogs may be a better avenue for companies to reach out to a wider audience, or to attract "eyeballs" for their products.

Third, the inclusion of archives and categorization of entries increased visit rate. This finding is consistent with the proposition that some people read blogs to seek specific types of information (e.g., discussion on a social topic, stock market news, etc.), and hence blogs can potentially be used as a means for knowledge sharing and dissemination. Alternatively, since archiving and entry categorization help organize the contents of a blog and enhance the ease of navigation for visitors, it is also possible that such improved usability attracted more people to visit the blogs (Nielsen, 2000).

Fourth, the use of blogging tools and technologies, and navigation tools had mixed influences on visit rate. Although a bottom navigation bar increased visit rate, a sidebar decreased it. One possible reason is that a sidebar reduces the available space to display the blog contents, and hence may annoy visitors who want to focus on reading the entries.

The inclusion of links, including *persistent links* (i.e., links that are always displayed on the blog page), *ad hoc links* inside blog entries, or links to personal photo galleries, decreased visit rate. Links provide a convenient way for people to visit other pages, and hence may distract visitors' attention. Although people may visit a blog with the intention of reading its contents, they may not necessarily stay on that site and could easily click away from the blog site to someplace else. Bloggers or companies that sponsor blog advertisements may want to evaluate the inclusion of links carefully if traffic is deemed important to them.

Surprisingly, the posting of a personal profile reduced visit rate. This could perhaps be due to a novelty effect: some people may browse blogs just to learn about other people or to make new friends, and the posting of a personal profile reduces the number of visits needed to achieve such purposes.

Figure 9.5 **The Random Effects Computed from the *Visit Rate* Equation**

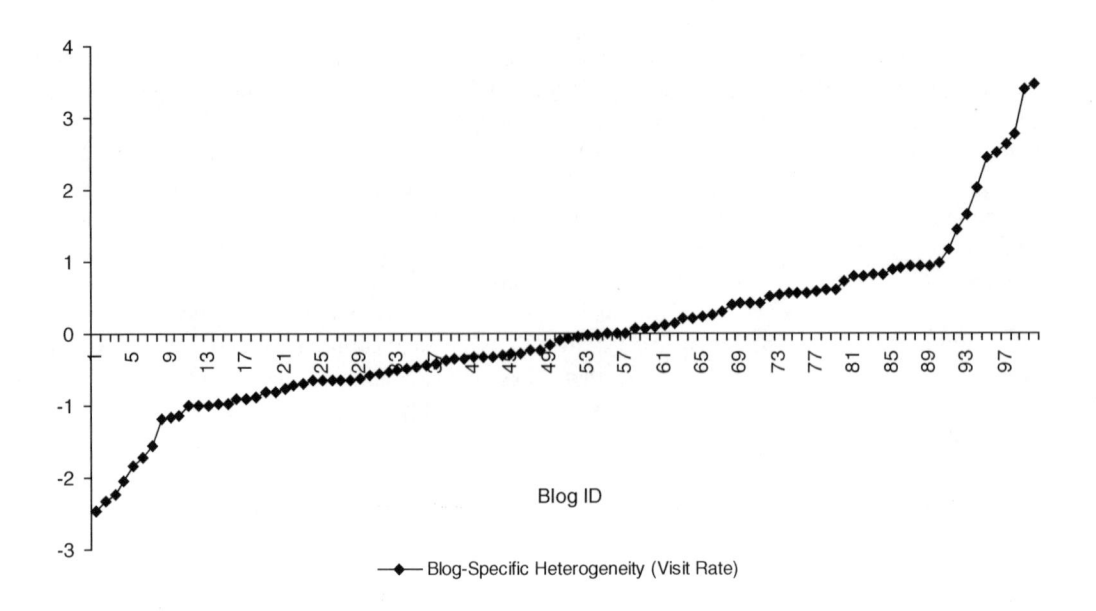

[Chart: Blog-Specific Heterogeneity (Visit Rate) plotted against Blog ID, ranging from approximately -2.5 to 3.5]

Finally, new entries, especially longer ones containing more links, caused visitors to write more comments, but they did not directly lead to more visits. It may be possible for bloggers to stimulate more feedback by enhancing the content or media richness of their entries. By doing this, more people may submit comments, which then indirectly raises the visit rate.[12]

Overall, our findings show that some people may read blogs to seek targeted information, but there are also people who are active in providing comments, which could be one key factor in dictating the success of a blog in terms of gathering more visits and gaining popularity. The use of blogging tools and technologies could matter, but only certain tools or features are relevant—we found no evidence that use of top navigation bars, tag boxes, and search engines, and inclusion of trackback features, affected blog visits. Most of the features that we now see on blogs are invented to empower people to track a discussion or locate some specific content, but apparently they are not equally useful from all visitors' viewpoints. Some technology features (e.g., sidebars) may in fact reduce individual's desire to visit a blog. Obviously, bloggers or blog hosts need to exercise judgment in selecting the right mix of blog site features (Du and Wagner, 2006).

Methodologically, the use of a random effects model allowed us to account for blog-specific heterogeneity that persists over time. More important, we were able to estimate the effects due to the blogging tools and technologies that otherwise would have been infeasible if we were to employ dummy-variable regressions. The random effects that we estimated from the visit rate equation are plotted in Figure 9.5. Evidently, the blogs that we studied differed quite significantly in terms of their ability to generate visits.

The Lagrange multiplier test in the fifth section confirmed that, in the case of *Visit Rate*, the random effects specification fits the data better than a simple OLS model with one overall constant. A quick comparison with the one-constant OLS model (the results of which are not reported here) showed that the estimated parameters in a random effects model could differ considerably in magnitude. Hence, unless the sample size is very large (in which case the point about estimator efficiency is moot), the use of random effects is recommended in future empirical research related to blogs. Indeed, the use of random effects models could well be the *only* feasible solution if some other model variables are correlated with blog-specific dummy variables.

Also, the results in Table 9.5 show that failing to account for endogeneity could lead to serious underestimation of the effect of the number of new comments on visit rate. So it is important for future blog research to develop a more in-depth understanding of the dynamics of the interactions between bloggers and visitors, and to use such knowledge to guide effective empirical estimation.

CONCLUSION

This chapter serves two purposes. First, we illustrate how econometric techniques can be applied in empirical information systems research to facilitate the analysis of massive amounts of data that comprise a large number of cross-sectional units and multiple time periods, and that cannot be systematically controlled by the researchers.[13] Such data are becoming available because of increased information transparency on the Internet, faster network transmission, and advances in Web bot and intelligent agent technologies, all of which make large-scale data collection from external sources much easier and affordable to a researcher. Our second purpose is to explore the communication dynamics exhibited in blogs—one of the fastest growing phenomena on the Internet. We reiterate our specific contributions and discuss the limitations of this research below.

Contributions

Using a set of panel data collected from 100 blogs for seven days in February 2006, we studied the visit and interaction patterns between bloggers and visitors, as a means of illustrating the nature of empirical advances and discovery of new information that are possible with interesting new sources of data that have become available on the Internet. Our methodology accounted for unobservable blog-specific effects, even when these effects were perfectly correlated with some independent variables and hence could not be estimated directly in the traditional dummy-variable fashion. Our methodology also explicitly allows for mutual influences between blog visits and comments, which has not received much attention in previous blog studies.

We found that blog popularity, in terms of actual number of visits, is systematically influenced by social and technological factors. People submit more comments in response to new entries, and these comments enhance the popularity of the blogs. Our findings also provide support for the notion that some people may read blogs to seek specific types of information. Hence, blogs could potentially serve as information repositories or an interaction medium as well. Future research should explore how blogs could be better used for different managerial or social applications.

Limitations

There are several limitations in this study. First, our snapshot was very short at just seven days, and only a demonstration of our approach, instead of a fully conclusive treatment of these issues. Hence, we were not able to assess the actual diffusion of the studied blogs. A longer time window, possibly in the magnitude of months or years, is necessary to gain further insights into the evolution of blogs, and to determine whether blog visits are subject to other social influences, such as word of mouth, fads, or the timing of a particular discussion topic. The number of blogs that we sampled was small compared with the size of the overall blog population too, and this may threaten the external validity of our findings. Future research should survey more blogs and observe each blog for a longer period of time to augment the knowledge gained in this study.

We also focused exclusively on objective data that we could directly obtain from the blogs that we studied or from Site Meter. We did not include other dimensions such as content quality or blogger reputation, however, and these are important variables that obviously will affect people's inclination to visit, read, and respond to blogs. The incorporation of random effects and the use of the standardized *Visit Rate* variable in our model should have captured the effects due to some of these qualitative variables. These two measures, however, could only account for blog-specific heterogeneity that persists over time. If the effects of the missing variables are temporal, then the use of random effects and standardized variables is insufficient, and the estimated parameters may be inconsistent. In this case, the only solution is to collect additional information on the missing variables. How to operationalize and measure these mostly qualitative variables is a key challenge for future research.

Finally, it is worth noting that an important assumption of the random effects model is that the random effects, in our case, the u_i and v_i in Equations 9.3 and 9.4, are uncorrelated with the independent variables. If this assumption does not hold (e.g., if a certain blog feature systematically increases the visit rate of some blogs more than the others), then the random effects specification will again lead to inconsistent estimates. In this case, the fixed effects model or instrumental variable regression should be used.

ACKNOWLEDGMENTS

The authors would like to thank the two editors, and seminar participants at the City University of Hong Kong for their helpful comments and suggestions, and the National University of Singapore for providing the resources needed for this research.

NOTES

1. During the dot-com boom, the values of many start-up companies were determined by the number of visits that they were able to obtain. Evidently, in the online world, traffic can sometimes be translated into a "currency" (Blood, 2002).

2. Although many blogs are able to generate good publicity and visits, a much larger number of blogs suffer from poor readership and are abandoned because visitors are overloaded by information or simply are not aware of their existence. In general, the popularity of blogs may follow a power law distribution (Shirky, 2003), and a *long tail* (Anderson, 2004; Brynjolfsson, Hu, and Smith, 2006) may well exist in blog traffic.

3. We will not distinguish *new visits* and *repeated visits,* as most online tracking sites do not report separate visit and revisit statistics. Hereafter, we use the term *visit* to refer to both visits and revisits. We used *visit rate,* which is defined as the number of new visits to a blog divided by its average number of daily visits, as the dependent variable, because visit rate is standardized. The number of new visits may consistently vary across blogs because of unobservable factors (e.g., some blogs may have been listed on more search engines), and hence it is not suitable for our purpose.

4. This is likely to be the case in future empirical blog research as well. Given the millions of blogs on the Internet, random or some other forms of sampling from the entire blog population is unavoidable.

5. FGLS is a standard econometric procedure to estimate the parameters with an unknown covariance matrix. In the case of a random effects model, specifically, Equations 9.3 and 9.4, the assumption of constant, nonzero variances for u_i and v_i would imply that OLS regressions are inefficient (i.e., the estimated parameters would be less precise if we do not account for these variances). FGLS uses the OLS estimator to compute an unbiased estimator of the covariance matrix of the parameters. This covariance matrix estimator is then entered, in a standard weighted least squares fashion, into the subsequent estimations to obtain efficient estimates of the parameters of interest (i.e., the effects of the independent variables). See the fifth

section for more details on estimating the random effects model. Up to this point we have not considered the endogeneity of visit rate and the number of new comments. We will return to that later.

6. For a more detailed discussion on the choices of instrumental variables, the interested reader should see Angrist and Krueger (2001).

7. blo.gs (www.blo.gs) is one of the largest portals that tracks active blogs from different sources. At the time when we composed our sample, blo.gs was tracking close to 68 million blogs, compared with Technorati.com's 30.4 million.

8. The 2SLS procedure, often called *instrumental variable estimation,* proceeds as follows. In the "first stage," the endogenous variable in question (in our case, the *Number of New Comments*) is regressed on all instrumental and other independent variables. The predicted values in this regression are computed, and are then used in the "second stage" (i.e., the original full regression) to replace the original endogenous variable in question. Essentially, the first stage serves to purify and remove unwanted variations in the problematic variable.

9. In our case it was impossible to estimate a fixed effects model, because some of the blog-specific dummy variables were correlated with the feature variables. The data matrix with blog-specific dummy variables was singular.

10. Estimation using an overall constant in Equation 9.2 produced results similar to those in Table 9.5, except that there was a decrease in the significance of the blog entry characteristics.

11. The possibility for blogs to form such an online community has been recognized by some news agencies. For example, MSNBC.com has used blogs to stimulate interesting debates on stem cell research, the death penalty, democratic nominees for the 2008 U.S. presidential election, and so on. The authors thank the editors for this observation.

12. We also regressed (by G2SLS with random effects) the *Number of New Entries* on the *Number of New Comments* and the *Cumulative Number of Visits,* and we found both coefficients to be positive and significant ($p < 0.01$). These results are consistent with previous research: one important motivation to blog is to seek feedback and opinions from others (Menchen, 2005; Nardi et al., 2004). We do not report the detailed statistical results for these findings to maintain brevity in this chapter.

13. Examples of cross-sectional units on the Internet may include blogs, the book titles contained in an online bookstore, the items that are auctioned on eBay, and so on.

REFERENCES

Adamic, L. and Glance, N. 2005. The political blogosphere and the 2004 U.S. election: Divided they blog. Paper presented at the Second Annual Workshop on the Weblogging Ecosystem: Aggregation, Analysis, and Dynamics, Chiba, Japan, May 10.

Advertising Age. 2005. Sony pays $25,000 a month for gawker blog, 76, 5 (January 31). Available at www.marketingtom.com/2005/02/index.html (accessed January 15, 2007).

Ajzen, I. and Fishbein, M. 1980. *Understand Attitudes and Predicting Social Behavior.* Englewood Cliffs, NJ: Prentice Hall.

Anderson, C. 2004. The long tail. *Wired Magazine,* October.

Angrist, J.D. and Krueger, A.B. 2001. Instrumental variables and the search for identification: From supply and demand to natural experiments. *Journal of Economic Perspectives,* 15, 4, 69–85.

Baltagi, B.H. 2001. *Econometric Analysis of Panel Data.* 2d ed. West Sussex, UK: Wiley.

Blood, R. 2002. *We've Got Blog: How Weblogs Are Changing Our Culture.* Cambridge, UK: Perseus Publishing.

Brynjolfsson, E.; Hu, Y.J.; and Smith, M.D. 2006. From niches to riches: Anatomy of the long tail. *Sloan Management Review,* 47, 4, 67–71.

Bucy, E.P., and Lang, A. 1999. Formal features of cyberspace: Relationships between Web page complexity and site traffic. *Journal of the American Society for Information Science,* 50, 13, 1246–1256.

Davis, F.D. 1989. Perceived usefulness, perceived ease of use, and user acceptance of information technology. *MIS Quarterly,* 13, 3, 319–340.

Delone, W.H. and McLean, E.R. 1992. Information systems success: The quest for the dependent variable. *Information Systems Research,* 13, 1, 60–95.

Du, H.S. and Wagner, C. 2006. Weblog success: Exploring the role of technology. *International Journal of Human Computer Studies,* 64, 9, 789–798.

Gelder, P.V.; Beijer, G.; and Berger, M. 2002. Statistical analysis of page views on Web sites. In A. Zanasi, C.A. Brebbia, N.F.F. Ebecken, and P. Melli, eds., *Proceedings of the 3rd International Conference on Data Mining Methods and Databases, Data Mining III.* Series: Management Information Systems, Vol. 6. Southampton, UK: WIT Press, pp. 979–988.

Greene, W.H. 2003. *Econometric Analysis.* Englewood Cliffs, NJ: Prentice Hall.

Gruhl, D.R.; Guha, R.; Kumar, J.; Novak, T.P.; and Tomkins, A. 2005. The predictive power of online chatter. In *Proceedings of the 11th ACM SIGKDD International Conference on Knowledge Discovery in Data Mining,* August 21–24. New York: ACM Press, 78–87.

Herring, S.C.; Scheidt, L.A.; Wright, E.; and Bonus, S. 2005. Weblogs as a bridging genre. *Information Technology and People,* 18, 2, 142–171.

Hindman, M.S.; Tsioutsiouliklis, K.; and Johnson, J.A. 2004. Measuring media diversity online and offline: Evidence from political Web sites. Paper presented at the 32nd Research Conference on Communication, Information and Internet Policy, National Center for Technology and Law, School of Law, George Mason University, October 1–3.

Hoffman, D.L. and Novak, T.P. 1996. Marketing in hypermedia computer-mediated environments: Conceptual foundations. *Journal of Marketing,* 60, 3 (July), 50–68.

Lim, K.H. and Benbasat, I. 2000. The effect of multimedia on perceived equivocality and perceived usefulness of information systems. *MIS Quarterly,* 42, 3, 153–179.

McAfee, A.P. 2006. Enterprise 2.0: The dawn of emergent collaboration. *Sloan Management Review,* 47, 3, 20–28.

McKinney, V.; Yoon, K.; and Zahedi, F.M. 2002. The measurement of Web customer satisfaction: An expectation and disconfirmation approach. *Information Systems Research,* 13, 3, 296–315.

Menchen, E. 2005. Blogger motivations: Power, pull and positive feedback. Paper presented at the *6th International and Interdisciplinary Association of Internet Researchers,* Chicago, October 5–9. Available at blog.erickamenchen.net/MenchenBlogMotivations.pdf (accessed January 5, 2007).

Nardi, B.A.; Schiano, D.J.; and Gumbrecht, M. 2004. Blogging as social activity, or would you let 900 million people read your diary? In J.D. Herbsleb, and G.M. Olson, eds., *Proceedings of the 2004 ACM Conference on Computer Supported Cooperative Work,* Chicago, November 16–24. New York: ACM Press, 222–231.

Nardi, B.A.; Schiano, D.J.; Gumbrecht, M.; and Swartz, L. 2004. Why we blog? *Communications of the ACM,* 47, 12, 41–46.

Nielsen, J. 2000. *Designing Web Usability.* Indianapolis, IN: New Riders.

Novak, T.P.; Hoffman, D.L.; and Yung, Y.F. 2000. Measuring the customer experience in online environments: A structural modeling approach. *Marketing Science,* 19, 1, 22–42.

Palmer, J.W. 2002. Web site usability, design and performance metrics. *Information Systems Research,* 13, 2, 151–167.

Shirky, C. 2003. Power laws, weblogs, and inequality. Entry on author's Networks, Economics and Culture mailing list, February 8. Available at shirky.com/writings/powerlaw_weblog. html (accessed January 18, 2007).

Simmons, E. 2005. The impact of the Weblog: A case study of the United States and Iran. Unpublished senior honor's thesis, Ohio State University, Columbus. Available at kb.osu.edu/dspace/bitstream/ 1811/371/1/ BlogImpact.pdf (accessed January 18, 2006).

Technorati.com. 2006. About us. Available at www.technorati.com/about/ (accessed December 25, 2006).

Trammell, K.D. and Keshelashvili, A. 2005. Examining the new influencers: A self-presentation study of A-list blogs. *Journalism and Mass Communication Quarterly,* 82, 4, 968–982.

Viegas, F.B. 2005. Bloggers' expectations of privacy and accountability: An initial survey. *Journal of Computer Mediated Communication,* 10, 3, 78–87.

CHAPTER 10

CHOICE-BASED SAMPLING AND ESTIMATION OF CHOICE PROBABILITIES IN INFORMATION SYSTEMS AND E-COMMERCE RESEARCH

JUNGPIL HAHN AND CHEN ZHANG

Abstract: As information systems (IS) and technologies proliferate, an unprecedented amount of business and individual activities have become mediated and captured by computers. Consequently, Internet technology has enabled academic researchers in information systems to access rich data sets (e.g., Weblog files, interpersonal communication history) that heretofore have been unavailable. These newly available data provide IS and e-commerce scholars with an excellent opportunity to observe individual activities online in an unobtrusive manner. Existing empirical methods, however, may be insufficient to analyze the Internet-enabled data. In this chapter we propose the application of choice-based sampling and weighted exogenous sampling maximum likelihood estimation to properly handle large-scale dyadic data sets representing infrequently occurring events. We then illustrate this empirical method using an example drawn from an open source software development context. The empirical advance associated with this approach is that it allows the researcher to analyze the influences of relational factors between the two entities involved in an event without excessive sampling cost and computation time. Through this research, we demonstrate that Internet technology not only brings along efficiency gains in research data collection, but also has the potential to help support the development of innovative empirical methods to analyze the data and eventually develop more in-depth explanatory theories.

Keywords: Choice-Based Sampling, e-Commerce Empirical Methods, Logistic Regression, Rare Events Response-Based Sampling, Weighted Exogenous Sampling Maximum Likelihood (WESML) Estimator

INTRODUCTION

As information systems (IS) and technologies proliferate and online activities rapidly grow, an unprecedented amount of transaction-related and product-related information that was either too difficult or too costly to obtain has become readily accessible to both practitioners and researchers. First, the interactions between consumers and e-commerce Web sites can be collected and stored in Web server log files. With business transactions increasingly being conducted online, consumer activities such as browsing, searching, ordering, and requesting support are captured and stored in a rich stream of digital records. Second, a vast amount of market information such as product information and price information have also been made available. For example, many online auctions reveal buyer, seller, and bid information to the public for both ongoing and completed auctions. Likewise, online travel agents such as Expedia.com (www.expedia.com) and Travelocity.com (www.travelocity.com) provide detailed information about product bundles.

Increasing online social interactions have also made more data available that reflect interpersonal activities. At the individual level, decreasing hardware costs, availability of software applications, and high penetration of high-speed Internet access have prompted many people to engage in social activities online. More and more social interactions have also become computer mediated in such formats as e-mail messages, instant messaging, and online communities exchanges, making these activities potentially recordable and usable for academic and marketing research. Furthermore, the increased prevalence of *user-generated content*—online content that is produced and published by users themselves (e.g., content on discussion forums, blogs, video-sharing sites or wikis)—has made even more data available to businesses and academic researchers. Related to user-generated content are user-led innovations such as *open source software development* (OSSD). Advances in computer-mediated communication have enabled software developers to collaborate on a project in a distributed environment, where interactions among developers are logged and observable by others.

Businesses, meanwhile, are faced with the growing need to extract useful information from the newly available, technology-enabled data to assist with their decision making. Internet-based sellers need to understand online consumer behavior to develop effective pricing, bundling, marketing, and other strategies. A recent Forrester Research report predicts that online retail will continue growing at a double-digit rate in the coming years, and that B2C sales are expected to reach $200 billion in 2009 (Mulpuru et al., 2006). However, despite the growth in consumer online spending, consumer overall satisfaction with online shopping experience has decreased (Johnson and Mulpuru, 2006). Meanwhile, consumers have become better informed due to easy access to online information and less sensitive to advertising. Additionally, online shoppers are becoming more price sensitive and concerned about security and privacy-related issues. Mulpuru et al. (2006) also report that the majority of online consumers consider themselves to be brand loyalists. Online retailers face even more challenges in understanding consumer behavior in order to better acquire and retain customers, especially high-valued and loyal customers. As a result, e-commerce companies have recognized customer information as one of their key assets and invested in learning more about their customers through data mining and customer relationship management applications.

From an IS and e-commerce research perspective, Internet technologies have not only facilitated research data collection through automated data collection techniques but also have generated an incredible amount of data for research purposes and are precipitating changes in how we can go about studying a variety of communication, organizational, and business phenomena (Kauffman and Wood, Chapter 2, this volume). Some of the new data sources utilized by researchers include online product reviews (Chevalier and Mayzlin, 2006), Internet clickstream data (Hahn and Kauffman, 2006; Moe, 2006), online collaboration activities (Roberts, Hann, and Slaughter, 2006), and online auction data (Bapna, Goes, and Gupta, 2003, 2004; Pavlou and Gefen, 2005). These data sets usually contain a large number of observations due to relatively lower data collection costs. More important, researchers now have the ability to capture individual behavior and e-commerce transactions embedded in realistic situations. For example, the consumer search process that leads to purchase decisions is now directly observable. In addition to data about ongoing events, data about past activities and transactions may also be collected by researchers.

As we will show later, these new data have interesting peculiarities that present challenges as well as opportunities for researchers in information systems and e-commerce. Empirical advances in methods are needed to overcome the challenges and to take advantage of the opportunities. For example, many of these newly available data are large-scale dyadic data representing rare events, where the availability of appropriate analysis techniques is limited. Although some estimation methods have been applied to analyze rare events data in IS and e-commerce research (Cameron and Trivedi, 1986, 1998; Dai and Kauffman, 2005; Greene, 2000; Maddala, 1983), we propose the application of *choice-based sampling* and the *weighted exogenous sampling maximum likelihood* (WESML) *estimator* to more accurately and efficiently analyze such large-scale data sets representing discrete and infrequent, yet important, events. We provide an illustration of this method in an open source software development context. Specifically, we study the impact of developers' collaborative relations on how project teams are formed. This study will shed light on the self-organizing process of these teams embedded in a social network. Our assessment of the formation process of open source software development teams is made possible by the fact that online collaborative activities among software developers can be captured and observed by researchers. Traditionally, software development activities are coordinated through face-to-face interactions. Advances in communications technologies have enabled software developers to collaborate online, where most of their activities and communications are recorded and archived.

Our proposed empirical method can be applied to further examine a number of economic phenomena such as consumer choices and information search. Consumer choices have been studied extensively in the economics literature. Traditionally, research on consumer choice has been based on experiments and surveys. As most consumer online activities are captured and stored by e-commerce companies, researchers may be able to observe consumer choice behavior in online environments in an unobtrusive manner. Choice-based sampling and its associated estimation method have great potential to help researchers gain a deeper understanding of online consumer choice behavior and to assist them with developing and testing economic theories of individual choice. Additionally, consumer search behavior, which has been studied extensively in the economics literature (Diamond, 1987; Rothschild, 1973; Stigler, 1961; Weitzman, 1979; Wilde, 1980), can also be investigated by applying choice-based sampling to Internet clickstream data. For example, researchers can examine consumers' tendency to search for information across competing retailers' sites as well as their search patterns within an e-commerce site as their responses to search results are recorded in clickstream data.

The chapter is organized as follows. The second section identifies the type of data made available by Internet technology. To illustrate how to overcome the methodological difficulties imposed by the technology-enabled data, we propose an innovative application of choice-based sampling and WESML estimator. After introducing the empirical method in the third section, we apply the method to an open source software development context in the fourth section. After identifying other potential e-commerce and IS areas where the method may be applicable in the fifth section, we conclude in the sixth section with a discussion of our contributions and the limitations of our recommended approach.

RESEARCH DATA IN THE INTERNET ERA

In this section, first, we benchmark IS and e-commerce research against marketing research to examine the shift in types of research data available to researchers. Next, we identify the characteristics of the Internet technology-enabled data that require empirical advances to better handle these data.

Data used in marketing research have gone through some fundamental changes due to the emergence of new technology. Before the creation and wide adoption of scanner technology, for example, the main data sources used by marketing researchers were experiments, surveys, and panel data (Bearden and Shimp, 1982; Cavusgil and Nevin, 1981; Churchill and Surprenant, 1982; Huber and McCann, 1982; Jeuland, 1982). Since the mid-1980s, research on UPC scanner data has been actively conducted by marketing scholars. Scanner data combined with other household data and marketing activities opened up an array of research opportunities to better understand marketing variables and to develop empirical methods (Baron and Lock, 1995; Bucklin et al., 2002; Guadagni and Little, 1983). About a decade ago, Internet clickstream data became available when Web-based information systems were able to track and store detailed information about e-commerce transactions and usage. Compared with scanner data, clickstream data can provide much more information about the interaction between consumer and e-commerce Web site (Bucklin et al., 2002). Correspondingly, in recent years an increasing number of papers have been published in marketing utilizing clickstream data. For example, Moe (2003) develops a typology of online store visits based on shoppers' underlying objectives and empirically tests it on Internet clickstream data obtained from an e-commerce site. Bucklin et al. (2002) survey clickstream research in the marketing literature and discuss future research opportunities that can advance understanding of consumer choice behavior. They suggest this new source of data requires researchers to develop new choice models based on new assumptions to understand and predict online consumer behavior, which is different from offline consumer behavior.

Similarly, data sources used in IS research are also going through some fundamental changes. Data used in many IS studies have traditionally been collected through various sources such as surveys, archives, laboratory experiments, and case studies. Pinsonneault and Kraemer (1993) give a review and assessment of survey methodology used in IS research. Collecting survey data involves eliciting subjective reports from respondents about the characteristics, actions, beliefs, or attitudes concerning a phenomenon of interest. Although survey research has several advantages, such as result generalizability, being able to predict behavior, and being able to objectively test theoretical propositions, survey data typically provide only a snapshot of behavior and offer limited understanding of the behavioral context (Runkel and McGrath, 1972). Although collecting archival data does not require researchers' direct probing of the subjects, the data may have some limitations in their construct validity, measurement accuracy, and criteria consistency. Case studies generally provide more detailed information about a phenomenon within its real-life context and can help with framing research questions to be examined quantitatively. However, conducting case studies is very time consuming and labor intensive, limiting the number of cases being studied and the representativeness of the case to the general population. Laboratory experiments enable researchers to maximize deliberate manipulation of variables of interest and to examine causal relations between variables. However, the results may not generalize beyond the artificial context of the experimental conditions.

As pointed out by Kauffman and Wood (Chapter 2, this volume), Internet technologies have provided academic researchers with vehicles for extending existing data collection methods and testing existing and new theories within a revisionist philosophy of science. Online surveys are not only less expensive and faster than traditional paper-based surveys, they can also provide validated answers using accuracy checks during the survey process. Online experiments also have the potential to involve a larger number of subjects at a lower cost. They may also offer greater convenience because experimenters and subjects do not need to be collocated during experimental sessions, and hence experiments can be conducted around the clock. Overall, Internet technologies can improve the efficiency of the research data collection process by reducing cost and increasing speed.

Moreover, advances in technology have not only extended existing data collection techniques but have also created a large amount of data that were heretofore unavailable. Consider some of the data that have become available in recent years:

- Online transaction and product-related data, such as price and sales information. Specific examples include auction data from Onsale.com (Bapna, Goes, and Gupta, 2003, 2004; Easley and Tenorio, 2004), uBid.com (Easley and Tenorio, 2004), and eBay.com (Vishwanath, 2004; Zeithammer, 2006), product information from online travel agents (Clemons et al., 2006; Johnson et al., 2004), and product information from online booksellers (Brynjolfsson, Hu, and Smith, 2003).
- Online consumer reviews, such as book reviews (Chevalier and Mayzlin, 2006) and beer reviews (Clemons, Gau, and Hitt, 2006).
- Online interpersonal communication and file-sharing data, such as Usenet discussions (Godes and Mayzlin, 2004), listservs (Butler, 2001), and P2P file-sharing activities (Asvanund et al., 2004; Gopal, Bhatacharjee, and Sanders, 2006).
- Open source software development data provided by SourceForge.net (Grewel, Lilien, and Mallapragada, 2006; Hahn, Moon, and Zhang, 2006; Howison and Crowston, 2004; Roberts, Hann, and Slaughter, 2006; Stewart and Gosain, 2006; Stewart, Ammeter, and Maruping, 2006).
- Internet clickstream data obtained from online retailers (Hahn and Kauffman, 2006; Moe, 2003; 2006; Montgomery et al., 2004), commercial Web sites (Bucklin and Sismeiro, 2003), and sponsored-content Web sites (Chatterjee, Hoffman, and Novak, 2003).

These data enabled by Web technologies have some attractive characteristics that most traditional research data, such as survey data and archival data, do not have. First, the data are captured during the activities, helping researchers observe individual-level behavior in a direct yet unobtrusive manner and analyze it without having to take it out of its context. Second, it is relatively easier to have sufficient observations in the sample due to an abundance of data. Third, computer-mediated activities can be captured in their entirety together with activity histories. For example, researchers can obtain historical information about past interactions and observe the online social context accumulated from past activities. In e-commerce research, clickstream data have become available about consumer purchasing behavior as well as consumer browsing behavior; these data would not have been available through traditional data collection means. Fourth, the data are usually at a lower level of granularity. For instance, individual-level and product-level data are available from clickstream data, offering researchers more flexibility in aligning their unit of analysis with different research objectives.

On the other hand, the nature of existing forms of online data may require researchers to develop methodological innovations to be able to analyze such data accurately and efficiently. For example, many of these newly available data are large-scale dyadic data that represent rare events for the following reasons.

First, advances in IT have dramatically increased the processing and storage capabilities of Web-based information systems. Online transactions and activities take place around the clock, resulting in a large number of records and large-scale data sets available for research.

Second, the data often represent *dyadic interactions* between an individual and an information system (e.g., online purchasing) or between two individuals (e.g., online social networking). Because data are automatically captured for each online event or interaction, the granularity of the data is usually much finer than the granularity of data collected from traditional direct-probing methods, such as surveys or instruments. Hence, researchers are able to observe occurrences of individual actual events instead of summaries of events. In addition, Evans (1963) proposes that selling be modeled as a dyadic relationship and that the sale is a product of the dyadic interaction of a salesman and a potential customer rather than a product of either party's individual qualities. The same is true for online selling and interpersonal communications, since the purchase and communication event takes place between a retailer and a consumer or between two people, which in this case signifies a dyadic relationship between two parties. Furthermore, data captured at the dyadic level can help us investigate phenomena at a micro level rather than at an aggregate level. For example, with aggregate data we can investigate research questions like: "What are the factors that influence customers' online purchasing behaviors?" However, with micro-level data we can examine different questions: "What are the factors that motivate a customer to purchase a particular product and not some other product?" In summary, Internet-enabled data are often dyadic in nature, and this structure gives rise to some challenges and opportunities that are worth exploring.

Third, an event of interest to researchers may occur very infrequently, mainly because data represent actual occurrences of events. For instance, besides examining the relationship between customers and products in general, we can investigate the relationship between specific customers and specific products. Although at an aggregate level, the relationship between two types of entities need not necessarily be rare, the specific relationship between a particular entity and another particular entity is likely to be rare given the large number of possible choices of entities involved in a dyadic relationship.

For instance, online auction data consisting of seller-buyer dyads, with the event of interest being "placing a bid," may help researchers examine the factors contributing to buyers' bidding decision. Online communication data in a knowledge exchange context may consist of dyadic pairs between a knowledge seeker and a knowledge provider and the event being studied is the exchange taking place. Product-consumer dyads in clickstream data may also be used to examine an individual consumer's decision rules for choosing which product to browse or to consider buying. Similarly, in open source software development data, project-developer dyadic data may be used to investigate criteria used by developers to decide in which projects to participate.

Although some estimation methods have been applied to analyze rare events data in IS and e-commerce research (Cameron and Trivedi, 1986, 1998; Dai and Kauffman, 2005; Greene, 2000; Maddala, 1983), these methods may not be sufficient to analyze large dyadic data sets with rare events. We will explain in greater depth below the reasons behind this assessment. In the following section we propose the application of choice-based sampling and weighted exogenous sampling maximum likelihood estimator as a way to improve our capabilities to analyze such large-scale dyadic data sets representing discrete and infrequent events.

MAXIMUM-LIKELIHOOD ESTIMATION FOR CHOICE-BASED SAMPLING

Rare events data have often been of great interest to researchers in fields such as political science, social science, public relations, and epidemiology (Davies, 2002; King and Zeng, 2001a; Sorenson and Stuart, 2001). They represent events that occur very infrequently in a population, such as outbreaks of wars, presidential vetoes, and rare disease infections. The dependent variable is usually a binary variable that represents the occurrence of an event. The unit of analysis is typically a dyad representing the relationship between two entities. For instance, Davies (2002) analyzes directed dyads that identify both the initiator and the target of a conflict. The binary dependent variable indicates whether there has been an international conflict between the two countries. The data set in Sorenson and Stuart (2001) consists of dyads of a venture capitalist and a target company with the dependent variable representing whether the venture capitalist invests in the target company.

Although rare events data have also been studied in econometrics and information systems (Cameron and Trivedi, 1986; Dai and Kauffman, 2005; Maddala, 1983), the unit of analysis is an entity instead of a dyad between two entities. As a result, the dependent variable is a count variable that only takes non-negative integer values denoting the frequency of an event occurring to an entity. For example, Cameron and Trivedi (1986) give an application of their modeling strategies in which the dependent variable is the number of consultations that an individual has with a doctor or a specialist in a two-week period. Their research focus here is on the association between an individual's insurance level and her healthcare use. In other words, the entity of interest is an individual, not the relationship between an individual and a doctor. Hence, although some estimation methods such as Poisson regression and negative binomial regression have been applied to analyze rare events data in which the dependent variable is a count variable, these methods are not sufficient to capture the impact of those factors specific to the parties involved in the event or the factors related to the other party.

Therefore, with dyadic data and a binary dependent variable, logistic regression seems to be appropriate since logistic regression is widely used to investigate the association between explanatory variables and a binary response variable. However, with rare events data, this statistical technique may underestimate event probabilities and lead to biased parameter estimates (King and Zeng, 2001b). One reason for such unreliable estimates is that the maximum likelihood estimators obtained by logistic regression are biased not only in samples with fewer than 200 observations but also in large samples where the proportion of positive outcomes in the samples is very small. Random sampling, in which the selection rule is independent of all other variables, and exogenous stratified sampling, in which the values of the dependent variable are randomly selected within categories defined by predictor variables, often generates too few instances of the event in the sample to make logit analysis an optimal approach. On the other hand, a sample large enough to consist of sufficient events may be either too expensive or impossible to obtain.

Among the alternative data collection strategies that have been proposed in political science, one strategy to overcome these problems is choice-based sampling or response-based sampling. Unlike random sampling and exogenous stratified sampling, *choice-based sampling* selects observations based on values of Y. Compared with observations where the response variable is 0, observations with a response variable of 1 carry much more information for the estimation of the factors influencing the occurrence of an event. The strategy is to construct a sample by collecting a fraction α of the observations with $Y = 1$ (the events or cases) and a fraction β of the observations with $Y = 0$ (the non-events or controls), such that α is much larger than β. A precondition for adopting this strategy is that the population fraction of 1s is either known or can be estimated. With rare events data, considerable resources can be saved in data collection when this sampling approach is used.

King and Zeng (2001b) also identify some potential problems that researchers need to avoid when sampling on the dependent variable. First, the sampling design for which the weighted estimation method is appropriate requires independent random selection of event and non-event observations. Second, for the sampling design to produce valid inferences, researchers need to ensure no inadvertent selection on X (i.e., independent variables) for the cases and the controls. In other words, the cases and the controls cannot be selected differently for the explanatory variables. Third, researchers should be cautious about using an explanatory variable as a dependent variable in a supplementary analysis. Fourth, determining the optimal trade-off between more observations versus more predictor variables is application-specific. Generally speaking, the optimal number of non-event observations depends on how much additional value the explanatory variables can have compared with the cost savings of collecting fewer observations.

Although choice-based sampling can ensure there are enough occurrences of events in the sample, it makes the standard maximum likelihood estimation procedure inappropriate because it will yield inconsistent and asymptotically biased estimates (Manski and Lerman, 1977; Manski and McFadden, 1981). A statistical basis for the estimators is needed. Two broad categories of estimators—*weighted estimators* and *intercept-corrected estimators*—have been proposed for maximum likelihood estimation in choice-based sampling. King and Zeng (2001b) suggest a *weighted exogenous sampling maximum-likelihood estimator* (Manski and Lerman, 1977) that is obtained by maximizing the following weighted pseudo-likelihood function:

$$\ln L_w = \frac{1}{\alpha} \sum_{\{Y_i=1\}} \ln(\frac{1}{1+e^{-x\beta}}) + \frac{1}{\beta} \sum_{\{Y_i=0\}} \ln(1 - \frac{1}{1+e^{-x\beta}})$$
$$= -\sum_{i=1}^{n} [(1/\alpha)Y_i + (1/\beta)(1-Y_i)]$$

where the weight for each sample observation is computed based on the sample and population proportions of 1s as a result of choice-based sampling.

Choice-based sampling has been used for dyadic data in a number of studies in international relations and political science over the past few years. Davies (2002) empirically tests the effects of domestic strife on the likelihood of an international conflict using a two-country dyad as the unit of analysis. Compared with a monadic study whose unit of analysis is country-year, that study examines the impacts of initiator-related factors as well as target-related factors and initiator-target-related factors, such as geographic distance, relative power, and joint democracy.

Sorensen and Stuart (2001) examine the impact of social structural factors in interfirm networks on the financing relationships between venture capitalists and startup companies by analyzing a dyadic data set. Due to the computational difficulty in analyzing all potential dyads corresponding to millions of matrix cells and the rarity of the investing event, the authors adopt a choice-based sampling strategy. The sample consists of all dyads representing the actual funding relationship as well as a matched sample of nonevents. To account properly for the effects of the sampling procedure, they adjust the coefficient estimates with logistic regression for rare events data as suggested by King and Zeng (2001b).

Within the past few years, a handful of management researchers have also started using choice-based sampling. For example, Singh (2005) investigates the effects of interpersonal networks on knowledge flow among patent inventors. In the sample, an event refers to a patent's actual citation of another patent. Since citations between any random pair of patents are extremely rare with only a few actual citations among a large number of potential citations, he follows the empirical strategy outlined in King and Zeng (2001b) and constructs a choice-based sample. WESML estimators are then calculated as suggested by Manski and Lerman (1977). Sorenson and Fleming (2004) adopt a similar approach to investigate the role of publication in accelerating the rate of technological innovation by analyzing citation patterns.

In the marketing literature, Malhotra (1984) recommends that choice-based sampling be used when the choice data can be purchased or obtained from point-of-sale surveys. Further examples include transportation mode choice (Currim, 1981, 1982) and college choice (Manski and McFadden, 1981).

In summary, choice-based sampling is most appropriate when there is a large dyadic data set representing an infrequently occurring event and when research is focused on the relational properties between the two entities involved in the event. The method not only reduces sampling cost and computation requirements, it also yields more accurate estimates when the WESML estimator is used. As discussed earlier, many Internet-enabled data contain a large number of observations at the dyad level and the occurrence of events, such as browsing and purchasing, is relatively rare.

ILLUSTRATION: OPEN SOURCE SOFTWARE DEVELOPMENT

We next illustrate the application of choice-based sampling and the associated WESML estimator in the context of IS and e-commerce research. As argued previously, an example of one type of data made possible by Internet technology-based capture of online collaboration activities involves open source software development. Traditionally, systems development activities are conducted by developers who are in the same location, and mainly coordinate their efforts through face-to-face interactions. Advances in communications technologies have enabled software developers to collaborate on projects online, where most of their activities and communications are observable to others.

Research Background and Main Hypothesis

Since the early 1990s an alternative model of software development, the *open source software development model,* has gained popularity as a viable approach to developing software (Raymond, 2001). Open source software refers to software whose source code is available to users so that they can read, modify, and redistribute new versions of the software. Unlike traditional software development teams that are formed by managers based on developer skills and experience, in most cases OSSD teams are formed by developers self-selecting into projects without monetary incentives. Usually an OSSD project starts out with a developer or a small group of developers who want to create a software product that meets their personal needs. Other developers may join the project at a later time. Open source software project success depends partly on successfully attracting and retaining volunteer developers. One of the main reasons for the failure of some OSSD projects is the lack of developers in the project teams, or the inability of the project to bring together a critical mass of developers (Lerner and Tirole, 2001; O'Reilly, 1999; von Krogh, Spaeth, and Lakhani, 2003). Although research on OSSD motivations has shed light on why individuals contribute time and effort to the development of open source software, it remains unclear how developers evaluate projects at an early stage and choose which particular project to join. Because attracting developers early is critical to the take-off and success of OSSD projects (Raymond, 2001), it would be valuable to understand individual developers' joining decisions in order to provide more actionable insights. Familiarity based on past interactions and work relationships has been identified as one important factor in work group formation (Hinds et al., 2000; Zander and Havelin, 1960). The goal of this analysis is to explore how prior project collaborative ties affect which newly initiated open source software projects developers will choose to participate in.

Earlier works on open source software development have mainly been case studies of some large-scale and well-known projects such as Apache and Linux (Gallivan, 2001; Koch and Schneider, 2002; Mockus, Fielding, and Herbsleb, 2002; Moon and Sproull, 2002). While they offer interesting insights into the phenomenon, the generalizability of their findings is limited because these projects may not be representative of the majority of open source projects. Since the introduction of SourceForge.net in the early 2000s, it has become an attractive data source for open source software development research. It is the world's largest open source software development site providing tools and resources for managing open source projects' code contribution, communications, and so on. Furthermore, it captures and stores developers' activities in its data repository accessible to interested academic researchers. The abundant data provided by SourceForge.net have given scholars many opportunities to conduct research on open source software development. Many empirical studies were conducted based on large-scale data sets collected from SourceForge.net (Crowston and Howison, 2005; Grewal, Lilien, and Mallapragada, 2006; Hahn, Moon, and Zhang, 2006; Krishnamurthy, 2002; Stewart and Gosain, 2006).

Our exploration into the formation process of open source software development teams is made possible by the availability of data related to developers' past communication and collaboration activities at SourceForge.net. We can infer developers' ties formed in past collaborations based on their past projects' data. More specifically, if both developers were participating in the same project at the same time, we assume that they have formed a collaborative tie between them. In summary, online OSSD collaboration data enabled by Internet technologies provide us with an opportunity to investigate the impact of developers' past relationships on the team formation process.

In this application, we investigate the impact of past collaborative ties on the team formation process. We propose that the existence and the strength of a prior collaborative tie between the project initiator and a developer positively influence the probability that the developer will join the project team. Developers' prior collaborative ties are captured by observing developers coparticipation in other projects hosted on SourceForge.net.

Data Collection

To test our research hypothesis, we use the developer-project dyad as the unit of analysis. Because we are interested in the impact of past relationships between a developer and a project initiator, using dyadic pairs in our analysis is likely to be more appropriate than using monadic data. We can control for the factors related to the joining developer, the project initiator, and both the joiner and the initiator.

To construct the sample, we first collected project and developer data from SourceForge.net's monthly data repository hosted at the University of Notre Dame (www.nd.edu/~oss/). As the largest repository of open source applications on the Internet, SourceForge.net currently provides free hosting to more than 130,000 projects and more than 1.4 million subscribers. We selected all public OSS projects newly registered on SourceForge.net between September 13, 2005, and October 14, 2005, yielding 1,780 observations. We also captured data on the OSS project initiators. After revisiting these projects in November 2005, we were able to identify the developers who had subsequently joined the project in the first one to two months. Furthermore, in order to identify the previous collaborative ties of the developers, we collected data on other projects that each developer had participated in prior to joining the focal project. Based on this data, we constructed affiliation matrices of developers and projects that depict the existence of the relationship ties between developers.

In addition, due to the unavailability of some project and developer information required to operationalize measures of fit between developers' technical skills and project technical requirements, we constructed the choice-based sample using a subset of the sample projects described above. Sample selection was based on availability of project and developer information required to operationalize measures of fit between developers' technical skills and project technical requirements. First, we included only those projects that explicitly defined technical details such as programming language, domain of software, and operating system platform. Second, we restricted the sample of SourceForge.net developers to those who had participated in at least one project by October 2005. As only a small percentage of developers make their technical skill profiles publicly accessible on SourceForge.net, we inferred the developers' technical skills from their past project experience. The final data set used for hypothesis testing consists of 938 projects and 173,523 developers.

Measures

Dependent Variable

The dependent variable is a binary variable that represents whether a developer joins a particular project within the first one to two months of project initiation (*Join*).

Independent Variable

To test the effects of prior collaborative ties on the formation of OSSD teams, we capture the existence of a past collaborative tie between a developer and a project initiator using a binary indicator variable (*HasTie*).[1]

In addition, the quality and strength of the tie between the developer and project initiator may depend on the nature of their past collaborative experiences. We computed measures of past collaboration quality using factor analytical methods based on data about developers' past projects' performance. Two factors emerged from the analysis. The first factor, *TieStrengthProd*, represents tie strength based on whether the outcome of the past collaboration between the developer and the project initiator was positive. The second factor, *TieStrengthProc*, represents tie strength that is dependent on the process of coordination such as whether or not the developer collaborated as administrator with the project initiator in past collaborations.

Control Variables

First, we controlled for project initiator-related characteristics that may have an impact on developers' joining decisions. It may be possible that potential OSS developers will prefer participating in projects initiated by people who are perceived to have higher status. Such status perceptions are influenced by the extent to which the initiator is perceived as being embedded within a network of developer collaborative ties, that is, the relative perceived centrality of the project initiator within the OSS developer network. Hence, we measured a project initiator's social capital based on the number of developers in the open source software development network with whom she has had previous collaborative ties prior to project inception (*InitiatorTieAmt*). In addition, it is likely that developers with prior open source project experience will have superior knowledge of OSS development and management processes, increasing the likelihood that the project outcome will be successful. Therefore, we measured the experience of project initiators using absolute participation duration at SourceForge.net (*InitiatorExpTime*) as well as the number of projects in which the initiator has participated in the past (*InitiatorExpPartic*).

Second, we captured additional developer-level characteristics that would affect developers' decisions to join a particular project. We measured the experience of developers in terms of number of projects (*DevExpPartic*) they participated in and total participation duration (*DevExpTime*) at SourceForge.net. Third, we considered the technical fit between developers' skills and the focal project's requirements in order to control for the impact of developer expertise and interest on project selection. These were captured in three variables that reflected whether the technical details in terms of topic (*MatchTopic*), programming language (*MatchProgLang*), and application

Table 10.1

Summary of Measures

Variable	Operational definition
Join (DV)	Binary variable, which equals 1 if the developer joined the project within the first one or two months of project initiation, 0 otherwise.
HasTie	Indicator variable that is equal to 1 if the developer has past collaborative ties with the project initiator, 0 otherwise.
TieStrengthProd	The strength of a collaborative tie approximated by the product of the collaboration.
TieStrengthProc	The strength of a collaborative tie approximated by the process of the collaboration.
InitiatorTieAmt	The number of collaborative ties that the project initiator has prior to project inception, calculated as the natural log of the number of distinct developers (+1) who have collaborated with the project initiator on OSS projects at SourceForge.net.
InitiatorExpTime	The project initiator's experience in terms of the natural log of the number of days since she registered on SourceForge.net.
InitiatorExpPartic	The project initiator's experience in terms of the natural log of the number of prior projects (+1) that he/she has participated in on SourceForge.net.
$DevExpTime_T$	The developer's experience in terms of the natural log of the number of days since he/she registered on SourceForge.net.
DevExpPartic	The developer's experience in terms of the natural log of the number of prior projects (+1) that he/she has participated in on SourceForge.net.
MatchTopic	Indicator variable that is 1 if the developer's prior OSS projects' topics match the project's topic, 0 otherwise.
MatchProgLang	Indicator variable that is 1 if the developer's prior OSS projects' programming languages match the project's programming language, 0 otherwise.
MatchOS	Indicator variable that is 1 if the developer's prior OSS projects' operating systems match the project's operating system, 0 otherwise.
Duration	Duration of the project's life (log of days)
DescDetail	The level of details in project description as measured by the natural log of the number of characters in the project description.
AcceptDonation	Indicator variable that is 1 if the project has been set up to accept donations from users, 0 otherwise.
TopicPopularity	Popularity of the project's topic as measured by the proportion of developers working on the top 1,000 projects within the topic category.

platform (*MatchOS*) of any of the projects in which the developer had previously participated matched the details of the new project.

Last, we controlled for other project attributes that would influence developer joining decisions. These included attributes of the project that would affect the visibility of the project to potential developers such as whether the project has been included in the OSSD community SourceForge. net software map *(TroveDefined)*, the lifetime of the project *(Duration)* and the popularity of the project application domain measured as a proportion of developers for the top 1,000 projects who work on this domain *(TopicPopularity)*. Other project attributes we measured are the level of details available in the project description that would facilitate information gathering required for making a joining decision (*DescDetail*) and whether the project is set up to accept donations from users (*AcceptDonation*). A summary of the measures computed for the empirical analysis is shown in Table 10.1.

Results

To test hypotheses at the developer-project dyad level, we adopted the technique of choice-based sampling or endogenous stratified sampling (King and Zeng, 2001b; Manski and Lerman, 1977).[2] The strategy is to choose a fraction of the developer-project dyads representing the joining event and to choose a much smaller fraction of the nonevent pairs. We used our sample of projects ($N = 938$) and selected all developers who have joined these projects as the event sample. In addition, we matched each dyad in the event sample with six control dyads as the control sample while ensuring that the control sample has similar (or dissimilar) characteristics to the event dyads. Four of the control dyads were used to control for the match between project requirement and developer skills in terms of software topic, programming language, and operating system as well as the existence of prior collaborative social ties. In addition, we selected two random dyads for each event dyad to ensure that developer-project pairs with no joining event are also included in our sample. Overall, the sampling procedure produced a sample of 3,885 dyads.

Corresponding to the choice-based sampling technique, we adopted the weighted exogenous sampling maximum-likelihood (WESML) estimator (Manski and Lerman, 1977) as a validated approach adopted in prior literature (Singh, 2005). The WESML estimator is calculated by maximizing the weighted pseudo-likelihood function that weighs each observation in the sample with the number of population observations that it represents. For example, the weight of a sample dyad that represents 100 potential dyads in the entire population is 10 times the weight of a sample dyad that represents 10 population dyads. In addition, because the same developer may be included in multiple project developer dyads, we calculated the standard errors without assuming independent errors among observations.

To investigate the robustness of the estimation for the choice-based sampling procedure, we drew 1,000 bootstrap choice-based samples to derive the bootstrap mean and the confidence intervals for each parameter estimate. Table 10.2 summarizes the descriptive statistics and Table 10.3 presents the pairwise correlations of the measures for the developer-project dyad sample. The highest correlation among the independent variables is between *InitiatorTieAmt* and *InitiatorExpPartic* ($\rho = 0.652$, $p < 0.001$).[3]

At the developer-project dyad level, we hypothesize that a collaborative tie between the developer and the project initiator (β_1) and the strength of such a tie (β_2 and β_3) will have a positive impact on developer decisions to join a project. We use WESML to estimate the parameters for the following logistic regression model:

$Pr(y = 1) = \alpha + \beta_1 HasTie + \beta_2 HasTie \cdot TieStrengthProd + \beta_3 HasTie \cdot TieStrengthProc + \beta_4 InitiatorTieAmt + \beta_5 InitiatorExpTime + \beta_6 InitiatorExpPartic + \beta_7 DevExpTime + \beta_8 DevExpPartic + \beta_9 MatchTopic + \beta_{10} MatchProgLang + \beta_{11} MatchOS + \beta_{12} Duration + \beta_{13} DescDetail + \beta_{14} AcceptDonation + \beta_{15} TopicPopularity + \varepsilon$

The results of the logistic regression are presented in Table 10.4 (see p. 264).

The variable *HasTie* has a significantly positive impact on the likelihood of developer joining ($\beta_1 = 7.244$, $p < 0.01$), suggesting that a developer is far more likely to join a project that has

Table 10.2

Descriptive Statistics (N = 3,885)

Variable	Mean	Std. dev	Min.	Max.
Join	0.14	0.351	0.00	1.00
HasTie	0.02	0.142	0.00	1.00
InitiatorTieAmt	0.56	1.041	0.00	5.64
TieStrengthProd	−0.01[a]	0.164	−2.56	3.32
TieStrengthProc	0.01[a]	0.226	−1.06	8.57
InitiatorExpTime	1.96	1.179	0.09	4.12
InitiatorExpPartic	0.52	0.632	0.00	2.77
DevExpTime	6.48	1.163	1.25	7.69
DevExpPartic	0.83	0.337	0.00	3.09
MatchTopic	0.14	0.351	0.00	1.00
MatchProgLang	0.15	0.354	0.00	1.00
MatchOS	0.19	0.395	0.00	1.00
Duration	3.97	0.164	3.62	4.22
DescDetail	5.05	0.547	2.94	5.92
AcceptDonation	0.08	0.273	0.00	1.00
TopicPopularity	0.13	0.083	0.00	0.62

[a] For developer-project dyads without ties, *TieStrengthProd* and *TieStrengthProc* are coded as 0.

been initiated by a past collaborator with whom he has had a past relationship. Furthermore, the interaction term between *HasTie* and *TieStrengthProc* has a positive and significant parameter estimate. The quality of ties associated with collaboration processes affects the strength of the relation between *HasTie* and the dependent variable, implying that a developer is more likely to join a project when the tie between the developer and the initiator is based on their prior positive collaboration experience. The interaction term between *HasTie* and *TieStrengthProd* is not significant though, indicating that the past collaboration process itself has a greater moderating influence on a developer's future joining decisions than the successful production of software. In summary, the results indicate that the existence and the strength of collaborative ties between the developer and the project originator associated with the past collaboration process positively impact the likelihood of the developer joining the project.

POTENTIAL APPLICATIONS IN IS AND E-COMMERCE RESEARCH

In this section, we propose some potential applications for our empirical methodology based on the characteristics of data sets that can be handled by the method.

Choice-based sampling together with WESML is most appropriate when:

- a data set contains dyads with two entities involved in the event;
- the event occurs very infrequently in the data set; and

Table 10.3

Correlations

Variable	(1)	(2)	(3)	(4)	(5)	(6)	(7)	(8)
(1) Join								
(2) HasTie	0.159***							
(3) HasTie · TieStrengthProd	−0.124***	−0.574***						
(4) HasTie · TieStrengthProc	0.122***	0.417***	−0.070***					
(5) InitiatorTieAmt	0.189***	0.184***	−0.079***	0.061***				
(6) InitiatorExpTime	0.010***	0.117***	−0.055***	0.047***	0.387***			
(7) InitiatorExpPartic	0.055***	0.142***	−0.075***	0.063***	0.652***	0.537***		
(8) DevExpTime	−0.602***	−0.002	0.041***	0.001	−0.135***	−0.000	−0.038	
(9) DevExpPartic	−0.131***	0.141***	−0.059***	0.091***	−0.052	0.003	0.001	0.352***
(10) MatchTopic	−0.015***	0.198***	−0.100***	0.106***	0.020	0.029***	0.019	0.117***
(11) MatchProgLang	−0.005***	0.206***	−0.097***	0.107***	0.025***	0.040***	0.024*	0.106***
(12) MatchOS	−0.067***	0.119***	−0.022*	0.072***	0.007	0.021	0.022	0.172***
(13) Duration	−0.032***	−0.010***	0.008	−0.005	−0.137***	−0.047***	−0.096***	0.050
(14) DescDetail	0.007***	0.002	0.000	−0.011*	−0.043***	−0.037***	−0.033	−0.001***
(15) AcceptDonation	−0.038***	−0.005**	−0.008	0.004	−0.049***	0.024***	−0.012	0.025
(16) TopicPopularity	0.002	0.024	0.003	0.032**	0.021	0.082***	0.021	0.006

Variable	(9)	(10)	(11)	(12)	(13)	(14)	(15)	(16)
(10) MatchTopic	0.256***							
(11) MatchProgLang	0.220***	0.216***						
(12) MatchOS	0.248***	0.212***	0.305***					
(13) Duration	0.039***	0.006***	−0.002***	−0.004***				
(14) DescDetail	0.005	0.037*	0.013	0.019	0.047*			
(15) AcceptDonation	0.018*	0.013	0.002	0.012	0.030*	0.071*		
(16) TopicPopularity	0.007	0.186***	0.019	0.054**	−0.011**	0.121***	0.018**	

Note: Significance: *** = $p < 0.01$, ** = $p < 0.05$, * = $p < 0.10$.

Table 10.4

Logistic Regression Results

Variable	Parameter estimate	Odds ratio
Constant	−2.521	—
HasTie	7.244***	1,399.211
HasTie · TieStrengthProd	−0.122	0.885
HasTie · TieStrengthProc	1.370***	3.934
InitiatorTieAmt	0.124***	1.131
InitiatorExpTime	−0.092***	0.912
InitiatorExpPartic	−0.462**	0.630
DevExpTime	−1.611***	0.200
DevExpPartic	−1.156***	0.315
MatchTopic	0.360	1.434
MatchProgLang	0.224	1.251
MatchOS	0.039	1.039
Duration	0.105	1.111
DescDetail	0.092	1.096
AcceptDonation	−0.435	0.647
TopicPopularity	−0.297	0.743

Notes: Model = logistic regression. $N = 3,885$. Parameter estimates and significance levels are derived from results of running logistic regression on 1,000 bootstrap samples.

Significance: *** = $p < 0.01$, ** = $p < 0.05$. Confidence interval 10.99 percent for model fit statistic *deviance:* (2.59, 2.74).

- the research objective is to investigate the factors associated with the relationship between the two entities.

In the management and sociology literature, choice-based sampling has been used by a number of researchers to examine how interfirm or interpersonal networks help shape the flow of exchange or the pattern of diffusion (Singh, 2005; Sorenson and Fleming, 2004). Similarly, in the IS discipline, as digital networks gain popularity with increasing participation in online communication and user-generated content, a similar method may be useful in shedding some light on how such virtual networks shape individual behavior.

Choice-based sampling can be used to study the interactions between digital networks and social networks for two reasons. First, data related to many, if not all, online communication activities, such as those in newsgroups and open source software development, are publicly available. Interactions among individuals have become more transparent over time. With the help of software agents that automatically gather such data from Web sites, researchers are able to gain access to both current and historical data, effectively capturing many of the activities in digital networks. Second, digital networks have a large number of participants whose time and efforts are not unlimited. Thus, the events being studied are likely to be rare especially in large-scale networks such as open source software developers' networks and other online collaboration networks.

One of the strengths of applying choice-based sampling to dyadic data is its ability to capture the characteristics specific to the relationship between two individuals in the network. For example, it may help identify the information diffusion patterns in online social networks such as collaboration networks. It can also assist researchers interested in empirically examining the matching process in online dating.

Choice-based sampling may also be used to examine online consumer choices with clickstream data. For example, in a traditional offline shopping environment, consumers' choice sets are rarely observable. The availability of data capturing consumer online activities has made it relatively easier to observe the choice sets by examining consumers' browsing history. Specifically it can help answer the question: "among all the available products, what factors attract consumers to product-specific pages and what decision rules do consumers adopt to make a purchase from their choice set." Furthermore, due to the rare event nature of the data, constructing a choice-based sample between multiple products and multiple consumers may help online retailers better target the right products for the right consumers.

Furthermore, clickstream data usually reveal not only consumer purchase decisions but also consumer search behavior, which has been studied extensively in the economics literature (Diamond, 1987; Rothschild, 1973; Stigler, 1961; Weitzman, 1979; Wilde, 1980). Consumer search behavior is theoretically modeled as an economic process in which a consumer's decision to seek additional information depends on the expected utility gain achieved by that additional information (Diamond, 1987).

Online information searches sometimes take place at a single retailer's Web site. Prior to purchasing a product consumers often perform a search reflecting their criteria for desired product functionalities, manufacturers, prices, and so on. After the search query is executed and the consumer is presented with a list of matching products, he or she then chooses which product to select to obtain further information. Very often the query gives a number of choices that match the search criteria and the consumer is unlikely to read detailed information about each choice. In other words, the event of a consumer actually clicking on a product among a list of search results happens infrequently. Examining consumer search processes that lead to actual purchases will not only allow researchers to further validate the economic theory of search in an online environment, it may also have several practical benefits to online retailers. For example, a deeper understanding of consumer online search behavior can help an e-tailer to present search results in a way that caters to individual consumer's needs while at the same time maximizing the e-tailer's revenues.

In addition, with consumers' increasing online shopping experience, they tend to search across different retailers' Web sites in order to identify the best price or service quality or both. Choice-based sampling technique may be used to analyze consumer search behavior across multiple competitors using comparison shopping clickstream data. Results can assist retailers in developing their pricing strategies and benchmarking against their competitors to attract more potential purchasers.

CONCLUSION

Advances in information and Internet technologies have created the availability of an unprecedented amount of business and individual activities to be mediated and captured by computers. As a result, Internet technology has enabled academic researchers in IS and e-commerce to access rich data sets that were heretofore unavailable. These data sources provide scholars with an excellent opportunity to observe online actions in an unobtrusive manner. Furthermore, our understanding of phenomena is influenced by the progress in our reliable and systematic understanding of factual knowledge (Simon, 1980). However, our existing empirical methods may not be suitable for dealing with the inherent complexity in newly available data and for capturing the knowledge conveyed in the data. Therefore, depending on the research questions, researchers may need to borrow methods from other disciplines or invent new methods to handle the data.

In this chapter, we focused on the challenges in analyzing large-scale rare events data and proposed an empirical advance that can help overcome them. Although some estimation methods such as Poisson regression and negative binomial regression have been applied in existing IS research to analyze rare events data, these methods are not sufficient to capture the impact of the factors specific to the parties involved in the event or the factors related to the other party. Therefore, logistic regression seems to be appropriate for dyadic data with a binary dependent variable. To deal with the problems associated with applying logistic regression to randomly sampled rare-event dyadic data, we propose choice-based sampling method and weighted exogenous maximum likelihood estimator to optimize data collection efforts and to increase estimation reliability in subsequent data analysis.

We also suggested some potential applications of the proposed methodology in information systems and e-commerce research. In particular, choice-based sampling and the associated estimation technique provide researchers with a tool to study individual economic behavior such as consumer choice and consumer information search. In summary, as new data sources that fit within the umbrella of the empirical advances described in this study become available, scholars will have many more opportunities to study individual economic phenomena arising from the Internet age.

Nonetheless, there are several limitations of the empirical advance we propose in this chapter. First, two broad types of estimators have been proposed for choice-based sampling or response-based sampling—*weighting estimators* (Manski and Lerman, 1977) and *intercept correction estimators* (Huber and McCann, 1982; Manski and McFadden, 1981; Prentice and Pyke, 1979). Although weighting estimators such as WESML estimators can outperform intercept correction estimators given a large sample and misspecified functional form, intercept correction estimators may be preferred when sample size is small. Second, scholars have considered several alternative sampling strategies (Bueno de Mesquita and Lalman, 1992; Verba, Schlozman, and Brady, 1995). We should take these alternative strategies and associated statistical estimation methods into consideration in order to identify the most efficient and cost-saving sampling strategy. Third, choice-based sampling is usually applied to study phenomena at an individual level. Hence, it is less appropriate when researchers try to examine joint behavior or interdependent individual behavior (e.g., social norms, strategic interactions among individuals). Fourth, abundant data do not necessarily ensure high-quality data. The strengths of our proposed empirical method are contingent on the quality of the data under investigation. The Internet-enabled data may be complemented with data obtained through traditional sources such as surveys to confirm our research findings.

In conclusion, Internet technology not only brings along efficiency gains in research data collection, it can also assist us in developing new methodologies, identifying interesting research issues, and developing in-depth explanatory theories. The peculiarities of these new data present challenges and opportunities for researchers in information systems and e-commerce. We propose the application of choice-based sampling and weighted exogenous sampling maximum likelihood estimator to better handle large-scale dyadic rare-event data. This empirical advance can help researchers overcome some challenges and take advantage of the opportunities afforded by the newly available data.

ACKNOWLEDGMENTS

The authors thank the participants at the second International Conference on Open Source Systems, the MIS research workshop at Purdue University, as well as at the 2006 Academy of Management Open Source Software Research Development Workshop for insightful comments on our approach to understanding and empirically modeling team formation dynamics in open source software development. We also thank the editors, Rob Kauffman and Paul Tallon, who encouraged us to think further about the broader applicability of these ideas in the context of Internet-enabled data collection.

NOTES

1. Using a binary variable to capture the existence of a collaborative tie may not be able to distinguish between the ties developed from a long history of frequent interactions and the ties formed from a short history of less frequent interactions.

2. For our sample, the conventional logistic regression approach with random sampling is impractical due to the rarity of a developer's project joining event. For instance, with approximately 1,000 sample projects and 170,000 sample developers, there would be over 170 million (i.e., 1,000 × 170,000) developer-project dyads in total. However, of those possible dyads, only a very small percentage of dyads represent the event that a developer joined a project. Thus, pure random sampling from all possible dyads would make the sample size impractically large and lead to biased statistical estimation.

3. The number of ties correlated with initiators' prior experience is expected because the more projects in which developers participate, the more ties they will develop. We reviewed additional collinearity diagnostic statistics such as tolerance and variance inflation factor for *InitiatorTieAmt* and *InitiatorExpPartic*, the results of which suggested that multicollinearity is not a major concern.

REFERENCES

Asvanund, A.; Clay, K.; Krishnan, R.; and Smith, M.D. 2004. An empirical analysis of network externalities in peer-to-peer music sharing networks. *Information Systems Research*, 15, 2, 155–174.

Bapna, R.; Goes, P.; and Gupta, A. 2003. Replicating online Yankee auctions to analyze auctioneers' and bidders' strategies. *Information Systems Research*, 14, 3, 244–268.

———. 2004. User heterogeneity and its impact on electronic auction market design: An empirical exploration. *MIS Quarterly*, 28, 1, 21–43.

Baron, S. and Lock, A. 1995. The challenges of scanner data. *Journal of the Operational Research Society*, 46, 1, 50–61.

Bearden, W.O. and Shimp, T.A. 1982. The use of extrinsic cues to facilitate product adoption. *Journal of Marketing Research*, 19, 2, 229–239.

Brynjolfsson, E.; Hu, Y.J.; and Smith, M.D. 2003. Consumer surplus in the digital economy: Estimating the value of increased product variety at online booksellers. *Management Science*, 49, 11, 1580–1596.

Bucklin, R.E. and Gupta, S. 1999. Commercial use of UPC scanner data: Industry and academic perspectives. *Marketing Science*, 18, 3, 247–273.

Bucklin, R.E.; Lattin, J.M.; Ansari, A.; Gupta, S.; Bell, D.; Coupey, E.; Little, J.; Mela, C.; Montgomery, A.; and Steckel, J. 2002. Choice and the Internet: From clickstream to research stream. *Marketing Letters*, 13, 3, 245–258.

Bucklin, R.E. and Sismeiro, C. 2003. A model of Web site browsing behavior estimated on clickstream data. *Journal of Marketing Research*, 40, 3, 249–267.

Bueno de Mesquita, B. and Lalman, D. 1992. *War and Reason: Domestic and International Imperatives*. New Haven, CT: Yale University Press.

Butler, B.S. 2001. Membership size, communication activity, and sustainability: A resource-based model of online social structures. *Information Systems Research*, 12, 4, 346–362.

Cameron, A.C. and Trivedi, P.K. 1986. Econometric models based on count data: Comparisons and applications of some estimators and tests. *Journal of Applied Econometrics*, 1, 1, 29–54.

———. 1998. Regression analysis of count data. *Econometric Society Monograph*, no. 30. Cambridge: Cambridge University Press, 1998.

Cavusgil, S.T. and Nevin, J.R. 1981. Internal determinants of export marketing behavior: An empirical investigation. *Journal of Marketing Research*, 18, 1, 114–119.

Chatterjee, P.; Hoffman, D.L.; and Novak, T.P. 2003. Modeling the clickstream: Implications for Web-based advertising efforts. *Marketing Science*, 22, 4, 520–541.

Chevalier, J.A. and Mayzlin, D. 2006. The effect of word of mouth on sales: Online book reviews. *Journal of Marketing Research*, 43, 3, 345–354.

Churchill, G.A., Jr. and Surprenant, C. 1982. An investigation into the determinants of customer satisfaction. *Journal of Marketing Research*, 19, 4, 491–504.

Clemons, E.K.; Gao, G.; and Hitt, L.M. 2006. When online reviews meet hyper-differentiation: A study of the craft beer industry. *Journal of Management Information Systems*, 23, 2, 149–171.

Crowston, K. and Howison, J. 2005. The social structure of free and open source software development. *First Monday*, 10, 2. Available at www.firstmonday.org/issues/issue10_2/crowston/index.html (accessed May 20, 2007).

Currim, I.S. 1981. Using segmentation approaches for better prediction and understanding from consumer mode choice models. *Journal of Marketing Research*, 18, 3, 301–309.

———. 1982. Predictive testing of consumer choice models not subject to independence of irrelevant alternatives. *Journal of Marketing Research*, 19, 2, 208–222.

Dai, Q. and Kauffman, R.J. 2005. Partnering for perfection: An economics perspective on B2B electronic market strategic alliances. In K. Tomak, ed., *Advances in Information Systems and Economics*. Harrisburg, PA: Idea Group, 43–79.

Davies, G.A.M. 2002. Domestic strife and the initiation of international conflicts: A directed dyad analysis. *Journal of Conflict Resolution*, 46, 5, 672–692.

Diamond, P. 1987. Search theory. In J. Eatwell, M. Milgate, and P. Newman, eds., *The New Palgrave Dictionary of Economics*. London: Macmillan.

Easley, R.F., and Tenorio, R. 2004. Jump bidding strategies in Internet auctions. *Management Science*, 50, 10, 1407–1420.

Evans, F.B. 1963. Selling as a dyadic relationship: A new approach. *American Behavioral Scientist*, 6, 9, 76–79.

Gallivan, M.J. 2001. Striking a balance between trust and control in a virtual organization: A content analysis of open source software case studies. *Information Systems Journal*, 11, 4, 277–304.

Godes, D. and Mayzlin, D. 2004. Using online conversations to study word-of-mouth communication. *Marketing Science*, 23, 4, 545–560.

Gopal, R.; Bhatacharjee, S.; and Sanders, L. 2006. Do artists benefit from online music sharing? *Journal of Business*, 79, 1503–1533.

Greene, W. 2000. *Econometric Analysis*. 4th ed. Englewood Cliffs, NJ: Prentice Hall.

Grewal, R.; Lilien, G.; Mallapragada, G. 2006. Location, location, location: How network embeddedness affects project success in open source systems. *Management Science*, 52, 7, 1043–1056.

Guadagni, P.M. and Little, J.D.C. 1983. A logit model of brand choice calibrated on scanner data. *Marketing Science*, 2, 3, 203–238.

Hahn, J. and Kauffman, R.J. 2006. A design science approach for identifying usability problems in Web sites that support Internet-based selling. Working paper, MIS Research Center, University of Minnesota, Minneapolis.

Hahn, J.; Moon, J.Y.; and Zhang, C. 2006. Impact of social ties on open source software team formation. In *Proceedings of the Second International Conference on Open Source Systems*, Como, Italy, June, 307–317.

Hinds, P.J.; Carley, K.M.; Krackhardtm, D.; and Wholey, D. 2000. Choosing work group members: Balancing similarity, competence, and familiarity. *Organizational Behavior and Human Decision Processes*, 81, 2, 226–251.

Howison, J. and Crowston, K. 2004. The perils and pitfalls of mining SourceForge. *Proceedings of the 26th International Conference on Software Engineering (ICSE 2004)*, Mining Software Repositories Workshop, Edinburgh. Available at floss.syr.edu/publications/howison04msr.pdf (accessed February 1, 2008).

Huber, J. and McCann, J. 1982. The impact of inferential beliefs on product evaluations. *Journal of Marketing Research*, 19, 3, 324–333.

Jeuland, A.P. 1982. Brand choice inertia as one aspect of the notion of brand loyalty. *Management Science,* 25, 7, 324–333.
Johnson, C.A. and Mulpuru, S. 2006. Online retailers face a tough road ahead. Research report. Stamford, CT: Forrester Research.
Johnson, E.J.; Moe, W.W.; Fader, P.S.; Bellman, S.; and Lohse, G.L. 2004. Depth and dynamics of online search behavior. *Management Science,* 50, 3, 299–308.
King, G., and Zeng, L. 2001a. Explaining rare events in international relations. *International Organization,* 55, 3, 693–715.
———. 2001b. Logistic regression in rare events data. *Political Analysis,* 9, 2, 137–163.
Koch, S. and Schneider, G. 2002. Effort, co-operation and co-ordination in an open source software project: GNOME. *Information Systems Journal,* 12, 1, 27–42.
Krishnamurthy, S. 2002. Cave or community: An empirical examination of 100 mature open source projects. *First Monday,* 7, 6.
Lerner, J. and Tirole, J. 2001. The open source movement: Key research questions. *European Economic Review,* 45, 4–6, 819–826.
Maddala, G.S. 1983. *Limited-Dependent and Qualitative Variables in Econometrics.* Cambridge: Cambridge University Press.
Malhotra, N.K. 1984. The use of linear logit models in marketing research. *Journal of Marketing Research,* 21, 1, 20–31.
Manski, C.F. and Lerman, S.R. 1977. The estimation of choice probabilities from choice-based samples. *Econometrica,* 45, 8, 1977–1988.
Manski, C.F. and McFadden, D. 1981. Alternative estimators and sample designs for discrete choice analysis. In C.F. Manski and D. McFadden, eds., *Structural Analysis of Discrete Data with Econometric Applications.* Cambridge, MA: MIT Press, 2–50.
Mockus, A.; Fielding, R.T.; and Herbsleb, J.D. 2002. Two case studies of open source software development: Apache and Mozilla. *ACM Transactions on Software Engineering and Methodology,* 11, 3, 309–346.
Moe, W.M. 2003. Buying, searching, or browsing: Differentiating between online shoppers using in-store navigational clickstream. *Journal of Consumer Psychology,* 13, 1–2, 29–39.
———. 2006. An empirical two-stage choice model with varying decision rules applied to Internet clickstream data. *Journal of Marketing Research,* 43, 4, 680–692.
Montgomery, A.L.; Li, S.; Srinivasan, K.; and Liechty, J.C. 2004. Modeling online browsing and path analysis using clickstream data. *Marketing Science,* 23, 4, 579–595.
Moon, J.Y., and Sproull, L.S. 2002. Essence of distributed work: The case of the Linux kernel. In P.J. Hinds and S.B. Kiesler, eds., *Distributed Work.* Cambridge, MA: MIT Press, 381–404.
Mulpuru, S.; Temkin, B.D.; Stromberg, C.; Steinberg, J.; and Hult, P. 2006. U.S. e-commerce: Five-year forecast and data overview. Research report. Stamford, CT: Forrester Research.
O'Reilly, T. 1999. Lessons from open-source software development. *Communications of the ACM,* 42, 4, 33–37.
Pavlou, P.A. and Gefen, D. 2005. Psychological contract violation in online marketplaces: Antecedents, consequences, and moderating role. *Information Systems Research,* 16, 4, 372–399.
Pinsonneault, A. and Kraemer, K.L. 1993. Survey research methodology in management information systems: An assessment. *Journal of Management Information Systems,* 10, 2, 75–105.
Prentice, R.L. and Pyke, R. 1979. Logistic disease incidence models and case-control studies. *Biometrika,* 66, 3, 403–411.
Raymond, E.S. 2001. *The Cathedral and the Bazaar: Musings on Linux and Open Source by an Accidental Revolutionary.* Sebastopol, CA: O'Reilly and Associates.
Roberts, J.A.; Hann, I.H.; and Slaughter, S.A. 2006. Understanding the motivations, participation, and performance of open source software developers: A longitudinal study of the Apache projects. *Management Science,* 52, 7, 984–999.
Rothschild, M. 1973. Models of market organization with imperfect information: A survey. *Journal of Political Economy,* 81, 6, 1283–1308.
Runkel, P.J. and McGrath, J.E. 1972. *Research on Human Behavior: A Systematic Guide to Method.* New York: Holt, Rinehart and Winston.
Simon, H.A. 1980. The behavioral and social sciences. *Science,* 209, 4, 72–78.
Singh, J. 2005. Collaborative networks as determinants of knowledge diffusion patterns. *Management Science,* 51, 5, 756–770.

Sorenson, O. and Fleming, L. 2004. Science and the diffusion of knowledge. *Research Policy,* 33, 1615–1634.

Sorenson, O. and Stuart, T.E. 2001. Syndication networks and the spatial distribution of venture capital investments. *American Journal of Sociology,* 106, 1546–1588.

Stewart, K.J.; Ammeter, A.P.; and Maruping, L.M. 2006. Impacts of license choice and organizational sponsorship on user interest and development activity in open source software projects. *Information Systems Research,* 17, 2, 126–144.

Stewart, K.J. and Gosain, S. 2006. The impact of ideology on effectiveness in open source software development teams. *MIS Quarterly,* 30, 2, 291–314.

Stigler, G.J. 1961. The economics of information. *Journal of Political Economy,* 69, 3, 213–225.

Verba, S.; Schlozman, K.L.; and Brady, H.E. 1995. *Voice and Equality: Civic Voluntarism in American Politics.* Cambridge, MA: Harvard University Press.

Vishwanath, A. 2004. An empirical investigation into the use of heuristics and information cues by bidders in online auctions. *Electronic Markets,* 14, 3, 178–185.

von Krogh, G.; Spaeth, S.; and Lakhani, K.R. 2003. Community, joining, and specialization in open source software innovation: A case study. *Research Policy,* 32, 1217–1241.

Weitzman, M.L. 1979. Optimal search for the best alternative. *Econometrica,* 47, 3, 641–654.

Wilde, L.L. 1980. The economics of consumer information acquisition. *Journal of Business,* 53, 3, S142-S158.

Zander, A. and Havelin, A. 1960. Social comparison and interpersonal attraction. *Human Relations,* 13, 1, 21–32.

Zeithammer, R. 2006. Forward-looking bidding in online auctions. *Journal of Marketing Research,* 43, 3, 462–476.

PART V

LOOKING FORWARD: CHALLENGES, TRANSFORMATIONS, AND ADVANCES

CHAPTER 11

DEBATING THE NATURE OF EMPIRICAL E-COMMERCE RESEARCH

Issues, Challenges, and Directions

VIJAY GURBAXANI, HENRY C. LUCAS, JR., AND PAUL P. TALLON

Abstract: After more than a decade of e-commerce research, we reflect on the state of the research through the eyes of two prominent information systems (IS) researchers with backgrounds in organization theory and the economics of IS. Using the format of an unstructured debate, we examine progress toward a cumulative research tradition, identify challenges that continue to impact e-commerce research, and uncover new and exciting research possibilities. While there is a broad consensus that much has been achieved in this area of research since the mid-1990s, there is also a sense that the IS community has yet to develop a road map that can draw together the many strands of e-commerce research into a cumulative tradition. This chapter also addresses issues of research relevance for IS practitioners in light of the long lead times often seen in academic publishing and the possibility that some research may be driven more by the availability of data than by an overarching practical dilemma. Finally, the transformational aspects of information technology and e-commerce are identified as a promising area for future research.

Keywords: Academic Disciplines, Business Value, Causality, Cumulative Tradition, E-Commerce, IT Value, Research Opportunities, Research Road map, Senior Scholars' Debate

INTRODUCTION

At the first International Conference on Information Systems (ICIS) held in Philadelphia in 1980, Keen (1980) called for the embryonic information systems (IS) field to build a distinct identity around an IS reference discipline, to define a dependent variable around which future IS research could coalesce, and to build a cumulative tradition around issues of lasting relevance to practitioners. Attesting to the progress made in the intervening years, in 2004 on the occasion of the fiftieth anniversary of *Management Science,* Banker and Kauffman (2004) conducted an extensive survey of the IS literature across five separate *research streams:* decision support and design science, the value of information, human-computer systems design, IS organization and strategy, and the economics of IS and information technology (IT). The path to a cumulative research tradition is shown not only in how each of these research streams has developed, but in how they have combined to probe issues at the periphery of IS research—the application of real options to IT investment analysis and the use of value-at-risk

(VaR) models to identify worse-case losses from security breaches, data theft and loss are two examples showing how concepts from financial portfolio analysis can be applied to IS (Bardhan, Bagchi, and Sougstad, 2004; Benaroch and Kauffman, 1999; Tallon and Scannell, 2007). Recognizing the progress that IS has made since Keen's rallying cry and the many questions that remain unanswered after twenty-five years or that have arisen in the interim, in their conclusion, Banker and Kauffman (2004) issued a renewed call for relevant, impactful, and meaningful research as follows:

> We expect that future IS research will continue to be characterized by the study of problems in IS management, including systems analysis and design, the management of software and IT investments within the firm, the configuration of business processes and the formation of business strategies that rely on IT, and the continued use of IT to create unique capabilities for users, decision makers, work groups, organizations, and industry sectors. . . . IS research has the potential to inform managers and academicians about how to understand, interpret, adapt to, and effectively manage technologies that have been and currently are in use, as well as emerging technologies whose impacts are just being felt. If this capability can be brought to bear more strongly on the IS management function, there will be significant leverage to make one of the important business functions within the contemporary firm deliver on the promises that IT investments are supposed to offer. Clearly, however, there remains much more research to accomplish this. (Banker and Kauffman, 2004, 294)

Implicit in the above reference to *emerging technologies* are systems associated with e-commerce and the Internet in particular. While research on mobile technologies, net-centric organizations, and interorganizational systems—areas that can be broadly classified under the rubric of e-commerce research—is not new, extending as far back as research on markets and hierarchies (Gurbaxani and Whang, 1991; Malone, Yates, and Benjamin, 1987; Williamson, 1975), the commercialization of the Internet from the mid-1990s onward spurred a considerable research effort to understand this new phenomenon. Electronic commerce has been defined by various researchers to include not just the buying and selling of goods and services over electronic networks and the technology that supports such actions, but mechanisms that facilitate information exchange, collaborative work, and technology-mediated forms of communication (Kalakota and Whinston, 1996; Riggins and Rhee, 1998; Zwass, 1996). During the same time frame, IS journal editors began to notice an increase in the number of e-commerce-related journal submissions while there was also an acknowledgment of the need for special issues that went beyond research on interorganizational systems, for example, to identify particular aspects of e-commerce (Benbasat, 2001). Among the challenges facing the earliest e-commerce researchers, as indicated by Isak Benbasat, editor of *Information Systems Research,* in editorial notes in 2001 (Benbasat, 2001), was the task of convincing reviewers and editors that e-commerce research belongs in IS journals. Some researchers still grapple with this issue today when, for example, research on pricing is seen more as *marketing* than IS or when research on auction mechanisms is seen as *economics* and, hence, better suited to non–IS journals.

Echoing a comment made by Lyytinen and King (2004), a sense of unease involving our nascent IS identity has emerged as the boundaries of IS expand to include research that addresses how e-commerce is changing the ways that industries, corporations, and consumers interact with IT. At the same time, there have been calls by senior academics for IS to return to its core—the IT artifact—as a way to validate IS research and to form a separate identity from economics, marketing, or other disciplines (Benbasat and Zmud, 2003; Ives et al., 2004; Orlikowski and Iacona,

2001). Perhaps, more than an issue of identity, what we are witnessing is an exchange of ideas that Kuhn saw as critical to paradigm formation and growth. As Kuhn describes, "a paradigm can, for that matter, even insulate the community from those socially important problems that are not reducible to the puzzle form, because they cannot be stated in terms of the conceptual and instrumental tools the paradigm supplies" (1962, 37). Designing a more inclusive IS paradigm, one that is welcoming and inclusive of e-commerce research—even where it crosses functional boundaries—is less a reason to revert back to what might be viewed as the dominant IS paradigm (designed around a technical core) and more a cause for celebration, if the conceptual tools and techniques attributable to the wider paradigm are capable of resolving a wider array of research questions. Thus, extending the IS paradigm to include e-commerce need not be seen as a threat to the technical core.

In the context of debates as to the relevance or practicality of IS research, it might be argued that a considerable body of e-commerce research is distant from practitioners who face considerable pressure to keep pace with changes in IT (Benbasat and Zmud, 1999, 2003; Mohrman, Gibson and Mohrman, 2001). As was argued during an ICIS panel discussion in 1999, there is growing evidence that practitioners are oblivious to, and maybe even purposefully avoiding, IS research (Lyytinen et al., 1999). Given the tendency of IS researchers to refrain from issuing prescriptive advice and the long lead times often associated with academic publishing, e-commerce researchers may find their research falling on deaf ears, at least as far as practitioners are concerned. With practitioners struggling to keep pace with a constant stream of IT innovations, researchers are reminded of Keen's advice to avoid chasing the "next big thing" and to focus instead on understanding the technology that is already in place (Keen, 1980). Therefore, it would seem logical to ask whether the agendas of practitioners and researchers will ever intersect when research continues to focus on *what is* while practitioners are instead focused on *what could be*.

FOUNDATIONS OF A DEBATE

E-commerce now stands at an interesting point in its evolution. Among IS researchers, there is an ongoing debate as to the role of the IT artifact within the broader framework of IS research, the nature of e-commerce research, its relevance to practitioners, and its future direction.

Purpose

Accordingly, the editors of this volume felt that much could be uncovered by convening a debate between individuals from different theoretical domains, representing a behavioral or organizational theory perspective and the economics of IS perspective. Although both theoretical domains have tended to reach similar conclusions in areas such as the economic or business impacts of IT investment, they are generally seen as dissimilar and somewhat in competition with one another (Bakos and Kemerer, 1992; Chan, 2000; Tallon and Kraemer, 2007).

The aims of the debate are to discover the following: (1) how each domain considers the nature of e-commerce research in terms of progress toward a cumulative tradition; (2) how each considers the key issue of rigor versus relevance in e-commerce research; (3) publication strategies for reaching an audience that includes IS practitioners; (4) the identification of areas for future research. Such a debate will help to frame the state of the research, indicating a road map toward a cumulative tradition in e-commerce while also affording a greater appreciation or understanding of how e-commerce is shaping the world around us, whether from the perspective of consumers, firms, inter- or intraindustry rivalry, or the global economy.

The Participants and Their Backgrounds

The debate was centered around an unstructured exchange between two senior IS scholars, Henry C. Lucas from the R.H. Smith School of Business at the University of Maryland, an established researcher in the behaviorist tradition, and Vijay Gurbaxani from the Merage School of Business at the University of California, Irvine, who has been an active researcher in the domain of the economics of IS for over two decades. The debate, moderated by Paul Tallon from the Carroll School of Management, Boston College, was held in late 2004 at the International Conference on Information Systems (ICIS) in Washington, DC. This was followed by a brief e-mail exchange that helped to clarify each individual's position. As is customary in debates, the role of the moderator was to focus the debate around a set of core themes, namely: the extent to which there has been progress toward a cumulative tradition, the nature of e-commerce research, the relevance of e-commerce research for IS practitioners, and future research possibilities. An agenda listing these core themes was e-mailed to both participants in mid-2004. A brief e-mail exchange took place before the ICIS conference, as each individual staked out his position on each of the issues for discussion.

We provide an edited transcript of the debate—subdivided by theme—to allow readers to observe each individual's position, and if necessary, to draw their own conclusions on whether there has been any degree of progress toward a cumulative tradition in e-commerce research. Given the unstructured nature of the debate, the participants veered off theme at various points during the discussion. We have included these sidebar comments as they provide an important context for understanding the broader discussion of how e-commerce research has evolved over time. To assist the reader, we provide a summary at the start of each section of what was discussed and the conclusions generally reached, and so we begin the debate by asking: "Is there a cumulative tradition in e-commerce research?"

IS THERE A CUMULATIVE TRADITION IN E-COMMERCE RESEARCH?

Summary

Although there is a significant body of e-commerce research in the IS literature, the consensus arising from the debate is that a road map toward a cumulative tradition has yet to materialize. Instead, it appears that much of the research is opportunistic in the sense that research is triggered by the availability of data rather than by a research question that leads to a data collection effort. The path toward a cumulative e-commerce research tradition has been shaped in part by the fact that e-commerce research has been published in journals outside IS. As a result, some academics have begun to question the "ownership" of the research when it emerges that marketing faculty are often as active in e-commerce research as IS faculty. This issue could erode the technical core of IS leading to a splintering of IS as the research begins to divide into separate paths rather than coalescing around a central theme. We turn now to the opening segment of the debate.

Debate

Paul Tallon (Paul): I would like to turn first to a subject that has been debated within information systems for many years; it involves the dual issues of research trajectory and cumulative research tradition. If I think of the historical trajectory of IT business value research, for example, we moved from early work on IT use, through the discovery of a productivity paradox, to a debunking of the paradox by Brynjolfsson and others, to the point where we are now in a postparadox phase looking at how IT capabilities and idiosyncratic management practices drive value. Do you see a similar road map emerging within empirical e-commerce research so we can say something about the look and feel of the research as we go forward? Second, over time as that research has matured, what do you think has become the defining characteristics of that work? Have we become broader in our perspective or are we starting to look at narrower, more micro questions? [*Editors' note:* for a review of the literature on IT business value, see Dehning and Richardson (2002), Kohli and Devaraj (2003), or Melville, Gurbaxani, and Kraemer, (2004).]

Vijay Gurbaxani (Vijay): My perception of the empirical research in e-commerce is that it is somewhat opportunistic in that it revolves around the data that researchers have available to them or can acquire, and that frequently is what motivates the research questions. I think developing a road map would be extremely important because what you find are lots of empirical papers and lots of empirical presentations, often well executed and interesting, but it's not always clear what the context is, how these results carry over to other contexts, and so on. I think it is very important to identify the settings and conditions that drive our research results. I also think that positioning or structuring these results within a comprehensive road map will be extremely important and useful.

Henry Lucas (Hank): If I think about the impression that one gets from a lot of the e-commerce research to this point, it has been heavily influenced by studies on price: how much more or less do you pay for a book on the Internet than you would someplace else, why hasn't everything gone to one price, why are there still price differences and why do people sometimes not go to the lowest price vendor, and why are they not taking advantage of how inexpensive search costs are compared to the days before e-commerce? It's been a funny mixture of trying to show how basic economic principles apply and then contrasting that with consumer behavior. This has some implications for management but it's not clear that these papers have very many implications for management except that you can succeed without matching your competitors' price. I wonder if any of the e-commerce research has influenced Jeff Bezos, the CEO of Amazon.com, for example.

Vijay: I agree with Hank's comment on the influence of price. With reference to my earlier comment on opportunistic research, this form of pricing research is opportunistic to the extent that it's perhaps easier to get at pricing data. You can write agent-based software that goes out onto the Internet and collects reams of pricing data. However, we're not limited to pricing studies alone. For example, I saw at the 2004 Workshop in Information Systems and Economics that some researchers at MIT had a field experiment on the complementarity between the Internet and more traditional marketing channels (Brynjolfsson et al., 2004). Theoretical models that examine this complementarity have also been developed by researchers at Rochester's Simon Graduate School of Management.

Hank: The risk, though, in that type of research is that it could fall under the umbrella of marketing research.

Vijay: I agree. One thing that perhaps worries me more than it might worry others is that I feel we're setting ourselves up for a "tragedy of the commons" in that we're moving further and further away from our core in IS research. We need to ask ourselves who the target audience is for the managerial implications of our research and what the key issues are for this audience. It's not at all clear to me what the field of IS will look like in five to ten years.

Paul: If we're moving further and further away from our core, irrespective of how that core is defined, do you foresee the possibility of splintering within the IS discipline? Will the core attain a certain amount of identity so that as researchers move further and further away from the core, they will need to redefine themselves as being something other than mainstream IT?

Vijay: It's hard to say if different schools of thought will coexist over time or go their separate ways. I also agree, by the way, though I should be cautious here, that a lot of the marketing-like work in e-commerce is in many cases better done by people in our field than by people in marketing because I think we are better able to understand the technology. In some ways, we anticipate technology-enabled research questions more so than researchers in other disciplines. Even then, when we work on this type of research, we're still not focusing on what technological capabilities are necessary to make e-commerce initiatives successful.

Hank: I knew a dean who used to argue that IS would disappear as a separate discipline because it would be subsumed by other disciplines. His comment was that IS would go the same way as management science, which has been integrated into finance and marketing. He meant that there was no longer a management science "core." However, one of the things that he ignored was that it's not clear that you can easily understand information technology and infrastructure, or appreciate what it takes to build and deliver applications. We face a serious risk now in the falloff in enrollments of IS students. I'm sure some of this reduction is due to the dot-com bust, but it is a concern and if it turns out that our research could be done better by economists and people in marketing or other disciplines, we are in real trouble.

Paul: By implication, does that mean that people in finance or marketing could begin to target IS journals so that people in IS are no longer left to compete among themselves for that journal space?

Vijay: I don't know that they'll target IS journals but the questions will migrate to their domains rather than staying in our domains. I don't see it becoming a "turf war"—it just makes us less relevant.

Hank: An editor will say: "Don't send it to *ISR [Information Systems Research]*. It should go to the *Journal of Marketing Research* or *Marketing Science*."

Vijay: That's happening already. I've seen several e-commerce papers appearing in places like *Marketing Science.*

Hank: What you want to do is to try to bring that back into IS through implications for technology and implications for managers, not just how you market a product. There are a lot of issues in technology that people should study that are independent of whether you are in marketing, finance, accounting, or someplace else. If you look at our research, it doesn't always give you the impression that is the case: there is something in the field that's uniquely ours rather than someone else's.

Vijay: We don't take into account as much as I think we should such things as better predictions of the underlying technology models and what that enables. Let me give you an example. At a recent meeting of the Center for Research on Information Technology and Organizations (CRITO) Industry/University Consortium, which I direct at the University of California, Irvine (www.crito.uci.edu/consortium/index.asp), there was a presentation of a project on licensing models for software vendors. After the presentation, one of the sponsors from IDC, an industry analyst, raised his hand and said: "This is all very well but you're looking at old pricing models. This is how firms like Oracle used to price where vendors try to price discriminate based on number of employees, number of seats, and so on." The point that this person was making was that software vendors were moving to some form of utility pricing model. Increasingly, software is sold as a service, as vendors move to an ASP-like model. He felt that this project was really studying a dated scenario, and so the project was reconfigured to look more at utility pricing issues. These are some of the things where we in IS have an edge because of the technology slant. The other thing is that if we start talking about technology architectures, then we should have a head start over other domains. For example, how do service-oriented architectures and grid computing affect the kinds of problems that we ought to be considering? What do they do to the viability of IT and business process outsourcing? What does it do to technology infrastructure within corporations? Understanding how these technology trends enable business strategies and structures is really where we have a competitive edge. I suspect we have a better understanding of where technologies are going and what this means for businesses.

Paul: So as long as we retain some links to the technology core—to the artifact—should we still be able to retain our place at the table as an independent discipline?

Hank: Perhaps this is an oversimplification, but I've been concerned that as a discipline we study a lot of very narrow problems that aren't of interest to many people beyond the researchers who are doing the research. In fact, you can step back and ask how our field can be declining when the most exciting changes that have happened in the economy in the past twenty years are all based around technology. Our biggest selling point is the transformational aspect of the technology on business practices in e-commerce. As an example, you really need to try to do an insightful analysis to say that this technology is changing the entire financial securities industry. It has radically changed the full-service brokers. It has brought in a new entrant called the *online broker*. It has created new markets, so-called *electronic communications networks* or ECNs. It is leading to dramatic changes at the stock exchange, and yet, it's very hard to do credible research there that doesn't sound like arm waving. I even suggested that we need to study what economic historians do, and then to undertake studies like Paul David at Stanford University, who has studied the advent of QWERTY and the diffusion of electrical power. Such researchers don't have data, they don't have econometric models. This kind of research relies upon an intelligent and informed observer laying out an analysis that the reader can agree or disagree with. That ought to be exciting to people. You're really taking an old model and changing it into something new, but it's not amenable to some of the research traditions that we have in the IS field of collecting a lot of data and testing some sort of a model against that data.

THE NATURE OF E-COMMERCE RESEARCH

Summary

There is a risk that over time some e-commerce research will become repetitious and jaded—studies on pricing are cited as one example. Interesting examples of new and potentially ground-breaking research come when researchers consider how e-commerce is enabling industry transformation; Web-based markets for used books and cars are cited as examples of markets that have evolved through the use of e-commerce. The development of a road map toward a cumulative tradition could emerge from consideration of how e-commerce has transformed markets and corporations (hierarchies in a theoretical sense). There is equally a criticism that shallow theoretical arguments and a general lack of theory have made it difficult for e-commerce research to make substantive progress toward a cumulative tradition. While at some level all papers are required to test theory, the issue is whether they are testing the same theory or are instead testing a set of atheoretical hypotheses. A cumulative tradition can only arise when there is a solid theoretical basis. The debate continues with a more detailed consideration of these issues.

Debate

Paul: Could you point to a piece of research that strikes you as particularly groundbreaking—something that makes the IS discipline proud? How about something that exemplifies what e-commerce research should look like and that can serve as a foundation for new streams of research? Is there something that has special practical merit but is also academically appealing?

Hank: The issue of what determines exemplary research really depends on timing. The very first studies on e-commerce that looked at pricing were interesting. The 412th study that looked at price was less so. I see all kinds of interesting topics, though I'm uncertain as to exactly the best research methodology to study them. So, for example, I would never have guessed, except for very rare and antique items, that we would have a national used car market. That was the last place that I thought technology would have an impact. To me, all used cars were local within a ten-mile radius of the dealer. But now, some person in Maryland will buy a car from Southern California. For the right price, they'll fly across the country and drive it or ship it home.

Vijay: Actually, buying and selling of used cars has now morphed into an international market. I was watching a program on TV recently where they talked about buying cars in the U.S. and Japan and transporting them to Africa via Dubai! So there are several issues here. One is the fact that you have created a *clearinghouse.* One of the essential components is that if you impose a transaction cost of people flying to another city to actually check the car, it's not going to work. But if you have some rating agency that says: "I guarantee that this car falls within this band of quality," then people are willing to buy things like used cars sight unseen, and that's what's happening in this international market. They're selling these cars to developing countries at a premium that you wouldn't ordinarily get in a used car market in the U.S. or Japan.

Paul: But then if it works for cars, and granted, we only buy one car every three to five years, would it by implication then be more amenable to other products and services that we buy more frequently? One of the things that I'm thinking about is medication, ignoring for a moment the nontrivial regulatory issues.

Vijay: I think that when you have different prices in different markets, it's highly likely that there will be some form of arbitrage opportunity. It could be price arbitrage in some cases involving supply, if the car that you want is not available in your neighborhood but it is available somewhere else. But then you might have a point when it comes to medication given the wide price differentials in different countries and the possibility that different cocktails of drugs—AIDS drugs, for example—might be priced differently in order that these drugs can be affordable to those in developing countries.

Paul: Here's another example. Within the book-retailing world, books tend to be released in markets such as the U.K. and U.S. at different points in time. So, for example, a new hardback book that's going to be coming out in the U.S. in March 2005 could already be at the paperback stage in the U.K. and, as such, is already being heavily traded within used book circles in the U.K. So, by that definition, if there was a global mechanism whereby readers could source their books in the U.K. at used prices and resell them in the U.S. at a time when the new hardback version is already selling at a much higher retail price, there would be an opportunity for substantial profit. What makes this even more compelling is the fact that the pricing structures are often radically different across global markets. For example, within the academic book market, it's not unusual to see the same economics or finance book selling at a much lower price in Asian markets than in the U.S. Publishers insist that those books not be resold into the U.S. market, but it's highly likely that some will get through.

Vijay: You see this in the airline market as well where, for instance, the price of a round-trip ticket for Los Angeles–Bombay–Los Angeles is completely different than Bombay–Los Angeles–Bombay.

Hank: Wouldn't it be fantastic if Internet drugstores were able to force a price reduction for prescription drugs in the United States? That could happen. The senior lobby is very effective. It's not going to happen in isolation. It's got to have a bandwagon effect with politicians and seniors saying that they're no longer willing to pay these astronomical prices. If you believe the drug companies (which I have a hard time believing), we're essentially paying for all the research on drugs because other countries have capped their payments for drugs. We're paying for a lot of advertising for prescription drugs while the pharmaceutical companies are buying and licensing drugs from small start-up firms, rather than developing them themselves. The fact is that IT could be forcing that kind of industry transformation. As another example, take a look at the movie and entertainment industry. What you're going to find, I think, in the not too distant future, is that movies are going to open in every theater in the world on the same night.

Vijay: It's already happening in many cases. I'm amazed that the time lag between movies being released here and in India has shortened so dramatically because these bootleg DVDs are becoming available almost instantly. In the case of books, I bought a legitimate paperback copy of *The Da Vinci Code* in India and of course it's still only available in hardback here (as of December 2004).

Hank: Boeing and a couple of the other communications satellite companies have offered to finance the installation of digital projection equipment in theaters in the U.S. to get the business of transmitting digital movies. This would eliminate film and movie reels, so my advice is to short Kodak!

Vijay: The book example is kind of another example of the used car market. These are things that we couldn't have really conceived of before. We've always had campus fraternities buying used books and reselling them to the following year's students.

Hank: Right! There's a great mystery bookshop in Los Angeles near UCLA, but it's very local in its clientele. But now if you remove time, space, physical, and geographical limitations, its market could become substantially larger.

Paul: Taking it to the next level, I've seen very interesting applications of book retailing in the Irish-language market, where there are books that have been out of print for many years. What you see are old grimy backstreet bookstores going online and publishing their inventory. You also have some academic in the U.S. who has been searching high and low for a particular book but who hasn't been able to find it for years. Now suddenly, a relatively simple search engine is able to find what they are looking for.

Vijay: If you try to abstract away from these examples—you had asked earlier about a road map for e-commerce research—I don't know what the precise road map should look like, but Hank is talking about technology and transformation, and you can extend that into technology and markets, technology and processes, or you can change technology to e-commerce if you want to be more specific. I think that if we can identify important domains and important questions, we will be generating very useful outcomes.

Hank: The issue that we wrestle with all the time—it's very true in the business value of IT, a little less so in e-commerce, but it applies to all of our research—is the *causality question.* You can provide evidence, but the reader is going to have to judge for him- or herself whether they believe there is a causal mechanism operating. Let me go back to the interpretations of the QWERTY keyboard as to why that came about. That's somebody saying: "We think this happened because the first typewriters were mechanical and you wanted the keys that people pressed together to be far enough away that they didn't jam." That's a plausible explanation, but is that really what happened? Did that historian go back and find something in an engineer's notes that said that they needed to spread out these keys? Or did a designer hand the problem to a secretary and say, design us a keyboard? I guess since it's not a matter of life and death, nobody's too concerned about the authenticity of that explanation!

Vijay: That's hotly disputed, right, whether it was in fact intentional or not?

Hank: Right! So we're trying to say things like "technology lets you do X or Y," but then somebody asks "well, how can you prove that?" I can't prove it.

Vijay: That reminds me of one of the points that was made at the beginning of our conversation, where Paul mentioned that when you have extremely large data sets, the research seems to show significance on virtually any question that is asked. This I think is where theory becomes extremely useful because you have a model from which you're deriving predictions and to the extent that you find that your predictions are supported by the evidence, and people buy into your theory base and your model, then you increase the likelihood that they'll buy your results. You could find all kinds of relationships through data mining, for example, whether it be numerical fitting of forecasting models or something else. You can always generate a forecast but are you adequately capturing the underlying behavioral phenomenon? I think the same thing applies to the QWERTY keyboard. Do you essentially buy the core argument? Most of us probably do since we're all old enough to remember those jammed keys!

Paul: So what it's suggesting then is that even though access to data is a problem, a larger problem in the long term is theoretical grounding. It's not just about having a meaningful research question; it's more about having a firm theoretical basis upon which to test your data.

Vijay: I'm not sure though if the theory is actually a problem, but I think it is something that we need to reinforce. Too often you see these papers that contain really obscure relationships. At a high level, they probably make sense, but when the author says "every one of my propositions is supported," my reaction is to say, "you're either a genius, or you reverse-engineered this thing!" So theory is important, but there again we're not immune from back-stepping into a theory from a set of existing results. It's not theory driving data driving results necessarily; it is data driving results driving theory.

Hank: The other problem with theory concerns the instructions going to reviewers in the journals. They seem to say that every paper must create theory. If all we do is create theories, we are going to end up with a proliferation of theories with very little support because there will be one study for each theory. We haven't coalesced around some theories that we're willing to accept and to continue to do research on to refine and improve. We don't have a capital asset pricing model . . . we don't have a resource-based view model that neatly fits e-commerce. The closest thing we have to a theory, and it's extremely limited, is the *technology acceptance model* (TAM). If you look at the number and variety of papers that are generated on that model, I think you'll see that it's a very limited model.

Vijay: Even if you look at the IT productivity paradox or IT business value literature, everybody—or at least the economics of IS group—buys into the production function approach. However, the reality of the situation is that it's nice to document productivity impacts using this framework but you can't say anything useful to a CIO based on that, other than to say that IT is valuable. All of us know that IT is one of the most mismanaged assets around or—putting it another way—there is high variability in how IT is managed as an asset, but we rarely capture that in our empirics when we look to what's happening inside a specific firm.

Paul: But isn't that really a disconnect that appears in all research—whether it's the business value of e-commerce or anything else that involves large-scale regression? While we might be able to generalize across the entire population, when I go back to an individual CIO, I can only say: "Here's what we have learned in general, but in terms of your company, I can't really deduce whether the same relationship holds at that level of granularity or not."

Vijay: Correct, but I'm also saying that while we have a theory, the theory is limited in its scope so that it really doesn't allow you to address all of the issues that surround the theory, and that you really need to get into in order to really understand what's going on.

Hank: If you go back and look at the stream of Brynjolfsson and Hitt papers on IT business value and productivity, you're explaining a few hundred firms' performance with just four variables: IT labor, non–IT labor, IT capital, and non–IT capital. But you know that there's a lot more going on in those firms and so it's really only at a very high level that you can interpret this result. When I saw the very high rate of return on IT investment in those papers, I thought to myself that this is just incredible. Consider the number of IT projects that don't return what's promised, or the number of IT projects where there's no hope of a return because you're trying to comply with some regulatory mandate that does nothing for the bottom line other than keep your managers out of jail. There's some implicit cost of these nonperforming projects, but it's not captured in the regression analysis.

Vijay: Actually, for those types of reasons, we've backed off some of the results that first emerged in the IT productivity studies. The other thing that's not captured in there is that much of the IT investment is just to take care of depreciation. IT is one of your fastest depreciating assets.

Hank: Peter Weill and Marianne Broadbent did a series of studies in Australia, the U.S., Asia, and Europe, I believe, and out of that whole book, the number that stuck in my mind was something like 46 percent of IT investment went to infrastructure (Weill and Broadbent, 1998). It's very hard to show a return on infrastructure investment. That's a little like your "depreciation dilemma" if you're replacing your infrastructure with something else. You have to go out and buy ten new routers. Those routers will be used on all the systems that you're operating, so how do you allocate that investment to a particular system and calculate the return from that?

Paul: So then to go back to one of your earlier points about technology and transformation, the real benefit comes from transformation, not necessarily the installation of technology.

Hank: That's correct! The fact that you're doing business differently today than you could have in the past is important. One thing that I like from a business value perspective is options pricing, although it's probably a daunting task for the average company to do such an analysis before undertaking an IT investment. I like the framework that real options analysis provides when it says that technology gives you an option. The trouble is that I don't know what that option is going to be. At the University of Maryland, we've done an intensive study of the New York Stock Exchange (NYSE), which has been battered from all sides by other kinds of markets, ECNs, and others. The NYSE has used technology to maintain a better market share than have the NASDAQ market and others. They still manage to trade about 85 percent of NYSE-listed stocks, whereas NASDAQ has a much lower share. We had a referee ask us to prove that these investments in technology have helped the exchange maintain its competitive position. My reaction is to say that without the technology, they'd still be passing pieces of paper back and forth. How many shares could you effectively trade that way?

Vijay: That doesn't show up in any dependent variable measure of value added. This gets back to the idea of your survival prospects. The fact is that you're alive because you made appropriate investments but all that the analysis is going to say is that it somehow failed to increase profit.

RESEARCH RELEVANCE, DATA DISPARITY, AND VARIABLE MEASUREMENT

Summary

There is much interest among IS practitioners in grasping the results of e-commerce research, as evidenced by the success of commercial research outlets such as the Forrester Research (www.forrester.com), Gartner Group (www.gartner.com), and IDC (www.idc.com). These firms understand that in certain instances executives will pay to have relevant research results delivered in a timely manner. The issue facing many academics when it comes to publishing for an IS practitioner audience is one of incentives: there is a certain perception that this form of publishing can jeopardize one's academic career. Progress toward a cumulative tradition is also slowed not only by the fact that researchers do not have access to shared data pools but because the measurement of the underlying variables also is often complex and varied. Professors Gurbaxani and Lucas continue to debate these issues and offer their contrasting and insightful views.

Debate

Paul: Among the CIOs that I've spoken with, there is a common reaction to our research in that while they say that academics do great work, it's still difficult for the practitioner community to interpret and apply what we find in our research. There is a sense that we publish in academic journals, and we overwhelm the reader with math, which while necessary for an academic audience, immediately turns off the vast bulk of our nonacademic or IS practitioner readers.

Vijay: In finance, they have the *Financial Analysts Journal* (www.aimrpubs.org/faj/home.html), and it's not seen as a "big negative" to publish in it. The finance discipline expects every now and again that you will talk about why your research is important and what it means for practice. It's very different from information systems. For example, they provide numerical examples of how their methods are used and so on.

Hank: We have *MIS Quarterly Executive,* but I'm sure they have nowhere near the circulation of the *Financial Analysts Journal.*

Vijay: Sure, but I think that there's a certain homogeneity to the financial analyst profession that makes it easier for finance academics to identify their audience.

Paul: Even if the audience is well defined, I suspect that the finance discipline is also more mature than IS and so an audience knows what to expect from its journals.

Hank: You also have people who are used to doing research. The whole business of an analyst doing research on companies is well defined, even if it's not academic-style research. How much research does a CIO do though?

Vijay: But on the other hand, there's clearly a hunger for this knowledge. I have spoken at Gartner events on outsourcing and I'm amazed by how many people attend, paying high registration fees every single year to come learn this material. I think that some of the research that we have done in academia is very pertinent and relevant, and has improved over time because of this interaction, but we're dropping the ball in terms of getting it into the hands of IS practitioners.

Paul: The interesting thing that I've seen in some of the research that Gartner sells is its proximity to academic research. It has stripped away much of the minutiae that often defines academic research in order to expose the key underlying message. They're also more inclined to focus on frameworks, 2x2's, and simpler ways of understanding what otherwise would have been a very complicated idea. So perhaps with our way of thinking, we're shooting ourselves in the foot. So my question for you is: By narrowly defining our audience and meeting their relatively narrow expectations, are we closing ourselves off from a broader interpretation or application of our work?

Vijay: I have several responses. First, academics, as is appropriate, are trying to succeed in the academy. But what I think Gartner does better than academics—which is not surprising given who their audiences are—is recognizing the questions that people will pay to have answers to. We in the academic IS community are not very good at doing that and I think that is something we need to be a little more focused on, particularly as we face a similar challenge in demonstrating relevance in the MBA curriculum.

Hank: Part of the problem is that it takes us so long to do anything. Gartner can launch a study and have a report back on a topic within a month. Our research is old by the time we've spent a few years working on it, and companies have moved to a new model by the time we get our research out.

Paul: Part of the reason that it's taking us so long to complete a piece of research is because there are complex data access issues. So if we get to a point where we have access to common datasets such as IRI or Information Resources Inc. (www.infores.com/public/us/default.htm) and we somehow agree among ourselves that we are all going to direct our research against the same data set rather than spend more time and effort in collecting separate data sets, will that make it easier for us to do timely and relevant research?

Hank: Our colleagues in finance are looking at stock prices and everyone can agree on what database they need and that the collection of that data will be automatically handled by the exchanges. Our problem is that we don't have really common models. If you show me a database, it's likely not to include two or three of the variables that are important for what I'm studying. I can't think of a database now that would encompass the things that I want to have. In our field, you see a lot of primary rather than secondary data collection. Nobody is going to get any credit for being the data collector, making their career building databases for other researchers to use. I don't hold out a lot of hope for a common database that would serve the IS community broadly.

Vijay: I agree with that, but every now and then when you do see common data—you had mentioned earlier the Computer Intelligence InfoCorp or CII database in IT business value research—it can be beneficial. We in CRITO saw the CII database as a valuable data source that would enable a stream of research. CII collected data on site- and firm-specific IT variables, such as IT spending, number of mainframes, PCs, servers, and so on for several years. CII was later acquired by Harte-Hanks (www.harte-hanks.com), which has continued and refined the data collection process for these IT variables. We used a grant from IBM to bring that data into CRITO. Researchers including Erik Brynjolfsson and his colleagues at MIT have also obtained access to the same data set. However, the data are closely held because that's our licensing agreement with CII. But when you do see multiple researchers with access to the same data, you see the cumulative tradition unfolding. You see a sequence of papers coming out, often from the same sets of researchers. Paul had earlier talked about the IT productivity paradox question and how that matured over time. If you track the business value of IT stream of research over time, you will see that people have zeroed in on what the essential questions are and how to focus the research around them. Those questions and methods have become more sophisticated over time in terms of addressing the issues that reviewers brought up in some of the early papers. I think the central issue in this stream of research for all of us is that we are still not able to capture firm-specific effects. So what are the strategic opportunities for research there? I'm assuming the question is something like: "What is the value of IT or e-commerce to a firm?" You might have some systematic effects that demonstrate that IT is valuable, but what are the strategic opportunities available to the firm that has made them invest in that particular set of technologies? We're just never going to be able to get the kind of data that we want, and that will allow us to capture the context within which all this takes place.

Paul: Yesterday, I was on an ICIS panel discussing IT and dynamic capabilities (Pavlou et al., 2004), and the questions that the audience uniformly hit upon were: "How do you measure dynamic capabilities? How do you measure flexibility and agility, as particular forms of dynamic capabilities?" In response, we talked about IT and transformation and, in particular, about investing in IT infrastructure that has almost no value today but is going to enable a stream of technologies and future investments that hopefully will give rise to future value. We also talked about measuring the business value of e-commerce. If we measure value by looking at a historical context alone, rather than capabilities, there is a risk that we will miss a large part of the "value equation" through which IT delivers value.

Vijay: I want to go back to something that Hank said about options theory because I once built a model for a consulting firm that used that idea of looking ahead. My single biggest message from that experience was that nobody is going to price a real option correctly, but actually taking a large IT project and subdividing it into a sequence of stages adds a discipline to the process that you don't often find. You could do a net present value [NPV] on a very large project and conclude that it's negative or too risky depending on the risk premium you apply and so choose not to do it. You could also take the same project and say: "Well, I'm going to do Phase 1 and it's going to require X dollars in infrastructure and Y dollars in applications, but if this part fails, at least my IT infrastructure investment is reusable. I'm sure I can dream up something else to use it for, and so I abort the project. Alternatively, if Phase 1 rolls forward and is successful, then I could decide to invest two times Y dollars in Phase 2. When you break down a project this way, you get very different answers as to whether you should invest or not. You don't have to compute an exact value for the real option in order to gain these kinds of insights. To get back to your question about the business value of e-commerce, the other thing we need to study much more, since we're not doing enough at this point, is the whole notion of complementary investments in relationships with partners and so on, because you are now in an environment where the business value of an IT investment to me depends on what my partners do, and if those partners don't make complementary investments, I could end up wasting my entire investment or alternatively, it could be much more valuable if all of us make complementary investments. I don't think that we're looking enough at models of group behavior, which completely changes how we calculate ROI [return on investment] based on our assumptions of what our partners are going to do.

Paul: So then research that has as its dependent variable measures such as return on assets, and so on, while valid in and of itself, will perhaps be too narrowly defined.

Hank: You still see a lot of EDI [electronic data interchange] investment being made, despite what we see happening with XML [extensible markup language]. If your EDI works, there's not a whole lot of incentive to change it. You see a tremendous amount of cooperation among organizations even with something as basic as EDI.

Vijay: I believe that the measures are still useful, but we need to incorporate newer alternative measures as a supplement. On that note, we are seeing some interesting initiatives among the journals. There's an *MIS Quarterly* special issue on standards, for example (see vol. 30, August 2006). I think that's a good idea because standards are clearly a central issue in how you foster this kind of collaboration.

Hank: Because we want to be scientific, we have a fairly rigid set of standards for what we consider good research. Some of these research questions are very hard to address in that standard way. There needs to be a more cosmopolitan approach—maybe you could start a new journal of "unusual" results!

Vijay: That's actually a really good point. I just joined the editorial board of a journal that Uday Karmarkar at UCLA recently launched (personal.anderson.ucla.edu/uday.karmarkar/). The focus of this journal is going to be top-down to some degree where the editors suggest some of the questions that we would like to see addressed. We will then go to senior people in the IS field and remove the page-length restriction. You can say to authors that we're not interested in a *Management Science*-like paper. Instead, we're saying to them: "You are the expert. Bring together everything that you know on this topic. Your work will be reviewed. We'll give you lots of feedback along the way, but we're not going to hold you to the traditional standards." So I agree with Hank. How as a discipline do we become more cosmopolitan in the kinds of research that we do? How do we say to our field: "Here's a set of N important questions—go study them?" You can say right off the bat that at least some of these questions cannot be answered with some of the more traditional approaches that existing journals are inclined to favor, so we have to think in nontraditional ways, use altogether new empirical methods.

Paul: It's likely to take multiple years to even begin to answer those types of questions.

Hank: Absolutely! It may also mean that it's only limited to senior people in the field who will not perish if they don't have a *Management Science* or an *Information Systems Research* article that year on their record. The challenge is to get a large circulation for a journal of the kind that you're describing, and to get it circulating among both the practitioner *and* the academic community.

Vijay: That's true but I'm not certain how much traction a journal like that would actually have.

Hank: Going back to your earlier comment about the *Financial Analysts Journal,* it would be great if there is some way we could produce a journal that really spoke to practitioners. We've tried to go through the Society for Information Management (SIM) where the audience is CIOs, but maybe that's not the right group. Should we be aiming for a general manager rather than a CIO?

Vijay: I agree with that. For years we've been saying to companies that you shouldn't take your techie guys and promote them to CIOs—which, to be honest, is still what many companies are doing.

Paul: Aren't we targeting that IT managerial audience already with publications like *Communications of the ACM* (or *CACM* at www.acm.org/pubs/cacm/homepage.html)?

Hank: I bet you have five managers reading *CACM* . . . [wink]!

Vijay: CACM is aimed at computer science professionals, more so than IT managers.

Hank: The circulation is 80,000 or something like that, but they're all members of the Association for Computing Machinery (ACM), and so you really have to ask yourself what MBA is a member of the ACM? They've taken the journal and removed all of the academic material. Most of us who are doing this type of research are in business schools and we don't turn out people who are highly technical. They may have had a technical undergraduate education, but if you came through our MBA programs, you wouldn't be prepared to work in a technical capacity at a company.

Vijay: There is another test that we could apply, which is to simply ask each author who they think should read their article? Who cares about the implications of your work, or who should care? We don't ask that question often enough.

Paul: In another sense, we're underselling ourselves to an MBA audience and to those who are sitting in our graduate programs. Although we're producing research that perhaps has some practical merit, given the captive audience in our classrooms, we may be failing in our efforts to use that opportunity to sell our research to them by translating our research findings into teachable material. If we can pique the interests of our students, as they work their way up the managerial ladder, they might be more open to using the results of our research in a more practical sense.

IS THERE A CORE, ENDURING QUESTION IN E-COMMERCE RESEARCH?

Summary

While the search for value from IT remains an enduring issue in IS research, there is some disagreement that e-commerce research should be guided by one single question. The issue is that a cumulative tradition emerges when researchers are guided by a common question but, at the current time, there is little consensus as to what that question should be. This makes it difficult to conduct a meaningful meta-analysis. The debate as to what questions we should be asking in e-commerce research carries over to how we teach e-commerce. If there is one guiding question, the problem comes when we try to provide generalizable truths that can respond to the needs of different constituents: IT managers, business leaders, students, and so on. The next portion of this debate examines these questions.

Debate

Paul: People in finance, marketing, and certain other disciplines have an enduring question that persists across time. However, within the IS field, we're still so fixated on the latest innovations that we're unable to identify the core question that we should be trying to answer. There may be some perennial question deep within the IS discipline but it seems that we're too open to distraction from ever-changing events and new gadgets to be able to spend enough time identifying and then addressing that question. Do you think there is a core, enduring question within e-commerce research?

Vijay: I'm on a panel this afternoon organized by Vasant Dhar from New York University and the topic for discussion is whether there should be a single core question that drives the MIS core course (Dhar et al., 2004). Basically, the proposed core question is "Why do some companies succeed with IT while others fail?" What is being discussed is whether this is the question that should guide what our core courses ought to center on. This is further based on the notion that in finance you have a single question—which is roughly true—that asks how assets are priced. I'm not sure if we should have just one single question driving IT research but one thing to ask is: "How do you create sustained value with IT or e-commerce rather than focusing on the success or failure of individual companies?" I think that there are some enduring principles that are completely independent of what the technology of the day turns out to be.

Hank: We have, like a lot of disciplines, followed paths. If you've been around long enough, you'll recall that we started out with *management information systems.* Then we found out that we weren't really doing that and moved toward decision support systems (DSS), then on to *group DSS,* executive information systems (EIS), computer-aided software engineering tools, and so on. We've had enterprise resource planning (ERP) systems, databases, expert systems, fifth-generation computing, and now we're into e-commerce. As soon as the Internet was available for profit-making purposes in 1995, everyone started studying pricing on the Internet. I'm not sure what the enduring question really is, though I think Vasant Dhar and his colleagues' question really started back in the 1970s.

Vijay: The issue then is whether a core course should focus on a single question.

Hank: That I would have to disagree with, because I think if you're selling a core course to captive MBAs, you have to address a number of decisions that they're going to be involved in making, not just the success or failure of IT. Also, what's the definition of success or failure? When I started doing research on that in the 1970s, it was really about whether you got enough people to use IT. We had no notion of trying to assess value. It may or may not have been a useful system. In fact the company might have been better off without it, but it was implemented and it worked.

Vijay: Those were the old automation days where companies were trying to improve speed, accuracy of transactions—as far as objectives for IT investments are concerned, these were valuable. . . .

Hank: And you were clearly substituting capital for labor then, and the assumption was that labor was going to become increasingly more expensive, so you wanted to automate. This work was back in the day when there were huge price-performance improvements in technology. That was the way that the outsourcing business made money in the 1960s and 1970s—it was because of the decline in price. They would go for a ten-year contract and they would lose money for the first four or five years, but count on the fact that technology was changing. They would really only start to make a profit toward the end of the contract. I recently heard an outsourcer saying that they couldn't make any money off hardware and software. He said that the only way to make money is to operate more effectively than a company can by itself. So knowledge, skills, and expertise are their key resource. It's not about financial plays on the equipment.

Vijay: That's absolutely right! So why does a Fortune-100 company outsource? They already have considerable economies of scale, so it must really boil down to technology management expertise. I think a core question would be to ask, from a general manager's perspective: "How do you value an IT investment?" Then you can derive from that a set of underlying questions that are very interesting. For example: How do you discover new applications that create value? How do you source and deliver them? How do you ensure that people use them effectively in order to derive value? Those questions are enduring but yet change to reflect new kinds of functionality that emerging applications provide. We still struggle with how a company should engage in the discovery process. When new technologies are being developed, for example, how do you assess which ones to bring into the organization and how do you identify which ones are going to generate value?

Paul: So there's almost a paradox here in the way that we have set things up. Several questions arise from this. From the point of view of a doctoral student though, you have to drill down into this universe of questions to come up with a single issue that you feel is important and that will provide you with a stream of research papers for the years leading up to your tenure decision. However, what I hear both of you saying is that the really interesting questions are at a more macro level. So, maybe, we haven't yet acquired the discipline of abstracting back from our overly narrow research foci to say something meaningful about those more macro issues.

Vijay: It is worth comparing our traditions with the process by which pharmaceutical companies discover new drugs and assess their efficacy. If we're talking about a cumulative tradition, the thing that the medical field does really well is *meta-analysis* on all of the scores of data on clinical trials and field studies. Even though there have been some ethical issues recently, the field is conscientious and they conduct the aggregated analysis of studies on different groups to yield significant insights. For example, consider the Framingham Heart study (www.framingham.com/heart/). This study tracked thousands of people over a very long period of time, and kept releasing results along the way. At the end of that type of study, when you aggregate the results based on meta-analysis, you see some interesting things. I don't know if we in the IS discipline value meta-analysis enough. In part, we don't see a lot of it because we don't share data sets and so we don't make it easy to aggregate.

Hank: The IS discipline is also small. How many IS faculty members would you estimate there are in the world? We've got 2,000 to 3,000 members in AIS [Association for Information Systems]. . . .

Vijay: There are maybe 1,300 people here [at the 2004 ICIS conference in Washington, DC] and if you start looking at the number of serious researchers among that number, you have a very small number indeed.

Hank: You're absolutely right, it is a very small number of people and then if you go further and break that into subfields, it's going to be even smaller. For example, how many people are there who do econometric studies in e-commerce so that you would have a hundred good e-commerce studies to do a meta-analysis?

Vijay: You're absolutely right. There are probably twenty faculty interested in that type of work. . . .

Paul: So straight away, you're going to face a small sample size problem.

Vijay: And it's even worse than that because, of these twenty, they are not always doing studies that you can easily aggregate into a meta-analysis. They're often doing completely different things.

Paul: Plus, I'm sure that over time individual academics will tend to develop specific areas of research expertise—you become a *domain expert*. It's like creating a collage—you add little pieces to the frame but until you have all the pieces, it's very hard to form a cohesive picture—or at least a picture that we can all agree on. The essential challenge then is . . .

Vijay: We should all quit! [laughter]

Paul: So what it suggests then is that practitioners are looking for those grandiose answers to those larger, more macro questions, and we're still mired in the detail of our own little micro research worlds.

Vijay: In the CRITO consortium to which I referred earlier, we have several corporate sponsors. One communication challenge that I face as director—and it's exactly what Paul is describing—is that faculty tend to focus on presenting the contributions of their specific research efforts. Consider the perspective of the practitioners who support the research though. Imagine that you gave them an assessment of the state of knowledge in the field as we do in the literature review section of our papers. You could say to them: "This is a summary of what has been published on a particular subject, and here's a reasonable way to assimilate everything that's been said." That would be seen as highly valuable, since that's largely what they care about. They are less interested in the incremental results because they can't use them. If there's a paradox, that's the crux of it.

Hank: A financial analyst is hungry for data on a company, or anything that will give them an edge over another financial analyst at a competitor. Unlike analysts, CIOs are focused on the problem they've got today. I have not heard very much from CIOs by way of long-term projections or thinking about the environment that they will be facing. They are under immediate short-term pressures, often for cost reductions, while facing calls for improvements in service delivery from people above them. CIOs are not long-range planners.

Vijay: We also anticipate that the results of our research will only be published within four years, so that's not going to solve the problem of the day. As a result, being driven by what's topical is unlikely to help us speak to the practitioner community.

Hank: So we try to find generalizable truths, which may or may not be very helpful to a practitioner. Some people will say that CIOs are our target audience whereas others will say that it's general managers.

Vijay: I don't think we're ever going to get to the point of targeting a single constituency but it would be useful to try to be clearer about what it is that we're trying to do.

Paul: That brings me back to my earlier comment about dynamic capabilities. In some of the case studies that I've done, when I get an opportunity to discuss with CIOs some of the reasoning behind their e-commerce investments, they will say that they are being evaluated today on their ability to reduce the IT budget by X percent or to reduce operating costs by a specified amount. Consequently, being able to place bets in keeping with the notion of real options is something that's not really important to them right now. They have a belief that if they want to invest in groundbreaking applications by making a series of short-term bets, more often than not, they're likely to get it wrong. So, for future-oriented investments, they will not be able to deliver the immediate impacts that they so desperately need to satisfy their short-term goals. Thus, if you have CIOs who are thinking about staying in a job for two or three years, the last thing that they want to think about is pursuing investments that will mature and benefit the person who comes after them.

Hank: Another enduring question in e-commerce that is a critical concern for any manager or CIO today is legacy systems—and I don't just mean IBM mainframes or COBOL software. We had a speaker at the R.H. Smith School from Motley Fool (www.motleyfool.com/, an investment advisory Web site) a few years ago and he identified all of these legacy systems that they had put in only two years previously. At that time, the company needed something quick and dirty. So they just threw things together. Now they need to go back and engineer real software from this mess. The speaker made an observation, which I thought was very insightful: *a system is a legacy system from the moment you put it in.* So we can talk about e-commerce research, but there are some really practical problems for a company. What do I do when I've got ten subsidiaries that all want something different? Yet, we in the academic community would dismiss that problem as being theoretically uninteresting.

Vijay: If you think about ERP, we know from CSC Index's research that two-thirds of these projects fail. Even though I don't completely buy this, it's still a very high number. They define their *failure rate* as people who didn't meet their original stated goals regardless of how much benefit they got. If you look at this failure rate, what does the IS community have to say about ERP implementation?

Paul: . . . other than to revise your expectations downward . . .

Hank: Yes—or reengineer. That's another fad that we got onto for a few years. I like the sound of a new journal to get at these big issues.

Vijay: An alumna called me a year or so ago and said: "I loved the class I took from you. Here are all the things you taught me that I use everyday, and here's some stuff that you didn't teach me but that I need every day." She's an e-commerce product manager for a bank—which means that she selects the projects that are implemented in any given year. She receives requests from a whole bunch of people related to online banking. She said that the hardest thing she has to deal with is deciding which of those "fifty or so" projects she is going to fund, because she's only got enough funding for ten. So she asked me: "Which ones do I fund?" All of this discussion about what's the value of each project—how do you integrate a new application into your infrastructure, will each application work as intended, will people use it, what will it do for you competitively—are enduring questions that you can ask of almost any system but are incredibly difficult to answer. [*Editors' note:* for a relevant case study on IT spending and investment prioritization, see Austin, Ritchie, and Garrett (2005).]

Hank: We need to prepare our students for the kinds of decisions they are going to have to make. You may be an MBA in marketing or some other area, but you'd still better know something about technology and infrastructure because otherwise you're going to find yourself in a tough situation with no answers one day.

Vijay: All MBAs have corporate finance training. So they can create an NPV model and compute the numbers, but they have a limited sense of how difficult it is to understand how to generate these projections. In a corporate finance class, the data usually come with the question: here's a spreadsheet, now tell us what the NPV is. The hard part in our discipline is figuring out what the cash flows are for both costs and value. Even so, the harder part is recognizing that this assumes a set of conditions under which the system gets used and your competitors react to it in a certain way. How do you construct your NPV model in a way that focuses on whether the system will be integrated into the rest of the organization, whether it will be easy to use, and whether your managers and customers will use it? How do you even start to think about all this? It seems to me that the NPV part can actually be one of the easier parts even though it can be pretty difficult to come up with those numbers.

E-COMMERCE AND GLOBALIZATION: BEYOND THE FIRM LEVEL

Summary

Although e-commerce is traditionally thought of in business-to-consumer (B2C) or business-to-business (B2B) terms, e-commerce is also having a profound impact on the developing world and on economic growth more broadly. To the extent that the benefits of e-commerce can trickle down to the individual citizen, diffusion will depend to a large degree on the availability of infrastructure and training of end users. The debate concludes with a discussion of these global issues.

Debate

Paul: There's one final topic that I want to touch upon, and it's very different from the things that we've spoken about so far. The issues that we've addressed so far might be characterized as being predominantly at the firm level. The topic that I want to address is motivated in part by the keynote speaker[1] [at the 2004 International Conference on Information Systems] who spoke about some of the challenges facing the diffusion of technology within China. A question that came from the audience mentioned the notion of a "digital divide." The argument that the speaker posed was that China was going to move in the direction of "informating" its population, but by virtue of the disparity between the earnings of those living in the cities and those living in rural areas, it seemed that the rich would get richer and the poor would get poorer. Consequently, to the extent that there is a digital divide already in place, it would be amplified in the coming years. So, let's abstract back from what we see happening at the firm level to looking at what is happening at the level of an individual economy. For example, Singapore is holding itself out as a "digital island," and India is promoting technology in its schools, and so on. Suppose a government minister comes to you and says: "We're thinking of putting together a system of incentives that will enable our firms to invest in more technology, part of which may involve e-commerce-like investments." In this context, would you suggest that by giving firms short-term incentives, benefits will flow through to the economy as a whole?

Vijay: It's somewhat speculative, but I buy into the notion that benefits will diffuse down. If you look at what is going on in India, for instance, two examples come to mind. One is of fishermen in a village off the west coast who are now using satellite imagery to tell them where the fish stocks are located (BBC, 2004). They have learned how to get to the right Web page that shows them the relevant satellite image and that's where they all sail to. There's also a Harvard case—C.K. Prahalad has talked about this—it's called "ITC E-choupal," which translates to the "Village Square" (www.echoupal.com/default.asp and www.itcportal.com/ruraldevp_philosophy/echoupal.htm). These are soybean farmers who are now able to look at world prices for their produce. There is a teacher in each village who is helping the farmers to understand the prices for soybeans in different markets. The farmers were being ripped off by local traders because there was so much information asymmetry.

Hank: I've looked at the digital divide in the U.S., and one thing that has helped alleviate the divide is high-speed Internet access in libraries. So poorer, generally minority students, will spend a fair amount of time on the Internet, but it's all done through libraries, whereas better-off students of course have a computer and Internet connection at home. There's also a computer scientist who's created icon-driven kinds of PCs for illiterate people. There's also a great article about a developer who has organized an Internet connection involving a bicycle because this particular village didn't have power—one minute spent peddling on the bicycle gives you five minutes of

Internet time (Liddell, 2005). It's going to take a concerted effort in cases involving people who are really poor or underprivileged to erase the divide.

Vijay: You need intervention, I believe. Somebody has to subsidize the cost of the infrastructure.

Hank: I agree, and once the infrastructure is in place, you'll see things happening just as in your example of the village farmers in India checking for crop prices.

Vijay: An interesting aspect of the ITC E-choupal case is that ITC or the India Tobacco Company (www.itcportal.com/) has its own set of incentives (which they never quite talk about). They have built a very interesting system. They were looking for distribution into some of these very remote villages, although it was ultimately driven by their own profit motive rather than offering a public good, which may still be okay.

Paul: So it sounds then that if government is in the business of distributing grants and incentives, it ought to go more toward the public sector or public services, rather than the private sector?

Vijay: Not to the public sector necessarily, because that has overtones of "big government," which is often inefficient in developing countries. You may really want to empower some *nongovernmental organizations* or other organizations.

Hank: I'm not sure that e-commerce research is the issue for China or India. It's really an infrastructure issue, plus it's a teaching and training problem at this point. You can't just drop technology into a village square. There has to be someone there to help it succeed. There's a contrarian who has contributed to this development discussion with an article in *Scientific American* saying, "Wait a minute!"(Warschauer, 2003). They put kiosks in India with the computers well protected—all that was showing was the keyboard, but there was nobody there to show people how to use them, so the children were just playing games on the machines, and that's not what you want.

Vijay: The point about libraries reminds me of something else. You can look at telephones per capita—in India, for example, it's a very low rate—but what that doesn't acknowledge is that in some of these villages you have a phone booth that's staffed by someone 24/7—there's one of these every 100 meters or so in Bombay. There's some small entrepreneur running each of these kiosks. Each one could probably serve a thousand customers. By the way, they'll even take "hold" messages for a customer. It's voice mail with a difference—a personal touch! So traditional U.S.-based metrics don't translate very well into what the true access is in places like India. Even before that, it used to be when you had a phone at home, everybody on the same floor in your apartment building would stop by to use it.

Paul: But what it means is that the introduction of technology in these areas constitutes life-changing experiences for some of these people, whether it is the village farmers or the local fishermen.

Hank: Absolutely!

Vijay: Yes, I really think so! In many cases these are sources of higher value than what we're doing here.

Paul: Even in things like health care, there are interesting changes taking place on a global scale. For example, you can have access to outside sources of information if the local village doctor doesn't have that level of medical knowledge or awareness.

Vijay: One of my relatives was ill recently and I'm sitting here, literally in my hotel room checking WebMD (www.webmd.com/) and getting all of these diagnostics, trying to find out what's the U.S. "gold standard" of care, then calling the physician in India and asking: "Why aren't we using a particular diagnostic test or prescribing a particular medicine?" So it's really suggesting that there's some kind of information equalization going on.

Paul: In some ways that's actually scaring the doctors, when the patient comes into their practice knowing what they want, or at least thinking that they already know what's wrong with them. In days past, a patient knew they felt pain or discomfort, but had no way to diagnose what it could be. Self-diagnosis might be useful but access to all this online medical information could also pose problems of misdiagnosis by self-appointed experts whose expertise doesn't extend beyond WebMD.

Vijay: In India, there is very high variability in physician competence, as I mentioned before. It's important that a patient asks the right questions. It's really a matter of self-education, but then that brings us back to the digital divide. If the technology is not available, you might never know what questions you should be asking. It's a really dilemma for those in the developing world.

CONCLUSION: THE "STATE OF THE RESEARCH" IN E-COMMERCE

Although we observe much progress in the years since academics first embarked on a program of research in e-commerce, there is still some doubt as to whether the research has formed a cumulative tradition. Certainly, there are individual research domains—for example, in the areas of pricing, auctions, reputation, and trust mechanisms—that have taken on the appearance of a cumulative tradition with a core or classical body of work, an enabling theoretical foundation, and a compelling set of research questions. If there are barriers to the development of a broader cumulative tradition across e-commerce, it may come in the form of data-driven research, which although not devoid of a research question in a classical sense, is still not motivated *ab initio* by a research question and an accompanying theoretical argument. There is certainly nothing fundamentally wrong with this style of inductive research except that it may complicate the task of meta-analysis if research variables are inconsistently defined or measured, or if data are drawn from diverse populations. Progress toward a cumulative tradition is further challenged by the frantic pace of innovation in e-commerce and the uncertainty that this may cause for continued use of older-generation technologies. For example, toward the end of 2006, there was significant interest in the adoption and use of social networking Web sites such as Facebook (www.facebook.com) or MySpace (www.myspace.com). These sites are a logical extension of prior technologies such as chat rooms and instant messaging and yet their emergence poses both a risk and an opportunity to researchers as they struggle to come to terms with the core underlying phenomenon, without being sidetracked by the technical aspects of the innovation.

The issue as to the practical merit or relevance of e-commerce research is very much in evidence in this debate with questions being raised as to the incentives provided to IS academics to publish in more practitioner-oriented journals. More so than many areas of the social sciences, IS is inherently a practical, hands-on science. The success of for-profit research firms such as Gartner, IDC, and Forrester attests to the willingness of IT and business executives to pay for timely, actionable research. This does not mean that academic-style e-commerce research is irrelevant but it does call into question the ability of IS academics to reach out to practitioners in a timely manner with results that can affect the efficiency and effectiveness of their firms. Several journals such as *MIS Quarterly Executive, Communications of the ACM, Sloan Management Review,* and *IEEE Transactions* (including *Software Engineering, Engineering Management,* and *Knowledge and Data Engineering*) are known for asking their authors to be explicit about the practical implications of their research. Even then, there is still some question as to whether the findings from these studies are accessible to managers in a way that fosters closer relationships between research and practice. The experiences of the *CRITO Consortium*—a National Science Foundation–sponsored industry–university cooperative research center at the University of California, Irvine, shows the potential for delivering research that is responsive to practitioners and that is accessible by a lay audience, while remaining true to the rigorous standards of academic publishing.

The contribution of this debate, although presented solely through the perspectives of two senior academics, nevertheless finds a significant degree of commonality and shared insight across two different research domains, represented in this case by the more behavioral organization theory perspective and the more quantitative economics of the IS perspective. Each perspective acknowledges the significant progress in e-commerce research to date while being cognizant of the remaining challenges—challenges that speak to the costs and complexity of data collection, generalizability of results, the temporal nature of the systems under review, and the fact that e-commerce research is typically out-of-date soon after it is published. The challenge for researchers is not just to keep abreast of innovation and changes to the technical core but to understand the transformative capabilities of IT and e-commerce.

One example of these capabilities can be found in the brokerage industry, where the rise of online brokers such as Scottrade or E*Trade has had a dramatic effect on trading commissions. Equally, the rise of electronic communications networks such as Archipelago or ArcaIEx (which was involved in a reverse takeover of the NYSE in 2006) and Island/Instinet (now part of NASDAQ) highlight the potential for e-commerce to fundamentally alter the dynamics of established securities markets, potentially creating a direct link between buyers and sellers without the intervention of a specialist or market maker. Whether this transformational effect underscores an enduring objective of e-commerce and hence a primary focus for e-commerce research remains to be seen. Certainly, the issue of an enduring, core research question is important to identifying progress toward a cumulative tradition, as is the discussion of how e-commerce is moving the dominant IS paradigm away from its technical core to encompass research that may be seen by some as clearly belonging outside IS. How the IS field deals with this internal struggle—one that will ultimately define the field—will say much about how a road map to a cumulative tradition will unfold.

NOTE

1. From a speech by Cheng Siwei, vice-chairman, National People's Congress, People's Republic of China. Further information is available at the ICIS 2004 Web site: www.terry.uga.edu/conferences/icis2004/keynote.html.

REFERENCES

Austin, R.; Ritchie, W.; and Garrett, G. 2005. *Volkswagen of America: Managing IT Priorities.* No. 9–606–003. Boston, MA: Harvard Business School Press.
Bakos, J.Y. and Kemerer, C. 1992. Recent applications of economic theory in information technology research. *Decision Support Systems,* 8, 5, 365–386.
Banker, R.D. and Kauffman, R.J. 2004. The evolution of research on information systems: A fiftieth-year survey of the literature in management science. *Management Science,* 50, 3, 281–298.
Bardhan, I.; Bagchi, S.; and Sougstad, R. 2004. Prioritizing a portfolio of information technology investment projects. *Journal of Management Information Systems,* 21, 2, 33–60.
BBC. 2004. Fishermen get space guides. Available at http://news.bbc.co.uk/2/hi/south_asia/3492773.stm (accessed May 20, 2007).
Benaroch, M. and Kauffman, R.J. 1999. A case for using real options pricing analysis to evaluate information technology project investments. *Information Systems Research,* 10, 1, 70–86.
Benbasat, I. 2001. Editorial notes. *Information Systems Research,* 12, 1, i–ii.
Benbasat, I. and Zmud, R. 1999. Empirical research in information systems: The practice of relevance. *MIS Quarterly,* 23, 1, 3–16.
———. 2003. The identity crisis within the IS discipline: Defining and communicating the discipline's core properties. *MIS Quarterly,* 27, 2, 183–194.
Brynjolfsson, E.; Anderson, E.; Hu, J.; and Simester, D. 2004. Does the Internet complement other marketing

channels? Evidence from a large-scale field experiment. Available at http://opim-sky.wharton.upenn.edu/wise2004/program.htm (accessed May 20, 2007).

Chan, Y.E. 2000. IT value: The great divide between qualitative and quantitative and individual and organizational measures. *Journal of Management Information Systems,* 16, 4, 225–261.

Dehning, B. and Richardson, V.J. 2002. Returns on investments in information technology: A research synthesis. *Journal of Information Systems,* 16, 1, 7–30.

Dhar, V.; Sundararajan, A.; Brynjolfsson, E.; Johnson, K.; Gurbaxani, V.; Mendelson, H.; and Severance, D. 2004. Should the core information systems curriculum be structured around a fundamental question? In R. Agarwal, L. Kirsch, and J. DeGross, eds., *Proceedings of the 20th International Conference on Information Systems.* Atlanta, GA: Association for Information Systems.

Gurbaxani, V. and Whang, S. 1991. The impact of information systems on organizations and markets. *Communications of the ACM,* 34, 1, 59–73.

Ives, B.; Parks, M.; Porra, J.; and Silva, L. 2004. Phylogeny and power in the IS domain: A response to Benbasat and Zmud's call for returning to the IT artifact. *Journal of the Association for Information Systems,* 5, 3, 108–124.

Kalakota, R. and Whinston, A.B. 1996. *Frontiers of electronic commerce.* Redwood City, CA: Addison Wesley Longman.

Keen, P. 1980. MIS research: Reference disciplines and a cumulative tradition. In E.R. McLean, ed., *Proceedings of the Proceedings of the 1st International Conference on Information Systems.* Atlanta, GA: Association for Information Systems, 9–18.

Kohli, R. and Devaraj, S. 2003. Measuring information technology payoff: A meta-analysis of structural variables in firm-level empirical research. *Information Systems Research,* 14, 2, 127–145.

Kuhn. 1962. *The Structure of Scientific Revolutions.* Chicago: University of Chicago Press.

Liddell, C. 2005. Pedal power: Look Ma, no wires. Available at www.wi-fiplanet.com/columns/article.php/1454991/ (accessed May 20, 2007).

Lyytinen, K. and King, J.L. 2004. Nothing at the center? Academic legitimacy in the information systems field. *Journal of the Association for Information Systems,* 5, 6, 220–246.

Lyytinen, K.; Grover, V.; Linder, J.; Mendelson, H.; Senn, J.; and Sviokla, J. 1999. Making information systems research more relevant: Academic and industry perspectives. In P. De and J. DeGross, eds., *Proceedings of the Proceedings of the 20th International Conference on Information Systems.* Atlanta, GA: Association for Information Systems, 574–577.

Malone, T.W.; Yates, J.; and Benjamin, R.I. 1987. Electronic markets and electronic hierarchies. *Communications of the ACM,* 30, 6, 484–497.

Melville, N.; Gurbaxani, V.; and Kraemer, K.L. 2004. Information technology and organizational performance: An integrative model of IT business value. *MIS Quarterly,* 28, 2, 283–322.

Mohrman, S.; Gibson, C.; and Mohrman, A. 2001. Doing research that is useful to practice: A model and empirical exploration. *Academy of Management Journal,* 44, 2, 357–375.

Orlikowski, W.J. and Iacona, S. 2001. Desperately seeking the "IT" in IT research: A call to theorizing the IT artifact. *Information Systems Research,* 12, 2, 121–134.

Pavlou, P.; Bharadwaj, A.; El Sawy, O.; Gupta, A.; and Tallon, P. 2004. Linking information technology and dynamic capabilities: The elusive dancing partners. Twenty-fifth International Conference on Information Systems, Washington, DC. Available at http://aisel.isworld.org/pdf.asp?Vpath=/icis/2004/&PDFPath=2004pn03.pdf (accessed May 20, 2007).

Riggins, F. and Rhee, H.S. 1998. Toward a unified view of electronic commerce. *Communications of the ACM,* 41, 10, 88–95.

Tallon, P.P. and Kraemer, K.L. 2007. Fact or fiction? A sensemaking perspective on the reality behind executives' perceptions of IT business value. *Journal of Management Information Systems,* 24, 1, 13–55.

Tallon, P.P. and Scannell, R. 2007. Balancing cost and value-at-risk: The new challenge in information lifecycle management. *Communications of the ACM,* 11, 7, 65–69.

Warschauer, M. 2003. Demystifying the digital divide. *Scientific America,* 289, 2, 42–47.

Weill, P. and Broadbent, M. 1998. *Leveraging the New Infrastructure: How Market Leaders Capitalize on Information Technology.* Boston, MA: Harvard Business School Press.

Williamson, O.E. 1975. *Markets and Hierarchies.* New York: Free Press.

Zwass, V. 1996. Electronic commerce: Structures and issues. *International Journal of Electronic Commerce,* 1, 1, 3–23.

EDITORS AND CONTRIBUTORS

Daniel Almirall is a Ph.D. candidate in the Department of Statistics at the University of Michigan. His dissertation focuses on the development and application of causal models for longitudinal data with time-varying covariates and time-varying treatments. These include marginal structural models and structural nested mean models. His current methodological research interests lie in the broad area of causal inference with applications in information technology, depression, substance abuse prevention, patient-treatment matching, and social science, more generally. Recently, he won a "Distinguished Student Paper Award" for a dissertation-based paper, titled "Structural Nested Mean Models for Assessing Time-Varying Effect Moderation: An Illustration," presented at the International Biometric Society's ENAR Conference.

Indranil R. Bardhan is associate professor of management information systems and accounting and information management at the University of Texas at Dallas. He is also the director of the Center for Practice and Research in Software Management (PRISM). His research interests are in the areas of information technology valuation, business impacts of information systems on supply chain and firm performance, and software development. His research has been published in leading journals, including *Operations Research, Journal of Management Information Systems, MIS Quarterly, European Journal of Operational Research, Annals of Operations Research, Journal of Productivity Analysis, Journal of the Operations Research Society of Japan.* He has ten years of management consulting experience and has advised Fortune 500 executives on information technology strategy and systems implementation. He co-chaired the INFORMS Conference on Information Systems and Technology in San Francisco, California, in November 2005.

Bruce Dehning is an associate professor of accounting information systems at Chapman University's Argyros School of Business and Economics. He holds a B.S. in finance, an M.S. in accounting, and a Ph.D. in accounting from the Leeds School of Business at the University of Colorado. He received the American Accounting Association Information Systems Section Notable Contributions to the Literature Award in 2006, was named a Fulbright Scholar to teach in the Czech Republic in 2005, and was awarded the Wang-Fradkin Professorship at Chapman University in 2004. He has presented papers at numerous prestigious national and international conferences, and his research has been published in *MIS Quarterly, Journal of Operations Management, Journal of Information Systems, Journal of Strategic Information Systems, International Journal of Accounting Information Systems, Information and Management,* and other academic journals. Outside of academia he spent time in the insurance industry and as an accounting information systems consultant for small businesses.

Her-Sen Doong is an assistant professor of management information systems at National Chiayi University, Taiwan. Prior to his doctoral study, he worked as a project manager in the Software Incubator of the National Sun Yat-sen University and product manager in the software technology company. His current research interests are in the areas of negotiation support systems, human computer interaction, and electronic commerce. His papers have been published in the *International Journal of Electronic Commerce, Decision Support Systems, Group Decision and Negotiation,* and several international conference proceedings.

Vijay Gurbaxani is associate dean, professor of information systems and computer science, and director of the Center for Research on IT and Organizations Industry-University Consortium at the Paul Merage School of Business, University of California at Irvine. His research interests are in the economics of information systems. He is the author of the book *Managing Information Systems Costs* (Washington, DC: ICIT Press, 1990), and numerous journal articles. His research has appeared in *Information Systems Research, Management Science,* and *Communications of the ACM.* He received master's and Ph.D. degrees in business administration from the William E. Simon Graduate School of Business Administration, University of Rochester, New York, and an integrated five-year master's degree in mathematics and computer science from IIT, Bombay. His Ph.D. thesis won the prize for the best dissertation in a global competition sponsored by the International Center for Information Technologies. He was awarded the 2002 Outsourcing World Achievement Award in the academic category by PricewaterhouseCoopers and Michael Corbett and Associates.

Jungpil Hahn is an assistant professor of management at the Krannert School of Management of Purdue University, which he joined in 2003. He holds a B.B.A. and an M.B.A. from Yonsei University in Korea, and a Ph.D. in management information systems from the Carlson School of Management of the University of Minnesota. His current research interests include electronic commerce, human-computer interaction, systems design, and knowledge management. His research has appeared in such journals as *Information Systems Research, ACM Transactions on Computer-Human Interaction,* and *Electronic Markets.* He has also presented his research at leading academic conferences such as the International Conference on Information Systems (ICIS), the Hawaii International Conference on System Sciences (HICSS), the ACM Conferences on Human Factors in Computing Systems (CHI), the Workshop on Information Systems and Economics (WISE), and the Workshop on Information Technology and Systems (WITS). While earning his Ph.D. at the University of Minnesota, he received the Carlson School Dissertation Fellowship and the Excellence in Teaching Award. His primary teaching interests include systems analysis and design, database management, IT infrastructure, and principles of IS.

Kai-Lung Hui is an associate professor in the Department of Information Systems, Faculty of Business, at the City University of Hong Kong. He is currently on leave from the Department of Information Systems, National University of Singapore. His research interests include information privacy, product line design and pricing, new product introduction, and copyright and piracy. His research has appeared in the *American Economic Review, Management Science, MIS Quarterly,* and the *Journal of Management Information Systems,* among others.

Wolfgang Jank is assistant professor of management science and statistics in the Smith School of Business at the University of Maryland. He joined the University of Maryland in August 2001. His methodological research interests center around computational statistics, functional data analysis, methods for spatial and temporal data, Monte Carlo methodology, stochastic optimization and information visualization. He is interested in applications in electronic commerce, marketing, operations management, and aviation. He received his master's degree from the Technical University of Aachen (Germany) in mathematics on cluster analysis under Professor H.H. Bock. He received his Ph.D. in statistics from the University of Florida on stochastic estimation methods under Professor J.G. Booth. He is a member of the American Statistical Society, the Institute for Mathematical Statistics, the European Network for Business and Industrial Statistics, the Association for Computing Machinery, and INFORMS. He is also past president of the University of Florida's chapter of the statistical honor society Mu Sigma Rho.

Robert J. Kauffman is currently the W.P. Carey Chair in Information Systems at the W.P. Carey School of Business, Arizona State University. He was previously director of the MIS Research Center, and professor and chair in the Information and Decision Sciences Department at the Carlson School of Management, University of Minnesota. He has worked in international banking, and served on the faculty at New York University and the University of Rochester, before moving to Minnesota in 1994. His M.A. is from Cornell University and his M.S. and Ph.D. from Carnegie Mellon University. His current research focuses on senior management issues in IS strategy and business value, financial evaluation of technology investments, technology adoption, e-commerce and electronic markets, pricing strategy, and supply chain management issues. His research has been published in *Organization Science, Journal of Management Information Systems, Communications of the ACM, Management Science, MIS Quarterly, Information Systems Research, Decision Sciences,* and other leading IS, economics, and computer science journals, and has been presented at conferences. He has won outstanding research awards with his doctoral students and faculty colleagues at the INFORMS Conference on IS and Technology in 2003, 2004, and 2005, the Hawaii International Conference on Systems Science in 2004, and the International Conference on Electronic Commerce in 2005. In 2006, he also won an Outstanding Research Contribution Award from the IEEE Society for Engineering Management for an article on standards drift in technology adoption published in the *IEEE Transactions on Engineering Management* in 2005.

Mayuram S. Krishnan is Mary and Mike Hallman e-Business Fellow, area chair, and professor of business information technology at the University of Michigan Ross School of Business. He is also a co-director of the Center for Global Resource Leverage: India at the University of Michigan's Ross School of Business. His research interests includes corporate IT strategy, the business value of IT investments, management of distributed business processes, software engineering economics, and metrics and measures for quality, productivity, and customer satisfaction for software and other IT products. In January 2000, the American Society for Quality (ASQ) selected him as one of the twenty-one voices of quality for the twenty first century. His research has appeared in several journals, including *Management Science, Information Systems Research, Strategic Management Journal, Harvard Business Review,* and *Sloan Management Review.* He currently serves on the editorial board of the academic journals *Management Science* and *Information Systems Research.*

Hsiangchu Lai is a professor of information management at National Sun Yat-Sen University in Kaohsiung, Taiwan, Republic of China. She received her doctorate from Purdue University in

1989 and was a visiting scholar at the University of Texas at Austin in 1993–1994, and Concordia University, Canada in 2004. She has served as a department chair and been involved in many academic activities, including acting as a conference committee member, and as a reviewer of journal papers and research projects. She currently serves as an associate editor of *Decision Support Systems* and will be the program co-chair for the 2007 Group Decision and Negotiation Conference. Her research interests include auction mechanism design, negotiation support systems, and electronic commerce. Her papers have been published in *IEEE Computer, Group Decision and Negotiation, Decision Support Systems, International Journal of Electronic Commerce, European Journal of Operational Research, Journal of Computer Information Systems, Journal of Information Systems,* and elsewhere.

Yee-Lin Lai is a research assistant and a doctoral candidate in the Department of Information Systems at the School of Computing, National University of Singapore. She was a visiting scholar at the Haas School of Business, University of California, Berkeley, in 2005. She received her B.S. (with honors) in information systems from National University of Singapore in 1993. Her current research interests span the domains of privacy, framing, human–computer interaction, consumer behavior and choice, animation, Weblogs, and online gambling. Her research has appeared in the *Communications of the ACM* and the *Proceedings of the International Conference on Information Systems*. She also received an Honorable Mention for Best Student Paper for a co-authored submission to the American Marketing Association Marketing and Public Policy Conference in 2005.

Winston T. Lin is a professor of operations and management strategy at the School of Management, State University of New York at Buffalo. His current research interests are in the areas of information systems, multinational finance, and forecasting. He has published sixty articles in refereed proceedings and leading academic journals, including the *Journal of the Association of Information Systems, Communications of the ACM, Information and Management, Journal of Business and Economic Statistics, Financial Review, Journal of Financial and Quantitative Analysis, International Finance, Multinational Finance Journal, International Journal of Forecasting,* and *Journal of Forecasting*. He has presented papers at numerous national and international conferences. He also has been awarded significant research grants and awards, including a three-year grant from the Chiang Ching-Kuo Foundation of Taiwan for research on the comparative analysis of efficiency in major industries.

Henry C. Lucas, Jr. is the R.H. Smith Professor of Information Systems at the R.H. Smith School of Business, University of Maryland. He received a B.S. from Yale University and an M.S. and Ph.D. from the Sloan School of Management, MIT. His research interests include IT-enabled transformations, IT in organization design, electronic commerce, and the value of information technology. A prolific researcher, he has authored eleven books as well as monographs and more than seventy articles in professional periodicals on the impact of technology, information technology in organization design, the return on investments in technology, implementation of information technology, expert systems, decision making for technology, and information technology and corporate strategy. His most recent books include *Information Technology and the Productivity Paradox: Assessing the Value of Investing in IT* (Oxford University Press, 1999), *The T-Form Organization: Using Technology to Design Organizations for the 21st Century* (Jossey-Bass, 1996), and *Strategies for E-Commerce and the Internet* (MIT Press, 2002).

Sunil Mithas is an assistant professor at Robert H. Smith School of Business at the University of Maryland. He completed his Ph.D. at the Ross School of Business, University of Michigan. Prior to pursuing the Ph.D., he worked for ten years in various engineering, marketing, and general management positions with Tata Steel and Tata Ryerson. He is primarily interested in understanding how information technology (IT) contributes to firm performance and how firms can better manage their IT resources. His research has appeared or is forthcoming in *Journal of Marketing, Production and Operations Management, Journal of Management Information Systems, Statistical Science, Decision Support Systems,* and *Information Technology and Management.* His papers have won the Best Doctoral Paper Award at the INFORMS Conference on IS and Technology in 2004, and he also had a best paper nomination at the 2005 International Conference on Information Systems in 2005. His research has been featured by leading business publications such as *MIT Sloan Management Review, Bloomberg, Computerworld, InformationWeek,* and *Optimize.* He also won the Best Reviewer Award at the INFORMS Conference on IS and Technology in 2005.

Vernon J. Richardson is a professor of accounting and the Ralph L. McQueen Distinguished Chair in the Sam M. Walton College of Business at the University of Arkansas. He received his B.S., Masters of Accountancy, and MBA from Brigham Young University and a Ph.D. in accounting from the University of Illinois at Urbana-Champaign. He has taught students at the University of Arkansas, University of Illinois, Brigham Young University, University of Kansas, and the China Europe International Business School in Shanghai. He has published articles in the *MIS Quarterly, Journal of Operations Management, Journal of Management Information Systems, Journal of Accounting and Economics, Journal of Accounting and Public Policy, Financial Analysts Journal, Journal of Marketing,* and *American Business Law Journal.* He is currently an associate editor at *MIS Quarterly.*

Benjamin B. M. Shao received his B.S. in computer and information science and M.S. in information management from National Chiao Tung University, Taiwan, and his Ph.D. in management information systems from the State University of New York at Buffalo. His research interests include information technology impacts, IS security, e-commerce adoption, distributed/parallel processing, and software project management. His research has appeared in *Communications of the ACM, Computer Journal, Computers and Security, Decision Support Systems, European Journal of Operational Research, IEEE Transactions on Dependable and Secure Computing, IEEE Transactions on Systems, Man, and Cybernetics, Information and Management, International Journal of Production Research, Journal of the Association for Information Systems, Journal of Electronic Commerce Research, Journal of the Operational Research Society,* and the proceedings of the AMCIS, HICSS, and INFORMS conferences, among others. His work experience includes employing IT to reengineer business processes at a medical center and developing parallel algorithms in a research institute. He was recognized for teaching excellence by the Department of Information Systems Club as Professor of the Year in 2003 and 2005. He is a member of AIS, ACM, INFORMS, and Beta Gamma Sigma.

Galit Shmueli is an assistant professor of management science and statistics in the Decision and Information Technologies Department, at the R.H. Smith School of Business, University of Maryland. She holds three degrees in statistics, including a B.A. in statistics and psychology from Haifa University, as well as an M.S. and Ph.D. from Technion, the Israel Institute of Technology. Her research focuses on developing and using statistical and probabilistic methods in marketing, quality control, and biosurveillance. She collaborates with researchers from computer science, marketing, and industry. Before arriving at the Smith School of Business, she conducted research at Carnegie Mellon University. Two large-scale projects that she has worked on involved developing a detection system for bioterrorist attacks by tracking medication sales (a CDC and AHRQ project); and developing a flexible family of distributions for modeling count data that are frequent in marketing data sets. She has been invited to present her work at several conferences, and her work appears in publications such as the *Proceedings of the National Academy of Sciences,* and has been covered by W*all Street Journal, CNN.com,* among others. In her Ph.D. dissertation, she developed a method for the efficient computation of distributions that are related to runs and scans, and has applied these methods to various industrial applications. She continues her work in this area and developed a Web site that is frequented by industrial practitioners.

Rodney E. Smith is an associate professor at California State University, Long Beach. He holds a B.S. in mathematics from the University of Oregon, an M.S. in financial management from the Naval Postgraduate School, and a Ph.D. in management from the University of California, Irvine. He received the American Accounting Association Management Accounting Section Best Paper Award in 2005. He has presented papers at several American Accounting Association Annual Meetings, and his work has been published in the *Journal of Management Accounting Research* and the *Journal of Information Systems.* Prior to his academic career, he served twenty five years in the United States Coast Guard.

Ryan Sougstad has seven years of experience in client sales and marketing with the IBM Corporation, and recently completed a research internship with IBM T.J. Watson Research Center. He holds an MBA from the University of Texas at Dallas. He is currently in the doctoral program in Information and Decision Sciences at the Carlson School of Management of the University of Minnesota, and previously served as a faculty member at National American University in Rapid City, South Dakota. His research interests are centered on information technology valuation and portfolio management. His papers have appeared in the *Journal of Management Information Systems* and he has presented his work at the Hawaii International Conference on Systems Science, the INFORMS Main Conference, the E-Services Conference, and IBM.

Paul P. Tallon is an assistant professor of information systems at the Carroll School of Management, Boston College, and a research associate at the Center for Research on Information Technology and Organizations, at the University of California, Irvine. He received B.Comm. and M.Mgt.Sc. degrees from University College Dublin, and a Ph.D. in information systems from the University of California, Irvine. He previously worked as an IT auditor and chartered accountant with PricewaterhouseCoopers in Dublin, Ireland, and New York. His research has appeared in the *Journal of Management Information Systems, Communications of the ACM, Communications of the AIS,* the *Journal of Strategic Information Systems,* and the *Journal of Global IT Management.* His research interests include the economic, social, and organizational impacts of IT, strategic alignment, real options, IT portfolio management, and the economics of data management.

Charles A. Wood is currently an assistant professor of management at the Mendoza School of Business, Notre Dame University. He is a graduate of the University of Minnesota's Carlson School of Management, where he received a doctorate in information systems in 2001. His research interests lie in the area of electronic commerce, electronic auctions, buyer and seller reputation, and pricing in Internet-based selling. He received a best paper award in 2000 for his research on "follow-the-leader pricing" dynamics in e-commerce. His research publications have appeared in

Management Science, Information Technology and Management, Electronic Commerce Research and Applications, Managerial Decisions and Economics, and the *International Journal of Intelligent Systems in Accounting, Finance and Management.* He has presented his research at leading conferences in the fields of IS, marketing, computer science and economics, and is the author of multiple books on various topics in software development, database management, and computer programming.

Shun-Jian Yee previously was an undergraduate student in the Department of Information Systems, National University of Singapore.

Chen Zhang is a Ph.D. candidate in management information systems at the Krannert Graduate School of Management at Purdue University. She earned her MBA degree from Bowling Green State University in 2000 and her M.S. degree in computer science from Wright State University in 2002. Her current research interests include open source software development, virtual teams, innovation diffusion, and social aspects of online communities.

Ya-Ting Zhuang is currently a system programmer at the China Life Insurance Company, Taipei, Taiwan, Republic of China. She previously completed her master's degree under Professor Hsiangchu Lai in information management at National Sun Yat-Sen University in Kaohsiung, Taiwan, where she researched electronic commerce and group-buying-related issues. Her research has appeared in the Workshop on E-Business in 2004.

Robert W. Zmud is professor and Michael F. Price Chair in MIS, Division of MIS, Michael F. Price College of Business, University of Oklahoma. His research interests focus on the organizational impacts of information technology and on the management, implementation, and diffusion of information technology. He is currently a senior editor with *Information Systems Research* and *MISQ Executive* and sits on the editorial boards of *Management Science, Academy of Management Review,* and *Information and Organization.* He is a fellow of both AIS and DSI. He holds a Ph.D. from the University of Arizona and an M.S. from MIT.

SERIES EDITOR

Vladimir Zwass is the University Distinguished Professor of Computer Science and Management Information Systems at Fairleigh Dickinson University. He holds a PhD in Computer Science from Columbia University. Professor Zwass is the Founding Editor-in-Chief of the *Journal of Management Information Systems,* one of the three top-ranked journals in the field of Information Systems; the Journal has celebrated 25 years of its publication. He is also the Founding Editor-in-Chief of the *International Journal of Electronic Commerce,* ranked as the top journal in its field. More recently, Dr. Zwass has been the Founding Editor-in-Chief of the monograph series *Advances in Management Information Systems,* whose objective is to codify the knowledge and research methods in the field. Dr. Zwass is the author of six books and several book chapters, including entries in the *Encyclopaedia Britannica,* as well as of a number of papers in various journals and conference proceedings. Vladimir Zwass has received several grants, consulted for a number of major corporations, and is a frequent speaker to national and international audiences. He is a former member of the Professional Staff of the International Atomic Energy Agency in Vienna, Austria.

INDEX

Note: Italicized locators indicate figures and tables.

A

Abdul-Gader, A.H., 220
accounting-based performance measures, 136, 140–145, 149–150
accounts payable turnover, *141*
accounts receivable turnover, *142*
activity histories, 253
Adamic, L., 13
Adar, E., 13
adjustment methods, regression, 75, 78
advertising, *239,* 250
agent-based data collection, 54–56
airline market, 280
Allen, G.N., 32, 55
Alm, J., 49
Alvarez, S.A., 16
Amazon.com, 7, *9,* 277
American consumers, compared with Chinese, 213
analytical modeling, 37
Anand, K.S., 191
Angelou, G.N., 108
Angrist, J.D., 247n6
ANOVA, *204, 206, 208*
Apache, 257
Appatel Industry Magazine, 219
ArcalEx, 295
Arcelus, F.J., 123
Archipelago, 295
archival data, 252
Ariely, D., 48
Aron, R., 191
Arozena, P., 123
artificial intelligence, 43–44
Asia-Pacific region, 128, 130

asset value movement, 96, 98, *98, 99*
assets, proxies for, 107
Association for Computing Machinery (ACM), 287
Au, Y.A., 92
Aucnet, 49
auction markets. *See also* bidding behavior; group-buying auctions
   aggregation of data, 158, 182
   closed versus open, 50
   data collection for, 254
   descending price auctions, 182
   Dutch auctions, 49, 182
   economics of, ix
   "energy" of, 175–176
   item categories distribution, *169*
   net revenue of, 32
   public nature of, 32
   reputation systems, 50
   reserve price, 171–172
   shilling, 52
   transaction data available for, 249–250
   value perceived in, 194
   "winner's curse," 45
automated collection techniques, 250
average causal effect (ACE), 64, 67, 77
average treatment effect, among treated (ATT), 80–82
Awad, N., 176

B

Ba, S., 45
bad debt expense, *142*
Bagchi, S., 98, 104, 149
Bajari, P., 45
Banker, R., 63, 273
Banker, Rajiv, 64
Bapna, R., 48, 49, 52

Bardhan, I.R., 98, 104, 149
Barnes and Noble.com, 7, *9*
1Obase.com, *9*
Battese, G.E., 130
Baumer, D., 49
Beam, C., 48
Bearden, W.O., 191, 194
Belsie, A., 219
Benaroch, M., 92, 98, 99, 104, 107
Benbasat, Isak, 220, 274
Benjamin, R.I., vii
Bennett, M., 45
Bertrand competition assumption, 52
best practice frontier countries, 127
Bezos, Jeff, 277
bidding behavior. *See also* auction markets; group-buying auctions
  auction/market "energy," 175–176
  best price, 185
  bid histories, 159–160, *163*
  bid sniping, 48
  bidders, number of, 172
  buy-it-now option, 176, 185
  closing price, 185
  data visualization for, 16–19
  dynamic variables for, 157–159, *159*, 166
  early activity cluster, 169–170, *170, 171*
  final auction price, 173–174
  functional cluster analysis, 166–170, *171*
  functional data analysis, 175–176
  functional regression analysis, 171–174
  incentives for buying, 190–194
  last minute bidding, 160–161
  late activity cluster, 169–170, *170, 171*
  opening bids, *171,* 171–174, 176
  price dynamics, *167, 168,* 170
  reserve price, 171–172
  shilling, 52
  static dependent variables for, 157–159, *159*
  sub-price dynamics of, 160–161
  testing methods for, 194–198
  theories on, 48–50
  "winner's curse," 45
Big Words, *9*
binary dependent variable
  in rare events data, 255–257
Biswas, A., 191
Bitran, G.R., 192
Black, F., 90
Black-Scholes model, 92, 96
Blair, E.A., 191
blogs
  ad hoc links, 243
  advertisements on, *239*
  age of blog, 242
  archiving in, 243

blogs *(continued)*
  background on, 232–234
  characteristics of, 234, *235, 238–240*
  comments, new, number of, 231–232, 237, *238,* 242
  consumer attention to, 230, 243
  daily measures of, *240*
  data collection on, 237–242
  design of, 233, 242
  entry characteristics, 234, 240, 243, 244
  extent of, 229–230
  features of, 230, 232–234
  friends lists on, 243
  images, new, 242
  interactiveness of, 230, 232
  links in, 242, 243
  links to, 233
  motivation for, 230
  pages viewed, total, 237, *239*
  personal nature of, 233–234
  personal profiles on, 243
  photo galleries in, 242
  poor readership of, 246n2
  popularity over time, 236, 240–241, 245
  research model for, 234–237, 245–246
  spam blogs, 237
  statistics for, *239,* 239–240, *240*
  time spent per visit, 237
  traffice, predicting, 233
  usability of, 233
  visit length, *239*
  visit rate for, 231, 234–237, *238,* 241, 242, *244,* 244–245
blo.gs (Web site), 237
Boeing, 90
Bonds, Barry, 19
Bonferroni test, 220
BooksAMillion, *9*
bookselling, online, 7–14, *9,* 176, 253
Booth, P., 140
Borders.com, *9*
borrowing, cost of, 143
Boston College, 276
Bosworth, B.P., 116
bots (shopbots), 38
boys, computer use by, 50
Brinkmann, U., 45
Broadbent, Marianne, 90, 283
Browder, S., 219
Brynjolfsson, Erik, viii, 49, 116, 277, 283, 285
Bucklin, R.E., 252
Burk, D.L., 32, 55
business processes, 128, 150–151
business value of IT, viii–ix, *137,* 153n1, 277, 283, 285

Business Wire, 219
business-to-business (B2B) e-commerce sales, 32, 183, 191–192
business-to-consumer (B2C) e-commerce, 31–32, 250
Buy.com, *9*
buying pools, *185*
buy-it-now value, 176, 185
Buyukkokten, O., 13
Buzzell, R.D., 191
"BZST-Musings on Business and Statistics," 25n5

C

Cameron, A.C., 255
capital deepening, 116
Carlson School of Management, 7
Carroll School of Management, 276
case studies, 252
Catledge, L.D., 48
causality
 analysis of, *76,* 78–79
 average causal effect, 64
 individual causal effects (ICE), 66–67
 inference, 63–65, 67, 68
 observed data, 67, 69–71
 potential outcomes, 67, 69–71
 propensity score-based approach for estimating, 73–75
 stable-unit treatment value assumption (SUTVA), 69, 71
 terminology, 65–66
Center for Research on IT and Organizations (CRITO) Industry/University Consortium, 278
Chang, D.R., 130
Chen, J., 187
Chen, R., 45
Cheng Siwei, 295
Cherry, J., 48
Chevalier, J.A., 48, 176
China, 130, 183, 292
Chinese consumers, compared with American, 213
choice-based sampling, 251, 254–257, 261, 262, 264–265
Churchman, C. West, 15, 33–34
Clay, K., 50
Clements, N., 80
Clemons, E.K., 90, 91
Cleveland, W.S., 10–11
clickstream data, 251, 253, 254, 265
Clinton, M., 48
closed auctions, 50
Cobb-Douglas functional form, 131
Cochran, W.G., 74
Coelli, T.J., 130
comments, online, 32
Communicaitons of the ACM (CACM), 56, 287, 294
complementaries between countries, 130
Computer Intelligence InfoCorp (CII), 285
computer simulations, 37, *37*
comScore, 31–32
confounding bias, 68, 72–75
consumer behavior, xii, 250, 251, 253, 265
consumer reviews, 253
consumer's reference price, 208
contract manufacturing, 128
control subjects, multiple, 74
coproduction. *See* user-generated content
CoShopper.com, 183
Cox, D.F., 193
Cox, J.C., 91
Cox-Rubenstein binomial model, 91
CRITO Consortium, 290, 294
cross-country efficiency measurements, *122, 123, 125*
cross-country productivity measurements, 114, 120–126, *121, 124*
CSC Index, 291
C-Tribe.com, 183
Cunningham, S.M., 193

D

Da Vinci Code, The, 281
Dabrowska, D.M., 65
Dai, Q., 92
Dans, E., 48
data, quality of, 266
data aggregation, 158
data collection approaches
 agents for, 38–39, *40,* 40–41, *42, 46–47,* 48
 applications for, 262, 264–265
 code of conduct, absence of, 55
 cost of, 53
 data extraction, 55
 in international relations, 256
 limitations of, 53–54
 mechanisms for, 157–159
 for online auctions, 254
 online experiemnts, 39, *40,* 40–41
 online surveys, *40,* 40–41
 for rare events, 253–254
 Web log files, 39, *40,* 40–41
data envelopment analysis, *115,* 131
data protection, 49
data set partitioning, 15–16
data sets
 cross-sectional, 63–65
 increased size of, 3–15, 32, 36
data smoothing, 161–164, *164,* 173, 177–178

data visualizing, 10–14
Davamanirajan, P., 149
David, Paul, 279
Davies, G.A.M., 254, 256
Davis, G.B., 32, 55
DealPilot.com, 7
Dealtime, 7
DeBono, M., 219
Dedrick, J., 114, 128, 130
deduction, 15, 35, 36
Dell, 126
Dellarocas, C.N., 48, 55, 176
demand aggregation, 182, 183–187
DemandLine.com, 183
deregulation, 128
descending price auctions, 182
developers, attracting, 257, 259, *260, 262, 263*
Dewally, M.A., 48
Dewan, S., 45
Dhar, Vasant, 288
Dickinson, M., 90
Dickson, D., 104
"digital divide," 292–293
digital networks, 264–265
digital products, economics of, x
direct measures of business processes, 150–151
discounted cash flow (DCF), 91
distance functions, 118
Dixit, A.K., 91
Dodge, J., 219
dog, blog of, *233*
Doong, H-S., 45
Dos Santos, B., 91
Du, H.S., 233
dummy variable approach, 231
Dunnett's studentized maximum modulus distribution-based T3 test, 202, *205, 207, 209*
Dunnett's studentized range distribution-based pairwise mean comparison C test, 202, *205, 207, 209*
Dutch auctions, 49, 182
dyadic interactions, 8, 253–255
Dybvig, P.H., 220
dynamic pricing, 181–182, 190, 196, *196*

E
Earp, J.B., 49
Easley, R.F., 50
Eaton, D.H., 48
eBay, 16–19, 32, 48–50, 253
EBITDA, 142, *142*
eCampus, *9*
e-commerce research
  core question, existence of, 287–291
  cumulative tradition in, 276–279

e-commerce research *(continued)*
  by inquiry systems, 31–32, 44–45, *46–47*, 48–50
  nature of, 279–283
  repetition of studies, 279–280
  speed of, 290
e-commerce sales, 32
e-commerce spending, 31–32
economic activity
  IT enabled changes in, vii–viii, 117
economics
  of digital products, x
Economides, A.A., 108, 220
Ederington, L.H., 48
eDRILL, 55–56
efficiency change (TEC), 114, 119, *126,* 131
efficiency measures
  cross-country comparison, 127
  deterioration of, 124
  literature on, 116–117
  operating asset turnover, 143
  value chain profitability, *147*
Efollet, *9*
El Niño, 161
elasticity of substitution, 131
Eldridge, E., 219
electronic communications networks (ECNs), 279, 283
electronic data interchange (EDI), 286
electronic markets, ix
email communication, patterns of, 11–14
embedded options, 107
empirical regularities, 15
Engineering Management, 294
enterprise resource planning (ERP), 90, 140, 288
errors-in-variables problems, 150
estimand, causal, 67
E*Trade, 295
Etrana.com, 183
Europe, technology in, 130
European Union data protection, 49
Evans, F.B., 253
executive information systems (EIS), 288
Expedia.com, 250
experimental simulations, 37, *37*
expert systems approaches, 43–44

F
Facebook, 11, 294
factors of production, 131
failure of IT projects, 288, 291
Fan, M., 48
Färe, R., 123
farming, 292
Farrell, M.J., 118, 119
feasible consideration set, 102
feasible generalized least squares (FGLS), 237

Ferl, T.E., 45
Feurstein, M., 92, 104
Fichman, R.G., 92
Fiedler, K.D., 220
field experiments, 37, *37*
field studies, 37
52MarketPlace.com, 183
financial analysis, 283
Financial Analysts Journal, 284
financial trade markets, 283
finished goods inventory turnover, *142*
Finland, 121–124, *125, 126*
firm value, 143–145
Fisher, 117, 128
Fisher's least significant difference (LSD) test, *205, 207, 209,* 220
fishing, 292
Fleming, L., 256
forecasted final payment, 208
formal theory, 37, *37*
Fornell, C., 79
Forrester Research, 250, 283, 294
Framingham Heart, 289
friends list, 243
functional cluster analysis, 166–170, *171*
functional covariates, 175
functional data analysis (FDA), 161–166, *165*
functional data analysis, 175–176
functional k-medoids clustering, 178
functional principal components analysis, 174–175
functional regression analysis, 171–174, 178–179

G

Gambale, M., 219
Games-Howell test, 202, *207, 209*
game-theoretic approaches, 92
Gardyn, R., 50
Gartner Group, 283, 284–285, 294
general two-stage least squares (G2SLS) procedure, 232
generality, *37,* 37–38
generalized least squares (GLS), 231
generalized two-stage least squares (G2SLS), 242
Germany, 121–124, *125, 126,* 127
Gilkeson, J.H., 48
girls, computer use by, 50
global computer industry, 128
global IT production network, 128
globalization, 128, 292–294
Goes, P., 48, 49, 52
Gomez Advisors, 219
Gordon, M.E., 50
Gordon, R.J., 117, 126
graphs, 11
Graves, S., 90

Grewal, D., 194
gross profit margin, *141*
group-buying auctions. *See also* auction markets; bidding behavior
  approaches for, 183–187
  bargaining power base, 190
  "breaking the lot," 212
  versus buying pools, *185*
  consumer bid arrival, 190
  coordination within, 187–188
  decision time in, 193, 200–201, *203, 205,* 208, 210, 211
  defined, 181–183
  in different countries, 183
  discounts, *196,* 206, 208
  dynamic pricing in, 181–182
  expected price-drop effect, 187
  experiment illustrations, *214–217*
  incentive mechanisms, 190–194, *196,* 196–197, *198, 202–209,* 211
  initiators, 190
  joining time, *203–205*
  mechanisms for, 187–190
  models for, 182
  order size, final, 193–194, *202,* 206, *206, 207,* 210–211
  order size, planned, 192–194, *202,* 206, *206, 207,* 210–211
  orders, increasing volume of, 191, 193, 197
  participation externality effects, 187
  perceived value, 194, 206, 208, *208, 209,* 210
  positive participation network externalities, 190, 197
  price curves, 190, 196, *196*
  pricing strategies in, 187
  problems with, 183
  quantity-based incentives, 191, 193, *196, 198, 202–209,* 211, *217*
  questionnaire for experimental subjects, 218–219
  sequence-based incentives, 191, *196, 198, 202–209,* 211, *216*
  studies in, 189–190
  testing methods, 194–198, *199,* 208–213
  time-based incentives, 191, *196, 198, 202–209,* 211, *215*
  total quantity of sale items, 190
  traditional incentives, 191, *196, 198, 202–209, 214*
  uncertainty and consequence, 193
  variety of products, 190
group-buying Web sites, 48
Grover, V., 220
Gumbrecht, M., 243
Gupta, A., 48, 49, 52
Gupta, S., 192

Gurbaxani, Vijay
  airline market, 280
  background on, 276
  business value, ix
  core question in e-commerce research, 288–291
  entertainment, 281
  financial analysis, 284–287
  globalization, 292–294
  health care, 280–281
  pricing, 277–278, 280
  research issues, 277–279, 280–283, 286, 290–291
  used car market, 281
  value of IT, 116
Gustafson, N., 104
Guzzo, M., 219

H
Hahn, J., 45
Han, S., 192
Hancock, G.R., 220
Hardee's, 64
Hawthorne effect, 52
He, F., 45
health care, 92–97, 100–101, *105, 106,* 255, 280–281
Heckman, J.J., 80
Hegelian inquiry, 15, 35, *35. See also* hybrid theory construction
Heller, G.Z., 175
Henderson, C.J., 91
"hidden" phenomena, 52
Hitt, L.M., viii, 116, 283
Hofacker, C.F., 45
Holland, P., 65
homogeneity assumption, 68
Hong, W., 220
Hong Kong, 130
Hortacsu, A., 45
Houser, D., 49
Hsu, V., 45
Huber, P.J., 25n1
Huberty, C.J., 220
Hui, K-L., 8
human sleep data, 16
Hume, D., 65
hybrid theory construction, 15, 35, *46–47,* 50

I
IBM, 126, 285
IDC, 283, 294
IEEE Transactions, 294
inbound logistics, *138,* 138–140, *139*
income, quality of, *142*
India, 130, 183, 292, 293–294
India Tobacco Company, 293

induction, 15, 34–36
industrialization, policies for, 126–130
Information Resources Inc., 285
information science (IS)
  faculty members in, 289–290
  identity development of, 273–275
  research, direction of, 273–275
Information Systems Research, 274, 287
information versus knowledge, x
inputs (factors of production), 131
inquiring systems, 33–36, *35,* 44–50
instrumental variable regression, 232
Intel, 126
interactions
  information available on, 249–251
intercept-corrected estimators, 256
interdependences, 108
interfirm networks, 256
International Conference on Information Systems (ICIS), 64, 273, 276
international relations, 256
International Sectoral Database (OECD), 120
internet commerce, 189–190
interproject embedded options, 96
intraproject embedded options, 96
invariance assumptions, 68
inventory
  obsolescence, 139
  turnover, *141, 142*
investments in IT
  benefits, projected, *94*
  business value, contribution to, 136, 286
  business-to-consumer (B2C), 31–32
  characteristics of, 91
  embedded options in, 107
  and flexibility, 90
  partitioning of, 107
  performance benefits of, *149*
  prioritizing, 90
  rate of growth of, 89
  real options approach, 90–104, 107–108
  on technology, 135
  timing of, 91, 92, 108
IPv6 (Internet Protocol Version Six), xiii
Iraq, 25n8
Ireland, 126, 281
  IT industries, contribution to growth, 114, 117
IT literature, 273
ITC E-choupal ("Village Square"), 292, 293

J
James-Howell test, *205*
Jank, W., 16, 17, 19, 52, 175
Jap, S.D., 50
Japan, 121, *122, 123,* 124–127, 130
Jeffery, M., 98, 99

Jidoun, G., 219
Jin, G., 48
Jorgenson, D.W., 116, 126
judgmental tasks, 37, *37*
Juergens, M., 219
jump bidding, 50

K

Kafka, S.J., 219
Kambil, A., 91
Kane, M., 219
Kantian inquiry, 15, 34–35, *35. See also* theory verification/falisification
Kaplan, R.S., 107
Karmarkar, Uday, 286
Kasper, G.M., 220
Kato, A., 48
Kauffman, R.J.
  agent-based data collection, 54
  Bertrand competition assumption, 52
  bidding behavior, 45, 48, 50
  causality, inferring, 63
  data collection mechanisms, 39, 158, 252
  data extraction, 55–56
  data visualization, 13
  group-buying auction performance, 182, 183, 187
  on internet's effect on research, 32
  on IT investments, 90, 92, 104, 107
  pricing, 192
  randomization, 64
  shilling, 52
  survey of IT literature, 273
Kawamoto, D., 219
Keen, P., 273, 274
Keil, M., 92
Kim, N., 130
Kim, Y., 48
Kim, Y.G., 220
King, C., 219
King, G., 255
King, J.L., 274
Klein, M., 55
Klockars, A.J., 220
knots, 162
knowledge, value of, x
Knowledge and Data Engineering, 294
knowledge versus information, x
Koehler, G., 107
Kogut, B., 91
Konsynski, Benn, 64
Korea, 121–124, *125, 126*
  as supplier, 130
  technical efficiency in, 121
Kozar, K.A., 220
Kraemer, K.L., ix, 114, 116, 126, 128, 130, 252

Kriebel, C.H., 90
Krishnan, M.S., 79
Krishnan, R., 194
Kromrey, J.D., 220
Krueger, A.B., 247
Kuhn, 275
Kulatilaka, N., 91
Kumar, R., 92

L

labor productivity, 131
laboratory experiments, 37, *37,* 252
Lagrange multiplier test, 244
Lai, H., 45, 182
Lai, Y-L., 8
Lakshmanan, L.V.S., 56
LaRocca, M.A., 220
Laxminarayan, P., 16
Leader, L.R., 175
Lee, H.G., 49
Lee, J.N., 220
legacy systems, 291
Lehmann, D.R., 192
Leibnizian inquiry, 15, 34, *35. See also* theory generalization
Leithheiser, R.I., 220
Lerman, S.R., 256
Lester, S., 116
LetsBuyIt.com, 183–185, *186,* 219
Levene's test, *204,* 220
Levin, J.R., 220
Lewis, D., 65
Li, X., 92
licensing models, 278
Lima-Turner, K.D., 50
Lin, L., 92
Linden Lab, xii–xiii
LinkedIn, 11
Linux, 257
List, J.A., 48, 49
ListGrabber, 56
Livingston, J.A., 45
Lockean inquiry, 15, 34, *35. See also* theory building
log files, 39–41, *42, 47,* 249
log-transformed binomial model, 99, *99,* 109–110
Lomax, R.G., 220
"long tail," ix, 246n2
longitudinal research designs, 52
Lowengart, O., 194
Lucas, Henry C., Jr.
  background on, 276
  bookselling, 281
  core question in e-commerce research, 288–291
  e-commerce research, 277–283
  electronic data interchange (EDI), 286

Lucas, Henry C., Jr. *(continued)*
  financial analysis, 284–287
  financial trade markets, 283
  globalization, 292–294
  health care, 280–281
  legacy systems, 291
  on price, 277–278
  research, speed of, 285
  research relevance, 284–287
Lucking-Reiley, D., 48, 49
Luft, J., 104
Lyytinen, K., 274

M

Malhotra, N.K., 256
Malmquist, S., 118
Malmquist productivity index (MPI)
  cross-country comparison, *124–126*
  defined, 131
  and distance functions, 118
  and efficiency change (TEC), 119
  as empirical advance, 127–129
  and technilogical change (TCH), 119
Malmquist total factor productivity index (TFP), 117–118, 121, 123, 124
Malone, T.W., vii
Malu, D., 17, 19
management information systems, 288
Management Science, 273, 287
Manaster, S., 107
Manski, C.F., 256
Mara, J., 219
March, S.T., 32, 54, 55–56, 220
Margrabe, W., 91
market share, *141*
market-driven strategies, 127
marketing research, 251–252
Mason, R.O., 34
Massad, V.J., 48
massive quasi-experiments, 41, 43, 51–52
Matheis, M., 104
Matolcsy, Z., 140
maximum-likelihood estimation, 254–257
Mayzlin, D., 48, 176
McAweeney, M.J., 220
McGrath, J.E., 36, *37,* 188, 189
Mejias, R.J., 220
Melnik, M.I., 49
Melville, N., ix, 116
menu costs, ix
Merage School of Business, 276
Mercata.com, 181, 183
meta-research, *35,* 35–36
Mild, A., 92, 104
military actions, 25n8
Millsap, L., 45

minority students, 292
MIS Quarterly Executive, 284, 286, 294
MIT, 285
Mithas, S., 79
Mitroff, I.I., 34
Mobshop.com, 181, 183
modification statistics, 15
Moe, W.M., 252
Mohsenzadeh, H., 91
Monahan, J.P., 192
Mondschein, S.V., 192
Monroe, K.B., 194
Moonis, M., 16
Morey, R., 63, 64
Morris, A.H., 220
Motley Fool, 291
MSNBC.com, 247n11
Mulpuru, S., 250
multi-stage embedded real options, 98–99
multiunit English ascending auction, 182
multivariate regression trees, 175
Murphy, J., 45
MySimon.com, 7
MySpace, 11, 294

N

Nardi, B.A., 243
NASDAQ, 283, 295
negative binomial regression, 255
neoclassical growth theory, 116
nested log-transformed binomial model, 96–101
nested options models, 98, 100
net asset turnover, *141*
net present value (NPV), 89–90, *102*
Netherlands, 121–124, *125, 126,* 127, 183
New York Stock Exchange (NYSE), 283, 295
New York Times "bestseller list," 8
New York University, 288
newly industrialized economies (NIEs), 130
newsgroups, dynamics in, 176
Neyman, J.S., 65
"Nine Cents"/"Nine Dollars" models, 8, 10
non-government organizations, 293
NOPAT (net operating profit after tax), 139, 143
NOPAT (net operating profit after tax) Margin, 139, *141*
Norton, D.P., 107
Norway, *121–123,* 124, *125, 126,* 127
nose job, blog of, *234*
Noy, A., 48

O

observational data, *77*
Ockenfels, A., 48, 158
OECD, 120, 130
offshore outsourcing, 128

Olejnik, S., 220
Oliner, S.D., 116, 117, 126
Olsen, S., 219
1bookstreet, *9*
online broker, 279
online experiments, 39, *40,* 40–41, *42, 47,* 48
online judgement tasks, 39, *40,* 40–41, *42,* 45, *47*
online surveys, *40,* 40–41, *42,* 45, *47*
OnlineChoice.com, 183–184
Onsale.com, 253
open auctions, 50
Open Source Auction Network (OSAN), 183
open source software development (OSSD), 250, 253, 257–262, *263, 264*
operating asset turnover, 143
operating return on assets (OROA), 145
operating working capital turnover, *142*
operations processes, *138,* 138–140, *139, 141*
order size, 206
ordinary least squares (OLS), 231
Organization for Economic Cooperation and Development (OECD), 113, 114
outbound logistics, *138,* 138–140, *139, 141–142*
out-of-sample data, 16
outputs (factors of production), 131
outsourcing, 128
outsourcing business, 289
Ow, T., 32, 49, 56

P

pair-wide matching methods, 74
panel data, 252
Pareto-improving welfare gains, 191–192
Park, C., 48
path of influences, 4
Patsuris, P., 219
pattern recognition, 11–14
Pavlou, P.A., 45
performance analysis, 113–116, 119–120, *141–142,* 145–151
performance comparison, 144–145
PetroSilicon.com, 183
philosophy of science, 32–38
Pindyck, R.S., 91
Pinsonneault, A., 252
Pitkow, J.E., 48
plan-driven strategies, 127
PointSpeed.com, 183
Poisson regression, 255
political strife, 256
polynomial smoothing splines. *See* data smoothing
Poole, M.S., 35, 50
Porter, M.E., 138
positive participation externality effects, 197
Positran, 64
potential outcomes, 64, 82–83
potential outcomes framework (for causation), 65–66
Powell's, *9*
power law distribution, 246n2
PP&E turnover, *141*
PR Newswire, 219
Prahalad, C.K., 292
precision, *37,* 37–38
price comparison, 265
price curves, *168,* 190, 196, *196*
price data, "scraping," 7
price decline, 117
price discounting, 191–192
price dynamics, 160–161, 166, *167,* 170, 173–174
price-performance improvements, 289
pricing, studies on, *9,* 277–280
pricing strategies, 187
privacy, in online shopping, 49
process performance measures. *See* accounting-based performance measures
production process, 131
productivity
  cross-country comparison, 114, 120–126, *121, 125,* 126–129
  defined, 131
  efficiency change (TEC) affect on, 114
  literature on, 116–117
  Malmquist productivity index, 117–119, 121
  productivity growth, xi–xii, 127, 131
  productivity paradox, viii, 116, 276–277
  stochastic production frontiers, 115
  technical efficiency, 115
  technological change (TEC) affect on, 114
productivity paradox, viii, 116, 276–277
product-related data, 253
profitability, *147*
propensity scores, 73–75, *77*
PttBBS, 183

Q

quality of income, *142*
quasi-experiments. *See* massive quasi-experiments
Quelch, J.A., 191
QWERTY, 279, 281–282

R

Rafaeli, S., 48
Ramsay, J.O., 175
Ramsey, J.B., 175
random effects model, 231
randomization, 64, 71–72
rare events data, 253–257
Ratcliffe, S.J., 175
real options
  abandon option, 108
  analysis, 104, 107

real options (continued)
  discounted cash flow (DCF), 91
  embedded, 96
  game-theoretic approaches, 92
  hard and soft dependencies, 93–96
  implications of, 107–108
  interdependencies, *97*
  in IS research, 90–92
  model of, 96–99, 101–104
  multi-stage embedded, 98–99
  and net present values (NPVs), *102*
  pricing models for, *91*
  valuation models, 92
realism, *37*, 37–38
Regan, K., 219
regression, 75, 78
research, speed of, 285
research approaches, 36–38, *42*, 53–54
research data
  dyadic interactions, 253–254
  versus marketing research, 251–252
  technology-enabled, 252–254
research funding, 291
research methodologies
  artificial intelligence, 43–44
  expert systems approaches, 43–44
  massive quasi-experiments, 41, 43
  three-horned dilemma for, 36–38, *37*
research relevance, 283–287, 291
residual income model, 144
Resnick, P., 49, 50
response-based sampling. *See* choice-based sampling
retailers, online, 7–14, 253, 265
return on assets (ROA), 136, 140
return on equity (ROE), 136, *137*, 140–148, *148*, 151–152
returns to scale, 131
Reynolds, K., 48
R.H. Smith School of Business, 276, 291
risk management, xi
ROE decomposition, *141*
Rosenbaum, P., 74, 75, 79
Ross, S.A., 91
Roth, A.E., 48, 158
Rubin, D.B., 65, 74, 75
Rubin's model, 65
Rubinstein, M., 91
Rugullies, E., 219
Ruiz, C., 16
Runkel, P.J., 36, 188, 189
Russo, R.P., 52

S
Sadri, F., 56
Sadrian, A.A., 192

Salmon, W.J., 191
sample surveys, 37, *37*
Sandoval, G., 219
Scamell, R., 220
scanner data, 252
SchemaSQL, 56
Scheraga, D., 219
Schiano, D.J., 243
Scholes, M., 90
Schwartz, E., 92
Scientific American, 293
Scottrade, 295
"scraping" price data, 7
Seaman, M.A., 220
Second Life, xii–xiii
Segev, A., 48
Seifert, M., 45
selling, general and administrative expense, *142*
sensitivity analysis, 73–75, 103–104, *105*, 108
Serlin, R.C., 220
service-oriented architectures (SOAs), 90
Shah, S., 98, 99
Shanthikumar, J.G., 48
Shapiro, C., 220
Sheehan, K.B., 49
Sheffé's test, 220
Shepard input function, 118
Shepherd, M.M., 220
Sheshkin, D.J., 220
shilling, online, 52
Shmueli, Galit, 16, 17, 25n5, 52, 175
Shocker, A.D., 130
shopbots (bots), 38
SHOP2gether, 183
shopping, online, 32, 49
Sia, C.L., 220
Sichel, D.E., 116, 117, 126
Simon Graduate School of Management, 277
Simonoff, J.S., 162
Simonson, I., 48
Simpson's paradox, 158
Sims, C., 7
Singapore, 130, 292
Singer, 34
Singerian-Churchmanian inquiry, 33–36, *35*, 35–36. *See also* meta-research
Singh, J., 256
Site Meter, 237
Sloan Management Review, 294
Smith, J.A., 80
Smith, M., 49
Smyth, P., 11
social interactions, online, 249–250
social networks, 11–14, *14*, 264–265
software design, 54–55

Software Engineering, 294
Solow, Robert, viii, 116
Sorenson, O., 254, 256
Sougstad, R., 98, 104, 149
SourceForge.net, 257–259
spam blogs, 237
Spatt, C., 220
Speed, T.P., 65
spiders/spyders, 38, 158
splines. *See* data smoothing
spread (cost of borrowing), 143
stable-unit treatment value assumption (SUTVA), 69, 71
STAN Database for Industrial Analysis (OECD), 120
standard estimator, 71
Standifird, S.S., 48
Stanford University, 279
static dependent variables for bidding behavior, 157–159, *159*
statistics, 11
Stelin, S., 219
Stiroh, K.J., 116, 117, 126
stochastic production frontier, 113–116, *115,* 119–120, 131
Stokes, H.H., 25n2
strong ignorability, 73–75
structural equation model, 4, 15
Stuart, T.E., 254, 256
studies of association, 69
Subramanian, S.N., 56
substitution effects, 117, 130
Sullivan, B., 219
Supattathum, S., 220
supply chain management, xi, 145–148
support processes, *138,* 138–140, *139, 142*
surveys, 52, 251, 252, 266
Szajna, B., 220

T
Taiwan, 130, 183
Tallon, Paul, 92
　background on, 276
　data collection, 49
　financial analysis, 284–287
　globalization, 292–294
　health care, 280
　industrialization policies, 126
　real options, 114
　research issues, 276–280, 284–291
Tam, K.Y., 220
Tamhane's test, *205, 207, 209*
Tan, B.C.Y., 220
Tan, Y., 48
Tanaka, J., 219
Taudes, A., 91, 92, 104

technical change (TCH), 114, 119, 123, 124, *126,* 131
technical efficiency (TEC), 115, *122,* 123, *123,* 131
technology acceptance model (TAM), 4, 45, 282
Technorati.com, 233
temporal invariance assumptions, 68
Tenorio, R., 50
TETRAD, 15
Thaler, R.H., 191
theory building, 15, 34, *35, 46–47,* 48–49
theory generalization, 34, *35,* 45, *46–47*
theory testing, 15
theory verification/falsification, 15, 34–35, *35, 46–47,* 49–50
Thong, J.Y.L., 220
Thornton, A., 90
three-horned dilemma, 36–38, *37*
Tillotson, J., 48
time series data, 52
time-sensitive goods, sales of, 176
Tiwana, A., 92
Todd, P., 220
Törnqvist, 117, 128
total factor productivity, 131
transaction data, 32, 253
transaction utility, 191
translog functional form, 127–129, 131
travel e-commerce, 32
Travelocity.com, 250
Trigeorgis, L., 91, 99, 109
Triplett, J.E., 116
Trivedi, P.K., 255
truncated normal distribution, 131
trust theory, 45
Tsvetovat, M., 183, 187
Tucker, J.M., 48
Tukey's test, 220

U
uBid.com, 253
unions, 117
United Kingdom, 121–124, *125,* 126–127, 183
United States, 121–124, *125, 126,* 127, 130, 183
United States Department of Energy, 219
United States Department of Justice, 25n8
universities, safety at, 25n8
University of California, Irvine, 276, 278, 294
University of Maryland, 16, 276, 283
University of Minnesota, 7
University of Notre Dame, 7, 258
University of Rochester, 277
unobservables, 75
UPC scanner data, 252
Urbany, J.E., 191, 194

UseNet newsgroup lists, 32, 253
user browsing patterns, 176
user-generated content, xii, 250, 253

V

value, perceived, 187, 194, 206, 208, *208, 209,* 210
  perceived value, 206, 208
value chain analysis, *137,* 138–140, *141, 147*
value of IT technology, 137
van de Ven, A.H., 35, 50
Van Horn, T., 220
Varian, H.R., 220
variance decomposition, 8
Varsitybooks, *9*
vector autoregression model (VAR), 7
Verhoef, C., 90
Vingron, Martin, 3
Virginia Tech killings, 25n8
virtual worlds, xii–xiii
Visual Basic for Application (VBA), 44
Visualizing Data, 10–11
Viswanathan, S., 193
VolumeBuy.com, 183

W

Wagner, C., 233
Wang, B.
  data visualization, 13
  group-buying auction performance, 48, 182, 183, 187
  pricing, 192
Wang, Q., 193
warranty expense, 139, *141*
waste, 139
Web design, 45
Web log files, 39, *40,* 40–41, *42, 47*
Webby Awards, 220
Weber, B., 91
Weblogs. *See* blogs
WebMD, 293–294
weekend effect, 48
Wegman, E.J., 4–5, 25n1
Wei, K.K., 220
weighted estimators, 256

weighted exogenous sampling maximum likelihood (WESML), 251, 256, 261, 262
Weilbaker, D.C., 191, 194
Weill, Peter, 90, 283
Weiner process, 109
Whinston, A.B., 92
Wieder, B., 140
Wilcocks, L.P., 116
Wilcox, R.R., 220
Wilcox, R.T., 49
willingness-to-pay, 208
Wimpsett, K., 220
"winner's curse," 45, 49
Wood, C.A.
  Bertrand competition assumption, 52
  bidding behavior, 48, 49, 52
  data collection mechanisms, 54–56, 158, 252
  on Internet's effect on research, 32
  price competition, 50
Wood, Chuck, 7
Wooders, J., 49
work-in-process inventory turnover, *141*
Workshop in Information Systems and Economics, 277
WorldWide Retail Exchange (WWRE), 183, *184*

X

XML pages, 55, 56

Y

Yamagishi, T., 50
Yates, J., vii
Yee, S-J., 8
Yin, P., 49
Yoon, Y.S., 192

Z

Zeckhauser, R., 50
Zeng, L., 255
Zhang, D.S., 220
Zhang, X., 176
Zhu, K., 92
Zhuang, Y-T., 45
Zozaya-Gorostiza, C., 92
Zwirl.com, 183